THEOLOGICAL FOUNDATIONS
for
MINISTRY

Selected Readings for a Theology of the Church in Ministry

RAY S. ANDERSON, Editor

T. & T. CLARK, LTD.
EDINBURGH
AND
WILLIAM B. EERDMANS PUBLISHING COMPANY
GRAND RAPIDS, MICHIGAN

Copyright © 1979 by Wm. B. Eerdmans Publishing Co.
All rights reserved
Printed in the United States of America
for
Wm. B. Eerdmans Publishing Co.
255 Jefferson Ave. S.E., Grand Rapids, Mich. 49503
and
T. & T. Clark, Ltd.
36 George Street, Edinburgh, Scotland
ISBN (U.K. edition) 0-567-22355-8

Library of Congress Cataloging in Publication Data

Main entry under title:

Theological foundations for ministry.

   1. Theology, Practical — Addresses, essays, lectures.
2. Church — Addresses, essays, lectures. I. Anderson, Ray Sherman.
BV3.T44   262'.7   78-13613
ISBN 0-8028-1776-9

Contents

Part Four: THE CHURCH'S MINISTRY TO THE WORLD ON BEHALF OF JESUS

Epilogue

The Authors

RAY S. ANDERSON is Assistant Dean and Associate Professor of Theology at Fuller Theological Seminary in Pasadena, California.

KARL BARTH was Professor of Theology at the University of Basel, Switzerland, until his retirement in 1962. He died in 1968.

DIETRICH BONHOEFFER was a lecturer in Theology at the University of Berlin from 1932–33 and Director of the "Preacher's Seminary" for the Confessing Church in Germany at Finkenwalde from 1935–38. He was imprisoned for his underground activities and finally hanged, upon Hitler's orders, on April 9, 1945.

IGNACIO ELLACURÍA is Professor at the Universidad Centroamericana José Simeón Cañas, San Salvador, South America. He studied Theology at Innsbruck under Karl Rahner and Philosophy at Quito and Madrid.

KARN GRIFFEN received his Doctor of Ministry degree from Fuller Theological Seminary in Pasadena, California, in 1976. He presently serves as the Protestant Chaplain for Claremont Colleges in California.

HANS KÜNG is Professor of Dogmatic and Ecumenical Theology at the University of Tübingen in Germany.

KORNELIS MISKOTTE was professor of Dogmatics and Ethics at Leyden University in Holland. His book, *When the Gods are Silent,* was first translated into German in 1963 and when it appeared was called the "book of the decade."

HELMUT THIELICKE is Dean of the Theological Faculty and Professor of Systematic Theology at the University of Hamburg, Germany.

JAMES B. TORRANCE is Professor of Systematic Theology at the University of Aberdeen in Scotland.

THOMAS F. TORRANCE is Professor of Christian Dogmatics at the University of Edinburgh in Scotland.

W. A. WHITEHOUSE is on the Faculty of Theology at the University of Kent, Canterbury, England.

Part One:

A THEOLOGY FOR THE CHURCH IN MINISTRY

Editor's Introduction

THIS IS NOT THE INTRODUCTION TO ANOTHER THEOLOGY, FOR, TO paraphrase the apostle Paul, if anyone, even an angel from heaven, comes with another theology, let him be anathema! Those who are crying out for a "ceasefire" by the theologians so that the Church can get on with its ministry are making more and more sense. Let this not be considered a stone offered to those who are asking for bread.

Nor is this an argument that the Church ought to have a ministry. That fact is self-evident according to any definition of the Church. What we want to do is strengthen the foundations of the Church in ministry by going back and digging out the wells which our fathers dug when the land was given by promise, or, to change the metaphor, to hew out cisterns in the rock from which those who minister can find refreshment and renewal for the task.

Once every generation or so, the Church surely must pause to ask the question—what is the *nature* of the ministry which occupies us? But to ask this question necessarily drives us back to the foundational work of God himself in establishing a ministry of revelation and reconciliation in the world. It forces us to search for the fundamental paradigm of ministry as demonstrated in God's ministry for us and for our salvation. It is this search and struggle for understanding that legitimates the theological task of the Church. For one cannot inquire about ministry without inquiring about God and what he has said and done. The concern of Part One in this set of readings is to inquire into the nature of ministry by seeking the theological foundations of that ministry in the Word and deed of God.

Chapter 1 establishes the fundamental paradigm within which the entire project is placed. All ministry is God's ministry, in and for the sake of reconciling the world to himself. This ministry of reconciliation is upheld, on both the divine and human side,

3

through divine initiative and action. Considered carefully, this chapter will serve as a framework within which a theology for the Church in ministry can be developed.

Following this introductory chapter, the essay by Karl Barth on the place of theology defines theology as the proper discipline of the Church. In exercising this discipline, the Church takes stock of itself in accordance with the Word of God, under the tutelage of the inspired witness of response to that Word in the form of Scripture, and believingly experienced as the life of the communion of saints. Thus, enriched by the Holy Spirit, the Church takes up the task of theology in its ministry and for the sake of its ministry. Theology, therefore, says Barth, properly belongs at the center of the Church's life and ministry, and is thus "evangelical theology," because it speaks and acts concerning the "God of the Gospel," who is both the source and norm of theological existence.

The section by Helmut Thielicke, which then follows, develops the doctrine of the Holy Spirit as the starting point for evangelical theology, arguing that the "Cartesian self" with its subjectivizing tendencies must be displaced by the new creation of faith through the testimony and work of the Holy Spirit. For Thielicke, everything depends upon the question of whether the Word approaches and determines our method of knowing it, or whether we approach the Word with a view to appropriating it to our own situation. This "critical" question precedes the methodological question and decides the issue at the outset. Thielicke earlier in his book has outlined "Theology A," or Cartesian theology, as the theology of liberalism (Schleiermacher) and existentialism (Tillich, Bultmann), both of which assume the primacy of the human subject in the act of theologizing. By "Theology B," or non-Cartesian theology, Thielicke means that theology which affirms the incarnation of God in Christ, the cross of Christ, the resurrection of Christ, and the epistemological relevance of the Holy Spirit. It is "evangelical theology" in the sense that Barth uses the expression.

In his essay which follows, T. F. Torrance carries the development one step further by showing how theological language, as human response, is grounded in the objectivity of divine revelation, which includes both the divine Word and human response through the humanity of Christ. Torrance shows how faith, worship, the sacramental life of the Church, and Christian service are called forth and given a transcendent source through the incarnation. Torrance argues that this revelation as a historical actuality and possibility creates and confers rationality upon the creaturely order by overcoming the irrational structures of sin and oppression. Ministry, therefore, is a "reasonable service," through which Christ continues to minister to the world.

It will be the purpose of the first section to present an alternative to the customary dichotomy between "pure theology" and "applied theology." We will attempt to demonstrate that theology itself must be understood in terms of the mutual involution of revelation and reconciliation given in the gospel of Jesus Christ as a completed and yet continuing ministry of Christ, through the power of the Holy Spirit, in the life and witness of the Church as community.

1

RAY S. ANDERSON

*A Theology for Ministry**

INTRODUCTION

THE RECENT SPATE OF "ADJECTIVAL" THEOLOGY HAS BECOME A
matter of concern to those who question the utilitarian basis for such
movements. Has theology succumbed totally to the prevailing
winds of *praxis,* where movements write their conceptual basis for
existence as revolutionary manifestos meant to justify as much as
to compel? Or, to put it another way, does a political theology or a
black theology appropriate revelation to a concrete situation in
such a way that the immediate occasion becomes the authoritative
"text"? Has theology virtually become hermeneutics—where
self-understanding incorporates the data of revelation into one's
own experience and action? At the core of these questions is a
concern that the center of gravity has shifted from revelation as
determinative of truth in action, to action as determinative of truth
in revelation.

Yet, does one want to return to the concept of "pure" theology
as distinguished from "applied" theology, a dichotomy which
continues to plague the curriculum of theological education in
the guise of "practical" theology? To take another approach
in questioning—Can the Church tolerate the separation of the
theoretical task from the concrete situation of its own existence?
Will theologians be permitted to do their work in cool *absentia*
while pastors sweat out their existence in the steamy space of the
Church in the world? Does theological training end where practice
begins?

Obviously, these questions prejudice the case by exaggerating
the options. However, the point has been made. In too many cases,

*Portions of this essay were published previously as, "Producing Doctors
for the Church" in *Theology, News, and Notes* (October, 1977), pp. 3-4.

the seminary graduate considers his theoretical task to be finished and his education for ministry to take place through the relentless and unforgiving demands of feeding, healing, and, above all, pleasing the sheep. The danger in this is twofold: First of all, when theological thinking is practiced in abstraction from the Church in ministry, it inevitably becomes as much unapplied and irrelevant as pure. Secondly, when the theological mind of the minister is being educated primarily through experience, an *ad hoc* theology emerges which owes as much (or more) to methodological and pragmatic concerns as to dogma. The task of working out a theology for ministry begins properly with the task of identifying the nature and place of ministry itself.

A. THE NATURE OF MINISTRY

One fundamental thesis will control this discussion—the thesis that ministry precedes and produces theology, not the reverse. It must immediately be added, however, that ministry is determined and set forth by God's own ministry of revelation and reconciliation in the world, beginning with Israel and culminating in Jesus Christ and the Church.

All ministry is God's ministry. Jesus did not come to introduce his own ministry. His ministry was to do the will of the Father and to live by every Word that proceeds out of the mouth of God. God's initial act, and every subsequent act of revelation, is a ministry of reconciliation. Out of this ministry emerges theological activity, exploring and expounding the nature and purpose of God in and for creation and human creatures. Theology, thus, serves as the handmaid of ministry, proclaiming it as God's ministry and making known the eternal being of God. This knowledge of God, as Calvin reminds us in the opening paragraphs of his *Institutes,* leads us to a knowledge of ourselves. We cannot contemplate the nature of God in his revelation without contemplating our own nature and purpose.

Ministry cannot be construed solely as the practical application (or technique) which makes theological knowledge relevant and effective. Theological activity must emerge out of ministry and for the sake of ministry if it is to be in accordance with the divine modality. The "practice" of ministry, then, is not only the appropriate context for doing theological thinking, it is itself intrinsically a theological activity.

To say that all ministry is God's ministry is to suggest that ministry precedes and determines the Church. The on-going ministry of Jesus Christ gives both content and direction to the Church in its ministry. Jesus is the minister *par excellence*. He ministers to the Father for the sake of the world, taking the things of God and disclosing them faithfully to sinners, and taking sinners to himself and binding them graciously into his own Sonship to the Father. This ministry is as extensive as it is intensive. As the eternal Word which goes forth from the Father, Jesus continually discloses the depths of divine being as purposeful and loving in its relationship to the creature. This ministry continues through the inspired witness of the apostles, whose own ministry is foundational for this very reason. Thus, God's ministry becomes the dogma from which all insight into the nature and strategy of ministry issues and to which the Church must return in every generation to test its own concept of ministry.

The Church has no existence apart from being called into being through this ministry and equipped for it by the gift of the Holy Spirit. For the Church to seek a ministry of its own is to deny Christ's ministry and to turn aside to spurious activities which can never justify its own existence or redeem the world. Consequently, unless ministry takes a purely pragmatic turn, it is necessarily led to the theological activity of exploring the dogma of divine revelation which is given to us as the Word of God in Holy Scripture. This theological activity will be both exegetical and experiential.

The Holy Spirit unites the doing of ministry to the ministry which has already been accomplished in Christ, establishing a reciprocity between dogma and experience which continually discloses and disciplines. There is disclosed to the Church the nature of ministry in the context of its own situation. There are different ministries even as there are different gifts to the Church, but all ministries are forms of Christ's ministry, even as all gifts of the Spirit come from one Spirit. The experiential component in ministry is necessary to identify and confirm gifts for ministry.

As Christ's own ministry is unfolded and proclaimed, the Church discovers its own ministry, and its members their own particular ministry. Christ continually discloses his ministry in concrete situations. This disclosure is the source of all true innovation and creativity in ministry. Thus, dogma does not stifle but stimulates creativity.

Christ's primary ministry is to the Father for the sake of the world, not to the world for the sake of the Father. This means that the world does not set the agenda for ministry, but the Father, who loves the world and seeks its good, sets this agenda. This Christological, and actually Trinitarian, basis for ministry rules out both utilitarianism, which tends to create ministry out of needs, and pragmatism, which transforms ministry into marketing strategy. It links the Church and the theological seminary in a mutual commitment to learning and healing. For God's ministry is at once revealing and reconciling with respect to the world.

B. MINISTRY AS REVELATION AND RECONCILIATION

It is common in contemporary theology for Cartesian and Kantian assumptions to demand that revelation be appropriated to the human subject. It was the distinguished French philosopher René Descartes, in the middle of the seventeenth century, who formulated the dictum—I think, therefore I am. This principle not only led to the objectification of that which was experienced outside of the mind itself, but located the only source of certainty in the subjective act of thought. As applied to theology, this principle dictated the conclusion that the objectification of God as a phenomenon of experience necessarily shifted the decision with regard to the reality of God to the human subject.

But it remained for Immanuel Kant, a century later, to cut the connection between the act of thinking and the ultimate being of that which is thought. Pure reason, said Kant, can only be extended to objects of possible experience, and can never be extended beyond the objects of sense-perception to "things in themselves." In his *Critique of Pure Reason,* Kant expounded a "rational faith" which was expressed in terms of the moral law. By placing the source of the moral law in the pure principle of reason, that is, in the noumenal realm, he made revelation inaccessible to reason, and therefore unverifiable. Kant thought that in effectively "disobjectifying" God (revelation), the reality of God would no longer be conditioned by the relativism and doubt which the Cartesian principle entailed.

This agnosticism concerning objective knowledge of God set the agenda for modern theology. Holding that a determination of the truthfulness, or objective validity, of divine revelation is impossible and yet that revelation should continue to be normative for theological discussion, modern theologians made distinctions between truth and meaningfulness and between knowledge and faith, and they viewed these distinctions as advances rather than losses for theological thought. While denying that revelation is true and can be objectively experienced (i.e., can be known), they never-theless affirmed that revelation is meaningful, that is, that it leads to coherence and authentication of the self. They viewed faith, then, simply as a means to self-understanding. Their position was really one of theological solipsism, for it referred all statements about God to the judgment of the human person.

The point in this all-too-brief excursion into philosophical theology is to establish a critical reference point for the discussion of ministry as God's ministry. Given the assumptions of a Carte-sian approach to revelation, coupled with a Kantian agnosticism concerning objective truth, it would be impossible to sustain the thesis that God's ministry is determinative for, and is the dogmatic basis for, the ministry of the Church. Rather, one would be com-pelled to assert, as do many contemporary theologies, that the ministry of the Church is determinative for God's ministry. Rec-onciliation thus becomes the dogmatic basis for revelation. The world sets the agenda for the Church, and all things become true to the extent that they are useful and actually work. Hence, utilitarianism and pragmatism become prevalent in the literature of the Church concerning its ministry in the world.

It is the objective of this essay to offer an alternative to this methodology and these conclusions, without pausing to demon-strate the fallacious and unfortunate assumptions which underlie the Cartesian paradigm as a basis for a theology of divine revela-tion.[1] The development of this alternative will properly be a dog-matic task. That is, it will require us to set forth the nature of revelation and reconciliation as God's giving of himself to us in Jesus Christ. As such, our task will be what Karl Barth calls "scientific theology." It will require us to allow the nature of reality, as it discloses itself to us, to determine our method of knowing that reality. It will necessitate our viewing the object of knowledge as free to disclose itself to us on its own terms. Thus, by subordinating or relativizing the knowing subject to that which is known, our scientific theology will present an alternative to the Cartesian paradigm. It will be the reader's responsibility to deter-mine which paradigm is more compelling.[2]

1. I have set forth a more systematic critique of Cartesian theology in *Historical Transcendence and the Reality of God* (Grand Rapids: Eerdmans, 1975), pp. 39–77. Cf. also, Helmut Thielicke, *The Evangelical Faith* (Grand Rapids: Eerdmans, 1976, 1977), Vols. I and II.
2. For a helpful discussion of an alternative to the Cartesian paradigm in the form of a more heuristic approach, one should read the article by Richard Gelwick, "Discovery and Theology," *Scottish Journal of Theol-ogy*, XXVIII, No. 4 (1975), 301–321.

Upon reading the account of God's self-disclosure through the history of salvation as given to us in Holy Scripture, it can be stated as an axiom that revelation and reconciliation are reciprocal movements of a single event. This is to assert that God reveals himself to the creature in such a way that a knowing relation is established and upheld from both sides by God. This axiom precludes the possibility that divine self-revelation occurs in such a way that it presupposes a creaturely capability and disposition to grasp it and complete it by way of a response that is not itself produced by the event of revelation. Or, to put it another way, to say that revelation produces the appropriate response on the part of the human creature is to say that man bears the image and likeness of God (Gen. 1:26–27). It is a dogmatic assertion of biblical theology that the *imago Dei* is an endowment rather than an innate disposition of the creature. Adam does not bear the divine image because he is human; he becomes human as a result of the divine fiat, portrayed as a divine inbreathing (Gen. 2:7).

If reconciliation is supposed to represent that movement by which man is conformed to the Word of God and through which man is constituted as possessing health and holiness, then it would be meaningful also to suppose that this is what is meant by ministry—the reconciling of man to God. However, in asserting axiomatically that reconciliation is reciprocal to revelation, it must be made clear that reconciliation is not a movement which originates with the fall. That is, the fundamental paradigm of revelation includes reconciliation as an original movement of response. This can be expressed more clearly in the following diagram:

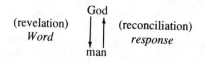

In this diagram the Word is creative of the response. As such, the Word of God is self-authenticating in its demand for recognition and response. Adam *ought* to respond because he *can* respond. Because the divine Word posits a correspondence of the creature to God in the form of a divine image and likeness, the Word reveals God in terms that are creaturely and human. The Word does not need to be appropriated by a human action; it becomes a human Word while retaining its transcendence. The human response does not condition or determine the divine Word, for the Word has itself a divine correspondence by virtue of the image of God through which Adam knows himself. This is what Calvin meant when he said that knowledge of God necessarily involves knowledge of self.

The temptation story (Gen. 3) suggests that deviation from the Word occurs when an independent criterion is adopted as a basis for making a judgment concerning the divine Word. The temptation comes in the form of a question, "Has God said?" What the question implies is that the concrete Word of God for which obedience is the proper response, is now conditioned by a verdict based on an abstract knowledge of truth to which the divine Word must correspond. In deciding to eat the forbidden fruit, a decision against the self-authenticating Word is made in favor of the universal principle which holds that the good, the true, and the beautiful can be established independently of one's experience of the divine Word. The Word, which comes through a historically and temporally conditioned event of revelation, is set aside in favor of a non-historical and timeless truth which appears to be accessible through human thought alone. The Cartesian principle of the primacy of the human mind is taken up over and against the historical Word. This act is the fall.

The fact that God does not abandon the creature who attempts to establish an autonomous existence, is a testimony to the original grace which underlies the creative act. Reconciliation, as a movement initiated by God, does not originate outside of the event of revelation itself. Because the divine Word and the human response are reciprocally related, so that one cannot be considered apart from the other, revelation and reconciliation participate in the same fundamental paradigm. Because the fallen experience is the typical experience by which all persons experience their selfhood (this too is a dogmatic assertion, though it appears also to be experientially validated), God's Word of revelation involves the ministry of reconciliation. That is, the Word is saving in its revelatory nature. This is not to deny that there is a general revelation. But, as Paul makes clear in Romans 1, a revelation of God through creation only serves as an indictment against unbelief. The Word which saves as it reveals does not presuppose a positive attitude, but a negative one, which must be overcome. To assert that the Word is revelatory without also producing reconciliation violates the fundamental paradigm. Furthermore, it tends to sustain the autonomy of the fallen self in its attempt to render a verdict over the Word itself, based on something other than the Word. It is the paradigm of revelation and reconciliation which establishes the nature of ministry as God's ministry and brings that ministry as both an act of judgment and grace to the human situation.

C. MINISTRY AS JUDGMENT AND GRACE

We have established the postulate that all ministry is God's ministry, for the Word of revelation is always a creation *ex nihilo*. The Word of God which goes forth to create, brings into being that which *is* from that which *is not* (Heb. 11:3). The creative Word does not presuppose existing substance or capability outside of itself. In the divine fiat, "Let there be," there is the implied negation of all that would seek to exist outside this Word. What then comes into existence rests solely upon the creative and sustaining Word. Herein is both the grace and judgment of the Word.

Out of his freedom, God moves to create. This is his grace—to bring into being what had no possibility of being, that is, to make possibility out of impossibility. But this grace militates against any encroachment upon God's freedom. For the creature to assert a possibility based upon some creaturely or created nature, independently of this Word, would cause it to come into opposition to and under judgment of the Word. To assert that ministry is both a Word of judgment and grace, then, is to follow faithfully this paradigm and to assess critically every motivation toward ministry which seeks some possibility outside of the revealing and reconciling Word.

The original possibility of a human response to the divine Word is posited by the Word itself. In the creation narrative (Gen. 1–2), the human creature emerges as a result of a divine initiative which bestows an image or likeness of the divine Word itself (Gen. 1:26–27). While other creatures are created "after their own kind," the first man, Adam, knows himself only as he knows the Creator and responds to him. There is no humanity of a creaturely sort which has the "choice" of responding to the divine Word. The very response, which can be considered to be reflexive in nature, is itself the endowment of humanity. Adam speaks with God because he is human, and he is human because he speaks with God. To this extent, Adam's humanity is self-authenticating. It is not as though an independent criterion exists by which Adam can verify his humanity in terms of likeness to God. Adam is free to know himself for what he is as he knows himself in relation to God the Creator. The dignity which he possesses, which marks him off from all other creatures, is an alien dignity. It is a dignity which has its antecedent in something other than a creaturely nature, though it can only be known and experienced as a creaturely nature.

In the second creation narrative (Gen. 2), the human creature is presented as a solitary being—the male. Despite the fact that the Creator provides a supportive environment and a meaningful task, the verdict of God himself is that "it is not good for the man to be alone." But then it is as though some possibility is sought within creatureliness to fill this void. God creates and brings the other creatures to Adam, one by one, so that he can name them. Certainly, in this act of naming there is also implied a search on the part of Adam for a counterpart to his own being. And yet, not even the Creator himself could find a suitable counterpart within the possibilities of existing creation. It is as though at the very outset we are warned against an overly optimistic reliance upon some technique or some technician which could intensify or alter existing creaturely being so that it could fulfill and complete itself. God, as the master technician, is unable to find sufficient possibilities within the creature for the human self to complete itself. It is only when the single male is put to sleep and the creative Word itself operates in such a way that the divine likeness and endowment is divided into a complementary existence, that that possibility is actualized. Out of impossibility, God's Word becomes God's ministry. Adam responds, "At last, this is bone of my bone and flesh of my flesh." This grace of God is a verdict rendered upon every attempt to circumvent that Word and to provide an alternative response. It is revelation that provides the reconciliation. God's ministry takes what is impossible and creates possibility. But it does this in such a way that the creature himself is incorporated into the new possibility. It is "bone of my bone and flesh of my flesh." Adam is not himself set aside. There is no judgment against him, but a judgment for him and against all that would only inevitably betray and fail him.

This fundamental paradigm is reiterated in the event of Abraham. There is no hint given as to how Abraham verifies the divine summons which leads him to leave his kindred and homeland for a land which is unknown to him (Heb. 11:8). Because this paradigm suggests that the Word of God is self-authenticating, one suspects that he hears and obeys the Word because it is the Word of God. Implicit in this Word is a judgment against all the questions which could be raised in hopes of verifying the Word on some basis independent of the Word itself.

But there is more. To Abraham and Sarah the promise is given that through their heir a blessing will come upon them and upon all nations (Gen. 12:1-4; 15:1-6; 17:1-8). However, it is seemingly impossible for this promise to be fulfilled. Sarah is not only barren, but she is past the age of bearing children. Yet, Abraham and

Sarah believe the promise and attempt to appropriate it to their situation, that is, to understand it as meaningful and attempt to live by it. It seems reasonable to Abraham that the means by which the promise could be effected would legitimately take into account the human possibilities. Thus, Abraham views the opportunity to have an heir of his own loins through the servant-maid, Hagar, as a means of acting in obedience, given the imperative of the revelation itself. So, from the union of Abraham and Hagar, Ishmael is born, and for thirteen years Abraham lives with assurance that the promise is being fulfilled and that the Word is completed by this response.

However, the Word of the Lord again comes to Abraham, saying that his wife Sarah, who by this time is ninety years old, will conceive a child who will be the true heir of the promise. To Abraham, this is incredible and unnecessary. For thirteen years, Abraham has taught Ishmael that he is the answer to the promise, the heir that can fulfill God's Word. "O that Ishmael might live before thee!" cries Abraham. But the response is "No, but Sarah your wife shall bear you a son..." (Gen. 17:18,19). All that Ishmael has been taught must now be untaught. The Word of grace that will enable Sarah to conceive supernaturally is also a judgment against the natural possibility. Isaac is the son of promise and the divinely provided response to the Word itself. True enough, Abraham and Sarah must come together in an act of human love in order that the child be conceived, and Sarah must carry and nourish the child in her own womb. But this only establishes again the truth that the divine Word is not a judgment against the creature, but against that presumption of the creature which will inevitably lead to failure. The human act is given a place in the new creation of God and thereby finds the completion of its own authentic being.

Israel herself becomes the historical paradigm for this truth. In her election to be the people of God, the Word which reveals is also the Word which reconciles—but it is a Word of both judgment and grace. For the sake of the covenant which Jahweh has established, there is a judgment against the presumption by which a human possibility is viewed as a means to the fulfillment of Israel's goal. Again and again, the strategy of survival which depends upon military alliances, cultural assimilation, and religious syncretism is disowned by God. Israel is the chosen one who must suffer and die, in order that she might be created anew and given a response to the Word which will not fail. The remnant will come as a "root out of dry ground," and as a green shoot from the stump of the tree. The barrenness of Israel must be demonstrated in order that the promise may be shown to rest upon divine aid. God's ministry of reconciliation comes as a judgment against everything that would condition this divine Word.

From creation *ex nihilo,* from the barren womb of Sarah, and from the impotency of Israel, the paradigm moves through the virgin womb of Mary and the grave of Jesus, where it reaches its final utterance in the resurrection. The miracle of the virgin birth is a judgment against the possibility of the creature producing its own word of revelation and reconciliation. For Jesus himself, the argument rages. "Take this cup from me," says Jesus, but only if it is thy will. Implicit in this prayer is the plea—Cannot my Ishmael live before you? Is not there sufficient reason in all of my good works to warrant a verdict of righteousness? But the answer is the same—No, for this purpose I have come to this hour (John 12:27). There can be no resurrection without a death. God's ministry of reconciliation brings a judgment against the possibility of a creaturely response that can complete the Word of revelation. When Jesus stands outside of his own tomb on Easter morning, there is only discontinuity with that which stood against the Word. Continuity is maintained with all that he was, is, and shall be. His new humanity does not disannul the original humanity, but completes it.

The Sabbath of God is a summons and permission for the creature who is elected by God to stand free of the tyranny of the sixth day. In the sixth day, nature determines destiny, and what is becomes the verification of what shall be. Bound up in the "solidarity of the sixth day" (a fine phrase of Thielicke's), the human person experiences the Word of God as a liberating Word. It is a Word which gives permission to escape the determinism of the sixth day, of nature alone, and to receive a new destiny, that of eternal fellowship with the Creator. In bringing this Sabbath to its completion, Jesus, through his resurrection from the dead, provides the hermeneutical paradigm for all understanding of divine revelation. To seek to appropriate divine revelation to the understanding and situation of the creature is hopelessly to imprison it within the determinism of the sixth day and to subject it to futility. It is against this fatal tendency toward appropriation of the revealed Word that Helmut Thielicke inveighs (Chapter 3). For in the act of appropriating revelation to the self-understanding of the human creature, the revelation is not only altered in its content and character, but is stripped of its reconciling power. The act of appropriation as an epistemological movement, incorporates revelation into a human situation and then seeks to render a verdict upon it from a finite, creaturely perspective. This act, as Thielicke points out, is Cartesian in form, whether it takes place as a rationalist or existentialist movement. The moment that revelation is only a possibility which must be actualized by the believing subject, the believer is left without an objective basis for a life of faith. While Ishmael seems more objective to Abraham than the Word, which still insists upon its own incarnation on its own terms, the child is hopelessly subjective with respect to the divine Word itself. Ishmael is not the ministry of God, and therefore cannot be the revelation of God. What the Word produces becomes the actuality which verifies what the Word says. Isaac is God's actuality, and therefore becomes Abraham's possibility. Thus, Isaac can never really betray Abraham in being subject to the inevitable threat of death. In being received supernaturally from a barren womb, he can be received again from the dead (Heb. 11:19). Because Abraham's faith has already taken into account a human impossibility, Abraham does not stagger in unbelief at the seeming impossibility of offering Isaac as a sacrifice. The Word of God is not only self-authenticating, it is self-actualizing. It brings into being what it demands.

D. MINISTRY AS ACTUALITY AND POSSIBILITY

It ought to be clear at this point that to introduce a creaturely and human possibility as the basis on which the Word of God can actually be heard and obeyed, is to violate the fundamental paradigm of revelation and reconciliation itself. The implications of this fact for a theology of ministry ought also to be quite obvious. If ministry is viewed as the actualizing of the possibilities which exist because the gospel reveals to us a new order of being, it will inevitably flounder in the shallow waters of its own impotence. But ministry, as our thesis originally stated, precedes and determines not only theological reflection but the very existence and life of the Church.

To elaborate upon this thesis is to enlarge the scope of Christology as a discipline of theological reflection. A Christological perspective of ministry is that of ministry which has been accomplished and which continues to be accomplished through the Holy Spirit, who indwells and actualizes the life of the Church. To say that actuality precedes possibility, is to say that God has actually given and upheld both sides of the ministry of the Word.

Through the incarnation of the divine Logos (John 1:14), the ministry of bringing the Word of God to human creatures was accomplished as well as the bringing of the human creature into conformity with that Word. In his ministry of revealing the Word, Jesus stands among us as the God who is for man. He discloses the depth of divine love and grace in terms that are fully accessible to finite, human creatures. To know Jesus is to be confronted with the reality of God himself. This fact was the concern of the fourth-century doctrine of the *homoousion* as argued against the Arians, who denied the essential deity of the incarnate Logos. To confess anything less than that Jesus of Nazareth is of the same essence as the Father, with respect to his deity, is to deny the actuality of revelation as a divine Word which stands on the creaturely side with us. The concern of Arius was to make the divine Logos more understandable from the perspective of created rationality, but as the orthodox theologians at Nicea clearly saw, this concern betrayed Christian faith at its very core by substituting a possibility for an actuality, with respect to the saving effect of the Word. A divine revelation which awaits appropriation to a contemporary world-view or metaphysical structure of reality, achieves recognition and acceptance at the cost of sacrificing its objective and transcendent content.

In bringing the Word fully into human flesh, the incarnation unites the finite and creaturely with the infinite and uncreated reality of God himself. That is, revelation does not exist between God and man as an abstract entity which is something else than either God or man, but exists as God himself exists—personally and concretely in relation with man. The possibility of knowing and expressing the Word of God in human thought-forms and in historical events follows upon the actuality of that event in the incarnate life of Jesus. The fact that the incarnate Word inevitably acquires a human language and culture may be considered by some to be an embarrassment and limitation for that Word. But those who follow this line of thinking will only be confronted by the embarrassment and limitation of being unable to grasp a divine revelation which has been stripped of its humanity and temporality. The ministry of proclamation, for example, will be radically determined by how one understands the incarnation. If the Word of God stands only as an abstract or existential possibility, separated from the historical context in which it originally came, then the ministry of proclamation will have no dogmatic basis for its content. Scripture will necessarily be appropriated to the latest style of cultural interpretation and hermeneutics; the act of making meaningful will itself be the primary source for revelation. Proclamation will seek to actualize all possibilities in hope of producing an event of revelation.

On the other hand, for those who take the incarnation seriously, proclamation has already occurred in the Word made flesh. All subsequent proclamation has its possibility based on this actuality. The event of revelation does not rest upon the inspiredness of the proclaimer or the existential moment for the hearer, but exists in human language and historical event as the dogma of Jesus Christ incarnate. As Karl Barth so well put it, "It is not He that needs proclamation, but proclamation that needs Him."[3] If the hermeneutical task be that of ascertaining the meaning of that which is revealed, then one could say that revelation has incorporated (appropriated) the human situation into its own occurrence as historical event. Revelation is not just the Word of God to Abraham; it *is* Abraham. As Abraham becomes drawn into the sphere of the Word, no distinction can be made between the Word of God which came to Abraham, and Abraham's history as a history of that Word. Thus the written record of this history is revelatory precisely because it is revelation's history.

Surely this is what it means to say that the Holy Spirit will take the things of Christ and make them known to us (John 16:13-14). As a theological discipline, the hermeneutical task of the Church is to continue to search out and seek to be conformed to the hermeneutical structure of revelation itself, as given in Holy Scripture. Thus, the ministry of the Church necessarily involves theological reflection and a correction of its own inevitable tendencies to create ministry for its own justification.

But if actuality can be asserted concerning revelation as a Word of God for man, what of reconciliation as response to that Word? Here too, a Christological understanding of ministry is helpful. Not only is Jesus the God who is for man, but he is also the Man who is for God. Not only is he the one who brings the Word and bears the Word fully in his own humanity, but he is also one who bears the Word and faithfully lives in obedience to it. At every point he is tempted, such as we are (Heb. 4:15), but he steadfastly lives by every Word that proceeds from the mouth of God (Matt. 4:4). With regard to a human will disinclined to conform to the will of God, Jesus bends that will back into conformity to the divine will at every point. Coming not to destroy the law, but to fulfill it, he completes all of the demands of the divine Word through his life of obedience and faith. Being conceived of the

3. *Church Dogmatics,* IV/1 (Naperville: Allenson, 1969), p. 227.

Spirit in the virgin and anointed by the Spirit at his baptism, he sanctifies the humanity which he assumes as his own and creates the actual sanctification of that humanity through his atoning death and resurrection.

The good news which he announces is based on his own self-testimony as the faithful servant of Jahweh. His gospel invitation—"Come unto me"—is no burden to be applied to weak humanity and no yoke to be thrown on the necks of struggling disciples, but rather is an offer to assume his burden and his yoke. It is easy because he actually has borne it and continues to bear it.

In preaching the gospel of the kingdom, Jesus opens up his own life of fellowship with the Father, as the avenue upon which the weary, the crippled, the blind, and sinners can walk in grace and glory. He breaks down partitions between races and ideologies and creates new bonds of fellowship for old enemies. Through him the reconciliation of the world to God actually occurs (II Cor. 5:19). The ministry of reconciliation given to the Church has its possibility firmly rooted in this actuality. Otherwise, it would be a cruel hoax.

Thus God upholds the event of revelation from both sides. The ministry of disclosing the Word to the world is upheld by the reality of the incarnate presence of Christ in the world. All exegetical, hermeneutical, and homiletical work as the proper theological activity of the Church, is supported and made possible by this incarnation. The ministry of reconciling the world to this Word of revelation is upheld by Jesus' incarnate life of obedience and faithful response to this Word. All of the healing, teaching, and saving ministry of the Church is supported and made possible by this incarnation.

In this way it can be said that ministry precedes and creates the Church. All ministry is Christ's ministry of faithfulness to the Father on behalf of the world. The sending of the Holy Spirit continues this ministry; it does not constitute the creation of another ministry (John 16:7-15). To the extent that the Church understands this ministry of God, it will understand its own existence and ministry in the world.

Every Ishmael struggles for recognition, however. And in a sense, as long as Ishmael stands before us, we will have difficulty hearing and believing the Word of God. "The discovery of truth," said John Macmurray, "must be from the subjective side a process of disillusionment. . . . We all confess to the desire to get at the truth, but in practice the desire for truth is the desire to be disillusioned.''[4] Illusions die hard. Theological illusions have the strongest resistance.

Every pragmatic principle of ministry must be subjected to the critical dogmatic test: Has it gone through the death and resurrection process? Have we allowed the ministry as such to reveal to us its impossibility before we have assumed its possibility? Does the Church understand that it only exists because of Christ's ministry? Does Christ's ministry continue to exist in our ministry as both the presupposition and the goal?

This essay bears the title, ''A Theology for Ministry''; perhaps it should be retitled, ''Toward a Theology for Ministry.'' For at best, only an attempt has been made to point the way toward the development of such a theology. The chapters which immediately follow may be viewed as the ''unteaching of Ishmael,'' for they focus upon the place of theology and the nature of revelation as a Word of God to man and the response of man to that Word. It is always the task of the Church, admonished Barth, to give account of its theology in light of the contemporary situation and the dogma of Christ's ministry of reconciliation. Who better is prepared to do that, and who can less afford to ignore that task, than those who are ministers of the gospel of Christ?

4. *Reason and Emotion* (London: Faber and Faber, 1935), p. 22.

2

KARL BARTH

The Place of Theology

THEOLOGY IS ONE AMONG THOSE HUMAN UNDERTAKINGS TRADI-
tionally described as "sciences." Not only the natural sciences are
"sciences." Humanistic sciences also seek to apprehend a specific
object and its environment in the manner *directed* by the phenomenon itself; they seek to understand it on its own terms and to speak
of it along with all the implications of its *existence*. The word
"theology" seems to signify a special science, a very special
science, whose task is to apprehend, understand, and speak of
"God."

But many things can be meant by the word "God." For this
reason, there are many kinds of theologies. There is no man who
does not have his own god or gods as the object of his highest
desire and trust, or as the basis of his deepest loyalty and commitment. There is no one who is not to this extent also a theologian.
There is, moreover, no religion, no philosophy, no world view that
is not dedicated to some such divinity. Every world view, even
that disclosed in the Swiss and American national anthems, presupposes a divinity interpreted in one way or another and wor-
shiped to some degree, whether wholeheartedly or superficially.
There is no philosophy that is not to some extent also theology.
Not only does this fact apply to philosophers who desire to
affirm—or who, at least, are ready to admit—that divinity, in a
positive sense, is the essence of truth and power of some kind of
highest principle; but the same truth is valid even for thinkers
denying such a divinity, for such a denial would in practice merely
consist in transferring an identical dignity and function to another

object. Such an alternative object might be "nature," creativity, or an unconscious and amorphous will to life. It might also be "reason," progress, or even a redeeming nothingness into which man would be destined to disappear. Even such apparently "godless" ideologies are theologies.

The purpose of these remarks is not to introduce the world of these many theologies with their many gods. We will not compare them historically or offer critical conjectures regarding them. No position will be taken on behalf of one against all the others, nor will the others be subordinated and related to this one. There is no apparent reason why these many theologies should have anything essential in common with that which we want to discuss under the title "theology"; nor is it clear how we could fruitfully set them in relation to our task. Among themselves they have one thing in common, something that immediately casts a significant light on the gods to which they are dedicated. Each one of them considers and represents itself as the best theology because, even should it not be the only right one, it claims to be still more right than the others. From the very beginning, as the fable of the three rings suggests, we should beware of participating in this competition. In one of his plays the German poet Lessing compares the claims of the Jewish, Mohammedan, and Christian religions to the claims of three brothers. Each one of them had received a precious ring from the hands of their dying father. Each claimed to have received his father's one and only precious ring, rather than an exact copy of it. The warning contained in this fable is obvious, even if we do not choose to follow Lessing's opinion that perhaps the genuine ring was lost and nothing else but imitations were left in the brothers' hands. The best theology (not to speak of the only right one) of the highest, or even the exclusively true and real, God would have the following distinction: it would *prove* itself—and in this regard Lessing was altogether right—by the demonstration of the Spirit and of its power. However, if it should hail and proclaim *itself* as such, it would by this very fact betray that it certainly is *not* the one true theology.

For this reason we will dispense with any comparison or evaluation that would separate or synthesize various theologies. Instead, let this simple pointer suffice: the theology to be introduced here is *evangelical* theology. The qualifying attribute "evangelical" recalls both the New Testament and at the same time the Reformation of the sixteenth century. Therefore, it may be taken as a dual affirmation: the theology to be considered here is the one which, nourished by the hidden sources of the documents of Israel's history, first achieved unambiguous expression in the writings of the New Testament evangelists, apostles, and prophets; it is also, moreover, the theology newly discovered and accepted by the Reformation of the sixteenth century. The expression "evangelical," however, cannot and should not be intended and understood in a confessional, that is, in a denominational and exclusive, sense. This is forbidden first of all by the elementary fact that "evangelical" refers primarily and decisively to the Bible, which is in some way respected by all confessions. Not all so-called "Protestant" theology is evangelical theology; moreover, there is also evangelical theology in the Roman Catholic and Eastern orthodox worlds, as well as in the many later variations, including deteriorations, of the Reformation departure. What the word "evangelical" will objectively designate is that theology which treats of the *God of the Gospel*. "Evangelical" signifies the "catholic," ecumenical (not to say "conciliar") *continuity and unity* of this theology. Such theology intends to apprehend, to understand, and to speak of the God of the Gospel, in the midst of the variety of all other theologies and (without any value-judgment being implied) in distinction from them. This is the God who reveals himself in the Gospel, who himself speaks to men and acts among and upon them. Wherever he becomes the object of human science, both its source and its norm, there is *evangelical* theology.

Let us now attempt to describe evangelical theology. An account of its most important characteristics will serve as a prelude to clarify the uniqueness which it derives from its object. Among these characteristics there is none that, *mutatis mutandis*, presupposing the requisite changes, could not and would not have to be the characteristic of other sciences as well. Although we will not expand upon this observation here, we will indicate the extent to which these general characteristics are specific characteristics of *theological* science.

In the first place, it was not Lessing who originally forbade evangelical theology to award itself the prize in comparison with other theologies or, what is more, to pass itself off in any one of its forms as divine wisdom and doctrine. For the very reason that it is devoted to the God who proclaims himself in the Gospel, evangelical theology cannot claim for itself that authority which belongs to him alone. The God of the Gospel is the God who mercifully dedicates and delivers himself to the life of all men—including their theologies. Nevertheless, he *transcends* not only the undertakings of all other men but also the enterprise of evangelical theologians. He is the God who again and again discloses himself anew and must be discovered anew, the God over whom theology neither has nor receives sovereignty. The separation and distinction of this one true God from all the others can only be continually his own deed. This deed cannot be reduplicated by any human science, not even by a theology which is dedicated explicitly to him alone. Even in this basic consideration he is, without doubt, a God wholly different from other gods. Other gods do not seem to prohibit their theologies from boasting that each one is the most correct or even the only correct theology. On the contrary, such gods even seem to urge their respective theologians to engage in such boasting. Evangelical theology, on the other hand, no doubt can and should base its thought and speech on the decision and deed by which God lets his honor pale all other gods; however, it would definitely *not* think and speak about such acts if, by this, it wished to win renown for itself according to the example of other theologies. For better or for worse, it must set forth and proceed along its own way, a way which is fundamentally and totally different from that of other theologies. All the same, evangelical theology must not lose patience when it is viewed and understood in the same categories as those others. It must even tolerate being compared and seen in relationship to them under the rubric "philosophy of religion" (though let me warn you that, for its part, it cannot join in this attempt). It can expect justice for itself only by the fact that God justifies it. It can give only him and not itself the glory. Evangelical theology is *modest* theology, because it is determined to be so by its object, that is, by him who is its subject.

In the second place, there are three subordinate presuppositions with which evangelical theology works. The first is the general event of human *existence* in its insoluble dialectic, which theology sees confronted by the self-proclamation of God in the Gospel. Secondly, there is the particular *faith* of those men who not only are allowed but are also ready and willing to acknowledge God's self-proclamation. They know and confess for all people and specifically for his chosen witnesses that God authenticates himself. Thirdly, there is the general and the particular presupposition of *reason,* the capacity for perception, judgment, and language common to believers as well as to all men. It is this capacity that makes it technically possible for them to participate actively in the theological pursuit of knowledge, an endeavor directed to the God who proclaims himself in the Gospel. However, this does not mean that theology would be ordered, much less even allowed, to choose for its object and theme—in place of God—human existence or faith or man's spiritual capacity (even if this should include a special religious capacity, a "religious a priori"). Such topics—if made dominant—would render homage to theology's unique theme only subsequently and incidentally. They could not avoid also arousing the suspicion that "God" might be, after all, only a mode of speaking, comparable to the symbolic role of the King of England. Theology is well aware that the God of the Gospel has a genuine interest in human existence and, in fact, awakens and calls man to faith in him; it knows that in this way God claims and arouses man's entire spiritual capacity, more, in fact, than his spiritual capacity. But theology is interested in all this because it is primarily and comprehensively interested in God himself. The dominant presupposition of its thought and speech is *God's* own proof of his existence and sovereignty. If theology wished to reverse this relationship, and instead of relating man to *God*, related God to *man,* then it would surrender itself to a new Babylonian captivity. It would become the prisoner of some sort of anthropology or ontology that is an underlying interpretation of existence, of faith, or of man's spiritual capacity. Evangelical theology is neither compelled nor commissioned to embrace such an undertaking. It bides its time and confidently lets things take their course, whatever the way in which existence, faith, the spiritual capacity of man, his selfhood, and self-understanding may present themselves in confrontation with the God of the Gospel who precedes them all. With respect to those subordinate presuppositions, theology is, for all its modesty, in an exemplary way a *free* science. This means it is a science which joyfully respects the mystery of the freedom of its object and which, in turn, is again and again freed by its object from any dependence on subordinate presuppositions.

In the third place, the object of evangelical theology is God in the *history* of his *deeds.* In this history he makes himself *known.* But in it he also *is* who he is. In it he has and proves, in a unity which precludes the precedence of one over the other, both his existence and his essence. The God of the Gospel, therefore, is neither a thing, an item, an object like others, nor an idea, a principle, a truth, or a sum of truths. God can be called the truth only when "truth" is understood in the sense of the Greek word *aletheia.* God's being, or truth, is the event of his self-disclosure, his radiance as the Lord of all lords, the hallowing of his name, the coming of his kingdom, the fulfillment of his will in all his work. The sum of the truths about God is to be found in a sequence of events, even in all the events of his being glorious in his work.

These events, although they are distinct from one another, must not be bracketed and considered in isolation.

Let it be noted that evangelical theology should neither repeat, re-enact, nor anticipate the history in which God is what he is. Theology cannot make out of this history a work of its own to be set in motion by itself. Theology must, of course, give an account of this history by presenting and discussing human perceptions, concepts, and formulations of human language. But it does this appropriately only when it *follows* the living God in those unfolding historical events in which he is God. Therefore, in its perception, meditation, and discussion, theology must have the character of a living *procession*. Evangelical theology would forfeit its object, it would belie and negate itself, if it wished to view, to understand, and to describe any one moment of the divine procession in "splendid isolation" from others. Instead, theology must describe the dynamic interrelationships which make this procession comparable to a bird in flight, in contrast to a caged bird. Theology would forfeit its object if it should cease to recount the "mighty works of God," if it should transfer its interest instead to the examination of a material God or merely godly matters. Regardless of what the gods of other theologies may do, the God of the Gospel rejects any connection with a theology that has become paralyzed and static. Evangelical theology can only exist and remain in vigorous motion when its eyes are fixed on the God of the Gospel. Again and again it must distinguish between what God made happen and will make happen, between the old and the new, without despising the one or fearing the other. It must clearly discern the yesterday, today, and tomorrow of its own presence and action, without losing sight of the unity. It is just from this point of view that evangelical theology is an eminently *critical* science, for it is continually exposed to judgment and never relieved of the crisis in which it is placed by its object, or, rather to say, by its living subject.

In the fourth place, the God of the Gospel is no lonely God, self-sufficient and self-contained. He is no "absolute" God (in the original sense of absolute, i.e., being detached from everything that is not himself). To be sure, he has no equal beside himself, since an equal would no doubt limit, influence, and determine him. On the other hand, he is not imprisoned by his own majesty, as though he were bound to be no more than the personal (or impersonal) "wholly other." By definition, the God of Schleiermacher cannot show mercy. The God of the Gospel can and does. Just as his oneness consists in the unity of his life as Father, Son, and Holy Spirit, so in relation to the reality distinct from him he is free *de jure* and *de facto* to be the God of *man*. He exists neither *next to* man nor merely *above* him, but rather *with* him, *by* him and, most important of all, *for* him. He is *man's* God not only as Lord but also as father, brother, friend; and this relationship implies neither a diminution nor in any way a denial, but, instead, a confirmation and display of his divine essence itself. "I dwell in the high and holy place, and also with him who is of a contrite and humble spirit, . . ." (Isaiah 57:15). This he does in the history of his deeds. A God who confronted man simply as exalted, distant, and strange, that is, a divinity without humanity, could only be the God of a *dysangelion,* of a "bad news" instead of the "good news." He would be the God of a scornful, judging, deadly *No*. Even if he were still able to command the attention of man, he would be a God whom man would have to avoid, from whom he would have to flee if he were able to flee, whom he would rather not know, since he would not in the least be able to satisfy his demands. Such a god might be embodied in deified "progress," or even more likely by the progressive man.

Many other theologies may be concerned with such exalted, superhuman, and inhuman gods, who can only be the gods of every sort of bad news, or *dysangelion*. But the God who is the object of evangelical theology is just as lowly as he is exalted. He is exalted precisely in his lowliness. And so his inevitable No is enclosed in his primary Yes to man. In this way, what God wills for man is a helpful, healing, and uplifting work, and what he does with him brings peace and joy. Because of this he is really the God of the *euangelion*, the Evangel, the Word that is good for man because it is gracious. With its efforts, evangelical theology responds to this gracious Yes, to God's self-proclamation made in his friendliness toward man. It is concerned with God as the God of *man*, but just for this reason, also with man as *God's* man. In evangelical theology, man is absolutely not, as Nietzsche has put it, "something that must be overcome." On the contrary, for evangelical theology, man is that creature destined by God to be a conqueror. Strictly speaking, therefore, the word "theology" fails to exhaust the meaning of "evangelical theology," for one decisive dimension of the object of theology is not expressed clearly by it. This dimension is the free love of God that evokes the response of free love, his grace (*charis*) that calls for gratitude (*eucharistia*). "Theoanthropology" would probably express better who and what is at stake here, with the provision that this should never be confused with "anthropotheology." Let us stick, therefore, to "theology," as long as we do not forget that this theology is "evangelical" in the special sense we have just discussed. Since it is "evangelical," it can by no means be devoted to an inhuman God, for in that case it would become *legalistic* theology. Evangelical theology is concerned with Immanuel, God with us! Having this God for its object, it can be nothing else but the most thankful and *happy* science!

I would like to forgo any special explanation of the word "introduction," which appears in the title of this work. At the same time, I wish to refrain from any discussion (which would be both polemic and irenic) of the manner in which a similar task has been conceived and carried out by Schleiermacher, as a "Short Presentation of Theological Study," and by various others, as a "Theological Encyclopedia." Whether and to what extent an *introduction* to evangelical theology is offered here may become clear during the process by which I attempt to present it.

In this and the next three lectures we will undertake to determine the special *place* of that theology which, according to our previous explanation, desires to be evangelical theology. What concerns us is not the place, right, and possibility of theology within the domain and limits of general culture; especially not within the boundaries of the *universitas litterarum*, or what is otherwise known as general humanistic studies! Ever since the fading of its illusory splendor as a leading academic power during the Middle Ages, theology has taken too many pains to justify its own existence. It has tried too hard, especially in the nineteenth century, to secure for itself at least a small but honorable place in the throne room of general science. This attempt at self-justification has been no help to its own work. The fact is that it has made theology, to a great extent, hesitant and halfhearted; moreover, this uncertainty has earned theology no more respect for its achievements than a very modest tip of the hat. Strange to say, the surrounding world only recommended to take notice of theology in earnest (though rather morosely) when it again undertook to consider and concentrate more strongly upon its own affairs. Theology had first to renounce all apologetics or external guarantees of its position within the environment of other sciences, for it will always stand on the firmest ground when it simply *acts* according to the law of its own being. It will follow this law without lengthy explanations and excuses. Even today, theology has by no means done this vigorously and untiringly enough. On the other hand, what are "culture" and "general science," after all? Have these concepts not become strangely unstable within the last fifty years? At any rate, are they not too beset by problems for us at present to be guided by them? All the same, we should certainly not disdain reflecting on what the rest of the academic world actually must think of theology. It is worth considering the place of theology within the university; discussion may be held about the reason and justification for locating this modest, free, critical, and happy science *sui generis* in such an environment. But for the present moment, this question may be considered secondary. Compared to it, other questions are much more pressing. Who knows whether the answer to such secondary questions might not be reserved for the third millennium, when a new light may perhaps be cast on theology and its academic *ambiance?*

The "place" of theology, as understood here, will be determined by the impetus which it receives from within its own domain and from its own *object*. Its object—the philanthropic God Himself—is the law which must be the continual starting point of theology. It is, as the military might say, the post that the theologian must take and keep, whether or not it suits him or any of his fellow creatures. The theologian has to hold this post at all costs, whether at the university or in the catacombs, if he does not wish to be imprisoned for dereliction of duty.

The word "theology" includes the concept of the *Logos*. Theology is a *logia*, logic, or language bound to the *theos,* which both makes it possible and also determines it. The inescapable meaning of logos is "word," however much Goethe's Faust felt that he could not possibly rate "the word" so highly. The Word is not the only necessary determination of the place of theology, but it is undoubtedly the first. Theology itself is a word, a human response; yet what makes it theology is not its own word or response but the Word which it hears and to which it *responds*. Theology stands and falls with the Word of God, for the Word of God precedes all theological words by creating, arousing, and challenging them. Should theology wish to be more or less or anything other than action in response to that Word, its thinking and speaking would be empty, meaningless, and futile. Because the Word of God is heard and answered by theology, it is a modest and, at the same time, a free science. Theology is *modest* because its entire logic can only be a human *ana-logy* to that Word; analogical thought and speech do not claim to be, to say, to contain, or to control the original word. But it gives a reply to it by its attempt to co-respond with it; it seeks expressions that resemble the ratio and relations of the Word of God in a proportionate and, as far as feasible, approximate and appropriate way. Theology's whole illumination can be only its human reflection, or mirroring (in the precise sense of "speculation"!); and its whole production can be only a human reproduction. In short, theology is not a creative act but only a praise of the Creator and of his act of creation—praise that to the greatest possible extent truly responds to the creative act of God. Likewise, theology is *free* because it is not only summoned but also liberated for such analogy, reflection, and reproduction. It is authorized, empowered, and impelled to such praise of its creator.

What is required of theological thought and speech, therefore, is *more* than that they should simply conduct, direct, and measure themselves by that Word. It goes without saying that they must do that; and it is equally true that such concepts are relevant to the relationship of theology to the witnesses of the Word, of whom we will speak next. But for the relationship of theology to the Word itself, such concepts are too weak. The idea that autonomous man should be concerned with the response to the Word and its appropriate interpretation must be completely avoided. It cannot be simply supposed that man naturally stands in need of, and is subject to, the authority that encounters him in the Word. Before human thought and speech can respond to God's word, they have to be summoned into existence and given reality by the creative act of God's word. Without the *precedence* of the creative Word, there can be not only no proper theology but, in fact, no evangelical theology at all! Theology is not called in any way to interpret, explain, and elucidate God and his Word. Of course, where its relationship to the witnesses of the Word is concerned, it must be an interpreter. But in relation to God's Word itself, theology has nothing to interpret. At this point the theological response can only consist in confirming and announcing the Word as something spoken and heard prior to all interpretation. What is at stake is the fundamental theological act that contains and determines everything else. "*Omnis recta cognitio Dei ab oboedientia nascitur*" (Calvin).[1] Not only does this Word regulate theology and precede all theological interpretation; it also and above all constitutes and calls theology forth out of nothingness into being, out of death into life. This Word is the *Word of God*. The place of theology is direct confrontation with this Word, a situation in which theology finds itself placed, and must again and again place itself.

The Word of God is the Word that God *spoke, speaks,* and *will*

---

1. "True knowledge of God is born out of obedience."

speak in the midst of all men. Regardless of whether it is heard or not, it is, in itself, directed to all men. It is the Word of God's *work* upon men, for men, and with men. His work is not mute; rather, it speaks with a loud voice. Since only God can do what he does, only he can say in his work what he says. And since his work is not divided but *single* (for all the manifold forms which it assumes along the way from its origin to its goal), his Word is also (for all its exciting richness) simple and single. It is not ambiguous but unambiguous, not obscure but clear. In itself, therefore, it is quite easily understandable to both the most wise and the most foolish. God works, and since he works, he also speaks. His Word goes forth. And if it be widely ignored *de facto,* it can never and in no place be ignored *de jure.* That man who refuses to listen and to obey the Word acts not as a free man but as a slave, for there is no freedom except through God's Word. We are speaking of the God of the Gospel, his work and action, and of the Gospel in which his work and action are at the same time his speech. This is his Word, the Logos in which the theological *logia,* logic, and language have their creative basis and life.

The Word of God is Gospel, that is, the good word, because it declares God's *good* work. In this Word, God's work itself becomes speech. Through his Word, God discloses his work in his *covenant* with man, in the history of its establishment, maintenance, accomplishment, and fulfillment. In this very way he discloses himself (both his holiness and his mercy) as man's father, brother, and friend. At the same time, however, he discloses his power and his eminence as the possessor, Lord, and judge of man. He discloses himself as the *primary* partner of the covenant—himself as *man's* God. But he also discloses *man* to be his creature, the debtor who, confronting him, is unable to pay. Man is lost in his judgment, yet also upheld and saved by his grace, freed for him and called by him to service and duty. He discloses man as God's man, as God's son and servant who is loved by him. Man is thus the other, the secondary, partner of the covenant. The revelation of the primacy of God and the station of man in the covenant is the work of God's word. This covenant (in which God is man's God and man is God's man) is the content of the Word of God; and God's covenant, history, and work with man are the contents of his Word which distinguish it from all other words. This Logos is the creator of theology. By it, theology is shown its place and assigned its task. Evangelical theology exists in the service of the Word of God's covenant of grace and peace.

What follows now is in no wise different from what has been said already, but it now says the same thing *concretely*. Theology responds to the Word which God *has spoken, still speaks,* and *will speak again* in the history of *Jesus Christ* which fulfills the history of Israel. To reverse the statement, theology responds to that Word spoken in the history of *Israel* which reaches its culmination in the history of Jesus Christ. As Israel proceeds toward Jesus Christ, and Jesus Christ proceeds out of Israel, so the Gospel of God goes forth. It is precisely the particularity of the Gospel which is its universality. This is the good Word of the covenant of grace and peace established, upheld, accomplished, and fulfilled by God. It is his Word of the friendly communion between himself and man. The Word of God, therefore, is not the appearance of an *idea* of such a covenant and communion. It is the Logos of this *history*, the Logos, or Word, of the God of Abraham, Isaac, and Jacob, who, as such, is the Father of Jesus Christ. *This* Word, the Word of this *history*, is what evangelical theology must always hear, understand, and speak of anew. We shall now try to delineate what this history declares.

First of all, this history speaks of a God who calls his own people to himself. Out of a tribal community which exemplifies all mankind, he calls his own people by acting upon it and speaking to it as *its* God and treating and addressing it as *his* people. The name of this God is *Yahweh:* ''I am who I will be'' or ''I will be who I am'' or ''I will be who I will be.'' And the name of this people is Israel, which means—not a contender *for* God, but—''contender *against* God.'' The covenant is the encounter of this God with this people in their common history. The report of this history, although strangely contradictory, is not ambiguous. This history speaks of the unbroken encounter, conversation, and resultant communion between a holy and faithful God and an unholy and unfaithful people. It speaks of both the unfailing presence of the divine partner and the failure of the human partner that should be holy as he is holy, answering his faithfulness with faithfulness. While this history definitely speaks of the divine perfection of the covenant, it does not speak of its human perfection. The covenant has not yet been perfected. Israel's history, therefore, points beyond itself; it points to a fulfillment which, although pressing forward to become reality, has not yet become real.

At this point, the history of *Jesus*, the Messiah of Israel, commences. In it the activity and speech of the God of Israel toward his people, rather than ceasing, attain their consummation. The ancient covenant, established with Abraham, Isaac, and Jacob, proclaimed by Moses, and confirmed to David, becomes in Jesus Christ a new covenant. The holy and faithful God of Israel himself now calls into existence and action his holy and faithful human partner. In the midst of his people he lets one become man and espouses the cause of this man totally. With him he expresses the same solidarity that a father has with his son; he affirms that he, *God*, is identical with this *man*. Certainly, what is fulfilled in the existence and appearance, in the work and word of Jesus of Nazareth, is the history of God and his Israel, of Israel and its God. But the fulfillment of Israel's history is not its own continuation, as though God should raise up and call a new Moses, a further prophet, or a hero. Its fulfillment, instead, is the indwelling of God in this man, working and speaking through him. Anything less than this, obviously would be too little to fill up that vacuum. What the history of Jesus Christ confirms in the consummation of the history of Israel is *this event* in which the God of Israel consummates the covenant established with his people. The history of Jesus Christ is rooted deeply in the history of Israel, yet it soars high above Israel's history. It speaks of the realized unity of true God and true man, of the God who descends to community with man, gracious in his freedom, and of man who is exalted to community with him, thankful in his freedom. In this way "God was in Christ." In this way this one was and is the one who, although expected and promised, had not yet come forward in God's covenant with Israel. And in this way the Word of God was and is the consummation of what was only heralded in the history of Israel: the *Word* become *flesh*.

The history of Jesus Christ took place first and foremost for the benefit of Israel. It was the history of the covenant of God with Israel which attained its consummation in that subsequent history. And so God's Word, which was fully spoken in the history of Jesus Christ when it became flesh in him, remains first and foremost his concluding word to Israel. This ought never to be forgotten! Nevertheless, Israel was sent precisely as God's mediator to the nations; and this remains the meaning of the covenant made with it. The presence of God in Christ was the reconciliation of the world with himself in this Christ of Israel. In this consummating history, God's Word was now spoken in and with this, his work, which was done in and upon Israel. His Word remains a comforting announcement to *all* fellow men of the one Son of God, an announcement calling for repentance and faith. It is God's good Word about his good work in the midst, and for the good, of all creation. It is a Word directed to all peoples and nations of all times and places. The task of evangelical theology, therefore, is to hear, understand, and speak of the consummation of God's Word, both its intensive and its extensive perfection as the Word of the covenant of grace and peace. In the Christ of Israel this Word has become *particular*, that is, Jewish flesh. It is in the particularity of the flesh that it applies *universally* to all men. The Christ of Israel is the Saviour of the world.

This whole Word of God in Christ is the word to which theology must listen and reply. It is God's Word spoken both in the relation of the history of Israel to the history of Jesus Christ and in the relation of the history of Jesus Christ to the history of Israel. It is the Word of God's covenant with man—man who is alienated from God but who nevertheless is devoted to him, because God himself has interceded for man.

If theology wanted to do no more than hear and relate this Word as it appears in the *conflict* between God's faithfulness and man's unfaithfulness, theology would not respond to the whole Word of God. Should it limit itself to the conflict which would be characteristic for the history of Israel as such, theology would completely miss the central truth of this Word. The fact is, there is no history of Israel in itself and for its own sake. There is only the single history which, though it has its source in God's good will in overcoming Israel—the "contender with God"—nevertheless hastens toward a goal. It hastens toward the history of Jesus Christ, the establishment of the human partner who, for his part, is faithful to the divine partner. In Israel's history there is no message that does not point beyond itself, that does not express its character as the Word of the divine partner at work in it. Every such message strives toward its consummation in the message of the history of Jesus Christ. Already containing this message within itself, Israel's history is to this extent already Gospel.

Theology would not respond to the whole Word of God if it wished only to hear and to speak of the Word become flesh. It would totally miss the truth of this Word if it proclaimed simply and solely the history of Jesus Christ, the Saviour of the world. As if the reconciliation of the world with God were made at the expense of, or in abstraction from, the promises given to Israel! If theology wishes to hear and repeat what God has said, it must remain attentive to what *happened* in Israel's history. What happened was the fulfillment and accomplishment of the *reconciliation* of Israel. The old, untiring, but now weary contender with God was reconciled by the will of the one true God. All the same, it was in this *Jewish* flesh that the Word of God now went forth into the whole world. "Salvation is from the Jews" (John 4:22). The covenant of God with man consists neither simply in the one nor simply in the other, but rather in the succession and unity of both forms of the history of the work of God. Similarly, the Word about this covenant goes forth in the same unity, since it is the Word of the selfsame God spoken both in the history of Israel and in the history of Jesus Christ. Their succession and unity form the whole Logos, and it is this unity of which evangelical theology must hear and speak. When theology fulfills this command, it takes and holds its post. To use a remarkable expression of Paul's, theology is then *logike latreia*. Not theology *only*, but among other services rendered in the church, theology *specifically* is committed to offer "reasonable service" to God.

A more precise determination of the place of evangelical theology requires that we take note of a definite (although not statistically definable) group of human beings. These enjoy a *special* and singular, indeed a unique, position in their relation to the Word of God. But their position is not special by virtue of a particular aptitude of sentiment or attitude toward the Word or by the fact that it might earn them particular favors, gratuities, or honors. Instead, it is special by virtue of the specific historical situation in which they are confronted by this Word, by the particular service to which the Word called and equipped them. They are the *witnesses* of the Word. To be more precise, they are its primary witnesses, because they are called directly by the Word to be its hearers, and they are appointed for its communication and verification to other men. These men are the *biblical witnesses of the Word,* the prophetic men of the Old Testament and the apostolic men of the New. They were contemporaries of the history in which God established his covenant with men. In fact, they became contemporary witnesses by virtue of what they saw and heard of this history. Other men, of course, were also contemporary witnesses of this history. But the prophets and apostles became and existed as eyewitnesses of those deeds done in their time, and *hearers of the Word* spoken in their time. They were destined, appointed, and elected for this cause by God, not by themselves; they were also commanded and empowered by him to speak of what they had seen and heard. They speak as men who in this qualified sense were *there*. The Logos of God in their witness is the concrete concern of evangelical theology. Though this theology has no direct information about the Logos, it nevertheless has, with the utmost certainty, this indirect information.

The prophetic men of the Old Testament witnessed Yahweh's action in the history of Israel, his action as father, king, lawgiver, and judge. They saw his free and constructive love, which nevertheless was a consuming love; in Israel's election and calling they beheld Yahweh's grace, and in his kind but also severe and wrathful direction and rule over this people they saw his untiring protest and opposition to the conduct of Israel, the incorrigible contender with God. Israel's history spoke to the prophets. In the manifold forms of this history they heard Yahweh's commands, judgments, and threats as well as his promises—not confirmations of their own religious, moral, or political preferences, or their optimistic or pessimistic views, opinions, and postulates! What they heard was, instead, the sovereign voice of the *God of the covenant:* "Thus says the Lord." This is the God who is constantly faithful to his unfaithful human partner. It was his own Word which these witnesses were enabled, permitted, and called to echo, either as prophets in the narrower sense of the term, or as prophetic narrators, or occasionally as lawyers, or as prophetic poets and teachers of wisdom. In giving their witness they, of course, listened to their predecessors as well, appropriating in one way or another their answers and incorporating them into their own. It was Yahweh's Word itself, as it was spoken in his history with Israel, which they brought to the hearing of their people. Naturally, each prophet also spoke within the limits and horizon of his time, its problems, culture, and language. They spoke, first of all, *viva voce,* but they also wrote down these words or had them written down so that they should be remembered by succeeding generations. The Old Testament canon is a collection of those writings which prevailed and were acknowledged in the synagogue. Their content was so persuasive that they were recognized as authentic, trustworthy, and authoritative testimonies to the Word of God. Evangelical theology hears witness of the Old Testament with the greatest earnestness and not merely as a sort of prelude to the New Testament. The classic rule is *Novum Testamentum in Vetere latet, Vetus in Novo patet:* the New Testament is concealed within the Old, and the Old Testament is revealed by the New. As long as theology preferred to neglect this rule, as long as it was content to exist in a vacuum by claiming exclusive orientation to the New Testament, it was continually threatened by a cancer in its very bones.

Nevertheless, theology must obviously focus its attention on the *goal* of the history of Israel, on the *prophetic* Word spoken in this history, on the *history of Jesus Christ* as it is witnessed to by the apostolic men of the *New Testament*. What these men saw and heard, what their hands touched, was the fulfillment of the covenant in the existence and appearance of the one human partner who was obedient to God. This fulfillment was the Lord who as a servant lived, suffered, and died in the place of the disobedient; the Lord who uncovered but also covered their folly, taking upon himself, and taking away, their guilt, uniting them and reconciling them with their divine partner. In the death of this Lord they saw the old contender *against* God overcome and vanquished, and in the life of this Lord, another man come forward, the new contender *for* God. In him they saw the hallowing of God's name, the coming of his kingdom, the fulfilling of his will on earth. In this event in time and space, in the "flesh," they were allowed to hear the Word of God in its glory, as a pledge, promise, warning, and consolation to all men. By Jesus' commission the apostles were sent out into the world in order to attest to all men that Jesus is this Word of God.

Once again, the subject and strength of their commission were neither their impressions of Jesus, their estimation of his person and his work, nor their faith in him. Instead, their theme was God's mighty Word spoken in Jesus' resurrection from the dead which imparted to his life and death power and control over all creatures of all times. The apostles spoke, told, wrote, and preached about Jesus as men who were in this way directly illumined and instructed. They spoke as men who had behind them the empty tomb and before them the living Jesus. Let it be noted that, *apart from* Jesus' history as the mighty Word in which God's reconciling act was revealed, the apostles lacked all interest in any other aspect of his history. They ignored any reality that might have preceded this history of salvation and revelation. There *was* simply no such reality; therefore they could not know or be concerned with any such hypothetical reality. Jesus' history was real, and real to *them,* pre-eminently as a history of salvation and revelation. For them, Jesus' reality was exclusively linked to their proclamation and based on his self-proclamation as *Kurios,* Son of God and son of man. It was neither a "historical Jesus" nor a "Christ of faith" which they knew and proclaimed, neither the abstract image of one in whom they did not yet believe nor the equally abstract image of one in whom they afterward believed. Instead, they proclaimed concretely the one Jesus Christ who had encountered them as the one who he was, even when they did not yet believe in him. Having their eyes opened by his resurrection, they were able to tell who he was who had made himself known to them *before* the resurrection. A twofold Jesus Christ, one who existed *before* and another who existed *after* Easter, can be deduced from New Testament texts only after he has been arbitrarily read into them. From the viewpoint even of "historical criticism," such an operation ought to be considered profoundly suspect. The origin, object, and content of the New Testament witnesses were and are the one history of salvation and revelation in which Jesus Christ is both God's deed and God's Word. Before and behind this history, all that the New Testament witnesses could reflect and contemplate was its commencement in the history of Israel as evidenced by the Old Testament. To *this* preceding history, and to this alone, they were constantly oriented. The New Testament *canon* is a collection of testimonies, fixed in writing and handed down, which relate the history of Jesus Christ in a way which proved itself authentic to the communities of the second, third, and fourth centuries. In contrast to all kinds of similar literature these communities approved the canon as the original and faithful document of what the witnesses of the resurrection saw, heard, and proclaimed. They were the first to acknowledge this collection as genuine and authoritative testimony to the one Word of God, at the same time taking over, with a remarkable naturalness and ease, the Old Testament canon from the synagogue.

We shall now attempt to clarify how evangelical theology is related to this biblical witness to the Word of God.

First of all, theology shares with the biblical prophecy and apostolate a common concern for human response to the divine Word. The witnesses of the Old and New Testaments were men like all others, men who had heard the Word and witnessed to it in a human way—in speech, vision, and thought that were human and conditioned by time and space. They were *theologians;* yet, in spite of having an identical orientation to an identical object, as theologians they differed widely from one another. Anything other than *their* intention, anything more or less than that, cannot be the substance of evangelical theology. In its study of the two Testaments, what theology has to learn as much as anything else is the method of a *human* thought and speech as they are oriented to the Word of God.

All the same, in the second place, theology is neither prophecy nor apostolate. Its relationship to God's Word cannot be compared to the position of the biblical witnesses because it can know the Word of God only at second hand, only in the mirror and echo of the biblical witness. The place of theology is *not* to be located on the same or a similar plane with those first witnesses. Since the human reply to the Word will in practice always consist partially in a basic question, theology cannot and dare not presume that its human response stands in some immediate relationship to the Word spoken by God himself. At that moment when everything depended on being present, scientific theology, as defined earlier in these lectures, is completely absent.

The position of theology, thirdly, can in no wise be exalted *above* that of the biblical witnesses. The post-Biblical theologian may, no doubt, possess a better astronomy, geography, zoology, psychology, physiology, and so on than these biblical witnesses possessed; but as for the Word of God, he is not justified in comporting himself in relationship to those witnesses as though he knew more about the Word than they. He is neither a president of a seminary, nor the Chairman of the Board of some Christian Institute of Advanced Theological Studies, who might claim some authority over the prophets and apostles. He cannot grant or refuse them a hearing as though they were colleagues on the faculty. Still less is he a high-school teacher authorized to look over their shoulder benevolently or crossly, to correct their notebooks, or to give them good, average, or bad marks. Even the smallest, strangest, simplest, or obscurest among the bibical witnesses has an incomparable advantage over even the most pious, scholarly, and sagacious latter-day theologian. From his special point of view and in his special fashion, the witness has thought, spoken, and written about the revelatory Word and act in direct confrontation with it. All subsequent theology, as well as the whole of the community that comes after the event, will never find itself in the same immediate confrontation.

Once and for all, theology has, fourthly, its position *beneath* that of the biblical scriptures. While it is aware of all their human and conditioned character, it still knows and considers that the writings with which it deals are *holy* writings. These writings are selected and separated; they deserve and demand respect and attention of an extraordinary order, since they have a direct relationship to God's work and word. If theology seeks to learn of prophecy and the apostolate, it can only and ever learn from the prophetic and apostolic witnesses. It must learn not this or that important truth but the one thing that is necessary—and with respect to this one thing on which all else depends, the biblical witnesses are better informed than are the theologians. For this reason theology must agree to let *them* look over its shoulder and correct its notebooks.

In the fifth place, the peg on which all theology hangs is acquaintance with the God of the Gospel. This acquaintance is never to be taken for granted; it is never immediately available; it can never be carried about by the theologian in some intellectual or spiritual pillbox or briefcase. The knowledge of Immanuel, the God of man and for man, includes acquaintance with the man of God. That he is Abraham's God, Israel's God, man's God—this is Yahweh's marvelous distinction from the gods of all other theologies. Theology has Immanuel—true God, true man—as its object when it comes from the Holy Scriptures and returns to them. "It is they that bear witness to me." Theology becomes evangelical theology only when the God of the Gospel encounters it in the mirror and echo of the prophetic and apostolic word. It must also grasp God's work and word as the theme and problem of *its* thinking and speaking, in the same way that the Yahwist and Elohist, Isaiah and Jeremiah, Matthew, Paul, and John saw and heard this Word. Many other things, much that is interesting, beautiful, good, and true, could also be communicated and disclosed to theology by all sorts of old and new literature of other kinds. But with respect to the theme and problem that make it theological science, it will, for better or for worse, have to stick to this literature, the Holy Scriptures.

Nevertheless, in the sixth place, theology confronts in Holy Scriptures an extremely polyphonic, not a monotonous, testimony to the work and word of God. Everything that can be heard there is differentiated—not only the voices of the Old and New Testaments as such, but also the many voices that reverberate throughout both. It should be noted that the primary and real basis of this differentiation does not lie in the various psychological, sociological, and cultural conditions which existed for each witness. There is, of course, such a preliminary basis for differentiation in the profusion of biblical witnesses, in the various factors influencing their purposes and points of view, in the variety of their languages and the special theology of each. The primary basis, however, lies in the objective multiplicity and inner contrasts sustained within the motion of the history of the covenant which they recount and affirm. This motion is all-inclusive; it encompasses even its smallest elements, reflecting the interplay of unity and disunity between God and man as the witnesses disclose them. Therefore, although theology is certainly confronted with the one God, he is One in the fullness of his existence, action, and revelation. In the school of the witnesses theology can in no way become monolithic, monomanic, monotonous, and infallibly boring. In no way can it bind or limit itself to one special subject or another. In this school theology will be oriented to the unceasing succession of different loci of the divine work and word, and in this way theological understanding, thought, and speech will receive their definite place. In the school of these witnesses theology inevitably begins to wander, though always with the same goal in mind. It migrates from the Old Testament to the New and returns again, from the Yahwist to the priestly codex, from the psalms of David to the proverbs of Solomon, from the Gospel of John to the synoptic gospels, from the Letter to the Galatians to the so-called "straw" epistle of James, and so on continually. Within all of these writings the pilgrimage leads from one level of tradition to another, taking into account every stage of tradition that may be present or surmised. In this respect the work of theology might be compared to the task of circling a high mountain which, although it is one and the same mountain, exists and manifests itself in very different shapes. The eternally rich God is the content of the knowledge of evangelical theology. His unique mystery is known only in the overflowing fullness of his counsels, ways, and judgments.

Theology responds to the Logos of God, in the seventh place, when it endeavors to hear and speak of him always anew on the basis of his self-disclosure in the Scriptures. Its searching of the Scriptures consists in asking the texts whether and to what extent they might witness to him; however, whether and to what extent they reflect and echo, in their complete humanity, the Word of God is completely unknown beforehand. This possibility must be seen and heard again and again, and this knowledge must be won from it and illuminated repeatedly. The open, candid question *about this Word* is what theology brings to the Bible. All other questions are only conjoined and subordinated to this question; they can present only technical aids to its solution. Nowadays, of course, the "exegetical-theological" task is often said to consist in the translation of biblical assertions out of the speech of a past time into the language of modern man. The remarkable assumption behind this project, however, seems to be that the content, meaning, and point of biblical assertions are relatively easy to ascertain and may afterward be presupposed as self-evident. The main task would be then simply to render these assertions understandable and relevant to the modern world by means of some sort of linguistic key. The message is all very well, it is said, but "how do you tell it to the man on the street?" The truth of the matter, however, is that the central affirmations of the Bible are not self-evident; the Word of God itself, as witnessed to in the Bible, is not immediately obvious in any of its chapters or verses. On the contrary, the truth of the Word must be *sought* precisely, in order to be understood in its deep simplicity. Every possible means must be used: philological and historical criticism and analysis, careful consideration of the nearer and the more remote textual relationships, and not least, the enlistment of every device of the conjectural imagination that is available. The question *about the Word* and this question alone fulfills and does justice to the intention of the biblical authors and their writings. And in passing, might not this question also do justice to modern man? If modern man is earnestly interested in the Bible, he certainly does not wish for its translation into his transitory jargon. Instead, he himself would like to participate in the effort to draw nearer to what stands *there*. This effort is what theology owes to modern man and, above all, to the Bible itself. "What stands there," in the pages of the Bible, is the witness to the *Word of God*, the Word of God in this testimony of the Bible. Just how far it stands there, however, is a fact that demands unceasing discovery, interpretation, and recognition. It demands untiring effort—effort, moreover, which is not unaccompanied by blood and tears. The biblical witnesses and the Holy Scriptures confront theology as the object of this effort.

When theology confronts the Word of God and its witnesses, its place is very concretely in the *community*, not somewhere in empty space. The word "community," rather than "Church," is used advisedly, for from a theological point of view it is best to avoid the word "Church" as much as possible, if not altogether. At all events, this overshadowed and overburdened word should be immediately and consistently interpreted by the word "community." What may on occasion also be called "Church" is, as Luther liked to say, "Christianity" (understood as a nation rather than as a system of beliefs). It is the commonwealth gathered, founded, and ordered by the Word of God, the "communion of the saints." These are the men who were encountered by the Word and so moved by it that they could not withdraw themselves from its message and call. Instead, they became able, willing, and ready to receive it as secondary witnesses, offering themselves, their lives, thought, and speech to the Word of God. The Word cries out for belief, for this acceptance in recognition, trust, and obedience. And since faith is not an end in itself, this cry of the Word means that it demands to be proclaimed to the world to which it is directed from the outset.

First of all, the Word insists upon being annunciated by the choir of its primary witnesses. The community represents the secondary witnesses, the society of men called to believe in, and simultaneously to testify to, the Word in the world. In this community, theology also has its special place and function.

"I believed, and so I spoke." This attitude, taken over from the psalmist by Paul, indicates the situation peculiar to the entire community as such, and in the last analysis to each one of its members. The community is confronted and created by the Word of God. It is *communio sanctorum*, the communion of the saints, because it is *congregatio fidelium*, the gathering of the faithful. As such, it is the *coniuratio testium*, the confederation of the witnesses who may and must speak because they believe. The community does not speak with words alone. It speaks by the very fact of its existence in the world; by its characteristic attitude to world problems; and, moreover and especially, by its silent service to all the handicapped, weak, and needy in the world. It speaks, finally, by the simple fact that it prays for the world. It does all this because this is the purpose of its summons by the Word of God. It cannot avoid doing these things, since it believes. From the very beginning the community also expresses itself in spoken words and sentences by which, according to the summons of the Word, it attempts to make its faith audible. The work of the community consists also in its testimony through oral and written words, i.e., in the verbal self-expression by which it fulfills its commission of preaching, teaching, and pastoral counseling. And here begins the special service, the special function, of theology in the community.

In the area between the *faith* of the community and its *speech* a problem arises. What is the proper understanding of the Word that founds faith, the proper thought about this Word, the proper way to speak of it? Here "proper" does not mean pious, edifying, inspired, and inspiring; neither does it mean something that would satisfy the categories of everyday reason, thought, and speech. Although such properties would certainly be well suited to the speech of the community, they have no decisive significance for what this speech must achieve. What is at stake is the *quest for truth*. Take note that the quest for truth is not imposed on the community by the outside world (as the community in modern times permits itself, to a large extent, to be persuaded). The quest is not imposed in the name and authority of some general norm of truth or some criterion that is generally proclaimed as valid. Instead, it comes from within, or, more precisely, from above; it comes from the Word of God that founds the community and its faith.

The question about truth, therefore, is not stated in the familiar way: is it true that God exists? Does God really have a covenant with man? Is Israel really his chosen people? Did Jesus Christ actually die for our sins? Was he truly raised from the dead for our justification? And is he in fact our Lord? This is the way fools ask in their hearts—admittedly such fools as we are all in the habit of being. In theology the question about truth is stated on another level: does the community properly understand the Word in its purity as the truth? Does it understand with appropriate sincerity the Word that was spoken in and with all those events? Does the community reflect on the Word painstakingly and speak of it in clear concepts? And is the community in a position to render its secondary testimony responsibly and with a good conscience? These are the questions posed for the community, questions that are really urgent only for the people of God, and with regard to which no positive answer can ever or anywhere be taken for granted. Even the most able speech of the most living faith is a human work. And this means that the community can go astray in its proclamation of the Word of God, in its interpretation of the biblical testimony, and finally in its own faith. Instead of being helpful, it can be obstructive to God's cause in the world by an understanding that is partly or wholly wrong, by devious or warped thought, by silly or too subtle speech. Every day the community must pray that this may not happen, but it must also do its own share of earnest *work* toward this goal. This work is *theological* work.

There is no other way. In principle the community and the whole of Christianity are required and called to do such work. The question to be unceasingly posed for the community and for all its members is whether the community is a true witness. This question concerns, therefore, not only the community's speech but also its very existence. The community speaks in the surrounding world by the positions it assumes on the political, social, and cultural problems of the world. But the question of truth also concerns the community's order of worship, discipline, constitution, and administration, as well as its quiet ministerial work (which is perhaps not so quiet at all).

Since the Christian life is consciously or unconsciously also a witness, the question of truth concerns not only the community but the individual Christian. He too is responsible for the quest for truth in this witness. Therefore, every Christian as such is also called to be a theologian. How much more so those who are specially commissioned in the community, whose service is preeminently concerned with speech in the narrower sense of the term! It is always a suspicious phenomenon when leading church-men (whether or not they are adorned with a bishop's silver cross), along with certain fiery evangelists, preachers, or well-meaning warriors for this or that practical Christian cause, are heard to affirm, cheerfully and no doubt also a bit disdainfully, that theology is after all not their business. "I am not a theologian; I am an administrator!" a high-ranking English churchman once said to me. And just as bad is the fact that not a few preachers, after they have exchanged their student years for the routine of practical service, seem to think that they are allowed to leave theology behind them as the butterfly does its caterpillar existence, as if it were an exertion over and done with for them. This will not do at all. Christian witness must always be forged anew in the fire of the question of truth. Otherwise it can in no case and at no time be a witness that is substantial and responsible, and consequently trustworthy and forceful. Theology is no undertaking that can be blithely surrendered to others by anyone engaged in the ministry of God's Word. It is no hobby of some especially interested and gifted individuals. A community that is awake and conscious of its commission and task in the world will of necessity be a theologically interested community. This holds true in still greater measure for those members of the community who are specially commissioned.

It is fitting that there should be a special theological activity, just as there are special emphases in other tasks of the community. The special theological science, research, or doctrine concentrates on the testing of the whole communal enterprise in the light of the question of truth. It functions to a certain extent vicariously and even professionally. Moreover, it is related to the community and its faith in roughly the same manner as jurisprudence is related to the state and its law. The inquiry and doctrine of theology, therefore, are not an end in themselves but, rather, functions of the community and especially of its *ministerium Verbi Divini*. Theology is committed directly to the community and especially to those members who are responsible for preaching, teaching, and counseling. The task theology has to fulfill is continually to stimulate and lead them to face squarely the question of the proper relation of their human speech to the Word of God, which is the origin, object, and content of this speech. Theology must give them practice in the right relation to the quest for truth, demonstrating and exemplifying to them the understanding, thought, and discourse proper to it. It must accustom them to the fact that here nothing can be taken for granted, that work, just as prayer, is indispensable. It also has the task of exhibiting the lines along which this work is to be conducted.

Theology would be an utter failure if it should place itself in some elegant eminence where it would be concerned only with God, the world, man, and some other items, perhaps those of historical interest, instead of being theology for the *community*. Like the pendulum which regulates the movements of a clock, so theology is responsible for the reasonable service of the community. It reminds all its members, especially those who have greater responsibilities, how serious is their situation and task. In this way it opens for them the way to freedom and joy in their service.

But in order to serve the community of today, theology itself must be rooted in the community of yesterday. Its testimony to the Word and the profession of its faith must originate, like the community itself, from the community of past times, from which that of today arose. Theology must originate also from the older and the more recent *tradition* which determines the present form of its witness. The foundation of its inquiry and instruction is given to theology beforehand, along with the task which it has to fulfill. Theology does not labor somewhere high above the foundation of tradition, as though Church history began today. Nevertheless, the special task of theology is a *critical* one, in spite of its relative character. The fire of the quest for truth has to ignite the proclamation of the community and the tradition determining this proclamation. Theology has to reconsider the confession of the community, testing and rethinking it in the light of its enduring foundation, object, and content.

The faith of the community is asked to seek understanding. Faith seeking understanding, *Fides quaerens intellectum*, is what theology must embody and represent. What distinguishes faith from blind assent is just its special character as "faith seeking understanding." Certainly, the assumption behind all this will be that the community itself may have been on the right track in the recent or remote past, or at any rate on a not altogether crooked path. Consequently, fundamental trust instead of mistrust will be the initial attitude of theology toward the tradition which determines the present-day Church. And any questions and proposals which theology has to direct to the tradition will definitely not be forced on the community like a decree; any such findings will be presented for consideration only as well-weighed suggestions. Nevertheless, no ecclesiastical authority should be allowed by theology to hinder it from honestly pursuing its critical task, and the same applies to any frightened voices from the midst of the rest of the congregation. The task of theology is to discuss freely the reservations as well as the proposals for improvement which occur to it in reflection on the inherited witness of the community. Theology says *credo*, I believe, along with the present-day community and its fathers. But it says *credo ut intelligam*, "I believe in order to understand." To achieve this understanding, it must be granted leeway for the good of the community itself. There are three points at which this freedom becomes important.

First of all, a tacit presupposition in our last lecture on the immediate witnesses of the Word of God was that we know *who* these witnesses are. We presupposed that both the community and theology know the identity of these witnesses who, since they are immediate, are authoritative for the community and its service. A further presupposition was that we know which scriptures must be read and interpreted as "holy" Scripture and acknowledged and respected as the theological norm. In fact, we do know this, for theology is a service in and for the community and springs from the tradition of the community. In this matter theology clings to that confession which is perhaps the most important and portentous of all Church confessions of faith, i.e., it clings to the selection of the various writings that confirmed themselves to the community as genuinely prophetic and apostolic witnesses. It was this selection that was unanimously accepted by the community of the late fourth century. The character of these writings as such witnesses is what the fathers of those days recognized and confessed by faith in God's Word, whose image and echo they perceived in them. To this knowledge and confession the community of every succeeding century has also committed itself, and with it, on the whole, it has had good and trustworthy experience. It is just this traditional canon which theology must first of all simply risk as a working hypothesis, for the decisive reason that it cannot refuse to join in that age-old act of faith if it is to be a service in and for the community.

The precise task of theology, however, is *credo ut intelligam*, "I believe in order to understand." In the fulfillment of this task, theology seeks to grasp and understand specifically one thing: the extent to which the canonical collection acknowledged by earlier generations actually *is* the canon of *Holy* Scripture. But how can this question be decided other than through knowledge of the content of those writings? How else can the rightness of traditional respect for the canon be tested other than by activating that working hypothesis? How else other than by questioning the texts of the Old and New Testaments as to whether and to what extent authentic witness of God's Word may be actually heard in them? How else, therefore, than in the careful investigation of those texts in the light of this question, by engagement in the exegetical circle that is unavoidable if those texts are to be understood? This investigation does not consist in premature anticipation but in expectation of an event, an event in which the authority of these texts announces itself. In this way theology sees, understands, and knows that the search for authentic witness to God's Word is fruitful only if pursued in the original canon. Theology knows also, however, that this search in the canon must be conducted with earnestness and total frankness. To be sure, theology always gropes to a great extent in the dark, with only a gradual, variable, partial knowledge. Nevertheless, even limited knowledge may convey, like a look through a keyhole, a glimpse of the riches of God's glory which is mirrored in the totality of the Biblical testimony.

In the second place, the thought and speech of the community have behind them a long history which is, in many ways, confused and confusing. The community's attention to the voice of the Old and New Testaments and to the Word of God witnessed by this voice was not always sensitive and accurate. It did not always withstand the temptation to listen to all sorts of strange voices as well, and often it listened almost entirely to them—to the voice of the old serpent. The dogmas, creeds, and confessions of the community are the documents of its resistance to this temptation and, at the same time, of its repenting return to its origins. They are the professions of its faith, formulated in opposition to all sorts of unbelief, superstition, and error. If theology did not take seriously the tradition of the community in the form of these documents of conflict, it would not be service in and for the community. In attempting to be equal to the quest for truth today, it must show both respect for the tradition and eagerness to learn from it. It must take note how one thing was occasionally defined and proclaimed as right and another anathematized as wrong *magno consensu*, by the consent of the majority of the fathers, during times of the beclouding of the Christian witness. Theology will often enough have occasion to wonder at the wisdom and determination of the decisions of the fathers that were made in their time and became significant for all times.

Nevertheless, the significance of tradition may not be simply taken for granted. *Credo*, indeed! But *credo, ut intelligam*. No dogma or article of the creed can be simply taken over untested by theology from ecclesiastical antiquity; each must be measured, from the very beginning, by the Holy Scripture and the Word of God. And under no circumstances may theology set out to appropriate creedal propositions merely because they are old and widespread and famous. If it is seriously committed to the quest for truth, it will forgo seeking the name and fame of an "orthodoxy" faithful to tradition. There is no heterodoxy worse than such orthodoxy! Theology knows and practices only *one* faithfulness. All the same, just this one faithfulness may perhaps prove to be also faithfulness to the confessions of the early Church and the Reformation for long stretches of the way, on the basis of the *intellectus fidei*, the understanding which is characteristic of faith.

Thirdly and finally, a brief comment is called for by the fact that the *history of theology* itself belongs to the tradition determining the community. As in all previous considerations, the *communio sanctorum* may and should be the starting point for understanding, even though this hypothesis is by no means easy to carry out (least of all in this case!). Nevertheless, the risk must be taken. The same hypothesis and risk apply particularly to the ruling theology of the past, whether of yesterday, of fifty, or of a hundred years ago. Time and again, the community grows used to living from what was said in it and to it yesterday; as a rule it lives from the Christian knowledge of yesterday. In the meantime, it is to be hoped, theology has advanced somewhat further, and what it supposes to know, what it ventures to think and to say *today*, will only seldom agree completely with what the fathers of yesterday thought and said. The far greater likelihood is that the newer theology will vigorously take exception to the fathers, especially to the immediate fathers. Even if this tension is justified by the vigorous nature of theological science, theology will still do well to keep in contact with its predecessors. For better or for worse, theology of yesterday is a bubbling source of the community and, above all, of theology itself. We will listen, therefore, with special attention precisely to those fathers of yesterday, interpreting them not only according to the critical rule, *credo ut intelligam*, but also in *optimum partem bona fide*, and making the best of them. By no means will we drop the problems which concerned them; instead, we will pursue them further, repeatedly meditating, considering, and reconsidering the very problems they posed, although at the same time no doubt putting them in the right perspective. Otherwise, theology might find the sons of today proving tomorrow to be enthusiastic rediscoverers and perhaps avengers of their grandfathers. The work of overcoming past weaknesses and errors, a work which was perhaps only apparently completed, would then have to begin all over again. May the good Lord preserve us from that!

We cannot overlook the fact that we ventured some very extraordinary statements in the last three lectures on the determination of the place of evangelical theology. Taken by themselves, of course, they may have been tolerably distinct and understandable, interrelated among themselves and also mutually confirming. Nevertheless, in their wholeness, as in their particulars, they were obviously statements that were not supported by what is usually considered sound evidence. They could not be derived from any points outside of the sphere of reality and truth which they themselves represented. They were not founded upon any results of a general science oriented to nature, man, the human spirit, or history, just as they had no dependence upon any philosophical foundations. Like the Melchizedek of the Letter to the Hebrews, each single sentence and all of them together were "without father or mother or genealogy." When we, nevertheless, ventured these statements, what power did we acknowledge? What is the power hidden within these assertions which establishes and illumines them? In other words, how does theology come to take and hold the place described by them—a place which seems to the onlooker to be situated in mid-air?

Let us recapitulate briefly in order to pinpoint this situation for ourselves. In our second lecture, "The Word," we ventured the statement that the history of Immanuel arose from the history of Israel and attained its goal in the history of Jesus Christ, and that this history, as such, was God's Word spoken to the people of all times and places. What a history! What a Word! What is the power that makes it so great a history and so bright a revelation? In our third lecture, "The Witnesses," we ventured the statement that there is a definite group of men, the biblical prophets and apostles, who directly heard the Word of that history. They were called by it to become its authentic and authoritative witnesses to the people of all times and places. How were these witnesses specially selected for such hearing? How were these men, no different from others, chosen for such proclamation? By what possible power? In our fourth lecture, "The Community," we ventured the affirmation that a whole group of men arose as secondary witnesses through the power of the Word spoken and entrusted to those earlier, primary witnesses. A community arose, the Church, destined and commissioned to proclaim the work and word of God in the world. What an extraordinary commission for a group of men! What is the power of their existence and action?

Obviously, all these assertions were ventured solely in order to describe the *place* of evangelical theology. Obviously, they had, as such, a strictly theological character and content. They could be only *theologically* guaranteed, only *theologically* intended and understood. What, then, is theology? According to these foregoing statements, by which we described its place, theology can be only theologically defined. Theology is science seeking the knowledge of the Word of God spoken in God's work—science learning in the school of Holy Scripture, which witnesses to the Word of God; science laboring in the quest for truth, which is inescapably required of the community that is called by the Word of God. In this way alone does theology fulfill its definition as the human logic of the divine Logos. In every other respect theology is really without support. While, seen from the viewpoint of an outsider, it hovers in mid-air, it depends actually upon God's living Word, on God's chosen eyewitnesses, and on the existence of God's people in the world. This dependence is its foundation, justification, and destination. The power of its existence is the power focused through those statements we have made about God's Word, God's witnesses, and God's people.

We will carefully refrain from speaking of a power *presupposed* either by us, in our theological assertions about the place of theology, or by theology itself in the form of any further theological statement. All would be betrayed, all would be false if we were to speak in this way. Theology cannot lift itself, as it were, by its own boot straps, to the level of God; it cannot presuppose anything at all concerning the foundation, authorization, and destination of its statements. It can presuppose no help or buttress from the outside and just as little from within. If theology wished to provide a presupposition for its statements, it would mean that it sought to make them, itself, and its work safe from any attack, risk, or jeopardy. It would presume that it could and must secure them (even if this presupposition was a tour de force, a *Deus ex machina* introduced in the form of a further theological statement). Precisely in this way theology would sell its birthright for a mess of pottage. Theology can only *do* its work. It cannot, however, seek to secure its operation. Its work can be well done only when all presuppositions are renounced which would secure it from without or within.

What can be arbitrarily presupposed, obviously stands at one's disposal. Were theology to *presuppose* the power sustaining its statements and itself (in the manner that mathematics presupposes the axioms supporting its theorems), then theology would assume *power* in its own right, superior to that first and fundamental power. Theology could then muster that power for its self-protection or at least place it on guard duty. The true power, which is powerful in its own right, defies being a potency which theology can possess and manipulate in its statements. Such presumed potency would be something like Münchausen trying to pull himself out of the bog by his own hair. In one way or another the very thing theology seeks (because in fact it needs it) would be lost whenever theology attempted to rely upon such an arbitrary presupposition.

We have to speak, therefore, of the real power that is *hidden* in theological assertions—hidden, unattainable, unavailable not only to the environment but also to the very theology which serves the community. This is the power *present* and *active* in what the affirmations of theology declare, in the history of salvation and revelation, in the hearing and speech of the biblical witnesses, in the being and act of the community summoned by them, and also in the work of theology when it testifies to these things. But this power is also totally superior to theology itself. It sustains and activates that whole event from the history of Immanuel down to the little tale in whose telling theology also, finally and at the last, has its existence and activity. In the telling of this tale, that hidden power prevents and forbids the slightest attempt to construct treacherous presuppositions. Most of all, it excludes the presumption that theology can vindicate itself. That power makes all arbitrary presupposing superfluous, since it is a *productive* power which replaces all safeguards stemming from other sources. It is power that produces security, of course—but just because its power is *creative* and *sufficient* to produce security, it is so effective that even the greatest theological master cannot, as it were, play with it as though it were one of his chessmen (perhaps the most powerful—the Queen). It is not endowed with a potentiality which the theologian knows and can exploit, as though he could overlook its origin, significance, and limits, The theologian does not have it in his control. This power is by no means a further theological assumption which he, much like a magician, could employ or not employ according to need or desire. He should be happy if, while brooding over his work, he heard the hidden power rushing, and finds his statements determined, ruled, and controlled by it. But he does not know "whence it comes or whither it goes." He can wish only to follow its work, not to precede it. While he lets his thought and speech be controlled by it, he gladly renounces the temptation to exert control over it. Such is the sovereignty of this power in the event of the history of Immanuel; such its sovereignty over and in the prophets and apostles; such its sovereignty in the gathering, upbuilding, and sending forth of the community; such its sovereignty as the hidden power of theological statements that describe and explain all this—statements such as we ventured in the three preceding lectures. No wonder that from the viewpoint of an outsider, these assertions seem to hover in mid-air, apparently crying for safeguards.

Is this true only from the viewpoint of an outsider? And do these assertions only *apparently* hover? It is precisely at this point that we must think further if we are to name this sovereign power by its true name. Is the phrase "hovering in mid-air" supposed to be something that characterizes theology only in its external aspect? Does it pertain to theology only apparently, as something probably harmful, from which theology should be acquitted as soon as possible? Still, "mid-air" could, above all, mean flowing, fresh, healthy air in contrast to all motionless and stagnant office air. And to "hover" in mid-air could also mean to be moved, borne, and driven by this flowing air. Who could actually wish that it were otherwise? It should be characteristic for theology to be borne and driven by this powerfully agitated and stirring air, not hindered by any safeguards existing ultimately and decisively in this very open air as its native habitat. All this should characterize theology if for no other reason than that such free mobility and movement are also the place of the community which lives from God's Word. On a higher level such motion is the place of the witnesses who directly hear and transmit the Word of God. And on a still higher level it is also the place where the history of Immanuel, as God's work, becomes God's Word. All this takes place in the realm of that freely moved and moving air, the gentle or stormy wind, the divine *spiratio* and *inspiratio*. According to the Bible, God's "spiration" and inspiration are the effective powers by which God discloses himself freely to men, making them accessible to himself and so on their part free for him.

The biblical name of this sovereign effective power is *ruach* or *pneuma*. And both terms mean, specifically, moved and moving air; they mean breath, wind, probably also storm, and in this sense, *spirit*. In the Latin *spiritus* and also in the French *esprit* this significance is rather clearly recognizable. In English the word should certainly not be reproduced by "Ghost" with its frightening proximity to "spooks." In German, unfortunately, *Geist* is a word which makes the dynamic significance of the biblical term altogether unrecognizable. Our use of the term, however, will be taken from the biblical axiom: "Where the Spirit of the Lord is, there is freedom" (II Cor. 3:17). The freedom of which we talk is God's freedom to disclose himself to men, to make men accessible to himself, and so to make them on their part free for him. The one who does that is the Lord God, who is the Spirit. There are also other spirits, those created good by God, such as the spirit natural to man. Moreover, there are demonic, erring, and disruptive spirits of annihilation which deserve nothing else than to be driven out. But none of these is that sovereign power of which we speak. Of none of them, not even of the best among them, can it be said that where it is, there is freedom. They must all be tested for the direction of their current, for their source from above or below. Above all, however, they must again and again be distinguished from the Spirit that, working in the *ambiance* of divine freedom, creates human freedom. In the Nicene Creed (as it was adopted by the Western Churches) the Spirit is called "the Holy One, the Lord and Giver of life," who "proceeds from the Father and from the Son, who together with the Father and the Son is adored and glorified." That is to say, the Spirit is himself God, the same one God who is also the Father and the Son; he acts both as Creator and as Reconciler, as the Lord of the covenant. As this very Lord, however, he now dwells, has dwelt, and will dwell in men. He dwells not only *among* them but also *in* them by the enlightening power of his action. It is that flowing air and moving atmosphere in which men may live, think, and speak wholly and entirely freed from presuppositions—for they are men who know the Spirit and are known by him, men called by him and obedient to him, his children begotten by his Word.

According to the second biblical saga of creation, God breathed into man "the breath of life," man's own spirit. This is the way the Spirit "spoke by the prophets," to use another phrase of the Nicene Creed. In this way John the Baptist saw the Spirit descend at the Jordan on the one who there, in solidarity with all sinners, accepted for himself the baptism of repentance. In this way the Spirit was the origin of the existence of the Son in the world of men—the Son who was *conceptus de Spiritu Sancto*, conceived of the Holy Spirit. In this way the spirit was the origin of the apostolate that proclaims the Son, as well as his nascent community. According to the Book of Acts, "suddenly a sound came from heaven like the rush of a mighty wind, and it filled all the house where they were sitting." By this power the disciples were enabled to speak of the mighty works of God and to be immediately understood even by those strangers who were present from every corner of the globe. It is in this manner that they spoke; and although they gave the impression of being drunk, it was as a result of this *spirare* and *inspirare* that the Word was understood and accepted by three thousand people. The Spirit *himself* was present, *God* the Spirit, the *Lord* who is the Spirit. This was his invasion, incitement, and witness to "what is in God" and "what has been given us by God," his power arousing and begetting the confession "Jesus is Lord!"

It was the Spirit whose existence and action make possible and real (and possible and real up to this very day) the existence of Christianity in the world. Up to this very day the Spirit calls into being the existence of every single Christian as a believing, loving, hoping witness to the Word of God. The Spirit does this certainly and irresistibly (for to wish to withstand him, when he steps in and acts, would be the one unforgivable sin), for he alone does this. "Any one who does not have the Spirit of Christ does not belong to him" (Rom. 8:9).

It is clear that evangelical theology itself can only be pneumatic, spiritual theology. Only in the realm of the power of the Spirit can theology be realized as a humble, free, critical, and happy science of the God of the Gospel. Only in the courageous confidence that the Spirit is the truth does theology simultaneously pose and answer the question about truth.

How does theology become the human logic of the divine Logos? The answer is that it does not *become* this at all; rather, theology may find that the Spirit draws near and comes over it, and that theology may then, without resisting, but also without assuming dominion over the Spirit, simply rejoice and obey its power. Unspiritual theology, whether it works its woe in the pulpit or from the rostrum, on the printed page or in "discussions" among old or young theologians, would be one of the most terrible of all terrible occurrences on this earthly vale. It would be so bad as to be without comparison with the works of even the worst political journalist or the most wretched novels or films. Theology becomes unspiritual when it lets itself be enticed or evicted from the freshly flowing air of the Spirit of the Lord, in which it alone can prosper. The Spirit departs when theology enters rooms whose stagnant air automatically prevents it from being and doing what it can, may, and must be and do.

The departure of the Spirit from theology can occur in two ways.

The first possibility is that theology, whether it is primitive or exceedingly cultivated, whether old-fashioned or, perhaps, most fashionable, will no doubt be practiced more or less zealously, cleverly, and probably also piously. In any case it will certainly be occasionally reminded of the problem of the Holy Spirit. Yet this theology does not muster the courage and confidence to submit itself fearlessly and unreservedly to the illumination, admonition, and consolation of the Spirit. It refuses to permit itself to be led by him into all truth. By such refusal, theology fails to give, in its inquiry, thought, and teaching, the honor due the Spirit of the Father and the Son that was certainly poured out over all flesh for its sake. One moment theology stands in out-and-out fear of the Spirit; in another it plays dumb, perhaps pretending to be better informed or else becoming obstinate in open opposition to him. As soon as the Spirit begins to stir within it, it suspects the danger of fanaticism; or it may rotate in circles of historicism, rationalism, moralism, romanticism, dogmaticism, or intellectualism, while "round about lies green and pleasant pasture."[2]

When theology poses and answers the question about truth in the above style and manner, it certainly cannot be serviceable to the community which, like itself, is totally dependent on the Holy Spirit. Its effect will be just the opposite! If theology is in the same situation as those disciples of John in Ephesus, who reportedly did not even know that there was a Holy Spirit, then theology must inevitably open the door to every possible, different, and strange spirit that aims at nothing other than to disturb and destroy the community, the church, and itself. Unpleasant consequences cannot and will not be lacking! Human criticism, mockery, and accusation, to be sure, cannot help theology when it is in this predicament. Only the Spirit himself can rescue theology! He, the Holy One, the Lord, the Giver of Life, waits and waits to be received anew by theology as by the community. He waits to receive from theology his due of adoration and glorification. He expects from theology that it submit itself to the repentance, renewal, and reformation he effects. He waits to vivify and illuminate its affirmations which, however right they may be, are dead without the Spirit.

The second possibility is that theology may know only too well about the rival power of the Spirit, which is indispensable to Christianity, to every Christian, and to it as well. Just because of this familiarity, theology may once again fail to acknowledge the vitality and sovereignty of this power which defies all domestication. In such a situation theology forgets that the wind of the Spirit

2. From Goethe's *Faust*, Part One (scene in "The Study").

blows where it wills. The presence and action of the Spirit are the grace of God who is always free, always superior, always giving himself undeservedly and without reservation. But theology now supposes it can deal with the Spirit as though it had hired him or even attained possession of him. It imagines that he is a power of nature that can be discovered, harnessed, and put to use like water, fire, electricity, or atomic energy. As a foolish church presupposes his presence and action in its own existence, in its offices and sacraments, ordinations, consecrations and absolutions, so a foolish theology presupposes the Spirit as the premise of its own declarations. The Spirit is thought to be one whom it knows and over whom it disposes. But a presupposed spirit is certainly not the Holy Spirit, and a theology that presumes to have it under control can only be unspiritual theology.

The Holy Spirit is the vital power that bestows free *mercy* on theology and on theologians just as on the community and on every single Christian. Both of these remain utterly in need of him. Only the Holy Spirit himself can help a theology that is or has become unspiritual. Only the Spirit can assist theology to become enduringly conscious and aware of the misery of its arbitrary devices of controlling him. Only where the Spirit is sighed, cried, and prayed for does he become present and newly active.

Veni creator Spiritus! "Come, O come, thou Spirit of life!"[3] Even the best theology cannot be anything more or better than this petition made in the form of resolute work. Theology can ultimately only take the position of one of those children who have neither bread nor fish, but doubtless a father who has both and will give them these when they ask him. In its total poverty evangelical theology is rich, sustained, and upheld by its total lack of *presuppositions*. It is rich, sustained, and upheld, since it lays hold on God's promise, clinging without skepticism, yet also without any presumption, to the promise according to which—not theology, but—"the Spirit searches all things, even the deep things of God."[4]

3. Title of a hymn by Heinrich Held, 1658.
4. At the conclusion of his delivery of the fifth lecture on "The Spirit," at Chicago and Princeton, Karl Barth added the following: "So much as an introduction to evangelical theology. But one thing remains to be added. Allow me to say it a little enigmatically and cryptically with the words of the Rebel General Stonewall Jackson, spoken at the hour of his death:
" 'Let us cross the river'—nobody knows whether he meant the Potomac or the Jordan—'and have a rest in the shade of the trees.' "

3

HELMUT THIELICKE
The Evangelical Faith

THE QUESTION AS TO OLD TRUTH HAS A "SPIRITUAL" BASIS. IF
faith and the resultant theological reflection look back, as we have
seen, to what the fathers believed, if they try to grasp and represent a tradition, this is not due to the conservative mentality of
those who believe, think, and confess thus. (The simple fact that
being conservative is a mentality is enough to disbar the term.) The
explanation is the very opposite. Looking back at the essence of
the gospel is required. It is grounded in the thing itself, not the
person. It thus gives rise to a certain conservative mentality.

Looking back is grounded in the thing itself to the extent that
faith and its reflection on what has happened once and for all relate
to the great acts of God which are the data of faith (cf. *ephápax* in
Romans 6:10; Hebrews 7:27; 9:12; 10:10). While it is true that the
faith given to me is a saving event which takes place now, an act of
the grace of God upon me, this saving act is not of the same rank as
what took place then, as God's conclusions of the covenant, as the
crucifixion and resurrection of Christ. Faith is only a subsequent
act by which what took place then is appropriated to me now. Faith
is simply a ratification of the covenant for me. This ratification
today, however, is grounded in the existing covenant. If I today
die and rise again with Christ (2 Corinthians 4:11; 2 Timothy
2:11), this presupposes that Christ has already died and risen
again. Hence faith is relativized. It has no specific weight of its
own.

This is why Luther liked to compare the subject of faith to a
mathematical point (WA, 40, II, 527, 9). Faith is not to be regarded as a psychological process and hence as a work. It is

From Helmut Thielicke, *The Evangelical Faith*, Vol. I, pp. 129–160,
193–205. © William B. Eerdmans Publishing Company, Grand Rapids,
1974. Used by permission of the Publisher.

defined exclusively by the one in whom it believes and to whom it relates itself.

The self-understanding and egocentricity of Cartesian theology threaten to banish this relativization of faith to forgetfulness by treating the present act of faith as equal to the past event on which it rests and even by making it the true content of the saving event. In spite of every safeguard it often seems that what is discussed is not the relation between the Christ-event of the past and its present actualization in faith but rather faith as itself the real point of the salvation event. Along these lines the work *Für und wider die Theologie Bultmanns* (2nd ed. [1952], p. 32) can even state that faith is the same work of God in me today as his work done once and for all in Christ for me yesterday, so that there is the closest possible union between faith and the salvation event (a supposed insight of the Reformation). Here one may hardly detect any relativization of faith. The priority of the past event is not maintained. Faith is given its own significance. It is now more and other than the subsequent response to God's assurance in the covenant that he will be gracious to me.

While Schniewind says that faith does not draw attention to itself (KM, I, p. 97; E.T. p. 72), but depends on encounter with a unique event, in many trends within Cartesian theology faith achieves a rank of its own. Even linguistically it is a subject and almost a personified hypostasis. In Ebeling and Fuchs it often seems to be a figure in salvation history which cooperates in the achievement of salvation. Thus Ebeling says that if faith is referred to Jesus, then Jesus is referred to faith (G. Ebeling, *Das Wesen des christlichen Glaubens* [1959], p. 50; E. T. *The Nature of Faith* [1961], pp. 45f.). Although he modifies this, the structure of his teaching shows that all christological and dogmatic statements are ultimately controlled by faith, and the decisive christological principle is that Jesus as the witness to faith becomes the basis of faith (*Wort und Glaube* [1960], pp. 314f.). Fuchs goes even further and has fewer safeguards than Ebeling. Thus faith participates in the resurrection of the crucified by publicly recognizing Jesus as Lord; Christ is risen when this confession is an expression of love (ZThK [1962], 1, pp. 42f.). Faith, then, is not subsequent to the event. It helps to bring it to pass, cooperating in the resurrection.

Are we pressing the point unduly if we say that on this view the past event is nothing without faith? But if we are right, then what Fuchs says is the direct opposite of Luther's doctrine of participation in the Lord's Supper even by the unworthy. The doctrine, which was aimed against Zwingli, argues that when the Word is preached and the sacrament is administered something always happens. Reception in faith is not what makes it an event; it is this whether with faith or without it. Faith plays a part only to the degree that it decides whether what happens is for blessing and not for condemnation, as with unbelief (cf. Form. Conc. Sol. decl., VII, 123). The point of the doctrine is thus to safeguard the fact that Christ's sacramental presence for me is not dependent on my faith (P. Althaus, *Die christliche Wahrheit,* II [1948], p. 393). Faith does not cooperate in the event. The event is a given factor; it takes place on me and to me.

This is the element in the thing itself, in the gospel, which forces us to look back at what happened then. To put it simply, we were saved nineteen hundred years ago.[1]

The function of protecting the givenness of the event when it is being actualized, of not allowing it to become pure present, of seeing to it that salvation history is always there before me, is a function discharged by the Holy Spirit. No matter what the Holy Spirit discloses to me, no matter into what truth he leads me (John 16:13), it will always be true that he will take the things of Christ (John 16:14), referring back to what took place in Christ's history, so that it is for me a given which establishes my faith without itself being established by this faith.

Even if this is not the place to develop a full doctrine of the Holy Spirit, the testimony of the Spirit is significant at this point in various ways. For this testimony obviously has something to say about the relations of "then" and "now," about the Christ-event and faith, about the relation of my self-understanding to what takes place to me and what is a given for me, in short, about the problem of appropriation and re-presentation.

The relevant aspects of the doctrine of the Holy Spirit in this regard are as follows.

1. Negatively, this reference back to the saving event finds expression in the fact that we do not make Jesus Christ our Lord in our own reason or strength. We cannot produce faith of ourselves. This is the work of the Holy Spirit (SC; LBK, 511, 6). This means, however, that the historical Jesus of Nazareth, through the Holy Spirit,[2] makes himself contemporary with us.[3] The natural man (*psychikós ánthrōpos*) does not perceive the things of the Spirit of

---

1. As pointed out, rather unexpectedly, by P. M. van Buren, *The Secular Meaning of the Gospel,* p. 169.
2. This is the point of the *filioque,* which found a place in theology from the time of Tertullian and which was then adopted into the Nicene Creed in the West (LBK, 27).
3. The Holy Spirit brings true "presence" (Form. Conc. Sol. decl., II; LBK, 8).

God (1 Corinthians 2:14). Hence he cannot produce the present which eventuates in faith. Nor can he reproduce the past in such a way that it is present for him and Christ becomes his (contemporary) Lord. In contrast, although it does not sound too well, one should rather say that Christ can reproduce himself and bring himself out of the past into the present.

This is the point of the Spirit's testimony. It means that the evidence of what we believe in is provided, not by faith, but by what we believe in itself, i.e., the given fact of the Christ-event. The Lord makes himself evident and hence he makes faith possible. Faith does not make the Lord evident. The Lord himself is the Spirit (2 Corinthians 3:17f.). He cannot be controlled, then, by the natural man.

The natural man cannot achieve re-presentation on his own initiative, i.e., by methodology or hermeneutical effort. The presence of the Lord in faith is a sovereign gift. Without this gift we have only a dead past and historical distance. The testimony of the Spirit is thus a protest against our own endeavor, preparation, thought, or work (CA, V; LBK, 58). Neither the preacher's planting and watering nor the hearer's running and willing can help if the Spirit does not himself achieve the re-presentation (Sol. decl., II, 55; LBK, 893, 55).

It is thus a mistake to try to bridge the gap to the given history with presuppositions of our own or subjective analysis. To do this is to expect to find possibilities of re-presentation. But concern about methodology, if it comes first and dominates the scene, is simply an expression of active preparation and is thus a latent protest against the monopoly of the Holy Spirit.

The doctrine of the Holy Spirit is for its part a protest against the Cartesian approach in theology, against beginning with existential analysis and preliminary hermeneutical questions. Hence we may well ask whether this is not the reason why the doctrine of the Holy Spirit seems to be so strangely awkward in Theology A, finding no real place in this type of theology.

The Augsburg Confession makes this point when it says that the Spirit is not a movement in creatures (CA, II, 6). The doctrine of the Holy Spirit does not invite introspection, the self-contemplation of the creaturely I. Instead, it directs attention away from the self.

The trinitarian description of the Spirit as a "person" is significant in this regard. Standing over against the human ego, the Spirit is God in person. He does not come into me in such a way as to be a movement within me. He remains an object of the prayer: "Come, Holy Ghost."

Some NT passages, if taken in isolation, might suggest that the Spirit is an inherent quality, e.g., Romans 8:4; 1 Corinthians 6:11; 1 John 3:9; 2 Peter 1:4. He seems here to be imparted to man almost as an indelible character. But we also find complementary statements in which the Spirit is more without than within, thus barring the way to any idea of his being simply a working or indeed a work in us. He is the one who works on us. We can safely speak of his work in us if the primacy of this "on us" is established (cf. G. Dehn, "Der neue Mensch," *Theologia viatorum* [1939], pp. 67ff., esp. 92ff.). This externality of the Holy Spirit will be even more plainly established under the next heading.

2. The Spirit's testimony does not just point us away from the self and its pre-conditions and activities. It also has the positive function of directing us to the self-evidence of the Word and of him to whom it bears witness. The Spirit orients us to Christ. He does not let us be bound to ourselves, i.e., to our carnality (Romans 8:9). For the Holy Spirit (*sphragízein*) is the seal of that which Christ signifies as a promise for the advance and consummation of the event of salvation (Ephesians 1:13; 4:30). Thus the Spirit points us away from ourselves to the past and the coming event of which Christ is initiator, content, and finisher.

How the Spirit refers us to this event that takes place outside the human psyche we are told by the Johannine Christ: "If I go not away, the Paraclete will not come unto you; but if I depart, I will send him unto you" (John 16:7). This means that the Spirit can be given only when certain events—the crucifixion and resurrection—have taken place which he will disclose to us. The "all truth" (*alétheia pásē*) into which he will lead us is not truth that goes beyond the promised and enacted events. It is truth which unfolds these events and applies them to me (John 3:27; James 1:17).

This work of the Spirit in pointing us away from self and "in me" to what takes place "on and to me" finds expression in certain NT metaphors which seem at first to locate the work of the Spirit in human subjectivity. One might quote, for example, the comparison of the body to a temple in 1 Corinthians 6:19. Exegesis might easily conclude from this that the Spirit is the center of our entelechy, i.e., that which fulfils us from within, the impelling core of the spiritual organism. But in fact the Spirit here is more like the eternal light burning in the temple. He points us to something outside, to what has taken place on and to us. We are redeemed at great cost (1 Corinthians 6:20). The dignity ascribed to us as a temple rests on the reference to him whose possession the temple is. We cannot be the temple of Christ and the temple of

Belial at the same time (2 Corinthians 6:16) because the references are in conflict. The temple does not point to itself but away from itself.

This metaphor has often commended itself as an illustration of the very differently slanted humanism (cf. W. von Humboldt) which makes the development of the human entelechy the real meaning of existence. Here the human temple is developed with architectonic symmetry and proportion. But instead of a sanctuary it becomes a museum. It has significance in itself, not in its external reference. Similarly the dignity of the human here is found aesthetically in its structure. But the dignity of the human in which the Holy Spirit dwells as his temple is defined by a dignity that is not its own (*dignitas aliena*).

This alien dignity shines forth the brighter when our own values are dubious and our humanist status is not so lofty. Thus it is by means of the weaker brethren that Paul shows that we are not to get too far ahead or to offend in relation to them. Christ died for them too. They too were bought with a price. They thus have a share in the dignity that makes them sacred (Romans 14:15; 1 Corinthians 8:11).

Christian humanism—if one may use the term—should not be concerned, then, with reason and conscience and similar marks of distinction from the animal kingdom. It should teach us to look at what is outside, at the dignity that is not our own, at what has taken place on and to us, and hence at what is a given factor for us.[4] When we are called the temple of the Holy Spirit, this external reference is in view. At issue is what is without, not within.

Lutheranism formulated this relation of the Spirit to the given and external event or word with a force that is not so easily matched in the Reformed statements. (This is because Lutheranism had to take issue more seriously with the sectarians.) The Schmalcaldic Articles say very definitely that only by and with the outward and prevenient word are grace and the Spirit imparted to anyone.[5] The work of the Spirit is to relate to us what this word tells us of the great acts of God, the forgiveness of sins, the resurrection of the body, and the life everlasting.[6] Only when we

---

4. In all such questions as euthanasia and abortion this factor of our alien dignity always arises for Christians, and it cannot be regarded as a variable or changeable functional value. The crux of the debate between Christian and Marxist anthropology lies precisely at this point (cf. ThE, Index, "dignitas aliena").

5. Art. VIII; LBK, 453, 3.

6. GC, Art. 3; LBK, 654, 41.

believe, then, can we receive him as the one who transforms us and kindles fervent love within us.[7]

When we say this, of course, we have to add what it is that we believe as thus disclosed and set at work within us by the Spirit. The Apology of the Confession of Augsburg offers here the memorable statement that we believe in God as a lovable object.[8] The human heart could not love the God of the law who simply commands and judges. Fervent love would be ruled out in such a case. This love is not something that has to be attained. It reflects subjectively what we experience transsubjectively as it happens outside us and to us, namely, that God is lovable.[9]

But how is God lovable?

God can be for me a lovable object only as this is attested to me, not as a mere assertion, but as a narrative of his self-demonstration as such, namely, in his mighty acts from the deliverance out of bondage in Egypt and through the wilderness to the warnings and promises of the prophets and finally the new covenant in the coming of Jesus Christ. The name of God that is proclaimed is also the name of his acts, of what has happened to us. God is there for us as we remember and look back upon the history which he has caused to happen to us and in which he has included us.

It is evident now how the Holy Spirit achieves re-presentation. He evokes faith, kindles fervent love, and opens up immediate access to God by illuminating the mighty acts of God as a nexus into which I am taken up and whose earlier stages are of contemporary or existential significance to me, so that in the simpler and more expressive language of Scripture I am pricked in the heart (Acts 2:37).

Peter's sermon in Acts offers an excellent illustration (Acts 2:14-36). He recalls what has happened. But the Spirit of Pentecost overcomes historical distance. He takes up those who are listening into the events. What the prophets foretold, what has now been fulfilled in the resurrection of Christ, is for the whole house of Israel (v. 36). It applies to "today," to "you." God can be seen in it as a lovable object. The natural man may have no organ to receive it (1 Corinthians 2:14). He can only remain at a historical distance. He can only relativize. But the Holy Spirit discloses it to

7. Cf. Luther's "Come, Holy Ghost" in EKG, No. 98, 1; Apol.; LBK, 185, 127.

8. *Ibid.*, 186, 129.

9. The author requests that the terminology used here not be related to the familiar controversy concerning the subject-object schema.

you. Love, confidence, and faith are thus imparted. Loving is not a subjective faculty; otherwise it would be under the law. Love is a reflection, the subjective side, of the fact that God encounters me as one who is worthy of love, and his history is for me a manifestation of this love.

Formally, there is a similarity here to the righteousness of God as an active righteousness in Luther's sense (cf. Schrenk in TDNT, II, 198ff.; H. Iwand, *Glaubensgerechtigkeit* [1941], pp. 55ff.). Understood thus, righteousness is not disinterestedly distributive, handing out rewards and punishments. It confers on man the possibility of being righteous before God, of sharing in God's own righteousness. We are righteous before him when we are in conformity with him. We are not in conformity with him, however, by our own works or efforts. These would give us claims and thus put us in a legal relation. They would make us partners with God. But this would not do justice to his Godhead. It would be a transgression of human creatureliness. I do justice to God and attain to conformity with his will only when I enter into what he wills to be for me, namely, a gracious God. I do so only when I trust his self-declaration as such, only when I have faith in him.

As, then, the righteousness of faith corresponds to God's righteousness, so love of God corresponds to God as lovable object. In both cases (the love of God and the righteousness of God) the genitive can be both subjective and objective. The very grammar thus shows that this is a relation of complementarity. I can view the same love and righteousness from the divine perspective and also from the human perspective. They point to one another. This is possible only because they describe a relation and not the state of an isolated person, whether God or man. Loving and being righteous imply relation. I come into relation with God as I accept him for what he wills to be and has shown himself to be in his mighty acts, namely, the one who loves me and has come to me in grace.

This is why the Holy Spirit works primarily, not through what is done in man so that he is "full of the Holy Spirit" (Acts 2:4; 4:8, 31; 6:3, 5; 7:55; 11:24; Ephesians 5:18), but through what is done on and to him, so that he is really "full" of the Holy Spirit. In other words, the Holy Spirit directs the one whom he enlightens away from himself to a history which is outside him even though it includes him, and to a word which is again outside him, so that it is an external word. If the Holy Spirit also works within to call and enlighten and sanctify, this is because the strange thing that comes from without also becomes proper to man (cf. Iwand, *op. cit.*, pp. 56ff.). There are two reasons for this.

The first is that God does not hold back but pours out generously. He wills to be there for me. But if he wills this so unreservedly, then "I am" means only what he is for me (Luther, WA, 54, 186).

The second is related to the first. "I am" can no longer denote my isolated and self-grounded entelechy. It tells of what God is for me and hence of what I am in consequence. It expresses a relation. I am the one who is brought under God's covenant and visited by God in judgment and grace.[10] This is what Luther has in mind when he says that God and we are in the same righteousness, as God also creates with the same word and we are what he creates, so that we are in him and his being is our being (WA, 5, 144).

The "I am" is thus a mode of God's being, not pantheistically, but in such a way that my being is determined by what God addresses to me. Christ is an exemplar of my existence.[11] A bold complementarity can thus be expressed: Christ is my sin and I am his righteousness.[12] The "I am" is a statement about being in relation, for in every dimension of life I am characterized by what God is for me. I am created, fallen, and visited. I am judged and blessed.[13] The I is thus determined from without by what is done on it, by what God is for it.

When things are viewed thus, it is impossible to begin with a self-understanding or pre-understanding. For this would mean excluding the I from that relation and seeing it as a prior entity. Who I really am I learn only from the word that proclaims to me God's condescension, his covenant, and his mighty acts. The Holy Spirit who discloses this word to me does not point me to myself but away from myself to the events by which I am what I am.

This is why the debate whether the Holy Spirit is a person or a power, a lord who encounters me or a force that works in me, is pointless. Whether we refer to him in one way or the other is connected with the complementarity of all theologico-anthropological statements, and these in turn are based on the relation which determines human existence.

In the same light one can also see why the Holy Spirit has a conservative aspect (not to be confused, as we have noted, with

10. W. Zimmerli, *Das Menschenbild des Alten Testaments* (1949), pp. 8ff.

11. For references cf. E. Wolf in *Jesus Christus im Zeugnis der Heiligen Schrift* (1936), pp. 214ff.

12. Cf. P. Althaus, *Die Theologie Luthers* (1962), pp. 180 and 199; E. T. 1966, pp. 203f., 227f.

13. Cf. G. Jacob, *Luthers Gewissensbegriff* (1929).

conservatism). He has this because he refers us to the external word and therewith to the history of God with us to which it bears witness. He summons as witness what God has done to the fathers, the patriarchs, prophets and apostles, and what they have testified to in the word, and handed down as a word to our own time. The Holy Spirit effects the *actualization* of the past. He makes it present as something that took place for me. He includes me in the history attested here. But it is an actualization of the *past*. He reminds me of what took place. He thus bears witness to the author of these events, the God of Abraham, Isaac and Jacob, and the Father of Jesus Christ.

In thus making God's history contemporary, though not reducing it to timeless ideas, the Holy Spirit honors all times, past as well as future, recollected as well as promised. Hence when Pascal says: "The God of Abraham, Isaac, and Jacob, not of the philosophers and scholars," he has in view the God who comes into history, the subject of mighty acts, not God as a timeless idea. Similarly one might say of the Holy Spirit that he is not the spirit of the philosophers and scholars, but the Spirit who leads into history and who brings history to us.

Thus *nous* and *pneuma*, the wisdom of the world and the historical manifestation of divine wisdom (1 Corinthians 1:18ff.), are always at odds with one another. The wisdom of the world (the rational spirit) contemplates itself and conducts its inquiry according to its own axioms and immanent principles, so that its picture of ultimate reality—whether called God or not—is formed according to these premises. The Holy Spirit, however, has in view the historical events by which God defines me as what I am, so that as I must believe these events, so I have the definition of myself only in faith. Not God alone, but man defined by God too, is the object of faith.

It was the conflict with the sectarians that led Lutheranism in particular to stress this link between the Spirit and history, along with the word that bears witness to it. Negatively this is a safeguard against the supposed spiritual revelations of enthusiasm, which, being direct, are not grounded in the external word, and are thus only contemporary and do not include recollection as well. We will append only a few of the many possible quotations from Luther to back up our thesis.

Spirit and letter (2 Corinthians 3:6f.) are not to be viewed as antithetical; the Spirit writes "the letters on our hearts" (WA, 47, 184). "God will not give anyone the Spirit apart from the word and the preaching office" (17, 135). The Holy Spirit kindles faith and illumines the heart, but "not without the outward office or the outward use of the sacraments" (43, 187). One cannot boast of the Spirit without having "the open and outward word." For "the Holy Spirit has set his wisdom, counsel, and all secrets in the word and revealed them in Scripture." A spirit that looses itself from these is not from God, but "from hell" (36, 501).

THE HOLY SPIRIT AS HE WHO CREATES ANEW AND YET ALSO LINKS TO THE OLD
The New Place of Self-Understanding

1. Problem of Continuity

We must consider at once an objection. This objection is an urgent one in relation to Cartesian theology. Against our thesis that the Holy Spirit does not let us begin with the axioms of our own self-understanding but turns our gaze on what has happened historically, this theology can advance a weighty argument which might be given the form of the following counter-questions.

How *can* I look outwards to let myself be defined by what takes place and to receive my self-understanding therefrom? This sounds as though I were a *tabula rasa*, a blank page to be filled only by the external word, the Word of God, while itself remaining passive. But this is surely an illusion. I am "someone" even before confrontation with that word. I have a definite self-understanding. I am of age. I am not a blank sheet. The Holy Spirit cannot ignore this, unless he avoids certain facts about me and is completely unrealistic. Are not my adulthood and my very humanity disregarded if it is assumed that the Holy Spirit causes me to be defined exclusively from without? Is not the external word degraded to a mere dictum if it no longer convicts me (convicting implies criteria), if it no longer calls me to conversion (conversion implies already being on a way), but simply fills an unresisting vacuum? If man is a vacuum and the Holy Spirit is the substance that fills it, we had better speak of physics rather than theology. A personal relation between God and man is impossible on this level. If this level is to be avoided, if the Word of God, the kerygma, is to encounter a concrete man with a specific self-understanding, then theological relevance must be ascribed to what is already there for the kerygma. It cannot be dismissed as belonging to the spirit of philosophy. Only as I take it seriously do I respect the claim of the kerygma that it can be appropriated by me, i.e., that it can enter into a specific relation to my self-understanding. Without this appropriation the kerygma remains outside or else it forces its way in as law, and is no true gospel. But the fact that it is gospel, that it tells of God's self-declaration as a lovable object, is the heart of the doctrine of the Spirit, of the non-Cartesian theology, that we are championing. A self-contradiction thus seems to arise. The spontaneity with which I accept God as a lovable object is endangered if the Holy Spirit ignores man's prior self, treats the process of appropriation as irrelevant, and puts enforced belief in the place of spontaneous faith. This perverts everything and indeed turns it into its opposite.

We have tried to express here all the essential arguments that arise out of our study of Theology A. Obviously we are at the very heart and center of the debate. It will thus reward us to give due weight to the counter-questions.

Undoubtedly these objections would be right if we had actually said that the Holy Spirit ignores altogether the data of natural existence, directs our gaze only outwards (in a nondialectical sense), and relentlessly confronts us with the proffered revelation. Even Barth, however, would never want his statement that the word creates its own hearers (by the Spirit) to be taken so one-sidedly and nondialectically.

We have thus to consider how it is that the Holy Spirit, in effecting a new creation (2 Corinthians 5:17; Galatians 6:15), does not ignore the given realities of the old creation or the natural man, but claims them and integrates them into the new creation. In so doing we may formulate our thesis as follows. While the prior self-understanding of man is not ignored in the Spirit's work and remains a theological theme, it is not accorded the same rank as in Cartesian theology. It is not the starting-point of theology in the form of existential analysis. It is the object of a retrospective glance and is thus a secondary theme.

The problem that concerns us has been discussed in modern theology under the title of the problem of a point of contact.[1] The question is whether and how far there are elements in our natural consciousness (or conscience) which make God's Word intelligible to us, which go to meet it, and which are thus the presupposition of possible appropriation of it. This raises the further question of the analogy between revelation and nature, the problem of analogy of being. It thus gives rise not merely to the

1. Cf. the famous debate between Barth and Brunner in *Natural Theology* (1946).

controversy between Theology A and Theology B[2] but also to that between Reformation and Thomistic theology.[3]

In this context we cannot go into the problem of analogy nor discuss the debate between Barth and Brunner in detail. We shall thus concentrate on the question of the point of contact to the degree that this impinges on the operation of the Holy Spirit as presented above.

In dealing with this question we shall study two models. The first is a philosophical one, that of the relation between the categorical imperative and the divine commandment. The second is a biblical one, the story of the Prodigal Son (cf. ThE, I, § 1605ff.).

2. Philosophical Model: The Commandments of God and the Categorical Imperative

In his doctrine of the categorical imperative Kant not only discusses the philosophical problem of autonomy[4] but also unintentionally makes a contribution to the theological doctrine of the law. Without expressly referring to it he adopts Paul's teaching that the law kills. It kills because it comes to me as an external command, so that it forces me instead of leading to spontaneous obedience. In this heteronomous function the law can only lead to protest (Romans 7:11). It forces me into self-assertion. According to Paul its goal of bringing me into harmony with God's will can be achieved only if it makes love possible for me. Love is spontaneity. In love I enjoy totality, whereas the law divides me into an assenting self and an opposing self (7:7ff.). But love as the fulfilment of the law cannot be achieved by the law itself. As noted, if I am to love, God must come to me as the object of love.

Along the same lines as Paul, Kant bases his ethics of autonomy on the thought that no claim of any kind, whether command or revelation, can legitimately hold me unless it is approved by the criteria of my own ethical consciousness and is appropriated with

2. In this regard the Barth-Brunner debate is not a good example, since Brunner is not a typical representative of Theology A. Nevertheless, the points raised there are a good illustration of the encounter in many ways.
3. In fact the Barth-Brunner debate has made the problem of analogy a subject of discussion interconfessionally as well as within Protestantism (cf. H. G. Pöhlmann, *Analogia entis und fidei* [1965]; H. Diem, *Theologie als kirchliche Wissenschaft* [1951], pp. 28ff.; G. Söhngen, *Die Einheit der Theologie* [1952], pp. 235ff.).
4. Cf. the author's *Das Verhältnis zwischen dem Ethischen und dem Ästhetischen* (1932).

the help of this approval. This condition must be observed if the dignity of my autonomy is not to be violated (which is anthropologically impossible) and the divine author of the law is not to be the epitome of tyrannical legalism and therefore of heteronomy (which is theologically impossible).

Thus Kant is dealing with the present issue. The self-understanding of the natural man, who thinks of himself autonomously, cannot be ignored if both the one who is claimed and that which claims are not to be subjected to tensions that will distort both. Obviously the Holy Spirit will not disregard these important realities. But if not, then we are face to face once more with the question whether we should not begin with existential analysis in the manner of Theology A, learning about the subjective conditions on which we can accept the claim. Does not Kant lead us back to the Cartesian starting-point?

This we must examine. The examination will show what weight or worth the question of the self-understanding of the natural man has when he is set under the claim of the Holy Spirit, i.e., when he is pointed away from self to the external word and comes to see that the natural man knows nothing of this word or Spirit, that the old man must die and become a new creature if he is to attain to understanding in this realm.

If, however, the Holy Spirit puts us to death and thus seems to create a *tabula rasa*, how can he make contact with anything? How can he treat anything as existent, and take it seriously as such? This is the crux of the matter. With it we turn to what Kant says about the structure of the ethical consciousness in the (theologically) old or natural man.

The structure of the natural conscience in virtue of which man is a subject and is responsible, having to give an answer, finds classical formulation in the categorical imperative. "Act in such a way that the maxims of your will can always be accepted as the principle of general legislation" (*Critique of Practical Reason*, I, § 7). We have intentionally said that conscience in the absolute finds classical formulation in this imperative. This has to be said because conscience is not referred here to a specific national or divine law. It is defined simply as a supreme court in man that seeks maxims that are worthy to be regarded as a general law and can thus be adopted by the conscience "with a good conscience" as the norm of the will. When conscience is described in this open fashion, with no specific content, the reference is to its intrinsic form.

Two points are important here. (1) Conscience bends only to a law which has the highest worth the human mind can think of, namely, that of universal validity. This means that the categorical imperative is ready for a law which stands above personal opinion or the fluctuating voices of purely subjective moral instincts. These might express the tainted remnant of opportunistic inclination and uncontrolled self-will. They must first be tested by the criterion of general validity, by the principle which is above all selfishness or individualism. A ray of man's divine likeness thus seems to shine in this world of the categorical imperative, for man himself is here the subject, the autonomous subject, the final criterion of the universal law, the author of the law. In this subjectivity or autonomy he experiences, as Kant says, the basis of his self-regard, of his dignity.

(2) Even more important perhaps is the further fact that the categorical imperative must accept a law into the will if it is to meet that rigorous demand, whether it be the heroic ethic of Nietzsche or the radical requirements of the Sermon on the Mount in Tolstoy. Here if anywhere it is an urgent question whether this uncompromising readiness for a final demand on and against man can serve as a point of contact for the law of God. Of what more radical and selfless readiness can we conceive even theoretically? Is not this man's supreme openness, his greatest receptivity? Is not the conscience, illumined by that imperative, one long waiting or questing for the unconditional command, one long readiness for obedience? How can God, the author of the law, have more open doors if he will only see it and seek entry here and introduce his command as a maxim into the will at this point? Is not the imperative the one legitimate place for an encounter between God's address and man's listening to the extent that this takes the form of a word spoken and heard, a word heard as a claim, so that it has to be lived out and practiced?

We shall come close to an answer to these questions if we recall the metaphysical basis of the categorical imperative: You ought and therefore you can (*ibid.*, § 6).

Heidegger, too, can say that in the conscience existence summons itself to its most authentic possibility of being.[5] An "ought" which demands what is impossible in principle, reaching out beyond the arc of possible human action, is nonsensical. It cannot be achieved. It cannot be the content of what is possible for me. Hence it cannot claim to be an "ought." Man's primal ethical instinct counts upon a relation between "ought" and "can." It is

5. *Being and Time*, pp. 318f.

thus evident that the imperative cannot ask of man what is beyond the unchangeable realities of his constitution and character. It can claim him only within this framework, within what he can achieve.[6] The imperative cannot challenge man as such, i.e., in his totality, along with his constitution. It can challenge him only insofar as he makes imperfect use of his constitution. Man himself, in his constitution and character, is the ethically indifferent presupposition of any ethics. His own place is thus secure.

The theological bearing of this comes to light when it is God's unconditional command that raises a claim to be accepted as a maxim into man's conscience, i.e., the categorical imperative. For God's command in its radical form—the command of love for both neighbor and enemy, the command not to covet (Matthew 5:43 par.; Luke 6:27, 35; Matthew 5:28)—certainly advances a claim to universal validity, but it does so in such a way as to question man himself in the very form of his existence, including his constitution and character. Indeed, it challenges the present aeon and all its structural laws.

We have to realize that if we fulfill this command, if we love our neighbor as ourselves, if we love our enemies, if we cease to covet, our whole history will come to a halt and we shall sink into the immobility of nonproductivity and starvation. For, to keep alive, this history needs the impelling forces of opposition, rivalry, oppression, passion, and conflict, so that fulfilment of the command is ruled out in principle by it.

For this reason the command, e.g., in the Sermon on the Mount, is God's assault on the present aeon with its laws and also on the total man to the degree that he is a representative of this aeon, to the degree that he *is*, i.e., in his given constitution, character, and structure, and not just in the sphere of his mobilized forces, of his capacity on the basis of his constitution.

I ought but I cannot. I cannot because I am what I am. This is the upshot of that assault. Man can alter himself only in his acts, not in his nature. The "I am" has determinative force for the "I will." This is why works cannot save. The "I will" cannot change the "I am." Good works do not make a good man, but a good man does good works, as Luther puts it.[7] Behind his works man is still the same man. Over this he has no control. Hence he has either to despair of God's total claim or to reject himself.

6. Cf. the author's *Geschichte und Existenz*, 2nd ed. (1964), pp. 66ff.
7. Thus the point in Luther's *De servo arbitrio (On the Bondage of the Will)* is that man is bound by the necessity of his own nature (cf. WA, 18, 634f., 709; E. T., pp. 102, 203f.).

Does this mean, then, that the Holy Spirit, when he refers us to the external word, transcends the conditions under which natural man exists? Are these conditions ignored? Do we not have the precise situation described by Theology A in its objections?

The problem is now somewhat clearer. We have stated that if there is in us a point of contact for God's revelation it will be found in the waiting, questing, and receptive conscience as described in the categorical imperative. Yet we have also seen that here, too, a chasm opens up with no bridge across it from man to God. For natural man in the grip of his autonomy lives in the illusion that if he ought he can. He cannot accept God's radical and unconditional law into his conscience because he is unable to hear and to recognize it as law, claim, attack. To demand that man and his world should be changed absolutely, that man should cease to be himself, that he should transcend the laws of life and existence, seems to make no sense at all—and sense is the chief maxim in this ethical view of things.

The "ought" which claims us in the law of God attacks the very basis of existence instead of limiting itself to the radius of ethical action within the framework of existence and on its basis. Hence it cannot be brought into harmony with man's self-understanding. Since it does not correspond to the ethical axiom "You ought and therefore you can," he cannot regard it as a command or an ought at all, and he cannot appropriate it as such.

A different explanation has thus to be found. Thus the divine command of love and the implied assault upon our whole world and our total existence might be viewed as the expression of universal pessimism or (as in Tolstoy) of a pacifism which is directed against the militant laws of reality. For, since man's natural ethos is indissolubly bound up with the illusion "You ought and therefore you can," and since this illusion is paradoxically made the criterion of all ethical reality, man in terms of himself and his own ethical maxims can never recognize God's law as ethical reality or a valid "ought," but necessarily has to dismiss it as illusion, as pessimistic illusion. For him it is thus unrealistic ideology, e.g., humanity expressed in ethical categories as pessimistic, pacifist, or some other humanity. Man's ethical self-understanding suffers here the fate of confusing illusion and reality. One might almost say that it suffers the fate of retrogression into a mythical worldview. When it finds a constitutive factor in man's disposition, in that which limits ontically the radius of his will, it adopts the mythical concept of cosmic matter as distinct from the belief in creation out of nothing. When this given matter qualifies my will and acts, zones of responsibility are changed into ethically neutral zones.

Yet everything depends on man's allowing the incursion of God's reality through the claim of the divine law to lead him to the very opposite view, namely, that the reality of the "You ought and therefore you can," and with it every other reality which is the basis on which he so confidently builds, is in fact an illusion. The illusion is that man is a subject who commands, and that he is thus at the center of his world, since it is he who draws its limits, making his own nature, the structure of the existence of the old man, the norm of all that can come to him as a claim or statement about his supposed possibilities.

When man protests against God's summons, therefore, he does so, not in the name of his reality, but in the name of the illusion he thinks is his reality. That he thinks he is fighting in the opposite direction, namely, against the fate of an unconditional demand and in the name of his own reality and aeon, is the sublime deception in the sin of illusion.

We have now achieved an important insight. The reality of man, e.g., his ethical reality, cannot be a systematic point of contact because it is a perverted and mythicized reality rather than the true one, because it is an illusion, and because it always isolates man. Only when God's prior reality is first disclosed to man does he learn to know his own reality.

This leads us to a first decisive conclusion. A given point of contact for revelation in the reality of man is impossible, since this reality arises only in faith, in revelation already enacted, and before that it can only be illusion in the sense described.

But this is not the end of the matter. It is still clear that God's law, or, more generally, God's claim, is addressed to the conscience of the natural man. This means again that it is addressed to man who by nature, by innate conscience, already has knowledge of an "ought," of obligation, of, e.g., the categorical imperative (cf. Romans 2:14f.). This is how man may be brought under obligation to God's law. And this still holds good even though the natural conscience and its categorical imperative are based on the "You ought and therefore you can," so that conscience builds a wall of partition between itself and God's law. Precisely for this reason contact between God's law and conscience cannot take place directly but only by way of a break. We shall now try to elucidate this.

If God as the author of the law makes contact with the natural "ought," if he compels the categorical imperative to adopt the command as a maxim of the human will, he does so only by challenging the natural "ought" and its illusion "You ought and therefore you can." The conscience is disquieted by God's law, not because it is aware of not having done, or having been able to do, all that it should, but because it begins to fear that it might be living in illusion and untruth, that its values and calculations are unfounded, that it is moving in the wrong direction. The result of this disquietude may be seen when the rich young ruler comes running to Jesus and falls at his feet (Mark 10:17). The presuppositions of his conduct were wrong. The confidence that his conscientious life would merit eternal life was misplaced. The unrest which impelled him was not just that he had not achieved perfection in his fulfilment of the law. He was now convinced that this fulfilment was itself defective (v. 20).

This, then, is the fear, the secret disquietude, of the natural conscience when confronted with the demand of God the Lord. If it acknowledges this demand—and of course it can refuse to do so—the presuppositions of its very existence are questioned. The categorical imperative itself withers when it is summoned before the new and unheard-of content of the law of God. For if it makes it the principle of general legislation, it transcends its own presuppositions, namely, the presuppositions of the "You ought and therefore you can." What seems to be gain to the categorical imperative is its undoing. God has crossed the boundary or horizon of its existence.

How he does this cannot be objectified, since the creative Spirit of God who brings it about cannot be integrated into the structure of the "old" existence. There is here no mere perfecting of what is there already. Who God is and what he does to me cuts right across my theories about him. These theories relate always to the fulfilment of given beginnings. But here the very foundations of my existence are opened up to new creation, to the Creator Spirit. This is something that has not entered the heart of man and cannot be grasped by the natural man (1 Corinthians 2:9, 14). It has no place on his list of categories.

It is now evident that we cannot speak of a constant point of contact which may be located in the reality of the natural man and which forms a steady continuum. The grace which gives rise to the new creature makes this creature wholly new by giving him a new and true reality. If we speak of a point of contact, this is an improper, though necessary, term. It is necessary because we cannot understand the judgment God executes in his law if we do not see this law as the great disrupting of the presupposed illusion of the "You ought and therefore you can" which thus serves as a contact. For the essence of this judgment is that it takes from man the illusion of ability in which he has taken refuge with his pretended "ought." The judgment thus presupposes the illusory relation of "ought" and "can" (as a point of contact). By transcending this relation it shows itself to be judgment and leads through the valley of despair to radical revisions and reorientations. Thus God's judgment is in some sense a summons, a "contact."

The very depths of the ambiguity of man's existence are exposed here.

On the one side man's existence is always a self-entrenching against God which tries to break off all contact. In this instance the means of entrenchment is the ethical illusion of "You ought and therefore you can." In this illusion man himself is the subject who commands; he is autonomous. Clearly this illusion is possible only in a certain attitude. This attitude—and here we come back to our starting-point and complete the circle—is one of refusing to acknowledge God, to praise him, or to be thankful to him, but of trying instead to stand on one's own feet (Romans 1:18ff.). In the present context this involves the illusion of not recognizing God's law as reality but of seeking a refuge in the illusion of autonomy, of the "You ought and therefore you can," against the reality of theonomy, of "You ought but you cannot."

On the other side man's existence means that at the very point where he deludes himself in the arrogant assurance of "You ought and therefore you can," he experiences the pain of "You ought but you cannot." The other aspect, then, is that at the very point where he began to invent God as a postulate and myth, as the metaphysical author of the "ought," and where God seemed to be adjusting only too smoothly to man's ability and supposed existence, man experiences God's assault on this existence in untruth. He learns that in this reality of his, God can live only on the cross, that he has to die on this cross, on this reality, and that there is a resurrection beyond this world and against it.

The final secret of the contact, then, is that God makes contact with man at the point where man digs in against him, at the nerve of man's curving in upon himself. The contact is thus a new creation and a new birth, and as such it is a transcending of the actual point of contact.

The miracle of the divine contact—and as a miracle it escapes all systematizing—is that God makes contact with man's attitude even though this is one of rejection and self-emancipation and even though there is in man no place which is independent of this attitude and which might serve as a neutral antenna to catch God's voice.

God creates anew the man to whom he speaks and whom he lifts up to sonship. We can know this event only as a miracle. For the miracle is characterized, established, and made relevant, not by how it happens, but by the one who performs it.

"Contact" is always an improper term because it secretly suggests the "how." It is used only for clarification. It should be written with chalk on the board and then at once rubbed out again.

If some of us are inquisitive like Nicodemus, and ask "how" these things can be, then the only possible answer is the "fact" that God so loved the world (John 3:4, 9, 16).

3. Biblical Model: The Parable of the Prodigal Son

The same dialectic of contact that we have seen in the philosophical model will also be found in Jesus' parable of the Prodigal Son in Luke 15:11-24.

Here again we note first the son's self-identity with which the father makes contact. It is his ontic privilege as a son, his specific biological relation to the father, which can lead him to ask his father for his inheritance, and which can cause the father to agree. Similarly, his reacceptance by his father when he returns penitent and empty-handed from the far country is essentially based upon the fact that the father is dealing with his son. The son has remained his son for all the alienation. His identity is not lost. His self persists. The father's action is unintelligible unless one notes this almost banal fact, the fact that on the son's departure and return the father makes contact with this persistent identity of the son, with this biological quality. This is the presupposition of all that the father does.

We are not dealing here with a pantheistic world-principle of love which embraces all creatures, which is indifferent to good and evil, to staying at home or going away, and for which there is no distinction between sons and servants or even men and animals. No, it is the son who returns. The ontic quality with which the father makes contact is a definite one that cannot be lost. It is biological sonship.

It is surely not a mistake to see in this specific relation of sonship, without which the father's action and contact would be hard to comprehend, a symbol of man's divine likeness. For this is what marks man off from other creatures and confers privileges on him. Only into man is the divine breath of life breathed to give him a part in God himself (Genesis 2:16). Only man is addressed by God as "Thou" (Genesis 1:28; 2:16f.). Other creatures can be described in terms of "It" (cf. ThE, 1, § 690-1174; E.T. I, pp. 47ff.). It is because man is a person in this sense, called to partnership with God and qualified as a "Thou," that—again in distinction from other creatures—he can fall and break up the partnership.

For the same reason he can also be redeemed. The visitations of God in judgment and grace, the redeeming work of Christ, apply to him and not to fish in the sea or birds in the air. For the presupposition of judgment and grace is that their recipient can be addressed. Judgment and grace "contact" his being as a person. They presuppose that he can speak and answer. Although we shall differ from Emil Brunner in many respects, he is surely right when he states the elementary and almost platitudinous truth that only human subjects and not sticks and stones (can) receive the Word of God and the Holy Spirit.[8]

The item of comparison between the divine likeness and the parable of the Prodigal Son is that man as a son and partner stands in a position of privileged identity in his relation to God and all God's dealings with him have this presupposition as their point of contact. This identity persists through every stage—at home, abroad, and on the return home. It is constant and cannot be lost. Even extreme alienation is possible only within this framework. The animal cannot fall. Man can. This is a mark of his dignity. This is why, even in the depths, he is still a king, though a king with a broken sceptre and stained purple (Pascal). His humanity has an indelible character. It is the same through every experience. It is thus a permanent point of contact for all that God does in grace and judgment, for all that the father of the parable does when he entrusts the son with his inheritance and grants him forgiveness on his return.

Nevertheless, the situation is completely falsified if we regard this identity as a fixture in relation to which the stages of the relation between God and man are simply variations. This would be to introduce the Cartesian I, which develops in several variations of self-understanding, which can be the I that emancipates and alienates itself and then comes back to itself. In this case the identity is one which plays the role of a substance and which thus

8. *Natural Theology*, pp. 23, 30. Cf. also Pascal's saying to the effect that only man knows his own misery; he is miserable in that he is, but he is great in knowing it (*Pensées*, No. 202). Hence thought constitutes the greatness of man (No. 158).

causes whatever happens to it to bring about accidental modifications of itself. The human self is on this view the constant point of reference and all the stages of its history are no more than modes of its self-understanding. In terms of the categorical imperative, the moral I of Kant maintains its identity and even the divine commands that come to it are only maxims which are integrated into the constant schema of its normative consciousness. We have seen, however, that the true situation is very different. When the commands of God, e.g., in the form of the radical requirements of the Sermon on the Mount, are accepted into the moral self-consciousness, the vessel that receives them is broken.

We are thus confronted with the paradoxical fact that we have to speak of an abiding identity, for otherwise we could not express man's answerability, and yet we cannot regard this identity as a fixture compared with which all that happens to it is mere variation, for otherwise we would deny to God's Word its creative quality and make it a mere cause of variations in self-understanding, a phenomenon of the immanence of the ego.

We thus have to use the concept of man's identity. But we cannot grant it normative rank. It is at most a conceptual instrument which is used only conditionally and provisionally. It thus shares the same fate as all the concepts used in theology. These cannot retain their original sense unchanged. They have to go through a process of dying and becoming. When they usurp normative rank—as "logos" did in the early Apologists—there is an alien intrusion into the kerygma and it suffers philosophical distortion.

The paradoxical way in which the concept of identity is used may be seen in the parable of Jesus.

If identity were straightforward (or nonparadoxical) the returning son could simply appeal to it. He would just have to make it known that he was the son to be able to make all the implied claims. But he does not do this. He makes it clear that he has forfeited the title. Twice we read: "I am no more worthy to be called thy son."

This formulation states the problem very precisely. It does not mean that he has ceased to be the son ontically. This would be absurd. It means two things.

First, he has lost the right to be "called" the son (even though he be it a hundred times). Calling implies recognition. A title carries with it an obligation. To do justice to the title of son, a son must act in a specific way in relation to his father. The son here has lost the title from this standpoint. He has not met the obligation.

He has in fact contradicted it. This is the paradox of his identity. He is the son and then again he is not. For what is a son who has lost the right to be so called? Can he be defined at all ontologically? Possibly as a potential son who has the chance of retrieving the title?

That this is not so is shown, second, by the confession of the returning prodigal: "I am not worthy...." He admits here that he can no longer appeal to his ontic quality as a son. He has lost the title in this second sense. For the title does not merely express an obligation that the son has to meet by acting as such. It also implies a claim that the son can make to the extent that he should be treated as a son. He has forfeited this claim. In giving up any appeal to the title of son, he expresses the fact: "I am no longer a son for thee; I no longer exist for thee." The father for his part confirms this: "This my son was dead" (v. 24). This means: "He was dead for me."

What is he ontically, then, apart from this "for me" or "for thee"? What is he "in himself"? We are back at the same question: How can a son of this kind be defined ontologically? What is a son who no longer exists for his father, who has dropped out of the relation that constitutes his being as a son? What is the point of any attempt to establish identity apart from that relation, to limit it to purely biological descent?

Now obviously the biological identity of the son (or the divine likeness of man) is a presupposition of the enacting of the story of the father and the son, or of God and man. But it is of no material significance for what takes place if it does not explain what takes place. It can do this, however, only if the identity of the son is going through different phases, if at the first it stands in the light of consciousness, then grows weaker and darker in the far country, and finally achieves its fulness again at the end in the identity of "bios" and "logos." Along these lines the son might appeal to at least his potential identity. But in fact he cannot do this, as we have seen.

Nor can we speak of mere variations of identity in which the constant subject is subjected to his changing self-consciousness. The one who is dead as a son is not a potential son. The idea of an entelechy that shrivels and then unfolds again, but is always centered on itself, is rejected here. The prodigal is not centered on himself when he is unable to appeal to himself. The dead man cannot claim that regard should be had to the seeds of possible development in him. If he is dead, he remains dead or has to be raised again. Raising again is the miracle that snaps the link between the old existence and the new.

Hence it makes no sense here to point to continuity or persistent identity. Nicodemus' question: "How can these things be?", being the impossible question of continuity, is rebuffed here too. Between the old existence and the new stands the miracle of a divine act, of the act of raising again performed by the Spirit. Between the two stands the miracle of the divine compassion, of a new creation.

Because new creation or a new creature is at issue (2 Corinthians 5:17; Galatians 6:15), identity is not just confirmed or filled out with the content of a new consciousness. The father in the parable does not simply act on a claim to the title of son, which in fact is not even made. Something completely new takes place that cannot be explained at all by the entelechy of the old existence. The miracle of raising again is performed on this identity. This miracle is not a creation out of nothing, for it is performed on the old self that still keeps its identity. Yet there is no discernible continuity between the former "living soul" and the present "life-giving spirit" (1 Corinthians 15:45ff.; cf. Ephesians 2:1, 5; 5:14).

It is worth noting that the very same problems arise in acute form in attempts to express the mystery of Christ's resurrection. This is a miracle which observes the gap between the old and the new. On the one side the risen Lord shows who he was, revealing his identity and displaying the marks of the nails (John 20:27). On the other side the continuity between what was sown in corruption and what rises again in incorruption is not demonstrable (1 Corinthians 15:39ff., 42).[9]

I *am* the son and yet I am also someone else. This is the paradox we need here, since identity has to be stated but is not self-evident. The best example of the paradox is Paul's "I live, yet not I, but Christ liveth in me" (Galatians 2:20). I am the one, yet not I, for something has happened that transcends the term identity but at the same time makes it unavoidable. For I need it to express the fact that I am the one upon whom this miracle of raising again takes place, and that this and only this is the miracle. Where there is to be seen in me no possibility of becoming new, where I am dead with no claim or chance of appeal, God has activated his own possibilities and the miracle of his fatherly mercy has taken place.

When we say that the concept of identity has been transcended but is still unavoidable, our interpretation of the parable has led us to the same result as did our study of the point of contact in terms

9. On the significance of identity and continuity in the theology of the resurrection cf. the author's "The Resurrection Kerygma," *The Easter Message Today* (1964), pp. 59ff., esp. 101f.

of the philosophical model. In the latter we had to use the concept of natural conscience, expressed in the categorical imperative, to envisage the encounter between God's claim and our consciousness. But we saw that the vessel was burst open by the new contents it had to receive. Conscience cannot adopt in continuous succession the norms of autonomy and the unconditional nature of God's demands. There can be here no sequence of self-consciousness on the same level. Hence conscience itself loses its continuity.[10]

Surveying our deliberations, we note that our earlier statement that man's identity consists in his responsibility or addressability, while still true, is obviously limited. It is dubiously ambivalent. It is so because the term addressability might suggest that there is in man himself a possibility of bridging the gap between the old and the new, that there are in him elements of regeneration which would lead in a very different direction from that of a new creation. It is also ambivalent because it might suggest that what takes place on and to man can be subordinated to the interpretative schema of addressable man.

Either way we should have serious misunderstanding. God's creative Word does not belong to the schema of addressability. It transcends man's capacity for word. It creates all things new. God's Word creates its own hearer. It is seen by no eye, heard by no ear, neither does it enter man's heart (1 Corinthians 2:9f.). Between the old man and this Word there is no bridge or continuity. This Word cannot be integrated into something already there. It creates.

Nevertheless we have to refer to what is there if we are to bear witness to the miracle that God raises from the dead. Death is what forces the idea of identity on us. It probably could not be limited or challenged more severely than it is by this truth.

The identity of the prodigal is not to be sought in a demonstrable link between the various stages in his story. As noted, this could only produce biological identity, which is irrelevant to the story, to his reacceptance. The true secret of identity is not to be found, then, in a demonstrable link, for there is no such link. Possibly his self-alienation was indeed so great that the inhabitants of the village could no longer recognize him on his return; they could no longer "identify" him. The secret of identity is to be found, rather, not in himself, but in the mind of his father, in his father's love. Here and nowhere else it is preserved.

10. P. Tillich is aware of this dialectic; cf. his discussion of "experience of the spirit" and "ecstasy" in *Systematic Theology*, III (1963), pp. 111f.

In this light we probably need to revise the usual concept of the divine likeness, which is constantly perceived, as in Thomism, in an indestructible continuity of human nature, so that it has to be insisted that man's nature is the same through the stages of innocence, fall, and redemption. If, however, man's real identity is hidden in the heart of God, this means that the divine likeness is not the sum total of man's demonstrable and persistent qualities. It is finally the image that God has of us.

This prepares the way for, and underlies, the christological concept that man's worth is not immanent; it is an alien dignity. What finally constitutes it is not demonstrable; it is an object of faith. Hence this dignity consists in what is done on and to us, not in us or anything we become. It consists in the fact that we are bought with a price, that Christ died for us (1 Corinthians 6:20; 8:11; Romans 14:15; cf. Deuteronomy 7:7; Proverbs 17:5; Malachi 2:11), and that our body is a temple of the Holy Spirit (1 Corinthians 3:16; 2 Corinthians 6:16; cf. ThE, I, § 817ff., E.T. I, p. 165).

DEATH OF THE OLD CARTESIAN SELF

1. Incorporation of the Self into the Salvation Events Instead of the Reverse

We are confronted by the unique and paradoxical situation that we have to speak of the identity of the human self before and after faith, in birth and new birth, and yet this identity is not objectifiable and the question regarding it is continually erased. If, however, the self is relativized as a theme of theology, the self-consciousness is called in question as the place of theological orientation. Thus the whole Cartesian approach is challenged.

To the degree that this finding is in line with Reformation theology, as we shall try to show, Hegel is in error when he says that the Protestant principle establishes self-consciousness as an essential element in truth, and that Descartes is its true initiator. Hence we are forced to protest when a Roman Catholic interpreter speaks of Luther's pre-philosophical Cartesianism and of the central place of the ego in his theology (cf. Hegel's *Sämmtliche Werke,* 3rd ed. [1959], pp. 328 and 258ff.; P. Hacker, *Das Ich im Glauben bei M. Luther* [1966], p. 13). In fact Luther relativizes the self (cf. E. Schott, *Fleisch und Geist nach Luthers Lehre unter besonderer Berücksichtigung des Begriffs totus homo* [1928], esp. pp. 50ff.; R. Hermann, *Luthers These "Gerecht und Sünder zugleich"*

[1930], esp. pp. 229ff.). This may be seen especially in his description of conscience and the subject of faith as a mathematical point (cf. WA, 40, 1, 21, 12; WA, 40, 2, 527, 9; WA, 40, 3, 527, 33 and in exposition W. Elert, *Morphologie des Luthertums*, I [1931], p. 72; E. T. *The Structure of Lutheranism*, I [1962], pp. 81f.).

This banning of the question of the self and self-consciousness (or self-understanding) to the theological periphery confirms our criticism of more recent theology when it gives such prominence to the problem of appropriation. This criticism may be summarized as follows.

By making this problem central theology pushes epistemological and methodological matters to the forefront. These are necessarily oriented to the subject's structure of understanding, as classically illustrated in Kant's Critiques. Discussing appropriation, they have to put the prior question of what is proper to man, of the self and its structure. We are thus trapped in permanent analysis of existence and introspective inquiry. This is what the Cartesian approach involves. Nor does it stop there. For this form of inquiry carries with it a filtering of the content of the kerygma. Only that which can become the content of my self-consciousness and which can be localized in the self and its categories is acceptable to my faith and understanding.

This fatal error can be avoided only if it is seriously admitted that the question of the self and self-consciousness can be relativized without dropping altogether the problem of identity. God's summons, the father's mercy, the work of the Holy Spirit, all reach back to my natural state. The miracle of the new birth is performed on those who have the first birth. Creative change takes hold of what is made. But being both "creative" and "change," it does not fit into the schemata of the old self nor submit to its conditions. It changes the schemata and the implied conditions.

"Who am I, and what can I thus appropriate in faith and understanding?" is not the real question. I learn who I am only from what happens to me and changes me. Not only does God's Word create the hearer. The hearer learns what he can hear only from this Word, not from preliminary self-analysis.[1] This puts the question of the self on the periphery where it ceases to be a real question and becomes a preliminary one in the true sense.

In this sense G. Bornkamm is right to take issue with Bultmann's attempt to present Paul's theology as anthropology,

---

1. Cf. Goethe's criticism of introspection (rather than action and experience) as a way of self-knowledge (ThE, II, 1, § 1386ff.).

i.e., to expound it from the standpoint of self-understanding.[2] In opposition Bornkamm advances the cogent thesis that what Paul is concerned about is not a new self-understanding but a new history and existence in and through which I am taken up into the history of Christ.[3] "Christ in me" precedes "I in Christ." The self is determined by what has taken place, and does take place, on and to me, by what is thus before me and outside me. This is what Cullmann has in view when to the thesis that I must appropriate the salvation event he opposes the Pauline thesis that in faith I am integrated into the salvation history enacted preveniently outside me and before me.[4] H. Iwand expresses it most forcefully of all when, following Luther, he says that encounter with God's Word as a believer does not mean that I draw God and his Word into my existence but that I can break away from my self-enclosed being and through the Word be drawn into God and his power and possibilities, so that I am born again. Only the believer can stand over against himself in this way, whereas in the theology and philosophy of the nineteenth century history, facts, speech, thou, and person were all sucked into the self-consciousness.[5] This bold thesis of Iwand that the believer integrates his existence into God's Word (not *vice versa*) and comes to confront the old, self-enclosed self sheds a new and unexpected light on the crisis of identity and on the theological status the question concerning it can claim.

2. Possibilities of the Salvation Event Instead of Possibilities of the Self

We are directed to the same crisis by another consideration to which the problem of appropriation necessarily gives rise.

If we venture to translate the term "appropriation" into the vocabulary of the NT we might say that it means hearing the voice of Christ as it applies to me (John 18:37). Now only he who *is* of the truth can hear this voice. What does it mean to *be* in the truth?

Of the many aspects of this being we shall select only one that is particularly pertinent here. It means to have dealings with the truth.[6] Now we have dealings only with persons. Persons cannot be manipulated. They are not at our disposal. They are not objects. I cannot take up any attitude I like to them. Persons with whom I

2. Cf. his article "Paulus," RGG, 2nd ed.
3. G. Bornkamm, "Mythos und Evangelium," ThEx, 26, p. 25.
4. O. Cullmann, *Heil als Geschichte* (1965), pp. 100ff.; E. T. *Salvation in History* (1965), pp. 118ff.
5. *Nachgelassene Werke,* I (1962), pp. 194f.
6. Cf. K. Kerényi, *Umgang mit dem Göttlichen*, 2nd ed. (1961), pp. 4ff.

have dealings advance a claim that can bring about a full subject-object interchange and incur commitment. I, too, am affected by these dealings. Thus to be in the truth is to let the truth work on us, to expose ourselves to it, to surrender to it, to let it shape our lives.[7] Only in this doing of the truth, which means surrendering to it and living with it, can it be manifested and have the chance to validate itself (John 7:17).

This confirms what we have been saying. Only if the validation of the truth takes place in dealings with it can appropriation cease to be a mere form of reflection which presupposes possibilities and methodological conditions in virtue of which the content of faith can be integrated into my self-consciousness. Now the possibilities are learned only in action, in dealings with the truth. The possibilities at issue here do not consist in potentialities of my own; they are the possibilities of the Word. For this reason we cannot calculate them. And since they are worked out on my own self by changing and regenerating it, the self, too, can no longer be calculated. Hence it cannot be a theme apart. The question of Nicodemus in John 3:4: "How can a man be born when he is old? Can he enter the second time into his mother's womb, and be born?", is falsely put, since it reckons only with possibilities enclosed in man's identity and produced by his entelechy. The further question: "How can these things be?", is tied to the same sphere. The answer of Jesus, however, presents the very different plane of events on which regeneration takes place, namely, the plane of God's possibilities. These cannot be calculated. They are like the wind; we do not know where it comes from or where it goes (3:8). In characteristic fashion we are then shown that incalculability applies not only to the moving of the Spirit, and hence to God's possibilities, but also to the one in whom these possibilities are worked out (the self): "So is every one that is born of the Spirit" (v. 8). The self experiences itself, and therewith the possibility of new birth, as it claims God's possibilities and is thus "outside" itself, living God's history rather than its own, confronting itself. Identity can be stated now only in the confession that God's mercy has visited me. In this "me" the self has become the other confronting itself. This is important when we look back.

We do not look back on possibilities that the I realized or that were elicited from within (in Socratic fashion). The I was grasped by God's possibilities. Thus it ceased to be an independent theme. The question of identity between the old and the new self is thus

7. Cf. G. Bernanos, *The Diary of a Country Priest* (1937), p. 109.

pointless. In other words, when Nicodemus asks about continuity in his question: ''How can these things be?'' he is missing the real theme. The question which he puts fatefully affects the horizon of possible answers. In it regeneration can be thought of only as an evolution or mutation of the entelechy of the self. But if it is described as the experience of God's possibilities, which it really is, then the question of the identity and continuity of the self is transcended by the knowledge that the old self has to die, that it does die like the grain of wheat (John 12:24), and that we are buried with Christ by baptism into his death (Romans 6:4; Colossians 2:12). The one who is snatched from death and raised again is not interested in what was raised again; he is interested in him who raised it.

Adopting this view, faith is not saying something new about the old themes. It is presenting new themes. In relation to the themes, too, it is true that ''old things are passed away.''

3. Identity of the Faithfulness of God Instead of Our Identity

A final aberration due to focusing on the self and self-consciousness must finally be described. We have said that this concentration leads to prior decisions about what God's Word can be. We now ask what kind of decisions these are. Thus far it has been said that they carry with them the postulate that the kerygma must be appropriated and that it must be subjected to the schema of self-understanding. What does this postulate mean for the understanding of God's Word? This is the crucial question these prior decisions raise.

To the degree that theological interest focuses on appropriation, faith becomes a matter of understanding.[8] Naturally it is a special type of understanding. Faith has its own niche in hermeneutics. Naturally, too, if faith is not to be a legalistic decree or implicit faith, it always involves understanding. The Spirit whose testimony leads to faith is a Spirit of understanding (cf. 1 Corinthians 2:9ff.). Hence faith and understanding are not to be sundered. The present problem is that they may be wrongly related, especially when the question of understanding, of understandability, and of the conditions of understanding is put under the rule of the Cartesian principle. For then it is assumed that what is to be understood is on the same plane as the one who is seeking to understand.

8. Cf. Bultmann's title *Glauben und Verstehen (Faith and Understanding)*.

It makes no difference in principle here whether the plan is the same because of a divinatory relation between the author and what is to be understood (as in Schleiermacher and Dilthey) or because of a thematic point of comparison which orients the inquiry, as in Bultmann (GV, II, p. 216). Paul Claudel uses the term "connaissance" for being on the same plane in this way. He construes it as "con-naissance," being born together, living on the same earth. When the question of understandability is integrated in this way into the question of faith, all possible acts of appropriation are determined by it. And since only the plane of the self is familiar, and thus constitutes the fixed point of orientation, what can be understood and accepted as credible is necessarily limited. It was perhaps because of this restriction of possibilities that Goethe had a distaste for epistemological questions, or at least for their primacy, complaining against Kant that he had gone too far; Goethe himself never thought about thinking (cf. R. A. Schröder, ThLZ [1949], p. 532).

If the principles of understanding are the criterion of what can be appropriated in faith, then God's Word becomes at once an interpretation. For, since understanding is a mode of interpretation, it seeks the Word of God which is to be understood on its own level, and thus treats it as an interpretative Word.

Regarded thus, understanding itself blocks the way to what really counts. For God's Word is not interpretative; it is creative. It brings forth being out of nothing. It thus transcends all analogies and all supposedly common planes. Unlike the Greek logos, God's Word is not related to a being which it discloses; it calls what is not into being (Romans 4:17). It is active, not interpretative. "He speaks and it is done; he commands and it stands fast" (Psalm 33:9). Being an active rather than an interpretative or "apophantic" word, God's Word changes the self rather than disclosing it. Hence it does not permit of prior principles of understanding. As the existence which is being understood is given up to death, so its principles of understanding are given up to death.

This means, however, that continuity and identity in the change from death to life are not to be sought in the principles of understanding which supposedly persist, nor in the human self as the Cartesian point of reference. They are to be sought outside the self in the faithfulness of God, in the image that he has of me, and in the tenacity with which he adheres to it. Identity is riveted to God's Word, which remains the same both in our world of sin and death and also in his world of life and righteousness (Iwand, *op. cit.*, pp. 200f.). Thus faith abandons the Cartesian approach and its axiom:

"I am I." It clings instead to the Word of him who proclaims himself as Yahweh: "I am who I will be" (Exodus 3:14), the God of Abraham, Isaac, and Jacob. Where the Word is active and creative, the only identity is ec-centric (*ibid.*, p. 202).

Again, while an interpretative word can only speak in terms of validity, the active and creative Word contains facticity. Regeneration takes place. New being takes place. The prior facts of salvation history are posited thereby. Since the Word effected them, and the Word produces faith and relates it to the facts, I cannot seek the mighty acts of God, the events and facts, outside the Word. Nothing is to be seen outside the Word and outside faith.

Hence faith does not have to reassure itself by first examining the facts which are its basis. It does not investigate before believing. If it does, it disparages the Word which posits the facts. It tries to establish a prior relation to reality on the basis of which it can prove that the Word has a real foundation and is in touch with reality. Faith can take this false path only if it grants normativity to the subject-object relation which underlies its "normal" understanding of reality. In this case the Cartesian I (the subject in the relation) again plays the part of a norm. Since, however, God's mighty acts are effected by the Word, I can have access to them only through the faith that this Word brings into being. Hence there can be no certainty concerning these acts apart from the Word and faith. One might also put it thus: The facts cannot be known by the old self; they are non-existent for its "mind" and "heart" (1 Corinthians 2:9).

This does not mean that faith discharges a kind of creative function by taking some of the raw material of history and giving it the religious significance of salvation history. If salvation history is not a datum for faith but the product of faith, deriving its significance from it, we are back in the sphere of Cartesian subjectivity, which can explain something that stands out from the raw state of facticity, that is laden with significance, only in terms of its own divinatory faculty, its interpretative power, or its charisma of investing with meaning. Indeed, it is only a nuance of the same thing, and not its opposite, when this kind of efficacious faith is understood, not as grounded in the constitution of the human self, but as imparted to the self as a gift of grace.[9] Many modern Cartesian theologians undoubtedly view it thus. But whereas Calvin says: "Take the word away and no faith is left" (Inst., III, 2),

9. For a good nontheological example of this, cf. Theodor Lessing, *Geschichte als Sinngebung des Sinnlosen* (1929).

they reverse the saying: "Take faith away, and no word is left" (cf. Iwand, *op. cit.*, p. 207). When faith does not project meaning, all that remains is naked facticity which has no word or meaning. In Cartesian thought, then, the word, as an interpretative word, can only be the contribution of him who interprets even though he does not produce this on his own initiative but it is evoked by what is without, by the history that encounters it, unleashing its possibilities in the same Socratic manner.

In the face of all this one has to realize that the relation of Word and faith or salvation event and faith is irreversible. God's creative and active Word precedes both faith and the event which as the sphere of God's mighty acts is the content of faith. This Word is pre-existent in relation to all these things. It is this Word, not faith, which makes events significant, which constitutes them salvation history, and which thereby takes them out of the ordinary flow of events.

One might also say that this Word discloses itself to be God's Word, and to be relevant to me. Faith does not cooperate in this regard. If it did it would not be the opposite of good works. It would itself be a work. It would thus lose its soteriological point.[10] In fact, however, it is the Spirit of God himself who confesses this Word, who bears witness to it as his own, and who causes the historical event to become preaching of God's mighty acts. Thus Peter's address at Pentecost makes it plain that the miracle of the Spirit unlocks the history. The history begins to preach. It points to the one who enacts it and causes it to be salvation history. Peter adduces known facts. But what they imply and express is not known. This is set forth when the Spirit validates them as the mighty acts of God.

When it is plain what the events contain as God's Word, they are marked off as a miracle from the rest of the historical nexus and they thus come to occupy a privileged position as salvation events, as the events of revelation and proclamation.

Ontically this separation entails the same breach of continuity as we have noted in the transition from the old man to the new. Hence there is no occasion to ask: "How can these things be?" in relation

10. From one angle Luther can call faith a good work (WA, 23, 29) and can even defend it as such against the papal view that it is a *habitus* (6, 206). Nevertheless, this has nothing to do with its real point, i.e., its function in justification. The justifying significance of faith does not derive from its reference to itself as a work but from its reference to its object; we are not to stay at ourselves or our faith but to crawl into Christ (10, I, 1, 126, 14).

to salvation events from creation to the coming again. This question is possible only if a continuous nexus is illegitimately presupposed—a nexus whose continuity can be objectified. Identity and continuity are irrelevant as conditions of being if we have to do with a creative Word which summons being out of nothing and then destroys what has been summoned out of nothing, gives it up to death, and raises it up again.

The Word is the origin of being. Hence I cannot integrate it into the continuity of being or of an interpretative event. How can something be put in a system when it is the very basis of this system?

The problem that the natural orientation of our epistemological functions causes us to search the field of being, when what is at issue is its basis, is brought to our notice by the doctrine of the pre-existence of Christ (John 1:1; Colossians 1:16; Hebrews 1:2), i.e., the statement that everything in heaven and earth is created in Christ. This has the following implications.

If we remain within the framework of our epistemological functions, we seek Christ in history; we seek the historical Jesus. Now the Word was truly made flesh (John 1:14). He came into history. He can thus be documented historically. Even secular history comes up against the historicity of Jesus of Nazareth. Yet he cannot be explained by the continuity of historical occurrence or integrated into it. This is at least true of what is said about him, of what the witnesses proclaim concerning him.

Quite apart from possible accretions, we are thus faced with the question of this extra element which transcends historical continuity. The alternatives (already intimated) are as follows.

Either the extra element can be put to the account of faith, which finds significance in normal events. In this case continuity is re-established. It is the closed correspondence between a historical event and our self-consciousness. Salvation history is a history which is characterized by this correspondence. Take this away (take faith away) and ordinary facts remain.

Or—the second alternative—the extra element is due to the appearance of something qualitatively different in Christ which escapes the continuity of occurrence because it is its basis. In this case we have a creative Word which lies behind the world, which makes possible all human speech, and which cannot therefore be understood as a special instance of human speech. If the incarnate Word can be heard, if even the individual sayings of Jesus strike home to us, we come into contact with the origin, which is God's creative Word.

The same applies in relation to the resurrection message. Here again we are faced with the question of the extra element which does not fit into the continuity of the normal historical nexus. Is the witness to the resurrection just a commentary on Good Friday (Bultmann)? Is it a concept of faith rather than its basis (W. Herrmann)? Or do we have here the "Let there be" of the creative Word which leads down to death and up from it again (1 Samuel 2:6), so that the continuity of the historical nexus is broken?

This question arises everywhere. It is ultimately the question of the significance of the human self as a point of theological reference. Our findings are these.

1. The philosophical model of the categorical imperative and the biblical model of the parable of the Prodigal Son have shown us that the identity of the self (conscience, the younger son) has to be considered if the miracle of change is to be attested, but it cannot be objectified.

2. It cannot be objectified because what happens to me in the reconstructive Word cannot be fitted into my schema of understanding; it transcends this schema. As the philosophical model shows, my conscience is given new axioms.

3. Thus the Cartesian self cannot serve as the point of reference in theological thinking. It allows no place for death and resurrection. Faith relates me to what is outside me, and this is unreasonable to the concept of identity. In faith I confront myself. Old things have passed away.

4. In contrast, the Cartesian approach clings to the possibility which the interpretative structure of the human subject seems to offer.

5. Since the question of the recognizable identity and continuity of the self through death and resurrection falls to the ground, the two concepts are related to what is outside me. Identity and continuity consist in the faithfulness of God, who stands by his Word.

6. Since this Word is active and not interpretative, since it summons what is into life, it is prior to faith and understanding, "pre-existent." The correspondence of history and the believing self does not give significance to the salvation event; the creative Word establishes this correspondence.

The Cartesian I is thus given up to death. It ceases to be an independent theme or to tell me through its conditions of consciousness what the theme should be. It becomes a theme only in view of what has happened to me and of that from which I am rescued. It is relevant only as a point of reference for what takes place for me as death and resurrection, as the miracle of transformation. Nor is this its own history. It is the event of the Word (and Spirit) into which it is caught up: "I live, yet not I, but Christ lives in me," or "I am in Christ."

This is the paradoxical way in which the theme of my identity can be discussed.

NEW CREATION BY THE SPIRIT: HERMENEUTICAL ASPECT
A Theological Epistemology

We have seen that in Cartesian theology there is a shift of emphasis. The image of empirical man himself, as reflected in his self-understanding, is of interest and achieves thematic rank. We have conceded to this theology that it does not have to stop at empirical man. Although some polemical confessionalism refuses to admit this, its intentions include kerygmatic address from outside. Thus God's Spirit is usually differentiated clearly from man's spirit.

We have also tried to show in various ways and from very different angles why these intentions are not realized in Cartesian theology. In a sphere of understanding which is dominated by the question of appropriation it is impossible to think in terms of the creative Word which creates a new creature and thus transcends the old creature and its schema of understanding. Exclusive focus on the question of appropriation means that the identity or continuity of the human self is proclaimed or accepted as a condition of acceptance or appropriation of the Word.

In contrast we have spoken of the death of the Cartesian I. With the help of the antitheses of letter and Spirit and flesh and Spirit we have depicted the change that the creative Word brings about and its implication for my identity. The drift of our inquiry has been: What does "I am" mean in relation to the spiritual man when he is "outside himself," when he has an alien righteousness, and when he stands over against himself? How does what is proper to the regenerate man relate to what is alien to him? How far can he identify himself with the spiritual existence which is the work of the Spirit?

The question of the work of the Spirit, which we have so far considered anthropologically in relation to the problem of identity, is one which must now be tackled from the hermeneutical angle.

In connection with the question of appropriation we have already seen how important the hermeneutical problem is. One might put it as follows: Do I draw the creative Word into my self-consciousness so that it is integrated into this and can no longer be regarded as a creative Word but only as one that modifies this self-consciousness? Or does the creative Word draw me into its sphere of influence, so that I am integrated into the salvation event which works on me, and to that extent am referred to something outside myself?

This question has a new edge in relation to the knowledge of God, or to theological truth in general. It is thus a significant one hermeneutically. This is evident the moment we give it the new form: Is this truth the content of an interpretative Word or of a creative and active Word?

If the former, it conforms to our self-consciousness which also seeks truth and which in its pre-understanding already has questions that are designed to elicit it. Even if kerygmatically imparted truth modifies the prior consciousness of truth, it still remains within the sphere of the possibilities of modification intrinsic to this consciousness.

If, however, theological truth is the content of an active Word, the situation is fundamentally different. In this case the Word itself first creates the possibilities of my understanding and acceptance. The Fourth Gospel states this when it says that only he who is in the truth hears the voice (John 18:37) and that only he who does the will of God can know the truth that Jesus' teaching comes from God and is not invented by himself (John 7:17).

Negatively this means that in and of himself man does not have any possibility of accepting the truth. In Paul's phrase, it has not entered the heart of any man (1 Corinthians 2:9) and the natural man does not perceive the things of the Spirit of God (2:14). In the situation of his inauthentic existence he can only suppress the truth of God, holding it down in unrighteousness (Romans 1:18). The ontic state of man shatters his noetic possibilities. His knowledge, and with it his relation to the truth, can be corrected only as his being is corrected. Truth can disclose itself only when the darkness of existence (Romans 1:21) ends.

We have no control, however, over this background of existence on which the possibility of knowledge depends. It is not the object of either a theoretical (cognitive) or a practical (ethical) operation. Man cannot make himself different from what he is. Since, however, this being is relation to God, he has no control over the knowledge of God which is bound up with it. Knowledge of the truth is fundamentally closed to being in untruth. There is no breaking free from this circle.

The positive implication is that God's truth is revealed to me only when the Word which contains it is understood by me as an active Word, i.e., when it alters the conditions of existence itself, when it frees me for being in truth, when it effects the conformity of existence which opens up for it the way to the truth of God. If knowledge is possible only to the degree that there is an analogy between him who knows and what he is to know—we shall return to this later—then one might also say that the active Word of God must first create the analogy of my existence in order that the truth of his Word may be intelligible.

If, however, I regard God's Word as an active rather than an interpretative Word, then I am again confronted by the question of identity. For the Spirit whom the Word imparts to me and through whom it accomplishes my regeneration breaks continuity with my old existence destroys it (2 Corinthians 5:17; cf. 1 John 2:8), and creatively summons up new possibilities that were not present in that existence. Without this breaking off of continuity with the old, the truth of God cannot be mediated. It would not be any the less true, of course, as the truth which is not imparted and not understood.

Truth may well be the same as that which discloses itself, which enlightens, and which is thus intelligible,[1] and we can accept this in relation to God's truth. It, too, is disclosure, being evident. But the question is: For whom is it disclosed, and to whom is it evident? The truth which is concealed from the natural man, or, paradoxically, the truth which conceals and "must" conceal itself from the natural man,[2] is true even apart from man. It is in this case evident only to God himself. It is restricted to the Logos who is as yet only with God (John 1:2). It is the wisdom which is with God before all self-disclosure (Proverbs 8:22; cf. Job 28:20ff.). Knowledge of God is self-knowledge here. Truth is God's knowledge of himself. If truth basically implies perceptibility, and if it thus presupposes transcendental apperception and hence a subject of perception, God himself is this subject. He alone is self-analogous.

This extreme concept of a truth which is truth only with and for God shows plainly what is meant by a creative and active Word

---

1. Cf. Heidegger's analysis of truth as nonconcealment.
2. This "must" is important in Luther's doctrine of the bondage of the will. The reference here is not to coercion from outside, which would destroy responsibility. It is to an inner necessity. I must accept this necessity and impute it to myself (cf. Cl, 3, 125, 23ff.; 3, 204, 30).

and by the testimony of the Holy Spirit. They mean that with a new fiat God summons me out of my forgetfulness of existence and the truth and transforms me by giving me a share in himself and his self-knowledge. The Spirit who explores the depths of Godhead (1 Corinthians 2:10) is God's own Spirit. Only he is analogous to himself, so that he alone can grasp the truth of his own profundity. But this Spirit is imparted to me to give me a share in God's analogy and to grant me the conformity which finds enactment in love (1 John 4:12).

Since the issue here is God's relation to himself, i.e., the truth of God in his self-knowledge, trinitarian statements are in order. For the self-knowledge of God in virtue of his self-analogy is not just pneumatological ("the Spirit searches the depths of deity"); it is also christological: Christ as the Son or Word of God knows the truth in the immediacy of that self-knowledge. When we belong to him we also share in this truth to which we would otherwise be closed. "No man hath seen God at any time; the only begotten Son which is in the bosom of the Father, he hath declared him" (John 1:18). "Not that any man hath seen the Father, save he which is of God, he hath seen the Father" (6:46). Here in the form of the one existence of the Son of God is the full conformity which gives access to God's truth. Here is no longer the indirectness of a mirror with its distortion; here is "face to face" (1 Corinthians 13:12). In Christ we are ordered to this conformity of the Son of God. As we can say: "We are his righteousness," so we can say: "We are his conformity with the Father." We have a share in the truth which he has—which he so has that he is it (John 14:6).

This brings us to the hermeneutical problem. I can understand the truth of God only through the Holy Spirit,[3] since the analogy which underlies this understanding is imparted through him. This analogy, however, is an analogy of being before it is one of understanding. The existence of this analogy points to the creative and active Word of God which renews this being in the miracle of the Spirit and causes it truly and authentically to "be."

To discuss this thoroughly we must first deal with some more preliminary questions.

1. Relation of Proclamation and Theology

If everything depends on whether we understand the Word to be interpretative or creative, the further problem at once arises:

3. The related christological statements show what was the theological concern of the western church when it adopted the double procession ("proceeding from the Father and the Son").

Where do we meet the decisive, active Word? A provisional answer to this question is that we meet it where it strikes us as an effectual Word in the sense that in the law and the gospel it breaks off the old existence and starts a new one, bringing sins to light and forgiving them, changing God's rejection into an acceptance which gives me a new future and makes me a new creature in the miracle of the Spirit.

This effectual Word is spoken in proclamation, preaching, and pastoral counseling. Theology as a reflective act can only be subsequent meditation on the faith that has arisen on this basis.[4] It thus has a part in the event of new creation. It considers what has happened, relates the event to the one to whom it occurs, and weighs the consequences for my understanding of self and the world, i.e., for the question of identity.

No matter what may belong to the sphere of theological reflection, it is always grounded in that which is the ground of the new existence itself. No matter how it goes in detail, its intention is always to describe the truth, God's truth. Since, however, disclosure of this truth is bound up with a specific state of existence, with being in the truth, theological reflection on the truth is also tied to this existential pre-condition. It can be pursued only on the basis of a state of existence which already has the break with the old existence behind it and which has been called to life by the active Word of the miracle of the Spirit.

This means that theology follows the proclamation of the Word; it cannot in principle precede it.

This is what Anselm has in mind in the prayer at the beginning of the *Proslogion*. Faith, which has its source in proclamation, takes precedence over theology (c. 1) so that we do not understand in order to believe; we believe in order to understand (cf. Augustine, In Joh. Tract., 40, 9). Knowledge only follows the faith which leads by way of hope to love.

The question arises here whether Cartesian theology has not in fact reversed this relation (although it does not have to do so). If theological inquiry is determined by analysis of pre-understanding and self-understanding, this surely decides what statements can be accepted as candidates for appropriation by this understanding. What can be called God's work is fixed in advance. What is set before me as God's word or work must be correlative to what my own consciousness has already indicated.

In other words, I do not first learn from God's active Word what

4. For a similar Roman Catholic view cf. K. Rahner, "Zur Frage der Dogmenentwicklung," *Schriften zur Theologie,* I (1962), p. 66.

his action is or can be and then go on to reflect on this experience of God's possibilities. I first reflect on what I can accept as the ostensible work of God. The order of precedence between theology and proclamation is thus reversed.

This raises the point whether our present plight is not due precisely to this reversal. We do not seek the rationale of proclamation after the event itself. In perverse fashion we first consult theological theory to find out what is the possibility of proclamation. This pre-vision is theological arrogance. Theology is here claiming a primacy for which it is quite unsuited. In the process it is terrorizing the community of those who are called to the miracle of the Spirit. It is bound to fail, for its whole enterprise is mistaken and it leaves out of its calculations the reality of the Spirit who precedes reflection. It is thus condemned to a permanent situation of preliminary inquiry.

This may be seen in the contemporary fixation on hermeneutical questions, i.e., on epistemology and methodology. All these are late disciplines which have their source in the scepticism to which the discovery and consolidation of the Cartesian I necessarily give rise.

Now obviously hermeneutics has a place. For scepticism must be acknowledged if it is to be overcome. It must not be repressed. Thus our reference to fixation on hermeneutics should not be construed as an attack on hermeneutics as such. There is certainly no need to be frightened by it. The real issue is its place in the total theological enterprise. This is where we have doubts. When the self-demonstration of the act of proclamation is not accepted, preliminary reflection on the possibility of proclamation, on addressability, and on the conditions of appropriation can go on forever. This means that we can never get away from hermeneutics.

A good illustration of the fact that method should be subordinate to fact is provided by the mistake that Schleiermacher made regarding the date of Plato's Phaedros. Under the influence of Schlegel Schleiermacher claimed that this was Plato's first work, his argument being that it deals with the methodological question why Plato uses dialog to expound his philosophy. We now know, of course, that the Phaedros was the last dialog. Only at the end does Plato consider methodology. He first exposes himself to being and on this basis "receives," as it were, his dialogical method. Encounter with being forces him, and at the end he asks why this is so, validating in reflection what he has done under the impulsion of being before any theorizing.

There is an analogy here to the relation between proclamation and theology. Theology puts its question on the basis of encounter with the proclaimed Word and exposure to it. Hermeneutics then investigates the question and its modalities and conditions. It is the epilogue in a process which is effected by the creative Word in the miracle of the Spirit. It is never a prologue.

Now it would be ungenerous to accuse even an extreme Cartesian theology of simply regarding hermeneutics as a prologue. One must obviously admit that its methodological deliberations are stimulated by problems that arise out of the summons of the kerygma. On the other hand the Cartesian I which is the abiding subject of appropriation seems to see to it that methodological questions are always at the forefront. In secondary authors these questions can easily become an intellectual exercise which never leaves any room for the real theme. The method of textual interpretation is learned—in case the text should ever be read.

Methodological questions are a transportation problem. Such a problem arises only when there is something to shift. To discuss it when there is nothing to move is absurd. But this height of absurdity seems to be common enough today.

It might well be, then, that God's Word is best preserved where we are simply exposed to it, where we are reached by its proclamation, and where methodological questions are naively, or unthinkingly, or perhaps even culpably ignored. If a secular example might help, the performance of Shakespeare's plays does not have to be postponed until a philological analysis has been completed. In fact, a good performance, which is quite possible without such an analysis, may ultimately contribute to it (cf. J. Kott, *Shakespeare heute* [1964]).

At this point we must pause and ask ourselves whether this order of proclamation and theology can actually be sustained. Can there actually be exposure to the proclamation of God's Word, and the work of the Word in the Spirit, without accompanying theological reflection? Indeed, is not God's Word itself theology as well as proclamation? If so, how can an order be established between the two?

If we are to see whether and how far God's Word is both theology and proclamation, and what this implies for the primacy of the active Word and the Spirit-event that is advocated here, we do best to start with the preaching situation and hence to investigate the problem as a concrete issue.

The Bible from which I take a text for expository proclamation is obviously intrinsic to preaching. But what if this book dissolves historically in my very hands? What if the *sola Scriptura* of the Reformation and the supposed self-interpretation of the Word by the Spirit prove to be so much waste paper? What if this Word is at best only a "witness" to which I for my part now bear witness? To be normative, does not this Word have to be God's Word and not just man's witness? To be God's Word, does it not have to have a unity—we use the term elastically and not in the sense of uniformity—which it is given by its divine author? Does not this mean that a canon which might contain a jumble of the authoritative and the non-authoritative, of God's active Word and man's interpretative word, of revelation and witness to revelation (or supposed revelation), would necessarily cease to be a canon? But does not the biblical canon, and with it its function as a text for my preaching, threaten to fall apart into widely differing elements? Do not the gospels, let alone the epistles, have different theological profiles? Have not the authors projected a distinct theological understanding into the traditional accounts of the historical Jesus, so that we often lose sight of the bond of union and have to ask ourselves which variant (that of Mark or that of Matthew) is to be decisive for us? Or should we allow the one to correct the other in our preaching?[5]

The reason why we find these different profiles is that the NT offers theology as well as proclamation. We have thus to ask what is the implication of this for our initial thesis that theology comes after proclamation, that before we can practice theology we have first to be reached by the Word of proclamation which renews our existence. If the kerygma as we have it in the NT manifests a combination of theology and proclamation, this seems to be a weighty indication that the material subordination of theology to proclamation does not have to find expression in a perceptible, chronological succession.

In fact there is no moment of pure proclamation just as there is no pure state of contemplation or feeling. As proclamation is appropriated and articulated and passed on, it is already caught up in reflection[6] and brought into relation to our stock of concepts, to the questions and states of our existence, to the situation of the hearers and much else.[7] This means that what is proclaimed and passed

---

5. Cf. the different accounts of the stilling of the storm in Matthew, Mark, and Luke.

6. Thus Karl Rahner observes that even though the initial degree of reflection may be small, it is never wholly absent (*op. cit.*, p. 78).

7. Cf. Tillich's concept of "correlation," *Systematic Theology*, I, pp. 59ff.

on—even and precisely when it takes the form of recorded facts that affect me directly like the history of Jesus—is always present in interpreted form. This process of interpretation is itself theology.

Thus Matthew in his account of the stilling of the storm accords only second rank to the miracle. It is not so much the basis of faith, as in Mark; it is rather an illustration of faith. Thus we have more than record and proclamation. A theological thesis about miracle is part of the record and proclamation.

Such theses vary. They introduce perspectives into the stories which, being different, threaten to destroy the unity of the stories. Does the unity of the kerygma remain behind this distinction in theological perspective? Is the canon still there when reflection has brought with it discursive deviation?

This has to be possible if we are to be able to preach the Bible in terms of the priority of the Word of proclamation and in so doing to tie it in with theological reflection. If it were not possible to find and invoke the underlying unity of the Word, then we should have to choose between the theologies offered in Scripture, e.g., in the NT. We should then be disciples of Paul, John, or Matthew, but not biblical Christians. We should have to abandon the *sola Scriptura*. For this makes sense only if it implies the "monopoly" of the active Word that comes to us, strikes us, and summons us to a new being.

In fact exegetes are always trying to find this kerygma which entails underlying unity, this address which stands behind the theologies of the synoptists and apostles and indeed the schemes of thought adopted from later Jewish apocalyptic, Gnosticism, and mythology. We need not discuss here the different ways in which the various schools of NT scholarship do this, whether by more conventional presupposition or by critical inquiry.

The crucial issue here—and it again leads on directly to the problem of proclamation—is that to a large extent, especially in Cartesian theology, the idea seems to be that kerygmatic unity must be found behind the many theologies and these must be interpreted in terms of the kerygmatic core. Now it may be granted that interpretation as a theoretical act is in fact one of various ways of fulfilling the task. It is no doubt the way that biblical scholarship should take. Our question is, however, whether it is not just one way of relating to the texts—a way which I cannot just decide to take but which depends on many conditions over which I have no control.

The decisive condition is that the texts have spoken to me. By the witness of the Spirit they have become for me an active and transforming Word. They have led me to the truth of being in which I can hear the voice. In short, faith is the decisive condition if interpretation is to be possible. Without it I cannot even begin to ask about the kerygmatic core, about what is unconditionally relevant to me. Before interpretation of the texts (according to their own meaning) can even begin, I must first come face to face with something over which I have no control, namely, that the texts interpret me, and that in so doing they transform me. It is only in this act of transformation that I learn that I am interpreted here, and that before God I have a completely different "image" from that held by my own prior self-consciousness.

The experience of being interpreted by the active Word of God presupposes that by the miracle of the Spirit this active Word changes the conditions of my being by bringing me into the truth of being. Only as I undergo its own interpretation can I myself interpret. Without this can I really relate scientifically to the texts, e.g., as an atheist or neutral religious scholar? To this question I can only reply in the negative if I espouse the thesis that I must approach the texts with a right relation, that I must have been addressed by them and transformed by the Spirit if I am to hear what is really said, that I must be in the truth to hear the voice. Only on this condition is scientific interpretation one of the possible ways of finding the kerygma behind the theologies.

Even then we must stress that it is only one possible way. We must not absolutize it as the only possibility. The normative way in the history of the church and its proclamation has in fact been a different one, namely, that of learning what God's Word is in the act of proclamation itself. In other words, qualification as the Word of God comes in practice.

To explain and defend this we should have to use many arguments that will come up later in the doctrine of the Word of God. Thus the relation of Word and Spirit plays a part here. In the present context it must suffice if we make only one reference, although this touches the nerve of the matter. We are speaking of the development of the canon.

The canon is the epitome of the unity of Holy Scripture and its focus on the active Word of the one God, the God of Abraham, Isaac, and Jacob, the Father of Jesus Christ. This canon did not come into being by theoretical interpretation of the available texts or by systematic investigation of their intention. No justification of the choice was offered in principle. The canon arose, and was then defined rather than constituted, as certain books established themselves in the practical proclamation of the church, while other candidates failed to do so.[8]

In the act or practice of proclamation canonical rank was brought to light. In other words, God acknowledged his Word. This means that in principle the canon is not closed on the Reformation view. We cannot say what might not prove to be canonical in the further course of proclamation.

From this it seems that only in the course of proclamation does it come to light what is in Scripture itself the proclamation behind the theologies. The crippling error which Cartesian tendencies have brought into theology obviously consists in the view that one has first to know what can count as proclamation, so that surreptitiously theological reflection takes precedence over proclamation.

In reality what we said about the subordination of interpretation to faith exposes the error. I can legitimately interpret the biblical texts in terms of the kerygmatic core only when I have been touched by this kerygma and have come to faith through the witness of the Spirit. But how can I believe without proclaiming? Is there faith without witness (Matthew 12:34; Acts 4:20)? Interpretation begins, then, as the counter-question of the man who is apprehended. Then everything is in order. Perversion arises when interpretation is not pursued as a counter-question into what empowers us for proclamation but takes on the rank of an *a priori* pre-construction which planes down proclamation and puts it under our own control. In this regard, something that our prior deliberations have already brought to light may be noted again. The program of interpretation in Cartesian theology was not proposed and planned. It simply arose on the basis of certain presuppositions. But having arisen, it makes the task of reflection a never ending one and by its failure to reach any conclusion it does permanent damage, achieving the very opposite of *parrhesia*.

At this point we may refer to an important distinction between the teacher and the student which works itself out in empirically discernible fashion too. In virtue of his practical and spiritual experience the teacher is in touch with kerygmatic realities. Even if this hermeneutical program may come very close to *a priori* pre-construction, there may always be seen in it an element of the counter-question, even if only in traces. This is not so in the

---

8. Cf. H. Diem, "Das Problem des Schriftkanons," ThSt, 32 (1952) and "Die Einheit der Schrift," ETh (1953), 9, pp. 385ff.

student, who enters the hall of theology through the vestibule of hermeneutical and methodological prolegomena. Here the counter-question yields to never ending reflection, and the perversion is complete.

The second generation is always the one that suffers in Cartesian schools. The homiletical efforts of students who are brought up in this theological climate, and who are frequently entangled in methodological and other preconsiderations, offer a good illustration. Students who are unsure of their matter always tend to take refuge in methodological questions. But here the material theological premises increase the tendency to such a degree that quantity is confused with quality and what we have called perversion results.

2. Truth Intended in Proclamation and Theology. Discussion of the Concept of Truth

a. Truth sui generis

The section on proclamation and theology developed a thesis which lies behind all our deliberations thus far. Our concern is with a particular style of truth. This is a truth that we cannot control, that has not entered the heart of man, that the natural man cannot perceive. It is a truth which leads me to being in truth and which thus transforms me. This transforming character of truth is what is brought to light by the active Word that mediates it. This Word is plainly the instrument of the miracle of the Spirit, bringing new birth and the new creation of the spiritual man.

This hermeneutics of the Holy Spirit means that the truth intended cannot possibly fall under the general categories which are the epistemological conditions for the usual definition of truth. We are thus confronted again by the familiar phenomenon in theology that when terms are transferred to theology they undergo a sharp modification of sense. Linguistically we still have the same word "truth," but it now denotes something very different.

The term still stands in analogy to what is usually called truth. Otherwise we should have to coin a new word and enter the hazy zone of glossolalia. Even after their "baptism" theological words still display their original meaning. We have here the same dialectic of identity and change as in the case of the person of the new and spiritual man. The new man is not a creation out of nothing. This is a miracle of change. He is made out of the existing material of the old man. Similarly the new terms are not a creation out of nothing. They are the old terms filled with new content.

There thus arises the unique dialectic in which we speak of

Christian truth, not as a special form of truth, but as truth *sui generis* both by nature and origin. But this includes rather than excludes the fact that we can define the relation between the theological view of truth and what is usually understood by truth in the secular sphere.

In this sense there seem to be three forms of truth which might be characterized as follows: (1) a truth which we can know; (2) a truth which applies to us; and (3) a truth which understands us before we can understand it.

(1) What we can know and express in a generally valid synthetic judgment must be objectifiable. What is discovered thus has the character of what is right. The right, as Martin Heidegger puts it,[9] says something suitable about an object. To be right it does not have to disclose its nature. When such disclosure takes place we have the true. The right is not yet the true. Only the true brings us into a free relation to what reaches us in terms of its nature.

This would bring us at once to a second form if we did not have to discuss, or at least to raise, an intermediate question. Does that which applies to us enter the picture only as we investigate the nature and significance of what is rightly known? Might it be that even that which is right can already reach us? A common view today is that it is our absolute right to collect knowledge, to extend indefinitely our knowledge of the right. As W. H. Auden points out, we agree that food and sex can be intolerable to excess, but we will not admit that intellectual curiosity is a desire like any other and that exact knowledge (the right) and truth are not identical. Perhaps we should be asking: What should I know? rather than: What can I know? Perhaps the only knowledge that can be true for us is that which we can measure up to in our lives. But this seems to us to be crack-brained and even immoral because it opposes the autonomy of the chain reaction of constant scientific inquiry.

Be that as it may, the question is whether even the question of the right as such (and not just that of nature and significance) does not have an existential reference, confronting us with the possibility that right knowledge and the technical use we make of it may be more than we can handle. In face of scientific knowledge it might well be that we are in the position of the sorcerer's apprentice. In face of possible space exploration it might well be that we are not by nature capable of exploiting the physical possibilities now open to us. It thus seems that there is no such thing as a neutral knowledge which does not affect our existence. Scholarship too, and

9. "Die Frage nach der Technik," *Vorträge und Aufsätze* (1954), 15.

even resolve upon it, provokes response and enforces the question of our attitude to it, of its significance for us, and of the way and end of our occupation with it.

Thus the transition from truth as knowledge to the second form of truth—truth as it applies to us—is a fluid one. The two forms are not sharply divided.

(2) This brings us to the second form, namely, truth as it applies to us.

This truth has to do with the meaning or nature of things, whether this denotes the meaning that sustains us or the meaninglessness that challenges us either by crushing us or by being so absurd that it provokes our powers of resistance and thus has a creative effect (cf. Camus and Benn).

Meaning and meaninglessness are always incarnate in persons. In the last resort being human describes the relation to the meaning or meaninglessness that either sustains me or threatens to crush me. Personal being is ontically characterized by concern in being for being itself.[10] There is in being a relation of being to being. One might almost say that being itself is such a relation. This relation is its truth. Plato saw this when he said that for him the question of truth is the question of authentic (as distinct from phenomenal) being and that the essence of a man results from the relation he either has or does not have to authentic being. On having or not having this relation depends his essential life or his subjection to confusion by appearance.

Since the relation of existence to being or meaning is not objectifiable, I can only understand personal life and not explain it. This distinction between scientific "explaining" and intellectual "understanding" was made by Dilthey.[11] In this context understanding as distinct from explaining means that insight into the life of another person demands a specific existential pre-condition, namely, that I represent in my own person the same structure of existence as that of the other person's life. Only because I myself have a relation of being and meaning can I see the other in the same relation. Only for this reason can I appreciate his boredom and emptiness, his anxiety, his defective being, or his fulness of being. Only for this reason can I understand that this other being, like myself, is summoned to grasp his destiny and risks missing it.

10. Cf. M. Heidegger, *Being and Time*, p. 32.
11. *Der Aufbau der geschichtlichen Welt in den Geisteswissenschaften, Gesammelte Schriften*, VII (1927; 3rd ed. 1961), pp. 71, 80ff., 86, 92, 141, etc.

Solidarity with the other under the same theme of existence makes understanding possible.

Dilthey in his work on the development of hermeneutics[12] works out psychologically the solidarity which makes understanding possible. It is the power of empathy, which is not unlike Schleiermacher's divinatory understanding. This ability rests on the kinship between expositor and author. It demands constant study enhanced by an empathetic life.[13] This ability, however, is only a psychological reflection of the ontological solidarity that exists between expositor and author as common bearers of personal life who share the same life and are in the same relation which constitutes the essence of existence. Bultmann is thus closer to the ontological secret of understanding when he describes it as a precondition that the expositor should have a living relation to what is directly or indirectly expressed in the text. In poetic, philosophical, and especially kerygmatic texts this is ultimate reality, to which both author and expositor stand related and which declares itself in intelligible fashion in the ciphers of the text. A certain "musicality" expressing the empathy of the receptive intellectual constitution may intensify and refine the process of understanding. But it can do so only within the ontic solidarity and can be no substitute for this. If there is no ontic solidarity, as may happen in face of an alien interpretation of existence, the "musicality" may produce aesthetic appreciation but will miss the heart of the matter. We see this in purely aesthetic interpretations and evaluations of Bach's religious works as these are found among those who enjoy them for purely secular reasons.

(3) Finally we must glance at the third form of truth. This is the truth that understands us before we understand it. In Pauline terms (1 Corinthians 13:12) it is the truth which we know as and after we are known by it. I can speak of the truth in this sense only when I see it incarnate in a person, in the king of truth (John 18:37f.). Apart from this I may well speak of a truth which discloses itself to me (cf. the literal sense of the Greek *alétheia*) or which applies to me. A truth which knows and sees me, however, can only be a living other that is resolved upon communication with me. This living other is not to be understood, of course, as one to whom I am related in the general solidarity of the same constitution of

12. *Gesammelte Schriften*, V (1924; 3rd ed. 1961), pp. 317–331, esp. 326f.
13. *Ibid.*, pp. 326f.; cf. Bultmann, *Glauben und Verstehen*, II (1952), p. 215.

being. It is not, as I am, in a relation to meaning or to ultimate truth. If it were, I might say that this other *form* had known me before I knew it, just as my mother did. But I could not say that the *truth* which is at issue here had known me before I knew it.

Christ's relation to the truth is in fact stated in a unique way which rules out even an enhanced form of ordinary solidarity with me. The exceptional character of Christ according to the NT consists in the fact that he does not just represent a relation to meaning (logos); he is the Logos. Truth is incarnate in him and identical with him. Truth is what he is; the ultimate reality which gives meaning appears in him, namely, the faithfulness of God which constitutes his truth according to Romans 3:3, which endures, on which one may rely, and which as *dikaiosyne* is opposed to human *pseudos*.[14] Christ does not merely proclaim to us the truth of God's faithfulness which sustains our life and gives it stability and meaning. He is this truth in bodily form present among us. He is thus characterized by "am" and "is" judgments which articulate being and not just doing. "I am the way, the truth, and the life" (John 14:6). "He is our peace" (Ephesians 2:14).

---

14. Cf. R. Bultmann, Art. *alétheia*, TDNT, I, pp. 242f.

4

THOMAS F. TORRANCE

The Word of God and the Response of Man[1]

BY THE WORD OF GOD IS MEANT NOT MAN'S WORD ABOUT GOD BUT quite definitely God's own Word as God Himself lives and speaks it—Word as personal mode and activity of God's Being. Yet we have to do with the Word of God only as it has been addressed to us and has actually reached us, Word that has called forth and found response in our hearing and understanding and living— otherwise we could not speak of it. We do not begin, then, with God alone or with man alone, nor even with God speaking on the one hand and man hearing on the other hand, but with God and man as they are posited together in a movement of creative self-communication by the Word of God. This is not Word in which God exists only in and for Himself or which He speaks to Himself alone, but Word by which He creates and upholds other realities around Him and gives them room for their relations with Him. It is the mode of His Being in which God goes forth to meet man, freely relating His divine Life to him within the conditions of his creaturely nature, and in which He sustains man in his meeting with God, enabling him freely to relate his human life to the majesty of the divine Nature. It is in this togetherness and open-ness between God and man that God's self-revelation to man takes place. A profound reciprocity is created in which God addresses His Word to man by giving it human form without any diminish-ment of its divine reality as God Himself speaks it, and in which He enables man to hear His Word and respond to it without any

1. Lecture given to the session of *Académie Internationale des Sciences Religieuses* at Liebfrauenberg, Goersdorf, France, on 11 October 1968, and to the Faculty of Theology, University of Louvain, on 14 October 1968.

From Thomas F. Torrance, *God and Rationality*, pp. 137–164. © Oxford University Press 1971. Reprinted by permission of Oxford University Press.

cancellation of his human mode of being. The nature of the reciprocity is such that in assuming human form the Word of God summons an answering movement from man toward God which is taken up into the movement of the Word as a constitutive part of God's revelation to man. Thus the Word of God communicated to man includes within itself meeting between man and God as well as meeting between God and man, for in assuming the form of human speech the Word of God spoken to man becomes at the same time word of man in answer to God.

It is of course in the revelation of God actualized in our historical human existence through the instrumentality of Israel and in Jesus Christ the Word made flesh, in whom that actualization of divine revelation was brought to its fulfilment in acutely personal form, that we learn this about the Word of God and the response of man. We do not derive it from an analysis of the concrete life-situations of ancient Israel or the objectified forms of proclamation and worship found in the primitive Church, but directly from the activity of the Word Himself who as the source of human being has penetrated through the barriers of its estrangement, opened it out to the light and understanding of God and established a two-way connexion between God and man in the incarnation where the human response is true and faithful to the divine revelation, and not in the last analysis just a refracted form of man's self-understanding. This is Jesus Christ, the Interpreter and Mediator between man and God, who, as God of God in unqualified deity and as Man of man in unqualified humanity, constitutes in the unity of His incarnate Person the divine-human Word, spoken to man from the highest and heard by him in the depths, and spoken to God out of the depths and heard by Him in the highest. He is not only the Word of God come to man and become man, but He who as man bears and is the Word of God, the Word not only as God utters it but the same Word as heard, uttered and lived by man, and who as such carries in Himself the vicarious actuality, and conveys in Himself the active possibility, of true and faithful response on the part of all men to God's Word. It is thus in the form of sheer humanity in all its lowliness, weakness and darkness that God's Word has reached us and made provision for free and adequate response on our part, but in such a way that far from being a dispensable medium to be discarded as soon as the target is reached, the humanity of the Word, God's condescension to be one with us in our humanity, remains the proof that in His own eternal Being He is not closed to us, and the manifestation of His freedom to unveil Himself to man and share with him His own divine Life.

It is upon this humanity of the Word in Jesus that we must reflect deeply if we are to penetrate into the inner relation between the Word of God and man's response, but we must not forget that He is word of man in answer to God only in that He is first and foremost Word of God become man. What did it mean, then, for the eternal Word of God, *as Word,* to take creaturely and human form, and thus to be heard *as word* by man?

I

In Himself the Word of God is quite independent of what He has made. As the creative source and ground of all finite being He maintains it in a binding relation to Himself but He is not bound to it through any necessary relation of being or operation such as that between cause and effect. He produces it freely by calling it into being out of nothing and gives it a reality of its own which He preserves and respects, and He Himself remains sovereignly free over against it. He does not impart His substance to it; His Life is not implicated in it; He does not communicate to it His divine nature—and therefore He is known and understood only on the free ground of His own self-subsistent Being. But He does give form and order to finite being, limiting, determining and enlightening it, and thereby makes it comprehensible. He confers upon it a created rationality different from, yet dependent on, His own transcendent rationality, and thus gives it an inner law of its own which is not self-explanatory, to be sure, but which endures before God as the truth and goodness of created being upheld by His eternal Word. It is into this created rationality (or *logos*) that the Word (or *Logos*) of God enters, assimilating it to Himself in the incarnation, in order to become Word to man through the medium of human word and in order to provide from the side of man for an appropriate response in truth and goodness toward God.

This created rationality takes two main forms, *number* and *word,* corresponding to impersonal and personal being. Different though they are, they come together in man, in the interrelation and inseparability of his physical and spiritual existence in space and time, and they operate together in the emergence of the universe as it is explored and scientifically built up through man's interaction with nature and as its inherent rationality is brought to co-ordinate expression in mathematical and verbal language. Number is the rationality of the creation in its form as determinate event, the rationality of immanence and necessity which is mute in itself but which may be brought to articulation through man in so far as he thinks it under the compulsion of the physical nature of things. Word is the rationality of the creation in which it reaches beyond its fixed and mute condition, the rationality of transcendence and freedom in which man as the crown and priest of creation has the function of shaping formal instruments through which he may bring being to disclose itself in accordance with its manifold nature. Both forms of rationality are needed, but it is in and through man alone that they emerge into the open, so that it is by man's grasp and handling of them that the creation, including man, attains to its full being. The development of scientific knowledge is not something alien to the creation, imposed upon it *ab extra,* but is part of its proper development and thus a manifestation of its inherent nature. Just as the creation is given to produce life in itself, so it is given to produce its own articulation and thus to rise above its mute and confined condition. Number cannot come to expression apart from word, that is, without the acquisition of language through which man can stand over against his environment, designating its features and presenting them to himself as objects for reflexion and computation in order that he may organize and enlarge his knowledge of the world. On the other hand, word cannot fulfil this role apart from number, that is, without the realm of the determinate and immutable which in virtue of its inherent rationality supplies the fixed medium for the development of intelligible systems of representation and at the same time acts as the external control required for consistency and universality in communication. Thus number and word find articulation in two co-ordinated levels of rationality in which each requires the other but in which word is the formal means by which the creation is delivered from being trapped in itself and is made open to what is above and beyond it. In this context the inherent rationality of the physical creation is seen not to be self-contained but to call for a transcendent rationality for its explanation and meaning.

Now the Word of God did not enter this sphere of created rationality as a stranger, for in the incarnation He came to His own, but He did enter into what was creaturely and contingent and therefore utterly different: and this *difference* must be taken into account. In the Creator Himself, Word, Person and Act are one and undivided, but in the creature they fall apart. With us word is different from act. We speak, but have to exert additional power in order to fulfil what we say in deeds. We act, but our acts are not personal in themselves. Our speech and our action do not coincide in the unity and power of our person. Act and person, word and person, word and act are all separate—they are not unrelated, but their relationship is conditioned by physical existence and is refracted and strung out in time. With God it is not so. He encounters us as One whose Word and whose Act belong to the self-subsistence of His Person. What He speaks takes place of itself, for it is filled with the power of His Person, the power by which He is what He is and by which He lives His own personal Life in absolute self-sufficiency and freedom. His power to act is not other than the power of His Person or the power of His Word. He is in Person identical with His Word, and His Word is itself His Act. However, when the Word of God condescended to participate in created existence in order to become Word to man, personally addressing him in the medium of human speech and physical event in space and time, He entered into the divided and finite condition of word, person and act and into the duality of number and word, that characterize created reality. He came as genuine man, physically conditioned in space and time, in whom willing, speaking and doing are different, who thinks and forms judgements, whose acts follow upon his decisions, whose words are in addition to his person and whose works are in addition to his words, but who in none of these things is self-sufficient, for as man he lives and thinks and speaks and acts only in inseparable relation to his fellow-men and in dependence upon the physical creation. Clearly, for the eternal Word of God to become understandable and communicable in the mode and character of word to man He had to share to the full in the space-time distinctions and connexions of human existence in this world and operate within the finite conditions of created rationality. This is not to say, of course, that He ceased to be the Word He is in the Creator, but rather that He appropriated human form within the frame of earthly life and action and speech in such a way as to take up the frail and finite conditions of the creature into Himself not merely as the earthen vessel of the Word of God but as His actual speaking of it to us. In Jesus Christ the word has become physical event in space and time, meets us in the indissoluble connexion of physical and spiritual existence, and is to be understood within the co-ordinate levels of created rationality. The unity in God between Person, Word and Act has been made to overlap and gather within its embrace the differences between person, word and act in the creature, so that they are allowed to mediate God's Word to man in time through a oneness between Christ's human utterance about God and God's self-utterance to man. Expressed otherwise, in the hypostatic union between the Word of God and the word of man, but in such a way that far from being displaced in some Apollinarian fashion the word of man is fully and finally established in its genuine humanity through the regenerating and humanizing work of the Word made flesh.

There is another side to all this, however, which is supremely important. When the Word of God became man, He came to His own, but His own did not receive Him, for although they derived their being from Him they had rebelled against Him and had fallen into darkness and enmity. Thus it was not only into our contingent and finite condition that the Word of God had to penetrate, but into our sin and alienation where we are subject to the thraldom of evil power, into our guilty existence under the sentence of divine judgement, and into the disintegration of our human being in death. He came, therefore, to share our lost and enslaved existence where it was breaking up under the corrosion of sin and guilt, disease and want, death and judgement, and to enter into the disordered state of our created rationalities in which finite distinctions are damaged and distorted into contradictions, in order to engage with the inhuman forces of darkness that had encroached upon the bodies and minds of men, to struggle with the perverse nature of an alienated creation, to meet the full hostility of evil by accepting and bearing it in Himself, and to make an end of it in His own vicarious life and death. But throughout all He by whom all men were made and in whom they consist lived as man on earth and in history a life of holiness, trust and love in filial obedience to the heavenly Father, thus carrying the human nature He had received from us through darkness, conflict, rejection and judgement into new being in His resurrection from the dead. By being completely and unreservedly God's Word incarnate in the fulness of grace and truth He was able from within our estranged and impaired existence to deliver man from subjection to futility and negation, recreate his relation to God, realize perfect humanity on the earth, and to offer in and through Himself man's true response in person, word and act to God the Creator. God's Word has reached and found common understanding and reciprocity with us through the anguish and passion of incarnation and atonement and through the rebirth of man in the integrity and wholeness of his physical and spiritual existence in the resurrection. In the whole life, death and resurrection of Jesus God Himself was directly at work affirming as good what He had made and making good His own Word in the creation of the world.

That is what was involved in every act of mercy and healing in which the commanding fiat of the Creator was found on the lips of

Jesus. As the Evangelists make clear in their reporting, the different miracles of Jesus were concerned with the saving of creation in its spiritual and physical conditions, but the way in which they took place, through His sharing in our earthly existence in all its distress and limitation, revealed that only through the full participation of the Creator with us in our creaturely and human life can atonement for sin and redemption from evil power issue in the actual restoration of what God has made. That is surely why the Fourth Gospel with all its immense stress upon the humanity and obedience of the Son opens with the Prologue in which we are told that the Creator Word has become flesh, Himself one of the creatures made through Him, in order to effect the enlightenment and regeneration of man by working within his creaturely existence and serving it from below and by sharing with him His own sanctified humanity. Without the incarnation of the Creator Word the fallen world would crumble away finally and irretrievably into nothingness, for then God would simply be letting go of what He had made and it would suffer from sheer privation of being. But the incarnation has taken place. Once and for all, the Creator Word has entered into the existence of what He has made and bound it up with His own eternal Being and Life embodied in Jesus Christ, yet without violating its creaturely nature. In this union of the Creator with the creature the eternal Word of God who is the ground of man's existence from beyond his existence has now become also the ground of his existence within his existence, undergirding and sustaining it from within its natural process in such a way as to establish his reality and meaning as human being and to realize his distinctive response toward God in the fulness of his creaturely freedom and integrity.

Let it be stressed, however, that all this is achieved by the Word of God, not merely as in the original creation by direct fiat, but by condescending to participate in finite being, submitting to its limitations and operating within its struggles and structures, thus fulfilling God's saving purpose for the creation in and through the inner determination of His incarnate life as Man on earth and in history. Such was the life and mission of Jesus Christ the Word made flesh who mediated between God and man, reconciling them in and through Himself, and so established a correlation and correspondence between God's self-giving and man's receiving within which alone God's revelation could be actualized in man and a true and faithful response could be yielded by man to God.

Here we arrive again at the point we noted at the outset, that in effecting His self-communication to man the Word of God assimilates the hearing of man to itself as a constitutive part of God's revelation, but now two things must be emphasized: Jesus Christ is Himself the hearing man included in the Word of God, and He is that in a final and definitive way. In the Gospels we do not have to do simply with the Word of God and the response of man, but with the all-significant middle term, the divinely provided response in the vicarious humanity of Jesus Christ. As the humanity of the Word through whom we have our being the humanity of Christ occupies a unique place in the creative ground of our humanity, and as the humanity in which atonement and reconciliation have been perfected it fulfils a representative and substitutionary role in all our relations with God, including every aspect of human response to Him: such as trusting and obeying, understanding and knowing, loving and worshipping. Jesus Christ is presented to us in the Gospels as He who in and through His humanity took our place, acting in our name and on our behalf before God, freely offering in Himself what we could not offer and offering it in our stead, the perfect response of man to God in a holy life of faith and prayer and praise, the self-offering of the Beloved Son with whom the Father is well pleased. And so to those who receive Him and believe in Him, power and freedom are given to become sons of God: not in virtue of any natural birth through the will of the flesh or the will of man, but in virtue of their birth from God, a rebirth from above. Now that God's saving grace has taken this way, in the provision of man's true and faithful response in the vicarious humanity of Jesus Christ, it thereby invalidates all other ways of response. Here there operates, so to speak, a theological form of Fermat's principle in accordance with which the selection of one among other possible paths in the formulation of natural law sets the others aside as unentertainable and actually impossible. In Himself God is transcendently free and able to create other possibilities—such as raising up children for Abraham from the stones of the Jordan—but the actual coming of His eternal Word into our contingent existence in Jesus Christ excludes every other way to the Father, and stamps the vicarious humanity of Christ to be the sole norm and law as well as the sole ground of acceptable human response to God. Hence the response to which man is summoned by the proclamation of the Word of God is not some arbitrary self-determination or independent self-expression on his part, but one derived from, grounded in, and shaped by the very humanity of the Word which originally gave him being as man and continues to sustain him in his human nature and spontaneity before God as well as in his engagement in the world of things and persons to which he belongs.

II

Hitherto we have been considering the fact that in order to be Word to man the Word of God became flesh, but now we must consider the fact that the Word came to *dwell* among us. That is to say, we have considered the relation of the Word of God to the response of man in terms of the humanity which the Word assumed in addressing him, and must now go on to consider the fact that in order to be heard and understood as Word it had to enter the speaker-hearer relationship within humanity and become speech to man, spoken and heard through the medium of human language. But language is rooted in a society and is kept alive by the exchange and development of thought that takes place through it. It is the currency of social being. Neither in God nor in man is word found in isolation but only in community. In God the Word subsists in the inner consubstantial relations of the Holy Trinity, and in man words have their existence in the public language of expression and communication developed by a community of persons bound together not only by a common world but by a common way of life and culture. Hence, if the Word of God is to enter the forum as speech to man through the medium of human words it must be directed to man in community, and if that Word creates reciprocity between God and man it must create a community of such reciprocity within human society as the appropriate medium of its continuing communication to man.

That is what happened between God and Israel, for the Word of God spoken to man did not operate in a vacuum but penetrated human existence in the particular life and history of one people elected as the instrument for the actualization of God's revelation in humanity and separated as a holy nation in whose midst God dwelt in an intimate way through the presence of His Word. The covenant relationship between God and Israel which this set up was a particularization of the one covenant of grace which embraced the whole of creation and constituted its inner bond and ground, and therefore carried in it the promise of a final universalization of God's revelation in which His Word would bring light and salvation to all the peoples of mankind and indeed a new heaven and a new earth.

Thus Israel became aware of itself as a people seized by the Word of God, and charged with messianic destiny. The same mighty Word that created the world and ultimately lay behind every event in nature and in history was at work in its midst creating corporate reciprocity and using the responses it provoked, whether of assent or dissent, obedience or disobedience, blindness or enlightenment, apostasy or reform, as instruments for its deeper penetration into Israel's existence and the means through which it became understandable and communicable to man. As the Word of God invaded the social matrix of Israel's life, culture, religion and history, and clothed itself with Israel's language, it had to struggle with the communal meaning already embedded in it in order to assimilate it to God's revelation of Himself. For new understanding to take root within Israel, it had to take shape within Israel's language, and therefore it had to remould the inner structure of the society within which that language had its home and had to determine the whole history of Israel in its physical existence. Hence through the impact of the Word there were initiated in the tradition of Israel priestly and prophetic movements which entailed critical revision of previous ways of life, worship, and thought in order to break through the barriers of naturalistic and pagan convention that obstructed knowledge of the living God. New forms of worship, thought, and expression had to be created as the context within which the Word of God could be heard and understanding of it could be established, but in order that this orientation toward God could be habituated in its mind and existence Israel had to be subjected to ordeal by history through a long struggle of the Word with the perverse nature of man as it was forced into the open in Israel's intimate experience of divine judgement and mercy. And so throughout Israel's tradition the Word of God kept pressing for articulation within the corporate medium of covenant reciprocity and progressively took verbal and even written form through the shared understanding and shared response that developed in this people. The historical dialogue between God and Israel, in covenant and controversy, was maintained by a concentration of the speaker-hearer relation in a prophetic nucleus within Israelite society through which the Word of God assumed decisive form in the mouth of men and impinged relentlessly upon Israel's life, interpreting its history, determining its direction, calling it out to be people or church of God, and opening its future toward the incarnation. Thus Israel became in a unique way the bearer of God's Word to mankind and His corporate prophet among the nations of history.

That Word was encountered in historic Israel as yet only in its 'formable' state (to borrow an old Augustinian expression), for it was still in process of taking shape in the habits of the human mind and speech. But throughout its historical reciprocity with Israel the Word of God kept creating formal and empirical correlates of its own self-utterance through which it extended its activity and speech in space and time. Although they were by no means exhaustive transcripts of that self-utterance they came to be deposited in the Old Testament Scriptures, for in and through them men continued to hear God addressing them directly and backing up His Word by the living power and majesty of His divine Person. In this dynamic mode the Word of God pressed on through the life and experience of Israel toward final and definitive form, but for that reason the scriptural forms inspired by the Spirit proclaimed far more than they could specify at the time and so by their very nature they pointed ahead to the full disclosure of the divine reality they served.

The whole fact of Israel entrusted with the oracles of God was itself a mighty response evoked by the Word of God out of the midst of history, but within Israel the Word of God was mediated in such a way that a divinely prepared form of obedient response was included within it. That is what we find in the prophetic message about the servant of the Lord through whose passion a new covenant would be inaugurated bringing redemption to Israel and a light to lighten the Gentiles, and that is what we find fulfilled at last in the birth of Jesus. God had adapted Israel to His purpose in such a way as to form within it a womb for the incarnation of the Word and a matrix of appropriate forms of human thought and speech for the reception of the incarnational revelation. And so Jesus was born of Mary, out of the organic correlation of Word and response in the existence of Israel, to be the Word of God made flesh in the life and language of man and to be that Word heard and expressed in the truth and grace of perfect human response to God. In Him God's Word has become speech to man through the medium of human words and speaks to men as man to man, for in Him God has graciously assumed our human speech into union with His own, effecting it as the human expression of the divine Word, and giving it as such an essential place in His revelation to man.

With the incarnation, however, we have moved into a decisively different situation from that which obtained in Old Testament times, for here the forms of thought and speech developed in ancient Israel are not only fulfilled but transcended and relativized by the final and permanent forms which the Word has taken in the life and teaching of Jesus Christ. That is the real ground for what Schleiermacher called 'the language-moulding power of Christianity'. It is not just a correlation between the Word of God and the transient response which it evokes, as the instrument of deeper and deeper penetration into human existence, which we have here.

Rather is it such a profound integration between Word of God and word of man that they can no longer be separated out from each other. The humanity of the Word, even in His distinctive individuality and physical particularity, is not something that can be discarded like outworn clothing that has served its purpose in the past, for it is constituted the actual address of God's Word to man and is indissolubly bound up with its material content. Hence the basic forms of human thought and speech in which the incarnational revelation is mediated to us cannot be made the object of independent investigation in themselves as if they could be abstracted from their historical context and factual reference, nor can they be understood primarily from their place in the social and religious matrix of Israel or Church as if they could be interpreted merely out of the subjective states of those who received God's revelation, but from their place in the normative and definitive structure of the Word made flesh in His solidarity with human and physical being in space and time.

At this point, we must remember that human language has its place in the interaction of man's physical and spiritual existence and functions through the co-ordinate levels of created rationality corresponding to determinate event and personal behaviour. The introduction of any dichotomy into that situation would take away the ground of signification and open up a chasm of meaninglessness. Far from doing anything like that, the incarnation of the Word overcame the inner disruption in man's existence that had resulted from his estrangement from God and established again the unity and wholeness of his being in space and time. Hence in Jesus Himself, word and deed, language and event, were inextricably interwoven in His revealing activity. His words were done as well as spoken and His deeds spoke as much as His words, for in Him God's Word had become physical, historical event, while the very fact and existence of Jesus was itself Word of God. This conjunction between language and event in the interaction of the Word of God with nature is very evident in the parabolic teaching of Jesus. The parable was chosen, not to provide detachable symbolic forms through which human thought could be lifted up away from this world into some transcendental realm of Word, but as the means of setting man's hearing of the Word squarely within this-worldly reality, for it is there in the concrete situations of our earthly existence that God Himself meets us and addresses us. Thus the parable operates through co-ordinating the conceptual and symbolic levels of language, in much the same way as we saw word and number to be co-ordinated in the development and articulation of our scientific knowledge of nature. As such it both reveals the applicability of the Word to our earthly existence and shows the significant place given to this world in the incarnation of the Word of God. The parables, however, direct us above all to Jesus Christ Himself as the mystery of the Kingdom of God in our midst, for it is in Him that the reality of God meets us within the reality of this world. He is the one place on earth and in history where we may have such reciprocity with God that we may hear His Word and see His Face. Thus in their conjunction of language and event the parables of Jesus correspond to and reveal His nature as Word of God manifest in the flesh. The real text of the New Testament Scriptures is the humanity of Christ. He is God's exclusive language to us and He alone must be our language to God.

We must now consider more fully the transition that took place in the historical existence of Jesus Christ from His being Word of God to man to His being also word of man to man, communicable within the medium of man's exchange in thought and word with his fellow man. In Jesus Christ, as we have seen, we are presented with God's Word to man and man's obedient response to God incorporated into God's Word as an essential part of it. As such, Jesus Christ is God's self-address to man, but this self-address in order to achieve its end had to penetrate, take form and domicile itself within the address of man to man, as the Word of Christ abiding among men. The reciprocity established between God and man in Jesus Christ had to create room for itself within the reciprocities of human society, and the Word of God which had come 'plumb down from above' had to deploy itself in the horizontal dimensions of human existence in order to continue its speaking and acting throughout history. This involved the formation of a nucleus within the speaker-hearer relations of men, corresponding to and grounded in the communion between God and man embodied in Jesus Christ, as the controlling basis among believers for the extended communication of the Word of God, and the translation of the self-witness of Christ into witness to Christ, answering the normative pattern of His obedient humanity, as the specific form for the proclamation of God's Word to all men.

That is what took place in the apostolic foundation of the Church and in the apostolic formulation of the *kerygma,* both as parts of one movement in which Christ's self-address to man evoked and inspired a response in word and deed which He assimilated into union with His own response to God and effected as the authoritative expression of His own *kerygma* in the world. Thus, in the apostles as the receiving end of His revealing and reconciling activity, Jesus Christ laid the foundation of the Church which He incorporated into Himself as His own Body, and permitted the Word which He put into their mouth to take the form of proclamation answering to and extending His own in such a way that it became the controlled unfolding of His own revelation within the mind and language of the apostolic foundation. The apostolic proclamation of Christ was so geared into His self-proclamation that it was used by Him as the shared and corporate medium of understanding and communication through which He brought His Word in human and historical form to bear upon mankind throughout the ages. Just as the response of man in Christ was made a constituent element in the Word of God to man, so the response of the apostles was assumed by Christ into oneness with His own to form the means by which the Word of Christ reached out into history. Thus, through the apostolic witness and proclamation, it was Christ Himself who was at work testifying to the mighty acts whereby He had redeemed the world and offering Himself to men as their Saviour and Lord.

This then is the New Testament proclamation of the Word of God which already includes within itself the kind of responses to which it summons mankind. The response of the apostles which had been taken up into the proclamation was of a second-order nature compared to that of Christ, for the primary text of the Word remained that of the humanity of Christ Himself. Hence the proclamation of the Gospel announces to us that the true and faithful response of man to God has already been made in the self-offering of Christ on our behalf, and holds it out to us as the divinely appointed and provided response in which we may share freely as through the Spirit we participate in the vicarious obedience of the Word made flesh. The place given to the response of the apostles in the *kerygma* is certainly of authoritative and critical significance for the whole history of the Church, but its purpose there is to enable us to stand with the original witnesses under the impact of the Word they received and to be drawn into the sphere of its effective operation where we, like them, may learn to repent and believe the Gospel, give thanks to God and live in communion with Him. Thus, far from obtruding themselves or their own spirituality upon us, the apostles serve the *kerygma* by directing us back to the representative and vicarious humanity of Christ as the creative ground and normative pattern for the actualization of every response to God on our part.

III

We must now give some attention to specific forms of response that are called forth by the proclamation of the Word of God and show their relation to the response of Christ.

(a) Faith

Faith is undoubtedly a primary form of response to the Word of God, involving the elements of trust, assent and belief; but since in the biblical context God Himself in His own Person stands behind His Word and pledges Himself to us in it, faith is also understood as the faithfulness of man answering to and dependent upon the faithfulness of God as its ultimate ground. God does not break His Word, for in His Word God remains true both to Himself and to those to whom He sends His Word. His Word always fulfils its intention, actualizing itself in deeds and events that correspond faithfully to it, thus manifesting itself as God's Truth. The same applies, *mutatis mutandis,* to the human sphere, in which truth is found wherever word and event coincide, and a man is reckoned true and faithful when his deed is as good as his word. Thus God is said to keep truth or faith with His people and they are required to keep truth or faith with Him. In this the biblical understanding, faith subsists in the mutual relation of faithfulness between God and man involving consistency between word and event.

In these terms the incarnation is to be understood as the mighty act of God in which His Word has become event in our flesh in such a way that the event corresponds perfectly with His Word. Jesus Christ is the Truth of God actualized in our midst, the incarnate faithfulness of God, but He is also man keeping faith and truth with God in a perfect correspondence between His life and activity in the flesh and the Word of God. In Him there is utter consistency between God the Word revealing Himself to man and man hearing, believing, obeying, and speaking His Word. Not only is He the incarnation of the divine faithfulness but the embodiment and actualization of man's faithfulness in answer to God's; but as such He offers to God, and is toward God in His own person and life, our human response of faith and obedience to God. If it was in His humanity in entire solidarity with us that Jesus Christ stood in our place, and gave to God an account for us in His life and death, in utter faithfulness to God and to man, then this includes the fact that He believed for us, offering to God in His vicarious faithfulness the perfect response of human faith which we could not offer.

That is what the Word of God proclaims to us in the Gospel, and therefore it summons us to respond by faith only as it holds out to us free participation in the faithful response of Christ already made on our behalf. Hence our response of faith is made within the ring of faithfulness which Christ has already thrown around us, when in faith we rely not on our own believing but wholly on His vicarious response of faithfulness toward God. In this way Christ's faithfulness undergirds our feeble and faltering faith and enfolds it in His own; but since His faithfulness enshrines within itself the faithfulness of God and the faithfulness of the Man Jesus, we are unable to disentangle our acts of faith in Christ from their implication in the eternal faithfulness of God.

Within this relation between the faithfulness of God and the faithfulness of man polarized through the incarnation of God's Word there is another primary aspect of faith that must be taken into account, that in which it answers to the Word as *Event* and credits Word and Event in their correspondence with one another as the Truth of God in action. This is the aspect of faith in which the intellectual elements are prominent. It takes place within the created rationalities of space and time into which the Word made flesh assimilated Himself, and therefore exhibits itself in ways that reflect those forms of rationality in respect of necessity and freedom, immanence and transcendence. Here on the one hand, where we are up against the concrete actualities in nature and history through which God meets us, faith is the *assent* which we are forced to yield when we react to the given facts in accordance with their immanent nature and intelligibility. This involves an act of rational judgement, but one demanded and controlled by the firm structure of the objective reality, the physical and historical event in which we hear God's Word. On the other hand, when we are engaged in personal encounter with God in which His Word penetrates into our existence, creates reciprocity with us, and invites our response, faith is the willing *consent* which we yield to the Word in recognition of His transcendent majesty and intelligibility. This involves an act of rational understanding in which our minds are opened to grasp what is beyond their natural power, but which they freely acknowledge on the ground of its divine nature and self-evidence, the Grace and Truth of God in Jesus Christ.

Of course, faith does not comprise two different acts but one movement of response in which there are elements of freedom and compulsion corresponding to the mutual involution of Word and Event in God's self-revelation in Jesus Christ. He is proclaimed to us in the Gospel as at once objective historical Fact and personal Word of God and thus encounters us in the *kerygma* with a determinate rationality in His Being, and an articulate rationality in His Word through which He is disclosed to us in His Being. As Word of God come in the flesh who cannot be other than He is, Jesus Christ is known only in accordance with the innermost necessity of His Being, but far from overwhelming us with the immediacy of His divine nature He graciously meets us in the midst of our worldly distinctions and relations through the medium of His human nature and word, giving us freedom to listen to Him and understand Him, respond to Him and follow Him. Nevertheless, even when we know Him freely through the Truth of His Word our minds fall under the compulsion of the Truth of His Being. This is what the New Testament calls 'the obedience of faith', which is the willing assent of our mind to the claims of His divine Reality and the responsible commitment of our will to the saving efficacy of His activity in the flesh. Since there can be no faith apart from the acknowledgment of the historical actuality and reality of Jesus Christ and of the divine authority of His self-revelation in our worldly existence, the humanity of the incarnate Word remains the firm basis and law of our response; but since He encounters us in the personal medium of word and requires of us a response in the same medium, faith does not come to fruition unless the inner assent spontaneously translates itself into articulate acknowledgment and thanksgiving, that is, in Pauline language, unless confession with the mouth accompanies belief in the heart.

(b) *Worship*

From the point we have just reached it should be evident that worship is the natural expression of faith; but, let it be added, expression of faith in its objective orientation in the humanity of Christ, rather than subjective self-expression on the part of believers. Like faith, worship comprises elements of freedom and necessity bound up with language which is its natural medium and the nature of that to which it offers response.

We recall that language is the system of verbal signs which we develop in order to grasp things and present them to ourselves in such a way that we can stand over against them and think about them, and allow them to disclose themselves to us in forms appropriate to them. This applies in different ways to the world of things and the world of persons, but in both we are engaged in the rationality of acting in accordance with what is not-ourselves and enlarging our knowledge of it. In the world of persons, however, it is particularly with inter-personal transcendence that we are concerned, in which we distinguish ourselves from each other and communicate with each other. This is also the role which language plays in our worship of God. Worship is essentially a dialogical activity in which we stand over against God even when we draw near to Him, distinguishing His transcendent nature from ourselves, while relating ourselves appropriately to His holiness and majesty and responding thankfully to the mercy He extends towards us. By meeting us and entering into dialogue with us through His Word the transcendent God creates space for our 'transcendence' over against Him and at the same time creates between us and Himself the rational continuity in which reciprocity and communion can take place. And since God's Word comes to us in and through the medium of human language, it establishes our communion with God in the creaturely freedom that obtains between human speaking and responding, and summons us to formulate our human responses to Him within that freedom.

If language is to serve its purpose adequately in any field, it must be rightly related to the realities which it is used to signify, but as soon as that relation is damaged the disclosure of reality through it becomes distorted and the language itself becomes obscure. That is our perpetual difficulty in worship. Since our language is rooted in human society, it is psychologically and socially conditioned by naturalistic patterns of thought and speech that have already developed in it and are not appropriate to God, so that if they are used in the formulation of our responses to His Word they inevitably make things opaque. That is why worship calls for a great deal of refined activity on our part in purifying and adapting our liturgical language until it becomes, as far as possible in our pilgrim state, a transparent medium for communion with God in which we do not obstruct self-discourse on His part and are made open for heuristic vision on our part.

Since liturgical activity of this kind requires to be controlled and shaped by the reality it serves, we are inevitably thrown back upon the objective self-disclosure of God in Jesus Christ, for He is the one place in our humanity where the divine Light shines through to us undimmed and unobstructed by damaged relations or distorting forms of thought and speech; but in Jesus Christ we are given more than the creative mould for our human responses, we are provided with the very essence and core of man's worship of God. In His life, death, resurrection and ascension He offered Himself through the eternal Spirit in our name and on our behalf, presenting us in

Himself to the Father, once and for all, so that He remains forever our sole offering in deed and word with which we appear before God. We do not draw near to God in worship either with our own self-expression or empty handed, but with hands of faith filled with the self-oblation of Christ, for He constitutes in His vicarious humanity the eloquent reality of our worship.

In His covenant with Israel God not only promised to be their God and required of them to walk before Him and be perfect, but gratuitously provided for Israel in the sacred cult the appointed way of response in fulfilment of His divine requirement. The prophets, some of whom came from the priesthood, insisted that this vicarious response had to be enacted by way of obedience into the life and existence of Israel in order to be efficacious reality, and pointed ahead to the Servant of the Lord as the chosen instrument for its actualization. That is precisely what took place in Jesus Christ in the whole course of His obedience from His birth to His death on the Cross, for He fulfilled in Himself the Word of God tabernacling among men, the covenanted way of response to God set forth in the ancient cult, and constituted Himself our Temple, our Priest, our Offering and our Worship. It is therefore in His name only that we worship God, not in our own name, nor in our own significance but solely in the significance of Christ's eternal self-oblation to the Father.

(c) The Holy Sacraments

Both Baptism and Eucharist are acts of human response to the proclamation of God's Word, but they are above all the divinely appointed and provided ways of response and worship. They are not sacraments of what we do but Sacraments of the vicarious obedience of Christ once and for all offered in His finished work, and for ever prevalent before the Face of the Father in the heavenly intercession and mediation of His Son. We do not baptize ourselves but are baptized out of ourselves into Christ who loved us and gave Himself for us, and are incorporated into Him as members of His Body. Therefore we do not come before God in the Eucharist on the ground of what we have done even by way of response to His Word, for we come with nothing in our hands but the bread and wine, to feed upon Christ's Body and Blood and find shelter in His sacrifice and oblation on our behalf. In both these Sacraments of the Gospel the emphasis is undoubtedly on the human response vicariously fulfilled for us in Christ, and hence even the form (or the matter) of the Sacrament in each case is

determined for us by dominical appointment. So far as the proclamation of the Gospel is concerned the Sacraments tell us that even
when we respond to its call for repentance and faith, it is nevertheless not on our repentance and faith that we must rely but solely on
that which Christ has already done and continues to do, freely
made available for us in and through the Sacraments. As such, the
Sacraments provide the natural basis within our daily physical
existence for free and spontaneous response to the Word of God in
which we do not have to keep looking over our shoulders to see
whether our response is good enough. The very fact that in our
response we are called to rely entirely upon the steadfast and
incorruptible response of Christ made on our behalf frees us from
the anxieties begotten of ulterior motivation and evokes genuine
freedom and joy in our responding to God. So far as the worship of
the Church is concerned the Sacraments tell us that liturgical language and activity derive their true form through assimilation to
the vicarious life and work of Jesus Christ and that they may truly
exhibit in themselves conformity to the normative pattern of worship in the humanity of Christ in so far as they make room for Him
and direct us to Him as the actualized essence and core of man's
true worship of God. That is why it is finally the Eucharistic
celebration in union with the proclamation of the Word that gives
shape to the Christian liturgy and mission.

Sacramental response has its place within the all-embracing response of faith to the proclamation of the Word of God and shares
with it an inner relation to the Word through their joint inclusion
within the covenanted faithfulness of God incarnated in Christ.
Although He is equally active in Word and in Sacrament, a significant distinction must be noted. The conjunction of the Sacraments
with proclamation means that Christ will not allow the Word proclaimed to return to Him void but insists on actualizing in us the
promises of redemption and regeneration that are extended to us in
it. Thus the Sacraments themselves proclaim that as the Word
made flesh Jesus Christ is effectively at work among us not only in
the unity of His divine and human natures but in the unity of His
spiritual and physical human being, healing and reintegrating
man's broken and divided existence. Thus whereas faith corresponds more to the activity of the Word as Word, sacramental
participation corresponds more to the activity of the Word as
Event, for by their nature the Sacraments have to do with our
physical as well as our spiritual being: we are baptized in body as
well as in soul, and it is into our bodies that we take the bread and
wine, feeding upon the Body and Blood of Christ and not just upon
His Word and Spirit.

Behind this lies the profound integration between redemption and creation which we have already discussed in the incarnate life and work of Christ. He came not only to make expiation for our guilt and to forgive our sins, but by overcoming the destructive powers of evil to remove the threat to our existence and to recreate our being as the human children of the heavenly Father. Although He entered into our fragmented and disintegrating existence and took His human nature from us, in His holy Humanity the rift between spiritual and physical existence which characterizes our fallen human nature has been healed. Thus He is not less real in terms of our this-worldly reality nor less historical in terms of our historical existence, but rather all the more fully real and all the more truly historical because He has vanquished in Himself the forces that corrode and demolish our worldly and human existence in space and time. That is the Christ who gives Himself to us in Word and Sacrament and grants us through the power of His Spirit to participate in Him, He who has already bound up our existence with Himself and who as the incarnate, crucified and risen Lord present within it, ever sustains it in its reconciled relation to God.

In this perspective the specific function of the Sacraments is seen to be directed to the tension between the physical and the spiritual that continues to characterize a world waiting for the redemption of the body and to the tension between the state of the world already redeemed by Christ and its state in the future consummation when He will return to make all things new. They erect in the midst of history the covenanted relation appointed by Christ which embraces those tensions within an indissoluble and enduring bond in Him, so that far from allowing them to become radical breaks which would plunge us into chaos and futility they make them to serve the redemptive and recreative purpose of God, just as in the Cross God made the terrible sin of men in the death of Jesus to minister to our healing and forgiveness. Thus like the miracles of Jesus the Sacraments are prophetic signs that have to do with the saving of creation. As the Sacraments of God's interaction with our physical existence in Jesus Christ they are the counterparts in our ongoing life to the deeds of grace and power in the historical life of Jesus in which He allied Himself with man against the forces of evil that had overtaken him, reclaiming lost humanity, not by accusing men in their sickness and sin but by shouldering the burden of their sickness and sin upon Himself, not by throwing the responsibility back upon them but by taking the responsibility upon Himself. As such, the Sacraments both call for and provide a response in which the interaction of the spiritual and the physical is exhibited here and now in anticipation of the new

creation. They will not allow us therefore to respond to the proclamation of the Word of God only in some intellectual or merely
spiritual way, for in and through them the movement of faith
reaches its fruition as lived and acted response to the coming of the
Word of God into our space and time, in thankful acknowledgment
of the fact that all our responses, physical and spiritual, are upheld
by Christ from within our existence and are enfolded in His one
all-embracing response to the Father on our behalf.

(d) Christian Service

Christian service is the form of our response in which we are not
partially but completely committed in the whole of our being before God, and which we discharge not occasionally but in the
whole of our life and work. It is the form of service yielded out of
an existence that has come under the compelling and commanding
reality of what has taken place in Jesus Christ on our behalf. It is
not to be thought of, therefore, as the spontaneous expression of
love arising out of an autonomous existence of the Christian, intrinsically intelligible in its own operation and enshrining its own
freely chosen motivation, but as *service,* the ministry of love
heteronomously grounded in the incarnation of the Word and taking its essential form from the pure self-giving of God in the
servant-existence and mission of Jesus. It is service in obedience to
His commandment of love, yet it is spontaneous and free response
because it is emancipated from the necessity of having to supply its
own intelligible ground and is cut free from all anxiety and ulterior
motivation by being grounded in the vicarious service of Christ in
His selfless fulfilment of the love of God for all men. But incorporating Himself among us in the form of a servant He has incorporated our servant-existence in Himself, and thereby He has
given it structure and shape, both through the obedience which He
rendered in our nature unconditionally to the Father and through
the love which in our nature He poured out in unrestrained compassion for all men. Thus Jesus Christ constitutes in Himself, in
His own vicarious human life and service, the creative source and
norm and pattern of all true Christian service. It is only in and
through this Jesus Christ that Christian service can be fulfilled in
which loving service looks for no reward beyond the knowledge
that it falls under the commanding reality of Jesus Christ and looks
for no thanks from those to whom service is rendered because it is
done out of thankfulness to Him.

We recall that in Jesus Christ the Word of God has established reciprocity with us in the conditions, structures and limitations of our creaturely existence and within the alienation, disorder and disintegration of our human being where we are subject to the wasting power of evil and the divine judgement upon it, in order to lay hold of our world and sustain it from below, to recreate its relation to the Creator and realize its true response to Him as God and Father of all. That is to say, in Jesus Christ the transcendent Rationality of God has planted itself within the created order where its bounds, structures and connections break down under the negation of evil, in order to reintegrate spiritual and physical existence by setting up its own law within it, and restore it to wholeness and integrity in the form, as it were, of a meeting of the Rationality of God with itself in the midst of estranged existence and in the depths of its disorder. In this way, the incarnation has affected the whole creation, confirming the primordial act of the Word in conferring order and rationality upon it.

That is the world in which Christian service is now fulfilled, the world of men whose very existence is sustained in its relation to God by the hidden presence of the incarnate, crucified and risen Christ within it, overcoming the negation and irrationality of evil, and the world of nature whose reality is maintained in its relation to God by the immanent presence of the Creator Word who will not suffer it to fall away into meaninglessness and futility. It is the world in which, through Jesus Christ the Word made flesh, man is reconciled to existence and nature is not alien to man, for all things, visible and invisible, are reconciled and gathered up in Him as their Head and Lord. Just as Jesus Christ, made of woman, made under the law, fulfilled His servant-existence within the created rationalities of this world, for our sake, so the disciples of Jesus Christ are sent by Him to fulfil their servant-existence, in the law to Christ, within the created rationalities of the world He has redeemed, for His sake—i.e. within the world of word and number, or of persons and things. We cannot divorce the one from the other, for even in ourselves spiritual and physical existence have been reconciled, so that it is in the wholeness of our new being in Christ that we must look out on the world of personal and impersonal nature. We cannot hold apart the ministry of love from the activity of science, nor may we pursue our scientific exploration of the universe except in obedience to the God of love. In both forms of created rationality we must fulfil our service as those who in and through Jesus Christ are connected up with the transcendent Rationality of God, but as those whose service is assimilated to the pattern which Christ instituted in Himself when He fulfilled His own ministry in the humility, selflessness and weakness of pure service, and entirely renounced the use of any kind of power which might betray the nature of that ministry as service.

If we are to follow this Jesus in the modern world we must surely learn how to apply scientific knowledge and method to such terrible problems as hunger, poverty, and want, without falling into the temptation to build up power-structures of our own, through ecclesiastical prestige, social success or political instrumentality, in order to make our ministry of compassion effective within the power-structures of the world, for then we would contract out of Christian service as *service* and betray the weakness of Jesus. On the other hand, if we are to engage in scientific exploration of the universe, in response to the Word of God incarnate in Jesus Christ by whom it was made, we must learn to respect the nature of all created things, using pure science to bring their mute rationality into such articulation that the praises of the Creator may resound throughout the whole universe, without falling into the temptation to exploit nature through an instrumentalist science in the interest of our own self-aggrandizement and lust for power, for then also we would contract out of Christian service as *service* and sin against the hiddenness of Jesus in the world. No doubt, the created rationalities of word and number are very different, as different as the world of persons and the world of things, but they both go back to the same source in the transcendent Rationality of God and they are both brought together in the incarnation of God's Word in Jesus Christ, for they are upheld and sustained by Him. Therefore our service in the realm of word and our service in the realm of number must be co-ordinated through Jesus Christ in our common response to the love of God.

Part Two:

JESUS' MINISTRY TO THE FATHER ON BEHALF OF THE WORLD

Editor's Introduction

IN PART TWO THE CHRISTOLOGICAL FOUNDATIONS FOR MINISTRY will be explored in the form of Jesus' ministry to the Father on behalf of the world. It must be clearly understood that we are not looking for "principles" of ministry drawn from the life of Jesus which can inform the ministry of the Church. This again would appropriate theology to the pragmatic and existential situation. For, obviously, principles are of interest to the extent that they work, or foster "success."

There is only one ministry—it is the ministry of Christ. All other ministry is rooted in this ministry and is the continuation of this ministry through the Church, in the power of the Spirit, and on behalf of the world.

Chapter 5 includes three brief selections from Karl Barth's *Church Dogmatics* which exalt the ministry of Christ to the Father as true Man. The service of man to God is not a service that man can do for or by himself, and yet, Christ, the Son of God, does this service as true Man. In this service Christ fulfills his own true office and is true to his own eternal being. It is his own work, and yet becomes the service of the creature offered up to the Creator. This service includes the reconciliation of man to God, since Christ not only is the one who commands obedience, but is also the one who obeys. As a result, a new community exists as Christ himself exists. This existence is actualized through the power and work of the Holy Spirit. The actuality of service to God thus precedes and determines its possibility.

In Chapter 6, T. F. Torrance traces out this theological foundation for the service and ministry of the Church by showing the continuity between Israel, as the vicarious servant, and Christ, as the "one Israelite" who gave form and content to the people of God. Thus, Torrance shows that the Church is rooted in the very person of Christ, not merely in his works.

This is a significant clue to the ministry of the Church—it is objectively rooted in Christ's own service to God on behalf of the world. The risen Christ continues to be determinative for the ministry of the Church. He determines the specific structure and leadership of the Church under the executive function of the Holy Spirit.

In Chapter 7, W. A. Whitehouse points out that the particular service which Christ rendered is scandalous to the self-esteem of the world, but perfectly consistent with the character of divine love. For a Christian to minister for and with Christ is to be a "fellow servant," bound into a corporate "priesthood" of which the Church is the visible embodiment.

Thus the scope of Christian ministry is Christologically determined, both extensively and intensively. The ministry of the Church, then, is not shaped by situational needs, nor confined to believers. Instead, it is shaped by divine will and extends to all people, just as Christ's presence does.

The concluding chapter of this section carries forth the implications of this theology of ministry by developing the "kenotic solidarity" of Jesus with the world. The self-emptying of Jesus (*kenosis*) indicates both the depth and length of divine love. It is itself a transcendent act of ministry, fully consistent with the inner relations of Son to Father. The ministry of Son to Father, as the inner life of the Trinity, becomes opened up to include creatureliness through the incarnation, and the sanctifying and perfecting of that creatureliness in the life, death, and resurrection of Christ. A "*kenotic* community" is created, by which disciples are bound into Christ's own life of service to the Father on behalf of the world. The Church in the world as a ministering community cannot then hold a condescending attitude—the "haves" reaching out to the "have nots." The ministry which is given to the Church, as a sharing in Christ's own ministry, has a transcendent source and power precisely because it is more than human solidarity; it is God's solidarity with the world through Christ.

The particular concern of Part Two is to point to the objective character of ministry as it is given to the world in the person and work of Christ. Here can be seen the importance of asserting the full humanity of Christ and the corresponding danger of the Apollinarian tendency to make Christ an object of worship and service rather than the one who performs, completes, and continues this worship and service in his own true creatureliness, with and for the sake of us creatures. (Cf. here T. F. Torrance's essay, "The Mind of Christ in Worship: The Problem of Apollinarianism in the Liturgy," *Theology in Reconciliation* [Grand Rapids: Eerdmans, 1976], pp. 139–214.)

5

KARL BARTH

The Lord Who Is the Servant

THE BEING OF MAN IS THE HISTORY WHICH SHOWS HOW ONE OF God's creatures, elected and called by God, is caught up in personal responsibility before Him and proves itself capable of fulfilling it.

I. JESUS, MAN FOR GOD

In this section we ask concerning the outline and form of our object, its character and limits, and therefore the special characteristics by which it is distinguished from other objects. In this first and comprehensive sense, we ask concerning the whole being and nature of man. Who or what is meant when we speak of man, not referring to God but to a creature of God, yet to this particular creature among all others? Which of the many realities distinct from God are we considering? In the first place, we pose the question from without—on the assumption that besides man there are many other realities distinct from God, many other creatures. To this extent we look back again to the first part of our investigation, to man in the cosmos. Who and what is man within the cosmos? On the basis of the conclusions reached we shall then have to consider and explain his being and nature as it were from within—his inner relation to God as the image of God, and in this relationship his humanity as such, man as the soul of his body, and finally man in his time. It is clear that even at this point we must keep all these later problems in view. For the moment, however, they will not concern us explicitly. Our present concern is with the problem itself which will then be developed in detail in these

Fom Karl Barth, *Church Dogmatics,* III/2, pp. 55-64; IV/1, pp. 158-159, 192-204; IV/3, pp. 706-721, 751-762. © T. & T. Clark Ltd., Edinburgh. Used by permission of the Publisher.

various problems. We are thus concerned only with the outline or form of man.

Even in this field we must desist from any attempt to give a direct answer to the anthropological question, and apply the christological basis of anthropology.

If in this question of the nature of man we look to the man Jesus as directly or indirectly attested in Holy Scripture, one answer which immediately presents itself is that the nature of man is to be observed and established in its history as determined by Him, in its continuous progress as resolved and executed by Him, through a series of conditions, actions, experiences, in the recurrence and confirmation of its identity through all these active modifications of its being. Who is Jesus? What is His humanity? The statements which Scripture makes concerning Him, the predicates which it applies to Him, the whole significance which it ascribes to Him— all these refer to His being as it is reaffirmed and expressed under specific and changing conditions. According to these statements He is wholly and utterly who and what He is in the continuity of this history.

"He is made unto us wisdom, and righteousness, and sanctification, and redemption," Paul writes of Christ in 1 Cor. 1:30. On the biblical understanding none of these terms denotes an idea, but they all refer to a history. In the same connexion it is no less significant that in John 14:6 Jesus speaks of Himself primarily and predominantly as the Way: not as the beginning or end of the Way; but as the Way itself. But even the self-descriptions which follow and explain this point in the same direction, viz. the Truth and the Life. In the Gospel of St. John ἀλήθεια does not mean the truth which is static, but the truth which imparts itself and discloses itself to others; and ζωή does not mean the life which is self-sufficient but the life which imparts itself and redeems from death. And the other Johannine passages in which Jesus describes Himself as the Light, the Door, the Bread, the Shepherd, the Vine and the resurrection, point to pure process, to a being which is caught up in its products, so that it is impossible to distinguish between this being as such and its products, or to seek and find this being in itself or apart from these products, but only in them. Eduard Schweizer (*Ego Eimi* . . . 1939) has shown that the Johannine Jesus does not simply compare Himself with these things in these so-called metaphorical sayings, but describes Himself as the true and proper object of all these conceptions, as the only legitimate bearer of all these titles, as the real subject of all these predicates, in opposition to the mistaken opinions of the naturally religious man; that they are all to be understood as pure self-attestations on the part of Jesus. This insight must be taken seriously. When Jesus points to His own person He points to the Way which is as such the Truth and the Life, to the true Light, to the one Door, to the heavenly Bread, to the faithful Shepherd. Hence in all these sentences "I am" means that My being and nature consists in what is suggested by all these words, concepts, titles and names. I am as I exist in the mode thus indicated. What we must note in these statements is first that He alone and no other is the Subject of these predicates; second that in Him alone these predicates rightfully find their full meaning and propriety; and third (our present concern) that who and what He is, He is in these predicates. Because in all these predicates it is a question of actions, of a history viewed from different angles, He is what He is in these actions, in this history. He is Himself what takes place as described in these predicates. He is the One who is to come, who has come and who will come. From whatever angle He is regarded, He is the One who comes. Hence He does not stand as Subject somewhere behind or alongside this coming; He is Subject as this coming takes place. The fact that He is Subject, and what He is as such, can be known only with reference in the light of this coming of His, and can be made known only by reference to it.

Jesus is wholly and utterly the Bearer of an office. Hence He is not first man and then the Bearer of this office, so that it might be possible to conceive of Him apart from this office, or as perhaps the Bearer of a very different office. On the contrary, He is man as He is the Bearer of this office. He is, as He is engaged in the fulfilment of it, in the exercise of its functions, in the claiming of its privileges and in the carrying out of its obligations. There is no neutral humanity in Jesus, which might give Him the choice of not doing what He does, or of doing something different in its place. He is, as He is active in a specific, and always in the same, direction.

He is always at work (ἐργαζόμενος), even on the Sabbath, as He confirms in Jn. 5:17 to the Jews who accuse Him. He must work as long as it is day (Jn. 9:4). In this respect there is in the New Testament no "not yet," or "not quite," or "no longer." As we know it is almost completely silent about the thirty years or so (Lk. 3:23) of the life of Jesus before His appearance in Galilee. Even the single exception, the story of Lk. 2:41ff. about the twelve-year-old boy who remains behind in the temple and is found "in the midst of the doctors, both hearing them and asking them questions" (v. 46), certainly does not mean that He was not yet the Messiah, Prophet, Priest and King, that He had not yet begun His ministry, that He received and entered upon His office only with His baptism in Jordan. His saying about the necessity of His being about His father's business (v. 49) is something which is not understood by His parents (v. 50), and refers already to His mission. And the remark in v. 51 that in Nazareth Jesus was subject to His parents, is certainly not intended to interest readers in the fact that before His public ministry He was a carpenter in Nazareth. This whole incident describes how He grows up into His office, His προκόπτειν (v. 52), but without calling in question what is said at the beginning of the chapter (v. 11), that He was born as Σωτήρ, Χριστός and Κύριος. Thus He cannot have become this at the baptism of John. All the three accounts of His baptism speak also of a visible and audible manifestation of His office, but not of His appointment to this office or equipment for it. Again, the descent of the Spirit upon Him like a dove does not mean that He received the Spirit for the first time, but in the words of Jn. 1:33: "Upon whom thou shalt see the Spirit descending, and remaining on him, the same is he which baptiseth with the Holy Ghost." And at least in Mt. 3:14 it is expressly stated that the Baptist recognised Jesus before His baptism, and on that account would have preferred not to baptise Him; and in v. 15, that Jesus' subjection of Himself to the baptism of repentance along with the people was intended to be a fulfilment of all righteousness, and thus an anticipation of the baptism (Mt. 20:22f.) with which He was to be baptised by the giving of His life as a ransom for many. Even less do the Evangelists envisage anything in the nature of a "conversion" of Jesus. All that Jesus might have been outside His office, or apart from its exercise, does not concern them. The remarkable saying of Paul in 2 Cor. 5:18: "Yea, though we have known Christ after the flesh, yet now henceforth know we him no more," might have been uttered in the name of all four Evangelists. Even in the mouth of Paul it certainly cannot have meant that we are no longer concerned about the fact that Jesus was obviously a man. Even Paul could not have been uninterested in the Christ who according to him too was crucified and rose again as man. But the four

Evangelists were not concerned about anything that this man may have been and done apart from His office as the Christ. If they had known this man in this respect ("after the flesh"), they knew Him so no more. They knew Him according to what they could testify of Him in their witness, i.e., only in this very different respect; only in and not apart from His work. Even when they say of Him that He was hungry and thirsty, that He ate and drank, that He was tired and rested and slept, that he loved and sorrowed, was angry and even wept, they touch upon accompanying circumstances in which we cannot detect a personality with its characteristic concerns and inclinations and affections independently of its work. Nowhere are we invited to compose from these indications a physical picture or even a character study of Jesus. Where necessary, these features accompany the description of His work, and it is always in the latter and never in the former—or in the former only in so far as they bear on the latter—that He Himself is recognisable and is really this man for the Evangelists. And it would be even more arbitrary if from the fact that Jesus was tempted and that He prayed, and that especially in the prayer of Gethsemane He questioned if He also reaffirmed His presupposed obedience to the will of the Father, we were to conclude that the Evangelists were alluding to interruptions of His work which had to be overcome. The Jesus who is tempted and prays is also— precisely and particularly—the Jesus engaged in His office and work. His work does not suffer any interruption. His history is not broken off, as it cannot begin or end anywhere outside. Even the titles Χριστός and Κύριος which the New Testament gives this man, say who He is by telling what He does. The only non-historical element which seems to remain is the proper name Ἰησοῦς. But this corresponds to the Old Testament Joshua, i.e., Yahweh saves. Hence it too tells a story, and it forms a fitting heading to the whole.

It would be extremely foolish to draw from all this docetic consequences, as though this Jesus whose being consists wholly in His work and history were not a real man. There is no doubt that He is a real man. He is born of a human mother; He lives and works as a man; He sees and hears as a man; He speaks in human language; He suffers and dies as a man. And if the four Evangelists conclude with the account of His resurrection, and if in the light of this all the New Testament witnesses look to Him as the One who sits at the right hand of God and will come again from the heaven to which He has ascended, this does not mean that they have ceased to think of the real man Jesus. But the real man Jesus is the working Jesus. They seem never to have thought of a human being beyond history or prior to history, or hidden from and transcending history, when they thought of the real man Jesus. They always found the real man Jesus in His work and history. It is not the mere fact that He is born as a man, that He speaks and therefore that He can obviously speak and think and perceive as a man, or that He suffers and dies as a man, which makes Him a real man as they see it. It is the fact that He is born as the Saviour, that He speaks words of salvation, and that He has therefore the thoughts of the Saviour and that He suffers death as the Saviour. To be sure, it is as the Son of God that He is empowered to act in all this as the Saviour. But this means that with His saving work He is empowered to be a real man. He is not a real man in spite but because of the fact that He is the Son of God and therefore acts as the Saviour. For this reason He remains a real man even in His resurrection and ascension and session at the right hand of God, and it is as real man that He will come again. No Christian of the apostolic age thought otherwise. Hence He is always to be identified with His history. He is always engaged in His office and work as Prophet, Priest and King, as the Evangelists describe Him. Where can we find any essence or quality in which He is not yet or no longer the Saviour? What point can we name from which He might equally well be the Saviour or not? And could such a neutral point indicate the true humanity of the true Son of God? The New Testament knows no such neutral point. Whether it looks back to Jesus or upwards to Him or forwards to Him, it knows only the One who was, is and will be the Saviour, and therefore it knows this man only in His work and history. And it is in this capacity that it knows Him as a real man.

The question may be asked whether He was not then a person like other human persons. Was He not a soul and had He not a body like them? Did He not live as a man with other men and with the same humanity as ourselves? Did He not have His time as we do? Even in relation to Him, therefore, do we not have to take account of a universal humanity? Indeed we do, but not a humanity prior to or outside His earthly history in which He was participant in this history under specific limitations and conditions; not a neutral humanity in which He might have had quite a different history; not a humanity which we can seek and analyse in abstraction from or otherwise than in His work. These are conceptions of the humanity of Jesus which the New Testament not only does not encourage but forbids us to entertain. For if it is true that even in

Jesus human nature has specific modes and features in which it is also our humanity, yet even more and primarily we must have regard to the fact that it is His nature—the human nature of the Son of God. He is a human person. He is the human soul of a human body. He is a man among men and in humanity. He has a time; His time. It is not the case, however, that He must partake of humanity. On the contrary, humanity must partake of Him. It is not the case, then, that He is subject to these specific determinations and features of humanity. It is not that He is conditioned and limited by them, but in so far as humanity is His it is He who transcends and therefore limits and conditions these features and determinations. As the nature of Jesus, human nature with all its possibilities is not a presupposition which is valid for Him too and controls and explains Him, but His being as a man is as such that which posits and therefore reveals and explains human nature with all its possibilities. But His being as a man is the whole of His action, suffering and achievement. His being as a man is His work. In this His work He has a human nature; He is a person, the soul of a body, man among men and in humanity; He has time. And it is not possible for us to know in advance what all this is and means; it is revealed in Him and therefore in His work. It is real and knowable only in relation to Him. Hence it cannot be known ontically or noetically as a neutral point. It is to be explained by Him, not He by it. It is revealed in His light, and not *vice versa*. The nature of human possibilities rests upon and is knowable by the fact that they are realised in Him. We therefore reckon with the fact that even in Him humanity has specific determinations and features in which it is also ours. But what these determinations and features are, and of what nature they are, is grounded in Him, and therefore in His work, and must therefore be investigated with reference to Him, and therefore to His work.

But we can clearly grasp this only when we consider the character and content of the history in which the humanity of Jesus is actualised. The formula that Jesus does not merely have a history but is Himself this history, that He not only does but is His work, may sound harsh and repulsive if we do not perceive what are the history and work in question. We have already had to anticipate the decisive definition. The work with which we have to do is the absolutely unique work of the Saviour, resolved and accomplished by Him alone. What Jesus does, and therefore is, is this work, which cannot be interchanged with any other, and can be His work alone. Not any work but this work is the object with which we find the New Testament witnesses exclusively concerned and with which they obviously wish to see their readers and hearers exclusively concerned as well.

Not that something agreeable happens, but that Yahweh saves, is the implication of the name Jesus. The other titles applied to Him point in the same direction. He is the Messiah who delivers Israel, and the Son of Man who triumphs over the beast-kingdoms. The self-designations of Jesus mentioned in John have the same reference. "Great joy shall be to all (the holy) people" is declared to the shepherds in Lk. 2:10 when they are told of the birth of Jesus. "He hath holpen his servant Israel, in remembrance of his mercy; as he spake to our fathers, to Abraham, and to his seed for ever" (Lk. 1:54ff.). It is with this particular intention that He has to come, and came and will come again. The statements of Jesus Himself about the purpose of His coming are in this respect particularly illuminating. He has come as a light into the world in order that no one who believes in Him should remain in darkness (Jn. 12:46). He was born and came into the world to bear witness to the truth (Jn. 18:37). He came to do so not merely in one but in many places (Mk. 1:38). He did not come to destroy the Law and the prophets but to fulfil them (Mt. 5:17). He did not come to be ministered unto, but to minister, and to give His life a ransom for many (Mt. 20:28). In so doing, and as a further consequence of His coming, He will kindle a fire on the earth (Lk. 12:49). Fire here undoubtedly means the same as in Mt. 10:34ff.; Lk. 12:51ff., where we are told that He came not to bring peace but a sword, i.e., διαμερισμός, a certain necessary division even between men who otherwise stand closest together. "For judgment I am come into this world," says Jesus at the climax of the story of the healing and confession of faith of the blind man (Jn. 9:39). Who stands to the right and the left of the Judge? The good and the bad? No, but the unseeing who see on the one side and the seeing who become blind on the other; sinners as those who are called, and the righteous as those who are not called (Mt. 9:13). This is the differentiation effected in the presence of Jesus. This is the division made, the fire kindled, when He comes to fulfil the Law and the prophets and to give His life for many. But the real purpose of His coming is not attained with this division. All these texts clearly point only to a temporary though necessary transition. Human roles are radically reversed when He comes. The first shall be last and the last first. But this is not the essential aim of His coming. Hence Jn. 12:47: "I came not to judge the world, but to save the world." That Jesus comes to bring about the ruin of any man is a thought which is wholly foreign to the New Testament. His coming brings destruction to the demons and only to the demons (Mk. 1:24). "The Son of man is come to seek and to save that which was lost" (Lk. 19:10); and even more emphatically: "I am come that they might have life, and that they might have it more abundantly" (Jn. 10:10). Salvation and life is what Jesus effects by fulfilling the Law and giving His life for many. It is as He does this that He becomes the Judge; for His intervention on behalf of all exalts the lowly and humbles the proud. It is as He does this that He destroys the demons and becomes the promise of the world. And the promise which is the meaning of His whole action, is salvation and life. "Unto you is born this day . . . the Σωτήρ" (Lk. 2:11). In the Pauline corpus this title, which was known at the time in other connexions, is applied to Jesus only in Phil. 3:20; Eph. 5:23 and the Pastoral Epistles. It seems on the whole to belong to the later elements of New Testament witness. But it is easy to see that in a comprehensive retrospect it necessarily forced itself upon the community of the apostolic age, since everything that Jesus had done and effected could be compressed into the terms σώζειν and σωτηρία, and finally into the personal name Σωτήρ.

Only of this saving work can we say what must be said of Jesus—that His work itself is one with His active person, and therefore that He the doer and His deed are indissolubly one. Of Jesus this must be said. For the work of Jesus is the work of the Saviour. And the saving work which brings deliverance and life consists materially in the fact that He gives Himself. We may not and must not understand by the title Saviour only the death in which He consummates the self-devotion of His life, but His whole existence. He is the Saviour, and is born as such, in the fact that He is for the many, for the world. We will return later to the significance of the fact that He is only as He lives for the many, for the world. The point which interests us here is that we cannot separate His person from His work, if only for the reason that it is in His person, because He gives nothing more nor less than Himself, that He accomplishes His work. He does not become the Saviour with something alien to Himself, but with His person, and not with a part of Himself but through His whole person. Whatever He is as man He is in this work of His. For this reason we cannot separate His person from His work—as should now be clearer.

How could He be the Saviour accomplishing this work—the work of self-sacrifice with which He brings life and salvation to the world—if He existed otherwise than in His work, or were to be sought and found elsewhere than in His work?

It is clear—we may remark in passing—that an important christological distinction customary in the orthodox dogmatics of the schools is seriously challenged by this fact. The usual procedure is to treat in two separate chapters *De persona Christi* θεανθρώπου and *De officio Christi mediatorio*. The distinction between *persona* and *officium* (who is He? and what does He do?) is logically correct and apparently unavoidable. But its application to this *persona* and this *officium* is impossible if it entails a real division rather than one made for the purposes of exposition. Orthodox dogmatics, however, could only act as if this were a real distinction. When it spoke of the divine-human person of Christ, it had to postulate this formally as the presupposition of His work: θεάνθρωπος *hoc est Deus et homo in una persona esse debuit, ut mediatorem inter Deum et nos agere possit* (J. Wolleb., *Christ. Theol. Comp., I, cap*. 16, 13). And when it spoke of the work of Christ the Mediator, it had to recognise: *Subiectum eius non solum est totus Christus, sed et totum Christi estque mediator secundum utramque naturam*, necessarily affirming that it began with His anointing by the Holy Ghost in the womb, and therefore with His incarnation as the beginning of His divine-human existence (J. Wolleb., *ib., cap*. 17, 4 and 6). In fact, this *persona* stands from the very first and wholly in this *officium*, and this *officium* is fulfilled in the mere fact that this *persona* is present. It is in this way—commensurate on both sides with the reality—that the New Testament speaks of Jesus Christ. Where there is a schematic division, however, the necessary consequence is that the mystery of the person of Christ is undervalued because the manner and scope of His work are not perceived directly, and conversely that His work is not understood because the point is missed that it has to be estimated as the work of this person.

But we have not yet touched on the decisive point, which we must now isolate and emphasise in and for itself. As the New Testament witnesses saw it, what conferred on the saving work of the man Jesus the character of an absolutely unique action, resolved and effected by Him alone, was quite simply that, while they did not doubt His true and genuine humanity, they had to regard it directly as God's own work. We cannot say that Jesus did not act in His own right, but in the name of another, namely God. We can describe the work of the prophets and apostles in this way. The position in regard to Jesus is both more complicated and more simple. He acts in the name of God, and therefore in his own name. He is distinguished from the prophets and apostles in the same way as He is distinguished from the most faithful of God's servants, namely, by the fact that He acts in His own cause as He acts in that of God. The saving work of deliverance and life is really the affair of God. Whose else could it be? What other being could have the mind or presumption or power to do this work? In what spirit but the Holy Spirit could the will to do so be born? In what power but the power of God could it be achieved? Only He who has created it can save that which is lost. When Jesus performs this work, God is revealed in Him. God acts as Jesus acts. The divine work is accomplished in the work of this man. And the work of this man consists in the abandonment of all other work to do the work of God.

The necessary interpretation of the name of Jesus may now be concluded with an emphasising of the Subject. "Jesus" means: "Yahweh saves." No other can render the help that Jesus renders. It is the work of Yahweh alone. For this is total help. It spells deliverance. Thus the scribes in the story of the sick of the palsy are quite right when they say in their hearts (Mk. 2:7): "Who can forgive sins but God only?" Similarly, the man born blind argues rightly when he observes (Jn. 9:33): "If this man were not of God, he could do nothing" (of what He is doing). Again, the witnesses of the resurrection of the young man of Nain (Lk. 7:16) are on the right track when they—ἔλαβεν δὲ φόβος πάντας—gave God the glory under the impression that a great prophet had arisen among them and that God had visited His people. And the confession of Thomas: ὁ κύριός μου καὶ ὁ θεός μου (Jn. 20:28), is not so completely isolated as might at first sight appear. In the Gospel of John we are given a good deal of enlightenment as to how all this is to be interpreted. What does Jesus do? He can do nothing "of himself" (Jn. 5:19, 30; 12:49). He cannot speak "of himself" (7:17; 12:49; 14:10). Never in any event, therefore, does He seek or do His own will (5:30; 6:38). Why not? Because there is One who, as we are repeatedly told, has sent Him; the Father. He is the Son of this Father. And so He says quite expressly: "He is greater than I" (14:28). It is because He is the One whom this Father of His has sent, because He has not come of Himself (8:42), that He can do nothing of Himself, that He cannot speak of Himself, and that He never in any event seeks or does His own will. There is no "own," no "of Himself," no neutral sphere, from which things might be sought or said or done as from the seat of a will distinct from that of His Father. But what then does He seek, say and do? He does His works by the command and authority and in the name of His Father (10:25). And this is amplified as follows: He sees the Father do something—for the Father also works (5:17)—and what the Father does the Son does in like manner (ὁμοίως, 5:19). And He speaks what He has heard from His Father (8:26). What the Father has commanded Him, that He does (14:31). He keeps the Father's commandments, as it is simply put in 12:49 and 15:10. Or, He does what pleases the Father (8:29). And in all this He acts as the Revealer of the Father who has sent Him. He declares the name of the Father; the name in which He speaks (17:6, 26). But as He does this He is not alone (8:16, 29). He does—and more immediate relations emerge at this point—the works which the Father has given Him to accomplish and fulfil (5:36; 17:4). Given! Thus the similarity of His work with that of the Father must be taken seriously. If it is really parallel to the work of the Father, if He really works ὁμοίως what He sees the Father work, there can be no possible dualism. The works done by the Son are those of the Father Himself, of the One who has sent Him, for the Father has given Him these works to accomplish in the Father's name and for the manifestation of this name (9:4; 10:37). The converse is also true. Because the Father dwells in Him, the Son, it is the Father who performs the works through Him (14:10). Thus the Son is not really alone in His action, but He who sent Him is with Him (8:29). Hence He is always one of two: ἐγὼ καὶ ὁ πέμψας με (8:16). The things of the Father are also His, as His things are only those of the Father (16:15; 17:10). He is not alone, but always one of two? There is more to it than that. He is in the Father, and the Father in Him (10:38; 14:10; 20:17; 21:23). This is the penultimate word. But the ultimate word is simply: "I and the Father are one" (10:30; 17:11, 22). This finally explains the confession of Thomas. If Jesus is the Son, and as such one with the Father from whom He comes and to whom He goes, then He is, no less than the Father, ὁ κύριος and ὁ θεός. The name ὁ κύριος is then to be interpreted by the concept ὁ θεός. Hence it can be said: "He that hath seen me hath seen the Father" (14:9; 12:45); "He that honoureth me honoureth the Father" (5:23); "He that hateth me hateth my Father also" (15:23); "He that believeth on me, believeth not on me, but on him that sent me'' (12:44). And on this ground Jesus did not hesitate to adopt the absolute ἐγώ εἰμι—spoken without predicate—of the Old Testament God (8:24, 58; 13:19). In the sense of Deut. 32:39, and also in the sense of these Johannine texts, the implication is: ''I am He who alone can help.'' He thus described and claimed as His own the δόξα reserved only for God (2:11; 11:40), as is affirmed by the Prologue: ''We beheld his glory'' (1:14).

The work of this man consists in His doing the work of God to the exclusion of all other works. And to be one with God in the accomplishment of this work is the being of this man to the exclusion of all other being. Hence the doing of the work of God does not mean for Jesus anything alien, anything imposed upon Him from without, anything added later to His own activity and thus limiting and supplanting it. He does not become estranged from Himself by the fact that in doing this work He is one with God, and in this oneness of being with God—to the exclusion of all other being—He has His own being. He would not be accomplishing His own work, but would become alien and unfaithful to Himself, if He were to do any other but the work of God. And it would not be His own but an alien being which did not consist in His oneness of being with God. He is Himself as He does the work of God and in so doing is one with God. Hence the fact that He does the work of God, and in so doing is one with God, does not mean that He Himself—the man as such—is subsumed in the process. On the contrary, it is in this way, in the doing of the work of God, and therefore in His oneness of being with God, that He is Himself, this man. It is in this way that He exists as a creature, which cannot be dissolved in its Creator, which cannot itself be or become the Creator, but which has its own reality and worth in face of the Creator, deriving its own righteousness from the Creator. It is in this way that the man Jesus—not although but because He is the Son of God—is the creature of God which, by fulfilling the will and doing the work of the Creator, and being one with Him, does not lose its existence as a creature. On the contrary, what it means when we say that God is loyal to His creature is revealed by this very fact. Jesus as a creature finds life and nourishment in the fact that He stands in this relation to the Creator. In this way He is a real creature. His glory consists in the fact that He stands so utterly in the service of God, and in this devotion He reveals His own true righteousness, the righteousness with which He is endowed by His Creator. Who and what man is, is manifest in its fullest significance in the fact that the Son of God has become man in Jesus, and that man is placed so wholly at the disposal of God in Him. It is in this that He is real man, and may be known in His reality.

*   *   *   *   *

The first aspect under which we shall try to consider the doctrine of reconciliation in this chapter is that of the condescension active and known in it, that condescension in which God interests Himself in man in Jesus Christ. We might put it in this way: the aspect of the grace of God in Jesus Christ in which it comes to man as the (sinful) creature of God freely, without any merit or deserving, and therefore from outside, from above—which is to say, from God's standpoint, the aspect of His grace in which He does something unnecessary and extravagant, binding and limiting and compromising and offering Himself in relation to man by having dealings with him and making Himself his God. In the fact that God is gracious to man, all the limitations of man are God's limitations, all his weaknesses, and more, all his perversities are His. In being gracious to man in Jesus Christ, God acknowledges man; He accepts responsibility for his being and nature. He remains Himself. He does not cease to be God. But He does not hold aloof. In being gracious to man in Jesus Christ, He also goes into the far country, into the evil society of this being which is not God and against God. He does not shrink from him. He does not pass him by as did the priest and the Levite the man who had fallen among thieves. He does not leave him to his own devices. He makes his situation His own. He does not forfeit anything by doing this. In being neighbour to man, in order to deal with him and act towards him as such, He does not need to fear for His Godhead. On the contrary. We will mention at once the thought which will be decisive and basic in this section, that God shows Himself to be the great and true God in the fact that He can and will let His grace bear this cost, that He is capable and willing and ready for this condescension, this act of extravagance, this far journey. What marks out God above all false gods is that they are not capable and ready for this. In their otherworldliness and supernaturalness and otherness, etc., the gods are a reflection of the human pride which will not unbend, which will not stoop to that which is beneath it. God is not proud. In His high majesty He is humble. It is in this high humility that He speaks and acts as the God who reconciles the world to Himself. It is under this aspect first that we must consider the history of the atonement.

That is why the title of this chapter is "Jesus Christ, the Lord as Servant." At every point we shall be dealing with the action and work of the Lord God. This is true in relation to the eternal decree, and the execution of the atonement once and for all. It is also true of the fruit of it brought forth by the Holy Spirit, and the existence of the Christian community and the human decision of faith. But because we are dealing with the true Lord God, because it is a matter of the atonement which was made and is made in His action and work, we have to do with Him in that form of a servant which as the true Lord He was capable and willing and ready to assume in order to exist in it, and in which He is the true Lord God and as such the true Reconciler of man with God.

That is why the title of our first section is "The Obedience of the Son of God." Our theme in it is Christology in the narrower sense of the word, a first aspect of the person of Jesus Christ acting for the world and us and of the work of Jesus Christ done for the world and us: how He was and is and will be very God in the fact that as the Son He willed to be obedient to the Father, and to become the servant of all and therefore man and therefore the One who fulfilled in His death the reconciling will of God; and how in the power of His resurrection He is all this for us by the Holy Spirit. In relation neither to His person nor to His work can we under this aspect say everything that has to be said about Him, or everything that makes the history of the atonement this particular history. It is a matter of the whole Christ and the whole atonement from this one standpoint. And obviously here—in dealing with the person and work of the true Son of the true God—we have to do with the indispensable basis and substance of all that follows.

* * * * *

We have seen already that if in faith in Jesus Christ we are ready to learn, to be told, what Godhead, or the divine nature, is, we are confronted with the revelation of what is and always will be to all other ways of looking and thinking a mystery, and indeed a mystery which offends. The mystery reveals to us that for God it is just as natural to be lowly as it is to be high, to be near as it is to be far, to be little as it is to be great, to be abroad as to be at home. Thus that when in the presence and action of Jesus Christ in the world created by Him and characterised *in malam partem* by the sin of man He chooses to go into the far country, to conceal His form of lordship in the form of this world and therefore in the form of a servant, He is not untrue to Himself but genuinely true to Himself, to the freedom which is that of His love. He does not have to choose and do this. He is free in relation to it. We are therefore dealing with the genuine article when He does choose and do this. Even in the form of a servant, which is the form of His presence and action in Jesus Christ, we have to do with God Himself in His true deity. The humility in which He dwells and acts in Jesus Christ is not alien to Him, but proper to Him. His humility is a *novum mysterium* for us in whose favour He executes it when He makes use of His freedom for it, when He shows His love even to His enemies and His life even in death, thus revealing them in a way which is quite contrary to all our false ideas of God. But for Him this humility is no *novum mysterium*. It is His sovereign grace that He wills to be and is amongst us in humility, our God, God for us. But he shows us this grace, He is amongst us in humility, our God, God for us, as that which He is in Himself, in the most inward depth of His Godhead. He does not become another God. In the condescension in which He gives Himself to us in Jesus Christ He exists and speaks and acts as the One He was from all eternity and will be to all eternity. The truth and actuality of our atonement depends on this being the case. The One who reconciles the world with God is necessarily the one God Himself in His true Godhead. Otherwise the world would not be reconciled with God. Otherwise it is still the world which is not reconciled with God.

But we must dig deeper if we are to understand the free love of God established in the event of atonement. If the humility of Christ is not simply an attitude of the man Jesus of Nazareth, if it is the attitude of this man because, according to what takes place in the atonement made in this man (according to the revelation of God in Him), there is a humility grounded in the being of God, then something else is grounded in the being of God Himself. For, according to the New Testament, it is the case that the humility of this man is an act of obedience, not a capricious choice of lowliness, suffering and dying, not an autonomous decision this way, not an accidental swing of the pendulum in this direction, but a free choice made in recognition of an appointed order, in execution of a will which imposed itself authoritatively upon Him, which was intended to be obeyed. If, then, God is in Christ, if what the man Jesus does is God's own work, this aspect of the self-emptying and self-humbling of Jesus Christ as an act of obedience cannot be alien to God. But in this case we have to see here the other and inner side of the mystery of the divine nature of Christ and therefore of the nature of the one true God—that He Himself is also able and free to render obedience.

We remember again the prayer in Gethsemane, and also the fact that in Phil. 2:8 His ταπεινοφροσύνη is explained in terms of a becoming obedient, and in Heb. 5:8 His suffering in terms of a learning of obedience. In Heb. 12:3 the fact that He suffered on the cross and despised the shame is described as a ὑπομένειν and in Heb. 2:18 as endurance in temptation. Rom. 5:19 tells us unmistakably that through the obedience of one many shall be made righteous, and in 2 Cor. 10:5 Paul shows us that it is his aim to bring every thought captive to the ὑπακοὴ τοῦ Χριστοῦ, an expression which surely has to be understood as a *Gen. sub.* as well as a *Gen. obj.* To the same context belongs the fact that there is at least one stratum in the tradition, still maintained in the 2nd century, in which Jesus Christ (Mt. 12:18; Ac. 3:13, 26; 4:27, 30) is not called υἱός, or rather this concept is given a particular nuance in reminiscence of David and the Servant of the Lord (Is. 53) and He is called the holy παῖς θεοῦ. We also remember the pitiless δεῖ of the Synoptic prophecies of the passion. And it should again be emphasised that the same Gospel of John which leaves no possible doubt about the deity of Christ in His unity with the Father no less plainly—and with particular reference to His way of suffering and death—represents Him as the One who is sent, who has a commission and who has to execute it as such, as the Son who lives to do His Father's will, to speak His words, to accomplish His work and to seek His glory.

Why is it so important to see that when we say all these things about the man Jesus we say them about God? Obviously because the being of Jesus Christ in humility, His suffering and dying, and therefore the act of atonement made in Him, are marked off by their characterisation as an act of obedience from the accidental events of nature or destiny. Jesus cannot go any other way than this way into the depths, into the far country. And if it is the case that as the Son of God He is not alone on this way, if the Father is on this way with Him (Jn. 16:32), if therefore in going this way He acts in the freedom of God, making use of a possibility grounded in the being of God, then the fact that He does so in obedience makes it plain that there is no question of God Himself being controlled by caprice or chance. The freedom in which God can be lowly as well as exalted, abroad as well as at home, our God in the hidden form of One who is accused and judged as well as in Himself (and known only to Himself) the Lord of glory—this freedom of which God makes use in His action as the Reconciler of the world is not simply an arbitrary ability. It is not a mere capacity to be now in this way and now in some other way, now above and now below. It is not a disorderliness and carelessness in God. But if "the Father's Son, by nature God, A guest this world of ours He trod" (Luther), if God made use of His freedom in this sense, then the fact that the use of this freedom is an act of obedience characterises it as a holy and righteous freedom, in which God is not a victim driven to and fro by the dialectic of His divine nature, but is always His own master. He does not make just any use of the possibilities of His divine nature, but He makes one definite use which is necessary on the basis and in fulfilment of His own decision. If this really happens, if God (in virtue of the richness of His divine being) does make it a fact in our history, in the created world and as a temporal event, that He "dwells in the high and holy place, with him also that is of a contrite and humble spirit," if in virtue of His true divine nature it is His own good pleasure actually in this condescension "to revive the spirit of the humble, and to revive the heart of the contrite ones" (Is. 57:15), then this is quite in order, since it is His own will which is done, His own plan and decision which is executed. In this happening we have to do with a divine commission and its divine execution, with a divine order and divine obedience. What takes place is the divine fulfilment of a divine decree. It takes place in the freedom of God, but in the inner necessity of the freedom of God and not in the play of a sovereign *liberum arbitrium*. There is no possibility of something quite different happening. When we are confronted with this event as the saving event which took place for us, which redeems us, which calls us to faith and penitence, we do not have to do with one of the throws in a game of chance which takes place in the divine being, but with the foundation-rock of a divine decision which is as we find it divinely fulfilled in this saving event and not otherwise. It is therefore worthy of unlimited confidence and only in unlimited confidence can it be appreciated. It can demand obedience because it is not itself an arbitrary decision but a decision of obedience. That is why it is so important to see that this is the character of the self-humiliation of God in Jesus Christ as the presupposition of our reconciliation.

But it is clear that once again, and this time in all seriousness, we are confronted with the mystery of the deity of Christ. Let us grant that this insight is right, that what the New Testament says about the obedience of Christ, on His way as a way of suffering, has its basis, even as a statement about the man Jesus, in His divine nature and therefore in God Himself. Does this make the mystery of His deity even more difficult and perhaps impenetrable? Or do we have in this insight the real key to an understanding of it, to the knowledge of it as an open secret?

We cannot conceal the fact that it is a difficult and even an elusive thing to speak of obedience which takes place in God Himself. Obedience implies an above and a below, a *prius* and a *posterius*, a superior and a junior and subordinate. Obedience as a possibility and actuality in God Himself seems at once to compromise the unity and then logically the equality of the divine being. Can the one God command and obey? Can the one God be above and below, the superior and the subordinate? If we speak of an obedience which takes place in God, do we not have to speak necessarily of two divine beings, and then of two beings who are not equally divine, the first and commanding properly divine, the second and obeying only divine in an improper sense? But what is divinity in an improper sense? Even if this second being which is divine in an improper sense is supremely distinguished by the true and proper God both in quality and in orientation to Him, is he not still on the side of the world created by Him and therefore of the reality which is distinct from Him, and therefore not qualified to be the subject of the reconciliation of the world with God?

Subordinationism of every age and type has committed itself to this questionable path. It has solved the mystery of the deity of Christ by dissolving it, by taking the statement about the deity of Christ only in an improper sense, by trying to understand it as the designation of a second divine being of lesser divinity—which, if we follow it through logically, necessarily means the hyperbolic description of a heavenly or earthly creature standing in supreme fellowship with God and to that extent itself supremely qualified. In favour of those who support this view we have to admit that they were obviously impressed by, and tried to take with full seriousness, the witness of the New Testament to the humiliation of Christ and therefore to His lowliness and obedience. But they regarded it as quite impossible to harmonise the assertion of His true deity with this witness. Obstinately preferring this witness, and in order to maintain it, they interpreted the assertion in such a way that its content was explained away and lost. They did not see that in doing this they destroyed the meaning and weight of the witness to the humiliation and the lowliness and the obedience of Christ. If the deity of Christ is interpreted in that way, this obedience acquires the character of an event in this world. But it was and is impossible to see how many can be made righteous by the obedience of a being which is not properly God, of a supremely qualified creature (Rom. 5:19). It was and is impossible to see what value or justification there can be for trying to bring every thought captive to the obedience of such a being.

A second alternative which presents itself is as follows. We must certainly accept and take seriously the whole sphere in which we have to speak of a divine obedience, in which, therefore, we have to reckon with an above and a below, a *prius* and a *posterius*, a superiority and a subordination in God. We must regard it as a definite sphere of God's revelation, of His speaking and activity and operation. But we must isolate this whole sphere by stating that in it we have to do only with a kind of forecourt of the divine being, with a divine dispensation (economy) in favour of, and with respect to, the particular nature of the world, not therefore with the true and proper and nonworldly being of God. There is, then, a commanding and an obeying divine being, but in a true equality, only as worldly forms or appearances of true Godhead, and therefore only in the sphere of the improper being of Godhead. But that is the weakness of this explanation. For obviously we have to ask what is this worldly, and purely economic, and therefore improper being of the true God. If His economy of revelation and salvation is distinguished from His proper being as worldly, does it bring us into touch with God Himself or not? Has He Himself really taken up the cause of the world or not? Has He really made Himself worldly for the world's sake or not? Obviously, according to this theory, He has not done so. In fact He has only acted as though He had done so. But if He has not, how can there be on this theory any reconciliation of the world with God?

We are referring to a solution—the direct opposite of Subordinationism—which has been attempted both in ancient and more modern times along the lines of Modalism. The main point of Modalism is to try to keep the true deity of the humiliated and lowly and obedient Christ, but to interpret the being of this Christ as a mere mode of appearance or revelation or activity of the one true Godhead, beside which there are the other modes of the ruling Father and also of the Holy Spirit. Sometimes, indeed, it is preferred, as it was originally, to identify God the Father with the true Godhead which does not appear in this world. On this view Christ is not deprived of true deity, but of any true and proper being. The drift is obvious. We must maintain the true deity of Christ as identical with the Godhead of the Father, but only in such a way that no hurt is done to His deity by His humiliation, lowliness and obedience. Hence the distinction between a proper and an improper being of God, an immanent and a purely economic. Hence the true deity of Christ only in this second sense, only in the forecourt of the divine being, only as a mode of appearance of the true Godhead which is untouched by this dualism of above and below. Unfortunately it was not noticed that in this way the meaning and relevance of the statement maintained against the Subordinationists were compromised, and it was no less emptied of force than on the opposite side where it was explained and ultimately explained away. For if in His proper being as God God can only be unworldly, if He can be the humiliated and lowly and obedient One only in a mode of appearance and not in His proper being, what is the value of the true deity of Christ, what is its value for us? It is as the humiliated and lowly and obedient One that He is the Reconciler. But can He reconcile if He has no proper being as the Reconciler, but only that of a form of appearance of the one true God, who has no part in the atonement?

These two attempts at a solution were often made in the 2nd and 3rd centuries in relatively harmless, because inconsistent and ambiguous, forms. We find both of them in acknowledged teachers of the Church: a kind of Subordinationism in Tertullian, for example, and a kind of Modalism in Irenaeus. Both were finally rejected as unsatisfactory by the Early Church. In their developed form (in the doctrine of Paul of Samosata, on the one hand, and that of Sabellius on the other) they were recognised to be heretical, being condemned as errors in which we cannot do justice to the mystery of the deity of Christ.

The questions raised by these two solutions are questions which we cannot evade. It will be wiser, then, not to try to circumvent the difficulty as these two solutions did, but to engage it in frontal assault.

Let us first review the three presuppositions which, at all costs, we must accept and affirm.

It is a matter (1) of determining the acting subject of the reconciliation of the world with God. According to the witness of the New Testament, when we have to do with Jesus Christ we are dealing with the author and finisher of this work, with the Mediator between God and man, with the One who makes peace between the two, with no other and no less than the One who has taken upon Himself and away from the world the enmity of the world against God and the curse which rests upon it, with the One who (we shall treat of this in the second part of the section) accomplishes the ineluctable judgment of the world in such a way that He Himself bears it in order to bear it away. We have to do with the One who has the competence and power for this work. In relation to the fact that He is the One who does this, the New Testament witness to His deity has to be understood and taken seriously as expressed in the different titles under which it speaks of Him. Everything depends upon our seeing and understanding as the New Testament does that He is the acting subject in this work. If we grant that we are at one with the New Testament in this, we must also follow it in seeing the true God at work in Him. In matters of the atonement of the world with God the world itself cannot act— for it is the world which is at enmity with God, which stands in need of reconciliation with Him. It cannot act even in the form of a supreme and best being produced by it and belonging to it. Anyone other or less than the true God is not a legitimate subject competent to act in this matter. At this point the subordinationist interpretation is evasive. And it has to be rejected as unsatisfactory. When we have to do with Jesus Christ we have to do with God. What He does is a work which can only be God's own work, and not the work of another.

But (2) it is a matter of the subject of the atonement as an event which takes place not only to the world but in the world, which not only touches the world from without but affects it from within to convert it to God, which is itself an event in the world. According to the witness of the New Testament, the world is not abandoned and left to its own devices. God takes it to Himself, entering into the sphere of it as the true God, causing His kingdom to come on earth as in heaven, becoming Himself truly ours, man, flesh, in order to overcome sin where it has its dominion, in the flesh, to take away in His own person the ensuing curse where it is operative, in the creaturely world, in the reality which is distinct from Himself. It is in relation to the fact that what He does in the atonement He does in this way, in the power of His own presence and action, that we have to take seriously the New Testament witness to the being of the one true God in Jesus Christ; the realistic and not the nominalistic sense in which it accords these titles to Jesus Christ, whatever they are and however their formulation may be taken. Again everything depends on our accepting and following out in all its realism the New Testament presupposition "God was in Christ." If we grant this—as the *credo* of Christian confession assumes—we have to follow the New Testament in understanding the presence and action of God in Jesus Christ as the most proper and direct and immediate presence and action of the one true God in the sphere of human and world history. If this is not so, then as the subject of the act of atonement He can only touch the world from without, not affect it from within, not truly convert it to Himself. It would not, therefore, be a real reconciliation of the world with Him. At this point the modalistic interpretation of the deity of Christ is evasive. And for that reason it must be regarded as unsatisfactory and rejected. When we have to do with Jesus Christ we do have to do with an "economy" but not with the kind of economy in which His true and proper being remains behind an improper being, a being "as if." We have to do with an economy in which God is truly Himself and Himself acts and intervenes in the world. Otherwise the atonement made in this economy is not a true atonement.

It is a matter (3)—and this is the connecting point—of the one true God being Himself the subject of the act of atonement in such a way that His presence and action as the Reconciler of the world coincide and are indeed identical with the existence of the humiliated and lowly and obedient man Jesus of Nazareth. He acts as the Reconciler in that—as the true God identical with this man—He humbles Himself and becomes lowly and obedient. He becomes and is this without being in contradiction to His divine nature (He is not therefore exposed to the postulate that He can become and be this only as a creature), but in contradiction to all human ideas about the divine nature. He becomes and is this without encroaching on Himself (He is not subject to the postulate that He can become and be this only improperly, in an appearance which is alien to His own being), but as a saving approach to us, an encroachment upon us which is authoritative and demands our conversion. According to the New Testament witness we have the presence and action not only of the man Jesus, but in the existence of that man the action and presence which is supremely proper to God Himself as the Reconciler of the world. God chooses condescension. He chooses humiliation, lowliness and obedience. In this way He illuminates the darkness, opening up that which is closed. In this way He brings help where there is no other help. In this way He accepts solidarity with the creature, with man, in order to reconcile man and the world with Himself, in order to convert man and the world to Himself. The God of the New Testament witness is the God who makes this choice, who in agreement with Himself and His divine nature, but in what is for us the revelation of a *novum mysterium*, humbles Himself and is lowly and obedient amongst us. In this respect, too, the New Testament witness has to be taken seriously. Everything depends on our accepting this presupposition, on our seeing and understanding what the New Testament witnesses obviously saw and understood, the proper being of the one true God in Jesus Christ the Crucified. Granted that we do see and understand this, we cannot refuse to accept the humiliation and lowliness and supremely the obedience of Christ as the dominating moment in our conception of God. Therefore we must determine to seek and find the key to the whole difficult and heavily freighted concept of the "divine nature" at the point where it appears to be quite impossible—except for those whose thinking is orientated on Him in this matter—the fact that Jesus Christ was obedient unto death, even the death of the cross. It is from this point, and this point alone, that the concept is legitimately possible.

We can now see the error which is common to the subordinationist and the modalist presentation and solution of the problem. Both suffer from the fact that they try to evade the cross of Jesus Christ, i.e., the truth of the humiliation, the lowliness and the obedience of the one true God Himself as it became an event amongst us in Jesus Christ as the subject of the reconciliation of the world with God. They evade it because they start from the assumption that it cannot be accepted as true. And they then err in their different ways as they try to escape the dilemma which they themselves have created, interpreting the obedient Christ either as some heavenly or earthly being distinct from God, or as a mere mode of appearance of the one true God. Both damage and indeed destroy the nerve of the New Testament knowledge of Christ. Both solve the christological mystery by juggling it away, and for that reason both show themselves to be quite useless.

They were both rightly rejected by the Early Church. We can add that in the first instance they could both be undertaken in good faith, because even serious and perspicacious theologians of both schools did not at first see that they were in fact taking offence where no offence must be taken, and that by trying to remove the offence they were compromising the very centre of all Christian knowledge. We can also add that the attempts had to be made because only then could their unsatisfactory character be exposed. If they had not been made, the possibility of evasion in one or other of these directions would have worked like an arrested fever in the thought of the Church. In the history of theology and dogma there have been many such blind alleys which had to be followed to the point where they proved to be such in order that they should no longer be confused with the right way, and in order to make necessary and to stir up a search for the right way. This is the relative necessity more than once ascribed to heresy by the fathers. In fact, Athanasius and Nicaea would not have been possible without the obscurities and errors of the 2nd and 3rd centuries.

It is another question to maintain, and to make again as we ought, the distinction between the right and the wrong path as it was made by Athanasius and at Nicaea. The blind alleys are always there, and have proved attractive again and again as they still do to-day. The warning signs set up at the entrance to them can easily be overlooked, and have often been overlooked. The right way found at that time can still be lost again, and has from time to time been lost. Subordinationism and Modalism, the teachings of Paul of Samosata and Sabellius, are not dead, and by nature we all of us incline to one or the other or perhaps both in some form. We have continually to seek afresh for the right way in thankfulness for what has been known and stated. That is what we have tried to do here. We shall not serve the cause of the recognition which is necessary in the Church to-day simply by retreating or paraphrasing or commentating on the decision which brought the controversy to the 2nd and 3rd centuries to a victorious end. We are reminded by Nicaea in which direction we have to look. Our own conclusions, which are formally independent of the dogma proclaimed there, have inclined us to look in the same direction. We will now try to go further in this direction, not losing contact with the dogma but again following our own path.

Is it a fact that in relation to Jesus Christ we can speak of an obedience of the one true God Himself in His proper being? From the three inalienable presuppositions just expounded it is plain that we not only can do so but have to do so, that we cannot avoid doing so either on the one side or on the other. We have not only not to deny but actually to affirm and understand as essential to the being of God the offensive fact that there is in God Himself an above and a below, a *prius* and a *posterius*, a superiority and a subordination. And our present concern is with what is apparently the most offensive fact of all, that there is a below, a *posterius*, a subordination, that it belongs to the inner life of God that there should take place within it obedience.

We have to reckon with such an event even in the being and life of God Himself. It cannot be explained away either as an event in some higher or supreme creaturely sphere or as a mere appearance of God. Therefore we have to state firmly that, far from preventing this possibility, His divine unity consists in the fact that in Himself He is both One who is obeyed and Another who obeys.

There is another thing outside of God, the world created by Him as the totality of the reality willed and posited by Him and distinct from Him. In this totality as His elect creature there is another person, His worldly counterpart κατ᾽ ἐξοχήν man, who, according to Gen, 1:27, is in his twofoldness as man and woman the image of God, the image primarily of His co-existence as Creator with the creature, His will not to be alone as God, but to be together with His creature, the God of His creature—yet not merely the image of this relationship *ad extra*. God did not need this otherness of the world and man. In order not to be alone, single, enclosed within Himself, God did not need co-existence with the creature. He does not will and posit the creature necessarily, but in freedom, as the basic act of His grace. His whole relationship to what is outside Himself—its basis and history from first to last—rests on this fact. For everything that the creature seems to offer Him—its otherness, its being in antithesis to Himself and therefore His own existence in co-existence—He has also in Himself as God, as the original and essential determination of His being and life as God. Without the creature He has all this originally in Himself, and it is His free grace, and not an urgent necessity to stand in a relationship of reciprocity to something other outside Himself, if He allows the creature to participate in it, if, as it were, in superfluity He allows its existence as another, as a counterpart to Himself, and His own co-existence with it. In superfluity—we have to say this because we are in fact dealing with an overflowing, not with a filling up of the perfection of God which needs no filling.

Primarily and originally and properly it is not the cosmos or man which is the other, the counterpart of God, that which co-exists with God. Primarily and originally and properly God is all this in Himself. He does not need on this account to divide into two gods of unequal divinity. That is how myth would have it, confusing the world and man with God, and carrying its own inner differentiation into the Godhead, speaking of the co-existence and reciprocity of a superior god in heaven and a subordinate goddess of earth. No, not in unequal but equal, not in divided but in the one deity, God is both One and also Another, His own counterpart, co-existent with Himself. We can say quite calmly: He exists as a first and as a second, above and below, *a priori* and *a posteriori*. To grasp this we have to free ourselves from two unfortunate and very arbitrary ways of thinking.

The first consists quite naturally in the idea that unity is necessarily equivalent with being in and for oneself, with being enclosed and imprisoned in one's own being, with singleness and solitariness. But the unity of God is not like this. It is, of course, exclusively His unity. No other being, no created being, is one with itself as God is. But what distinguishes His peculiar unity with Himself from all other unities or from what we think we know of such unities is the fact that—in a particularity which is exemplary and instructive for an understanding of these others—it is a unity which is open and free and active in itself—a unity in more than one mode of being, a unity of the One with Another, of a first with a second, an above with a below, an origin and its consequences. It is a dynamic and living unity, not a dead and static. Once we have seen this, we will be careful not to regard that mean and unprofitable concept of unity as the last word of wisdom and the measure of all things. And its application to God will be ruled out once and for all.

The second idea we have to abandon is that—even supposing we have corrected that unsatisfactory conception of unity—there is necessarily something unworthy of God and incompatible with His being as God in supposing that there is in God a first and a second, an above and a below, since this includes a gradation, a degradation and an inferiority in God, which if conceded excludes the *homoousia* of the different modes of divine being. That all sounds very illuminating. But is it not an all too human—and therefore not a genuinely human—way of thinking? For what is the measure by which it measures and judges? Has there really to be something mean in God for Him to be the second, below? Does subordination in God necessarily involve an inferiority, and therefore a deprivation, a lack? Why not rather a particular being in the glory of the one equal Godhead, in whose inner order there is also, in fact, this dimension, the direction downwards, which has its own dignity? Why should not our way of finding a lesser dignity and significance in what takes the second and subordinate place (the wife to her husband) need to be corrected in the light of the *homoousia* of the modes of divine being?

As we look at Jesus Christ we cannot avoid the astounding conclusion of a divine obedience. There we have to draw the no less astounding deduction that in equal Godhead the one God is, in fact, the One and also Another, that He is indeed a First and a Second, One who rules and commands in majesty and One who obeys in humility. The one God is both the one and the other. And, we continue, He is the one and the other without any cleft or differentiation but in perfect unity and equality because in the same perfect unity and equality He is also a Third, the One who affirms the one and equal Godhead through and by and in the two modes of being, the One who makes possible and maintains His fellowship with Himself as the one and the other. In virtue of this third mode of being He is in the other two without division or contradiction, the whole God in each. But again in virtue of this third mode of being He is in neither for itself and apart from the other, but in each in its relationship to the other, and therefore, in fact, in the totality, the connexion, the interplay, the history of these relationships. And because all division and contradiction is excluded, there is also excluded any striving to identify the two modes of being, or any possibility of the one being absorbed by the other, or both in their common deity. God is God in these two modes of being which cannot be separated, which cannot be autonomous, but which cannot cease to be different. He is God in their concrete relationships the one to the other, in the history which takes place between them. He is God only in these relationships and therefore not in a Godhead which does not take part in this history, in the relationships of its modes of being, which is neutral towards them. This neutral Godhead, this pure and empty Godhead, and its claim to be true divinity, is the illusion of an abstract ''monotheism'' which usually fools men most successfully at the high-water mark of the development of heathen religions and mythologies and philosophies. The true and living God is the One whose Godhead consists in this history, who is in these three modes of being the One God, the Eternal, the Almighty, the Holy, the Merciful, the One who loves in His freedom and is free in His love.

And His speaking and activity and work *ad extra* consist in the fact that He gives to the world created by Him, to man, a part in the history in which He is God, that there is primarily in the work of creation a reflection, in the antithesis of Creator and creature an image and likeness, and in the twofoldness of the existence of man a reflection of this likeness of the inner life of God Himself. And then supremely and finally (at the goal and end of His whole activity as established at its beginning) they consist in the fact that God Himself becomes a man amongst men in His mode of being as the One who is obedient in humility. In the work of the reconciliation of the world with God the inward divine relationship between the One who rules and commands in majesty and the One who obeys in humility is identical with the very different relationship between God and one of His creatures, a man. God goes into the far country for this to happen. He becomes what He had not previously been. He takes into unity with His divine being a quite different, a creaturely and indeed a sinful being. To do this He empties Himself, He humbles Himself. But, as in His action as Creator, He does not do it apart from its basis in His own being, in His own inner life. He does not do it without any correspondence to, but as the strangely logical final continuation of, the history in which He is God. He does not need to deny, let alone abandon and leave behind or even diminish His Godhead to do this. He does not need to leave the work of the Reconciler in the doubtful hands of a creature. He can enter in Himself, seeing He is in Himself not only the One who rules and commands in majesty, but also in His own divine person, although in a different mode of being, the One who is obedient in humility. It is the free grace of the atonement that He now not only reflects His inner being as God as He did in creation, that He not only represents it in a likeness as He did in the relationship of Creator and creature, but that He causes it to take outward form in itself and as such. In His mode of being as the One who is obedient in humility He wills to be not only the one God but this man, and this man as the one God. He does not owe this to the creaturely world. He does not owe it even to Himself. He owes it just as little and even less than He did the creation. Neither in the one case nor in the other—and even less in this case—can there be any question of the necessary working of an inward divine mechanism, or a mechanism which controls the relationship of God and the world. God gives Himself to the world in coming to the world as its Reconciler. But He can give Himself to it. He is His own master in such a way that He can go into the far country to do it. He does not need to cease to be radically and totally above, the first, in order to become radically and totally below, the second. Even below, as this second, He is one with Himself, equal with Himself as God. He does not change in giving Himself. He simply activates and reveals Himself *ad extra*, in the world. He is in and for the world what He is in and for Himself. He is in time what He is in eternity (and what He can be also in time because of His eternal being). He is in our lowliness what He is in His majesty (and what He can be also in our lowliness because His majesty is also lowliness). He is as man, as the man who is obedient in humility, Jesus of Nazareth, what He is as God (and what He can be also as man because He is it as God in this mode of divine being). That is the true deity of Jesus Christ, obedient in humility, in its unity and equality, its *homoousia*, with the deity of the One who sent Him and to whom He is obedient.

* * * * *

Looking back on what has been said thus far, we note first that there is no question here of any arbitrarily seen and fixed point in the void making possible no less arbitrary speculation and disposition concerning the antithesis arising on that twofold view. Jesus Christ is not a concept which man can think out for himself, which he can define with more or less precision, and with the help of which he can then display his mastery over all kinds of greater or lesser problems and therefore over the problem of this antithesis too. On the contrary, Jesus Christ is a living human person who comes and speaks and acts with the claim and authority of God, and in relation to whom there can be no question whatever of controlling and using Him to grasp or master this or that even in the sphere of thought. Hence the grace of God shown to the world in Him is not a principle which man can perceive, affirm and appropriate as such, and then logically develop and apply to transcend and overcome all possible antitheses, and therefore the one which now concerns us. It is rather a free and sovereign power and a free and self-disclosing truth. It is free because it finds actualisation in the sovereign, divine-human acts of the life and death of Jesus Christ. It is free because it is revealed in the resurrection of the same divine-human person of Jesus Christ. It is free as a Word spoken in the power of His Holy Spirit, who blows where He lists. What is there here to see and fix, to be the object of speculation and disposition? The grace of God addressed to the world in Jesus Christ is that which exists supremely, but quite uniquely, only as on the basis of God's eternal love and election and faithfulness it was and is and will be event, inaccessible to all human or even Christian *hybris*, recognisable only in gratitude for the fact that it is real and true, and in prayer for ever new recognition of its reality and truth. If we treat it otherwise than as an object only in the character of a supreme subject; if we regard it as if it were a product of our own thinking, a concept and principle and therefore an instrument with the help of which we can master and solve any problem, including a problem of the order of the antithesis of divine providence and human confusion, then we merely show that we are deceived in thinking that we are dealing with grace. We think and speak like poor heathen, no matter how earnestly we may imagine that we think and speak of it. Where grace is actually present and active, it is enveloped by the mystery of its royal freedom. For good or ill we who exist in this mystery must consider this when we describe and proclaim this grace as the third word which is entrusted to the community within world-occurrence and in relation to its course. Only then shall we avoid the confusion which means falsification from the very outset in the attempt to press forward to this third word.

We note further that there is no question of introducing into the discussion a kind of *Deus ex machina* or marvellous supernatural solution when we try to think further in terms of the grace of God addressed to the world in Jesus Christ. We do not introduce this element at all; we simply affirm that from the very outset it has been the presupposition of our question as to the Christian understanding of world-occurrence, and that it must now be brought into the forefront or the limelight if a correct and valid answer is to be given. From the very outset our concern is not with any view, but with that view which is disclosed and given to the people of God in world-occurrence as a required and legitimate view. If it were only that in the general terms of the philosophy of history, and on a neutral basis, we were discussing the relation of the two familiar principles of good and evil or light and darkness or whatever else we like to call them, then the introduction of what we term the grace of God addressed to the world in Jesus Christ would certainly mean the introduction of a *Deus ex machina* which would alienate the other participants in the discussion and rightly cause them to shake their heads and say that they can make nothing of the notion. But we are not in fact engaged in any such discussion. From the very outset we have been seeking the specifically Christian or theological view of world history, the view which has as its presupposition the prophetic witness entrusted as a commission to the people of God. But the unequivocal burden of this witness is that in Jesus Christ the grace of God was and is and will be addressed to the world. It is from the place which is appointed by the witness entrusted to it, which it has not chosen for itself, at which it cannot maintain itself, in which it was set and to which it is continually recalled, that the community looks first into the heights and thinks of the royal and fatherly overruling of the God at whose right hand Jesus Christ is seated, and then looks down into the depths and surveys the confusion of the men for whom the same Lord Jesus Christ has lived and died and risen again. From this standpoint it is not any antithesis but this particular antithesis which has engaged us. And from the same standpoint we are now quite right, indeed, we find it simple and self-evident, expressly to affirm and disclose this presupposition, understanding the view of history which concerns us, precisely its twofold aspect, in the light of this presupposition which is so peculiarly our own, leading it to its goal in the form most proper to it, and in so doing at least provisionally sketching to the world the witness which the community owes to the world engaged in that general discussion. To be sure, it will seem to the world that we are introducing a kind of *Deus ex machina*. But this need not trouble us, since it rests on the mistaken view that we, too, are engaged in that general discussion in which there is no place for the present line of argument. We can easily understand the world's attitude in this respect, for even to our own thinking, let alone that of the world, our presupposition always implies and is a new thing which as such may easily suggest a marvellous supernatural solution. We may even be confident in spite of this misapprehension, since we believe that this new thing has the power to break through the illusion and to disclose itself, as to us, so also to the world, and finally not merely to individuals but to all men, as the reality and truth which speaks for itself.

What does the people of God see in world-occurrence around it? To be sure, up above it sees first and last the glorious spectacle of its God, the Creator of the world and man, who as such is the Lord and Ruler of this occurrence. To be sure, down below it sees the dreadful spectacle of the man who has fallen away from God and fallen out with his neighbour and himself—so that he can and does achieve only confusion. To be sure, it sees the contradiction, the conflict, the *diastasis*, the riddle of this occurrence. And accordingly, to be sure, it sees no real synthesis resolving the riddle, no harmony between above and below, no relation between the positive will of God and the confusion of man, no possibility of understanding the one as the basis of the other, or the other as grounded in it. It accepts the twofold view. But it also sees that there is more to be said. What the Christian community has to think and say of world history in accordance with this twofold view cannot be its final thought or word. For the assertion of this antithesis and contradiction cannot possibly be its first thought or word in relation to world history. That by which it is itself created and sustained within world-occurrence as the people of God charged to bear witness to the work and Word of God, its own basis of existence, is a new thing in relation to that antithesis and contradiction. Originally and primarily it has to think on the basis of this new thing as its distinctive *a priori*, and it is only in this light,

therefore, that it can see and understand the antithesis and contradiction of above and below. It is precisely because it sees it from
this point that it must take it so strictly and exclusively, regarding
the lordship of God as so glorious and the confusion of man as so
dreadful, and finding it quite impossible to see them together or to
reduce them to a common denominator. It derives from this new
thing. It does not itself create it. It is what it is as and because this
new thing has introduced itself into world-occurrence and is of
itself so actual within it as its meaning and goal. It has not itself
discovered this new thing. It has no more discovered it than other
men or peoples. It cannot, then, master or control it. This new
thing—and this is what makes the community what it is as the
people of God created in world history—has revealed and made
itself known to it as the work of God for the world and His Word to
it. The task entrusted to the community is to attest this new thing to
the world. It did not come to it. On the contrary, the new thing
came to the community. It showed itself to it. It opened its eyes
that it might and should see it. Hence it does see it as the new thing
which is beyond the antithesis, yet also new within it. In relation to
the world-occurrence around it, it is this new thing which is its
final as it is already its first word.

Materially and to that extent neutrally we can and should describe it as the new thing. But this new thing which is manifest to
the community in the world around it is the grace of God addressed
to it. It sees the world in a new light to the extent that it knows that,
while the contradiction or antithesis is not removed and does not
lose its seriousness, it is relativised, loosened and in a definite
sense broken through by the fact that God not only confronts the
world as its Creator, Lord and Governor, but in this great superiority of His has turned to it as gracious Father, that apart from and
even in spite of its deserts He is kind towards it in the free omnipotence of His mercy, which necessarily means for the world that it is
not just obscured by the confusion of men who have fallen away
from God and fallen out with their neighbours and themselves, but
that in spite of this confusion of theirs the world is not bereft of
grace but exists under this gracious address of God. As described
in this way, the new thing which is event and revelation within
world-occurrence may be known as such. Neither in relation to
God's sovereign lordship nor to man's confusion can it be called
self-evident, and yet it is incomprehensibly valid. What opposes
that antithesis and contradiction, preventing the disruption of the
cosmos and shining over the abyss as the promise of peace, is the
grace of God, this grace alone, but this grace truly and effectively

as the grace of God, and therefore this grace as it implies a new heaven, the manifestation of the heaven from which God not only rules the world but in so doing has turned and continually turns to it in loving-kindness, and also under this heaven, in virtue of the loving-kindness with which God turns to it, a new earth. Even when it is stated in this way, we are thus giving a new and positive sign under which the community may see God and the world and therefore history.

But is not this description perhaps too general and pale to denote unmistakeably the new thing which discloses itself to the community in relation to history, and which the community has to attest to the world? Indeed, if it is described in this way, is it not possible that this new thing will easily give rise to the misunderstanding that, if the Christian community is really to appreciate the new thing disclosed to it, its gaze must still continue to vacillate, even under the new promise, between God on the one side and the world on the other, with the inevitable consequence that it can never come to rest on either side, that it can attain only a dialectical and not a simple assurance of the grace which unites God and the world? Indeed, how can the community really know it as the new *thing* if this material description is exhaustive? When described in this objective and neutral way, might not the concept of a God who has turned to the world in grace, and of a world which is participant in this gracious address—grace itself being obviously the overarching concept—easily give rise to the suspicion that after all it only denotes the product of further human speculation? Might it not represent yet another of the many bridge-building attempts which lead into the void? Might it not be simply giving a new and more hopeful name to the gulf between above and below, the gulf being hidden under the name grace, but still remaining open in fact, so that it is concealed or closed only in the dubious way already familiar to us? Under the biblical and Christian concept of grace, we might still have merely the play of a synthesising the product of which will certainly not be the new thing perceived by the people of God in world-occurrence. The new *thing*? Unquestionably the grace of God addressed to the world, and therefore a world which is participant in this grace, is the new thing perceived by the people of God. But do we not describe it in a way which is perhaps too equivocal, general, innocuous, dialectical, and therefore exposed to that suspicion, so long as we call it the new *thing*, however right we may be in fact to fill it with the concept of grace?

The new thing which the people of God perceives in world-occurrence is the new, unique person Jesus Christ. It is the grace of

God addressed to the world in Him. And this "in Him," the name of Jesus Christ, indicates more than the means, instrument or vehicle used by God in addressing His grace to the world. We cannot therefore look past Him, or look through Him as through a glass, to the true point at issue, namely, God's gracious address to the world as the true and proper thing intended under this name. He, the person who bears this name, is Himself God, the Son of the Father, of one essence with Him. He is Himself God in His gracious address to the world. He is Himself the grace in which God addresses Himself and which He addresses to the world. He is Himself the work of God in and on the world, and the Word in which this work declares itself to the world. He is Himself the true matter at issue. And it is as it looks at Him that His community in the world can see and understand world history in relation to Him. Once we realise this, the darkness and ambiguity in which we have been moving lighten and disperse. Looking to Him, the community does not look to a concept which intellectually removes the antithesis and contradiction of that twofold view, whether it be a concept invested by man on the one side or a concept supra-rationally introduced under the biblical and Christian title of grace on the other. It looks to the concrete event, once and for all in time, of His life and death and resurrection. Looking to Him, it is neither constrained nor enabled, neither commanded nor authorised, to look about excitedly either upwards to God on the one hand or downwards to man on the other. On the contrary, it calmly concentrates its gaze on the single place of this event. Looking to Him, it has to do with more than even the most glorious of promises and its fulfilment, with more than a positive sign of its thinking about God and the world, with more than a bridge over the gulf between them, with more than a new and more hopeful illumination of the human situation. It has to do with the true and radical alteration of this situation. This is what is meant by the grace addressed to the world in Him, by the new thing which is known by the community and which it has to attest to the world. This new thing is the event which alters the whole human situation and therefore world history. It is His existence, He Himself. It is He, the new person.

The new thing in Jesus Christ, in the power and truth of which He is the new person, consists quite simply in the fact that in Him—as the people of God in the world may know even though the world itself does not—we are concerned in the strictest sense with God, with His work and Word. This means, however, that we are concerned not only with God but also directly with humanity, and not only with a pure and ideal humanity but with the very impure, historical and sinful humanity which has fallen away from God and fallen out with itself, with the "flesh of sin" (Rom. 8:3), and therefore with the subject of the great confusion of world history. The event indicated by the name of Jesus Christ and identical with His person is that the true Son of God, of one essence with the Father, has in this One assumed humanity, and very concretely this humanity, to unity with Himself, that He not only became one with it and adopted its creaturely nature but took to Himself its whole sin as though He had committed it and were its Author, that in His death He bore it away instead, thus achieving in its place the obedience to the Father which the humanity of the first Adam had refused and still refuses. The reconciliation of the world with God, the justification and sanctification of man, of all men, before Him and for Him, the cutting off of human confusion at its root, the restoration of order in world-occurrence, is thus the event in question, the work and Word of Jesus Christ. The Christian community hears this Word, sees this work and knows this person as it hears and sees and knows the One whose call is the basis and meaning of its own existence. Hence what it perceives in this One is not merely an illumination of world history but its correction and reformation. The gulf is not merely bridged; it is closed. Man is not just comforted and admonished; he is rescued from destruction and renewed in the being assigned him by his Creator.

The hymn does not exaggerate: "Now to God His saints are pleasing; Now prevails a peace unceasing; Now all conflict is concluded." Nor does the other hymn: "All claim the devil once might make, Against the race for Adam's sake, Is hazarded and forfeit." How blind is the Christianity which sings such things but acts as though everything were otherwise!

For the open secret of what has happened in Jesus Christ is that in Him the transcendent God who yet loves, elects and liberates the world, and lowly man who is yet loved, elected and liberated by Him, are indeed distinct and yet are not separated or two, but one. In Him the covenant between God and man has not merely been kept by God and broken by man, but kept by both, so that it is the fulfilled covenant. In Him there is not the clash of two kingdoms, but the one kingdom of God in reality. This is the new thing which the Christian community has not sought and found at random, let alone invented in a fit of inspiration, but which has disclosed itself

to it and by which it has thus been found as the Word or call of
Jesus Christ has come to it and has been received by it. This
then—and we may return to our general description with no fear of
finding ourselves on the way of new speculation—is concretely the
grace of God addressed to the world which stands before the Christian community as it is confronted by world-occurrence around it.
This is the final thing which it has to think and say in relation to
this occurrence, because it is already the first thing, because it is
the source from which it derives its own existence and life.

The point to be grasped is that in Jesus Christ we do really have
the new reality of world history. The great test of the relationship
of the community and individual Christians to Him, of the
genuineness of their existence, is whether they see and are sure and
keep to the fact, and with childlike confidence avouch to the
world, that it is in Him that world history really and properly takes
place. This is not just a new opinion, view or theory about it which
has opened up before the community; it is the work of deliverance
and liberation which God Himself has accomplished and completed in and on the world, its reconciliation to Him, the fulfilment
of His covenant with man, the justification of man before Him and
his sanctification for Him, and therefore, as a result of the existence of Jesus Christ, the new reality of the world and man. It does
not see in Jesus only what might be, or ought to be, or one day will
be; it sees what is, what has come into being in Him and by Him.
How could it attest Him or believe in Him or know Him, what
advantage would it have over the world or what would it have to
say to it, if Jesus Christ were not unconditionally and unreservedly
for it the One in whom there has taken place once and for all this
alteration, the coming of the kingdom? Everything else the world
knows just as well as and perhaps better than the community. What
would it have to say to it if, perhaps because it did not know it, it
did not have this to say, attesting the absolutely new thing of the
lordship of God already established within it? It can and must
realise that Jesus Christ is the new person in whom this new thing
has already happened and is constantly shown to have already
happened. It can and must keep to the fact that what has happened
in Him has the dignity, power and validity of the first and last thing
in world-occurrence. Hidden though it may be from the world and
even the community, it will come to light as the reality of all
history. It is He, and therefore what has taken place in Him, which
will emerge as this reality rather than other things which claim its
attention, and exclusively so in the case of the world.

This does not mean that the twofold aspect of world-occurrence—*hominum confusione et Dei providentia*—is dissolved or dispersed. It does not mean that Jesus Christ has merged into world-occurrence and world-occurrence into Him, so that we can no longer speak of them as separate things. This would be Christomonism in the bad sense of that unlovely term. What it does mean is that according to the true insight of the people of God the twofold form of world history loses the appearance of autonomy and finality, the character of an irreconcilable contradiction and antithesis, which it always seems to have at a first glance. The twofold view loses its sting. It acquires a good and natural sense, being indissoluble and indestructible simply because God and man are still different even in their unity in Jesus Christ. It no longer points us to a menacing abyss. Hence we are no longer tempted either to invoke a *Deus ex machina* or to bridge it by speculative or dialectical juggling. It becomes relative to Jesus Christ, to what has already taken place in Him. The one Jesus Christ has already represented God to man and man to God. He has already championed the cause of God with man and the cause of man with God. He has already executed the decisive act of the fatherly and royal providence of God by the removal of human confusion. He has already restored order between God and man and concluded peace between them. He, and that which is accomplished in and by Him, is already the reality of world history precisely in its twofold form. His cross and empty tomb are already the sign of its true meaning. His Word already declares this meaning. His life is already the reality which takes place in it. His community knows this. It is unknown to the world, but already known to His community. For His call, which underlies and sustains it, has already made it known to it, and continually does so.

The restriction now to be made is not obvious, since it is connected with the by no means obvious fact that neither the world nor the people of God within it is at the end and goal of God's work, that even after the appearance of Jesus Christ and what has taken place in Him there is still time and history: time for the community to proclaim the Word of Jesus Christ and what has taken place in Him; time for the world to receive this Word; space for the history of the prophecy of Jesus Christ. The resulting restriction is that the reconciliation of the world to God, the fulfilment of the covenant, the reconstituted order between God and man and therefore the new reality of world history, is known even to the community only in Jesus Christ and cannot therefore be known to the world which does not participate in the knowledge of Jesus Christ. It cannot be known. Hence the restriction is not in respect of the new reality of world history as such. This has been created and introduced, and is present. It is lacking in nothing. In the life and death and resurrection of Jesus Christ everything has been accomplished and made new. This is what the community cannot and must not forget, let alone deny, but recognise and confess in spite of every appearance to the contrary. It can do this only in faith, not in sight; but the point of faith is to be aware and certain and confident of it. What would it mean to believe in Jesus Christ if it were not believed, and known and confessed in faith, that this has taken place in Him, that in and by Him world history has acquired this new reality, and that to this extent it has become the new history of a new world perfectly reconciled to God? The restriction applies rather to the revelation and knowledge of this new reality. Apart from Jesus Christ Himself it is still the hidden reality of world history. In this history itself, i.e., in its visible form, in its events, movements and relationships, in its rising and falling and intercrossing lines and series, it cannot be seen nor deduced even though we be dealing with what is called the history of the spirit. The form in which world history appears to us is at best only the twofold form of the antithesis and conflict of above and below. To blind eyes it is not yet the new reality, and to no eyes at all is it yet the new form of this new reality.

There are signs (cf. *C.D.*, III, 3, pp. 198ff.) of this new reality. There are distinct histories and historical constants in its history which stand in particularly close relationship to the event of the grace of God addressed to the world in Jesus Christ. There is, for example, the history of Holy Scripture, of the Church and of the Jews. Nor is the new reality of world history prevented from occasionally intimating itself as the first and final meaning of the whole even at what seems to be the farthest remove from the occurrence of the specific history of salvation. Perhaps it is only because of our stupidity that we do not more often and more strikingly see such intimations of its new reality. But these intimations are not declarations. If they can be the basis of meaningful gropings, they cannot form the foundation of knowledge. And in any case they are relevant only for those to whom the new reality of history has already made itself known directly in a very different way, though even by these, let alone by others, they are not to be overlooked nor interpreted differently. When we come to the other and more usual events of world history, we can only say that they may give both Christians and non-Christians cause for many suspicions concerning its meaning and interconnexion, but that these suspicions can never reach into the depth of its true reality nor have as their theme anything more than a variation on its familiar twofold aspect. In the light of what is seen in and may be deduced from world history, neither Christians nor non-Christians could suspect the reconciliation of the world to God in which the distinction between them is robbed of the sting of division, nor the divine covenant with man fulfilled by God Himself, nor the reconstituted order between the two, nor the kingdom of God inaugurated. If any do have inklings of these things, they are not to be restrained. But the Christian community in every age would be well advised not to erect its tents, let alone its houses, and especially not the temple, on inklings of this kind, if it is not to be guilty of the radical defection of attempted Christian philosophies of history and the related practical experiments, but to continue to see clearly that the transition from faith to sight is not in its own hands, that it is not therefore required, and that, since it is not required, it is not permitted. Sight is that which is not yet granted either to the world or to itself, namely, the perception of the new reality, of the one kingdom of God in world-occurrence itself. For the moment, even in the best of circumstances we can see this kingdom only in that twofold form and not in its true and proper sense.

The coming of the kingdom for which we now pray will be its manifestation, the final, universal and definitive manifestation of Jesus Christ and of what has already taken place in Him. For the community this will mean the transition from faith to sight. As yet, however—and this is the restriction which now concerns us—He Himself, and what has taken place in Him, and therefore the kingdom, is known only to the community, and to the community only in His appearance and person and not in world-occurrence as such, so that even the community must pray for the coming of the kingdom. To be sure, it is enough and more than enough that the new reality of world history is not hidden but is actually revealed and knowable in Him. Already, believing in Him, it does actually see in Him, in His appearance and person, the first and the last, the atonement already made in Him, the covenant already fulfilled, the order restored. This knowledge of the new heaven and the new earth already given in relation to Him distinguishes it, for all the restriction of its vision, from the rest of humanity which does not yet participate in the knowledge of Jesus Christ and what has taken place in Him. And it is this distinction which capacitates it for witness to the world, and commits it to this witness.

But knowing the new reality of world history even if only in Him and as hidden in Him, it is not merely enabled and authorised but also compelled and commanded to see world history as such very differently from the way in which the rest of humanity can see it. This is not because in relation to the events of yesterday, to-day and to-morrow, it has certain higher or deeper insights than others which it can weave into a Christian theory of the meaning and course of world history and then teach to others. We are thinking of something much more solid. As the new reality of world history is made known to the people of God in Jesus Christ, it is enabled, permitted and commanded to see things very differently in practice, to participate in world history very differently in its own attitude and action, than is the case with those who do not yet have knowledge of this new reality. Knowing Him whom others do not know, it sees it very differently to the extent that it now exists and participates in it very differently. And when we say "very differently" we do not mean this hypothetically, in the nature of an "as if," but in full and true reality on the basis of its knowledge of the true reality. Its faith may be only faith and not sight. But it is faith in Jesus Christ and therefore knowledge of what has taken place in Him. It is also obedient faith. It thus anticipates the appearance of that which already is but is not yet manifested. In its faith, which is both knowledge and obedience, it affirms already the transformation in which world-occurrence will be presented to it and to all humanity in the final, universal and definitive revelation of Jesus Christ, accepting the fact that this transformation has already taken place in His life and death and resurrection. Nor is this faith and anticipation an idle speculating and gaping. As obedience it is a resolute being and attitude and action. It is in this resoluteness that its view of world history will display the distinctiveness which makes it so different, so unique, as the Christian view. It is in this resoluteness that the people of God is already in its existence in world history a witness to the kingdom which it can see to have come already in Jesus Christ but towards the coming of which in direct and universal visibility it still looks forward. It is only in this resoluteness that it can and will properly discharge its ministry as a witness of Jesus Christ to the rest of man, as a people of those who see among the blind.

This is the resoluteness of a definite confidence. We refer to confidence in Jesus Christ and Him alone. But as such, in all its exclusiveness, this is true and total confidence. In world-occurrence the people of God sees no more than others. Even more soberly than others, it sees in it the great rift between above and below, between light and darkness. With even sharper eyes than others it recognises here the antithesis between the rule of God and the confusion of men. But it sees the same things differently. And the difference is real and indeed total to the extent that it always begins with the confidence, and may return to it, that in spite of everything the history which takes place is that of the world already reconciled to God. In spite of everything, the man who acts and postures on this stage, who in wickedness and folly, being blind to what he already is in Jesus Christ, thinks and speaks and acts, and arranges his sorry compromises, and sins, and causes so much suffering to himself and others, is the man who stands in the covenant with God which is already fulfilled. The order which is now so shamelessly and with such pregnant consequences attacked and violated, but which cannot be overthrown, is that which has been already and irrevocably restored. The people of God has no illusions about what goes on beneath its eyes, and not without its own participation. But it knows that in what takes place it is dealing with the passing and vanishing of a form of the world which is already judged, removed and outmoded by the coming and secret presence of the kingdom, so that, although it takes it seriously in all its consecutive and fading pictures, in none of them can it take it with ultimate, but only, as is proper, with penultimate seriousness. Or more positively, it knows that under, behind and in all that will be and is seen, there is concealed, and presses towards the light, the new form of the world which alone must be taken with first and final seriousness. Hence it can share neither the enthusiasm of those who regard the old form as capable of true and radical improvement nor the scepticism of those who in view of the impossibility of perfecting the old form think that they are compelled to doubt the possibility of a new form. It need judge no man either optimistically or pessimistically because in relation to all, whatever their virtues and accomplishments or their faults and blasphemies and crimes, it is sure of the one fact that Jesus Christ has lived and died and risen again for them too. In face of the disorder of historical relationships and interconnexions it can yield neither to reactionary spasms on the one hand nor to revolutionary on the other, because in relation to the reality of history already present in Jesus Christ it knows how provisional and improper is all the construction and destruction of man, or more positively how definitive and proper are the demolition and rebuilding which have already taken place in Jesus Christ and only wait to be manifested in the world on behalf of which they have been accomplished. This is the confidence with which the community confronts world history and the rest of humanity which does not share it. In world-occurrence it can neither fear for it nor be afraid of it, nor can it fear for nor be afraid of the humanity which acts within it as if it still had ground or presupposition on which to do so. But just because it cannot fear, it cannot hate, and therefore basically, whether it finds it easy or difficult, it can only love. At bottom and in the long run it can only be *pro*, i.e., for men, since God in Jesus Christ is and has decided for them. It cannot be *anti*, i.e., against even individuals. Obviously, it does not discuss or ponder its confidence. Nor does it experiment with it. What would become of it if it were regarded as marketable in this way? Nor does it resolve to maintain it. Since it is the community which has been called by Jesus Christ and which therefore knows Him, the decision has been made for it. It has no option but to maintain it. In all the necessity of its commitment to and orientation on Him, it can do no other. It thus maintains it, and it lives within world-occurrence with this great confidence.

But the resoluteness with which in Jesus Christ it sees what is and what is not, is necessarily also the resoluteness of definite decision. This brings us to the test whether it really believes in Jesus Christ or in a synthesis which is supposed to interpret and explain history and artificially to bridge the gulf which threatens in it. Faith in such a synthesis always has as its basis the desire to find escape from decisions in the supposed freedom of the Yes and No, of the As-well-as, of the neutrality which is fatally active in the origin of the combination of the good creation of God with nothingness and then again in the combination of this confusion with the world government of God. As the community sees and knows, the decision has been made in Jesus Christ which makes quite impossible the idle contemplation and assessment of world-occurrence from a spectator's seat high above the antithesis between God and sinful man. All mere meditation or discussion for discussion's sake is now ruled out. Serving both the glory of God and the salvation of man, the decision taken in Him is unequivocally and definitively a decision for the world government of God and therefore against the confusion of men, for the good creation of God and therefore against nothingness. In Him, in His obedience to the Father, God is unequivocally and definitively glorified as the Creator and Lord of the world. And in His self-offering for men the power of nothingness and the confusion of men are just as unequivocally and definitely set aside. The man who has fallen away from God and fallen out with his neighbour and himself, and who has thus surrendered to nothingness and caused confusion after confusion, has been crucified and done to death on the cross, and a new man, free in obedience to God, has been born and introduced. The act of God in Jesus Christ is a clear decision for this new man living at peace with God and therefore honouring the goodness of His creation. It is a clear decision for the new form of the world actualised in His existence. It is thus a clear decision against the old man and the old form of the world, which can only disappear now that they have been set aside. The community of Jesus Christ sees this decision taken in Him. It keeps to it. It follows it. It follows it in world-occurrence and therefore within the limits of its own possibilities. Yet it does follow it, not as an idle spectator, but in active obedience. It follows, not in one great absolute step, but in several small and relative steps. But it really does follow it. It cannot and will not accomplish the coming of the new man and his world and the perishing of the old man and his. It can only attest this coming. But it does this in resolute decisions for and against. It cannot and should not be otherwise than that where it does there should be provisional clarifications anticipating the great and conclusive clarity towards which it and the whole cosmos are moving. It is here that there is a cleavage of minds and ways and possibilities so far as this is possible prior to the last judgment of Jesus Christ. It may be that where two apparently equal and illuminating possibilities seem to offer, it will not mince matters but decide for the one and not the other, and therefore against the other. Conversely, it may not accept what seems to be the only possible course but pursue or seek a third way. But in any case, whether by declaration or impressive silence, whether by partisanship or rejection of partisanship or even the formation of its own party, it will resolutely participate. And in so doing it will always have regard to the decision taken in Jesus Christ; it will always look back to the triumph of the cause of God and man championed by Him; it will always seek to respect and assert His great Yes and No as it freely speaks its own little Yes and No; it will always look forward to the future, perfect manifestation of His victory, of the Yes and No spoken in Him. Looking backwards and forwards in this way, it will exclude any compromises in the little Yes and No which it can speak; it will refrain from excusing itself by its own uncertainty, ignorance and impotence; it will avoid all regressions into hesitation; and it will always be responsible and prepared, either engaging, or on the point of engaging, in resolute action within general world-occurrence. It can neither execute its decisions with a view to certain results, especially such as might seem good to itself, nor can it refrain from doing so in view of the unpleasant consequences which are always entailed, and least of all when these might seem to constitute a threat to itself. What it has been given to know in a certain situation on the basis of the new reality of history in Jesus Christ, it can never wrap up nor conceal nor keep to itself nor treat as if it were something indifferent, a mere matter of faith which can remain purely inward and individual and need not be followed by any specific conclusion or action. On the contrary, in concrete obedience and confession it will always do in world-occurrence that which men who do not yet know Jesus Christ neither do nor can do. It will take concrete account of the atonement made in Jesus Christ, the covenant fulfilled in Him, the order re-established in Him. It is always expected to do or to refrain from doing specific things. And as it executes its decisions in world-occurrence, it will undoubtedly change it. "Resolves genuinely taken change the world" (C.F. v. Weizsäcker). They do not do so absolutely conclusively or unequivocally. What the community can say and do in relation to the decision taken in Jesus Christ and in attestation of this decision, will always be relative. It can never consist in more than the erection of a sign. But the point at issue is that there should be this relative alteration of world history by the erection of signs. The community cannot and must not evade this if its faith is not an indolent or dead faith, if it is faithful with the little possibilities entrusted to it in relation to the new reality of history. No more than this is demanded. But this is unconditionally demanded. If it does not perform it, then it cannot have its true confidence in relation to world-occurrence. Indeed, the question whether or not it performs it is the test whether it believes in the living Jesus Christ or in the cheap grace of a synthesis which it has itself invented with a view to evading decision. If it believes in Him, it exists in the resoluteness of definite decisions in world-occurrence.

It exists finally in the resoluteness of a definite hope for world-occurrence. In the light of the grace of God addressed to the world, i.e., of Jesus Christ as the new reality of world history, and therefore unencumbered either by optimism or pessimism, it looks forward to the goal appointed, namely, to the revelation of the new reality of history which is as yet concealed. The confidence with which, right through whatever else it sees, it keeps to what it sees in Jesus Christ, is a quiet confidence in relation to what has already taken place in Him, but also a very lively confidence in relation to what applies and is, and to what does not apply and is not, on this basis. Otherwise it would not work out in the resoluteness of the decisions which it must constantly execute. Yet it is not exhausted by the movement in which it tries to follow, in relation to the immediate temporal future, the decision which has been taken in Jesus Christ. It is a resolute confidence even in relation to the future, to the goal of the totality of world history. The Christian community dares to hope in Jesus Christ and therefore it dares to hope for the world. It waits for Him who came once and for all yesterday, and who is and lives always and therefore to-morrow. In relation to Him it knows that the form of the world which now confronts it cannot last but will one day perish and be seen no more, and that its new reality will then appear and alone be seen by itself and all men—the world reconciled to God, the covenant fulfilled by Him, the order reconstituted by Him. It waits for Jesus Christ. It waits for Him to emerge from His concealment in world-occurrence and to show Himself to it and to the men of every age and place as the One He already is as its Lord. It yearns for this. It rejoices in it. For it sees it coming as the goal and end of world history. In relation to it, it hopes for history, not merely individual benefits, but the very best, and it does so with the same resoluteness with which it maintains its confidence and ventures and executes its decisions in relation to its present form. Resolute in its confidence and decisions, it cannot but hope, looking for the coming of Jesus Christ in His glory. Only in so doing, and therefore only in the resoluteness of its distinctive hope in Him and therefore its hope for the world and all men, can it and will it be capable of equally resolute confidence and decision.

In sum, when we ask what is world history we may say that for the people of God it is simply the sphere in which it has to exist with this resoluteness. In Jesus Christ this people sees it in the form of its new reality. In this form it is manifest to it in Jesus Christ from whom it derives, who is its Lord, and whom it has to attest to all other men. Apart from this one picture of Jesus Christ, the new reality of history is still concealed from it as from all men. What it sees as world history apart from this picture consists of the many pictures of a form which does not correspond to but contradicts its new reality, i.e., the form in which there is still a wide gulf between the providence of God which overrules it and the confusion of man which rules in it, the form of the history of a world which is as yet unreconciled and far from the kingdom of God and alien to it, of a man who is as yet unjustified and unsanctified. But already the Christian community sees it differently even in this form. For it is not deceived. It realises that in all these pictures in which it presents itself it does not have its true reality but a being which is already outmoded and condemned to perish in virtue of the new reality even now present within it. Hence it cannot fix its gaze on these pictures, however exciting they may be for good or evil, as though in any of them it had to do with first or final things. It is free in relation to all of them. It can take them in earnest only transitorily in their coming and going, knowing that they are all pictures of a transitory being. Again, it sees them all differently in the positive sense that, no matter how the pictures may change from day to day, it takes them seriously as the field where it must maintain the resoluteness to which it has been called and for which it has been empowered by the new reality revealed and not concealed in Jesus Christ, and which it has to express as the confidence grounded in Him, in the decisions determined by Him and in the hope directed to Him. The sphere in which it may do this is world history as seen by the people of God.

* * * * *

How does the Christian community exist or live or continue within world-occurrence? This is our third and final question in this context. What we are asking is how it comes about, how it becomes event and reality, that there not only can be but is the kind of people tacitly assumed in our answers to the first two questions, namely, a people elected and called to attest God and His Word and thus able to see and understand world-occurrence, and itself within it, as we have just described? Have we merely been spinning a hypothesis behind which the question of the existence of this subject is still open? To what extent have we good grounds to reckon with its existence and therefore to be sure of what we have heard concerning it? To what extent does this people, the Christian community, really exist?

We shall give an immediate and direct answer to this question. (Cf., for what follows, *C.D.*, IV, 1, pp. 660–668 and *C.D.*, IV, 2, pp. 651–660.) In a first general and comprehensive formulation our answer is to the effect that the Christian community exists in virtue of its secret. This means by way of delimitation that it does not exist in virtue of its own controllable power, freedom or capacity. It neither exists of itself nor can understand itself of itself. The power, freedom and capacity in virtue of which it exists cannot be understood as an element in general cosmic being. Or, as we may say more positively, the Christian community exists as it is called into existence, and maintained in existence, by its secret. It exists in this way alone, but in this way truly, indisputably and invincibly. It lives by its secret. Without it, it could only fall. But it cannot fall, for it stands with its secret. Its secret is its ontic and noetic basis, its noetic as its ontic and its ontic as its noetic, and in both cases its clear basis in the sense that it may be indicated and described in terms of its efficacy. This basis is identical with the will and work and Word of God. Hence it neither need nor can be established on the part of man, and for this reason and to this extent it cannot be perceived or explained. Yet it is identical with the will and work and Word of God as effectively addressed to the world and specifically to the community, and for this reason and to this extent it may be known in its operation for all its inscrutability and inexplicability. It may thus be indicated, named and described as its ontic and noetic basis. We can thus point to it. In virtue of it, the Christian community is what it is in the world, visible and yet invisible, in the world and yet not of it, dependent and yet free, weak and yet strong. In the light of it, it sees world-occurrence and understands itself. In relation to its effective operation we can point to it and point back to it, denoting, defining and describing. With this reference, then, we can answer our third and final question.

Two exalted names are both indispensable and adequate to denote and describe the basis and secret of the people of God in relation to the efficacy not concealed from it. Both in different ways are identical with the name of the God who has turned to it. Hence neither can be separated from the other, but each is necessary to elucidate the other. They are the names of Jesus Christ and the Holy Spirit. Jesus Christ acts and works and creates in and in relation to the Christian community by the Holy Spirit and therefore again in the mystery of God. The one effective action of God in this twofold form is the basis and secret of the Christian community. In making this reference and therefore in answering our final question, we may thus make two strictly related statements which mutually complement and elucidate one another.

The first is that the Christian community exists as called into existence and maintained in existence by Jesus Christ as the people of His witnesses bound, engaged and committed to Him. It exists in virtue of His calling. The power of His calling is the power of the living Word of God spoken in it. And the power of this Word is the power of His Holy Spirit. As this power shines as divine power and is at work in the world, there takes place in the world and its occurrence the new and strange event of the gathering, upbuilding and sending of the Christian community. As Jesus Christ in the power of the Holy Spirit, or the Holy Spirit as His Spirit, creates recognition, establishes knowledge, calls to confession and therefore quickens the dead, the existence of the community begins and endures. Hence its existence is absolutely given, imparted or presented to it by Him as the One who in the power of His enlightening Spirit, the *creator Spiritus*, is at work on it and in it. In relation to Him it has neither right nor claim to existence, and therefore no control over it. It cannot control its existence and therefore it cannot control itself. It does not exist in virtue of its own ability but only of His. It lives only as He, the living One, has controlled and still controls it. Its power and freedom and ability to be and live and persist in world-occurrence, it can treat only as His property for which it is responsible to Him, by the assignment of which it is set in His service, for the exercise and application of which it must render an account by continuing to be what it is and accepting and discharging its ministry. It exists as it belongs to Him, listens to Him and is obedient to Him. It really does exist, but only in this way, as the Christ community, as the branches in the Vine. "Without me ye can do nothing" (Jn. 15:5)—indeed, ye can be nothing except perhaps a pile of broken and withering branches that can only be burned. He is the secret, the basis, the Creator and Lord, of the existence of His people.

Thus the being of the people of God is grounded only in its God, and the being of the Christian community only in Jesus Christ as its Lord. We continually had to refer to the content of this statement in our previous deliberations, and especially in answering our second question as to the self-understanding of the community. How can it really understand itself in the first and final instance except as the people elected, called, commissioned, maintained and ruled by Him? Yet in relation to the question of the basis of its existence this statement needs to be decisively deepened, as is indeed demanded even by its provisional form. For it is neither an accident nor an act of divine caprice that Jesus Christ first calls certain men out of the common mass and constitutes and maintains them as the community of His witnesses in common adherence to Him. And while it is true and important that as His possession this community is wholly His creature called to existence and maintained in existence by Him, yet as a statement concerning the community, concerning this people in its relationship to Jesus Christ, this can only be the second and not the first and original thing that has to be said at this point. For the reconciliation of the world to God accomplished in Jesus Christ is first the history of a breaking through of God to man, and only secondly and in consequence a history of the relationship and intercourse between man and God. This order in the content of the witness entrusted to the community must also apply and emerge, however, in our present question as to the basis of its existence. That "ye shall be my people" is the consequence of the true and basic evangelical revelation: "I will be your God." If we might put it that way, it is the indispensable aspect of Law. The community exists as the people called by Jesus Christ and created by His call on the basis of the fact that first, i.e., in God's eternal election of grace, He has made Himself its Head and therefore made it ("elect in him," Eph. 1:4) His body, so that He now exists as its Head, as such as its Lord, and as such acts and works in and on it in the enlightening power of His Holy Spirit, and it for its part has its being, the being of His body, in and with His being as its Head. Hence it is from what He is in relation to it that what it is in relation to Him acquires its significance and weight and specific character, and not *vice versa*.

We say further that the Christian community exists as He, Jesus Christ, exists. It does not exist merely because He exists, because its existence is established and created by His election, vocation and governance. This is also true. But there is more to it than this. The first point, which includes the second, is that it exists as He exists, as to His being as its Head there belongs its own creaturely, earthy, human, historical and therefore distinct being as His body. It exists as its being is a predicate and dimension of His, and not *vice versa*. The being of Jesus Christ, then, is not, as Schleiermacher in his own brilliant fashion understood and explained, the supreme, decisive and distinctive predicate of His community, the model and historical point of connexion for its living piety. To be sure, it exists as it believes in Him, loves Him and hopes in Him. But the fact that it does these things is not the basis of its existence. It does not live by them, i.e., by its own activity, by its faith and love and hope. It does not derive from them. Nor does Jesus Christ for His part exist only as the community is what it is and does what it does. No, the community exists only as He exists. "Because I live, ye shall live also" (Jn. 14:19), is the right order. Hence we can and must venture to say that the being of the community is a predicate or dimension of the being of Jesus Christ Himself. In this full and strict sense it belongs to Him and is His property. This is the source of its life and existence. Hence it has no option but to exist in faith in Him, love for Him and hope in Him. It exists as He exists. For He does not exist without it. He alone is who and what He is. But He is not alone as who and what He is. He is it for Himself, yet not only for Himself, but also with His own, and by anticipation with all who will become His own when His own shall be manifested in accordance with their determination as such. He is it together with them, being not only very God but also very man, and as such representing all men to God and God to all men. As very God *solus* He is also very man *totus*, so that His being does not exclude but includes within itself that of His own. In Him it is true and actual that God alone is God, yet that as the only God He is not alone, but that as the Creator, Reconciler and Redeemer of His creature He has ordered and bound Himself to this other which is so wholly distinct from Himself. To this great context belongs our statement that the Christian community exists as Jesus Christ exists, that its being is a predicate, dimension and form of existence of His.

We must emphasise and maintain that it is a predicate. It is not, then, the only one. We have said already that He does not exist only as it exists. Otherwise the statement might be reversed in the sense of Schleiermacher, and there would be a great temptation to concentrate on the reversed formulation. Jesus Christ exists also, secondarily, in a definite sequence, but not exclusively, as His community exists. Primarily—and this is the first predicate of His being which we must always remember—He is the One who He alone is: not in isolation, for He is it for humanity and in the first instance for His community; but alone, and not together with it. In His baptism in the Jordan and on the cross of Golgotha He is again quite alone: in both cases for humanity and His community; yet in neither case with them. He alone is the eternal Son of God, who for our sake became flesh of sin like us, and for the reconciliation of the world to God was crucified and slain. He alone is the justification of man before God and his sanctification for Him. He alone is the life of all men and the light of their life. He alone is the Resurrected from the dead in revelation of the glory of His mission, of the act of God accomplished once and for all in Him. He alone is the Prophet, the Word of God. He is all these things for all humanity and in the first instance for His community which has to attest Him to humanity as this One, which He has called and equipped to do so by the enlightening power of His Holy Spirit. But He is not these things together with humanity nor together with His community. He was all these things in His once-for-all enacted work, in His person; and He is them now, in the time after His first *parousia* and before His second, up above in heaven at the right hand of the Father—He alone, i.e., with God alone, hidden in God, accessible to no aggression nor control from below on the part of the creaturely world, distinct from the being of humanity and His community as the Creator and creature are distinct. Clearly He is all these things in another and first predicate or dimension or form of existence of His being. For all these things which must be said of His being in this primary form of existence cannot be said of the being either of humanity or His community. How can it be said of the community that it was the incarnate Son of God, that it did what He did as such, that it represents humanity or even itself to God and God to humanity, that it is the justification and sanctification of man or even of the Christian before God and for Him, that it already has death behind it and that it has thus to reveal the glory of God and of Jesus Christ as its own? From its own depths within world-occurrence it can only lift up its eyes to Him in this first predicate of His being as man on earth lifts up his eyes to heaven, praying earnestly for His Spirit from above: *Veni, creator Spiritus!*, for the coming and revelation of His kingdom. To Him in this form of His existence it can only look and move as, "absent from the Lord" (2 Cor. 5:6), it waits with all creation for His appearance from heaven, for His coming forth from the hiddenness of God. It is comforting, alarming and helpful enough that it may and can do this. But it is obviously with reference to another predicate and form, to the first and basic form of existence of His being, that it does.

It may be asked parenthetically whether we do not have to take into account a third form of existence in addition to these two. What are we to make of what is said in Col. 1, namely, that "all things were created by him, and for him," that "he is before all things, and by him all things consist," or have their συστάς (vv. 16–17), and that "it pleased the Father . . . having made peace through the blood of his cross, by him to reconcile all things unto himself; by him, I say, whether they be things in earth, or things in heaven" (vv. 19–20)? How about the alteration of the whole situation of man and his cosmos as already accomplished in Jesus Christ in execution of this resolve? How about the remarkable step from the statement in Col. 1:18 that Jesus Christ is the Head of His body the community, to that of Eph. 1:22 that as the Head of all things He is given to the community? How about Jesus Christ as the new reality of world-occurrence to which we referred in answering our first question and which is still concealed in contrast to His present aspect? Does He really exist only as the One He alone is with God, and then as the One He is with and in His community? Does He not already exist and act and achieve and work also as the *Pantocrator*, as the κεφαλὴ ὑπὲρ πάντα, as the One who

alone has first and final power in the cosmos? Concealed though
He may be in the cosmos and not yet recognised by it as by His
community, does He not already exist in it with supreme reality,
with no less reality than He does at the right hand of God the
Father or in His community? In this respect we may recall the
striking doctrine of Calvin, on which research has thus far shed
little light, concerning the Holy Spirit as the principle of life
which rules not merely in the history of the saved community
but also in the whole created cosmos as such. Will not the future
coming forth of Jesus Christ from heaven, from the hiddenness
of God, mean also and at the same time His coming forth from
His hiddenness in world-occurrence? A strange stanza in the
strange Advent hymn: "O Saviour, rend the heavens apart,"
seems actually to reckon with this possibility. Obviously based
on Is. 45:8, it was retained in the tentative version of the new
Swiss hymnbook but deleted from the final version as presumably open to question on dogmatic grounds. It runs as follows:
"O earth, break out, break out, O earth, Let green on hill and
vale come forth, This little flower to birth then bring, Out of the
earth, O Saviour, spring." Do we not have here something true
and important which ought to be seen and sung? But if so, then
do we not have to conceive and declare a third form of existence
of Jesus Christ, a third predicate of His being, i.e., His being as
the *Pantocrator* who already reigns, as the principle of lordship
in world-occurrence? Our present concern, however, is with the
relationship of His being to that of His community, and therefore we may raise but cannot answer here this stimulating question.

In relation to the people of God existing in worldly form in
terrestrial and human history, and therefore in relation to the Christian community, we certainly have to say that the being of Jesus
Christ is not restricted to His being in the height and distance and
transcendence of God, that it is not exhausted by this first predicate, that it has more than this first dimension and form, that in His
being that of God Himself shows itself to be one which is not
merely otherworldly, but which also condescends mercifully to
this world. In the community it takes place that Jesus Christ Himself, the living Word of God, is present and revealed to certain
men together in world-occurrence as the One He is above in the
height and hiddenness of God. And it also takes place that by these
men together He is acknowledged, recognised, and confessed as

this Word from the height, as their heavenly Head, and that He is confessed by them together as the Lord of all humanity. These men in their own time and place here find themselves commonly ruled and determined by the fact that in speech and action He always comes to their time and place. In other words, they find themselves ruled and determined by the common recollection of His accomplished coming and the common expectation of the awaited coming which He has still to fulfil. In the witness commonly entrusted to these men there still shines here and now in world-occurrence the light of Easter Day, and there already shines the light of the last of all days, the one light of His life both behind and before. It is as this takes place that the community exists. It takes place to it and in it. It takes place in the form of the very human life, choices, speech and activity of the men united in it. It takes place in their particular human history which as such is also an element in human and secular history generally. It takes place in movements which are wholly creaturely and indeed, being made by sinful men, both capable and guilty of error. Yet it takes place as these movements, as the life, choices, thought, speech and activity of the men united here, follow the life movement of Jesus Christ as their model, either well or badly imitating, reflecting, illustrating and attesting it. It is precisely as this takes place that His community exists. It thus exists precisely as He Himself as its model is first present and alive in it, evoking, ordering and guiding its movements by His own, and as He Himself is also secondarily, or in reflection, illustrated and attested by the movements and in the being and activity of His community. We are thus forced to say that the community has its being as a predicate and dimension, and in a distinctive force, of His being. It exists as He alone lives with God, and yet as He who alone lives with God lives also in it, reflecting Himself in it, so that as the primarily active Subject He is not only above but also below, and below as the One He is above, present within it not merely as its recollected and expected but also as its present life. It exists as He does not exist abstractly in heaven, as a Head without a body, but is also with the community on earth, the heavenly Head of this earthly body. It thus exists as it, too, does not exist abstractly as a body existing only in worldly fashion in the world, but as it is His body, the body of this heavenly Head, a predicate or dimension of His being representing the merciful condescension of God to the world, His earthly-historical form of existence. This unity of its being with that of Jesus Christ, the existence of Jesus Christ in His singularity but also His totality, is the basis and secret of its existence.

According to the familiar Pauline formula, the community exists ἐν Χριστῷ. It exists as a fulfilment of the promise: "Where two or three are gathered together in my name, there am I in the midst of them" (Mt. 18:20), and: "Lo, I am with you alway, even unto the end of the world" (Mt. 28:20). Now obviously the first "I" does not indicate merely a third or fourth added to the two or three, and therefore a numerical increase; for we are significantly told: "I am in the midst." Again, the second cannot indicate merely the presence of a bystander or spectator who might give occasional support, for as the final saying recorded by the Evangelist it is linked with the commission given to the disciples and is obviously intended to show how it will be carried out, namely as during the intervening time which now commences Jesus is not far from His community but directly present with it. In both cases the "I" is the true and primary acting Subject in the Christian gathering and fellowship, constituting, maintaining and directing it by His presence and action. Hence those who hear it, hear Him; those who reject it, reject Him (Lk. 10:16). Similarly, in the last judgment all the peoples gathered around the Son of Man enthroned as King will be asked and judged according to their conduct to His brethren, His own (Mt. 25:31–46). In the time which now draws to its close, He the King was hungry and thirsty and a stranger and naked and sick and in prison as His brethren were. What did the peoples either do or not do to them? They did it, or did not do it, to Him, their King. Similarly, it is said to the persecutor of the community (Ac. 9:4): "Saul, Saul, why persecutest thou me?" Similarly, the giving of His body and shedding of His blood for the many is the true action, and He as the Doer of this work of atonement is the true Actor in the human event of the distribution and reception, of the common eating and drinking of bread and wine in the Lord's Supper. It is He who truly nourishes those who there receive and eat and drink bread and wine together. The establishment and realisation of His fellowship with them, the κοινωνία of His body and blood (I Cor. 10:16), is the true reality of their fellowship with Him and with one another as achieved in the Lord's Supper. In this action they proclaim His death till He comes (I Cor. 11:26). Hence this action as the reflection of His own can be directly equated with it: τοῦτό ἐστιν (Mt. 26:26 and *par.*). The Lord's Supper is truly the κυριακὸν δεῖπνον (I Cor. 11:20), as the first day of the week, the day of the resurrection of Jesus Christ and therefore the day of their assembling together, is the κυριακὴ ἡμέρα (Rev.

1:10). How else can we describe the relationship between Him and the community but by saying that He exists also in this predicate or dimension of His being, that therefore in this predicate or dimension, without ceasing to be the heavenly κεφαλή in the heights on the right hand of the Father, He Himself is also in the depths of world-occurrence, and that He is therefore σῶμα, this σῶμα, His ἐκκλησία. Hence it can be said quite clearly and definitely in I Cor. 12:27: "Ye are the body of Christ." As this His σῶμα, as this His earthly-historical form of existence, the community also exists as He does. It does not exist otherwise. But in this way it exists really, and indeed *realissime*. As the *unus Christus, solus* yet also *totus,* He is the basis and secret of its existence.

This first christologico-ecclesiological statement is to be understood as an elucidation of the second and more familiar pneumatologico-ecclesiological statement with which we began, namely, that the "Holy Ghost calls, gathers, enlightens and sanctifies all Christians on earth, keeping them in the true and only faith in Jesus Christ." The power of the act thereby denoted, of this dynamic event, of this mighty act of the Holy Spirit, is the power of the being of Jesus Christ in its relationship to that of the community as just expounded. In our statement that the Christian community exists as Jesus Christ exists, we have described the solid sphere and setting in which this act takes place, in which it becomes possible and actual. There is thus excluded any false idea that chance or caprice is at work in this happening. The order which underlies the free event of the grace which calls the community is thereby revealed, namely, the order of grace as the order of being.

Conversely, however, we can and should understand the second statement concerning the mighty work of the Holy Spirit, which is the basis of the existence of the community, as an explanation of the first and christological statement. Itself excluding a misunderstanding, the second statement tells us that the relationship of the being of Jesus Christ to that of His community is not static nor immobile, but mobile and dynamic, and therefore historical. As the act of the Holy Spirit which underlies the existence of the community takes place in the order of the being of Jesus Christ and His community, the latter existing as He exists, so this order of the being of Jesus Christ and His community is the order of grace, the order of the act of the Holy Spirit, the community existing as Jesus Christ causes it to exist by His Holy Spirit.

Both statements denote one and the same reality. But neither renders the other superfluous. Neither can be reduced to the other. Hence neither is dispensable. Again, neither can be separated from the other. Neither can be understood to be true except as elucidated by the other. In the present context, our concern is to formulate and fill out in detail the second, pneumatologico-ecclesiological statement in description of the one reality of the basis and secret of the existence of the Christian community in world-occurrence.

The Holy Spirit is the power of God proper to the being of Jesus Christ in the exercise and operation of which He causes His community to become what it is. In the power of His Holy Spirit as the creative power of the Word which calls it, it takes place that it exists as He, Jesus Christ, exists. As He wields this divine power of His in relation to it, its being eventuates as the second and earthly-historical predicate, as the second dimension and form of existence, of His own being, and He makes it in the strict and intimate sense the people of His possession, the Christ community.

What is this power of God? Our first point in characterisation is that this power, and therefore the Holy Spirit, is the power of the grace of God addressed to the whole world in the one Son of God and Son of Man in free, creative action in and on this people. As God is gracious to humanity, He creates, upholds and governs within it this particular people of witnesses, causing it to come to be and to exist as such, to exist as Jesus Christ exists, giving it a share in His being, endowing it with the power, freedom and capacity to do its human work, to bear the witness entrusted to it. If it enjoys and exercises this power, it is not its own, but an alien power addressed and ascribed to it, the power of the free grace of God being great enough—for this is the point of it—to impart, address and ascribe its own power to this people as its witness among other peoples. The event in which this takes place is the work of the Holy Spirit. As it takes place, this people exists, existing as Jesus Christ exists. As it takes place, its being is the predicate, dimension and form of existence of His being. As it takes place, it has the power to become His people and to take up and discharge its ministry of witness. It is thus also the free grace of God that it may exist as witness of this grace to all humanity and serve it with its human action. To the question how it comes to be this people, we may thus answer that the coming is not on its side at all. Its existence as this people comes freely to it. It could never become such of itself. Of itself it is only a people of blind, vain, stupid, perverted, defiant and despondent men like any other people. What is there to prefer it, what merit or dignity does it display, that it should have the right or the power to become and be this people?

If it were not the case as described in Ezek. 16:4–14, that as an abandoned infant, poor, naked and suffering, it is invested with this power as with the robe and insignia of royalty, then it could only continue to be that naked infant and die and perish as such. But the fact that it is invested with the robe and insignia of royalty, which are not its own, which it has not itself provided nor fashioned nor won, is the work of the Holy Spirit. The Holy Spirit is the divine power of free grace to clothe this infant. And the action or mighty work of the Holy Spirit is the event or occurrence of the clothing of this infant. It is the action in which the Christian community arises and consists by the creative Word of Jesus Christ, acquiring existence and being maintained in it.

This action of the Holy Spirit as the work of the free grace of God in Jesus Christ is the basis and secret of the existence of the Christian community. This is the second statement to be made in answer to our third and final question. We shall now try to shed light on it.

The Holy Spirit is the power, and His action the work, of the co-ordination of the being of Jesus Christ and that of His community as distinct from and yet enclosed within it. Just as the Holy Spirit, as Himself an eternal divine "person" or mode of being, as the Spirit of the Father and the Son (*qui ex Patre Filioque procedit*), is the bond of peace between the two, so in the historical work of reconciliation He is the One who constitutes and guarantees the unity of the *totus Christus,* i.e., of Jesus Christ in the heights and in the depths, in His transcendence and in His immanence. He is the One who constitutes and guarantees the unity of the first and the second predicates, of the primary and the secondary dimensions and forms of existence of His being. He is the One who constitutes and guarantees the unity in which He is at one and the same time the heavenly Head with God and the earthly body with His community. This co-ordination and unity is the work of the active grace of God. Its freedom, the freedom of God and His action and operation, should not be overlooked nor forgotten for a single moment when we venture, as we must, to see and confess Jesus Christ as the same on both sides, as the Head at the right hand of the Father and as the body in the being of the community in its temporal and spatial present and situation, and therefore as the *Kyrios* in His totality. His being in this unity, and therefore the secret and basis of the existence of His community, is not a datum or state. It is a history which takes place as Jesus Christ exercises His power, as this power is operative as the power of His calling Word, and therefore as the gracious power of the Holy Spirit.

The work of the Holy Spirit, however, is to bring and to hold together that which is different and therefore, as it would seem, necessarily and irresistibly disruptive in the relationship of Jesus Christ to His community, namely, the divine working, being and action on the one side and the human on the other, the creative freedom and act on the one side and the creaturely on the other, the eternal reality and possibility on the one side and the temporal on the other. His work is to bring and to hold them together, not to identify, intermingle nor confound them, not to change the one into the other nor to merge the one into the other, but to co-ordinate them, to make them parallel, to bring them into harmony and therefore to bind them into a true unity. In the work of the Holy Spirit there takes place that which is decisive for the calling and therefore the existence both of the individual Christian and of the Christian community, namely, that the light of the crucified and risen and living Jesus Christ does not merely shine objectively, but shines subjectively into fully human eyes and is seen by them; that His Word as the Word of God does not only go out into all lands and even to the ends of the world (Ps. 19:4), but here and now is heard by very human ears and received and understood by very human reason; that God's revelation of His accomplished act of reconciliation has its counterpart here and now in human faith and love and hope and knowledge, its echo in human confession at this specific time and place; that its creative freedom finds an equivalent in real creaturely freedom. In the work of the Holy Spirit it takes place that Jesus Christ is present and received in the life of His community of this or that century, land or place; that He issues recognisable commands and with some degree of perfection or imperfection is also obeyed; that He Himself actively precedes this people; that in its action or refraining from action there is more or less genuine and clear reflection, illustration and attestation of His action, more or less faithful discipleship in the life of this people, and therefore a fulfilment of its commission. In the work of the Holy Spirit there takes place in the Lord's Supper, in a way which typifies all that may happen in the life of this people, that which is indicated by the great τοῦτό ἐστιν, namely, that unity with its heavenly Lord, and the imparting and receiving of His body and blood, are enacted in and with their human fellowship as realised in the common distribution and reception of bread and wine. None of this can be taken for granted. It is all most strange and improbable. Indeed, from the human and even the Christian angle it is impossible. Yet on God's side it is not only possible but actual. If it may be perceived only in faith, which is itself the first of these counterparts or correspondents, in faith it may be perceived with clarity and certainty. In other words, it all takes place in the gracious act of the gracious power of the Holy Spirit which co-ordinates the different elements and constitutes and guarantees their unity. In virtue of this gracious act it is always true and actual that the Head does not live without His body nor the body without its Head, but that the Head, Jesus Christ, lives with and in His community, and the body, His community, with and in Him. In virtue of the gracious act of the Holy Spirit, who is Himself God, *Dominus, vivificans, cum Patre et Filio simul adorandus et glorificandus*, there exists and persists—this is the second answer to our third and final question—the people of His witnesses in world-occurrence.

6

THOMAS F. TORRANCE
Foundation of the Church[1]

THE CHURCH IS GROUNDED IN THE BEING AND LIFE OF GOD, AND rooted in the eternal purpose of the Father to send his Son, Jesus Christ, to be the Head and Saviour of all things. The Church does not exist by and for itself, and therefore cannot be known or interpreted out of itself. Both the source and the goal of the Church are in the eternal love of God which has overflowed in the creation and redemption of the world. God has not willed to live alone, but to create and seek others distinct from himself upon whom to pour out his Spirit, that he might share with them his divine life and glory, and as Father, Son and Holy Spirit dwell in their midst for ever. God will not be without his Church; the Church is nothing without God. But in God the Church exists as the supreme object of divine grace, and in the Church God is pleased to live his divine life and manifest his divine glory. That is the mystery and destiny of the Church, hidden from the foundation of the world, but revealed and fulfilled in the Incarnation of the Son of God and in his glorious work of redemption, for in Jesus Christ the Church as the redeemed people of God is the crown of creation living in praise and gratitude to the Creator and reflecting with all things, visible and invisible, the glory of the eternal God.

The Church does not derive from below but from above, but it does not exist apart from the people that make up its membership

---

1. Part of an essay written for the Faith and Order 'Commission on Christ and His Church', of the World Council of Churches; reprinted from *Scottish Journal of Theology*, 16.2, 1963.

From Thomas F. Torrance, *Theology in Reconstruction,* pp. 192–208. © SCM Press 1965; William B. Eerdmans Publishing Company, Grand Rapids, 1966. Used by permission of the Publishers.

or apart from the fellowship they have with the life of God. The Church is a divine creation but in the divine economy it did not come into being automatically with the creation of the world or all at once with the establishment in the world of a human society. The Church was formed in history as God called and entered into communion with his people and in and through them embodied and worked out by mighty acts of grace his purpose of love which he brought at last to its fulfilment in Jesus Christ. While there is only one people and Church of God throughout all ages from the beginning of creation to the end, there are three stages or phases of its life. It took a preparatory form before the Incarnation as in the covenant mercies of the Father one people was called and separated out as the instrument through which all peoples were to be blessed; it was given a new form in Jesus Christ who gathered up and reconstructed the one people of God in himself, and poured out his Spirit upon broken and divided humanity that through his atoning life and death and resurrection all men might be reconciled to God and to one another, sharing equally in the life and love of the Father as the new undivided race; but it is yet to take on its final and eternal form when Christ comes again to judge and renew his creation, for then the Church which now lives in the condition of humiliation and in the ambiguous forms of this age, will be manifested as the new creation without spot or wrinkle, eternally serving and sharing in the glory of God.

Because Jesus Christ through the Spirit dwells in the midst of the Church on earth, making it his own Body or his earthly and historical form of existence, it already partakes of the eternal life of God that freely flows out through him to all men. Because its existence is rooted in the sending of the Son by the Father to be the Saviour of the world, the Church lives its divinely given life in history as the servant of Christ sent out by him to proclaim the Gospel of God's love to the whole world and to be in itself as the reconciled people of God the provisional form of the new creation. It is therefore the mission of the Church by the witness of its word and life to bring to all nations and races the message of hope in the darkness and dangers of our times, and to summon them to the obedience of the Gospel, that the love of God in Jesus Christ may be poured out upon them by the Spirit, breaking down all barriers, healing all divisions and gathering them together as one universal flock to meet the coming of the Great Shepherd, the one Lord and Saviour of all.

1 THE PEOPLE OF GOD UNDER THE OLD COVENANT

The Church had its earthly beginning in Adam for then it began to subsist in the human society formed by God for immediate communion with himself. But in Adam the whole Church fell through disobedience, and its immediate relation with God was broken and interrupted by the barrier of sin and guilt. It fell not as a divine institution but in its constituent members, and therefore the Church upheld by the eternal will of God took on at once a new form under his saving acts in history.

In spite of their sin God did not give up his people but maintained with them a covenant of grace, in which he allied himself with his creatures as their God and Saviour, and committing himself to them in paternal kindness took them into communion with himself as his dear children. Therefore from generation to generation he sought to reveal himself to his people as they were able to apprehend him, and called them by his Word to a life of obedience and faith and righteousness. In the fulfilment of this purpose for the whole race God chose one people from among the others as the medium of his revelation and the special sphere of his redemptive acts leading throughout history to the fulfilment of his promise of salvation. Thus while the covenant of grace embraced all men, it was when God called Abraham and specifically promised him 'I will be a God to you and to your seed after you', that the Church began to be separated out from the nations and brought into definite form as the appointed sphere in history of God's revealing and redeeming activity through which all nations and all creation would be blessed.

It was with the redemption of Israel out of the bondage of Egypt and its establishment before God as a holy people in the ratification of the covenant at Sinai that Israel stood forth as the *Ecclesia* or Church of God. 'I am your God. Walk before me and be perfect. I am holy; therefore be ye holy.' This covenant was sealed with two major 'sacraments': circumcision, which inscribed the promise of God's blessing in the flesh and seed of his people and covenanted them to a life of obedience and faith; and the passover, in which God renewed his covenant, promising redemption from the bondage of sin and the tyranny of the powers of evil into fellowship with himself through a sacrifice which God himself would provide. Even in its Sinaitic form the covenant was essentially a covenant of grace. God knew that his people would be unable to keep the covenant, and to walk before him in obedience to his holy will, and so in his faithfulness and mercy he provided within the covenant a way of obedient response to his loving-kindness, and a way of cleansing and restoration to fellowship with himself. Not only, therefore, did he give his people his 'Word and Sacraments' through which he revealed himself familiarly to them and adopted them as his children, but he provided for them a Law which clearly set forth his will, and an order of worship and sacrifice in the cult which supplied his people in their weakness with a covenanted way of response to his will. Both of these were a testimony to the fact that mercy and judgment belonged to God alone, and enshrined the promise of messianic salvation.

In this way Israel came to be constituted God's Prophet among the peoples of the earth, that is, his Servant entrusted with the oracles of God and the promises of the Messiah, and to be equipped with ordinances to train it in the ways of righteousness and truth and faith. While the ordinances were temporary, belonging only to the preparatory economy of the divine covenant, the oracles and promises pressed forward throughout the whole history of Israel to their fulfilment in the Incarnation of the Word in Jesus Christ and in the establishment of his messianic Kingdom through a redemption that would embrace all races and nations in a new covenant of the Spirit and in one universal people of God.

When the Christian Church came to refer to itself as the *ecclesia* it was claiming continuity with the *qahal* or the People of God under the old covenant, but in so doing it clearly regarded the people before the Incarnation as the Church under the economy of the old covenant. It was the *ecclesia* or *qahal* that arose and existed through election, that was actively engaged in God's purpose of revelation and salvation, that was caught up in the mighty events whereby God intervened redemptively in history, and became involved in the forward thrust of the covenant toward final and ultimate fulfilment. It was the Church of God in its preparatory form in the tension and struggle of expectation, unable to be yet what it was destined to be when incarnation and reconciliation were fulfilled. Only with the consummation of the mediation between God and man in Jesus Christ could the people of God under the old covenant fully become Church in its permanent form in the Body of Christ. Nevertheless it was that one Church in the process of formation, waiting for its new birth in the resurrection and its universalization at Pentecost, while the mode and structure of its existence in the historico-redemptive movement of God's grace in Old Testament times were determinative of the Christian Church built upon the foundation of the prophets as well as the apostles.

(a) Israel was *the chosen people of God*, elected not for its own sake but for God's sake, in the fulfilment of his revealing and redemptive purpose. It was Church, therefore, not in the merely sociological or political sense of *ecclesia*; it was society formed not by human but by divine convocation. It was Church as act of God, as the community called into being by the Word of God, and constituted through union and communion with him. Yet by being separated out as covenant-community with an ordered life of its own, Israel was also established as a nation among the peoples of the earth. Thus there arose and persisted through the history of Israel a struggle between Israel and its Lord, between its 'ethnic' aspirations to be a nation like the other nations of the earth, and its 'laic' calling to be a people in covenant-communion with God. It was this conflict that plunged Israel into its long ordeal of suffering. Precisely because it was the bearer of divine revelation it could not be a secular nation like the others, and because it was elected for the fulfilment of God's redeeming purpose it had to be the holy people exercising a vicarious mission through which the whole race was to be transformed.

Nevertheless God used the suffering and ordeal of Israel to reveal himself more profoundly and give himself more completely in all his infinite faithfulness and love and his undeflecting will for the salvation of mankind, and at the same time to drive his revelation into the inner existence and understanding and life of this people in order to mould and fashion it into the vessel through which the Word was to be made flesh, reconciliation to be achieved, and the final revelation to be actualized in the midst of humanity. Hence already in the historical experience of Israel before the Incarnation the lineaments of the Church began to become manifest as the worshipping people of God called into being by his Word, with the mystery of divine election hidden behind the events of their history, and laden with the ministry of his revelation, and throughout it becomes more and more clear that as the creation and corporate election of God the Church exists prior to the individual members incorporated into it from generation to generation but that it will be brought to its fulfilment only through the death and resurrection of Israel in the body of the Messiah.

(b) Israel was called to be the *Servant of the Lord*, the one people within the Adamic race set apart for vicarious mission in the redemption of the many. Through the cult Israel had been taught that the covenant could be fulfilled only through an obedient response or sacrifice provided by God himself from within the covenant, but through the prophets Israel learned that such an obedient response had to be translated into its very existence and life and made to issue out of it. The election of the one for the many called for the election within the one people of a Servant chosen of the Lord who would fulfil in his own body and soul the covenant-will of God for his people, and fulfil the covenanted obedience of the people to God's will. This righteous Servant would mediate the covenant by bearing the sins of the people in himself and being cut off out of the land of the living for the sake of God's people, so that they might be pardoned and healed and restored to fellowship with God. The covenant thus mediated would be transformed to extend far beyond the bounds of Israel, for all nations would come at last under its light and salvation and share in the fellowship it bestowed between God and man.

The whole conception of the Servant represents the activity of God whereby he began to draw together the cords of the covenant in which he had bound Israel to himself as his covenant-partner; it represents the activity in which he began to narrow down the assumption of Israel into union with himself toward the point of the Incarnation where, in the midst of Israel, he was to assume man into oneness with himself in the ultimate act of reconciliation. But because the election of Israel as God's Servant was the election of man in his sinful existence and enmity to God, election involved the judgment of man in his will to isolate himself from God and in his refusal of grace. That was the reason for the suffering of Israel, for it involved the breaking and making of Israel as the Servant of the Lord. Thus the election of Israel as the Servant of the Lord meant that it was elected to be used even in its refusal of grace that through it the ultimate self-giving of God to man in spite of his sin and because of his sin might take place— elected, that is, to act in representative capacity for all peoples in their rejection of God's will; but the election of Israel as the Servant of the Lord meant also that out of Israel there was to come the Mediator to act in a representative capacity for all men, through whose rejection in suffering and sacrifice the redemption was to be achieved for all men, not least for Israel itself.

(c) Israel was called to be *the bearer of the Messiah*, the mother out of which should spring the new race. And so to the end of time it remains true that 'Salvation is of the Jews.' It is not only that Israel was called to be the bearer of the promises of God and therefore to be the messenger of hope, but that throughout her long history in her concrete existence in the flesh Israel always bore within her the seed of the messianic Saviour and of the messianic race. It was not least that organic union of Israel with Christ that constituted it Church and preserved it from extinction throughout all its ordeal of suffering, so that at last when it gave birth to the Messiah its whole historical life was gathered up in him and together with the Church of the Gentiles was constituted one New Man, the Israel of God, the universal Body of Christ.

But the transition from the people of the Old Covenant to the people of the New Covenant was only through the death and resurrection of the Messiah. Church of God though it was, the holy people bearing the Presence of God in its midst, yet Israel was concluded under sin with the Gentiles, in the solidarity of the whole Adamic race, in the one equal grace of God freely extended to all men. By condescending to be made flesh of our flesh in Israel, the holy Son of God incorporated himself into the continuity of man's sinful existence, taking on himself our body of sin under the curse of the law and the judgment of God, and even our body of death, that through his death and resurrection there might take place the death of the old man and the resurrection of the new, the destruction of the temple and the raising of it again, the cutting of Israel down to the very root, and the springing up of the new shoot, the Vine of Truth. Thus in the dying and rising of the body of Christ the old was translated into the new and the new was grafted into the continuity of the old.

The Christian Church must not forget that it has no independent existence, for through Christ it is grafted on to the trunk of Israel, nor must it imagine that God has cast off his ancient people or that the promises made to Israel as a people of divine election and institution have only a spiritualized fulfilment. Israel too as God's first-born son has part in the resurrected body of the Messiah, and together with the Gentiles grafted into it and sharing its riches, forms the one commonwealth of the people of God. All members of the Church are of the race of Abraham, and there is no messianic race but Israel.

At last in the fulness of time when a body had been prepared the Messiah came to do the will of God. John the Baptist as the messenger of the Covenant had been sent ahead of him to prepare the way. He stood on the boundary between the Old Testament and the New, proclaiming that the messianic Kingdom was at hand and that the covenant promises made to Abraham were about to be fulfilled, and through a baptism unto repentance for the remission of sins made ready a people prepared for the Lord. When Jesus submitted himself to John's Baptism and had the seal set on his messianic vocation by the voice from heaven, it meant that as the

Servant of the Lord and only Righteous One he identified himself with the people of God concluded under sin that through union with them in one body he might make their sin his own and make them participant in his righteousness. It was his consecration to the whole course of sacrificial obedience in life and death in which he healed and transformed the Church through death and resurrection in his own body. 'Christ loved the Church and gave himself for it; that he might sanctify and cleanse it with the washing of water by the word, that he might present it unto himself a glorious Church, not having spot or wrinkle or any such thing; but that it should be holy and without blemish.'

2 JESUS CHRIST AND HIS MESSIANIC COMMUNITY

From the very start of his public ministry Jesus came proclaiming the Gospel of the Kingdom of God and saying, 'The time is fulfilled, and the Kingdom of God is at hand: repent ye and believe the Gospel,' and set about at once calling people to himself in his mission to gather and redeem the people of God. With his advent and presence the transcendent Kingdom of God that had so long been the object of longing and prophecy had arrived and was active among men for their salvation. In the whole historico-redemptive activity of God in Israel the Kingdom of God and the people of God were essentially correlative conceptions, or rather two different aspects, of the one rule of God grounded in creation and made good in redemption. It was to be fulfilled through the saving acts of God in Israel but on fulfilment it would inevitably transcend the boundaries of Israel and take form as the universal kingship of God over all his creation. That Kingdom was to be ushered in with the coming of the Messiah, the anointed King, through whom it would be grounded on earth in the redeeming and raising up of a people who would enter into the Kingdom as its constituent members and be themselves the instrument through which the Kingdom would extend its rule over the ends of the earth. Small though its beginning was, grouped immediately round the person of the Messiah, it would grow and spread until all nations were brought under its rule. 'Fear not little flock, for it is your Father's good pleasure to give you the Kingdom.'

That is the context in which Jesus Christ and his messianic community are presented to us in the Scriptures—the Kingdom and the People of God alike are concentrated in him, while the life and mission of the Church, the people of the new covenant, are rooted in his sending as the Son from the Father and take their form and shape from his incarnate ministry on earth. It was the kind of person he was and the kind of mission he undertook which determined and gave form and structure to the messianic Kingdom and messianic people.

From his very birth Jesus was hailed as the Son of the Highest to whom the Lord would give the throne of his father David, and of whose reign over the house of Jacob there would be no end. He was born to be Saviour as well as King, for in his birth God had come to visit and redeem his people, raising up in Jesus a horn of salvation in accordance with his promises to the fathers and prophets since the world began, and in remembrance of his holy covenant. His coming was not only to restore the Kingdom to Israel and Israel to the Lord, but to bring a salvation prepared for all people, a light to lighten the Gentiles as well as the glory of God's people Israel. He was the Lord's Messiah or Christ, anointed to gather the people of God into one and save them from their sins.

That was the mission upon which Jesus publicly embarked at his baptism which was both his consecration as King and his consecration as the righteous Servant to bear the sins of the many. He who was baptized embodied the fulness of the Kingdom and the fulness of God's people in himself. His being was not only individual but also corporate, recapitulating in himself the chosen people and the messianic seed, and embodying in himself also the new humanity of the future. Jesus was not baptized for his own sake but for the sake of the whole people of God with whom he identified himself—on his side it was a vicarious baptism. He as the Son of God did not need to be anointed and endowed with the Spirit, but his baptism set forth the fact that it was our humanity in him that was baptized and anointed, and that it was in his capacity as a humble representative of the people that he was sanctified and consecrated to a special ministry. As the anointed Servant he was not the Messiah without his people, for he existed as Messiah to uphold and serve his people in giving his life a ransom for them, and establishing in them a new way of life. They were not the messianic people apart from him but only as they inhered in him, shared in his anointing, followed him and partook of his redemption. Hence it was for their sakes that he sanctified himself that they also might be sanctified through the truth and in him be consecrated together in one. 'Both he that consecrates and they who are consecrated are all of one: for which cause he is not ashamed to call them brethren.' Thus the goal of his mission to be the Saviour of the world included within it the sanctifying and gathering into one of the people of God, the raising up of the Church in its permanent and final form.

It was in the temptations immediately following his baptism that Jesus made clear the manner in which he was to fulfil his mission: not by acts of open divine majesty and compelling power but, Son of God though he was, by acts of humble service, in which he ranged himself with sinners in their weakness and lostness and bondage under the tyranny of evil and under the judgment of God, acting from their side toward God and only as such acting as God in their midst to save and deliver them. The ministry he had to fulfil before the face of the Father was at the same time the mission of redemption on which the Father had sent him. Hence he insisted on carrying out his ministry as a representative of the people into which he had incorporated himself, and within which he had been consecrated to the vocation of the Messiah, to the office of the *Christos*, the Elect One, the Servant, or the Son of Man, as he called himself. That is to say, he fulfilled his mission on earth as the supreme functionary of the messianic people, as Man holding messianic office and fulfilling a ministerial function.

Hence from his baptism Jesus advanced toward the Cross as the Son of God become Man, to carry out the mighty deeds of our redemption in the weakness of a man among men and in the form of a servant fulfilling a meek and lowly ministry. It was because he was incarnate that his ministry took a human form, and because he subjected himself with us under the Law that it took a servant-form. Because the Messiah and his people are essentially correlative and cannot be separated, the ministry which he came to fulfil he fulfilled as a human office within the conditions of the community he served and sustained by his personal ministry. He was the Son of Man who came not to be ministered unto but to minister. But because that was an office to which he was divinely appointed and consecrated, he exercised it as the Householder in charge of God's household, as the Steward of his people in the mysteries of the Kingdom, giving authority to God's servants within it and to every man his work.

In this way it is apparent that the Church of Christ was not just the holy society founded to perpetuate his memory, or to observe his teachings, or to proclaim his Gospel, but that it inhered in his being as the Incarnate Son, was rooted in his humanity as the historical Jesus, and grew out of the fulfilment of his ministry in the flesh. The Church of the new covenant arose out of the indivisible union of the Messiah and the people of God he came to redeem and raise up; it grew out of the concrete way in which he lived his divine life within their human existence thereby transforming their whole way of life; it took shape and form in every act that he performed, and derived its essential structure from the way in which he fulfilled his ministry on their behalf. This change in the people of God, the new birth or foundation of the Church in the messianic era, had two phases, one before and leading up to the crucifixion, and one after and arising out of the resurrection. Like the grain of wheat it had to be planted in the ground and had to die before it could spring up and bear abundant fruit.

The Rooting of the Church in the Person and Ministry of the Historical Jesus

Right from the start of his public ministry Jesus set about to restore the people of God by gathering followers or disciples round himself and building them up as the nucleus of the messianic community in whose midst the Kingdom of God was actively at work. This messianic office he fulfilled personally, not by mighty impersonal deeds, but by direct personal and individual ministry on his part. Hence we have the three arduous years of his personal ministry, in lowly, patient service; in preaching the Kingdom and summoning all to repentance, in seeking and saving the lost, in healing the sick and forgiving sins, in teaching all who had ears to hear and feeding them with the bread of life, in transforming their lives and communicating to them a new righteousness, in instituting in their midst the final Law of God, and moulding them into a structured community with its authoritative centre in himself.

The direct word and action of Jesus himself was essential in all this. As we have traditionally failed to see that the historical ministry of Jesus, his teaching and praying, his living and obeying, his miracles and parables, are an integral part of his atonement, so we have failed to pay sufficient attention to the essential and constitutive nature of his personal and individual ministry in the fulfilment of a special office laid upon him by divine authority for the building of the Church of God among his followers. The only comparison possible is with Moses. It was with divine authority that Moses delivered and reconstituted Israel, instituted the covenant at Sinai, promulgated its laws and installed men in office in the covenanted community. Moses' authority was supreme in Israel. But in Jesus there is not only a new Moses, but the Messiah himself, the Son of Man endowed with authority on earth to forgive sins and utter final commandments. Jesus fulfilled his office with an authority greater than that of Moses or any to which the Scribes and Pharisees appealed. It was the immediate authority of the Father which had been laid on him. He did nothing by himself, but acted only in accordance with the will and mission and Word of the Father who sent him, and therefore he resorted to prayer before all the major acts of his ministry. What he had to do and did was to found the new Israel and inaugurate the new covenant.

He laid the basis for the new Israel when out of the people prepared for the Messiah and out of the band of those he had called to be his disciples he chose twelve to be with him to be the inner nucleus of his Church. It was a tremendous act, for it meant that the longed-for age of salvation had come when the tribes would no longer be scattered but be gathered into one. Hence he formed and instituted them into one Body with himself, calling them to take up his Cross, and deny themselves, that they might have their centre of unity not in themselves but in him. He initiated them into his messianic secret, incorporated them into his messianic mission, sending them out to exercise his own ministry in preaching and healing, and granting them to be baptized with his baptism and to drink the cup which he was to drink, and even to watch and pray with him at the last in the Garden of Gethsemane.

As long before Elijah had gathered together twelve stones representing the twelve tribes of Israel to build an altar for sacrifice, Jesus gathered twelve living stones, such as the rock Peter, and built them round himself the Lamb of God to be offered in sacrifice. They were the many inhering in the one. They had one name in the Son of Man who came to give his life a ransom for the many. In the indissoluble bond between the one and the many, the Messiah and the People, the nucleus of the Church received its fundamental shape and form, and together the little flock went up to Jerusalem where it was to be given the Kingdom. Then there took place the Last Supper where Jesus inaugurated the new covenant in his Body and Blood, renewed the consecration of the disciples in himself, and in covenantal action appointed to them a kingdom making them a royal priesthood to sit with him at last on twelve thrones in his Kingdom.

Then came the crucifixion, the scattering of the disciples, the laying of the axe to the root of Israel, the destruction of the temple, the death of the Messiah. In the ultimate hour he was left alone, dying in lonely substitution on the Cross, the one for many. But in his death, the many who inhered in him died too, and indeed the whole body of sin, the whole company of sinners into which he incorporated himself to make their guilt and their judgment his own, that through his death he might destroy the body of sin, redeem them from the power of guilt and death, and through his resurrection raise them up as the new Israel, the new humanity, the Church of the new covenant, the one universal People of God. The death and resurrection of the Messiah brought the old economy in God's household to an end and inaugurated a new economy through union with himself in his risen body.

The Rebirth of the Church in the Body and Spirit of the Risen Jesus

The Church did not come into being with the Resurrection or with the pouring out of the Spirit at Pentecost. That was not its birth but its new birth, not its beginning but its transformation into the Body of the risen Lord quickened and filled with his Spirit. Jesus Christ had already gathered and built up the nucleus of the Church round himself, but because he loved it he gave himself for it that he might cleanse it and change it through the mystery of union with himself in death and resurrection. The form he had given it through his ministry was necessarily of a provisional character before the crucifixion and resurrection. He had prepared it for this hour, and therefore far from rejecting it he reaffirmed it, reconstituted it, and recommissioned it, giving it to participate in him now on the ground of his atoning work in a depth and fulness which was not possible before.

The Body had already been prepared, the people and the structure he had given them remained, but the Body was broken and humbled to the dust—it needed to be quickened by the Breath or Spirit of God. That had already happened to Jesus himself, the Head of the Body, for God had not allowed him to see corruption but had raised him bodily from the dead to be the new life-giving Adam, the Head of the new race. Now first upon the apostolic nucleus he breathed his quickening breath and then poured the Spirit out in fulness upon the whole Church, and so the Body prepared for Christ arose and lived. The Christian Church was born, the one Body of Christ incorporating the faithful of all ages before and after the Incarnation. It is a divine creation, not built by men on earth but deriving from the life of God above, existing prior to its individual members which it incorporates into itself, universal yet appearing in the world in visible form, grounded first upon the college of the Apostles and therefore prior to the local congregations which it assimilates to its order and through which it becomes visible from generation to generation. As such it is the immediate sphere of the operation of the Holy Spirit mediated to it through Christ, the anticipation and manifestation in the history of this ongoing world of the new creation at the end of time.

This Church does not exist by itself as a special creation of the Spirit nor does it have an independent life of its own. It is the Kingdom and Body of Christ and exists solely because of its organic relation to him. There is no Kingdom of the Spirit but only a Kingdom of Christ in and by the Spirit. The Church is not the Body of the Spirit, for there is no Incarnation of the Spirit, but it is the spiritual Body of Christ on earth and in history. It is the community of men and women with whom he identifies himself, which he united by the power of the Spirit to himself, and which in his grace he reckons and makes to be his own earthly and historical Body. It is what it is because of what Christ, the incarnate and risen Son of God, is; it is what it is because of its indissoluble bond with him who will not be without it. There is but one Christ who is both the Head and the Body, so that the Body cannot exist apart from Christ, or be divided without dividing Christ. Thus the Church has no independent existence, as if it were anything at all or had any life or power of its own, apart from what is unceasingly communicated to it through its union and communion with Christ who dwells in it by the power of the Spirit and fills it with the eternal life and love of God himself. It is quickened and born of the Spirit; it is filled and directed by the Spirit, but in order that the Church may be rooted in Jesus Christ, grounded in his incarnate Being and mission, and in order that it may be determined in its inner and outer life through participation in his life and ministry.

This means that through the Spirit the structure and functions of the messianic community which Jesus had gathered about him in the days of his ministry in the flesh continued to be determinative for the life and functions of the Church after the Resurrection and the Ascension. Jesus and his disciples shared in one messianic mission, but his role in it was utterly unique for he had a lonely and substitutionary work to fulfil. Jesus and his disciples formed one messianic Body, but his place in it was as Mediator, and Head and King, and their place in it was as the redeemed people, as members and servants. The crucifixion and resurrection made that likeness and difference completely clear, and it is that likeness and difference that constitutes the fundamental pattern of the Church's life and ministry in the world after the resurrection, and as it is unfolded and comes to view after Pentecost, i.e., in the apostolic structure of the Church. 'As the Father hath sent me, so send I you.'

Before the crucifixion Jesus took care to initiate his disciples into the same ministry as he was exercising, incorporating first the Twelve and then the Seventy into his own mission by sending them out to minister in the name of the Messiah as he the Messiah had been sent to minister in the name of the Father. The disciples were permitted to baptize, to go forth as his representatives bearing the kerygma of the Kingdom on their lips, and with authority to heal and forgive sins in his name; at the Last Supper the Twelve were solemnly washed and consecrated as his servants and prepared for office, and Jesus commanded them at the Supper to continue to fulfil this ministry until he returned, praying for them, in distinction from the rest, in the fulfilment of their special office; after the resurrection he forgave their failure and recommissioned them as his representatives, sending them out to follow his example in shepherding and feeding the flock, to be teachers and heralds of the Kingdom making disciples of all nations. The records make it clear that Jesus intended to leave behind a community with a structure and form and leadership, a community with a ministry shaped on the pattern of his own, and that while all men were called to be disciples and to engage in a ministry of witness to him, some were given special responsibilities and a special commission of pastoral care over his flock, endowed with an authoritative office to act in his Name. The constituent elements of the Church were all there, but now with the commissioning of the disciples as *Apostles*, and the pouring out of the *Spirit* at Pentecost the Church was given by its risen Lord the permanent form which he intended it to take throughout history until he came again.

The apostles had been specially trained through intimate association with Jesus, through initiation into the secret of the passion, through private instruction, in order that they might be the commissioned and authoritative witnesses to Christ. They were not intended by Jesus to pass on what they had received in precisely the same way they had received it—they had a special function 'in the Word' to perform in the tradition. Where Jesus proclaimed and confronted them with himself, they had to bear witness to him as the Son of God and Saviour. Where Jesus was present in person and acted, and let his presence and acts fulfil as much of his revelation as his words, the Apostles had to gather it all up and pass it on as communicable word. What is at stake here is the essential difference between Jesus, the unique Son of God, the only Saviour and Mediator, and those he came to save. The supreme importance of the Apostles lies in the fact that they were the chosen and trained instruments, endowed with the Spirit, to pass on the self-witness of Jesus (in word and act) translated into witness to him by men in history, for men in history. In the apostolic witness there took place once and for all, under the power of the Spirit, who quickened their understanding and opened their mouths, who brought all things to their remembrance and led them into the truth, that translation in an inspired act which has for ever since been the means of Christ's own self-revelation and communication to men. Thus the Apostles cannot be separated from what they passed on, or what they passed on from their function in passing it on. At the same time it is very clear that the power and authority of the witness of the Apostles do not lie in the Apostles themselves but in the self-witness of Christ which through the power of the Spirit operates in the apostolic witness to him as Saviour and Lord. This being so, we cannot separate the structure of the Church in history from the ministry of Christ's self-revelation through the Apostles.

What the Apostles had to do in regard to the witness, in translating the self-witness of Jesus into witness about him, required a corresponding change in the functioning of the ministry which Jesus had built up and left behind him, a change which he intended it to take. Thus as we are to see the relation of the witness of the Apostles to Jesus' self-witness, so we are to see the relation between the apostolic ministry to Jesus' own ministry in which it was rooted. Jesus intended the Apostles to become the wise master-builders or architects who would shape and build the mind and life and worship of the Church in him, and so lay once and for all the foundations of the historical Church in the life and ministry of Christ.

The important point here is to discern both the rooting of the apostolic ministry in the ministry of Jesus, and to discern the difference which comes about when the self-ministry of Jesus is translated into ministry in his name. It is the vicarious mediation of Jesus which is of fundamental importance here and explains why the Early Church worshipped the Father and ministered only in the name of Christ, and why they regarded Christ in the absolute and proper sense, as the only Minister of the Church before God, the only One who was appointed and anointed (*Christos*) for office in the Kingdom of God, the only One endowed with all authority in heaven and earth, the supreme Householder in God's Kingdom who at the end would hand over everything to the Father.

Grounded upon the Apostles and determined by their ministry, the ministry of the Church is both like and unlike the ministry of the historical Jesus. It is rooted in it and patterned after it, and in a real sense shares in it. But the ministry of the Church is also utterly different from that of Jesus, for it is directly related to Jesus as his ministry is directly related to the Father, and it is a ministry of redeemed sinners, whereas his ministry is that of the Redeemer. This essential and fundamental translation in the form of the ministry was carried out by the Apostles, so that all true Christian ministry is ever after determined at its root by the special function of the Apostles in their immediate relation to Jesus' ministry on the one hand and to the historical Church of forgiven sinners and its mission in the world on the other hand.

Thus it becomes apparent that in the new form given to the Church by the risen Lord, the ministry is part of the structure of the Church in a way similar to that in which the Messiah is indivisibly united to the structure of the People of God. The Christian Church is what it is because of its indissoluble union with Christ through the Spirit, for in him is concentrated the Church and all ministry. Because Christ fulfilled his ministry by sharing the life of the people of God, the Church is what it is through sharing in his life and ministry, living by the very Gospel it proclaims. Because the Person and Work of Christ, what he was and what he did, are inseparable, what the Church is in him and what it does in proclaiming him, its being and its ministry, are inseparable. As there is only one Christ and only one Body, so there is only one ministry, that of Christ in his Body. But Christ shares in it in his utterly unique way, as vicarious Redeemer, and Lord; the Church shares in it in an utterly different way as the redeemed people who as servants and heralds point away from themselves to Christ alone.

7

W A. WHITEHOUSE

Christological Understanding

I

To work in the personal service of another human being is, once more, the least coveted role in human society. Young persons may have to do this as part of their apprenticeship. Shop assistants and bus conductors must do it, but can protect themselves to some extent from the thought of indignity by 'serving the management' rather than the customers. Personal secretaries can bask in the dignity of their boss and enjoy the game of managing him—and can leave him for another if they are defeated or bored. Domestic servants, and more especially those who must serve their employers or their employers' 'guests' at table, are no longer in a worse position to look after themselves than are others engaged in direct personal service; but this occupation, lightly undertaken to earn money in a vacation, has revealed to many students the perils and indignities of being in personal service to their fellow men and women. They have tasted, in a greatly alleviated form and by uncommitted sampling, something which was a painful commonplace in Hellenistic society. It was scandalous for Jesus to interpret His own role, and to present the terms of discipleship, by using this model. But He did so, with the personal service of the table-waiter firmly in view.

Then, as now, the general idea of occupying oneself and expressing oneself in 'service' was not unacceptable. To serve a respected householder or farmer, to serve the community in the apparatus of government, to serve God from some niche in the religious establishment, these were possible ways of enriching

From James I. McCord and T. H. L. Parker, Editors, *Service in Christ,* pp. 151–161. © Epworth Press, 1966; William B. Eerdmans Publishing Company, Grand Rapids, 1966. Used by permission of the Publishers.

one's life and of giving to it value and meaning. (To serve a
commercial enterprise is a quite recent addition to the list of
worthy causes.) To serve one's mere fellow man who happens to
be in need was not, and is not, comparably worth while. If done at
all, it is done occasionally, as an act of condescension or as an act
of religious obligation. Judaism conjoined love of neighbour with
love of God. Indeed, any religion which expresses among other
things a community's will to survive is likely to prescribe some
form of neighbourly service to the needy. What is scandalous
about the teaching and example of Jesus is the suggestion, embodied in His choice of model, that those who follow Him must
spend themselves in direct personal service to any who call upon
them, without calculation and without any safeguards of dignity.
Their true dignity will emerge precisely in so doing, but it will not
commend itself as such to those wise in the ways of this world.
Nietzsche saw the point with rare clarity after it had been masked
for centuries by the dignities of 'Christendom'. The disciples of
Jesus will, it is true, be serving Him, serving, too, the 'cause'
which He embodies, and (so He assures them) serving God, by
putting their resources at hazard in this way. But faith and obedience may have to do without the comfort of being able to regard
Him, or His 'cause', or the God whose name He invokes, as
obviously adequate grounds from which to derive authentication
for such a programme of living.

The scandal is aggravated when one reflects on that aspect of the
public ministry of Jesus which particularly struck the theologians
of 'the Social Gospel' in the nineteenth century: His deliberate
turning to the poor and the incompetent rather than to the able and
influential. To help such lame dogs over their various stiles is a
humane procedure, and indeed may be an important safeguard for
the community against social collapse. But to make this the
corner-stone in a policy for world-regeneration is utterly 'unrealistic'. Those who call for personal service most loudly and most
frequently will always be 'the poor'. One need not hold them in
contempt (though the 'realistic' tendency is always in this direction), but to suggest that personal service to their manifold needs is
the lever which alone will avail to transform and regenerate the
world is folly. It is perhaps excusable and comprehensible and in
some mysterious way right, in a Jewish religious leader, who
identifies 'the poor' with 'the pious and therefore the oppressed';
but the actual conduct of Jesus can be neither justified nor explained in terms of that handy assumption. The 'poor' to whom He
turned were persons whom it is unrewarding to serve (even, one

might add, on that assumption); and to give Himself to them in the humble role of *diakonos* was to lay Himself open to degradation and wasteful self-destruction. In doing precisely this, the Son of Man gave up his own life. But He did so with confidence that this would provide 'for many' the means of procuring their emancipation (Mark 10:45).

Among 'the many', first and most evidently, are those who hear the news about Jesus Christ, leap to lose their chains, and therefore receive it as 'the word of the truth' (Colossians 1:5). In His case, they are persuaded, such spending of life in diaconal service has been authenticated, first in His own resurrection from the dead and now in His coming to them as their living Lord through the Holy Spirit to give them the freedom of faith. His lifetime of diaconal service was rooted in God. They do not, however, proceed by one short direct step to obey the injunction 'Go and do thou likewise' (Luke 10:37). This would be to step aside from one religion of righteousness by works to another one—to 'an impractical and inept idealism' which is even less appropriate to the condition of men and their world than whatever religion it is which they are ready to abandon. They do indeed turn to God from idols, to serve a living and true God (I Thessalonians 1:9)—a possibility to be joyfully welcomed in principle. But they serve Him first by the gratitude of faith; by acknowledging the grace with which He has emancipated them from the dominion of darkness and transferred them to the kingdom of His beloved Son 'in whom we have redemption, the forgiveness of sins' (Colossians 1:13–14).

Their gratitude is for services which they can neither repay nor emulate. In the servant-manhood of Jesus they recognize the Christ of God, the authority of God's anointed Servant; they see deeper, and identify this authority as the authority of God Himself in person, the Lord of all who has come to men as a neighbour in this world to serve them in their deepest need. His service to them has turned them into accepted fellow servants with Jesus, in a service to the world which God Himself is giving in His Christ. Yet they dare not say: 'I will therefore give myself as a Christ to my neighbour', until they have first suffered the judgement and transformation of human self-awareness out of which there emerges the qualifying clause: 'just as Christ offered himself to me'. Vivid in their minds is the picture of Christ giving Himself to His disciples in the diaconal service of washing their feet. At the heart of that episode is the word to Peter, who had found in Jesus a cause to serve and a master to emulate: 'If I do not wash you, you can have no part in me' (John 13:8). Those who are to serve must first let themselves be served. Only as beneficiaries of His unique personal service to them can they follow Jesus in freedom and light, being effectively emancipated from the darkness of this world's preoccupations. Among such preoccupations there is a certain interest in serving adequate causes or serving an adequate Lord, and the gratitude of faith includes testimony to the fact of having found such a Lord and such a cause. But the judgement and transformation in human awareness which Christian faith entails bring emancipation even from this subtle interest. In this life, believers are content to follow Jesus on the road of diaconal service whose end is the Cross. Those who make Christ's life their own believe that 'when Christ, who is our life, shall be manifested', they with Him shall also be manifested in glory (Colossians 3:4); and such hope provides in them a steady source of discipline and determination without which it is hardly possible to continue steadfast on so inglorious a road. But those who are to tread it must do so as men *prepared* always to find that it is intrinsically inglorious—though dignities, graces, and gratifications *may* be added, and to reject them when offered, to tread the road grimly wearing a hair-shirt for its own sake, is as bad in its own way as to depend on service being ennobling. Those who are prepared for the road have their feet washed by Him into whose death they are baptized; and this ever-renewed foot-washing means ever-renewed emancipation from ungenerous and self-regarding preoccupations including those of a religious kind.

Discipleship therefore means actually following Jesus in the paths of mundane personal service to those who call out from conditions of need however crude. The parable of judgement (Matthew 25:31–46) speaks to men in this world whose fellow men are physically short of food and drink, actually lonely and unwelcome in society, short of clothes, in poor health, locked up in prison. Discipleship is judged by the actuality of mundane service which makes its own quite concrete and practical difference to their condition. The service must be offered in its own right and for its own sake, but it is, in fact, set by God in a dimension deeper than humanitarianism or social therapy. Those conditions of deprivation, incompetence and bondage, are symbolically (and perhaps symptomatically) significant for the entire being and experience of every man in so far as he has not yet responded to the ministry of Jesus, Servant and Lord. He is ready to make our mundane service part of His own unique service; and what we have to offer may be viewed without presumption as a potential witness to, and vehicle for, the personal service which He alone can give. It bears witness, or may do so, in that it comes through servant-disciples who owe their freedom to services rendered; but more directly may it do so through its own intrinsic, but borrowed, grace.

'As our heavenly Father has in Christ freely come to our aid, so we ought freely to help our neighbour through our body and its works, and each should become as it were a Christ to the other that we may be Christs to one another and Christ may be the same in all; that is, that we may be truly Christians.' Luther's words express the hope of bringing the help of the Gospel, in, with, and under the practicalities of neighbourly help. It is not, in the last resort, for us to calculate for this; though what we can do 'through our body and its works' is never dissociated from what we simultaneously provide 'through our soul and its words', and we must reckon with the possibility that this will be used as God's vehicle for His own word. It is not, however, for the servant-disciple to assess what service is likely to be 'spiritually profitable', nor how to make it so. Like a waiter, he is at the beck and call of everyone in that part of the room where he happens to be. Their calls for mundane service must be answered with mundane efficiency 'through the body and its works.'

II

So far, with assistance from Luther's *Treatise on Christian Liberty,* we have considered how the Christian is conformed to his Lord as 'a perfectly dutiful servant of all, subject to all'. The prospect is scandalous to anyone who wishes to conduct his life as an essay in self-fulfilment. Such a person (and he is alive in all of us) may, when he becomes a Christian, conspire with his obituarist to produce a career which both can regard as 'self-fulfilment in a lifetime of service'. By so doing he will have distorted in practice what he ought to have been giving. The neighbourly personal service open to an individual under the Cross is piecemeal. It lacks the self-justifying cohesion to which so satisfying an epitaph seeks to draw attention. An obituarist is professionally obliged to disregard the fact that a really Christian life is a life broken and thrown away. This is not to deny that God may grace such a life with fullness and dignity in His own way, and that hints of this may be vouchsafed even in this world's experience. It serves merely to stress the truth that a Christian 'lives not in himself but in Christ and his neighbour . . . in Christ through faith, in his neighbour through love'.

But Christ whose accepted fellow servants Christians are is

more than an exemplary individual. In Him, so faith acknowledges, the Son of God assumed the role of King and Priest whose
office it is to make all creatures relate with God and with one
another in mutual grace and self-giving. Taking the form of a
servant, born as a man, humbled in obedience even unto death on a
cross, He is now exalted, to be owned as Lord by every creature,
to the glory of God the Father (Philippians 2:7–11). His service to
'the many', which at present only believers accept and acknowledge, imcorporates their emancipated lives into 'a royal priesthood, a priestly kingdom'. Of this, the Church is the visible embodiment. To live in Christ by faith is to take one's place in the
community of His Church. The discipleship of each individual,
called to live in his neighbour by love, is caught up into a corporate
service which has direction, scope, and shape of its own. It is in
this fellowship of service that believers receive their high
privilege, granted by grace and secured only through the Holy
Spirit, that God's own service to His world in the person of Jesus
Christ should be mediated through their persons and their actual
worldly service.

Before saying any more about this, a word of warning must be
interposed. It is improper to treat participation in the Church's
corporate service as one element, perhaps optional, in the whole
service to which individuals are called. A calculated risk has been
taken in this essay by adopting an order of discussion which might
suggest such a view. It is more nearly true to regard the individual's personal service to his fellows as the developed expression of
his Church membership—but not if this leads him to distort his
service to men in life's common ways by twisting it into some kind
of service to the Church and making it ecclesiastically meritorious.
The discipleship of each individual is caught up into the corporate
service of the Church and is constantly renewed, as we shall see, at
that centre; but each service, corporate and individual, has its own
distinct and proper shape. There is some truth in the impropriety of
viewing participation in the Church's special and limited service as
one element in the individual's total service. Luther took risks here
when he fought to make plain the freedom with which a Christian
man gives himself in service. It is, I believe, still necessary to do
so.

The *direction* of all Christian service is sufficiently indicated by
the phrase: 'a diaconal service of reconciliation' (2 Corinthians
5:18, to be understood in the light of all that precedes that verse
from 3:4 onwards, and with attention to chapters 8 and 9, where
there is lavish and varied use of 'diaconal' terminology).

The *scope* of reconciliation is the whole creation, viewed from

Christ as its centre and now brought by his service under His dominion. To live in Christ by faith is therefore to have one's own small being rooted in the principle which gives cohesion to all things; in Him all the fullness of God has chosen to dwell, that through Him God may reconcile to Himself all that is (Colossians 1:17, 19–20).

The first question is about the scope of the Church's own distinctive service. Its members have usually been unwilling to demarcate at all rigidly the frontiers of this new visible community; yet for some purposes it is proper to define them, and this rather precarious human decision can be safeguarded against the twin perils of arrogance and indifference if it is accompanied by recognition that the sphere of the visible Church and the sphere of Christ's Lordship do not in all respects coincide. The expression of Christian faith and life in diaconal service has for its scope a sphere of operation which transcends the apparent frontiers of the visible Church, but is nevertheless encompassed by Christ. He has defined this sphere, and He has done it not by first identifying Himself with the Church but first by identifying manhood with Himself. No human experience is alien to Him, and inasmuch as you do or do not render diaconal service to any human neighbour in need, you do it or don't do it to Him (Matthew 25:44f.).

It is rightly said that there is a mystery here, a mystery of the presence, in the person of each actual needy neighbour, of the Lord 'to whom to refuse anything is a monstrous sacrilege' (Calvin's comment on Matthew 25:40); and that Jesus wants his disciples to know about this mystery, so that their actual service may be cleansed from all taint of patronage and all will to impose. It is rash, however, to try to develop an understanding of this mystery—in terms, perhaps, of some 'identity-mysticism'—lest the service should come to seem rewarding in a religious sense to him who gives it, when nothing more can be at stake than its being actually helpful to him who receives it. Yet Calvin's moralizing, however valid, may not be quite sufficient to bring out in the right way this mystery and its power to safeguard the quality of 'obedient' service. Eschatological parables, as Hoskyns said, serve to strip us naked of transient preoccupations and little moral busynesses, so that ultimate facts and duties stand out in luminous simplicity. In this parable we hear how our lives are set in a fellowship of diaconal service where Jesus, the Christ of God, makes the call of the needy His own call and makes the answering word or gesture or helping hand His own as well. In Him it is all being justified, reconciled to God and sanctified, so that in the end it may be glorified.

The Church does not monopolize this fellowship of service; it knows about it and must bear explicit witness to it. It must do so by being itself a fellowship of service, in a way and a shape which are the more eloquent for being special and limited. This, however, raises a complicated question about scope which must be noticed before leaving that topic for the third one, which is shape. New Testament evidence about the Church's effort to express itself as a fellowship of service frequently suggests that such an effort, made as it is by believers, must be made in terms of the needs of believers. This is intelligible in the circumstances and it poses no great problem in a community which all the time is addressing itself with success to the task of drawing others in. With Christians for whom the whole of their society was 'Christendom', no problem is raised at all. For us, however, the Church is a community whose domestic life can all too easily be shut off from the main stream of society, so that a self-contained expression of diaconal service within the fellowship of the Church has no witnessing power and is spoiled in its very character by a taint akin to incest.

In the course of transition from 'Christendom' to present post-Christendom conditions, the Church has retained an interest in special activities and institutions through which, from the early days of 'Christendom', it tried to extend diaconal service into the whole fabric of society. It now has to reckon with a general verdict that these are rightly conducted under an aegis other than its own. It may, indeed, concur with that verdict. The Church's special interest in these activities and institutions is not so central as it once was to its own, or anyone else's, concern. They are residual lines of penetration for the Church with its distinctive witness, but they cannot be regarded in this light without embarrassment.

This is germane to the question about *shape* for the Church's life as a fellowship of service. There is something to be said for working towards an answer beginning from need and not from willingness to serve, and beginning from need outside the Church's domestic life. Since face-to-face personal service to persons is a vulnerable and wearing occupation, the Church ought not to relax its corporate concern that teachers, doctors, nurses, welfare officers, prison visitors, be raised up from its own membership, to help in manning the relevant services and maintaining their quality. But a distinction between these vocations to service and those open to an accountant, an assistant in a public library, a saleswoman, or a garage mechanic, is not easily drawn under modern social conditions—and neither should we expect it to be, when the 'waiter' model for diaconal service is kept in mind. The residual lines of penetration do not stand out with their former distinction.

Alongside all such lines of direct personal service to persons, furthermore, there are the great service-complexes of the national establishment and of industry and of semi-public and private administrations—new material for theological evaluation only in the sense that this has traditionally been confined to 'the State' in its varied manifestations, but now requires revaluation in a wider context and with more attention to the 'personal' nature of service in these complexes. There is a give-and-take of service between the Church and all parts of this worldly network. The problems involved are treated elsewhere in this symposium. They are mentioned here simply as a reminder of the rather puzzling conditions under which the Church must try today to shape its own life as a fellowship of service, and, in its *special and limited way,* be eloquent of the truth which it knows about through the Gospel of Jesus Christ. Traditions inherited from the apostolic age and from the epoch of Christendom are neither sacrosanct nor sufficient in new circumstances, though to consult such traditions, as preceding essays have helped us to do, is rewarding.

It is as a fellowship of believers that the Church must still shape its own life. In the conduct of its own peculiar affairs it can learn a great deal about human needs and do experiments in the art of meeting them as a fellowship of believers. But as such it lives all the time in an open commitment to serving unbelievers, serving *with* unbelievers, and being served *by* unbelievers. No aspect of its domestic structure is insulated from the effects of such a commitment, least of all its structure for diaconal service.

When we move right into the Church's domestic life it is plain first of all that its members are united in a fellowship of service to God offered through Jesus Christ. This is personal service offered to a neighbour, for in Christ God has given Himself to His people as their God and as such He has become their neighbour. But He is not a neighbour who needs either man's work or His own gifts returned. He asks for faith. Faith expresses itself in worship; and worship is the surrender of human interests, in adoration, to a Lord whose influence upon the being and well-being of the worshippers they wholly accept and wholly trust. Because God blesses human beings in all acts of worship where self-preoccupation is lost in praise of His goodness, their 'service to Him' is transmuted into a new experience of 'being served'. In this experience they are turned afresh towards neighbours on the other side, so to speak; towards their fellow men whose cause God has made His own in Jesus Christ.

Our human neighbour does need our resources; and if they are laid open to *him* in an offer of personal service, no one can say what he will do with them—and with the person in whom they inhere. In this direction there is no question of faith in one's neighbour, no worship of humanity, no unconditional devotion even to its more worthy preoccupations. In direct association with the Church, as contributor to its special and limited service, the Christian participates in a service to men which has been distinguished since very early days (Acts 6:2) as 'preaching the word of God' and 'serving tables'. In both respects the Church demonstrates by Christian discipleship how men can belp one another, having first been helped by Christ. To divorce the two distinguishable aspects is always wrong. But it is right to observe that it is through the second motif, 'serving tables', that the Church's special witness to diaconal service has been explicitly developed.

Christians who seek precise bearings from the New Testament for the shape and structure of obedience must take what comfort they can from experts in this field. It is evident that in New Testament times the Church paid explicit attention to the actualities of personal diaconal service, and shaped its life accordingly. How it did so is not very clear. Some of its members, presumably those who most obviously filled a role of personal assistants to their fellow men, attracted to themselves the title *diakonos* (Philippians 1:1; I Timothy 3:8–13); and *diakonia* is evidently the name (not, of course, in all cases) for one special activity among others, presumably of a 'table-serving' kind. It is difficult to see what more should be made of the evidence than what stands in *A Platform of Church Discipline Gathered out of the Word of God,* presented to the Synod at Cambridge, New England, in 1649. 'The office and work of the Deacons is to receive the offerings of the church, gifts given to the church, and to keep the treasury of the church: and therewith to serve the *Tables* which the church is to provide for: the *Lord's Table,* the table of the *ministers,* and of such as are in *necessitie,* to whom they are to distribute in simplicity' (cf. VII, par. 3). It is also difficult to hold back an opinion that something has gone wrong when such deacons are regarded as inferior personal assistants to the 'priestly and ruling' ministers, with servant-status less essential to the fundamental structure of the Church than that of the clergy proper.

To be unconcerned about structure, to confine concern in the case of deacons to their clerical status, to assume that the economic realities of the Church's life (treasury-keeping) may casually be conformed to the world's current practices—all these attitudes may cloak a fundamental lack of concern for the *actuality* of diaconal service within and beyond the Church's domestic life. If so, they betray the Gospel and depart from original apostolic tradition. Less heinously, they could be merely symptoms of a high-minded attitude to sordid practicalities—which has its endearing side, though it is sinful and imperceptive. To suppose that the Church is engaged in a 'spiritual service', which in principle is not impaired if its resources for practical mundane support are abused or squandered or left unused, is to work with false distinctions and ill-conceived priorities. It is tempting to say that, in this matter at least, the Church may find some significance in the lack of adequate help from tradition, and should let the contemporary situation structure its theology and its practice. After all, the whole point is to *serve;* and usually this means to be imposed upon, without imposing. But tradition, critically consulted, may help to renew and inform a concern for structure within the Church; and though, in diaconal service, it must be prepared for being imposed upon by men in their actual needs in the world as it is, its action must everywhere bear the stamp of standards imposed from a kingdom not of this world.

III

Luther's *Treatise on Christian Liberty* was a christological demonstration that God's truth about His world and about human living shines out in Jesus Christ, but had been obscured and opposed in mediaeval ecclesiasticism. Luther helped it to shine out again as light; light in which men may find and develop genuinely human lives. To do this work of theological clarification is to give personal service to persons—and to invite obloquy by doing so, whether it be done with Luther's epoch-making incisiveness or with Barth's daunting thoroughness. Barth has provided the same positive help, but with thorough-going attention to the ways in which this truth is obscured and opposed in modern humanitarianism. In his *Church Dogmatics,* Volume IV, Parts 1, 2 and 3, he demonstrates how men live as beneficiaries of the Lord who became Servant, the Servant who became Lord; and how, by our engagement in diaconal service, His justification of us and His sanctification of us are concretely shown forth in prophetic declaration. Faith working through love expresses the hope in which man as such is called to live. This hope is true to a world where man is to live as the accepted partner of God, purged from the pride and healed from the sloth which corrupt his authentic humanity; and in this hope, truth prevails over falsehood. The truth shines out as a light in which all may live, and to the hidden realities of righteousness by faith and sanctification in love there is added the visible testimony of wisdom—knowledgeable practice. Authentic humanity comes to us from its source in Christ Jesus, whom God made our wisdom, our righteousness and sanctification, our emancipation (I Corinthians 1:30); and in us, as in Him, the substance of knowledgeable practice is diaconal service.

'The true community of Jesus Christ is the society in which it is given to men to see and understand the world as it is, to accept solidarity with it, and to be pledged and committed to it' (*Church Dogmatics*, IV, 3, p. 780). Experience of this will vary with time and with place. Those who at present speak about it from a place in radically secularized societies tend to stress (cf. Hromadka) the unhelpfulness of 'high-sounding doctrines, lofty ideals or moral demands and aims' and ask for greater readiness 'to follow Christ's example of serving at the lowest levels of humanity'. Readiness so to do should not, perhaps, entail complete neglect of service on other levels, including those where doctrines, ideals, demands, and aims are very much to the point; though it is right to observe that men sick from the effects of an ideological diet are not helped by having a rival ideological diet served up to their tables, particularly one which they have already rejected as debilitating. In every cultural situation at present wise diaconal service must have a more helpful content than that.

Barth's balanced and penetrating account of the world as it is, and of humanity pledged with Christ to solidarity with it and to service, rests on preparatory work done in Volume III, Part 2, the theological account of man as the creature of God. Those who are ready to be helped by Barth, but are not prepared to let him do their thinking for them, must make an effort to relate what he has to suggest (in Volume IV) about the actualities of life in service to his earlier analysis of manhood as being-in-encounter. To understand how man *is with* his neigbbour and in limited ways *can be for* his neighbour, is to know the conditions of service. It is also to appreciate how, in diaconal service, the Church and the Christian should be *at their most human*.

Secular humanitarianism, like mediaeval ecclesiasticism, bears its own witness to God's truth, even while suppressing it by pride and wickedness. And secular humanitarianism may help the Christian community to learn (if it will learn from no other source) that it must come out from behind the protective masks of religiosity and self-interested ecclesiasticism and act with the unadorned integrity of generous men. The eleven-page discussion of possible confusions between 'humanity' and 'Christian love' (III, 2, pp 274–85) gives salutary help in this matter. Christian diaconal service, though proceeding from love and renewed by love, is *essential humanity;* it stands or falls by that criterion, a fact easily obscured when it is conceived explicitly as the outworking of Christian love.

God's truth shines out and prevails in the wisdom of diaconal service; and, in a special and limited way, this fact can be focused in Church Order, which itself should at all points be eloquent of the Gospel. Church Order expresses the full life of the Body of Christ, and the expression of this particular aspect has to be related to the total structure by which that is done—a total structure which may be shaped by a central Papacy, an Episcopal Bench, a hierarchy of Church Courts, or a network of localized Church Meetings and Synods. My own experience falls within the last of these areas, and, unlike most professional theologians, it includes service as a deacon (and vivid youthful impressions of the diaconal practice observed in the village church where I grew up) in a pattern of Church Order derived by way of seventeenth-century Congregationalism from Calvin at Geneva. The practice involves the 'social diaconate' of an elected group of men and women, whose humanity is certainly unadorned, but displays in rough and ready ways varying from person to person some integrity which warrants election. These men and women prepare the Table for the Lord's Supper, carry the food on it to the congregation, receive the collection, and entrust to one of their number the charge of giving quiet help from that money to anyone known to be in particular distress. In the village church where I grew up breaches in human relationships within the congregation were healed more often by the deacons than by the minister, and it was they who cared most effectively for the lapsing and the lapsed. It was they who saw to it, often in the absence of a minister, that congregational activities were maintained and financed. They knew better than any minister how to deal with local mischief-making, a matter of some importance when the congregation, along with two others of different Church Order, was a focus of village interest. They also knew how to deal with patronizing or imposing interventions from higher ecclesiastical sources, intent, in most instances, on marshalling financial and economic resources in their own way, which often seemed to be neither Christian nor consistent with human dignity.

From this special and limited domestic Church experience, deacons were equipped to go out, as many did, to public positions of social responsibility and to care in a humanly acceptable way for persons and their affairs outside the Church. Such special diaconal service was also a help to all Church members who went out in their company.

8

RAY S. ANDERSON
The Man Who Is for God

*from its very conception this gift was doomed
to sprinkle the earth—
    was it water or blood?
too great a need and too much love
conjugate the new verb—a sacrifice presumed
to be a senseless act devouring alike
    the giver and the gift.
    a crucifixion of logic
upon the tree of knowledge of good
    and evil, therein lies a god entombed
    too holy to be allowed to live.
earth drinks in its thanksgiving feast—
    is it water or blood?*

*the finest gifts are not always consumed
upon the parched altars of ravenous thirst.
renunciation is itself a sacrament exhumed
from eternal immutability: god the dispersed
gathered up again in those who have communed.
out of all our eucharists, this is the first.*[68]

THE SIMPLICITY OF THE INCARNATION AS AN IDEA OF GOD IS
shattered upon the cross. We had grown accustomed to thinking of
ourselves as not more than an 'arm's length' from God, and what-

---

68. 'An Elegy For God—Based on II Samuel 23:15-17', R. S. Anderson,
an unpublished poem.

From Ray S. Anderson, *Historical Transcendence and the Reality of God*,
pp. 168-186. © Geoffrey Chapman Publisher, London, 1975; William B.
Eerdmans Publishing Company, Grand Rapids, 1975. Used by permission
of the Publishers.

ever that entailed for us in terms of either fear or comfort; and then we heard his cry: 'My God, my God, why hast thou forsaken me?'[69] There is now, it appears, more depth and more distance involved in the 'Word becoming flesh' than was first conceived. The problem is, it is not a matter of taking the Word deeper into the flesh, for that is simply (simply!) to reveal the transcendence of God in a still more profound humanity. What we are confronted with here is the question of how we can continue to speak of the transcendence of God at all in the face of this cry of dereliction. We now see that *kenosis* is not too strong a word to speak of the one who, though existing in the form of God, took the form of a servant, and humbling himself, 'became obedient unto death'.[70] And we can now understand the dilemma which drove the kenoti-cists to the desperate expedient of suggesting that what was involved in this humbling unto death was, at least in part, a renunciation of divine transcendence altogether.[71] Has transcendence been driven back beyond the veil of the humanity, and has our attempt to show that the transcendence of God is historical, been driven off course, or even turned back in an utterly hopeless way?

It would, of course, be premature to conclude that this is the case. The argument has been constructed too slowly and carefully to be abandoned at the first real encounter with that which we suspected would have to be faced sooner or later. What remains to be seen, is whether or not the inner logic of the Incarnation in its two levels of understanding can now be integrated in a meaningful way; and specifically whether or not the transcendence of God can be found in such human helplessness.

It should be made clear at the outset that what is involved is not merely the resolution of an apparent antinomy between humiliation and glory, as, for example, E. Käsemann attempts in taking an eschatological view of the unbroken unity between Jesus and the Father.[72] Nor are we to seek the solution in the concept of a

69. Matthew 27:46.

70. Philippians 2:6–8.

71. It was W. F. Gess who argued that for there to be a unity of self-consciousness in Christ, the Son of God had to lay aside his consciousness of relation within the Trinity in becoming the human soul of Christ. Gess held that in becoming flesh by an act of self-divesting, the Son of God allowed his eternal self-consciousness to be extinguished in order to regain it as man. See *God and Incarnation in Mid-nineteenth Century German Theology,* C. Welch (ed.), p. 305; also cf. F. Weston, *The One Christ,* p. 119.

72. *The Testament of Jesus,* SCM Press, London, 1968, pp. 11ff.

'paradoxical identity' to which R. Bultmann resorts, in order to hold together the divinity and the humanity of Jesus by reducing the historical dimension to a *kerygmatic* word.[73] The 'scandal' of the cross is not made more existential, and thus more powerful in its effect, by making the death of the incarnate Logos into a crucifixion of logic. That is ultimately to cast faith back on its own resources, and destroys the ontic character of salvation. It is the question of transcendence which keeps us on track because it raises again the question of the subject. When we ask: *Who* is the man who died, the man who cried out in his abandonment by God?— we can only answer: the same one who was the Word, the eternal Subject. And so it comes down to a matter of the transcendence of God. Can the 'God who is for man' be, at the same time, the 'Man who is for God?'

The question will be taken up in the following manner. First, we will examine the problematic of covenant response with respect to the way in which Jesus worked out this response in both his life and death. Then we will consider what this reveals to us about the nature of God, particularly in regard to his transcendence through both Son and Holy Spirit; and finally, saying something about the implications of this understanding of transcendence for man himself.

In the earlier discussion of the problematic of covenant response,[74] it was shown that intrinsic to the covenant of creation, was the possibility of man's freedom to affirm the transcending limit of his existence through his created logos. Thus, the creation of man in the image of God is itself an act of transcendence on the part of the Creator by which man is given the possibility and the freedom to respond. This response is both an affirmation on man's part of the reality of his own created nature and an affirmation on God's part of the transcendent act which makes it possible. The inner logic of Incarnation was then shown to include this basic structure as its fundamental rationality. The importance of this for our discussion can now be shown in greater detail.

When it is said that there is such a thing as genuine, or authentic humanity, the validity and the rationality of this statement rests upon the transcendent reality of God which gives to the created logos its own freedom, and thus its own reality. While man is, therefore, 'Other' than God, because he is related to him as crea-

73. *Theology of the New Testament*, Vol. II, Charles Scribner's Sons, New York, 1955, pp. 47ff.
74. See my *Historical Transcendence and the Word of God*, pp. 135f.

ture to Creator, this 'Otherness' is constituted by the transcendence of God himself, so that God would not have to renounce, or restrict his transcendence in order to himself become that 'Other'—that is, to become man.[75] Because the relation is problematic to the creature does not mean that it is also problematic for the Creator. The eternal Logos can act as a created logos, even though this possibility is not reversible.

There are two things that are important to distinguish here: *first*, the subject of covenant response is constituted human, not in virtue of its freedom from God, but in virtue of its freedom for God. What it is to be man, therefore, cannot be abstracted from what it is to be God. The image binds the two together.[76] However, because the image is grounded in transcendence, the response remains problematical to man in the sense that he does not possess it in an autonomous way. The covenant response is therefore a human response, not merely because the subject is a creature, but because it is an affirmation of the transcendence of God as the limit, and, therefore, the centre of creaturely existence. *Second*, the subject of covenant response can therefore be immediately as well as mediately human. That is, the response from the side of the creature (a human response) can be made as well by the eternal Logos as the created logos, or, one could say, as well by God as by the image of God. It is the transcendence of God which is active in constituting the image of God in its reality. The point which I wish to make here is that the eternal Logos can take humanity to himself, and in and through that humanity make a real covenant response towards the Father because the Logos is also the eternal Son. This would appear to avoid the Apollinarian tendency towards monothelitism by constituting the covenant response in a creaturely will towards the Creator, while at the same time stopping short of Nestorianism which tends to restrict a human response to a merely human subject. When humanity is not defined in static, substantialistic terms, but in a dynamic, relational sense, a truly human act is thus constituted by that creative power and

75. 'Other', as distinguished from 'other' (lower case), refers to the Other as a personal subject, as another *Agent,* and not to another *thing*. In this context, there is no implied reference to the Other being a divine subject as distinguished from a human subject through the capitalization. The Other can be either the divine or human Subject acting as a personal agent.

76. Another way of stating the distinctive quality of 'being human' in terms of the image of God is to ground humanity in *ek-static* personhood. See my *Historical Transcendence,* p. 240, n. 29.

love which transcends it by limiting it.[77] This would also seem to offer us a way through the question which tormented the kenotic Christologists—namely, the question of the proper subject of the manhood of Christ. The more important question as to how both human covenant response and the divine transcending limit which constitutes that response can be understood as one act of God will be taken up shortly.

The covenant response which man did not make in Adam, remained to be worked out through the humanity of Israel. This, which we have shown to be the second part of the logic of the Incarnation, has as its pre-history the 'one Israelite', the man who is for God.[78] When the 'Word became flesh', not only was the limiting transcendence brought into human, historical existence in an absolute sense, but the covenant response was at the same time being worked out through this Man who was for God. This constitutes a preliminary statement of that which we could expect to be the case based on the inner logic of Israel's relation to God. It remains to demonstrate how this was the case in the person of Christ.

Perhaps a comment is in order at this point concerning the slogan which has been wrested from Bonhoeffer's later writings: Jesus—the man for others.[79] There is no lack of truth in the statement that Jesus had an ultimate concern for others. But this does not reach the fundamental truth of the fact that, first and foremost, Jesus was the man who was for God; or rather, one should say, that

77. My argument for this rests upon the doctrine of the image of God as explicated by the person of Jesus Christ. In this case I am making certain anthropological assertions based on Christological conclusions. As this is consistent with my general methodology, I see no reason why these assertions are not valid for the purpose of my exposition. While not accepting all his conclusions concerning the need for the divine Logos to restrict his deity in becoming the subject of the manhood of Christ, I think Bishop Weston has stated the case well when he says: 'I think the fundamental error of all who seek a human or divine-human subject of manhood lies in the false belief that the ego of manhood must, in some sense, be necessarily a man. . . .If man be God's image, may not the Son of God be presumed to possess, at least, all those characteristics that are essential to man's ego?' *The One Christ,* Longmans, Green, and Co., London, 1914, pp. 107-108.
78. See *Historical Transcendence,* p. 144.
79. What Bonhoeffer actually says is: 'Encounter with Jesus Christ. The experience that a transformation of all human life is given in the fact that "Jesus is there only for others". His "being there for others", is the experience of transcendence'. 'Outline for a Book,' *Letters and Papers From Prison,* p. 381. Paul van Buren is one among several others who

first and foremost he was the God who was for man, and as this, he also was the man who was for God.[80] The language of ultimate concern expressed in terms of co-humanity simply does not grasp the profound truth of the Incarnation, nor does it expose its inner logic. If Jesus is only a man for others in an ultimate sense, the cross becomes a monstrosity where Jesus crucifies his own manhood in an ultimacy that only carries the whisper of an ethical ideal. The transcendence of co-humanity cannot be computed to a 'higher power' and so become the transcendence of God. Our first parents learned this to their sorrow, and *nonetheless* were not left without a way of making a response through the cultus which God himself provided. It is this response on the part of man to God, rather than merely response of man to man, that marks both the style and the content of the life of Jesus Christ.

The 'community of reciprocity' which was portrayed in the life of Israel, that is, a covenant with God with its appropriate form of covenant response, can be seen as the rationale of the Incarnation. Jesus, as the 'one Israelite', unites humanity with the will and Word of God. From the beginning to the end, he is one person, his actions are not different from his innermost heart. He *is* the truth, even as he *does* the truth.[81] That which was true *of* him became truth *in* him. The unity of the Word with flesh was grasped by him as the single truth of his life. His early years of growth were years of growth into this knowledge and into this responsibility. A growth, not merely into 'adulthood', but growth of the covenant response itself in two dimensions. *First*, an increasing solidarity with human 'flesh', so that by the end he was identified with the lowliest and with the lost. In this growth of his own identity with humanity, he increasingly began to bear the sicknesses, the in-

---

interprets Bonhoeffer here to mean that one can see in this kind of a Jesus an alternative to the 'God hypothesis': 'To experience God, he wrote [i.e., Bonhoeffer], means to meet Jesus Christ. To be in a relationship to God means to live for others, sharing in that form of life which was Jesus Christ's. . . .For to live with God, *"vor und mitt Gott"*, is, as we have said already, to meet Jesus Christ, to live a new life of "being-for-others". Again, the frame of reference is the same: the biblical story of "the man-for-others".' *Theological Explorations,* p. 114.

80. It is upon this humanity of the Word in Jesus that we must reflect deeply if we are to penetrate into the inner relation between the Word of God and man's response, but we must not forget that He is word of man in answer to God only in that He is first and foremost Word of God become man.' T. F. Torrance, *God and Rationality,* p. 139.

81. Cf. John 14:6: 'I am the way, and the truth, and the life.'

juries, the weakness and the condemnation of the god-less. His saying: 'Come to me, all who labour and are heavy laden, and I will give you rest,'[82] was not merely an offer of an easier way, but was a self-conscious 'yoking' of himself to their lives. 'Take my yoke upon you, and learn from me,'[83] continued Jesus, and here we see the *second* dimension of his growth: a deepening passion for the union of flesh with God through the supreme word-act of love. 'I have a baptism to be baptized with; and how I am constrained until it is accomplished!'[84] That which we tend to think of as an 'act of reconciliation' and centred in the death upon the cross, was not a 'transaction' which took place above and distinct from his own person. This 'reconciling' work is already at work through the growing covenant response which Jesus is working out through the unity of Word and flesh. The concept of growth here must not be confused with a growth of self-consciousness either in terms of his deity or his mission, that is, a growth in what we would call 'personality'. Rather, the growth is a life of perfect and active obedience to the will of the Father—a progressive 'working into' the estranged flesh of humanity and also a progressive 'working out' of that same humanity, a will that perfectly conforms to the will of the Father.[85]

82. Matthew 11:38.
83. Matthew 11:39.
84. Luke 12:50. As an example of the way in which this progressive deepening of Jesus' own passion for the unity of the Father's will with humanity as the single purpose of his own life proceeds, one should take note of the structure used by Luke to portray this process. There are at least four phases in this progression, each introduced by the literary landmark 'on the way to Jerusalem'. The first is at Luke 9:51: 'When the days drew near for him to be received up, he set his face to go to Jerusalem.' This is followed by 13:22: 'He went on his way through towns and villages, teaching, and journeying towards Jerusalem'; 17:11: 'On the way to Jerusalem he was passing along between Samaria and Galilee'; and 19:28: 'And when he had said this, he went on ahead, going up to Jerusalem.' Within each of these sections, a progressive intensification of tension between Jesus and the authorities takes place, while at the same time his own life and ministry is narrowed down to a determination to die at Jerusalem, if need be, to complete the 'baptism' by which the Spirit has united Word to flesh and so bring man to the truth of God. See Luke 9:57-62; 13:31-35; 17:33.
85. The theme of growth is a predominate emphasis in the thought of Irenaeus, both with respect to the true nature of man: that is, creation is growth into the image of God; and with respect to the person of Christ: that is, the Incarnation is the completion of creation through the growth of the man Jesus into that which he actually is—the second Adam. 'For thou, O

That which takes place on the cross is no different in kind from that which has been taking place throughout his life incarnationally. The steadfastness of his obedience to God and his dependence upon his Father's will was perfectly manifested from the beginning. But with his increasing solidarity with estranged humanity, the dimensions of that obedience and that dependence deepened and widened. So that, by the end, his obedience was from the 'other side' of that gulf brought about by man's wilful estrangement. The steadfastness and obedience in his Baptism was a 'younger' response than his steadfastness and obedience in Gethsemane, though perfect in its unity with the Father. The very truth of that response on the part of man to God had not yet been driven by untruth into the wilderness to be tempted, into the temple to be scorned, onto the dusty roads and into the cold nights to be wearied, and last of all, into the hands of his enemies to be betrayed, spat upon, and nailed to the cross, there to be himself estranged and banished from the face of God.

The cry from the cross, 'My God, my God, why hast thou

---

man, are not uncreated being nor didst thou always co-exist with God, as did His own Word; but now, through His pre-eminent goodness, receiving the beginning of thy creation, thou dost gradually learn from the Word the dispensations of God who made thee . . . this Being alone is truly God and Father, who formed this world, fashioned man, and bestowed the faculty of increase on His own creation.' *Irenaeus Against Heresies,* Ante-Nicene Christian Library, T. & T. Clark, Edinburgh, 1868, Vol. I, pp. 214, 219 (II/25/3; II/28/1). The motif of growth for Irenaeus follows the scheme of child-son-man. Adam awakens to his existence much the same way as a child comes to discover his own existence. Thus, instead of Adam being created as 'completed' man, he is to 'become man' through his human growth which will culminate only with the final realization of his destiny, which is actually to be in the 'likeness and image of God'. Cf. G. Wingren, *Man and the Incarnation,* Oliver and Boyd, Edinburgh/London, 1959, p. 26. Between the child (Adam) and the man (perfected humanity) stands the Son, Jesus, as the Son of God, in bearing Adam's flesh brought the humanity of Adam (all men) into a state of health (possibility of growth) and removed the 'injury' which occurred through the fall. The relation of Jesus' 'growth' to the creation of man is completed in the resurrection: 'The Father accomplishes His first decree for Creation in the life which Jesus lived. Uncorrupted human life ends in *resurrection*—lordship over death—by the same inner necessity which brought Adam's perverted life to end in death—the destruction of the power of life. The conflict which Jesus had to undergo for His life to be fully human and the reverse of Adam's embraced the Resurrection also, and not merely the period up to his death.' *Ibid.,* p. 127.

forsaken me?', is the full measure of the distance from which the covenant response had to come, even as it was also the full measure of the dimensions to which the Incarnation had to reach. But the cry of astonishment and horror must not be abstracted from the logic of the Incarnation and made into a kenotic Christology on its own terms. It must be understood within the dynamic of covenant response, where the solidarity of the Word with the heart of the Father was as deep and irrevocable as the solidarity with the estranged flesh of humanity. It is the 'Man who is for God' who utters the God-forsaken cry, and because of this, and only because of this, this cry becomes the covenant response. And with it, the created image is restored, and the way of authentic human freedom opened up. Through a life of sonship which even the death of an estranged man could not shatter, he brought freedom to a humanity in bondage.

This gift of freedom and covenant—which in cultic language is called atonement—is intrinsically bound up with the Incarnation from beginning to end, and comes to man, not merely through a legal imputation, as though a transaction takes place 'over the head' of Jesus, but is given in the humanity of Christ himself. As the second Adam, he is also the last Adam. The covenant response has been worked out to the end (the eschaton), and thus is both historical and eschatological; it is both the first and the final covenant response. As the Man who is for God, the covenant of creation finds its fulfilment in his person which is also his act. He received the Spirit upon humanity by taking estranged humanity back into the 'Father's house'.[86] The gift of the Spirit is thus the gift of completed covenant response, it is the gift of freedom which has its ontic structure in the person of Jesus Christ where the

86. Along with the concept of growth in the thought of Irenaeus, there is the concept of the Word and the Spirit as the 'two hands of God' which 'formed' the first man in the image and likeness of God, and also work to 'prepare' man in the Incarnation to attain that image and likeness. Cf. *Irenaeus Against Heresies,* Vol. I, p. 377 (IV/pref. 4); p. 442 (IV/22/5); and Vol. II, p. 58 (V/1/3). The relation of the Holy Spirit to the humanity of Christ is pictured by Irenaeus as having a 'preparatory' function in the Spirit's dwelling in the human race: 'For God promised, that in the last times He would pour Him [the Spirit] upon His servants and handmaids, that they might prophesy; wherefore He did also descend upon the Son of God, made the Son of man, becoming accustomed in fellowship with Him to dwell in the human race, to rest with human beings, and to dwell in the workmanship of God, working the will of the Father in them, and renewing them from their old habits into the newness of Christ.' *Ibid.,* Vol. I, p. 334 (III/17/1). Cf. also p. 442 (IV/20/5), and Vol. II, p. 44 (IV/38/3).

transcending limit meets the covenant response in a completed and living unity.[87]

The question which we asked at the outset was, To what extent can we still speak of transcendence in the face of the cry of dereliction from the cross? This now seems possible to answer in two ways. *First*, the covenant response which Jesus worked out through his life of obedience was totally human in an immediate sense. That is, it was a life directed towards the limiting transcendence of the Father by the divine Logos in utter solidarity with estranged human flesh. From this, I would argue that the covenant response worked out by Jesus was an act of the transcendence of God through the divine Logos. I have already shown how this can be understood in such a way that the humanity of the covenant response is no less real, even though the divine Logos be the subject of that human response.[88] Second, the gulf between estranged flesh and God revealed through the experience of Jesus on

87. Cf. here the gift of the Holy Spirit after the resurrection (John 20:22). When the ontic structure of the gift of freedom by the Spirit is said to be constituted by the 'living unity' of transcendence and response in Jesus, the matter of the resurrection is brought into view. It is beyond the scope of this book to take up the problems of the resurrection from the standpoint of both textual and historical criticism, but it is not irrelevant to my argument to say that the resurrection of Jesus is presupposed to be a reality of an ontic nature which preceded the testimony of the gospel accounts. The Incarnation, therefore, continues to be the ontic structure for the gift of the Spirit through the living person of Jesus Christ. The final chapter of *Historical Transcendence* shows how the resurrection of Christ is the eschaton of all humanity.

88. The assertion made earlier (*Historical Transcendence,* pp. 157, n. 42, 170f.) that the eternal Logos can make an immediate human covenant response from the side of the creature without falling into the error of Nestorianism involves a merging of both a creaturely will and a divine will in a dynamic and personal life of obedience. Rather than starting with two 'wills', one human and one divine, and then proceeding to think of them as one act, I would rather begin with the one person Jesus Christ whose personhood is constituted as eternal Sonship acting towards the Father from and as creaturely being. What this involves, though it is not yet made clear, is an intra-divine transcendence with an intrinsic cosmic structure concretized as the image of God in man through the dynamic power (*exousia*) of Logos and Spirit. What I have called 'historical transcendence' might then be said to be the extrinsic reality of an intrinsic structure which is the nature of God himself. Thus, instead of positing two distinct realities which create a dualism between God and the cosmos, we would be led to think of one reality (God) who expresses himself intrinsically (eternally) and extrinsically (creatively).

the cross does not obliterate the covenant response of Jesus worked out in the flesh, but exposes the real dimension of estrangement from which that covenant response had to be made. In this sense, the 'God-forsaken' experience is integral to the covenant response as the lesser is included in the greater.

To be God-forsaken is a lesser dimension of reality than to be God-created. If this were not true, the transcendence of God would itself have a limiting reality other than God himself. The Incarnation then is the greater love which includes within it the lesser evil of estrangement. It is the greater act of belief which includes within it the lesser act of unbelief. What I am saying is that Incarnation as an act of God is the act of his transcendence, and, as such, from the 'far side' of man's estrangement towards the centre, the limit which gives freedom and life. Jesus Christ, then, is both the 'far side', indeed, the furthest side of God's transcendence, as well as the centre of God's transcendence. We must remember that in the creation covenant, the distance between Creator and creature was set at its absolute limit. In other words, the space between God and man was set as the space of God's transcendence. The estrangement of man through a failure to make covenant response and taking over the limit for himself, cannot *increase* that distance and so pass beyond God's transcendence.[89] Therefore, it is still possible for a human covenant response to be made, even when the estrangement is absolute, *as long as* transcendence is in view. For it is transcendence as the limit which gives covenant response both its possibility and its actuality.[90] In Christ, when the 'Word became flesh', transcendence did 'come into view', so that what was humanly impossible for the created logos was now humanly possi-

89. The suggestion that a doctrine of universalism is implied if 'nothing can pass beyond God's transcendence', is probably indefensible, although not thereby established. To consider the alternative, that something could pass beyond God's transcendence, involves an equally serious problem, and in my mind, a totally unacceptable conclusion—that God does not transcend total reality or total possibility. It would be an interesting exercise to explore the language of the Apostles' Creed concerning the 'descent into hell', and see if this is not, in fact, a way of speaking of the transcendence of God through the *kenosis,* and so a way of considering hell itself to be the lesser evil within the greater love of the Incarnation. I do not think that what I am setting forth here is in any way a 'minimizing' of the reality of what it is to be 'God-forsaken', but rather, is a way of 'maximizing' what it is to be 'God-created'.

90. Whether there is an 'eclipse of God' possible of such a nature that transcendence 'never comes into view', and thus an eternal estrangement takes place, I am not prepared to say, and furthermore, do not consider it relevant to the argument I am making.

ble for the uncreated Logos. It is in this way that the *kenosis*, the self-emptying, of Christ can be understood as the transcendence of God.

What remains inexplicable, at least to the extent that we have considered transcendence, is how transcendence can be conceived of as being active on 'both sides' of the gulf of absolute estrangement. Or, how Christ can be both the limit and the response to that limit. What is forced upon us, is the implication that if the transcendence of God is the greater love within which the lesser evil of estrangement is included, the cry of God-forsakenness from the cross took place *within* the relation of Father and Son. To be precise, within that eternal relation. If there were no other hints in the history of revelation, the *kenosis* itself would seem to demand a doctrine of the Trinity. The inner logic of historical transcendence appears to have its roots in the intra-divine structure of God's own being. Some tentative explorations in this direction should at least be made.

The doctrine of the Trinity has already been brought into consideration by the earlier suggestion that the *kenosis* could not have represented an ontic cleft within the Godhead, and that the penetration of the Word into flesh must, therefore, be considered to be an *intra-* rather than an *extra-*trinitarian movement of divine transcendence.[91] As Barth so well puts it, the Son who goes into the far country in order that man may return home, does not do this without the Father, for he and the Father are one.[92] One of the most fruitful insights into this relationship between Father and Son, even at the furthest extremity of self-emptying on the part of the Son, is the life of prayer which Jesus experienced. The prayers of Jesus exhibit two things: first, the intimate communion which he possessed with the Father in virtue of his sonship. That is, prayer was for him an intimacy of communion brought into the flesh, not merely a necessity of communication occasioned by the flesh.

> I thank thee, Father, Lord of heaven and earth, that thou hast hidden these things from the wise and understanding and revealed them to babes; yea, Father, for such was thy gracious will. All things have been delivered to me by my Father; and no one knows the Son except the Father, and no one knows the Father except the Son and any one to whom the Son chooses to reveal him.[93]

91. See *Historical Transcendence*, p. 240.
92. *Church Dogmatics*, IV/2, p. 43.
93. Matthew 11:25–27.

The second thing which the prayers of Jesus reveal is that prayer is possible from the 'far side' of estrangement, as well as from the 'near side' of intimacy. Though Jesus prays 'in the flesh' and subject to all the limitations and even contradictions of the flesh, not least of which is the disinclination of estranged flesh towards God, he not only *can* pray through a nature which is common to ours, but he *does* pray. And there is no force, demonic or delusive, which can break that communion. His prayers unfolded the life of the eternal Son with the Father out into the world and brought the tattered and tormented edges of all creation into that life. At least two of the words from the cross were prayers—'Father, forgive them'; and, 'Father, into thy hands I commit my spirit'—and there is no reason to think that the cry of dereliction was not also a prayer: 'My God, my God, why hast thou forsaken me?' If in that moment, the estranged flesh was brought into that space between the Son of God and the Father, so that the face of the Father was eclipsed from the face of the Son, we are given a new and terrible glimpse of the depths of divine transcendence.

Whatever the depth of the humility, or humiliation, which the Incarnation demanded of the eternal Son, we are not to conclude that there was any 'way of humility' here which was not intrinsic to the eternal life of the Son with the Father.[94] When we see God for us, we see him *as he is*.[95] This 'way of *kenosis*' which we see as the movement of the Son towards the Father in the Spirit, is not a *kenosis*, or a self-emptying in the form of a renunciation of the nature of God himself, but is a self-emptying precisely because self-renunciation is the very nature of God himself. Here, self-

94. It should be noted here, that if one makes a distinction between the Incarnation and the humiliation, as Bonhoeffer does (*Christology,* p. 111), then the humiliation is related to the bearing of sinful flesh while the Incarnation is related to created manhood. Thus, humiliation becomes an act of the Incarnate one and is restricted to the period prior to the exaltation. With this distinction, and in this case Bonhoeffer is following the traditional Lutheran Christology, one is left with a humiliation which is not intrinsic to the Son's eternal relationship with the Father, unless the Incarnation itself is presumed to include the humiliation, in which case the distinction would seem to be irrelevant.

95. Cf. K. Barth, *Church Dogmatics,* IV/2, who says: 'We can only say that in its great inconceivability—always new and surprising when we try to conceive it—this reason is holy and righteous and worthy of God because it corresponds to the humility of the eternal Son as it takes place in supreme reality in the intra-trinitarian life of God Himself; and although it cannot be deduced from this, in the light of it can be recognised as a reason which is in itself both clear and well-founded.' p. 43.

renunciation must be understood in a positive, and not a negative sense. It is the renunciation of a negative self-existence, in the form of a 'separate' kind of existence, which constitutes the eternal relation of Father, Son and Spirit. Thus, the Incarnation of the Son of God is the same Spirit of positive self-renunciation which is the very nature of divine existence. It is actually the dynamic dimension of love as activity.

Therefore, this movement of God 'outside of himself' to become flesh, and so bring estranged humanity into eternal and perfect unity with himself, demands that we now understand the nature of God in such a way that 'outside of' is also 'within'. At this point, our language, with its 'opticizing' tendencies, becomes too rigid for the dynamic and fluid inner logic of the transcendence of God, which is an *intra*-active personal reality of love and not just an *inter*-active force. When the eternal Subject prays to the eternal Subject, as a son talks with a father, we can hear what we cannot see—the intra-action of divine communion with one of the voices speaking out of history.[96]

96. For the assertion implied at this point, that the structure of the Trinity which is disclosed to us through the redemptive activity of Christ and the Spirit through the Incarnation is also the inner structure of the eternal Trinity, cf. Karl Rahner, *The Trinity,* who has as the basic thesis of this book: 'The "economic" Trinity is the "immanent" Trinity and the "immanent" Trinity is the "economic" Trinity.' p. 22. Rahner argues that the true and authentic concept of grace interprets grace as a *self*-communication of God in Christ and in his Spirit. Therefore, what we know of God as grace *is* the nature of God, and not merely a created 'mode of being' which would not actually reflect his own nature. What Rahner calls the 'immanent' Trinity is what I have called the eternal relation of the Son and Spirit to the Father. What he calls the 'economic' Trinity I would now call the transcendent Trinity. That is, the immanent Trinity is historically revealed as an intra-trinitarian communion which transcends itself to inter-act with man. This follows from my basic thesis that when God acts, he transcends himself to act in and with history. Where I would like to question Rahner further is what he means by the Incarnation of the Son as an act which takes place 'outside' the intra-divine life of the Trinity (*ibid.*, p. 23). If he only means that the Son becomes the Incarnate Word while the Spirit and the Father do not, then I could agree. But if he means that the humiliation of the Son involved an act on the part of one person in the Godhead to the exclusion of that intra-divine action which is constitutive of the nature of God, I could not agree. And I do not think that this is what Rahner would want to say. And this is borne out by what Rahner later says: ' . . . the immanent and the economic Logos, are strictly the same.' (*Ibid.*, p. 33.) This basically supports what I have already said concerning the fact that there is no 'way of humility' for the Son which is not already intrinsically part of his relationship with the Father.

When that voice which speaks out of history is heard to be the voice of the eternal Son of God, then the subject of that manhood is the transcendence of God fully and actively revealed within history.[97] But the inner logic of historical transcendence is not simply the inter-action of history and transcendence, but the intra-action of divine transcendence, with history and humanity now given speaking parts! History is not devaluated, nor humanity violated by its active participation in this divine transcendence. For the covenant of creation was established out of the transcendence of God and destined to this end.[98] What I am suggesting here is that the *kenosis* seems to expose to us a relation between the Son and the Father in which each 'transcends' the other. This is what I have called an intra-divine transcendence. While this way of putting it is not a very happy choice of expression to state the inner relations of the triune God, as it would appear to divide the unity of God into a plurality of persons, I would like to hold to the use of transcendence as a word which expresses activity rather than simply 'nature', or 'being'. This *activity* of communion *within* the unity of the Godhead becomes absolutely distinct through the Incarnation, as the Son, Father and Spirit act in particular ways which presuppose the activity of each other. It is this *activity* of the Son with respect to the Father, an activity which I have pointed to in the prayers of Jesus, which I choose to call the *intra*-divine transcendence of God.

We can say, then, that the first result of our tentative exploration

97. That controversy over the person of Christ which took place in the 16th century between the Reformed and Lutheran theologians had the truth on both sides. The Reformed Christology which stressed the eternal Logos who existed *totus intra et extra,* wished to maintain the transcendence of the Incarnation outside of the flesh, while the Lutheran Christology which stressed the eternal Logos *totus intra* wished to maintain the transcendence of the Incarnation within the flesh. The resulting kenotic controversy foundered hopelessly on a scholastic methodology which could not conceive of divine transcendence in dynamic and trinitarian terms. It was the *kenosis* itself which could have permitted them to come to a new understanding of the doctrine of God, if their concepts of the nature of God had not already been so rigidly formed. T. F. Torrance holds that the thought patterns which prevented them from grasping the dynamic of transcendence was a 'container' concept of space. *Space, Time and Incarnation,* pp. 28ff.

98. Cf. here, Ephesians 1:3–10, especially verse 4: ' . . . even as he chose us in him before the foundation of the world, that we should be holy and blameless before him.' Paul appears here to have grasped this fundamental relation of transcendence to the covenant of creation, and sees its fulfilment in the new covenant which Jesus effects in a final, or eschatological sense.

into the inner logic of the trinitarian structure of historical transcendence has been the discovery that divine transcendence is, first of all, an intra-active personal reality which can have an historical as well as an eternal dimension. The exploration can now be carried one small step forward by suggesting that in the Incarnation there is also an *inter*-active personal reality of divine transcendence through which a community is established between the eternal Logos and humanity. The *inter*-action as distinguished from the *intra*-action of divine transcendence suggests that, while there is a real 'otherness' between God and man constituted by God's transcendence of man as limit, there is also a structure of real inter-relatedness between God and man. The *inter*-action between God and man which has its ground in the created image, is a reality of relation constituted by the transcendence of God, but it is not the *intra*-action of divine transcendence itself. That is to say, the community of relation between the Creator and creature is 'other' than the community of relation which exists between the Father, Son and Holy Spirit. Although it must also be said that the former is the image of the latter. Consequently, I would say that the transcendence of *inter*-action is the image of the transcendence of *intra*-action.

Now what does this mean? It means that just as the Son could make the covenant response through his own humanity, taking humanity into the intra-divine movement of Son to Father, so he could make that response in and for our humanity through a community of relation—or inter-action—with humanity itself. For there exists intrinsic to humanity itself the real image of a community of relation. This image, which is grounded in the intra-divine transcendence, provides the basis for solidarity, or a community, between the humanity of Christ and the humanity of every other person.

This community of inter-action can be clearly seen as an integral part of the Incarnation itself. From the very beginning of Jesus' ministry, he gathered around himself a little flock of 'learners', the twelve, who would not only share his teaching, but share his life and inevitably share his sufferings. Not only were they summoned to share his life, but he entered into *their* existence as well. Baptized by John, Jesus placed himself into a solidarity of community with the 'sinners'.[99] While one could see obvious significance in the twelve as the re-constitution of a new Israel, there appeared a more profound basis for their existence after the 'point of no re-

99. Matthew 3:13–17.

turn' at Caesarea Philippi. 'From that time Jesus began to show his disciples that he must go to Jerusalem and suffer many things from the elders and chief priests and scribes, and be killed, and on the third day be raised.'[100] Not only would he not be dissuaded from this by a loyal but misunderstanding Peter, he made no attempt to break the bond which he had established between them and himself, but instead drew it all the tighter by sharing with them his own kenotic way: 'Then Jesus told his disciples, "If any man would come after me, let him deny himself and take up his cross and follow me".'[101] Here was a concept of community which cut deeper than any form of social or fraternal bond. This was more than co-humanity. Their own humanity was being prepared for a gift which they could not possibly have understood, though he gave them intimations: 'I will pray the Father, and he will give you another Counsellor, to be with you for ever, even the Spirit of truth.'[102]

But now it is Gethsemane and Calvary. And the little flock draw back in horror and fear. An unbridgeable chasm seems to be opening up between them and him, made all the more impossible by his words: 'Take, eat; this is my body....Drink of it, all of you; for this is my blood of the covenant,...'[103] He was giving them himself, and yet he was giving himself up to death. He was going where they could not follow, and yet he was not going to leave them desolate, but would come to them.[104]

When the *kenosis* is followed as it makes its way deeper into the humanity of Jesus' flesh, there is also to be discerned a progressive development of a kenotic community which cannot be understood purely in terms of the Incarnate Word. By that I mean that the transcendence of God which we have seen to be operative in covenant response exposes the intra-divine transcendence of the eternal Son in relationship to the Father. But now, with the growth of this little community around Jesus, there emerges a dimension to the *kenosis* which calls for a third dimension of intra-divine transcendence. The Son is leaving, but his little flock will not be alone. They are to receive the 'one he will send to them', and then not only will he be with them, but the Father as well.[105] 'Here we are forced to see that the *inter*-action between Jesus and his little

100. Matthew 16:21.
101. Matthew 16:24.
102. John 14:16.
103. Matthew 26:26, 27.
104. Cf. John 13:33; 14:18–19.
105. John 14:18–19.

flock has its place in the *kenosis* as the *place* where Spirit forms the true community between God and man. But this community is formed by transcendence, for it is brought into the intra-divine transcendence so that it is also the *place* where Father and Son make their 'home'.[106] When it was earlier suggested that the 'existence-form of Spirit is flesh', we can now see how this is realized in the community of lived transcendence. For Spirit needs *place* in which to work out the intra-divine transcendence which belongs to the historical reality of the Incarnate Logos.[107]

What we see happening in the life of Jesus, along with his covenant response, is the self-conscious way in which he takes man 'into community' with him. The way of humility is not just

---

106. John 14:23. Cf. T. F. Torrance: '. . . the Spirit is the presence of the Transcendent Being of God.' *God and Rationality,* p. 175.

107. For a more penetrating analysis of the concept of 'place' as a two-dimensional 'house of being', one should see the essay by William Kluback and Jean T. Wilde included as the Introduction to Martin Heidegger's book, *The Question of Being,* Vision Press, London, 1959. Kluback and Wilde argue that Heidegger can be faulted for disregarding the importance of the practical, or horizontal dimension of man's existence, and that his concern with ontological existence (spirit) is at the expense of the historical level (the state, or political existence). 'Place' is not merely a conjunction of time and space, but the structure of being where transcendence (spirit) has concrete reality: ' "Place" places man in that dimension which reveals the revealing meaning of being. Man is involved in "place" in two dimensions, horizontal and vertical. The horizontal dimension is determined by his political relationship. Vertically, being is a dimension hiding the uniqueness of Being, but at the same time it is the place of Being. "Place" places man in such a way that it reveals the external bounds of his existence and at the same time the depths of his freedom and reality. . . . The two dimensions appear in separation but are housed in unity and reveal each other to each other' (p. 19). With this concept of 'place,' the state is the 'house of man' in which he is lifted from his exclusive individuality into a higher totality, from which he receives meaning and to whose end he is inseparably united. With the substitution of community for state, one can find here an interesting paradigm for a way of understanding how 'community' is the 'place' where the intra-divine relationship of the triune God has its 'house' in man. And also, how man can live from this 'place' of transcendence, and yet not be drawn out of the historical reality of his 'place' in the world. One can also see in this an explanation for the fact that, while Judas had no 'place' with the little flock, despite his fellowship in the flesh, Peter did, despite his wavering in the flesh. With the giving of the Holy Spirit, that which had only been ambiguous and precarious now becomes concretely the Body of Christ—the 'place' where transcendence is placed into the world.

the way of the Son, but it is the way of sonship. It is the 'place' where the intra-divine transcendence is concretized as an inter-acting community between God and man. The self-emptying is not just a vicarious act on the part of one for the many, but is itself essentially an act of community. It is first of all an act of intra-divine community in which the Son moves towards the Father in the Spirit. But this is at the same time divine transcendence which *inter*-acts with humanity and binds men into community by bind-ing them to God himself. This 'law of *kenosis*', then, which is intrinsic to the intra-divine community, and which is the 'mind of Christ', forms the ontic structure of the community to which men are called in Christ. This ontic structure is, in fact, the intra-divine transcendence of Father, Son and Holy Spirit concretized in his-tory through the Incarnation. Thus, Paul appeals to the Christians at Philippi to 'have this mind among yourselves, which you have in Christ Jesus, who, though he was in the form of God, did not count equality with God a thing to be grasped, but emptied him-self, . . .'[108] When *kenosis* is seen as the form of intra-divine com-munity, the appeal is not merely to an ethical type of individual self-renunciation, but the appeal is to this kenotic way of life, which is the way of community.[109]

We can no longer be in any doubt about this: it is not lowliness or suffering, or even humility, which is divine in itself and as such.[110] The tendency, which was even a temptation to Bonhoef-fer, to make the divine way of kenosis reversible, is to distort the transcendence of God itself.[111] There is no 'power in weakness' which, by itself, transcends the world and offers an ontological

108. Philippians 2:5-7.
109. For a fine commentary on the 'law of humbling' which is found throughout the New Testament, and which reflects the kenotic way of divine Sonship, see K. Barth, *Church Dogmatics*, IV/1, pp. 188ff.
110. There is no lowliness which is divine in itself and as such. There is therefore no general principle of the cross in which we have to do with God (in principle). The cross in the New Testament is not a kind of symbol of an outlook which is negatively orientated, which speculates *à la baisse*. The limits of humanity are one thing, but God's visitation of us in the limits of humanity, in our creatureliness, in our humanness, in our sinfulness and mortality, in the incarnation of His Word and the crucifixion of His Son, that is quite another.' K. Barth, *Church Dogmatics*, IV/1, pp. 191-192.
111. E. Bethge says of Bonhoeffer: 'The belief in the power of weakness was one of Bonhoeffer's most basic insights, and he was to hold to it throughout his theological life. . . .In the interpretation of the weak Word, we are close to the profoundest thought ever expressed by Bonhoeffer.' *Dietrich Bonhoeffer*, p. 374.

vision of Christ. Nor can one simply make the way of humility an ontic form of existence and thereby reach the transcendence of God. This is what it means to say that the divine way of *kenosis* is not reversible. The virtue of Christ was not a superior humility and a more ultimate and self-less suffering, but it was his Sonship which was his eternally, and which he worked out through his humanity. This is why I have said that the ontic structure of community is not in co-humanity, not even in a co-suffering-humanity, but rather, it is in the intra-divine transcendence concretely given in the Incarnation. While this may well have been implicit in Bonhoeffer's thought, his failure to explicate it in terms of 'this worldly' transcendence cut the top off his Christology and paved the way for a 'post-Bonhoefferian' concept of transcendence with its ontic structure located in co-humanity. While there is a dimension of co-humanity to Christ's Sonship, because his humanity was also ours, his Sonship became a way of suffering and humiliation in order to make good the covenant response. So that the particular way of humility for Christ was not what was left after stripping himself of divine transcendence, but what was there when divine transcendence in the form of eternal Sonship brought man into total and final obedience to the Father. The inner logic of historical transcendence is then, first of all, the intra-divine transcendence of Sonship worked out through the humanity and history of the Incarnation, which is the existence-form of the creature. This is the transcendence of the 'God who is for man'. In this way, the *kenosis* brings the limiting transcendence of God, as a transcendence which is already community, into inescapable proximity to man.

But having said 'first of all', there obviously is a further truth implied in the logic of historical transcendence. This too is revealed through *kenosis* in the form of an *inter*-active transcendence by which community is created *between* God and man. The covenant response worked out through the estranged flesh which the eternal Son assumed, became a 'community of covenant response' through the inter-active transcendence of the Spirit. The kenotic way which is intrinsic to the nature of God, and thus is the way of intra-divine transcendence, is no special way which the Son of God took so that man could go 'another way'—the way which leads to individualism. But it is the way of unity with God, it is the way of freedom, it is the way of life, it is the way of the Spirit, and as such, it is the way of lived transcendence. This is the transcendence of the 'Man who is for God'.

And so there does appear to be a rationale for the transcendence of God. The basic 'grammar' of this transcendence is given to us in the inner structure of the Incarnation. Which, as we have seen, is the inner structure of the intra-divine communion of God himself. That is, from the depths of our humanity, the Son meets himself in the Father through the Spirit. The 'grammar' of the language of transcendence, thus, is decidedly trinitarian, and, therefore, ontologically derived from the intra-divine transcendence of God himself.

The reality of God comes to us as an activity of transcendence in which God acts as the divine personal agent whose own nature is to inter-act with his creation and his creature. The argument for the basic thesis that transcendence is the act of a personal agent, who is concretely embodied in the act and the inter-action, can now be brought to its conclusion. But the conclusion is not the end. For establishing a rationale for historical transcendence carries with it the imperative of a continuing action.

Where in the world is the 'place' of the Spirit? Where in the world is the limit which man can love, so as to find the centre again? And what does it mean that the reality of God is a 'lived transcendence?' These are the questions which will rise again after the rationale of historical transcendence is tidied up in its neat little package. And these are the questions which carry more than a little concern, not only for the 'little flock', but for the one who has already given thanks—

> *god the dispersed*
> *gathered up again in those who have communed.*
> *out of all our eucharists, this is the first.*

Part Three:

JESUS' MINISTRY IN THE SPIRIT FOR THE SAKE OF THE CHURCH

Editor's Introduction

WE HAVE SEEN THAT ALL MINISTRY IS THE MINISTRY OF Christ—his service to the Father which becomes a reconciling ministry on behalf of the world to which he belongs by his own incarnational solidarity with man. However, this ministry does not end with the resurrection and ascension of Christ. It is the will and prayer of Christ (John 17) that his ministry continue through those whom he has received from the Father and in whom he and the Father will come to dwell through the Holy Spirit. "As thou didst send me into the world, so I have sent them into the world" (John 17:18). This verse becomes the "hinge" on which the ministry of Christ turns in to the world. The Church is the predication of Jesus' continued ministry in the world. Thus, as Barth says, Jesus Christ is the community; the community is not Jesus Christ. He does not live because and as it lives, but it lives and grows because he lives and increases.

It is crucial for us to understand at this point that the Church does not exist by virtue of any historical or human predication, but rather it exists as the predication of the on-going ministry of Christ in the world. Thus, it is proper to say that it is ministry which creates and sustains the Church, rather than the Church which creates and sustains ministry. The Church knows itself as it discovers and enacts this ministry.

The material in Part Three has been divided into two subsections. In the first one, five chapters are devoted to the upbuilding and upholding of the Church for ministry. In the second one, there are three chapters on the ordering and equipping of the Church for ministry.

In Chapter 9, Karl Barth carefully lays the foundation for the existence and growth of the Church in the life of Christ himself. The life of the Church as community takes place as the power and operation of the Holy Spirit quickens and assembles believers. The upbuilding proceeds from the completed work of Christ to the upbuilding of community—a provisional representation of the new humanity in the midst of the old. The Church is a theological and confessional fellowship, a community of prayer and worship, of service, of proclamation and hope, existing in solidarity with the world.

This community, says Barth, takes place as *growth,* both extensively and intensively. Growth is the mark of life. Jesus is the immanent power of that life and his own "increase" in the world is the content of the growth. Thus growth is the mark of a healthy and ministering Church.

This community of saints, adds Barth, always faces dangers and needs to be upheld against them, from without and from within. The world is not only around the Church, but within it. Thus, to the degree that the Church does not live by the grace of God, it dies. The marks of its death may be either alienation (secularization) or self-glorification (sacralization). In its own right it is destructible, but as the community of Christ, it is imperishable. Christ upholds the community as his own body through both Scripture and the Holy Spirit.

In Chapter 10, the Church is presented as the "presence" and the "powerlessness" of Christ in the world. This "presence" has both form and power, but is not dependent upon the world for either. The transcendent presence and power is first of all *"kenotic"* in the sense that there is a continuation of Christ's own ministry of solidarity with the world for the sake of its reconciliation to the Father. It is also *"ek-static"* in the sense that it is not an "earth-bound" community, but is determined by and reaches out toward its source of existence in the Creator. This "lived transcendence" is manifested in the concrete acts which "break out" of the constraints imposed by sin and solidarity with the world.

We see here that the Church is upheld in its ministry of reconciliation by its life of transcendence. That is, it exists as the life of Christ, who, in giving himself to the world, lives in intimate communion with the Father. Another way of putting it is to say that Christ's divine service (*leitourgia*) is always *to* the Father *as* one who binds himself to man. This leads us to see that worship cannot be isolated from a ministry of solidarity with the world. The very nature of worship issues out of the history of salvation and is rooted in it.

Consequently, we must consider the event of divine worship as the "law of divine service" (Chapter 11). This divine service, says Barth, embraces and orders the whole life of the Church and is objectively rooted in the event of the historical life of Jesus; from Bethlehem to Golgotha, this on-going life of service to the Father on behalf of man continues in the Church. In public worship, the Church "casts off its anonymity," and the hour strikes, calling the "conspirators" into visible, but provisional, representation of the event of Jesus Christ. This worship takes place as confession in human words, as the fellowship of the baptized, nourished by the body and blood of Christ, who, as the host, presides at his own table. This "liturgical root," says Barth, is the law of the Church, holding it fast to its head, and is the source of its own self-determination as well as the source of correction, discipline, and renewal.

In a well-focused essay (Chapter 12), James Torrance shows how all worship is the on-going worship of the one true worshipper—Jesus Christ. We are graciously called and enabled to participate in his worship in the communion of the Spirit. Thus, worship is a recapitulation of the history of salvation, a manifestation of the Church in the world and a foreshadowing of the judgment and renewal of the world.

The concluding chapter in this first subsection focuses on the Holy Spirit as the agent of worship and of renewal. Here T. F. Torrance stresses the recreative power of the risen and glorified humanity of Christ. The Holy Spirit insists upon a "transparency" which continually brings into judgment the opaqueness and self-assertiveness of the Church, calling it back to the treasure, not the earthen vessel. The descent of the Spirit at Pentecost, says Torrance, lifted the Church out of itself and made it participate in the uncreated life of the Trinity through its union with Christ. The Church does not possess the Spirit, but the Spirit possesses the Church, and enables it to be the continuing ministry of reconciliation which Christ sustains in the world.

In Chapter 14, T. F. Torrance moves us into the second subsection, The Ordering and Equipping of the Church for Ministry. Here Torrance introduces the concept of a "third order," as the proper order of the Church. This new, or third, order is contrasted with the old order of a fallen creation and a subsequent attempt of the creature to "order" existence on its own terms in an attempt to conform to the law of the Creator. What Torrance wishes to make clear is that this third order is the only order in which the divine Word and the human response are already complete in the form of Jesus Christ. This new order is the economy of redemption through which Christ blends the will of the Father and the response of man into one continuous act of obedience and faithfulness. This new order of Jesus Christ is a divinely provided response to the divine law and, as such, is a "perfect order."

The actual order of the Church, however, will be provisional and ambiguous. The Church exists in the old order and continually carries the "disorders" of the fallen creature into its work of the new creation. Although the new order, as it exists concretely in space and time, is genuine, it is nevertheless provisional and ambiguous because of its eschatological dimension. That is, the new order, as it presently exists, cannot be viewed by us as infallible, for infallibility can never be a predication of a historical or human perspective. Whether the Church *is* the community of Christ remains a predication of Christ, through his own ministry and presence in the Church. Thus, the humanly determined order of the Church is a necessary and valid function, but it must be accompanied by repentance and a spirit of humility.

Christ, who consecrates himself so that those whom he sends into the world may be consecrated (John 17:19), is the servant of reconciliation and, as such, occupies the "office" of minister of reconciliation. Chapter 15 discusses the implications of this fundamental truth in terms of Christ's ministry through his whole Church and its ministers. In this essay, baptism is seen to be the qualifying act of consecration and ordination for ministry. Christ's own baptism constitutes his "ordination" to the ministry of reconciliation, and thus our baptism "into Christ" summons us to a life of service and ministry. Each baptized believer is "ordained" into the apostolic, charismatic, and sacrificial ministry of the Church.

This ordination, while not precluding subsequent ordination for special tasks, is foundational for the ministry of the Church. It is important to note, according to this discussion, that special ordination is a setting apart within and for the ministry of the Church, not above and apart from it. Here there is a distinction made between "office" and "occupation," with the office of ministry being held by each baptized person and the occupation being held by those who are set apart by a subsequent act of ordination.

The equipping of the Church for ministry, then, is brought about when Christ presents his gifts to the whole Church through the Spirit. Hans Küng helpfully draws out the implications of this viewpoint in his discussion of the Church as a community of the Spirit (Chapter 16). The Spirit is an eschatological gift, says Küng, which binds the Church into the death and resurrection of Christ, and grounds the Church in the redemptive mission of Christ. As the temple of the Spirit, the Church is under the reign of the Spirit, who, through the "charisms" given to the Church, orders and equips the Church for ministry. These *charismata* are ordinary, not exceptional; they are diverse and unrestricted with respect to office, and find an expression of unity in the edification of the community.

In an intensely practical manner, then, the ministry of Christ in the Spirit upbuilds and upholds the Church for ministry, equipping it with the necessary gifts to be the continuing service of Christ, and ordering it in conformity with the apostolic nature of Christ's own mission. The purpose of this third part is to develop a theology of ministry which provides the Church with a basis for its own self-understanding as a Church which exists *as* ministry, not merely *for the sake of* ministry. The Christological basis for this ministry is identical with the foundation of the Church itself and offers a continuing criterion for correction, renewal, and reconsecration to ministry.

THE UPBUILDING AND UPHOLDING OF THE CHURCH FOR MINISTRY

9

KARL BARTH

The Growth of the Community

WE HAVE BEEN CONSIDERING HOW FAR THAT WHICH IS CALLED
the Church, and claims and seems to be the Church, is really the
true Church. That is, how far does it correspond to its name? How
far does it exist in a practical expression of its essence? How far is
it in fact what it appears to be? How far does it fulfil the claim
which it makes and the expectation which it arouses? We have
given the general answer that it is the true Church in the event or
occurrence or act of its upbuilding as a community. Our next task
is to explain the concept of this event of upbuilding, unfolding it in
its most important dimensions.

It will repay us if we first interpret it in terms of the credal
concept of the *communio sanctorum*. The upbuilding of the community is the communion of saints.

> I may again refer to a book by Dietrich Bonhoeffer. This is
> the dissertation which he wrote and published—when he was
> only twenty-one years of age—under the title *Sanctorum com-
> munio, Eine dogmatische Untersuchung zur Soziologie der
> Kirche,* 1930. If there can be any possible vindication of
> Reinhold Seeberg, it is to be sought in the fact that his school
> could give rise to this man and this dissertation, which not only
> awakens respect for the breadth and depth of its insight as we
> look back to the existing situation, but makes far more instruc-
> tive and stimulating and illuminating and genuinely edifying
> reading to-day than many of the more famous works which have
> since been written on the problem of the Church. As Ernst Wolf
> has justly remarked in his preface to the new edition of 1954,
> many things would not have been written if Bonhoeffer's expo-

From Karl Barth, *Church Dogmatics,* IV/2, pp. 641–676. © T. & T. Clark
Ltd., Edinburgh. Used by permission of the Publisher.

sition had been taken into account. I openly confess that I have misgivings whether I can even maintain the high level reached by Bonhoeffer, saying no less in my own words and context, and saying it no less forcefully, than did this young man so many years ago.

If we are to use it in interpretation of the concept of "upbuilding" the term communion must be given the strict sense of the Latin *communio* and the Greek κοινωνία. Communion is an action in which on the basis of an existing union (*unio*) many men are engaged in a common movement towards the same union. This takes place in the power and operation of the Holy Spirit, and the corresponding action of those who are assembled and quickened by Him. Communion takes place as this divine and human work is in train; as it moves from its origin in which it is already complete to its goal in which it will be manifest as such. Communion takes place in the sphere of the incomplete between completion and completion, i.e., between union and union. At each stage of its fulfilment it is itself *per definitionem* incomplete. It takes place in the completion, the *unio*, from which it comes and to which it goes. In the measure that it takes place at this centre among many men, and their participation in this fulfilment, there also takes place the fact that these many are together and act in common, so that they are united among themselves—not because their unity has still to be established, but because it has taken place already, and they come from it together, and together move toward the revelation of its concealed reality. As they look backwards and forwards from this unity to the same unity, they are united, and are together, and act in common. In this communion there takes place the upbuilding of the community.

It is the saints who are and act in this communion. The saints are men who exist in the world, and after the fashion of the world, but who, in virtue of the fact that they come from the union presupposed in the event of their communion and move forward to its revelation, are integrated and engaged in self-integration. The saints are men who are gathered by the power and work of the Holy Spirit and appointed to do the corresponding work. They live and act in the occurrence of this communion, and therefore in mutual conjunction. As they now live and act on earth, in time, at the heart of world history (or as they have lived and acted, for those whose life is over have not dropped out of this fellowship), they are still the *communio peccatorum*, members of the race of Adam, participant in the transgression and fall and misery of all men. But in spite of this, and in triumph over it, they are already distinguished from all other men, constituting in face and on behalf of the world the *communio sanctorum*—a provisional representation of the new humanity in the midst of the old. These men—the saints—who live and act in the communion of the one Holy Spirit, and therefore in communion one with another, are Christians.

But what makes them Christians? In a final description of the basis of their particular being and action, we can and must reply that it is God's eternal election, His love directed towards them and embracing and activating them in this particular way, which makes them Christians, not only as individuals in their solitariness, but also in their common life, and therefore all together as a people of single descent. For the moment, however, we are concerned to know what it is that distinguishes their being and activity as men on earth and in time. What is the distinctive thing which becomes a historical event in their fellowship? To see this, we have to remember the twofold sense in which the Church is called the *communio sanctorum* in the creed. The genitive certainly indicates that it is the communion of the *sancti*, i.e., of those who are sanctified by the Holy Spirit, of all Christians of every age and place. But it also means—and apart from this we cannot see what it is that makes them *sancti* in their human being and activity—communion in the *sancta*: the holy relationships in which they stand as *sancti*; the holy gifts of which they are partakers; the holy tasks which they are called upon to perform; the holy position which they adopt; the holy function which they have to execute. From this standpoint the *communio sanctorum* is the event in which the *sancti* participate in these *sancta*. We may thus give the place as the fellowship of Christians in the knowledge and confession of their faith. It undoubtedly takes place also and even basically—if we understand the terms in their comprehensive sense—as a theological and confessional fellowship. It takes place as the fellowship of their thankfulness and thanksgiving. It takes place as the fellowship of their penitence (leading to conversion), but also with the joy without which there cannot be this penitence in the conversion of the saints. It takes place as the fellowship of prayer, which, even when it is in the secret chamber, cannot be a private talk with God but only the prayer of the community. It takes place, in relationship to the world, as the fellowship of the need of those who are moved by the burdens of the world, and the promise given to it, as their own innermost concern; yet also, in this relationship, as the fellowship in arms of those who are determined, in order to be true to the world and meaningfully to address themselves to it, not in any sense to be conformed to the world. It takes place as the fellowship of service in which the saints assist and support one another, and in which they have also actively to attest to those outside what is the will of the One who has taken them apart and sanctified them. It takes place as the fellowship of their hope and prophecy looking and reaching beyond the present, but also looking and reaching beyond every temporal future. Above all, of course, it takes place as the fellowship of their proclamation of the Gospel, of the Word by which they are gathered and impelled and maintained. For this reason, and because it takes place as the fellowship of prayer, it takes place as the fellowship of divine service—a liturgical fellowship. And in and above all these things it takes place as the fellowship of worship, of the silent or vocal adoration and praise of Almighty God. We do not claim that this is an exhaustive list, but these are the *sancta* with which we are concerned in the being and action of the *sancti*, of Christians, and therefore in the *communio sanctorum*. The *sancti* are those to whom these *sancta* are entrusted. They are not entrusted to any of us as private individuals. They are entrusted to us all only in conjunction with others. In this way, but only in this way, they are entrusted to each of us personally. Thus the *communio sanctorum*, as the upbuilding of the community, is the event in which, in the being and activity of ordinary sinful men, in a *communio* which is still and always a *communio peccatorum*, we have to do with the common reception and exercise of these *sancta*.

On the presupposition that the upbuilding of the community takes place in the communion of saints, we may now address ourselves to the proper task of this section. This is to see and understand the dimensions in which this event takes place.

In this sub-section we will take an inward look and try to understand the character immanent to this event as such. To describe this, we will venture the proposition that it takes place as a growth.

The term growth (αὔξειν, αὐξάνειν) is one which in the New Testament is parallel to the main concept of οἰκοδομή. Sometimes, indeed, the two seem to cross and the idea of growth seems to confuse the sense in which the Bible speaks of building. In fact, however, it clarifies it. And we have already been forced to touch on it in our treatment of the thought of building, when we recalled the seed which grows of itself in Mk. 4:26–29. The term denotes the distinctive character of this οἰκοδομή. It points to its secret. The community does not grow only because and as it is built by God and men. In this sense we can say of any other building that it grows. In this particular building the growth is primary. God and men build the community in consequence, confirmation, concretion and glorification of its growth. It grows, and its upbuilding manifests the fact that it does so. This is the secret of its construction.

Growth is an image taken from the organic world. Its use does not mean that the communion of saints is an organism, any more than the use of that of building denotes that it is an edifice. If we press them logically, the two images are mutually exclusive. In fact, however, the image of growth elucidates that of building. It shows us that the occurrence of the communion of saints, and therefore the upbuilding of the community, takes an analogous form to that of organic growth. The *tertium comparationis* is its augmentation, extension and increase from within itself; its development without any outward or alien assistance in the power of its own form and direction; the αὐτομάτη of Mk. 4:28. The secret of the communion of saints is that it is capable of this expansion and engaged in it. That human planning and speech and faith and love and decision and action are also involved according to the divine will and order is also true. This is not compromised by the reference to the secret of the growth of the community. But in itself this is no explanation of the secret, nor can it call in question the reference to it. That the community as the communion of saints grows like a seed to a plant, or a sapling to a tree, or a human embryo to a child and then to a man, is the presupposition of the divine as well as the human action by which it is built. It grows—we may venture to say—in its own sovereign power and manner, and it is only as it does this that it is built and builds itself. The fact that the saints become, that they are conceived and born and then live and act in the *communio* of all these *sancta* and therefore in mutual *communio*, is something which from first to last is primarily and properly a growth.

As I see it, not merely the parable of the seed which grows secretly but also that of the sower (Mk. 4:30–32 and par.) refers to the community existing in the last age of world history. Growth is a process which takes time. To what can the parables refer if not to the kingdom of God come in time and proclaimed in time? It is in this form, and only in this form, that the kingdom can be compared to a seed which grows irresistibly larger until it reaches its full stature. As long as it has a history, the kingdom of God has its history in the community which exists in history. The two parables tell us that the history of the community, because and as it comes from the kingdom of God as the communion of saints, and moves towards this kingdom and proclaims it, is the history of a subject which grows of itself.

But before we probe the matter more deeply we must ask in what this growth consists.

The most obvious, although not necessarily the final answer, is not to be summarily rejected—that the communion of saints shows itself to be fruitful in the mere fact that as it exists it enlarges its own circle and constituency in the world. It produces new saints by whose entry it is enlarged and increased. Of course, we are not told, even by the parable of the seed, that it will become constantly greater in this way so that all living men may eventually become Christians. What we are told is that it has the supreme power to extend in this way, that it does not stand therefore under serious threat of diminution, and that as a subject which grows *per definitionem* it has an astonishing capacity even for numerical increase. It is not self-evident that this should be the case; that it should have this capacity; that there should always be Christians raised up like stones to be Abraham's children. The more clearly we see the human frailty of the saints and their fellowship as it is palpable both at the very outset and in every epoch, the more astonishing we shall find it that from the very first and right up to our own time it has continually renewed itself in the existence of men who have been reached by its feeble witness and have become Christians in consequence. It is no doubt true that its power in this respect has been largely denied through the fault of Christians, or its exercise confined to a limited sphere. But it is also true, and perhaps even more true, that it has always had and demonstrated this capacity. It has propagated itself even where everything seemed to suggest that this was quite impossible. It has continually, and often very suddenly, assumed new forms—sometimes for the better, sometimes not for the better, but without forfeiture of its essential and recognisable essence. For always, directly or indirectly awakened and gathered by its existence, there have been Christians, and therefore men who have come to this fellowship and then lived and acted in it. As these men—often in the strangest places, and the very last that one would expect—have arisen and come to it, i.e., have discovered, and confirmed the fact, that they belonged to it, the community has grown. It does not matter whether the growth has been big or little. The fact remains that it has continually grown. And it still grows. It has the power to do so.

The New Testament itself knows and emphasises this primitive, if we like, but not really non-essential aspect of the growth of the community, or its immanent power to grow in this sense. The Book of Acts is particularly relevant in this connexion. When Peter gave his witness on the day of Pentecost, some 3000 people were added to the Church, receiving the Word and accepting baptism (Ac. 2:41). The joyful worship of the community had as its consequence that the Lord added daily to the Church those who are saved (2:47). Very soon the number of those who had heard the Word and come to faith had jumped to about 5000 (4:4). Further increase created the administrative problem solved by the commissioning of Stephen, and his fellows (6:1f.), and this in turn resulted in a further increase in numbers (including a great company of priests), but also in the persecution which claimed Stephen as the first Christian "martyr." The remarkable expression used in 6:7 is that "the word of God increased; and the number of the disciples multiplied greatly." The phrase occurs again in 12:24, and also in 19:20 where it is added that "it prevailed," i.e., for the winning of others. Similarly we are told in 16:5 that the faith of the Churches in Asia Minor was strengthened, and that they increased in number (in membership) daily. What Luke has in mind in these passages is the αὐξάνεσθαι καὶ πληθύνεσθαι over the whole earth promised to the first man in Gen. 1:23 (LXX), and also of the growth and increase of the people of Israel in Egypt (Ex. 1:7 and Ac. 7:17), which for its part was the fulfilment of the corresponding promises already given to the patriarchs. It is clear that for Luke, with his universalistic outlook, this was an important matter. The community exists in universal history, and it undoubtedly has the power to multiply in this history and therefore extensively (or, as we may say with Luke, numerically), and thus to grow in this sense.

On the other hand, it would clearly be quite inappropriate to understand this distinctive power of the community only, or even predominantly, as a power for extensive growth. It is obviously vital to it, as a society existing in history, that it should continually increase and extend its numbers. It has constant need of more saints if it is to fulfil the purpose of its temporal existence. Its task is so varied and comprehensive that it can never have enough. But the process of numerical expansion is not as such unequivocal; the less so when the increase is most imposing, but basically even when it is only slight. Where there is expansion, is it really to the saints that other saints are added, becoming disciples and witnesses with them? Or is it merely a question, as in other human societies, of men drawing large crowds and thus enjoying success? Is the growth in virtue of a power absolutely distinctive to the community of saints, or merely in terms of a dynamic which might also be, and is, that of the *communio peccatorum* as well? A power which has only an abstractly extensive effect is certainly not the power which characterises the community; and in the same way a growth which is merely abstractly extensive is not its growth as the *communio sanctorum*. Thus it can never be healthy if the Church seeks to grow only or predominantly in this horizontal sense, with a view to the greatest possible number of adherents; if its mission to the world becomes propaganda on behalf of its own spatial expansion. It has to attest the Gospel. It has to seek a hearing and understanding for the Gospel's voice. It cannot do this without exerting itself to win new witnesses. But this cannot become an end in itself. It knows of only one end in itself—the proclamation of the kingdom of God. And it has to achieve this, not merely in its words, but in its whole existence. In the service of this end in itself it will necessarily also be an end to win new witnesses and by their addition to increase extensively. But it will not forget that it is a great and rare matter when a man comes to faith; when he becomes a witness of the Gospel, a saint, a Christian. As it is out for the existence of as many Christians as possible, it will have to resist the temptation to win them by diluting the wine with a little water. It will certainly be disturbed and sad, but it will not be horrified, that the increase in the number of Christians is not so easy; that it does not go forward indefinitely; that a clearly defined limit always seems to be set to it. It will not imagine that, as itself only a race of men with others charged to give a provisional representation of the new humanity at the heart of the old, it will ever in its present historical form embrace the totality or even the majority of men. It will never equate itself in its present form with the *eschaton* which comes to it afresh from God. It will not, therefore, be of the opinion that it can and should actualise this *eschaton* here and now. It will be confident that the power of growth operative within it will not fail in this world, accomplishing no less, if no more, than that which is right and necessary here and now in accordance with its own law. It will thus allow this power to rule and give itself to serve it. But always it will be more concerned about the quality than the quantity of those who are already Christians, or who may become such. And it will be even more concerned about the realisation of its own communion; the common reception and exercise of the *sancta* by the *sancti*.

It is no reproach to Luke, but it must be noted that he is the only one of the New Testament writers who is so obviously concerned about the numerical increase of the community. And the question may well be raised whether the few places in which he speaks of an increase of the Word of God, while they have this undeniable immediate reference, do not point also in a different direction. At any rate, it is worth noting that it is the same Luke who in the Gospel has recorded the saying about the little flock to which the kingdom is given (12:32), and also the saying which is quite unparalleled in the New Testament in respect of the implied restriction in the extensive increase of the community: "Nevertheless, when the Son of man cometh, shall he find faith on the earth?" (18:8). In this bleak utterance it is shown to be questionable whether He will find and encounter the faith of anyone at all, even the faith of the community. How, then, can there be any question of the totality, or even the majority, of men standing in the Christian faith? We can thus learn from Luke himself that the Lucan view has its limits—although we have also to learn from him that the personal and extensive and quantitative increase of the community is a serious and necessary problem. For the rest, on a right understanding there is no contradiction between increase in this sense and the fact that in relation to the world the community must always recognise and confess that it is a little flock, knowing only too well what it is to sigh with Ps. 12:1 (in the familiar Prayer Book version): "Help me, O Lord, for there is not one godly man left: for the faithful are minished from among the children of men."

Of course, a rather different and wider conception may easily insinuate itself in the context of the legitimate concept of the extensive growth of the community, and of this we can only say that it has to be rejected out of hand. Can it really be characteristic of the communion of saints to increase in consequence and prestige and influence and outward pomp in the world around; to command increasing authority and esteem for itself as a recognised force, both from the state and from all other human societies; to win an assured and generally acknowledged place in the structure and activity of worldly politics and scholarship and literature and art? We need hardly demonstrate or bemoan the fact that the Church has often acted as if a positive answer had to be given to this question. But the very opposite is the case. The Church has the promise that "the gates of hell shall not prevail against it" (Mt. 16:18), but it has no promise to this effect. Its glory will be manifest when that of its Lord is manifest to the world. In the time between it is thankful for all the necessary space that it is granted in the world to fulfil its task. But the enlargement (or diminution) of this space has nothing whatever to do with its nature or commission. Its enlargement is not promised, nor its diminution demanded. It has its hands full with the task of filling it in the service of its cause according to measure in which it is given (whether great or small). It will not be surprised or annoyed if it is pushed into the corner; or if sometimes it is forcefully deprived (*per fas* or *nefas*) of its outward majesty and pushed even more into the corner. It is always seriously mistaken if it tries to grow in this dimension. The Church of Jesus Christ can never—in any respect—be a pompous Church.

The true growth which is the secret of the upbuilding of the community is not extensive but intensive; its vertical growth in height and depth. If things are well—and there is no reason why they should not be—this is the basis. The numerical increase of the community indicates that it is also engaged in this very different increase. But the relationship cannot be reversed. It is not the case that its intensive increase necessarily involves an extensive. We cannot, therefore, strive for vertical renewal merely to produce greater horizontal extension and a wider audience. At some point and in some way, where it is really engaged in vertical renewal, it will always experience the arising of new Christians and therefore an increase in its constituency, but perhaps at a very different point and in a very different manner and compass from that expected. If it is used only as a means for extensive renewal, the internal will at once lose its meaning and power. It can be fulfilled only for its own sake, and then—unplanned and unarranged—it will bear its own fruits. As the communion of saints takes place, the dominant and effective force is always primarily and properly that of intensive, vertical and spiritual growth.

This is the power in which the saints increase in the reception and exercise of the holy things entrusted to them; in which as *sancti* they increase in relation to the *sancta* commonly addressed to them, and by them to others. In this relation there is enacted a history. For it is not just a step or two but a whole wide way from the lower to the higher, which in turns becomes a lower to that which is higher still, and so continually. Where do we not have to make this way from good to better faith and knowledge and confession, to better thought and penitence and joy, to better prayer and hope and proclamation and worship or any other *sancta*, in short from good to better communion of the saints in holy things? The power immanent in the community is the power of this history, and therefore the power to go this way (or these many ways) as we should, not as individual Christians but together as the community in which there is mutual admonition and encouragement and warning and comfort and assistance and support. It is as the community goes this way, or these ways, in its immanent power that it knows inward increase and extension and expansion—inward growth.

But we must not understand the matter too much in pedagogic terms, as though there were a general curriculum of instruction which must be followed point by point with a view to passing an examination, and which has actually been followed in the course of Church history. For the *sancti* of the different times and places in which their *communio* is achieved, what is lower and higher and higher still, what is good and better in relation to the *sancta* may differ very widely in detail. Old aims may drop away altogether, and new ones arise and force themselves on our attention. There may be remarkable inversions in recognised and apparently immutable evaluations. Everything may take a very different course here and now from what it did there and then. Nor can there ever be any question—we are referring to the community in time and on earth, and therefore engaged in pilgrimage as also a *communio peccatorum*—of achieving the highest and best in any of these relationships; of a point at which the community, or some Christians within it, think that they have already brought their lambs to safety. We have always to reckon with the fact that the community, and all the Christians living and acting in it, are continually set on the way—and rather ungently sometimes if they are disposed to slumber. We have also to accustom ourselves to the thought that on all the ways on which Christendom journeys we shall be constantly faced, not only by the limit of its creatureliness and sinfulness, but also by the fact that, as in respect of its outward extension, so also of its inward growth, there is a limit which it cannot and should not pass because it is not ordained to give a perfect but only a provisional and therefore imperfect representation of the new humanity, God having reserved the definitive and perfect representation for His kingdom which comes in the final manifestation. The community of the *sancti* has to respect this limit of its relationship to the *sancta*. Finally, we have also to accept the fact that even within this limit the inward growth of the community may often have the appearance of its opposite: of apparent pauses; of narrow straits in which it seems to be hemmed in inwardly by steep walls with no way of escape or advance; of apparent retrogressions in which even that which has been believed and known and confessed or given seems to be taken away again, but which have to be passed through and endured and suffered in order that there may be real growth and increase and expansion. Nothing is more astonishing than the true, intensive, spiritual growth of the communion of saints on earth. In Church history— but who really knows how it really happened and does happen?—we are given a glimpse of the power which is continually at work in new and often contradictory and interrupted but ongoing processes of growth. To conclude, we may observe that this force effects even the spiritual increase of the communion of saints according to its own law. To be sure, it is the power of growth immanent in the community itself—and we have still to consider what this means. But its rule and efficacy are not according to the plans and efforts of Christians. It is a matter of their spiritual growth, and not therefore of a growth which they themselves can direct. It will continually have for them the greatest of surprises, sometimes glad and sometimes bitter. In moments when it is resolved to offer ''reasonable service,'' the plans and efforts of Christians will have to be ruled by it, and not the reverse. To their own astonishment it will continually exalt the lowly, enrich the poor, give joy to the sad and make heroes of the feeble. The rule and efficacy of the power of this growth can never be measured, foreseen or assessed by the ordinary standards of history, even when Christians try to think of their own history in relation to that of the world. It leads the community on a new and distinctive path through world history. But it *leads* them, and as it does so the community grows, either with or without repercussions in world history. And as it grows spiritually, there is no compulsion but it may also grow in the first way, extensively and numerically.

It is hard to decide formally which of these two directions in the growth of the community is denoted by the parables in Mk. 4:26–29 and 30–32. It would be foolish, however, to argue that in their exposition there can be no other understanding than that illustrated in Acts, so that in view of these passages we can speak quite freely of the extension of the kingdom of God over the whole earth, or the evangelisation of the world in our own or the next or the next but one generation. The rest of the New Testament obviously points in the second of the two directions. Αὐξάνειν in 2 Cor. 10:15 means growth in faith, as does also 2 Thess 1:3, which speaks of increase in love as well. In Col. 1:10f. it is increase in the knowledge of God—with strengthening in endurance and joyful patience. In 2 Cor. 9:10 it is the growth of the fruits of righteousness, and in 2 Pet. 3:18 growth in grace. The πληθύνειν of 1 Pet. 1:2 and 2 Pet. 1:2 points in a similar direction. In 1 Cor. 15:58 περισσεύειν is increase in the work of the Lord, with a corresponding steadfastness and immovability. In 2 Cor. 1:5 it is the increase of comfort, in 2 Cor. 4:15 of thanksgiving, in 2 Cor. 8:7 of faith, the word, knowledge and zeal, in 2 Cor. 9:8 of grace for every good work, in Rom. 15:13 of hope (by the power of the Holy Spirit). In Phil. 1:9 it is the enrichment of love in knowledge and understanding, and in Col. 2:7 it is again the deepening or enlarging of thanksgiving. Similarly, the expression προκοπὴ τοῦ εὐαγγελίου in Phil. 1:12f. does not seem from the context to refer to numerical increase but to the strengthening of the attitude of the community which Paul expects from his presence within it. In short, the progress of the Church—to adopt a term which has gained a peculiar currency in the ecclesiastical politics of Basel—denotes in the New Testament primarily and predominantly, although not exclusively, spiritual progress; the progress of the *sancti* in their relationship to the *sancta*. Progress means that they go forward together on the appointed way from their origin to their goal. The New Testament sees that where there is the communion of saints this progress may be expected. And it finds in this progress the true form of the growth which the community has to owe to the power immanent within it. It is in this happening that there is actualised its true nature and essence; its appointment to give a provisional representation within the old humanity of the new humanity sanctified already in Jesus Christ.

It is legitimate and even incumbent to gather together what has to be said about the occurrence of the communion of saints, in so far as it consists in its growth (both horizontal and vertical), in the simple statement that the community *lives* as the communion of saints. Growth is the expression, fulfilment and mark of life. The power by which the community grows is the immanent power of life. As we recognise the life of the community in its growth, and its power of life in its power to grow, we are brought face to face with the question which has not yet been answered in this discussion—that of the nature of this indwelling or immanent power of the community. We may give a preliminary answer in the second and very simple statement that the community lives as the communion of saints because and as Jesus lives. Jesus is the power of life immanent within it; the power by which it grows and therefore lives. This is what we must now explain.

In the thesis at the head of the section we have spoken of the Holy Spirit as the quickening power by which Christianity is built up as the true Church in the world. But as we made it clear, it is Jesus the Lord who is at work in this quickening power of the Holy Spirit. And we must now take up again that which we have already said, and maintain that according to the normative view of the New Testament the Holy Spirit is the authentic and effective self-attestation of the risen and living Lord Jesus; His self-attestation as the Resurrected, the living One, the Lord, the exalted Son of Man, in whom there has already been attained the sanctification of all men, but also the particular, factual sanctification of Christians—their union with Him and therefore with one another. In the Holy Spirit as His self-attestation we know Him; which means again that we know Him as the Resurrected, the living One, the Lord, the exalted Son of Man, in whose exaltation all men are sanctified, and especially, factually and concretely Christians, who are distinguished in the first instance from all other men by His self-attestation and therefore by their knowledge. In the Holy Spirit as the self-attestation of Jesus they thus know themselves in and with Him; themselves in their union with Him, and also with one another, in the fellowship of faith and love and hope in which they express themselves as His and find self-awareness as this people which has a common descent. It is in this sense that the Holy Spirit as the self-attestation of Jesus is the quickening power by which Christianity is awakened and gathered and built up to a true Church in the world. As the self-attestation of Jesus the Holy Spirit achieves the *communio sanctorum* and causes it to grow (intensively and extensively). It lives by His power—from the very first and on all its way and ways in the realisation of the relationship of the *sancti* to the *sancta* right up to its goal at the end of all history when it will meet the *eschaton* which will be the *eschaton* of the cosmos. But to understand this in all its fulness of meaning we must be clear that the Holy Spirit by which the community lives and becomes and was and is and will be is the self-attestation of Jesus.

The power with which He works is not, then, merely a remote

operation of Jesus. It is this. Risen from the dead, ascended into heaven, seated at the right hand of God the Father, Jesus is remote from earthly history and the community which exists in it. He is unattainably superior to it. He is separated from it by an abyss which cannot be bridged. He is even hidden from it in God (Col. 3:3)—and with Him, of course, the true life of the community. He (and its true life) cannot be violated or controlled by it. If in spite of this He is still at work in earthly history, and in the community as it exists in it, by the quickening power of His Holy Spirit, we can certainly call this His operation at a distance. From the point to which there is no way, from heaven, from the throne, from the right hand of God, from His hiddenness in God, He overcomes that abyss in the Holy Spirit, operating here from that exalted status, working in time, in which the *communio sanctorum* is an event and has its history in many events, from the eternity of the life which He has in common with God. The man Jesus has also that form of existence, so that it is quite true that His action towards His community in the quickening power of the Holy Spirit is a remote operation.

But this is only the one aspect of His action, and if we are to understand it as the power of growth and life which does not only reach it from the majesty of God, touching and impelling it from without, but also as that which indwells and is immanent to it, it is the second aspect which we must now consider. It is to be noted that this does not replace the other. The first aspect remains. The man Jesus is above, superior even to His community and remote from it in absolute transcendence; and with Him, so too is its own true life. He has and maintains also that heavenly form of existence characterised by His unique fellowship with God. He exists also at the right hand of God the Father where we men, even we Christians, are not; where even the *communio sanctorum* is not. Thus the Holy Spirit, too, is the power which quickens from above, from a distance, from God; from the God who dwells in light unapproachable. But the second aspect has also to be considered. For what does it mean to speak of there and here, height and depth, near and far, when we speak of the One who is not only the true Son of Man but also the true Son of God, the man who, exalted by the self-humiliation of the divine person to being as man, exists in living fellowship with God? It certainly does not mean that these antitheses are removed and obliterated and equated in Him. But since God is not limited to be there, since He is not the prisoner of His own height and distance, it certainly means that in the man Jesus who is also the true Son of God, these antitheses, while they remain, are comprehended and controlled; that He has power over them; that He can be here as well as there, in the depth as well as in the height, near as well as remote, and therefore immanent in the *communio sanctorum* on earth as well as transcendent to it. He can have an earthly-historical form of existence as well as a heavenly-historical. He can create and sustain and rule the *communio sanctorum* on earth. He can exist in it in earthly-historical form. We speak of His heavenly form of existence, of the form in which He exists in the height and distance and hiddenness of God, when with the New Testament we speak of Him as the Head of His community. But we speak of His earthly-historical form of existence, of the form in which, in the sovereignty of the same God, He also exists here and now with sinners in this history which has not yet concluded, when again with the New Testament we speak of the community as His body (cf. on this concept *C.D.*, IV, 1, pp. 662–668). And in both cases, and either way, we speak of the one man Jesus Christ. It is He who is both there and here. It is He who is both the Head and the body. Similarly, the life of Christians as the life of those sanctified in Him is one. With Him as its Head it is hidden in God, but with Him it is also provisional, manifest in the temporal being and activity of the community on earth. Similarly, His Holy Spirit is one. As the quickening power which accomplishes sanctification, He comes down with utter novelty and strangeness from above (as described in the story of Pentecost) and thus constitutes an absolute basis and starting-point. But as the same power He also rules and works in the events, in the sequence and multiplicity, of the temporal history of the *communio sanctorum* which is still the *communio peccatorum*, in all the relativities of that which is called Christian and ecclesiastical and even theological life. All this depends, however, upon the fact that first and supremely the one man Jesus Christ Himself exists both in the first form and also in the second: not in any contradiction of the one to the other and therefore to Himself; but because in the one, therefore also in the other, and thus in the whole glory of His being as the true Son of God and Son of Man. Our present concern is with the second form: His earthly-historical form of existence; His body; the community in which, as the One who is with God, He is also with us as the true Son of God and therefore the true Son of Man, in whom we are already united and sanctified.

For a better understanding, let us return to the equation that the Holy Spirit, as the power which quickens the community, is the self-attestation of Jesus. Thus the only content of the Holy Spirit is Jesus; His only work is His provisional revelation; His only effect the human knowledge which has Him as its object (and in Him the knowing man himself). But as the self-attestation of Jesus the Holy Spirit is more than a mere indication of Jesus or record concerning Him. Where the man Jesus attests Himself in the power of the Spirit of God, He makes Himself present; and those whom He approaches in His self-attestation are able also to approach Him and to be near Him. More than that, where He makes Himself present in this power, He imparts Himself; and those to whom He wills to belong in virtue of this self-presentation are able also to belong to Him. In the Holy Ghost as His self-attestation He reveals and discloses Himself to certain men living on earth and in time as the Holy One who represents them before God and therefore in actuality, and also grants them the knowledge that He is theirs; the Holy One in whom they also are holy, and are His—holy in His holy person. He reveals and discloses and grants to them the knowledge of His unity with them and their unity with Him. In this knowledge they find that even on earth and in time they are with Him, and therefore at unity with one another. It is in this way, by this self-attestation, self-presentation and self-impartation, that He founds and quickens the community, which is the mighty work of the Holy Spirit.

In virtue of and in the occurrence of this mighty work, the community lives and grows within the world—an anticipation, a provisional representation, of the sanctification of all men as it has taken place in Him, of the new humanity reconciled with God. Thus it can never be understood as a society which men join of themselves and in which they are active in the pursuit of their own ends, however religious. They are united only by and with Jesus, and only in this way with one another, and only for the fulfilment of His will and purpose. Nor can the community be understood as an organisation set up by Him, a machine for whose efficient functioning it has to provide, thus having its essential existence in its offices. It exists only as the mighty work of Jesus is done on earth, and as it allows it to take place in itself, and through itself in the world. It can be understood only with reference to Him, and only in Him can it recognise itself in its true actuality. It *is* only in Him. Even in its human being and action and operation it is from Him and by Him. It cannot recognise and take itself seriously in anything that is not from Him. What He is not, it is not, and in what He is not it is not His community, but can only be alien to itself, and withdraw in shame before Him and become small and as it were disappear. It does not live apart from the mighty work of His self-attestation. It lives as He Himself lives in it in the occurrence of this mighty work; as it is the earthly-historical form of His existence, His body, standing at His disposal, and ruled and impelled by Him, in all its members and their various functions.

This brings us back to the statement which was a kind of axiomatic starting-point, anticipating all that was to follow, at the beginning of the prolegomena of our *Church Dogmatics* (I, 1, p. 3)—that the being of Jesus Christ is the being of the Church, and its self-understanding and proclamation and practice and enquiries and conclusions and internal and external politics and theology must all be directed accordingly.

We cannot avoid the statement that Jesus Christ is the community. Nor do we refer only to Jesus Christ in His form as its heavenly Head, in His hiddenness with God. In Jesus Christ as the Head it can only believe. Here and now it can only look up to Him from the depths as its Lord. It can only love Him as the One whom it has not seen (1 Pet. 1:8). It can only wait for His revelation: "Amen. Even so, come, Lord Jesus" (Rev. 22:20). It can only move towards Him. Thus the statement cannot be reversed. It is a christological statement, and only as such an ecclesiological. The community is not Jesus Christ. It is not the eternal Son of God, the incarnate Word, the Reconciler of the world with God. The justification and sanctification of all men did not and does not take place in it, but only its provisional representation, its attestation by a handful of sinful men amongst others—saints who are holy only in the fact that He is, and has revealed and disclosed Himself to them as the Holy One, and that they have been recognised and confess Him as such. There does not belong to it the power of the sending and outpouring and operation of the Holy Spirit. It does not "possess" Him. It cannot create or control Him. He is promised to it. It can only receive Him and then be obedient to Him. There can be no thought of the being of Jesus Christ enclosed in that of His community, or exhausted by it, as though it were a kind of predicate of this being. The truth is the very opposite. The being of the community is exhausted and enclosed in His. It is a being which is taken up and hidden in His, and absolutely determined and governed by it. The being of the community is a predicate of His being. As it exists on earth and in time in virtue of the mighty work of the Holy Ghost, it is His body; and He, its heavenly Head, the incarnate Word, the incomparable Holy One, has in it His own earthly-historical form of existence; He Himself, who is not yet directly and universally and definitively revealed to the world and it, is already present and at work in it. The community is not Jesus Christ. But He—and in reality only He, but He in supreme reality—is the community. He does not live because and as it lives. But it lives, and may and can live, only because and as He lives. "Because I live, ye shall live also" (Jn. 14:19). The sequence and order are all-important. But in this sequence and order it may and must be affirmed that Jesus Christ is the community.

We may say the same with reference to the central New Testament concept of the kingdom of God. The kingdom of God is the lordship of God established in the world in Jesus Christ. It is the rule of God as it takes place in Him. He Himself is the kingdom of God. Thus we cannot avoid a statement which Protestantism has far too hastily and heedlessly contested—that the kingdom of God is the community. We do not refer to the kingdom or dominion of God in its completed form in which it obtains for the whole world in the person of the one Son of Man, the one Holy Spirit, and in which it will be directly and universally and definitively revealed and known at the end and goal of all history. We refer to it in the guise of the new and obedient humanity, as in the historical time which moves towards this end it is provisionally and very imperfectly but genuinely actualised where in virtue of the mighty work of the Holy Ghost there is an awareness of its incursion and therefore the communion of saints. The community is not the kingdom of God. But—proclaimed and believed in its earthly-historical form of existence by sinners among sinners, as the unholy may become the saints of God in an awareness of its coming—the kingdom of God is the community. It is not for nothing that it comes from the resurrection of Jesus Christ as its first revelation, and goes towards its final revelation in the return of Jesus Christ. As the kingdom of God itself is on the way from the first to the last revelation, it is the community. As the kingdom or rule of God is engaged in this movement, it creates the sphere corresponding to it and is to be found on this way too. And this takes place in the mighty work of the Holy Spirit founding and quickening the community. The community is not the kingdom of God, nor will it ever be before the kingdom encounters it, and is revealed to it, in its glory at the end of all history. It prays for the coming of the kingdom, that encountering it in its true and perfect form it may be directly and universally and definitively revealed. But already on this side of the end, even in the form of the community which prays for its coming, the kingdom is really on earth and in time and history. The community would be nothing if it did not come from the kingdom and go towards it; if the kingdom were not present in this transitional movement. The community can only follow it in this transition; otherwise it surrenders its particularity and betrays its reality as the communion of saints. Its proclamation can only serve the self-proclamation of the kingdom of God which is present here and now because it has come and comes. If it does not stand in this service it is absolutely nothing. If it does, for all its unpretentiousness it is greater than all the greatnesses of world history, for it has to speak the final word among all the words spoken by men and to men.

In sum, there is a real identity, not present *in abstracto*, but given by God and enacted in the mighty work of the Holy Spirit, between the Holy One, the kingdom of God as perfectly established in Him, and the communion of saints on earth, which as such is also a communion of sinners. Thus the power of this Holy One, of Jesus Christ as the heavenly Head, in whom God's rule is perfectly established, is also the indwelling power of life and growth which is immanent in the community on earth. It is in the light of this identity that we have to understand everything that needs to be said concerning its life and growth (both in the extensive and the intensive sense). He, Jesus Christ, must increase (Jn. 3:30), and He does in fact increase. The kingdom of God grows like the seed. It is for this reason that the community also grows— the fellowship of men who with open eyes and ears and hearts come from Jesus Christ, from the kingdom of God, and move towards Him. It grows as it gives Him room to grow, and to the extent that it "decreases," as the Baptist said of himself. It lives because and as its Lord lives. It lives wholly and utterly as His people.

We will verify what we have said by the direct utterances of the New Testament—and first in relation to the concept which has been prominent in the later part of our deliberations, that of the kingdom of God. We have already proved from Mk. 4:26–29 and 30–32 that it is something which grows, so there can be no doubt that it is a temporal and historical subject. But apart from Jesus Christ what subject can be meant but His community in which the kingdom is proclaimed and believed and prayer is made for its coming? Again, we are told in Lk. 12:32 that it is the good pleasure of the One whom the disciples may call Father to give (δοῦναι) the kingdom to them, the little flock. What can this mean except that it is already present in this little flock, so that it is not merely to be in the exalted Son of Man in heaven, but wonderfully yet genuinely on earth among men in the heavenly power of Jesus Christ? Again, what can entry into the kingdom of God mean in passages like Mk. 9:47 and 10:24 or Jn. 3:5 except to become a disciple and therefore to enter the community? To do this, we have to be "fit" for it, according to Lk. 9:62, and this is not the case if we set our hand to the plough and look back. Again, we are told in Lk. 17:20f. that the kingdom of God does not come μετὰ παρατηρήσεως, i.e., in such a way that we can establish its presence directly, indicating it with a Here or a There; nevertheless it is ἐντὸς ὑμῖν, "in the midst of you" (not with the invisibility of a mere idea, but in concrete if hidden form, so that the Pharisees see it and yet do not perceive it). The primary reference is to Jesus Himself, but according to the mind of the community which preserved the saying there is also a reference to itself in its wonderful but genuine existence as the provisional form of the kingdom in the world. The kingdom of God is used in the same sense in I Cor. 4:19f., where Paul says that the kingdom of God is not ἐν λόγῳ but ἐν δυνάμει, and that it is by this standard that he will measure certain folk when he comes to Corinth. The same is true of Rom. 14:17, where the kingdom of God is said not to be a matter of eating and drinking, but of righteousness, peace and joy in the Holy Ghost. We may also refer to what is said in Col. 4:11 about Paul's συνεργοὶ εἰς τὴν βασιλείαν τοῦ θεοῦ. Again, the reference can only be to the kingdom of God as provisionally actualised in history and therefore in the community when in I Cor. 15:24 it is said that Christ will finally deliver it up to God the Father. It is to be noted that the concept is not usually given this sense. Hence Augustine's general equation of the *civitas Dei* with the Church is quite impossible. But the references in the passage mentioned (and we could easily strengthen them from the synoptic parables of the kingdom) are emphatic enough to warn us against a general and indiscriminate rejection of Augustine's identification. Apart from the absolute, christological and eschatological meaning of the term there is also an applied and relative and historical, and in this case the kingdom is in fact the Church. In this restricted sense the pietistic and Anglo-Saxon version of the Kingdom of God may well have a place.

Yet, as Origen and Tertullian rightly perceived, on the New Testament view the kingdom or lordship of God is absolutely identical with Jesus Christ. *He* is the kingdom—the αὐτοβασιλεία. It is as His lordship that it is set up as the lordship of God in the world. The βασιλεία cannot be separated from Him any more than it can from God. This is true in the absolute sense. It is also true in the relative, to the extent that the kingdom is also the community. We read in Mt. 18:20: "Where two or three are gathered together in my name (συνηγμένοι εἰς τὸ ἐμὸν ὄνομα—probably a play on the confession which characterises the Christian συναγωγή), there am I in the midst." What does this mean? Does it mean only that He comes and is present as a third or fourth? Does it not mean rather that He is present and at work in the gathering of the two or three, as the centre which constitutes this circle? Is not this also the sense of Mt. 28:20: "Lo, I am with you alway, even unto the end of the world" (ἕως τῆς συντελείας τοῦ αἰῶνος). What is meant by the μεθ' ὑμῶν? Does it mean that He is there as an interested spectator who occasionally gives friendly help? Does it not mean rather that when and as they act in accordance with His orders in the time which hastens to the end He is present every day to sustain and protect and save in His mercy, to accompany them in His omnipotent *concursus,* to rule them by His will which alone is holy—Himself the primary and proper Subject at work with and amongst them? That is why it can be said implicitly in Lk. 10:16: "He that heareth you heareth me." That is also why the nations assembled for the Last Judgment in Mt. 25:31–46 are asked by the Son of Man concerning their attitude to His brethren and judged accordingly. What they have done, or not done, to the least of His brethren, they have done, or not done, to Him. It is not merely that there is a solidarity between Himself and His brethren. But He Himself is hungry and thirsty and a stranger and naked and sick and in prison as they are. That is why it is said to the persecutor of the community in Ac. 9:4: "Saul, Saul, why persecutest thou me?" And that is why the eucharistic action as the crowning act of worship—τοῦτο, this, i.e., the common eating and drinking of the disciples according to His command—is no more and no less than His body and blood (the κοινωνία of His body and blood according to I Cor. 10:16). This action then, accomplished εἰς τὴν ἐμὴν ἀνάμ-νησιν, is the direct proclamation of His death until He comes (I Cor. 11:21). In this provisional form as the action of the community, it is His own action; the work of His real presence. Here and now He Himself is for them—His offered body and His shed blood—the communion of saints thanking and confessing Him in this action.

Similarly the formula ἐν (Ἰησοῦ) Χριστῷ, which is so common in the Pauline Epistles, indicates the place or sphere in

which (determined absolutely by it) there takes place the divine
working, creating and endowing which moves the apostle and
his communities, and also the divine revealing, questioning,
inviting and demanding, and the corresponding human thanking
and thinking and speaking and believing and obeying. The ἐν
Χριστῷ denotes the place where the *sancta* are proffered and
the *sancti* are engaged in the realisation of their *communio* with
them and therefore with one another. Jesus Christ *is,* and in His
being the apostles and communities are. For this reason, directly
or indirectly everything that is said about the being of Jesus
Christ can be only an explication of the being of Jesus Christ,
and everything that is said about the being of Jesus Christ
applies directly or indirectly to the being of Christians. A single
presupposition emerges, and for Paul and His communities this
is not a hypothesis or theory (and therefore not a problem); in
the light of Easter, and in a present because renewed confrontation with the revelation of Easter Day, it is as self-evident as the
air which they breathe. For this presupposition is simply the fact
that the crucified Jesus Christ lives. But He lives—and this is
now the decisive point—as the *totus Christus.* And this means
that, although he lives also and primarily as the exalted Son of
Man, at the right hand of the Father, in the hiddenness of God
(with the life of Christians), at an inaccessible height above the
world and the community, He does not live only there but lives
too (in the power of His Holy Spirit poured out from there and
working here) on earth and in world history, in the little communities of Thessalonica and Corinth and Philippi, in Galatia
and at Rome. He does not live primarily in their knowledge and
faith and prayer and confession, or in their Christian being, but
as the place in which all this can and may and must and will
happen, in which they are Christians; as the air which they
breathe, the ground on which they stand and walk. As we are
told in Jn. 15:4f., they have no being or life apart from Him,
just as the branches are nothing apart from the vine but can only
wither and be burned: "Without me ye can do nothing." But
they need not try to do anything without Him. He *is* the vine,
and they *are* the branches.

Thus we are brought back from every angle to the main
statement that the community lives, not only because, but as
Jesus lives, the kingdom of God in person. It is He who lives as
it lives and grows as it grows. Thus the προκοπὴ τοῦ
εὐαγγελίου (Phil. 1:12) is His work. He is the προκόπτων,
the One who strides forward, the inner man who renews Himself

from day to day (2 Cor. 4:16), the Subject of all progress in the Church. It is as He indwells the community and is immanent to it (as the Head to the body) that it grows: from Him as its Head, but also in and with Him as He has in it His body; the earthy-historical form of His existence.

It remains only to conclude the discussion of Eph. 4:11–16 which we left unfinished in the previous sub-section. It is the final phrase (in v. 16) which particularly concerns us.

We saw in v. 15 that Christians are summoned, ἀληθεύοντες ἐν ἀγάπῃ (in a life by and for the truth which unites them in love with their Lord and with one another), to grow up into Him who is the Head—Christ. He is called the κεφαλὴ τῆς ἐκκλησίας in Eph. 5:23. And we have seen that according to 1:20–23 He is primarily the Head of all things. God has raised Him from the dead, set Him at His own right hand in the heavenly world, and exalted Him over every ἀρχή and ἐξουσία and δύναμις and κυριότης, over every name that may be named, not only in this world, but also in that which is to come. He is the πληρούμενος τὰ πάντα ἐν πᾶσιν—the One who fills what would otherwise be the inevitable emptiness of all things in all their various forms. It is as such that God has given Him to be the Head of the community, and to Him as such that He has given the community as the body. He cannot and must not be without it as the *totus Christus*. It is His πλήρωμα (1:23) to the extent that it is only with it, only as He also lives and reigns in it, that He is the ἀνὴρ τέλειος (just as it is only with Him, as filled and ruled by Him, that all things can consist). But in this heavenly form, as the Head of the cosmos and also the Head of the community, He is absolutely future, because not yet revealed, both to the community and the cosmos. And its own form as the σῶμα and therefore the πλήρωμα of this Head is still future, because not yet revealed, to the community. It believes in Him as its Head. It looks and moves up towards Him from the depths and distance as to the One who exists in this heavenly form. And believing in Him it believes also in itself as His σῶμα and therefore His πλήρωμα. But it does not see this. It is still on the way to this future when it will be revealed that He is the πλήρωμα of all things and it is His πλήρωμα; that He is the One who rules the world and it is ruled by Him; that He and itself with Him, as the *totus Christus,* is the ἀνὴρ τέλειος. Of course, all this—the *totus Christus*—has not still to evolve or to be made. In accordance with the predetermination of God, He has been instituted as such once and for all: not only in His relationship to the community but also in His relationship to the cosmos; and both not merely in heaven but also on earth; yet not visibly on earth even to Christians, and to that extent only in the sphere of the future. Thus, the community *is* His body, the πλήρωμα without which He would not be that which He has been appointed by God.

This is the point of the summons of 4:15: αὐξήσωμεν εἰς αὐτόν. How can the community be summoned to grow up into him? How can it do this? According to v. 16 it can do it because its growth is already taking place quite apart from its own action, and it is to this, and the deduction to be drawn from it, that attention is directed in this summons. It is ἐξ οὗ that we are now told that this takes place. And this ἐξ οὗ refers back to Christ who is the Head of the community. It thus grows, we must reply, from the One to whom (εἰς αὐτόν) it is summoned to grow. What is it that grows ἐξ οὗ? It is the σῶμα itself. This is the subject of the statement that follows: τὸ σῶμα ... τὴν αὔξησιν τοῦ σώματος ποιεῖται. The parallel in Col. 2:19 agrees with this in substance, although in this case the verb is αὔξει, and it has the remarkable accusative τὴν αὔξησιν τοῦ θεοῦ, signifying that the body fulfils the increase which comes from God and is grounded in Him and given by Him. The only possible meaning even of this sharpened form of the paradox is that the body accomplishes its own growth. And it is more closely defined as its own growth in Eph. 4:16 (and the parallel in Col. 2:19). The whole body accomplishes its αὔξησις as it is "fitly joined together and compacted by that which every joint supplieth, according to the effectual working in the measure of every part." It is clear that what is envisaged here is the unity and differentiation of the community as conditioned by the unity and differentiation of its gifts, according to the express account given in I Cor. 12:4–31 and more briefly in Rom. 12:3–8. Thus the subject of the statement is not a mythological *soma* but the community as it exists historically in history. It is this which fulfils its own growth—the αὔξειν which is described in Col. 2:19 as an αὔξειν τὴν αὔξησιν τοῦ θεοῦ. The conclusion shows that in this there is also envisaged the concrete action of Christians, the ἔργον διακονίας for which they are prepared according to v. 12. For the community grows εἰς οἰκοδομὴν ἑαυτοῦ ἐν ἀγάπῃ. Because and as it grows, it is edified as previously described—a term which also includes the fact that, working in human fashion in all its members and their mutual relationships, it has its own part to play and therefore edifies itself. The αὔξάνειν to which Christians are summoned in v. 15

is, of course, identical with this action. But what is the "increase" presupposed in this action? How is it that the community has not first to accomplish its own growth in obedience to this summons, but is accomplishing it (ποιεῖται) already, so that it is on this basis that it can be summoned to growth, i.e., to its own edification in love? There can be only one answer. Because and as Jesus Christ is its Head, it is already His body, although He is not yet revealed and therefore future to it in this quality, as it is also to itself. His being is its being. It has its being from him (ἐξ οὗ) who is in heaven at the right hand of the Father. Because He as the Head is present to it as His body, in virtue of His life and growth it too grows infallibly, demanding the consequence of human action but not compromised by the problematic nature of this action. It is not thrown back on its own resources in this action. It grows ἐξ αὐτοῦ and therefore εἰς αὐτόν. It accomplishes its own growth—in virtue of His real presence.

3. THE UPHOLDING OF THE COMMUNITY

Communio sanctorum! We now turn to another and as it were outward aspect—that of its constitution and the possibility of its effective action in the world around. And we will try to understand its history as the history of its gracious preservation. As in the concept of "upbuilding" which dominates the whole discussion, and the particular concept of the "growth" of the community which we have just analysed, so in that of its "upholding" we have to consider both the divine and the human side of the happening under review. Here, too, both God and men (Christians) are at work: God in His omnipotent grace; and Christians (if only they were it in this sense!) in the gratitude which corresponds to the grace of God. But in this case it is best from the very outset to see these two aspects together at the place where they are originally together, understanding the whole occurrence (in the light of what we have already learned from its character as growth) as a Christ-occurrence; the work of the *totus Christus*. Our particular theme at this point must be the human weakness of the communion of saints on earth, but its preservation in defiance of this weakness. How could it be upheld were it not that it exists in Christ, and the Lord is its strength?

It is surely relevant to quote in this connexion the magnificent definition of the *Heidelberg Catechism*, which might well have been used as the thesis for our whole section. *Qu.* 54: "What dost thou believe concerning the holy, universal Christian Church? *Answer*: That from the beginning of the world to its end the Son of God assembles out of the human race an elect community to eternal life by His Spirit and (His) Word in the unity of true faith, that He protects and upholds it, and that I am a living member of the same, and will continue to be so to all eternity." Note who is the acting subject in this definition. It is not a believing people which has to gather and protect and uphold itself as such. It is not a ministry controlling the Word and sacraments. It is not the Virgin Mary as a patroness who has already ascended into heaven and there represents it and acts for it. It is the Son of God. He it is who sees to it in spite of everything the Church is. We may add to this first definition the explanation of the request: "Thy kingdom come," in the answer to *Qu*. 123: "Rule us therefore by Thy Word and Spirit that we may be subject to Thee, maintain and increase Thy Church, and more and more destroy the works of the devil, and every power that vaunts itself against Thee, and all evil counsels that are devised against Thy holy Word, until the perfection of thy kingdom is attained in which Thou shalt be all in all."

The communion of saints needs defence, protection and preservation because it is in danger. It was always in danger. As long as time endures, it will always be in danger. For it is a human society among men. It belongs to the sphere of very different human societies—domestic, political, economic, social and academic—which have no thought of orientating from and to Jesus Christ and the kingdom of God which has come and comes, but the existence and activity of which is intersected in the most diverse ways by that of the community. And what is the community itself, from the standpoint of its human constitution and its own human action, but a part of the world? It is given to exist as such in its own peculiar fashion, not as though its existence were an end in itself, but in order to be a witness and messenger pointing the world around to the truth of God which has relevance and validity for it too, to Jesus Christ and its own true reality which is unknown and ignored and even denied both in theory and practice; in order to be a provisional representation of the new humanity, and therefore in the words of 2 Pet.1:19 to be a light shining in a dark place, to the salvation of all those who dwell there. To be this light in the world is its task even as that which in its human constitution and action is only a part of the world. The danger in which it finds itself is obvious. In order to be what it is commissioned to be, in order merely to maintain itself in the world, let alone to do justice to its commission in the world, it must be the true Church, engaged in its upbuilding as such, and therefore, as we have seen, living and growing. But its life and growth are continually menaced. They are threatened both outwardly by the world and inwardly by itself (in so far as it is a part of the world in its human status and activity). The question is whether it will be able to overcome this danger, to be upheld in it.

We will consider first the danger which threatens from without. In both the forms to be mentioned it is a matter of the restriction of what we have called its extensive growth and therefore the vital upholding, i.e., the constant renewal of its human position. In both forms the danger arises from the fact that it is not self-evident, or to be expected as a matter of course, that the world will accept at once the existence of this little fragment of it, or other human societies the existence of this particular society. For it claims both a very different origin and a very different goal. But how can the world and other human societies fail to be alienated if it does this seriously and effectively, if it exists within it as a living and growing community, and if it looks like making itself prominent both by the audible presentation of its universal message and if possible by the increase of its adherents? Will they not feel that they are unsettled and questioned and disturbed and perhaps even menaced by it? Its message is sufficiently revolutionary (as the community itself knows better than anyone) to make this a very understandable reaction. It proclaims Jesus Christ and therefore a new and different humanity; the dominion of God over all other dominions; the great freedom and necessity of conversion, of the *vivificatio* which inevitably involves *mortificatio*; discipleship and the cross. To hear this willingly and not unwillingly, or even thoughtfully and not with scorn and anger; to accept the Christian community if not seriously to receive its Word: this is not a human possibility, but (as the community itself knows better than anyone) that of the Holy Spirit who moves where He wills and whom no one can command. Where this possibility is not given, the community must be reconciled to the fact that in some form it will meet with the resistance and even the counter-attacks of the outside world; that it will find that it is itself unsettled and questioned and disturbed and even menaced; that its presence will be bewailed and deplored and unwanted, its activity ridiculed and misunderstood and suspected, and its propagation, i.e., the vital renewal of its constituency, represented as a danger and as far as possible hampered even to the point of definite attempts to prevent it. It will be accused of *odium humani generis* and it will be assailed by *odium humani generis*. Its only prospect may then be the ghetto and in the near or distant future its external repression and extinction: the less certainly in proportion as it is not perhaps the true Church; but all the more surely in proportion as it is a living and (even externally) growing community. Though its external growth may not be all that striking, a living community will always have to reckon with the fact that it must be in some form a community under trial and perhaps even under the cross.

The first form in which this may happen consists in the fact that it comes under pressure from the world around which seeks either to do away with it altogether or at least to reduce it to a more innocuous form. It is not perhaps required to surrender to error or unbelief, or to suspend its activity, or to disband, or to deny its confession, etc., but only to practice greater reserve, to adopt a more positive attitude to the dominant spiritual and unspiritual powers of the world, to make a few concessions which may well appear at first sight to be nonessential, to accept certain restrictions and adjustments the extent of which may well be a subject for discussion. In the first instance, the word "persecution" is probably far too dramatic for what takes place. The pressure is not exerted equally. It falls heavily only on a few, perhaps only on the more responsible and active of its members, and in such a way, in proportion as it is not really a living *communio*, that the majority of its members are hardly aware of it at all. More massive attempts may, of course, follow. There are means—and they will be used—to stop its mouth, or at least to make its voice more or less lifeless. Perhaps there will be the attempt to separate its most important spokesmen from it, and it from them. Perhaps it will be isolated from the rest of the world, its connexions with wider circles, especially with the younger generation, being restricted or broken, so that it is reduced to a cult, and as such pushed aside and made an object of ridicule and scorn and even hatred. Perhaps all the counter-measures it might take will be made difficult or even impossible. Perhaps in our own time the campaign will be conducted by the many-headed monster of the press, even by what are called its more responsible sections (themselves directed by the invisible forces which it has to serve). Or it may be the state, either in the background or the foreground, and perhaps in the form of an omnipotent state-party, that has a hand in it and even organises the whole affair, and is able to do it very energetically through its public and secret organs and the force which it can bring to bear indirectly on individuals and relationships. And it may well be that many Christians come to realise (for the first time) that it costs something to be a living member of the living community; that it will mean decision and act and quiet but also open endurance; and that the question has therefore to be faced whether it has been a good thing to confess oneself a Christian, or whether it is wise to continue to do so. Perhaps it is going to affect the most important relationships in life. Perhaps it is going to hinder advancement, or to involve the loss of profession or livelihood. Perhaps in the near future it may even mean one day the forfeiture of liberty, and in the more distant future—who knows?—of life itself. "And though they take our life, Goods, honour, children, wife, Yet is their profit small; Let these things vanish all. . . ." Let these things vanish all? It sounded very well when we sang it—so long as we had only to sing it. But now that it may be required in fact? Will there not be many who allow that it is not to be taken literally? Yet the community on earth, the *communio sanctorum*, lives in the persons of these many Christians who are so terribly assailed and harassed; of the *sancti* who both as a whole and as individuals are also *peccatores*, and in whom the spirit may be willing enough but the flesh is weak. The *communio* itself is assailed as they are assailed. It can grow only as there takes place the *communio* of these members in relation both to the *sancta* and to one another. Will it take place and maintain itself even in these circumstances, in a situation in which each one is concretely faced by the question whether it is not better to yield to the pressure of the world around, to contract out of the common movement? Will it be upheld in these circumstances and not come to a general standstill, so that the community as such is brought to dissolution, death and destruction?

But the external attack may also take a very different form, and it is hard to say whether in the long run this second form is not more dangerous to the constitution of the community. Experience old and new shows that more brutal or refined persecution may well have the opposite effect from that intended. The community is strengthened under pressure. The separation of the chaff from the wheat means new and stronger growth. Even from the human standpoint there is consolidation in defiance of oppression by violent or subtle tyrants. In any case, it is not always or everywhere that the world around expresses its hostility or ill-will to the existence of the community in the form of this type of pressure. It is natural for Christians to dramatise unnecessarily figures like Nero and Diocletian and Louis XIV and Hitler and other modern dictators with their "anti-God" movements and new state-religions, but there have not really been so very many of them in the course of the Church's history. On the other hand, it may well be that the hostility and ill-will of the world express themselves differently. The world does not allow itself to take seriously the disturbance caused by the existence of the community. It quietly accepts it. It uses the most terrible weapon of intolerance—toleration. It meets it with sheer indifference. It may well be regarded by the world as the wiser—or wisest—course to leave Christianity alone, to go its own ways as if it were not there, simply opposing to it the *factum brutum* of its own secular spirit and methods, of its own sure and secular technics and economics and politics and art and science and way of life. There can thus be presented to it in action the fact that things work out very well after the fashion of what the community describes and attacks as sin; that we are here on solid ground; and that there is no need of the fantastic knowledge of our beginning and end in God, of the grace of God and our reconciliation with Him, of a renewal of humanity already accomplished and universally relevant, in short of Jesus Christ and the quickening power of the Holy Spirit. This may well be, and often is, the reaction of the world to the existence of the Christian community. And it is powerful enough even though it never considers giving itself the superfluous trouble of oppressing the community. For what is the result of this type of attack upon it?—now that there is no planned or purposeful but only the factual opposition of a world preoccupied with its own concerns, and completely uninterested in its message, and assuming that its action is quite irrelevant to what the world regards as important and opposes to it as such; now that the world carries its toleration, or scorn, to the point of laying occasional claim to the ministrations of the community to give light and colour to its practical atheism—as concerts and theatres and art galleries are used for its adornment—in the forms of baptisms and confirmations and weddings and festivals and national days of prayer and the like; now that it has nothing to fear in the world but also nothing to hope, or to fear only that is is absolutely superfluous, like the fifth wheel which is obviously not essential to the movement of a car; now that it does not have the consolidating and winning power of persecution because the world does not persecute it, but quietly or hurtfully ignores it. How will it be with Christians, and how will they maintain themselves, when, with no particular malice and perhaps even with friendliness, the world treats them in this way? What will be the meaning for them, from this standpoint, of their Old and New Testament, their worship, their mission, their whole

Christian thinking and willing and action? "Where is now thy God?" (Ps. 42:10). Will the saints continue to believe and love and hope when they are harassed in this manner? Will they not be possessed by the desire to leave their own sphere for that where the lord *Omnes* is at work? How can the community continue to grow? How can it maintain itself? Will not the occurrence of the *communio sanctorum* be arrested and cease for lack of breath? Will the community be upheld and not disintegrate in face of this neutral but for that reason all the more weighty attack?

We will proceed at once to consider the danger which threatens from within. It is not now a matter of its constitution but of the effective action which corresponds to its nature. Here, too, we shall have to speak of two forms of the danger. But first we must refer to that which is common to it in both forms. In both forms it arises out of the fact that the community in its human activity is a part of the world. The world, therefore, is not just around it but—in all its members—within it. But the world is the flesh of sin, the old man in all the variations of his pride and sloth, with all his possibilities and works. There is no single form of sin, of the rejection of God's grace, which cannot entice the *communio sanctorum*, and which in its history has not in fact enticed and overcome it. The enticement may come from without, caused by the pressure exerted or simply by the impression made upon it by the world around. But the men outside are no different from those inside—within the community. The saints are not, as it were, artless children unfortunately led astray by wicked rascals. They themselves are wicked rascals. They are only too ready to follow those outside. Indeed, they sometimes set those outside a bad example. Basically, the enticement which threatens the community is always the same. Stimulated from without and welcomed from within, it may suddenly or gradually feel that the requirement is too hard that its action should be wholly directed by what the *Heidelberg Catechism* calls that progressive subjection to the will of God; that its own life and growth (in subtraction from it!) should be stimulated and determined by the fact that it is in the power of the Holy Spirit of Jesus Christ Himself who lives and grows in it. It may feel that it knows better and distrust the grace of God by and in which it lives. It may grow tired of it like a spoilt child. Coveting majesty and greatness for itself, it may repudiate the sovereignty in which it wills to rule in it. It may long for the solid bases, the clear principles, the success of promising methods, the sober or enthusiastic realism, which it sees in other human societies. There is no thought of treason or deviation, of heresy or apostasy. To give way to this desire, the community need not wish to become pagan or godless, let alone actually to become this—which is not so simple a matter. It is simply a matter of relaxing a little its friendlessness in the world, the incongruity of its existence as compared with that of other human societies. It is merely a matter of taking the tension out of the relationship; of trying to find a suitable form in which to be a worldly community as well as a Christian. An inclination in this direction will always exist and show itself in the assembled *sancti* to the extent that they are also *peccatores*. We can only say that in proportion as this inclination gathers strength and achieves dominance in the community it will also relax its relationship to the Holy Spirit and His gifts, and the intensity of its growth will decline, its substance evaporate, and its existence become problematical both to itself and to the world around. In proportion as it will not live by the grace of God, it begins to die. At the end of this development it will still seem to be there as a Church both in its own eyes and in those of the world around. But in reality it will not be there. The more it is enticed in this direction, the less need it be the community under affliction and even the cross. But then (however imposing may be its outward aspect) it can be only the community in corruption, in a process of inner decomposition.

Again, there are two forms in which this may happen. It may fall victim either to alienation (secularisation) or self-glorification (sacralisation).

I was led to this distinction by a remarkable passage in the essay by Heinrich Vogel, "Wesen und Auftrag der Kirche" in *Bekennende Kirche* (for the sixtieth birthday of Martin Niemöller), 1952, pp. 49–50. Vogel rightly emphasises the fact that the one form usually involves the other, so that it is not difficult to see the face of the one in the other. All the same, it is as well to consider them apart.

The community is betrayed into alienation when instead of or side by side with the voice of the Good Shepherd to whom it belongs it hears the voice of a stranger to whom it does not belong but to whom it comes to belong as it hears his voice. This is something which does not have to happen, but which can happen in so far as it is in the world and forms a part of it. It does not have to happen, for it is not alienated by the mere fact that it belongs to the framework of the habits and customs and views of the men of this particular time and place and speaks their language and shares their general limitations and aspirations, rejoicing with them that do rejoice and weeping with them that weep (Rom. 12:15). Alienation takes place when it allows itself to be radically determined and established and engaged and committed and imprisoned in this respect: in its knowledge by the adoption of a particular philosophy or outlook as the norm of its understanding of the Word of God; in its ethics by the commandment of a specific tradition or historical *kairos*; in its attitude to existing world-relationships by a distinctive ideology or by the most respectable or novel or simply the strongest of current political and economic forces; in its proclamation by allowing itself to be determined by what seems to be the most urgent and sacred need in its own particular environment. It is always alienated when it allows its environment, or spontaneous reference to it, to prescribe and impose a law which is not identical with the Law of the Gospel, with the control of the free grace of God and with the will of Jesus as the Lord and Head of His people. As and so far as it hears this law as a law, it does not hear the voice of the Good Shepherd but that of a stranger. It hears the voice of the world in one of its phenomena, accommodating itself to it, being "conformed" (Rom. 12:2) to its pattern, and therefore belonging to it. It is to be noted that this may often happen in weakness and therefore in the form of a movement of retreat or flight, or an attempt at self-preservation, in face of the all-powerful world. But it can also take the form of offensive action in which, by hearing the world and subjecting itself to its laws, the community seeks to live and grow and assert itself in it, conquering the world at the very points where it lets itself be conquered, subjecting it to its own law, or even to that of God and Jesus Christ, and thus acting *in maiorem gloriam Dei*. It will usually be argued that it is a question of mediation, of bridging the gap between those outside and those inside, of works of "sincerity" on the one side and serious and necessary attempts to win the world for Christ on the other; or that it is a question of the translation of the Christian into the secular at the command of love; or conversely of a translation of the secular into the Christian, of a kind of baptism of non-Christian ideas and customs and enterprises by new Christian interpretations and the giving of a new Christian content, or of a minting of Christian gold on behalf of poor non-Christians. And it is all very fine and good so long as there is no secret respect for the fashion of the world, no secret listening to its basic theme, no secret hankering after its glory; and, conversely, no secret fear that the community cannot live solely by Jesus Christ and the free grace of God, no secret unwillingness to venture to allow itself to live and grow simply from its own and not a worldly root as the *communio sanctorum* in the world (not against the world but for it, not in conflict but in what is, rightly considered, the most profound peace with it). Where there is this respect, this listening, this hankering, this fear and unwillingness, it always means the secularisation of the community. Secularisation is the process at the end of which it will be only a part of the world among so much else of the world; one of the religious corners which the world may regard as necessary to its fulness but which do not have the slightest practical significance for its manner and way. Secularisation is the process by which the salt loses its savour (Mt. 5:13). It is not in any sense strange that the world is secular. This is simply to say that the world is the world. It was always secular. There is no greater error than to imagine that this was not the case in the much-vaunted Middle Ages. But when the Church becomes secular, it is the greatest conceivable misfortune both for the Church and the world. And this is what takes place when it wants to be a Church only for the world, the nation, culture, or the state—a world Church, a national Church, a cultural Church, or a state Church. It then loses its specific importance and meaning; the justification for its existence. But its secularisation—the entry on the steep slope which leads to the abyss in which it is only the world—is its alienation. And it consists of mere men—Christians, of course—who are only flesh, and in whom there may be at any moment a triumphant insurgence of the inclination and desire for alienation. It certainly needs to be kept from corruption, from the declension by which it is threatened in this form.

The other form of this decay is its self-glorification. Its aim is still to develop and maintain itself in the world. But in this case it tries to do it, not by self-adaptation, but by self-assertion. It now has a highly developed consciousness of itself in the particularity of its being and action in the world. It now discovers that it has good reason to regard and represent itself as a world of its own within the world. In its own structure and dignity, grounded on the well-known secret of its existence, it is ultimately no less imposing than other factors. Indeed, in virtue of its secret, it is really the most imposing of all. It certainly knows the lordship and glory of Jesus Christ. And it discloses itself to be His body, the earthly-historical form of His existence, His ambassador to all other men, the representative of His right and claim to the world. It thus renounces any feelings of inferiority as compared with other societies and forms of life. It rejoices and boasts in its own vital and constructive power, in its own being as the incomparable *communio*: the *communio* of the *sancti* in their relationship to the *sancta*; the *civitas Dei* on earth, which cannot be confused with any other society, but towers over them as once cathedrals did over the little towns clustering round about them. Is not this the case? Is it not right? The answer is that this is indeed the case, and that it is perfectly right, but that the terrible thing is that by trying to be right (in itself) it can set itself in the worst possible wrong. We have seen already that, although Christ is the community, there can be no reversing this important statement. The community is not Christ, nor is it the kingdom of God. It is the very last purpose of the lordship and glory of Jesus Christ (which it has to proclaim) to exalt these little men, Christendom, above all others; to set them in the right against the world; to invest them with authority and power; to magnify them in the world. If the community nevertheless permits itself this reversal, it sets itself most terribly in the wrong. It makes itself like the world. And in so doing, by trying to be important and powerful within it instead of serving, by trying to be great instead of small, by trying to make pretentious claims for itself instead of soberly advocating the claim of God, it withdraws from the world. It is not inevitable that it will try to do this. But it may very well do so, thus setting itself in the wrong and supremely jeopardising its true life and growth. For if it does, its own common spirit replaces the Holy Spirit, and its own work the work of God—its offices and sacraments, its pure preaching of the Gospel, its liturgies and confessions, its acts of witness and love, its art and theology, its faithfulness to the Bible, its sovereign communities or collegiate governments or authoritarian heads with or without their vestments and golden crosses, its institutions and the specific events of its encounter with God's revelation, its whole *Kyrie eleison*, which is no longer a cry for the mercy of God and in which it does not even take itself literally, let alone allow the world to do so. And the result is the development in the world—for why should not Christians too enjoy some measure of worldly success?—of ecclesiastical authorities which in some degree, greater or smaller or even very small, are self-exalting and self-established. In this respect we are not thinking only of the Pope and his Church, but of what can happen in even the tiniest sects. We are thinking of what can and does always and everywhere happen in a hundred different forms; of the slipping of the community into the sacralisation in which it not only cuts itself off from its own origin and goal and loses its secret by trying to reveal it in itself, but also separates itself for its own pleasure from poor, sinful, erring humanity bleeding from a thousand wounds, trying to impose itself where it owes its witness, and denying and suppressing its witness by witnessing only to itself. Sacralisation means the transmutation of the lordship of Jesus Christ into the vanity of a Christianity which vaunts itself in His name but in reality is enamoured only of itself and its traditions, confessions and institutions. Sacralisation means the suppression of the Gospel by a pseudo-sacred law erected and proclaimed on the supposed basis of the Gospel. Sacralisation means the setting up of an idol which is dead like all other images of human fabrication; which cannot hear or speak or illuminate or help or heal; in which the man who has discovered and created it cannot in the last resort admire or worship anyone or anything but himself. Sacralisation as well as secularisation (and the two are very closely related) means the end of the community. But the men—Christians—who constitute the community are flesh, and it is only too natural that they should have an inclination and desire in this direction. Indeed, the surprising thing is that the community has not perished long since in consequence of this particular inclination. In this respect too—and supremely—it stands in need of preservation.

This is the danger, or the complex of dangers, by which the Christian community and its constitution and action are threatened in the world. There is no lack of examples, both from history and our own day, to prove its reality. The world and man being what they are, both *extra et intra muros*, the dangers are unavoidable. And to some extent they threaten the Church from all four quarters. If for the time being one of them is, or seems to be, warded off and overcome, the only result is that the opposite one usually threatens all the more seriously. There are no final safeguards against any of them. Each has the tendency continually to present itself in new forms, and then to evoke a new form of the others by way of reaction. We may thus compare the Church both past and present to a boat betrayed into the very heart of a cyclone, so that there is every reason to fear that at any moment the very worst will overtake both the boat itself and its helpless and unskilled crew. How often outward pressure or the isolation of the community has been so bad, its alienation or self-glorification so blatant, that we could only think that it was all over—*finis christianismi!* Nor is there any point in concealing the fact that each of the dangers which threatens the community, and especially all of them in their inter-action and co-operation, have the power to destroy it. Both outwardly and inwardly it is not merely a matter of human wickedness and sloth, severity and weakness, error and confusion, but in and behind all these the downward movement of a world on the point of perishing, the power of nothingness lashing out wildly in its final death-throes in this last time which is the time of the community, the violence of chaos which knows that its hour has come and, knowing that it cannot hurt the One who has trodden it underfoot, makes its last and supreme attack on His human attestation in an attempt to suppress and falsify and destroy it. If it has no power against the lordship of God established in Jesus Christ, the signs are all in favour of the fact that it will still enjoy a long and easy mastery over afflicted and anxious Christendom. All kinds of relative considerations and provisional consolations and partial defensive movements are no doubt possible and legitimate and demanded in face of this multiple threat. But we must not allow any illusions to blind us to the fact that finally and properly and incisively only one knowledge, and only one Subject of knowledge, can be of any avail against it. No one and nothing in the whole world is so menaced as Christianity and its constitution and action and future. No one and nothing is so totally referred for its upholding to a single and superior "hold" or support.

It is no accident that of all the books of the Old Testament the Psalter has always been found the most relevant. This is not in spite of the fact, but just because of it, that in so many passages it echoes the people of the covenant trembling for its preservation in final extremity before its all-powerful enemies. The Christian community always has good reason to see itself in this people, and to take on its own lips the words of its helpless sighing, the cries which it utters from the depths of its need. It turns to the Psalter, not in spite of the fact, but just because of it, that as the community of Jesus Christ it knows that it is established on the rock (as powerfully attested by the Psalms themselves), but on the rock which, although it is sure and impregnable in itself, is attacked on all sides, and seems to be of very doubtful security in the eyes of all men and therefore in its own.

That is why—to mention only a single passage—we catch the same notes in verses like Eph. 6:10-20. What is called for here is not merely patience and confidence and boldness but something very different—ἐνδυναμεῖσθαι in the Lord and in the power of His might (v. 10), and therefore ("to be able to stand against the μεθοδείαι of the devil") the putting on of the πανοπλία τοῦ θεοῦ. No other equipment can be used, then, than that with which God Himself takes the field, and the whole of this equipment is needed (v. 11). For the conflict of the community is not just with flesh and blood, and definitely not just with the corruption of man both without and within, but (v. 12) with principalities and powers, with the great and generally accepted presuppositions which rule the world in the continuing darkness of this age, with the spirits of evil which seem to strive against it even from heaven itself. If it is to offer resistance in the evil day, if having done all it is to stand, it has no option but to take to itself the armour of God (v. 13). Listening to His truth, subjection to His righteousness, a readiness for His Gospel, faith in Him, the salvation which is in Him and comes from Him—this is how the equipment is described in vv. 14–17. And its last and supreme piece is "the sword of the Spirit, which is the word of God." Finally (vv. 18–19)—as a clear reminder that in all this we have to do with God's own equipment, so that there can be no question of self-evident triumph on the part of those of God's warriors who seize it—the passage closes with a simple call to prayer and watchfulness "with all perseverance and supplication for all saints," including himself, the apostle adds, that to him too (for it is not self-evident even in his case, or something peculiar to him) "utterance may be given," to open his mouth boldly and joyfully to make known the mystery of the Gospel. It is with this exclusive confidence that the community looks for its preservation from the danger which engulfs it. We remember that it is in Ephesians that the glory of the community is so finely described. But if we re-read the first two chapters and Eph. 4:11–16 from this standpoint, we shall understand that the reference is to the glory of the community as it is genuinely threatened in the world.

If the radical jeopardy in which the community stands is not perceived, it will be difficult to understand the statement to which we must now proceed—that although it is destructible, it cannot and will not actually be destroyed. It is indeed destructible. It belongs to the creaturely world, which is the world of flesh, the world of the perishing man who is assailed by nothingness and all its demons, the world of death. With all that men think and imagine, will and do, plan and achieve along Christian lines, it is part of this world. Like so many other constructs and kingdoms and systems it might well have had its time and then disappeared. It might well have come to an end. It has no miraculous power to protect it against this fate, guaranteeing in advance its continuance in the world, the *perpetuo mansura est* of the *Conf. Aug.* VII. It might have been destroyed. But it cannot and will not actually be destroyed. It may be hounded into a corner, and reduced to the tiniest of minorities, but it cannot be exterminated. It may be destroyed at one point, but it will arise all the stronger at another. It may be ignored and humiliated and scorned by the world which rushes past it in triumphant hostility, but it cannot and will not break under this burden. On the contrary, it will reach a height which will put to shame the superiority of the superior. Its own sloth and dissipation may result in its secularisation, but this will never be so radical that even in its most serious alienation there does not remain an element which resists that which is secular—a remnant from which in some form a sudden or gradual counter-movement can and will always proceed. It may stage some form of the masquerade of sacralisation and suffer the consequences, but at some point, even in all the false glitter with which it is surrounded, the genuine light of the Gospel will again strangely shine out among the *sancti* united round the *sancta*, and the constitution of the *communio* will be maintained. In short, the community may often be almost overwhelmed by the danger which threatens from without and within; but it will never be completely overwhelmed. It may become ill—and where and when was it not dangerously ill? in what great or small society? at what time of resurgence any less than in ages of decline?—but it cannot die: *non omnis moriar*. There will always be a strange persistence: remarkable reformations and prophetic renewals, notable discoveries followed by notable reversions to its origins and equally notable advances into the future. To be sure, this will all stand in the shadow of the destructibility of all human (even Christian) works both old and new, but it will also be an indication of the presence of the indestructible beyond all human works. Neither the wise and powerful of this world, nor the weak forms of Christianity itself, will succeed in setting a term to the community before its time is up and it has attained its goal. In spite of every opposing force it will always still be there, or be there again; and in some hidden way it will always be as young as in the first days, mounting up with wings as eagles. The gates of the underworld (Mt. 16:18) will open up powerfully against it, but will not in fact swallow it up.

But why not? Do not all the indications suggest that it might do this, and that it ought to have done so long since? All the individual Christians—great and small, good and bad—in whom the community has lived, and who have lived in the community, in all ages within the last time, seem not to have been immune against this power to the extent that they have come like all flesh and then departed, having played their various parts in the faith and error and superstition and unbelief of the community, in its action and passion. And we cannot too confidently say that any of the societies and dogmas and cults and traditions and institutions of the

Church have enjoyed any obvious immunity against this power. How much artificial conservatism, and how many later interpretations and constructions, conceal the sober fact that even what seem to be the most solid forms in which the community has existed and still exists in time are no less radically subject to decay and destruction than all other forms of human historical life! They may go back four or ten or fifteen centuries, but their continuity does not constitute a solid basis on which we may know the truth of the promise of Mt. 16:18 and dare to confess it in spite of all appearances to the contrary. At very best, it can only be a sign of its truth and therefore of the upholding of the community. And at worst it may even be a product of human anxiety, obstinacy and mendacity, and thus a very misleading indication of this truth. It is certainly not in and by the strength of continuity itself, any more than by that of the existence of individual Christians, that the communion of saints is upheld.

How, then, is it upheld, and how is the promise kept? In reply to this question, our safest plan is to begin with the simple fact that right up to our own day the Old and New Testament Scriptures have never been reduced to a mere letter in Christian circles, but have continually become a living voice and word, and have had and exercised power as such. To be sure, they have sometimes been almost completely silenced in a thicket of added traditions, or proclaimed only in liturgical sing-song, or overlaid by bold speculation, or searched only for *dicta probantia* in favour of official or private doctrine, or treated merely as a source of pious or even natural and impious morality, or torn asunder into a thousand shreds (each more unimportant than the other) by unimaginative historico-critical omniscience. But they have always been the same Scriptures and the community has never been able to discard them. Scriptures? A mere book then? No, a chorus of very different and independent but harmonious voices. An organism which in its many and varied texts is full of vitality within the community. Something which can speak and make itself heard in spite of all its maltreatment at the hands of the half-blind and arbitrary and officious. There are many things—even things supposedly taken from Scripture—to which we cannot return once we have discovered and sufficiently admired them. But in some way there has always been a return to the Bible. There are many things which sooner or later become mere repetitions and therefore hollow and empty and silent. But the Bible has always spoken afresh, and the more impressively sometimes when it is surrounded by all kinds of misuse and misunderstanding. That Scripture upholds the community is not something that Christians can fabricate by their own Bible-lectures and Bible-study or even by the Scripture principle, but it is something that Scripture achieves of itself. It often does it by very strange and devious ways. It may not do it directly, to the shame of its most faithful and attentive readers, but in the form of an echo awakened in the outside world, so that its readers have to begin to study it in a new way. But at some point, as a fellowship of those who hear its voice, the threatened community begins to group and consolidate and constitute itself afresh around the Bible, and in so doing it again finds itself on solid ground when everything seems to totter. It is the Holy Spirit who upholds the community as it is He who causes it to grow and live. But according to the defiant saying in Eph. 6:17 the "sword of the Spirit" which protects and defends it is the Word of God. And according to what is often the reluctant recognition of the community of all times and places the Word of God has always been heard in its one, original and authentic form where Scripture has again made itself to be heard and created hearers for itself. Thus when the harassed community prays for its preservation its prayer must always take the concrete form: "Preserve us, Lord, by Thy Word," with the concrete meaning: By Thy Word attested in Scripture. The preservation of the community takes place as it is upheld by this prophetic and apostolic word, or as it is led back as a hearing community to this word. And so we can only say to Christians who are troubled about the preservation of the community or the maintaining of its cause that they should discard all general and philosophico-historical considerations (however unsettling or cheerful) and hear, and hear again, and continually hear this word, being confronted both as individual and united hearers by the fact that the community certainly cannot uphold itself, but that all the same it is in fact upheld, being placed in the communion of saints as this continually takes place in the hearing of this word. With the flowing of this stream, however low or sluggish its waters may sometimes be, the communion of saints takes place, and is therefore upheld.

But the reference to Scripture obviously cannot be our final and decisive answer to the question of the sure and reliable mode of its preservation. The word of all the prophets and apostles put together can only be a witness which requires—and does not lack—verification by the One whom it attests. It is in the power of this verification that Scripture is the instrument by which the Church is upheld. As the One whom it attests verifies its witness, it is He who primarily and properly upholds the Church. He verifies Scripture simply by the fact that He is its content; that as it is read and heard He Himself is present to speak and act as the living Lord of the Church. There concretely, as the One who was and is and will be according to the word of the prophets and apostles, He exists for the world and community of our time—the last time. There concretely, i.e., in the form attested there, He is revealed and may be known. There concretely He encounters Christians and therefore the world. From there concretely His Holy Spirit comes and works and rules. It is thus true already that from there concretely the Church is upheld by the Holy Spirit. But it is upheld only as He who is attested in Scripture does this; as He Himself is there not merely as letter but as Spirit and Life; as He is not past and inactive and silent, but the Son of God and Man, and Saviour of the world, who is present to-day, and acts here and now, and speaks with His own. It is because He is within His community, conducting its cause (both for itself and therefore for the world) in face of the great impending danger, that the destructible Church cannot in fact be destroyed; that the mortal Church cannot die; that the gates of hell cannot swallow it up. It stands or falls with Him. But He does not fall, and so the Church cannot fall. It can only stand. It can and must and will rise again even though it falls. He cannot deny Himself, or be untrue to Himself. And as the One who cannot do this, He upholds the community, and it is always upheld—simply by the fact that He is who He is, and that in it we always have to do with Him, because it is His body, the earthly-historical form of His existence. The outward and inward threat which overhangs the community, the whole onslaught of the chaos which He has mortally wounded, is no match at all for Him. It cannot defeat Him, nor can it separate Him as the Head from the community as His body. He, as the *totus Christus*, cannot die. That is why the community of His harassed and anxious saints also cannot die.

Confidence in its cause and continuance and future and triumph depends absolutely upon the fact that it is always confidence in Him; that renouncing all other helpers it keeps only to Him who is not only a Helper but already the Conqueror, the Victor, the death of death, and who as such is not apart from but with His saints. For the community everything depends upon its readiness not to try to be anything more or better or surer than His people, His body, and to live and grow as such on earth. In every deviation from confidence in Him, it can only be deceived as to its preservation, and know that it is doomed and lost. There is no objective need, or even possibility, of concern and anxiety or despair concerning its preservation. This can arise only when there is deviation; when search is made for other helpers; when there is a desertion of the

Victor by whom the community—even though it may be threatened on all sides, even though it may be under assault or the cross, even though it may be secularised or sacralised—is objectively victorious, and thus able at all times to throw off every fear. There is objective need to rejoice in its actual preservation. As the community does this, it is in a position to take up its human responsibilities with new thankfulness, seriousness and soberness, not folding its hands, but when it has prayed, and as it continues to do so, going boldly to work as if it were not threatened by any dangers. *Fluctuat nec mergitur.* The One who is attested and attests Himself in the Bible will never have any other message for His threatened community than that it should be confident, not because it has no reason for anxiety as it exists in the world, but because of the counter-reason which radically removes this reason—that He has overcome the world (Jn. 16:33).

10

RAY S. ANDERSON

Living in the Spirit

1 'THE KENOTIC COMMUNITY'

But how is the Presence known? How tested? And what is this life with which man then is dowered? In the midst of a world constantly, sullenly, wilfully, despairingly denying this life of persons as the one historical reality, where is this community of which you speak? And how, even if there is such a community, may it possibly continue in life amid such hostile and perverse circumstances?[1]

'THE WIND BLOWS WHERE IT WILLS', SAID JESUS, 'AND YOU HEAR the sound of it, but you do not know whence it comes or whither it goes; so it is with every one who is born of the Spirit.'[2] The reality of the wind is in the snap of the sail, the wing of the gull curved motionless between earth and sky, in the pull of a kite string in the hand, and in the dance of the leaves on an autumn day. The form of life *is* the reality, not as aesthetics would have it—where the impression is captured in an image—but as the sailor has it when the boat leaps forward, or as the child has it when the kite string tugs in his hand like a living thing. Not every form has the breath of wind in it—for a form can die, and can even have a kind of beauty in death—but every wind of spirit finds its reality in a form of life.

To speak then of Presence without also speaking of form is to

---

1. R. G. Smith, 'History is Personal', *Collected Papers*, p. 11.
2. John 3:8.

From Ray S. Anderson, *Historical Transcendence and the Reality of God*, pp. 227–251. © Geoffrey Chapman Publisher, London, 1975; William B. Eerdmans Publishing Company, Grand Rapids, 1975. Used by permission of the Publishers.

lose touch with reality. It is to take leave of one's senses, in the most sensible use of the word. The style and shape of life in its most tangible form is the reality of spirit which gives substance to faith. 'If a brother or sister is ill-clad and in lack of daily food, and one of you says to them, "Go in peace, be warmed and filled", without giving them the things needed for the body, what does it profit?'[3] These 'works'—food and clothing—constitute the reality of spirit according to James: 'For as the body apart from the spirit is dead, so faith apart from works is dead.'[4] Disembodied love is a state of mind, and thus does not exist at all. Disembodied spirits have a particular terror for us—especially in the dark—but there is really no certainty that they exist, except in our minds. If there is such a thing as a disembodied act or presence of God as Spirit, could one love it, or be comforted by it? What is the form of God in the world—what is the life-form of Spirit?

This, of course, is Bonhoeffer's question: 'What is the form of Christ in the world?'[5] It is the question of the reality of God for a world which has 'come of age'. We have seen how Bonhoeffer attempted to answer that question by grounding the reality of God in the pole of 'this-worldly transcendence'—that is, in man's basic social relations—while at the same time attempting to sustain the other pole of transcendence in a personal union with Christ centred in the secret discipline. As a result, for Bonhoeffer, the experience of transcendence in terms of one person's transcendence of another became the life-form of the historical transcendence of God. In effect, this makes man's historical existence the form in which one seeks the historical transcendence of God as Spirit. Thus, the Spirit of God (and so the person of Christ) *is* the reality of the form of trancendence within history, and consequently, one can speak of a religionless Christianity. Beginning with the problem, as was done at the outset of this chapter, this appears to be a quite valid way of attempting a solution. However, in proceeding to expose the inner logic of God's relation to the world, particularly through the Incarnation, we found it necessary to assert that the transcendent ground for the life of the Spirit in the world is the historical existence of Jesus Christ as the eternal Logos. The Incarnate Word is the *form* for the reality of Spirit. The historical transcendence of God has

3. James 2:15–16.
4. James 2:26.
5. This is the phrase chosen by John A. Phillips for the title of his book on Bonhoeffer's thought: *The Form of Christ in the World.* For the general idea of this form of expression, cf. D. Bonhoeffer, *Letters and Papers From Prison,* pp. 279–280.

only one form—that of the Incarnate Son. This was God's act in the world which, abstracted from all other human acts, remains itself both human and historical, and yet, an act of God. This is God's historical transcendence because it is the life of God *with* man in history and not just through man. We were therefore led to conclude that the Spirit has no history of his own, but has the form of the Incarnate Son.[6] As a result, we must say that the work and act of the Spirit is more like a re-formation of human existence in the form of Christ.

This life-form of the Spirit in the world has its transcendent ground in the life-form of the Incarnate Word—Jesus Christ—and its concrete ground in the historical existence of the 'new man' who lives in the Spirit.[7] Therefore, and on this point hangs the argument of this book, the transcendence of God is a reality of Spirit in which the historical existence of the man in whom the Spirit dwells is re-formed according to the form of Jesus Christ, the Incarnate Word, who is at once the image of the invisible God and the image in which man is created.[8] This reality of Spirit cannot be called the historical transcendence of God, for that belongs uniquely to the life of the Incarnate Word, but should rather be called a lived transcendence by which the reality of God impinges upon the world through the historical existence of the man who lives in the Spirit of God.

There are three implications of this which I wish to work out as a way of showing how historical transcendence is completed in lived transcendence, or, one could say, how Christology flows into Ecclesiology. These three implications constitute the theme for the final three chapters of *Historical Transcendence:* (1) lived transcendence is a community of life in the Spirit which takes the form of both a kenotic and ek-static existence; (2) lived transcendence is a reality of life in solidarity with the world which has both an incarnational and evangelical existence among men; and (3) lived transcendence is an eschatological life in God in which history and faith are bound up in the relation of the penultimate to the ultimate. While these three implications will each touch upon the nature and the mission of the church, the discussion will stay within the bounds of a critique.[9] That is, the overriding concern will not be

6. See my *Historical Transcendence and the Word of God,* pp. 218ff.

7. Cf. Ephesians 2:14–22.

8. Colossians 1:15; 3:10.

9. That is, a critique in the sense that Kant sought to clarify the nature and function of reason, rather than in developing an organon of reason. Cf. *Critique of Pure Reason,* pp. 58–59.

with methodology, but with the imperative essence of the transcendence of God as it has been disclosed to us through the Incarnation. As such, these implications constitute more of a preparation for a doctrine of the church, or perhaps even a canon, according to which the church may work out and place into execution the doctrine of its own existence in the world.

Turning then to the first implication, namely, that lived transcendence is a community of life in the Spirit, it can be said that this life is a life of *kenotic* community. Here again, it must be made clear that we are not searching for a clever way of introducing yet another alternative way for the church to find a new form of expression in the world. A kenotic *way* of life simply does not grasp the fundamental content of the life of the Spirit, and thus fails to touch the imperative essence of that life itself. What is even more dangerous is that the assumption of a kenotic way of life on the part of the church in the world occludes the very truth which the *kenosis* discloses, and envelopes the ego of the church ever more securely in a posture of humility. A life which is devoted to self-emptying can be a life committed most powerfully to a manner of self-existence.[10] It is most understandable that the natural reaction to a power-full church is a radical call for a power-less church. But, while the way of poverty and powerlessness is indeed a more attractive virtue than a spirit of acquisitiveness and superiority, that way is a temptation because of its very attractiveness. When the right hand knows what the left hand is doing (Matthew 6:3), it is difficult, and probably impossible, to keep the 'subtraction' from becoming an addition.

When the kenotic life of the Spirit is equated with a kenotic principle of self-emptying, the church can be confronted with a challenge that it cannot possibly understand, much less put into practice. It is easy to sympathize with Bonhoeffer's impatience with the church, particularly when writing from a prison cell, but his final thoughts concerning the future of the church invoked a kenotic principle without coming to grips with the reality of kenotic community:

10. I would want to distinguish here between a 'posture' of humility, which effects an attitude as a means to achieve an idealist form of *kenosis*, and a concrete life of humility which involves commitment and discipline. For example, I would consider Bonhoeffer's emphasis upon obedience and discipleship not merely a kenotic 'way of life', but kenotic living itself in the most concrete sense of the word. The humility of the kenotic life cannot be sought for and achieved, but comes more as humiliation arising out of obedience in the concrete situation.

The church is the church only when it exists for others. To make a start, it should give away all its property to those in need. The clergy must live solely on the free-will offerings of their congregations, or possibly engage in some secular calling. The church must share in the secular problems of ordinary human life, not dominating but helping and serving. . . .It must not under-estimate the importance of a human example (which has its origin in the humanity of Jesus and is so important in Paul's teaching); . . .[11]

My argument is not that what Bonhoeffer suggests may not need to take place; rather, I question the superficiality of what appears as a very radical proposal. If by the church Bonhoeffer has in mind a specific group of people, and if they accepted his suggestion as the truly kenotic way of life and disposed of all their worldly endowments, what then? The example which this dramatic act would produce would not exist for long without some reinforcement. As an example, it may have some negative value in terms of the indictment which it pronounces against every form of misrepresentation of Christ through the seeking of power and privilege in the world, although the real value of this in terms of producing a positive result is questionable. But there is little here of an example of the kenotic community which lives in the Spirit. Many churches would only discover that without their endowments, institutions and programmes, they would have very little in common as a fellowship of believers. This, of course, is not thereby to justify the existence of a church which depends upon such outward forms for its survival. I simply do not find such an approach very helpful in making clear the fundamental reality of lived transcendence in terms of kenotic community.[12]

11. 'Outline For a Book', *Letters and Papers From Prison*, pp. 382–383.
12. More recent attempts to use the kenotic theme as a principle for renewing the church reveal a genuine concern for a more authentic Christian community, but tend to use *kenosis* as a way to re-pristinate an original and more spiritual concept of Christian faith. D. M. MacKinnon says: 'But the issue of *kenosis* and Establishment is in the end an issue of spirituality. To live as a Christian in the world today is necessarily to live an exposed life; it is to be stripped of the kind of security that tradition, whether ecclesiological or institutional, easily bestows.' *The Stripping of the Altars*, The Fontana Library, Collins, London, 1969, p. 34. MacKinnon has in mind the particular form of institutionalism represented by the Anglican Church, and he appeals to what he calls the 'law of *kenosis*' as the way to a more vital Christianity. He grounds this concept of *kenosis* in the 'initiating act of the whole incarnate life', and suggests that there is relevance in the

The question is not, it seems to me, how the church can assume a kenotic way of life—for that assumes that there is such a thing as the church prior to and apart from a kenotic community—but, of where one locates the reality of the church itself. A life of kenotic community is not a way of life which will put new life into a dying institution if its primary virtue is a renunciation of privilege and power for its own sake. There may well be a genuine kenotic life which *appears* similar to this way of life, but its source and its (ultimate) power comes from another Spirit. In a word, the life of kenotic community is a life of *transcendence*.

When we probe the depths of *kenosis*, as we have done in *Historical Transcendence*, we discover that what appears as a way of life through self-emptying on the part of the man Jesus, and thus looks to an observer like a God giving away his divinity, is actually a quality of life intrinsic to the relation of Father and Son which is exemplified by the Son's human obedience even unto death.[13] From the furthest side of human estrangement, the intradivine transcendence exposed itself as a community of love which overcame the estrangement and reclaimed the estranged ones by inclusion in the divine life itself. The Holy Spirit, who was 'being accustomed' to dwelling in human flesh, as Irenaeus puts it,[14] through the intimate union of the Son with humanity, becomes one

---

concept for the 'articulation of an essential as distinct from an economic Trinity' (p. 17). This is a hopeful direction, and while MacKinnon does not elaborate upon this he does reaffirm the notion of *kenosis* as pointing to the 'deepest sense of the mystery of the incarnation' in a later writing (' "Substance" in Christology—a Cross-bench View', *Christ Faith and History,* S. W. Sykes and J. P. Clayton, eds., Cambridge University Press, 1972, p. 297). Robert Adolfs, from whom MacKinnon draws inspiration for the kenotic theme, has a good deal more to say about the way in which a 'law of *kenosis*' can be applied to the juridical and ecclesiastical power structure of the church, with specific reference to his own communion, which is Roman Catholic. Here again, the emphasis is upon practical modification to the existing structure of the church (many of them highly appropriate to any type of modern church) without really showing how this can take place other than by imposing a concept in such a way that 'a change of heart' takes place: 'One final question still remains to be answered—how is this change of direction towards the kenotic Church to be accomplished? It will certainly not be brought about by any 'measures' or by reorganization. It will above all be the result of a *metanoia*, a change of heart or conversion, the development of a new mentality, a kenotic attitude.' *The Grave of God,* A Compass Book, Burns and Oates, London, 1967, p. 149.
13. See my *Historical Transcendence,* Chapter V, especially pp. 179ff.
14. *Ibid.,* p. 175, n. 86.

with the kenotic *form* as explicated by the Son in his humanity and thus creates a kenotic community which is itself an image or likeness of the intra-divine community. This became visible through the way in which Jesus brought his 'little flock' with him into the depths (and heights) of his own kenotic experience. They were partakers of his suffering, and thus bearers of his own glory.[15] There was then, along with the historical transcendence of God through the life of the Son, already a lived transcendence of kenotic community through the life of the Spirit. We have earlier observed how the transcendence of God in a living way became more and more identified with the Spirit during the final period of Jesus' life.[16] The form in which the Spirit would express the power (*exousia*) of the living God had already been determined through the life of the Son. It was not the ideal form (Platonic) of which the material and human form was only a shadow, but it was the kenotic form (Incarnational) in which the intra-divine transcendence of God exposed its own reality. To say, then, that the transcendent form of the Spirit is the life of the Son is not to imply that there is any ideal form of a transcendental kind which determines the real life of the Spirit, but the form is a reality of historical transcendence. It is necessary to make this clear to avoid falling into the error of idealism whereby the kenotic life of the Spirit becomes a principle by which man determines his own existence, or a 'law of *kenosis*' by which the church achieves its own renewal. If one cuts loose from the historical transcendence of the man Jesus, the life of the Spirit tends to become idealized and confused with self-consciousness (Schleiermacher).

If we were to express the fundamental meaning of *kenosis*, then, it could be said to be the intrinsic character of divine love itself, and thus conceived as an activity rather than as essence. The intrinsic character of this love has its clearest explication in the life of the Incarnate Logos, but this also clarifies the nature of man as created in the image of God. The dogma of *kenosis* tells us that the transcendence of God is as real in the image of God as for God himself. *Kenosis* can be, therefore, another way of understanding the image of God, or of stating the true nature of man. *Kenosis* means that man has his true nature completed when he participates in the intra-divine transcendence (love), and that this participation does not involve the repudiation or violation of that which is truly human.

15. John 17:10.
16. See *Historical Transcendence*, pp. 182, 211.

The life of the Spirit, therefore, is the transcendence of God understood kenotically. That is, even as the Spirit was active in the Incarnate Logos, making possible a genuine human response and participation in the divine life, the Spirit continues to act in this *form* by re-forming man into the form of Christ. But this is also the *real* form (if not the actual) of man's intrinsic nature as the image of God. And by suggesting that the real form of man's nature as the image of God is not always realized in actuality, I do not mean to introduce a philosophical distinction between the real and the actual, but to point to an actual estrangement, which, because it is estrangement from the reality of community with God, is a real estrangement which man experiences from his own true nature. Man's estrangement is real, and not merely actual (in a phenomenological sense) because man is grounded by the nature of his own being in the transcendence of God. Therefore, one could say that man's real form of authentic existence is to be found in the person of Jesus Christ. In him the real and the actual were never split apart. This is what it means to speak of the 'sinlessness' of Jesus. He experienced the reality of fellowship with God with no actual deviation from that reality, even from the furthest side of man's estrangement. In its most positive sense, this is what kenotic community means.

It can now be said that the particular character of the kenotic way of life is not an ethical pattern of life modelled after the style of Jesus, nor is it a kind of suffering or self-renunciation which seeks to emulate Christ. And still less is it a programme for poverty, by which the church seeks to re-form itself in the shape of the destitute. I say that these do not constitute the particular character of kenotic community, as though one could use these methods as means to a higher end. In the kenotic community, life in the Spirit is the end, and not the means to an end. Because the kenotic community has first of all radicalized the presence of the Other in terms of my own existence, the Other in his concreteness becomes my end, and never my means to an end. The reality of the Spirit for me, thus, cannot take the form of my own historical existence and so confirm me in a state of perfectionism, with its corresponding intolerance of the Other, or reduce me to a state of hopelessness, unable to escape my actual limitations. But the Spirit can assume the historical existence of the Other in the kenotic community as the form of reality for me, so that now I can find my real existence in my actual relation to him. The Other then becomes the form of Christ for me as the Spirit assumes that particular historical existence in which Christ is re-formed. Because I meet my own real existence when I act in love towards the Other, I see beyond his actual existence with its limitations and immaturities. I do not merely tolerate him, I see his reality as a person. We are touching again upon what was earlier alluded to as an 'unfinished' aspect to covenant response in creation. That is, if man's 'transcending limit' represented as the tree of knowledge of good and evil should be said to become 'enfleshed' through the creation of woman, so that man could then 'love his limit' as himself, this pointed towards the transcendence of Spirit in the form of an 'enfleshment' recognized in a community of relation. As the Spirit re-forms the Other in the form of Christ, I can love the Other as the transcending limit of my own existence in the flesh.[17]

This only explains the particular character of the kenotic community, and shows how the kenotic community can be re-formed in the likeness of Christ without denying or falsifying the actual life of persons. This explains how one can speak of the presence of Christ in the kenotic community—he is really there in the historical existence of the Other who gives concrete form to the Holy Spirit—without resorting to a mystical, and consequently, a subjectivizing way of thinking.[18] And finally, this shows, as Professor MacKinnon rightly points out, that the ultimate significance of Christian community is kenotic—that is, it is received, not imposed.[19] It is the gift of the Spirit which Christ himself promised, so that his followers should not be *alone*.[20]

There are quite clearly two things implied in the character of kenotic community as it has been explicated above. *First*, the kenotic community is formed of actual people who have their place in the community, not by virtue of their capacity to love or their maturity of spirit, but by virtue of their common humanity with Christ and the reality of the Holy Spirit which comes as a gift.

---

17. *Ibid.*, pp. 142–143.
18. While I would not want to discount a genuine mystical dimension to theology, and to Christian experience, I am questioning here the kind of mysticism which operates out of an antithesis between spirit and matter, and consequently seeks to 'transcend' the world of sense-experience in order to know God in an immediate sense of oneness of spirit which has no cognitive or temporal structures. Cf. T. F. Torrance who says: '. . . an experience in which the mystic is said to take leave of his senses is to be discounted, that is, an experience in which cognition is not *rationally* mediated through the senses or which uses sense-experience merely as a spring-board to enter a realm that transcends it altogether. That is a form of *docetism.*' *Theological Science*, p. 189.
19. *Stripping the Altars*, p. 40.
20. John 14:15–17.

When the Holy Spirit assumes the historical existence of the other man as the form of Christ for me, a cripple is no less real than a whole person. *Second*, and this follows from the first, the kenotic community offers to each person, to the extent that he is able to bear it, an actual growth into the reality of his own personhood, which is the capacity to live in love.

It is the transcendence of God which constitutes each person in the kenotic community; first of all, through the historical transcendence of the Son of God by which the appropriate human response is made from the furthest side of human estrangement, so that the weakest of human flesh *already* possesses a place of participation; and then through the Holy Spirit who takes each person's actual life into fellowship with Christ. This life in the Spirit has its ground in the historical life of Christ himself, but has concrete expression in the life of the community itself—such as it is.

Such as it is! And here we come to the heart of the matter. For the fundamental truth of the kenotic community is not revealed to the theologian at his desk, but to the pastor in the midst of his people. It is one thing to say that the kenotic community is formed of actual people, it is quite another thing to know how actually sick, how actually weak, how actually unable to love, and how actually unlovable actual people can be! But here is where the kenotic community establishes its real character, for it dares to include those who have the capacity (and often the compulsion) to destroy the community itself, and even more, it dares to offer love as a possibility of growth. The same Spirit who led Jesus to choose Judas as one of his intimate followers prior to the resurrection, baptized Ananias and Sapphira into the kenotic community of lived transcendence.[21] Here we see that the true kenotic community is marked, not by whom it is willing to renounce, but whom it is willing to receive. But there is more implied in this 'receiving' than a blind spot in the centre of one's vision. For the 'being received' is a participation in lived transcendence, for such is the nature of kenotic community.

The kenotic community thus touches man at his most vulnerable spot—his willingness to receive the Spirit of God and to enter into fellowship with Christ. Here again we can see just how the transcendence of God acts through a kenotic movement. The one who discovers that he is received into the community by virtue of his common humanity with Christ, and not by virtue of any 'qualify-

21. Acts 5:1-11.

ing' efforts of his own, does not stand in the circumference at some distance from the transcendence of God in the community, but is immediately placed in a relation of transcendence through the reality of Spirit who assumes the form of the Other's concrete existence. There are two marks of visibility for the transcendence of God at this point. One is the visibility of historical transcendence in the revelation concerning God's act in Jesus Christ as contained in the Scriptures. This is a form of visibility which assumes an audible form as the Word of God is 'heard', and yet, one is ultimately confronted by the historical existence of the Word as Jesus Christ. The other form of visibility is the presence of the Spirit in the concrete life of the other person in the community, or, one could say, in the concrete existence of the community itself.[22] These represent the 'two poles of transcendence' which come together in the kenotic community as two visible and concrete realities, each of which 'places' the person in a relation to God's transcendence.[23]

It is at this point, however, that the one who is 'received' in this kenotic way is touched at the crucial point of his own 'receptivity'. To receive the Spirit of God in this way, represents a radical and devastating confrontation with one's actual situation of spiritual autonomy, which we have already called estrangement from fellowship with God. To receive now means a reversal of the Ego and a 'turning towards' the transcendence of God with openness and a 'change of mind' (*metanoia*) which represents a conversion to God

22. Lesslie Newbigin, in his book, *The Household of God*, SCM Press, London, 1953, lays great emphasis on the visibility of the church: 'The Christian community is precisely as visible as the Christian man.' p. 29. He suggests that Luther 'abandoned his deepest insight of justification by faith' when he substituted the unbiblical distinction between the visible and the invisible church (p. 127). I would think that Newbigin would agree that to speak of an invisible church is to retreat from the reality of the kenotic community. The more critical question, it seems to me, is the question of the distinction between the 'Christian man' and the non-Christian man in terms of the kenotic community. This will reappear as an area of concern in the next chapter [of *Historical Transcendence*].

23. I only wish to note here that I see the two poles of transcendence as *both* concretely placed in history, contrary to Bonhoeffer (see *Historical Transcendence*, p. 218). For Bonhoeffer, the historical transcendence of God was concrete and represented by the presence of the Other, while the personal transcendence of Christ through the Spirit was immediately related to this historical transcendence through faith. I would give a more cognitive dimension to faith by seeing revelation in terms of the content of Scripture as well as the immediate relation of Spirit.

in the deepest sense of the word. It seems clear from the character of kenotic community as it has been exposed, that a conversion 'experience' cannot be demanded as the qualifying act on the part of a person for his belonging to the kenotic community. This has some very important implications. But it must also immediately be said that participation in the kenotic community does involve receiving as well as being received. And it may well be that only after 'being received' for a considerable length of love (one would naturally say 'time', but these 'lengths' have a duration which only love can measure!) can a person muster the strength and the will to receive. This is, of course, what is entailed in the second aspect of the character of the kenotic community: it offers to each person, to the extent that he is able to bear it, an *actual* growth into the reality of his own personhood, which is the capacity to live in love.[24]

There is, I think, something which can be said about the form, if not the structure, of the church at this point which arises directly out of the character of kenotic community. We have seen that the kenotic community is the 'place' where both poles of God's transcendence come together in such a way that man is 'placed' in a living fellowship with God so that his *actual* existence is taken seriously in terms of his *real* personhood. The kenotic community can be said then to be the 'home of personhood' where man is both received as a person and then, at the same time, receives his personhood. The word which I am searching for in attempting to interpret this in terms of a form for the church could be best expressed as 'domestic'. The home or domicile for man is community with God. There he receives his true personhood. In this sense of the word, domestic refers to the total context in which the Spirit of God works to create man's personhood. The Spirit can be known as the 'domesticating' Spirit of God, who creates the place where man *learns* to receive his personhood. It is not too difficult to interpret the creation story (as given in Genesis) domestically. The world is for man his domicile, his home with God, in which he is a participant with God in the creative process. All the while, man is learning to receive and growing towards his true personhood.[25]

I should think that it would be helpful for the church to see its

24. See *Historical Transcendence*, p. 234.

25. This recalls for us the central motif in the theology of Irenaeus, who sees Adam as the child who finds his completion in the man Jesus. This is brought out especially in G. Wingren's work on Irenaeus, *Man and the Incarnation*, pp. 49, 127.

true form as contiguous with that of the domestic shape of creation itself, and thus understand the redemptive dimension as integral to the creative, rather than as an end in itself. It would also seem that the immediate implication of the domestic motif of the kenotic community for the church in a practical sense would be the recognition of the need to help each person receive the Spirit of God and so live in the transcendence of a communicating and loving personhood. The question which would appear to have priority, and thus the determining question for the shape of the church's ministry, is the question: why is this person unable to receive? Assuming that the church is a genuine kenotic community where the transcendence of Word and Spirit are both concretely given and active, the church can creatively (in the true theological sense) take up the domestic functions of kenotic community by seeing actual persons as real persons, and providing the necessary (or perhaps overcoming the hindering) conditions for growth in true personhood. In Pauline language, the church thus is a 'household' of faith, gives itself to the 'edification' of the body, and identifies the particular domestic functions as 'gifts of the Spirit'.[26]

This 'domesticating' function of the kenotic community should then take into account the actual life of the person in the world. Rather than opposing a religious life to a secular life, or splitting a person's commitment between his life-work and his 'church-work', the domestic Spirit of kenotic community relates a man creatively to his place and function in a created world. It is not the least of the values of the kenotic community to suggest that it works to redeem the world, not by speaking with a posture of authority to issues, but by domesticating man himself to a life in the Spirit. But what the concept of kenotic community has to offer the church is a way of seeing that a true life in the Spirit is not alien to man's creative vocation in the world.

For the kenotic community, poverty is not that which it gives away, but that which it receives; powerlessness is not in the abandonment of a place in the world, but in refusing to let go of the weak for the sake of the strong; humility is not in taking less than the world, but in receiving more than the world can give. The kenotic community has no Presence other than its own existence, or rather, God's presence to himself in its existence. It has no sacristy to be profaned, no temple to be destroyed, no Prince to be exiled—or ignored; and it has no answer to the question put at the beginning of this chapter. For *such as it is*, it is the transcendence of God. The answer is in the wind.

26. Galatians 6:10; I Corinthians 12:1–11; 14:12.

2 'THE EK-STATIC COMMUNITY'

In a world of fugitives
One who moves in the opposite direction
Will appear to run away.[27]

Being something of an anarchist at heart (the Spirit blows where it wills), I have a notion that a domestic Spirit is not necessarily a house-bound Spirit, nor is kenotic community necessarily an earth-bound fellowship. At this point, an important corrective needs to be applied, lest domesticity be misconstrued as slavery, and life in the Spirit be reduced to life with one another. Will a parable help?

Imagine that geese could talk, Kierkegaard once said, and that they had arranged things so that they too could have their church services and their worship.

Every Sunday they would assemble together and a gander would preach.

The essential content of the sermon was the exalted destiny of geese, the exalted goal for which the creator has destined geese (and every time his name was named all the geese curtsied and the ganders bowed their heads). With the help of their wings they could fly away to far countries, blessed countries, where they were really at home: for here they were just like exiles.

And so every Sunday. Then the gathering broke up, and every goose waddled home. Then the next Sunday off they went to the service again, then home again. That was all. They throve and grew fat, they became plump and tender. . . .

That was all. For while the sermon sounded so exalted on Sundays, on Mondays they would tell one another of the fate of the goose who wanted to take his high destiny seriously, with the help of the wings the creator had given it. And they spoke of the horrors it had to endure. But they prudently kept this knowledge among themselves. For of course to speak of it on Sundays was most unsuitable, for as they said, in that case it would be obvious that our service would be a mockery both of God and of ourselves.

There were also among the geese some that looked ill and thin. Of them the others said, 'You see, that's what comes of being serious about wanting to fly. It is because they are always

27. R. G. Smith, 'J. G. Hamann and the Princess Gallitzin', *Philomathes,* Robert Palmer and Robert Hamerton-Kelly (eds.), Martinus Nijhoff, The Hague, p. 339.

thinking of flying that they get thin and do not thrive, and do not have God's grace as we do. That is why we get plump and fat and tender, for it is by God's grace that one gets plump and fat and tender.'[28]

So it is with Christians, adds Kierkegaard; they conclude that the domesticating grace of God is not meant to take seriously the wings of the spirit, for to do so emaciates one's well-being and destroys one's peace as an earth-bound creature. Whereas, in fact, the wings are meant to be used—man has spirit, and thus is destined to live a transcendent life.

For all of its visibility and concreteness, then, life in the Spirit is a lived *transcendence*. The kenotic community is earth-related, for it exists in the same flesh as that of Jesus of Nazareth, but it is not earth-bound, for it lives in the same Spirit as did Jesus. When we explored the kenotic life which Jesus lived, we saw that with the deepest penetration of humanity and from the furthest side of human estrangement, he lived in unbroken communion with the Father. His prayers were considered as evidences of this extra-human relation on the part of a genuinely human person. If his relation to humanity as the eternal Logos can be called a *hypo-static* relation, that is, as the particular man Jesus he was the bearer of human nature in its totality, one then could designate his movement toward the Father as an *ek-static* relation. These two aspects cannot be separated in such a way that Jesus could be considered a 'person' by virtue of either his hypo-static or his ek-static being; rather, as Dr. John Zizioulas says,

> *Ekstasis* and *Hypostasis* represent two basic aspects of Personhood, and it is not to be regarded as a mere accident that both of these words have been historically applied to the notion of Person. Thus the idea of Person affirms at once both that being cannot be 'contained' or 'divided', and that the mode of its existence, its *hypostasis*, is absolutely unique and unrepeatable. Without these two conditions being falls into an a-personal reality, defined and described like a mere 'substance', i.e., it becomes a thing.[29]

28. *The Last Years,* 'Journals 1853–55', edited and translated by R. G. Smith, The Fontana Library, Collins, London, 1965, pp. 292–293.
29. 'Human Capacity and Human Incapacity', *Scottish Journal of Theology,* 28, 1975, pp. 401–447. Dr. Zizioulas, in developing an ontological concept of personhood, suggests that, rather than man being a human person by virtue of what is possessed *qua* individual, man's true humanity is expressed in his movement towards community in God. This 'ek-static'

movement constitutes personhood, not merely personality: 'Man's personhood should not be understood in terms of "personality", i.e., of a complex of psychological or moral qualities which are in some sense "possessed" by or "contained" in the human *individuum*. On the contrary,
being a person is basically different from being an individual or "personality" in that the person can not be conceived in itself as a static entity, but
only as it *relates* to. Thus personhood implies the "openness of being",
and even more than that, the *ek-stasis* of being, i.e., a movement towards
communion.' *Ibid.*, p. 6. If one follows Dr. Zizioulas here in thinking not
of person as 'being' (*ousia*) but as 'presence' (*par-ousia*), the notion of
being 'present to God' through direct communion underlines what I have
termed 'covenant response'. Therefore, the question of the divine Logos
constituting a truly human response is not simply a question of the 'being'
of Christ and the 'being' of God (i.e., a question of an ontic cleft within
God), but a question of the movement (*ek-stasis*) towards community in
God from the standpoint of the creature in union with (*hypo-stasis*) the
divine Logos. The concept of *ek-stasis* as the distinctive dimension of
personhood has its roots more in the definition of person suggested by
Richard of St. Victor than that of Boethius. Richard held that a person is an
incommunicable existence of an intellectual nature (*person est in-
tellectualis naturae incommunicabilis exsistentia*). Dr. Heribert Mühlen
shows how this concept of person was taken up by Johannes Duns Scotus
and developed ontologically as the *ex-sistentia* of a triune God (*Sein und
Person nach Johannes Duns Scotus,* Dietrich-Coelde-Verlag, Werl.,
Westf., 1954, pp. 4ff.). The two basic questions which Dr. Mühlen frames
as the outline of his study show in what sense *ek-static* human personhood
is ontologically derived from the *ek-sistence* of God himself: 'Is the essence of man only a standing and a resting on one's own basis (*in sich
ruhender Selbstand*) and a having of oneself in one's own power, or does
there not rather belong in addition to the essence of man, the "whence"
and the "whither" (*das Woher und Wohin*) of his existence? Is not the
essential thing for man and the ek-static (*ek-statische*) in the sense of
Richard of St. Victor, the relation to the origin, to the "whence" of his
existence, a relation which "stands out" of itself (*aus sich herausstehende
Bezug*)?' p. 6. The retention of the hyphenated form of ek-stasis is meant to
retain, in a visible way, the etymological construction of the word and so
reinforce the ontological derivation of the concept of person in the sense of
a dynamic 'standing out of' one's self towards the 'whence' of essential
being. In this way I hope to get behind the familiar connotation of 'ecstatic'
as the experience of being 'beside one's self' and reserve for the word
'ek-static' a more restricted and technical connotation as the movement of
being towards its ultimate and original source. For this reason, the preposi-
tion is separated slightly from the stem of the word to denote the 'whence'
of personhood, a fundamental fact, as Dr. Mühlen suggests, which must
not be lost sight of: 'Person ist aber nicht nur durch Sistenz, durch
Selbstand, charakterisiert, sondern ebenso durch den Bezug zum
Ursprung. Dies drükt die Präposition "ex" aus: . . . Personales Dasein ist
begründet durch das Woher des Wesens.' *Ibid.*, p. 5.

The idea of Personhood, then, which we are led to consider through this understanding of the person of Christ, includes the reality of Spirit as the ek-static reality of Word. When I have defined lived transcendence as kenotic community, these two aspects of Personhood must be included. That is, the kenotic community is constituted a community through both the hypo-static union of Word and flesh, which is the reality of the Incarnate Word, and the ek-static reality of Spirit. The kenotic community is not itself a hypo-static union of Word and flesh, that is, it is not the bearer of humanity in its totality in a unique and unrepeatable existence, it is not another Incarnation; but it is constituted in community with God through its humanity which it has in common with the humanity of the Incarnate Word. We have said that each person has his 'place' in the kenotic community by virtue of his humanity. The transcendent grounds for this 'being placed' in community is the hypo-static union of Logos with humanity in the person of Christ. Therefore, when the Spirit assumes the 'form' of the historical existence of the one who is Other to me in the community, that 'form' of the Other in his actuality becomes the real presence of Christ for me through the Spirit.

But now it must be made clear that this kenotic community is not thereby an 'introverted' community (fat geese) and earth-bound in the sense that the transcendence of co-humanity constitutes its limiting possibility. The domesticating work of the Spirit is not directed towards group dynamics and the adjustment of one person's life in terms of the other, but is directed towards the *receiving* of Spirit so that the ek-static reality of Spirit may issue from human hearts and hands and voices as one life expressed in relation with God.[30] My purpose in using a word such as ek-static is to point towards a reality which is the opposite of an introverted experience, where life is turned back upon itself. The introversion of love works as a fragmenting and destructive force within community. A spirit of introversion either serves to particularize community into a disruptive individualism, where the Ego of personhood is intensified in its opposition to other hypostatic entities, or it can produce quite another effect (and the two may well be related as cause and effect) in the form of a tyrannical collectivism where the Ego of personhood is hypostatized into one entity—the social or political unity which exists as the end towards which all personal life exists as means.[31]

30. Cf. I Corinthians 12:4–13; Ephesians 4:4–6.
31. One could also say that Capitalism and Marxism share a common anthropology which leads to two quite dissimilar political and economic

It is for this reason that I prefer the concept of ek-static community to that of charismatic community as a way of representing the transcendence of Spirit. The gifts of the Spirit (*charismata*) can tend either towards a hypo-static or an ek-static function. When they function primarily as an intensification of the hypo-static basis of community they produce disorder and confusion. In this case there is a tendency towards the individuation and division of personhood. The early church was not immune to this problem.[32] For this reason, Paul attempts to restore balance, not by seeking the suppression of the charismatic expression of Spirit, but by giving priority to the ek-static expression of Spirit. The ek-static community is a community united in one Spirit and thus participates in the life of God. The practical expression of this is love (I Corinthians 13), for 'God is love, and he who abides in love abides in God, and God abides in him'.[33]

Because love is not something which one person 'does to another', but is rather a dimension of reality in which God and man have communion, love can also be an extra-human reality and, thus, is the ek-static life of Spirit. The transcendence of Spirit means that God abides in every *work* of love. The food and clothing which are given in love become the life and reality of Spirit. But because the life of Spirit is ek-static, it also means that every work of love abides in God. The ek-static community is thus able to bring creation itself into relation with God. For the created world has no ek-static life of its own apart from Spirit. It is dumb and lifeless when it comes to an expression of love and response towards the Creator. Creation can only have 'presence' towards God as God 'meets himself' in his creation. Once again, we are touching upon that which I have alluded to earlier as the 'intrinsic cosmic structure' of historical trancendence.[34] That is, the intra-divine transcendence of God, which is but another way of expressing the trinitarian reality of God in dynamic terms, has an extrinsic *par-ousia* in the form of the presence of God as Creator in creation. Creation requires the Creator in order to exist in reality, but it does not possess the divine life as an immanent spirit in such a way

systems. The one divides man up against himself, the other sacrifices man as individual to man as a social unit—both fall short of true personhood because they lack the ek-static dimension.

32. This would seem to be the precise nature of the problem in the church at Corinth. I Corinthians 12:1–14:40 becomes quite revealing when read in the light of the hypo-static/ek-static tendencies.

33. I John 4:16.

34. See *Historical Transcendence,* p. 175, n. 87.

that the relation is an extra-trinitarian reality. This would constitute creation as a reality 'outside' of the reality of God himself. In which case, creation plus God would constitute a greater reality than God himself. But, when the Creator-creature relation is understood as the extrinsic reality of the intrinsic transcendence of God in his triune nature, creation can be real in itself and at the same time, as Barth says, through the Holy Spirit creation is 'present' to God in the form of the relation of God to himself.[35] In the historical transcendence of God through the Incarnation, there lies exposed this intra-divine transcendence by which God meets himself from the side of creaturehood. All creation now has the possibility of its *ek-stasis* through the redemption of man from the introversion of the divine image. The ek-static community may thus be said to serve as the 'priest of creation', for only man, as he lives in the Word and Spirit of God, has his personhood completed in a relation which passes 'beyond' creation to the Creator.[36] The ek-static community has a cosmic dimension—it is itself the 'horizon of revelation' for all of creation.[37]

35. *Church Dogmatics,* I/1, pp. 515ff. Barth says: 'The creature indeed requires the Creator in order to live. He thus requires relation to Him. But this relation he cannot create. God creates it through His own presence in the creature, i.e., in the form of the relation of Himself to Himself. The Spirit of God is God in His freedom to be present in the creature, and so to create this relation, and thereby to be the life of the creature.' *Ibid.,* p. 516. I think that Barth would see the relation of Spirit to creation as the immanence of God, a view which I have earlier criticized (see *Historical Transcendence,* p. 150, n. 11). The difference may only be semantical, but I see no reason not to speak of God's 'meeting himself' in the creature as God's transcendence when it is understood as intra-divine transcendence such as is revealed in historical transcendence. This enables one to speak of solidarity with the world, while at the same time he speaks of the absolute difference, or of God's freedom. The gain in this conceptuality, it would appear, is that one can avoid dialectical language in speaking of God and man, and also can think in terms of a genuine natural theology without diminishing the transcendence (grace) of God. For if a natural theology is constituted in the transcendence, rather than in the immanence of God, it remains problematical in the sense that God remains free in being known by man in an intelligible way.
36. Cf. John Zizioulas, 'Human Capacity and Human Incapacity', p. 12.
37. This seems to be the meaning behind Paul's interpretation of the fall. When man turned his ek-static capacity back on creation itself (Romans 1:25) instead of the Creator, creation is subjected to a mute bondage to its own inarticulate nature and can only wait for man to once again liberate it through an ek-static life of the Spirit: 'For the creation waits with eager longing for the revealing of the sons of God; for the creation was subjected

The introverted community of man seeks distinctiveness in its autonomy over and against nature, and, as a result, either worships nature, or, as is more typical of our technological age, exploits it in the name of creativity. The emergence of a genuine ecological concern in the wake of such a despoiling of creation by man, has by and large exposed the Christian Church's own introversion. Here again, a charismatic community lacks both the desire and the theological tools to engage with ecological concerns creatively if it does not understand the ek-static relation of Spirit to creation. On the other hand, the ek-static community can come to the aid of ecological conservationism and supply the only possible transcendent grounds for such a concern. Lived transcendence then, as life in the Spirit, does not produce a division between man and creation, neither does it confuse the relation by identifying man with creation, but it turns creation back towards the Creator by giving creation its ultimate place in Being, that is, by giving creation an ek-static dimension through Spirit, so that God abides in the work and the work abides in God—through love.

The implications for the church are staggering and perhaps incomprehensible when considered in the light of traditional Western Christianity.[38] From the time of Augustine, the Western Church

to futility, not of its own will but by the will of him who subjected it in hope; because the creation itself will be set free from its bondage to decay and obtain the glorious liberty of the children of God. We know that the whole creation has been groaning in travail together until now; and not only the creation, but we ourselves, who have the first fruits of the Spirit, groan inwardly as we wait for adoption as sons, the redemption of our bodies.' Romans 8:19–23.

38. The tradition of the Eastern Church as represented in the theology of Eastern Orthodoxy, in contrast to the Western Church with its Augustinian tradition, seems to provide a more congenial theological framework for the understanding of this concept of the ek-static community and its cosmic dimension of man's relation to God. For Eastern theology, both cosmology and anthropology are dynamic and inter-related. V. Lossky says that man is situated at the juncture of the intelligible and sensible spheres, and through him the created world can find its true destiny of 'deification' (*theosis*) as man unites created with uncreated being through relation with God. Lossky cites St. Maximus (580–662 A.D.) as saying that the human person was called 'to unite by love created with uncreated nature, showing the two in unity and identity through the acquisition of grace.' *The Mystical Theology of the Eastern Church,* James Clarke and Co., Cambridge and London, 1968 (1957), p. 126. A more comprehensive statement of the cosmological implications for Eastern theology is given by Timothy Ware (*The Orthodox Church,* Penguin Books, Middlesex, 1963) who shows how

has been struggling with the doctrine of the 'Two Cities'. The City of God was basically set in opposition to the City of Man; what could be redeemed from the world was baptized into communion with God and the remainder left to destruction—or even worse, to be plundered by the redeemed citizens of the heavenly city who exercised a sort of 'eminent domain' over its resources. If the church is to link up again with creation, and ecology is only one aspect of this relation, the Spirit which has been so largely introverted in terms of both worship and ministry must become truly ek-static in the widest possible sense. The place where this can begin is with the kenotic community, for only here are both Word and Spirit united in a living transcendence of creative personhood.

In light of what has been said, one is led to question the way in which Bonhoeffer seemed to restrict the devotional and religious life of the community of Christ to the 'secret discipline' (*Arkandisziplin*). While Bonhoeffer referred to the 'secret discipline' on only two occasions in his letters from prison,[39] it was not as peripheral for him as this infrequent mention might appear. E. Bethge, who himself was a student of Bonhoeffer's at Finkenwalde, tells us that Bonhoeffer associated the concept of the 'secret discipline' with the early Christian practice of excluding the uninitiated, the unbaptized catechumens, from the second part of the liturgy in which the communion was celebrated and the Nicene Creed sung.[40] Later, when Bonhoeffer moved so deeply into the possibilities of 'religionless Christianity', he was concerned for what would happen to

---

the Byzantium period was an attempt to accept and apply the full implications of the Incarnation to every facet of material and worldly life. The world was conceived as a living *icon* of the heavenly Jerusalem in that all created things were redeemed by the assumption of a creaturely humanity by Christ (pp. 43–50). Eastern theology tends to include creation in a sacramental and doxological movement towards God in a way that makes the eucharist not only the dynamic centre of all life, but incorporates all material life into this centre through the use of *icons* (pp. 269–302). The sanctuary of the Orthodox Church is divided from the rest of the interior by a solid screen called the *iconostasis*; this screen, covered with *icons*, serves as the meeting place between heaven and earth (pp. 266–267). The *icons* represent the first fruits of creation's redemption through the Incarnation, and thus point to the cosmic dimension of Eastern Orthodox's ecclesiology (pp. 239–240). One could almost say of the Eastern Church that it is more of an *icono-static* community than an *ek-static* one. However, I have only meant to show that, in contrast to the West, the East has a cosmic and dynamic concept of the redeemed community.

39. *Letters and Papers From Prison*, pp. 281, 286.
40. *Dietrich Bonhoeffer*, p. 784.

the worship of the Christian community. The events of worship, the sacraments, prayer and meditation, Bonhoeffer held, properly belong to the centre of the life of the Christian community, and, as such, are to be 'screened off' from the world. The 'creative events of the Holy Spirit' were centred in the inner life of the worshipping community, and Bonhoeffer wished to avoid 'cheapening' these events by exposing them promiscuously to the world.[41] However, his concern seemed to be that the world should be protected from religion as much as that the community of Christ be protected at its centre from the world. It was not that Bonhoeffer wished to erect spatial barriers between the church and the world—he had long since discarded that from his thinking;[42] rather, he felt that by making the cultic life private he could remove altogether the public barrier between the church and the world.

However, what Bonhoeffer has virtually done is to separate the ek-static life of the community from its kenotic life. What this does is restrict worship to a cultic event in which only the initiated participate. One lives in the world as if there is no God, and in the cultus as if there is no world! This dialectic between the 'secret discipline' and 'worldliness' cannot be sustained when one considers that the kenotic community is also the ek-static community— for Word and Spirit cannot be split apart.

On the other hand, if we consider the alternative, that the kenotic community as the ek-static community includes a cosmic dimension, the worship of the church as well as its work gives creation its place in the life of the Creator. The redeemed community should not be considered as only a community with a cultus, for it is the community in which creation finds its ek-static fulfilment. It is the ones who do not receive the Spirit who are actually the 'cultic' community, for they are the ones who are 'screened off' from creation's true expression. Does this not also raise the question of a basis for a so-called 'religionless Christianity' when the 'events of the Spirit' are restricted to a discipline hidden from the world? While I would not be happy about the idea of considering the kenotic community as a religious community, if religion means a cultic posture as against a life of faith, on the other hand, I do not see how the kenotic community can even be Christian if the ek-static dimension is restricted to a hidden life. This appears to be an introversion of the Spirit of the worst kind. What a creative worship should actually be, remains for the church to discover in

41. *Ibid.,* pp. 785, 786.
42. *Ethics,* pp. 203, 205.

its own context. But I do not think this implication can be avoided if creation is to begin to find its ek-stasis in Christian community. There will be, it is true, a certain tension between the kenotic community in its ek-static form and the world which awaits its final redemption. This question of what it means that the kenotic community is not really 'earth-bound' constitutes the question for the final chapter of *Historical Transcendence*. There is an eschatological tension which Paul clearly speaks of (Romans 8:19–23), and which is true for the kenotic community as well as for all of creation. But if worship constitutes the ek-stasis of all creation through the kenotic community, especially in the form of the 'first fruits' of the Spirit, worship needs its windows open towards the world as well as towards God. It would seem that worship is most truly Christological when it ceases to be a private redemptive cult and begins to express the first fruits of redemption as the ek-stasis of creation through man in the Spirit. If kenotic community has its roots in the world, then the created world cannot be denied its place in the worship of the Creator.[43]

43. I am well aware that I have raised the question of what constitutes true worship without intending to answer it in terms of specific forms. George F. Regas ('Explorations in New Liturgy for Man of the Future', *Theology, News and Notes,* Fuller Theological Seminary, March, 1972, pp. 16–18, 22) points to one dimension of contemporary worship which is attempting to take this seriously when he says: 'For centuries the sense of the reality of worship has been diminished in proportion to the way attention to man's sensory environment has been allowed to diminish. It is imperative that within the liturgical life of the Church we renew our appreciation of the body, the depths of emotion and the power of the visual arts. The Church must do more to bring the sensory world into our midst and celebrate it and discover the glory of being human and the intimate presence of God in creation' (p. 18). But I am not sure that I follow him in his conclusion when he says: 'Corita Kent said it beautifully: "If we left it to the Spirit, there would be nothing left in Churches but Jesus and dancing" ' (p. 22). He is on solider ground when he refers to William Kuhn's book, *Environmental Man,* in which liturgy is related to man's total environment. This 'environmental interface' allows man to meet God in the 'facticity of an objective world, a world of colour and texture and form, a world of sensory impressions' (p. 17). However, I am uneasy about liturgical renewal which adds to the triangular relationship of individual, community, God, a fourth dimension of environment. I am not sure that a rectangle is any more ek-static than a triangle. Closer to what I would want to say, although it does not suggest so much by way of form, is the essay by James B. Torrance, 'The Place of Jesus Christ in Worship', *Church Service Society Annual,* May, 1970, pp. 41–62, in which he says: 'God has made all creatures for His glory. The lilies of the field in their beauty glorify God

The consideration of the kenotic community as also the ek-static community enables us now to see that the distinction between 'community' and 'society' so common in recent theological as well as philosophical writings is not as helpful as it might be. In particular, the identification of the church as 'community' as opposed to other human social relations as merely 'society' does not stand up to the character of lived transcendence as we have seen it develop. Bonhoeffer, again, sought to make the distinction by thinking of community as 'will for meaning' and society as only constituted by a rational, or purposive will.[44] He further elaborated this distinction by holding that society is the concretion of metaphysical social relationships while community is the concretion of moral and social relationships.[45] The implication of Bonhoeffer's distinction was that society could never form a communal type of relations apart from the moral dimension which is acquired when Christ becomes identified with society through a life of personal faith. All community for Bonhoeffer was community in Christ, and, therefore, the world could never have community, but only a common or rational purpose.

Emil Brunner is another theologian who sought to identify the form of the church in the world with a distinctive type of community. Although it must be said that his concern was not so much to make a distinction between community and society as to make a distinction between the *Ekklesia* (community) and the Church as an institutional and legal entity.[46] Brunner, who was clearly influ-

---

with a glory greater than that of Solomon, but they do not know it. The sparrow on the housetop glorifies God in its dumbness, but it doesn't know it. The universe in its vastness and remoteness glorifies God but it doesn't know it. But God made man in His own image to be the Priest of creation, to express for all creatures the praises of God, so that through the lips of man the heavens might declare the glory of God, that we who know we are God's creatures might worship God and in our worship gather up the worship of all creation' (p. 41). The central thesis of Torrance's essay on worship is that Christ is the one true worshipper who now by his Spirit leads us in our worship. 'The writer of the Epistle to the Hebrews describes our Lord as the *Leitourgos* (Hebrews 8:2)—"the leader of our worship," "the minister of the real sanctuary which the Lord pitched and not man", . . . The Worship of Christ is thus the worship which gathers up the worship of Israel and replaces it, and it is this Worship which is the substance of all Christian worship' (pp. 43–44).

44. *Sanctorum Communio*, pp. 56ff.
45. *Ibid.*, p. 119.
46. *The Misunderstanding of the Church*, Lutterworth Press, London, 1952, p. 107.

enced by the writings of Ferdinand Ebner and Martin Buber, found the I-Thou relation to be particularly expressive as a way in which man finds his authentic personhood. While this provides a basically anthropological basis for his concept of community, he would also say that apart from an 'encounter' with God which produces a corresponding 'answer' of faith, man is not in community apart from the proclamation of the *Kerygma*, and the reception of the Holy Spirit.[47] In effect, then, man is only capable of social relations and not true community apart from this encounter.

From a more philosophical perspective, John Macmurray holds that community is possible only when society moves beyond its common organic and functional unity and begins to relate out of motives which are 'intentional':

> A community, however, is a unity of persons as persons. It cannot be defined in functional terms, by relation to a common purpose. It is not organic in structure, and cannot be constituted or maintained by organization, but only by the motives which sustain the personal relations of its members.[48]

Macmurray, therefore, would maintain that true personhood is only possible when man is related intentionally to another person. Because the self is basically an agent who acts, personhood can only exist when there is a community of acting agents who intentionally relate out of love.

The common principle which unites these three concepts of community, despite their differing emphasis as to what community signifies, is the idea that true personhood, and thus true humanity, is primarily achieved through a relation of persons and not through any other level of social existence. In Brunner and Bonhoeffer there is a strong tendency to see in community the concretion of personhood in a particularly theological way. But because community is defined along relational terms, the distinctives of personhood are centred in the degree of inter-relatedness (love) which is now possible because of either faith or the presence of the Holy Spirit. Bonhoeffer would emphasize the ethical aspects of this inter-relatedness, while Brunner would see the distinguishing characteristic as fraternal. The tendency for all such emphasis on community as inter-relatedness in contrast to human society in its functional forms, is to maintain that human social relations cannot achieve this degree of personhood apart from faith in Christ, how-

47. *The Christian Doctrine of the Church, Faith, and the Consummation*, Dogmatics, Vol. III, Lutterworth Press, London, 1962, p. 41.
48. *Persons in Relation*, pp. 157-158.

ever it is understood. Unfortunately, this kind of qualitative distinction made at the level of inter-relatedness is difficult to sustain, if, indeed, it can even be made in the first place.

Certainly one would want to say that man is more truly personal and therefore more genuinely human when he exists in a community of relation than when he merely organizes himself into a society. But would one want to say that all community is Christian, or that only Christian faith produces community? The question, again, is of how one understands the transcendence of God. If man is only truly man when he exists in a relation to the transcendence of God, does community itself as human inter-relatedness constitute that transcendence? I suspect that this was the case for both Bonhoeffer and Brunner, though Bonhoeffer moved towards the proposition that all true community was Christ, while Brunner approached it more kerygmatically, stating that Christ produces community through faith.[49]

I have used the word 'community' as the basic form of lived transcendence in the Spirit because I believe it to be the fundamental character of man's true personhood. But if man's personhood is constituted by the transcendence of God, as we have already established, then true personhood is community which participates in

49. I have not included the concept of community as held by Karl Barth in this discussion because, though he taught that there was an 'inner circle' and an 'outer circle' constituted by the elect community (*Gemeinde*) living within the larger circle of 'world occurrence', his concept of the church was so strongly eschatological that one could not say that he saw community in strictly historical terms. (Cf. *Church Dogmatics*, II/2, p. 196; III/4, p. 490; I/1, p. 514.) The 'time' of the community (the church) for Barth was the 'time between the times', that is, the time between the ascension and the final *par-ousia*. The community as the 'event' of the Kingdom points to the fulfilment, for Christ himself is already totally present, but on the other hand, it is provisional and weak. Because it is the life of Christ himself in the world, it has no form or power of its own, but rather exists to serve and to die. As 'event', the community *is* the Body of Christ, not merely a symbol or representation of that Body. But this is precisely why the church cannot have a history or be simply an 'event' in the daily life of the Christian. Because the 'event' of the community is the event of Christ himself in solidarity with the world, and yet, acting over and against the world, the event of the community is eschatological. Through the community, Christ continues to speak and act in a 'creaturely' way in history, but without having a history, that is, without being a predicate of history (cf. *Church Dogmatics*, I/1, p. 514). See also Colm O'Grady, *The Church in the Theology of Karl Barth*, Geoffrey Chapman, London, 1968, especially pp. 91ff., 106ff., 190ff., 246ff.

the life of God. Therefore, an ontology of community can only be explicated on a trinitarian basis. That is, man's capacity for community becomes an incapacity when viewed from a strictly anthropological perspective. Man does move towards community, and, I think one must say, does experience community, but he experiences community as merely a 'capacity'. However, the dimension of God's transcendence, as the constitutive element of community, can only be known as incapacity from the standpoint of man himself. Yet, this is a 'capacity' which expresses itself as a movement towards community, of which the interpersonal is evidence.[50] Through the Incarnation, the transcendence of God made human community both kenotic and ek-static. Through Word and Spirit, God entered human community to the depths of its incapacity, and from that depth raised a response to God which completed community through a union of man with God. In this sense, the ontological structure of community can be said to be trinitarian.

Because Word and Spirit can never be separated, the kenotic community is at the same time the ek-static community. Which is to say, the ek-static community reveals to the community of man its *incapacity* which it can only experience as a capacity for community. Therefore, the Spirit of God does not produce a qualitatively *better* human community, and enter with the claim that only in the Spirit is there community at all, but on the contrary, the Spirit speaks from the incapacity of community to complete itself, and speaks to God for community on the basis of the community of humanity with the Incarnate Word. Rather than making the distinction between community and society, and hoping thereby to distinguish between the church and the world, the distinction is solely one of the Spirit, and it is the distinction between the ek-static community, which experiences community as incapacity (thus as grace), and all other community, which experiences community as

---

50. Inter-personal transcendence, therefore, cannot be a 'form' into which divine transcendence is poured, but is a capacity which reveals an incapacity for divine transcendence. I have drawn the concept of capacity/incapacity from the essay by Dr. John Zizioulas, 'Human Capacity and Human Incapacity': 'All that we have tried to say so far by looking at human capacity and human incapacity from the angle of Personhood shows that in being a Person man has his capacity *in incapacity*. This means that he is essentially dependent on communion and that ultimately, because of the idea of ontological presence implied in this communion, he can be fully in communion, only if he overcomes the tragic element of absence which is the inevitable form in which the presence of being is offered to him as a creature.' p. 10.

capacity. It would seem to follow from this that the kenotic community is not the point at which a distinction is to be made within the human community, but that it is rather the Spirit producing the ek-static dimension of community where the distinction arises. Having established the true distinctive of the kenotic community as its life in the Spirit, there will now emerge a new freedom to consider the implications of the relation of the transcendence of God to the world through a lived transcendence which seeks to close the circle of transcendence by living in the world.

If it is true that the world is 'a world of fugitives', the Christian is a 'Christ' among fugitives, and the church, to some extent at least, must become the 'fugitive' church.

'As thou didst send me into the world, so I have sent them into the world.'[51]

---

51. John 17:18.

11

KARL BARTH

The Event of Divine Worship

WE ARE LOOKING FROM THE SAME PLACE AND IN THE SAME DIREC-
tion, but more concretely, when in a rather bold expression we
describe the law which has to be sought and established and executed in the community as liturgical law. Church law has an original connexion with the particular happening of Christian worship.
It is here that it has its original seat. It is in the act of worship that it
is originally found and known. It is to worship—as the order of
divine service—that it is originally applied. It is from this point
that it embraces and orders the whole life of the community. At an
earlier point we have described and emphasised public worship as
the centre of the whole life of the community; as the true act of its
upbuilding. The time has now come to give our reasons for this
emphasis.

The necessity and central significance of this happening—or this
particular service, as we may now call it in retrospect of our first
point—have their immediate derivation in the basic law (the
christologico-ecclesiological concept) of the community in virtue
of which it is the body whose Head is Jesus Christ. According to
Holy Scripture Jesus Christ is the One who exists in a history—His
own particular history—within universal history. In virtue of His
resurrection from the dead He will be this One, and therefore the
Head of His community, in every age and to all eternity.

Our first emphasis must fall on the fact that He is the One who
exists in His *history*. The One who is the Head of the community is
the man who not only went but still goes and always will go the
way from Bethlehem to Golgotha. The One who goes this way is
manifested on Easter Day as the living Lord, and His Spirit, His
quickening power, is the Holy Spirit, who has created and rules

From Karl Barth, *Church Dogmatics,* IV/2, pp. 695–710. © T. & T. Clark
Ltd., Edinburgh. Used by permission of the Publisher.

and upholds the Christian community. The being of the Head of the community is the event of the life of this man.

But we must also emphasise the fact that He is the One who exists in this *particular* history. The event of this life is indissolubly connected with His name. It is the event which exhausts itself in this name—concrete, limited in time and space, singular and unique. It is this event and not another; a "contingent fact of history," to use the phrase of Lessing.

It is in this way, i.e., in Jesus Christ, in His particular history, that there was and is and comes true God and true man, the humiliated Son of God and the exalted Son of Man, the One who fulfils the covenant between God and man, the Reconciler of the world with God, the Word which was in the beginning with God and will also be His final Word, His eternal Word. In heaven, hidden in God, He whose being is this once for all act, this particular history, is the Head of His community.

If His community then, created and ruled and upheld by His Holy Spirit in the time between His resurrection and His return in glory, is His body, the earthly-historical form of His existence; if this is its basic law, it is inevitable that His particular history, both as history and in its particularity, should be actively and recognisably reflected and represented in its life.

Hence it is not enough, but conflicts with its basic law, if it is merely present in the world as His legacy and endowment, as an establishment and institution founded and ordered by Him, and therefore as a mere phenomenon. It is true that it is His valid and living bequest to this intervening time. It is also true that it cannot be this living bequest unless in obedience to Him it takes all kinds of forms and establishes all kinds of institutions. But as His living bequest, as the body of which He is the Head, it is itself history. The Christian community is not a mere phenomenon, however distinguished. It is an event. Otherwise it is not the Christian community. It is another question that in this event it takes different forms and establishes different institutions. The fact remains that it is not itself a foundation or institution. In correspondence with the hidden being of Jesus Christ Himself, it is an earthly-historical event, and as such it is the earthly-historical form of His existence.

But it is also not enough, and conflicts with its basic law, if in its life there is no correspondence to the particularity of His history. By the event of the Christian community there certainly can and must be understood the more general truth that as the human fellowship of those who are elected and called and sent, who believe in Him and obey Him, it is comprehensively at work in time and space as its members belong together in virtue of their relationship with Him, and are inwardly and perhaps outwardly united, and meet occasionally on the basis of their common convictions and interests and hopes, and take certain steps together, and give various forms of assistance to one another and to those outside, in view of that which they have in common. In actual fact, there is no doubt that for the most part they live in dispersion, each one in his own place and occupied with his own needs and concerns as a Christian, although grouped in various ways with other Christians. And in this form, they will not be recognisable either to themselves or others as the concrete *communio sanctorum* in time and space. To be sure, the Christian community is an event even in this form. Its history does have this character and aspect. It has a real existence submerged in this way under the secularity of its environment. It wears also the working clothes of an anonymity which is broken only occasionally and haphazardly. It is a secret conspiracy whose members are largely unknown to one another, or meet only rarely, and cannot regard it as over-important—because its hour has not yet struck—to manifest it even to themselves, let alone to others, in its full dimension. The inward life of Christians will, it is to be hoped, shine out—decisively in the private or combined attitude and action and abstention of individuals—even though they may be "scorched by the sun outwardly." We refer to the everyday life of Christians, which must not be undervalued, although it has often been one-sidedly and thoughtlessly exalted. It is legitimate and necessary that the community should exist in this form. For one thing, it belongs to the everyday life and traffic of the world. But more than that, its Head is the One in whom God took the world to Himself, and therefore the everyday life of all men and of Christians. It is not enough, however, if the community exists only in this form. If this is all, if it does not correspond to the particularity of its Head Jesus Christ and of His history, it does not attest the concrete, unique and limited actuality of this history, nor does it attest Him as the One who exists individually as this man and not another. In its representation of His history there is lacking the offence and the glory of the fact that it is a "contingent fact of history."

This is where the particular happening of worship is supremely relevant. The event of the community takes place in other ways. And conversely, divine service in this particular sense of the term is not a continual but a particular event within the total event "community." As the total event "community" stands out from the world within the world, so divine service stands out from the total event "community" within this event. And it is only as the community has its distinct centre in its worship that it can and will stand out clearly from the world. But this is necessary as in its history there is to be a representation of the particular history of its Head, an attestation of Jesus Christ.

In divine service there takes place that which does not take place anywhere else in the community. In divine service the sabbath intervenes between six working days on the one side and six more on the other. In it it exchanges its working clothes for its festal attire. It is now an event as community. Unpretentiously but distinctly it stands out from the secularity of its environment in which it is for the most part submerged. It now casts off the anonymity of that which is distinctive and common to it; the occasional and haphazard and private character elsewhere assumed by its manifestation. It now exists and acts in concrete actuality and visibility as the congregation to which many individuals—each from his own human and Christian place in dispersion—come together to one place at one time in order that together, occupying the same space and time, they may realise the *communio sanctorum* in a definite form. There can be no doubt that not merely their life in the world, but their own everyday life as Christians as it was lived yesterday and will be resumed to-morrow, is now left behind. There can be no doubt that the hour for which the conspirators otherwise wait in dispersion has now struck, even if only provisionally and not definitively. The dimension which embraces individual Christians and Christian groups is now visible to themselves, and in their common action to the world around. This is the distinctive feature of this action within the wider context of the life of the community; the feature by which it is distinctly shown to be the centre of its life, not to be confused with the everyday either of the world or of Christians. It is shown to be its centre because here—and in this way only here—the community exists and acts in direct correspondence to its basic law, in a particular and not merely a general historicity. In divine service it becomes and is itself a witness to its own being, to its determination in the world, to the factuality of its existence. And in divine service it exists and acts prophetically in relation to the world to the extent that in divine service—and here alone directly—there is a serious discharge of its commission to be a provisional representation of humanity as it is sanctified in Jesus Christ. We must not be too pretentious and say that divine service or any of its parts is an "eschatological event." It is quite sufficient, and startling enough, to say that on its journey between the resurrection and the return the community achieves in it this representation provisionally but in concrete reality, so that it is only here that it exists and acts in its true form. From this centre of its life there can and must and may and will be also true Christian being and action on the circumference, in the Christian everyday. From it there can and must and may and will be general law and order. Thus from its liturgical root Church law must be understood as a law which (1) is ordered by divine service; (2) is continually to be found again in it; and (3) has itself the task of ordering it. We shall now consider the problem from these three standpoints.

We must begin by asserting (1) that all law in the Church has its original seat in the event of divine worship, and that it is primarily established in this particular happening. Where two or three are gathered together in the name of Jesus, i.e., by the fact that the name of Jesus is revealed to them, He Himself is with them and among them (according to Mt. 18:20). The saying has unmistakeable reference to the gathering (''synagogue'') of the community. If the saying is right, it means that in that which is done and takes place in the coming together of these men their King and Lord is present and at work; the One who is as such the source and guarantee of the law which obtains for them. As they have not met by accident, or gathered together arbitrarily, but have been brought together by the revelation of His name, they are not left to their own devices in their common action, but their King and Lord Himself gives them direction and orders and commands, and consolation and promises. It is He who gives the freedom for what takes place. Because and as He, the righteous One, is present in their gathering, there takes place in it that which is lawful and right for these men, His own, in spite and even in defiance of the imperfection and corruption of their action, in which they set themselves wholly or very largely in the wrong. It is quite out of the question that the community assembled for public worship can exalt itself in this action, or even try to do so, to be itself the source and guarantee of the law which obtains within it. The men assembled, even if they act in His presence and under His direction and as those who are comforted by Him, are always sinners and therefore never righteous or in a position to establish a valid law or right by their action. They themselves are not and will never be the King and Lord. They are only His people; worthy only as He makes them worthy to be witnesses in their activity to His presence, and therefore to the right established and made a law for them by Him. That He does this in their assembly, that He Himself is the right or law which underlies and shapes and orders this event of divine service, is the secret of this action which makes it the original seat of all their law. Essentially and decisively there are in this action four concrete elements in which, in spite and even in defiance of all the imperfection and corruption of the human action of Christians, Jesus Christ and therefore the law of the *communio sanctorum*, the right which obtains for it, is really present.

First, where two or three are gathered in His name, they speak with and to one another in human words. They do not do this merely because speech is the characteristic vehicle of human fellowship, but because from the very first this particular fellowship has its meaning and substance in the fact that there is something specific which calls for common utterance and must be declared by those who have been brought to this fellowship. In general terms, it is a matter of the common confession of the One who has brought them together by awakening them all to know Him and believe in Him and love Him and hope in Him. This knowledge and faith and love and hope, or rather the One who is known and believed and loved by them and the object of their hope, impels the two or three to make this common confession as He gathers them together. They hear Him together as the Word of God addressed to them, and they cannot do this without making their common human response. But they also owe this response to one another; for the mutual ratification and confirmation, consolation, correction and renewal of their knowledge and faith and love and hope; for the *mutua consolatio fratrum*. And they cannot make this response merely in private, or in the accidental, local and optional encounters in which Christians may speak with and to one another. They can and may and should make it in this way too. But under the impulsion of the Word of God, the human response to this Word calls for something public. The unity of knowledge, faith, love and hope, and of the One who is known and believed and loved and the object of their hope, calls for the unity of their confession. Confession may well be the confession of individual Christians or groups of Christians. But it cannot be only this. Indeed, it cannot really be this unless it is first the confession of the community, and flows into the confession of the community, in which the human response to the Word of God is the common word of all, and the *mutua consolatio fratrum* does not take place in a corner between individuals but is the objective and obligatory work of all to all. This common response in the common hearing of the Word of God, the confession commonly spoken and received in the renewal of the common knowledge, is the first element in the public worship of Christians. It may include the common recitation of a creed. It will certainly involve singing. But it will take place decisively in free witness, bound only to its object, as the Word of God is proclaimed and published and taught and preached and heard by the community according to the commission of its Lord. As this is done, that which is lawful and right takes place in and for the community. It is constituted as a fellowship of confession: not in the power or weakness of the human words spoken and received but because these words are an answer to the Word of God; because in these human words spoken in power or weakness it is a matter of witness to Jesus Christ; because it is He who wills that they should be spoken; because He Himself is present where they are spoken and heard by those whom He has gathered. Thus in the confession of the community that which is lawful and right takes place, and the community is constituted, even though—and when is this not the case?—it sets itself in the wrong with its human speaking and hearing; even in impotent witness and poor proclaiming and publishing and teaching and preaching. The right may be totally or partially concealed. Failing to see it, it may not be set to rights by it. But these are later questions. What is unquestionable is that in the liturgical act of confession as such we have to do with that which is lawful and right in the community and has to be perceived and practised as such. As the community gathers, and there is not merely speech but confession in this gathering, it is already constituted even though it may not be aware (or clearly aware) of the fact, and however it may constitute itself, and thus give expression to its law, on this foundation.

Second, where two or three are gathered together in the name of Jesus they will mutually recognise and acknowledge that they are those who are gathered by Him as their one Lord, and regard and receive one another as brothers because they are all brothers of this First-begotten. Who really belongs to them? Who is awakened by the quickening power of the Holy Spirit, and therefore a saint, and as such a member of the communion of saints, a brother of those united with him in this fellowship? They all see and judge one another with human eyes and not with those of God. They do not see into the heart. They can only trust one another. And which of them, looking even into his own heart, can give more than a human judgment that he himself is awakened by the Holy Spirit and a true member of the communion of saints, so that he belongs to this assembly? This, too, and above all, is something that he can know only in trust. The Christian community is built on the fact that this trust is permitted and commanded: the mutual trust in which one recognises and acknowledges the other as a brother belonging to it; and the trust that each must have concerning himself for glad and confident participation. It is in this authorised and commanded trust that the community gathers for divine service. How would its members stand in relation to one another and themselves if they did not have it, or if they arbitrarily assumed it on the basis of their own fancied knowledge of themselves and one another? In these circumstances they could only assemble and at once disperse again. But they have this trust, which is not grounded in their own opinions of themselves and one another, even though they can see only that which is before their human eyes, and they know that appearances may deceive. What do they see? They cannot see the Holy Spirit who has awakened and assembled them, nor can they see the knowledge and faith and love and hope to which He has awakened themselves and the others. They cannot see one another as brothers. But they see that these men, and they themselves, are baptised—in the one new name common to them all, in the name of Jesus, and therefore the name of the Father, the Son and the Holy Ghost. They see only that these men, and they themselves, are those who have obviously begun to know the salvation of the world enclosed in this name, and therefore their own salvation; to know themselves as people who stand in absolute need of it—of the forgiveness of their sins, of justification and sanctification, of conversion. They see only that these men, and they themselves, have come to the community with the desire and request for this salvation; that they have confessed this name with their lips; that they have asked for baptism and therefore for recognition as members of the body of Jesus Christ, and acceptance into the body of Jesus Christ; and that this recognition and acceptance have been granted in their baptism, not in the name of the community, but in the name of its Lord. They see these others and themselves accepted only as those who are baptised, and in the frame of mind in which they came to baptism, as beginners in this knowledge, with this desire and request, as those who make this confession with their lips. But in respect of others and themselves they hold to the fact that they all come from the fact that they are baptised in the name of the Lord. Because they all stand under this sign in the name of the Lord, they accept the sign. Hence they are permitted and commanded to do that which of themselves they have no right or power to do—to take these others and themselves seriously as members of the body of Jesus Christ, and to be with them gladly and confidently in the congregation. As this takes place, there takes place that which is lawful and right in the community. It could not take place were it not for the presence in the midst of the One who has brought them together; were it not that baptism is His permission and command, and therefore the sign which not merely gives us good reasons for that trust but makes it an act of obedience undertaken in perfect confidence. And so our second point is that the Christian community is a fellowship of baptism. That is to say, when it comes together in the name of Jesus, in all its members it does so in virtue of baptism; and it is in the freedom given and received in baptism that it holds its public worship. Whatever else may be said either for or against itself or its members, coming and coming together from this point it is already constituted and is in the right, even though it may set itself a thousand times in the wrong against this right.

Third, where two or three are brought together in the name of Jesus, it is in order that they may be unitedly strengthened and preserved to eternal life. Eternal life is their human life, but as their true life, hidden and glorified with God. They assemble as members of the Christian community, and celebrate divine service, to be prepared for the attainment of their life in this form. In going, or coming, to public worship they perform a movement which has a wider, typical significance. For all men are ordained to eternal life. The question of strengthening and preservation, of preparation to attain it, is thus necessarily a question which concerns them all. Christians are those who are awake to the question. Impelled by it, they hasten together; together because they know that the answer to this question can be received only unitedly in the Christian community as the provisional representation of the whole race for which it has already taken place and which needs to receive it. They know the truth about human life—their own life too, and especially their own. They know that it is the wonderful gift of God the Creator, to be enjoyed in thankfulness and lived out by man in daily prayer and labour in his allotted span. They know, too, that it is a life which is encumbered and radically jeopardised by the pride and sloth of man towards God and his fellows; a forfeited life. But they also know that it is a life which is inflexibly ordained to be eternal life; life in concealment and glory with God, and therefore true life. They know all this as they are brought together by the revelation of the name of Jesus, and united to the community where He is present in the midst. And so they go and come to Him as they go and come to the community, concretely participating in its assembly. They seek the answer to this question of the attainment of eternal life; the answer which is given in Him, which is He Himself. They hunger and thirst to be prepared, to be strengthened and preserved, for the eternal life which in defiance of the frailty of the present form of their life is His work, and can be only His work. The promise with which they are brought together is that He will give them food and drink, that in the life in which they too are surrounded by death He will provide, and will Himself be, their wayside sustenance. And so they go and come to the gathering of the community to seat themselves, and to eat and drink, as brothers and sisters at the table where He Himself presides as Lord and Host, and they are His invited and welcome guests. They go and come to the Lord's Supper. In so doing, they do the very thing which they also do for the strengthening and preservation of creaturely life; just as when they talk with and to one another they do something which is ordinarily done by men when they meet. They eat and drink. But as in their speaking in the community it is not a matter of the private and optional exchange of human convictions and opinions, but of the common utterance of the confession, so in the eating and drinking of the Lord's Supper it is not a question of the nourishment of one here and another there in company with neighbours, but of the eating of one bread and the drinking from one cup, of the common nourishment of them all, because it is He, Jesus Christ, who brings them to it, who invites them, who is the Lord and Host, who is Himself, indeed, their food and drink. It is thus a question of their nourishment by Him. It takes place in the fact that, as often as they here eat and drink together, He proffers and gives Himself to them as the One He is, as the One who is absolutely theirs; and conversely, that He continually makes them what they are, absolutely His. He strengthens and upholds them in their existence as those whom He, the Crucified and Risen, accompanies in the valley of the shadow. More strongly, He strengthens and upholds them in their existence as His body and its members, and therefore to eternal life in the concealment and glory of God. He constitutes Himself their preparation to attain this. It is to be noted how the event of His own life is reflected and repeated in the event of the Supper (as in that of confession and baptism). In remembrance of Him there takes place here and now exactly the same as took place there and then between Himself and His first disciples, immediately prior to His death and resurrection. Provisionally in the place of all men, the community in its reaching out in all its members for eternal life necessarily lives by and in the fact that in its life here and now there may be this reflection and imitation. And the fact that this takes place is again the right or law established in divine service. The community may set itself in the wrong against it. It has continually done so, and will continually do so again. From the standpoint of the community itself, of the company assembled round the table of the Lord, what takes place will always be highly problematical. Yet in spite of this it is a fellowship of the Lord's Supper, united by Him both with Him and also, because with Him, in itself; *communio sanctorum* as a fellowship of the sure and certain hope of eternal life. In its worship, which is also communion in this concrete sense, this is made palpable and visible; as is also, in the event of this communion, the law or right which indwells it in spite of all the wrong committed by it, and which in this special form demands that it should be observed in every aspect of its life.

Fourth, where two or three are gathered together in the name of Jesus, they are called by Him to pray with one another. Those gathered by the revelation of His name are men who are wholly referred and directed to God. That they are referred to God is something that they have in common with all men. But they are also directed to Him. They know that in the last resort they are not in their own hands and under their own control. They know that they are only creatures and not the Creator. They know also that they are God's sinful creatures; that because of their own corruption their activity is a corrupt activity. They thus know that they cannot avert the sorrow and suffering of the world; that they cannot avoid their own misery; that they cannot alter the human situation; that they cannot accomplish the reconciliation of the world with God as a genuine transformation; that they cannot hallow God's name as they should; that they cannot bring in the kingdom of peace and salvation; that they cannot do His will. Hence they know that they cannot and will not of themselves receive their daily bread, know the forgiveness of their debts, withstand temptation and overcome evil and the evil one. They know that they can only pray that these things should happen. They will do so in faith and love and hope, and therefore not indolently but in practical act and activity to God's glory. Yet in principal and as the climax of everything else they can only pray, seeking Him and calling upon Him that He should begin and execute and complete all the things for which they find themselves quite inadequate even in their most zealous and eloquent action. The decisive work and the driving force in their daily defensive and offensive action will consist in their surrender; the decisive work of their hands in the fact that they lay all things, both great and small, in the hands of God. They know that all that man can do can be helpful only in the renunciation of all self-help, and the cry to God that He will be the helper and help of man and all men. But they know that they may pray for this, and be certain that their prayer is heard. They have freedom and joy for this. And so they meet to pray with one another. They also pray, of course, individually and in small groups. But this is not enough, just as their private speech and their individual opinions of one another and their meals in one another's houses are not enough, but the confession and baptism and Supper, in short the action, of the community are also needed if everything is to be lawful and right. The prayer of Christians, too, demands that it should find its true and proper form in the prayer of the assembled community; in the united calling upon God: "Our Father, which art in heaven. . . ." The reason why it must be united is not merely that it is easier and finer and more consoling to pray in company than individually—for this is an open question. It is because those gathered to the community may pray with the One by whom they are united and who is Himself present in the midst—their predecessor in prayer. The distinctive value and importance of the "Our Father" as the Lord's Prayer consist in the fact that in it Jesus ranged Himself alongside His disciples, or His disciples alongside Himself, taking them up with Him into His own prayer. The "We" of this prayer is the We to which the Lord attaches Himself with His people. The We in which He does this is the We of the community. And the We of the community has its concrete form in its coming together. That is why Christian prayer demands that it should be the prayer of the assembled community as well as the prayer of individuals and groups. That is why the prayer of individuals and groups can be true and serious calling upon God only as it derives from the prayer of the assembled community. To be true and serious, to be the prayer which is heard by God, it must first and last be the prayer of the One who as the true Son has the authority and power truly to address Him as Father. As His brothers and sisters, as the children of God in His name, Christians can and may call upon God as Father. As and because their prayer is that of His brothers and sisters, it does not need any particular art or power or intensity. Because it is prayed in fellowship with the First-begotten, it is a spreading out of the totality of man's true need, and a reaching out for the totality of what God will be for him and give him. Prayed in fellowship with Him, it is never in vain. It is always rightly addressed and prayed with the certainty of being heard and answered. In prayer prayed in the assembled congregation, there is done again that which is lawful and right. As it is prayed as the prayer of the Lord Himself, for all the poverty and thoughtlessness and uncertainty and distraction from which it will suffer on the lips of Christians, the right of God is set up on earth. For it is right before God that He should be called upon as He may be called upon by the assembled community in the prayer of its Lord. The community is constituted as it prays. And as it faces the many-sided question how it is to constitute itself, it will always hold and return to the fact that it is already constituted; that the public worship in which it prays as the community, for all the weakness with which it may do so, is the place where that which is lawful and right for it both outwardly and inwardly already takes place, in its concrete life as a fellowship, not only of confession and baptism and the Lord's Supper, but also of prayer.

But in our explanation of the fact that Church law is liturgical we must now go on to state (2) that it is originally to be sought and found and known in the occurrence of Christian worship. Church law has this in common with all human law—and it is itself human law in the fact—that it must be found and known. The direction in which it is to be sought, in which we have to look when drawing it up, is already fixed; for here as elsewhere we have to turn only to Jesus Christ, the Lord and Head of the community as He is attested in Holy Scripture. It is solely and exclusively in the light of His relationship to it, which is its basic and constitutive law, that we can consider what is lawful and right in the Church. But the concrete form of His relationship to it, and therefore the concrete form of its basic law, is His own presence and lordship in its assembling for divine service in the occurrence of confession, baptism, the Lord's Supper and prayer. This being the case, we have to consider all questions of that which is lawful and right in the Church in the light of its assembling for public worship and therefore of this fourfold occurrence. In the formulation of all statements about Church law we have thus to look first in this direction. This does not mean, of course, that the community should orientate itself by its own action, making this a law and unfolding it as such. It cannot try to be its own Lord and King and Lawgiver: not even in its liturgy; not even if this is ever so old; and not even if it is sincerely thought to be in supreme agreement with this or that biblical precedent. In this respect we have to take into account at every point the human weakness and confusion of its own action; the wrong of Christians contradicting the right of their Lord. But we have also and even more so to take into account Jesus Christ Himself present in their human action as the Lord of their confession, of their coming from baptism and going to the Lord's Supper, of their united calling upon God. He is their law; He, the One who is attested in Holy Scripture. We do not therefore violate the

Scripture principle when we say that the divine service of Christians is the concrete source of our knowledge of Church law. If the Lord present and active in divine service is its law (and therefore the law of the whole life of the community), it is clear that when we ask concerning Him as the Lord present and active in the divine service of Christians we are again referred wholly and utterly to Holy Scripture. But He who is attested in Scripture is the basic law, normative for that which is lawful and right in the Church, in the form in which He is present and active here at the heart of the Church's life.

The lordship of Jesus Christ in His community takes place as in divine service it makes to His summons the response of its confession. To this confession there must correspond even formally that which is regarded as law in its life. The propositions of canon law must follow the confession of the community, expounding and applying it with particular reference to the order of its human action. They themselves will not be liturgical (whether in the form of confessional statements, hymns, proclamation or preaching). Nor will they be theological. They will be juridical statements orientated by the liturgical event of confession and based on theological reflection. They have to fix the rules of the human shaping of the existence of the community as these are required by its message and commensurate with it. Whether they are right or not will be decided by the question whether and how far in their establishment and execution the community is committed and faithful to its message, or to the One who has entrusted its message to it; whether and how far they are calculated to free and bind its members by keeping them to their faith as their response to the Word of their common Lord; whether and how far they are adapted to reveal practically to those without the distinctive nature of the Christian community as grounded in its doctrine and preaching. Not directly but indirectly true Church law is necessarily "confessing," i.e., it is human law drawn up in view of the confession and therefore of the man who confesses it, and thus to be executed with this reference. The confessing community needs this confessing law, for its existence in the world is worked out and expressed in human and therefore in sociologico-juridical form, and as a community it is faced at this point by the question of obedience. If it does not ask concerning this law, this can only mean that it does not ask concerning the obedient fulfilment of its confession—at the very place where this is most directly commanded. In true Church law the community undertakes to fulfil its confession first in relation to itself. If the lordship of Jesus Christ is an event within it, this is something which has to be attempted.

The lordship of Jesus Christ in His community takes place as the community, assembled for public worship, comes in all its members from baptism in His name. We have seen that the confidence which each can and should have in respect of all others and himself rests on the permission and command received by the members in their baptism. But all the propositions of canon law rest on this confidence. In the community men trust that in spite of the dubious nature of all human seeking and finding they are summoned and able to seek and find these propositions. Their establishment and formulation take place, therefore, in this confidence. Without it they could not take place at all. Again, in the community there is trust that the propositions sought and found in this way will have sufficient authority for each and all to claim acceptance and respect. Even in their application the only appeal can and will be to this confidence. Negatively, this means that the competence of Church law (in contrast to all other) cannot at bottom be proved, because all possible determinations of its competence (e.g., of the authority of its assembly or representatives or other officers) can be reached only in the confidence that the few or the many are authorised in virtue of their baptism. Thus the definitions of canon law (in contrast to all other) are not at bottom enforceable, because even the greatest rigour with which they are asserted can consist only in their power to claim the confidence and obedience of those concerned. No true Church law can be established or executed apart from the common recollection of baptism and therefore apart from this mutual confidence. Conversely, the confidence which, having its basis in baptism, enables this law to be established and executed—far from being a hindrance—gives to it a spiritual power which no other, no worldly, law can ever have.

The lordship of Jesus Christ in His community takes place as the community, assembled for public worship, goes to the Lord's Supper and therefore to the common nourishment which the Lord provides on the way to eternal life. Drawn up and applied with reference to this happening, its lawful ordering necessarily acquires the character of a common ordering of the present life of the men assembled in it. We recall at this point the thought of the *communio* of the *sancti* in and in relation to the *sancta*. There are no *sancta*, no gifts and powers of knowledge and love, which any one of the *sancti* can and should have and use and enjoy alone and not with some of the others and even all the others. Even in the particular form in which they are his he can have them only in interchange with others. In the Lord's Supper, when it is rightly administered, there is no distinction of persons in the distribution of the bread and wine, but all eat the one bread and drink from the one cup and are strengthened and preserved to eternal life by the one Lord and Host. And this is something which has to be brought out in true Church law, and safeguarded against the disruption of its spiritual life into the private spheres of individuals, or of certain pious or more pious or wholly pious groups. Naturally, there can and should be all kinds of active fellowships for the promotion of specific ends and in the discharge of specific tasks which cannot be the particular concern of all but only of those specially called or endowed for the purpose. But the idea of an *ecclesiola in ecclesia*, of a special *communio* within the one, always involves either openly or tacitly an abandonment or relativisation of the one. No *ecclesiola*, however, can find any basis or authority in the Lord's Supper, to which all come with the same hunger and thirst, and at which all are equally nourished with food and drink. It may sometimes be the case that the living and true Church has to arise and is compelled and empowered to take new shape in a dead Church or a false. But in an order of fellowship derived from the Lord's Supper there can be no place for a true Church within the true Church. And we have to remember especially that in the Lord's Supper it is distinctively a question of outward and inward, visible and invisible, physical and spiritual nourishment at one and the same time. Where the human mind normally separates these two spheres, in the action of the Holy Spirit, and drastically in the action of the Lord's Supper, they are comprehended and united. And the eternal life to which the community is strengthened and preserved in the Lord's Supper is the glorification of the whole of human life. Thus the Church order to be derived from the eucharistic action will necessarily embrace, protect and claim the life of the community and its members as it is now lived in its totality and therefore at one and the same time in its physical and spiritual nature. It will aim at the living fellowship of Christians in both spheres. In each respect it will make the strong responsible for the weak, the healthy for the sick, the rich for the poor. It will make Christians answerable for one another and for the continuance of the community, outwardly no less than inwardly. It will claim the help of all in both spheres. And it will promise help to all in both spheres. It will remind the community that what is lawful and right in the Lord's Supper is lawful and right everywhere: fellowship in heavenly and therefore also in earthly things; the *communio* of the *sancti* in and in respect of the *sancta*.

The lordship of Jesus Christ in His community takes place as the community assembles in public worship for prayer as the fellowship of those who are referred only to God, and therefore directed wholly to Jesus Christ. They address God as "Our Father" as they are freed to do so by the Son who has Himself the power to address Him in this way. From this standpoint the law which holds sway in the community must always be the law of men who have been freed to do this and have therefore become brothers. What has to be expressed in canon law is that they are united to one another both as a whole and individually by the fact that they all have equal need of God and all have equal access—with the same certainty, directness, fulness and worth. There will necessarily be stronger and weaker, older and younger, higher and lower brothers, and in their common life the law valid in the community will have to give them as such the necessary directions. But it will also have to make clear that the necessary differentiations not only cannot harm but can only strengthen the brotherly unity in which they are together in calling upon the Father in the name of the one true Son of God; in which—with the exception of this One, the First-born—none can argue that he has any less need of God or claim any higher access; in which none can try to be a mediator between God and others, or commend or impose himself upon them as one who is directly commissioned by God, or be accepted and proclaimed as such by others. In the community canon law cannot possibly establish a "hierarchy" because this term contains and evokes the idea of a ruling for which there is no place among brothers. Its task is to show in what way the one can be to the other a real brother: stronger, older and higher perhaps; but a brother all the same, with the same need of God and the same access; and therefore, without any essential precedence and claim but only in the name of the First-born and as His human witness, able to be a true helper and adviser, and therefore, with an actual and not an institutional authority, a leader and teacher and pastor. The man who most seriously and unreservedly ranges himself with others, even the most lowly; who most sincerely gives himself to the depths where the sun of the Father shines on good and evil, the just and the unjust, the wise and fools; who with them (and as one of them) can most humbly and joyfully call upon Him from these depths—he it is, and only he, who proves his call to be a true leader in the community. And he does this by the fact that he really is a leader and does not merely claim to be such, or receive investiture with the dignity of leadership. The freedom of the Holy Spirit, to order the christocratic brotherhood in this way, not preventing but guaranteeing the actual leadership of one brother in relation to another, poses the task and concern of true Church law.

Our final statement in defining Church law as liturgical law is that in divine service it not only has its original seat and its source of knowledge but also (3) its true and proper theme. It has to guard its peculiar basis and source. Even public worship as the centre of the life of the community is at every point a human action. It is men who confess, who baptise, who administer the Lord's Supper, who pray "Our Father." Hence this whole occurrence is not protected from misunderstanding and abuse. In this respect the community has its treasure in earthen vessels. It cannot escape the risk involved. Nor can it console itself with the reflection that everything human is imperfect, or the recollection that its sins are forgiven. The grace of sanctification, and therefore of Jesus Christ generally, is surely alien to it if it does not try to counteract the continual menace and process of a profanation of that which is holy by its own human and therefore unholy hands; if it does not resist to the best of its ability and conscience. It is to do this that it asks concerning true Church law as the true ordering of its worship. It is well aware that only He who is present and active within it as its Lord has the authority and competence to order this and therefore to protect it against perversion. Its human ordering can thus consist and take place only in an obedient regard for His. It cannot refuse this. It cannot, therefore, regard its liturgy as inviolable because inerrant. It cannot shelter it (least of all for reasons of piety) from the critical question whether it is rightly done, or whether it might not be done differently and better. For this reason its concern for Church law as the ordering of divine service must be unceasing.

12

JAMES B. TORRANCE

The Place of Jesus Christ in Worship

GOD HAS MADE ALL CREATURES FOR HIS GLORY. THE LILIES OF the field in their beauty glorify God with a glory greater than that of Solomon, but they do not know it. The sparrow on the housetop glorifies God in its dumbness, but it doesn't know it. The universe in its vastness and remoteness glorifies God but it doesn't know it. But God made man in His own image to be the Priest of creation, to express for all creatures the praises of God, so that through the lips of man the heavens might declare the glory of God, that we who know we are God's creatures might worship God and in our worship gather up the worship of all creation. Man's chief end is to glorify God, and creation realises its own creaturely glory in glorifying God through the lips of man.

But nature fails of this purpose because of the failure of man. Instead of songs of joy the whole creation groans in universal travail, waiting for the fulfilment of God's purpose in the lives of men. Does God then abandon His purposes for man and for all His creatures? Does God leave all nature to be subject to vanity and futility and forget He has made man in His image?

The good news of the Gospel is that Jesus comes to be the Priest of Creation, to do for men what man fails to do, to offer to God the worship and the praise that we have failed to offer, to glorify God by a life of perfect obedience, to be the One true servant of the Lord, in whom and through whom we are renewed in the image of God and in the worship of God. Jesus comes, as our Brother Man, to be our great High Priest, that He might carry on His loving heart the joys, the sorrows, the prayers, the conflicts of all His creatures, that He might reconcile all things to God, that He might intercede for all nations as our eternal Mediator and Advocate, that He might

From James B. Torrance, *Church Service Society Annual,* No. 40, May, 1970, pp. 41–62. Used by permission of the Author.

stand in for us in the presence of His Father, when in our failure and bewilderment we don't know how to pray as we ought, and forget to pray. By His Spirit He helps us in our infirmities.

In that He is the Head of all things, He makes us His Body, and calls us to be a royal priesthood, a corporate priesthood to offer up spiritual sacrifices, that we might be identified with Him and participate with Him in His great priestly work and ministry of intercession, that our prayers on earth might be the echo of His prayers in heaven. Whatever else our worship is, it is our liturgical Amen to the Worship of Christ.

Christian worship, therefore, is our response to God for all that He has done for us in Christ. It is our self-offering in body, mind and spirit to the One True Offering made for us in Christ, our response of gratitude (*eucharistia*) to God's grace (*charis*), our sharing by grace in the heavenly intercession of Christ. Therefore anything we say about worship—the forms of worship, its practice and procedure—must be said in the light of that to which it is a response. It must be said in the light of the Gospel. Therefore as a Reformed and reforming Church we must ask ourselves: Do our forms of worship convey the Gospel? Are they the appropriate response to the Gospel? Do they help people to apprehend the Worship and Ministry of Christ, or do they hinder? Are they transparent or are they opaque? To answer these questions we have to look at the *meaning,* the *content* of worship, before we can decide whether our traditions and procedure in worship are adequate. If our worship is to be intelligent, meaningful worship, we must look at the realities which evoke from us and demand from us an intelligent, meaningful response. So the Apostle says in Romans 12:1—after expounding the content of the Gospel in the first eleven chapters—"With eyes wide open to the mercies of God, I beg you my brothers, as an act of intelligent worship (*logike latreia*), to give Him your bodies as a living sacrifice, consecrated to Him and acceptable by Him" (J. B. Phillips).

JESUS IS THE ONE TRUE WORSHIPPER

The writer of the Epistle to the Hebrews describes our Lord as the *Leitourgos* (Hebrews 8:2)—"the leader of our worship", "the minister of the real sanctuary which the Lord pitched and not man". As such the *leitourgia* of Jesus is contrasted with the *leitourgia* of men. This is the worship which God has provided for men, and which alone is acceptable to God. In old Israel, the priests sought to fulfil their God-given ordinances of worship (*dikaiomata latreias*) but their worship only foreshadowed the true Worship and Self-offering of Christ on our behalf. "But now Christ has come . . . and offered Himself without blemish to God, a spiritual and eternal sacrifice; and His blood will cleanse our conscience from the deadness of our former ways and fit us for the service (*latreuein*) of the living God" (Heb. 9:11–15; 10:1–25). Our risen and ascended Lord is still "the High Priest over the House of God", the Minister of the sanctuary, the One true Worshipper who leads us in our worship. The Worship of Christ is thus the worship which gathers up the worship of Israel and replaces it, and it is this Worship which is the substance of all Christian worship. So Calvin expounded it at the time of the Reformation in the *Institutes*, Bk. II: chs. 9–11ff; IV: chs. 14–17 and also very fully in his Commentary on the Epistle to the Hebrews. This was the heart of his interpretation of baptism and the eucharist, as of all worship, viz. that Christ's Baptism is our baptism, set forth in our water baptism; that Christ's Sacrifice is our sacrifice, set forth at the table; that Christ's Worship is our worship, set forth in our worship and prayers. This is the heart of the Reformed doctrine of Justification by Grace, that Christ is made unto us wisdom and righteousness and sanctification and redemption—that Christ's Righteousness is our righteousness apprehended by faith.

Jesus' whole life in the Gospel story was a life of worship. As a boy, in the Lucan account, He heard the call of God, and offered His life in obedience to God. "Did you not know that I was bound to be in my Father's House?" He said to his parents when they found Him in the Temple. He grew in wisdom and stature, in favour with God and men, daily offering Himself in prayer and communion in the service of God and of men, praying at times all night on the mountainside, before facing the duties of the coming day, praying at the great turning points and crises of His life, at His baptism, when He chose the twelve, at the Last Supper, in the Garden of Gethsemane, on the Cross, offering as man to God a life of unbroken obedience. His whole life of self-offering culminated in the One True Sacrifice of obedience and love on the Cross, which alone is acceptable for all men, for all nations, for all time, "the offering by which He has perfected for all times those who are sanctified" (Heb. 10:14). In John's Gospel, the life and ministry and signs of Jesus are set in the context of the festivals and worship life of Israel, to show the meaning of the ministry of Jesus and of the true worship of Israel (cp. O. Cullmann: *Early Christian Worship*).

JESUS AS MEDIATOR IN WORSHIP

Here lies the mystery, the wonder, the glory of the Gospel, that He who is God, the Creator of all things, and worthy of the worship and praises of all creation, should become man and *as a man worship God,* and as a man lead us in our worship of God, that we might become the sons of God we are meant to be.

This thought emerges clearly in several ways in the New Testament. It is the theme of the Servant passage in Philippians 2:5-11. In confessing "that Jesus Christ is Lord, to the glory of God the Father", we confess that He is God and man. Together with the Father and the Spirit He is the object of our worship, the One to whom every knee shall bow but yet as the Incarnate Son, He is the One who worships the Father for us and with us. There is duality in unity in the predicate "Lord". He is Lord as our Creator, and He is Lord as the Leader of our humanity. He is Lord as the One whom we worship, and He is Lord as the Leader of our worship.

This again finds explicit formulation in the doctrine of the Mediator. So the Apostle, in I Timothy 2:1-6, in exhorting that "petitions, prayers, intercessions and thanksgivings be offered for all men" goes on to add at once, "For there is one God, and also one mediator between God and men, Christ Jesus, himself man, who sacrificed himself to win freedom for all mankind . . ." (N.E.B.). We intercede in the name and through the ministry of the Mediator.

In the language of the Epistle to the Hebrews, Jesus is the Mediator of the New Covenant (8:6; 12:14). As High Priest, Jesus Christ *represents God to men and represents men to God* in His own person. The Epistle to the Hebrews, which says so much about worship, is significant in that in its High-Priest Christology, it lays such stress on the vicarious role of the humanity of Jesus in worship, ministry, sacrifice and prayer, while always seeing this as the ministry of the Incarnate Son of God. Jesus Christ is both the Apostle of God and the High Priest in our confession of faith. So Professor W. Manson writes: "Christianity as known to the writer is the confession of Jesus Christ as our High Priest, and this for him is as momentous as the confession 'Jesus is Lord' is for St. Paul . . . And if the confession also proclaims Jesus to be our 'Apostle' it should be remembered that in Judaism the high-priest on the Day of Atonement was recognized as the *Shaliach* (the apostle, commissioner) not of men but of God" (*Epistle to the Hebrews,* p. 54; cp. Strack-Billerbeck, III, pp. 2-4). The High Priest is appointed by God to act for men. "For every High Priest is taken from among men and appointed their representative before God, to offer gifts and sacrifices for sins'' (Heb. 5:1). The role of Representative Man is, in the argument of the Epistle, assumed by the Incarnate Son of God. God in Jesus is the Leader of our worship. He fulfils for us His own holy ordinances of worship, in providing One in whom and through whom we can draw near to God.

Such is the wonderful love of God, that He has come to us in Jesus Christ, and in Jesus assumed our life (the life of all men), underwritten our responsibilities, offered for us a life of worship and obedience and prayer to the Father, taken to Himself our body of death, vicariously submitted for us to the verdict of 'guilty', died our death and risen again in our humanity, so that by the grace of God, His life is our life, His death is our death, His victory our victory, His resurrection our resurrection, His righteousness our righteousness and His eternal prayers and self-offerings to the Father our prayers and offering in the presence of the Father. So we are accepted in the Beloved, and discover our status as sons.

HIS WORSHIP IS OUR WORSHIP—BY GRACE

What we have said above is that *by grace* God gives us what He demands. *He draws near to us* to give Himself to us in wonderful love and communion, in an act where *He draws us near to Himself* in Christ. We are accepted by God, not because we have offered worthy worship, but in spite of our unworthiness, because He has provided for us a Worship, a Way, a Sacrifice, a Forerunner in Christ our Leader and Representative, and our worship is our joyful Amen to that Worship. This is the heart of all true Christian worship. It is our response of faith to God's grace. So we worship God ''through Jesus Christ our Lord'', and pray ''in the name of Jesus Christ''.

According to the Shorter Catechism, ''Prayer is an offering up of our desires unto God, for things agreeable to His will, *in the name of Christ,* with confession of our sins, and thankful acknowledgement of His mercies''. But we can only pray in the name of Jesus, because already Jesus has *in our name* offered up our desires to God, *in our name* lived that perfect life agreeable to the will of God, *in our name* confessed our sins by His death upon the Cross, *in our name* made the one great thank-offering as when at the Last Supper Jesus took bread and gave thanks on behalf of all men and all nations for the Father's mercies. So in prayer we come by grace alone, in the name of our great High Priest, believing that we are accepted in Him who bears our names on His heart.

Calvin and Knox both constantly interpreted worship in terms of our Lord's High Priestly ministry over against mediaeval conceptions of the priesthood and Pelagian conceptions of grace. The *sole Priesthood of Christ* in the Church was their constant theme. So they spoke about justification in Christ, justification by the blood of Christ, for the content of grace is Jesus Christ, given to us by God to do for us what we can never worthily do, and they spelt this out in terms of worship and prayer. So they interpreted our Lord's High Priestly prayer in John 17, seeing behind it the liturgical symbolism of the Day of Atonement in Old Israel. That was the day in the year which gathered up the worship of every other day. On that day an offering was made to God which gathered up all the other offerings made daily in the sanctuary. On that day the worship of all Israel was led by one man, the high priest. He was the Representative of all Israel, standing in solidarity with them. This was symbolised by the fact that he bore the names of the twelve tribes inscribed on his breastplate. For their sakes he consecrated himself for his priestly work of offering and intercession, confessed the sins of the people over the head of the sacrificial lamb, and in the name of the people entered into the Holy of Holies. There he intercedes with God for the people, and then returns to the people from God to pronounce the Aaronic blessing of peace. Two statements can be made about the liturgical significance of that action. (1) When the high priest entered into the Holy of Holies, all Israel entered *in the the person of the high priest*. (As Calvin says in his Commentary on Hebrews 6:19, ''in the person of one man all entered into the sanctuary together''.) (2) When the high priest entered within the veil with the blood of the victim and interceded for Israel, God accepted all Israel *in the person of the high priest*. That twofold statement expresses the thought of God's covenant relationship with Israel being mediated *in the person* of the priest. As Mowinckel puts it, ''the covenant was concentrated in the person of the high priest''. Calvin was not slow to interpret the person and work of Christ as the Mediator of the New Covenant in these terms, which are significant for our understanding of *sola gratia* and the theology of worship. So we can make two similar statements about the ministry of Christ as our *Leitourgos*. (1) When Christ assumed our humanity, for our sakes consecrated Himself, in our name suffered, died, rose again, ascended to the Father, *we* suffered, died, rose again, and ascended to the Father *in Him*. We have entered into the presence of God in the Person of our High Priest. (2) Because Jesus has assumed our name, confessed our sins, died our death, risen and ascended in our humanity to intercede for us, *God* has accepted us *in Him*. These two statements, taken together, present the New Testament teaching that all God's covenant relations with us in worship, in prayer, in forgiveness, reconciliation and in sanctification are mediated to us in and through the Person and Ministry of Christ. The New Covenant is concentrated in Him. This, it seems to me, is the heart of the Reformed approach to the theology of worship. Great emphasis is placed on the role of the representative priestly humanity of our Lord. Cp. Calvin, *Institutes* 2, XV, 6. "For we, though in ourselves polluted, in Him being priests (Rev. 1:6), offer ourselves and our all to God, and freely enter the heavenly sanctuary, so that the sacrifices of prayer and praise which we present are acceptable and of sweet odour before Him, . . . etc".

HIS WORSHIP IS OUR WORSHIP—IN THE COMMUNION OF THE SPIRIT

Jesus draws us into Himself—into His life of prayer to the Father, in an act of memory, in a life of communion—through the Holy Spirit.

(a) Jesus taught us to call God "Father", and in our prayers to say "Our Father..." All true prayer is gathered up in that one word, and a very large part of our Lord's teaching was devoted to putting content into that word, as in the parables and the Sermon on the Mount. But Jesus not only *taught* us to pray "Father". He Himself is the living embodiment of that prayer. His life on earth was one of unbroken communion with the Father. He put content into the word by *being* among men the true Son of the Father, from the boyhood incident in the temple in His "Father's House" to the last word from the Cross, "Father, into Thy hands..." So He could say, "I and the Father are one", "he that hath seen me hath seen the Father", etc. As the early Fathers put it, He who was the eternal Son of the Father by nature became the Son of Man, that we sons of men might become sons of God by grace. He became what we are that we might become what He is. In that earthly life of communion, we are given a glimpse (as in John ch. 17) into the eternal communion of the Trinity. But the Son of God became our brother man that He might lift us up into that life of wonderful communion, and so He sends His Spirit into our hearts and puts His prayer into our lips whereby we too can pray, "Abba,

Father''. So in the communion of the Spirit our prayers on earth are the echo of His prayers in heaven, and by grace we are given to participate in His intercessions for all men. So in our corporate worship we are called to be a royal priesthood, bearing on our hearts the sorrows and cares and tragedies of our world as our heavenly High Priest does. So by grace we are given to participate in the life, ministry, sufferings, death, resurrection and heavenly intercessions of Him who is the Head of the Body.

(b) Jesus said to the disciples, "I will pray the Father, and He will give you another Comforter... and He will bring all things to your remembrance". At the Last Supper, Jesus said, "This do in remembrance of Me''. The word *anamnesis* (as Prof. J. K. S. Reid has reminded us in an article in the *Church Service Society Annual,* May, 1960) is of rich liturgical significance in the Bible. It does not mean simply an act of recollection of some remote date of bygone history, as every schoolboy remembers 1066 A.D. Rather it means remembering in such a way that we see our participation in the past event and see our destiny and future as bound up with it. So when Jews remember the passover and the exodus from Egypt, they do not think of it simply as an irretrievable date from over 3000 years ago. Rather they remember it in such a way that they confess "*We* are the people whom God brought out of the land of Egypt, for *we* were Pharaoh's bondmen''. "*We* are the people with whom God made His covenant, saying 'I will be your God and you shall be my people'. That mighty act of God in delivering Israel was *our* redemption'' (cp. op. cit., pp. 8ff.). Thus Israel lives by this kind of historical memory. Today, at this point in her historical existence, she stands related to that historical point of departure as an elect covenanted people in the faithfulness of her ever present Lord. This is no doubt what gives her her historical continuity and sense of identity through the centuries. Understandably, therefore, this is central to her cult, in which she recapitulates the saving acts of God. "Remembrance, then, occupies a place of first importance in the celebration of the Passover. It is a remembrance that finds expression, both words and acts; and to ask whether the words or the acts were the more important element is probably an idle question. But it is very significant that the verbal expression is so marked a feature of the rite itself, appearing as it does both as *Haggadah* (the telling of the whole paschal story) and in the *Hallels* (singing of praise for the deliverance effected at the time of the Exodus). Nor can it escape notice that the transmission is given careful verbal direction and definition'' (p. 7). "In cultic remembrance.... the past is rendered present; there is a re-*present*-ation of the past so that it lives again in the present time. This, for lack of a better word, we may call a *presentifying* of the past'' (p. 10).

So at the Last Supper, we do not merely remember the Passion of our Lord as an isolated date from 1900 years ago. Rather we remember it in such a way that we know that *we* are the people for whom our Saviour died and rose again, *we* are the people whose sins Jesus confessed on the Cross, *we* are the people for whom God has made a New Covenant in the blood of Christ. *We* are the Israel of God, to whom God has said, I will be your God and you shall be my people. We are the people whose sorrows and cries Jesus bears on His Kingly heart as He intercedes for us, and constitutes Himself the eternal Memorial for us before God. We are what we are today by the grace of God because of what God did for us then.

This work of memory, of realising our participation and fellowship in the sufferings of Christ, is the work of the Holy Spirit, who brings these things to our remembrance, interpreting to us the meaning of these events. We remember Christ—yet it is not so much we who remind ourselves of these events, but Jesus Christ who brings the things of His Passion to our remembrance through the Holy Spirit, as our ever living and ever present Lord, who is in His own Person our Memorial in the presence of the Father. In other words, our memorial is the earthly counterpart of the heavenly Memorial. Christ in constituting Himself as our Memorial before the Father, by His Spirit lifts us up with our acts of presenting our memorials before God. So the Lord's Supper, like the Passover, is both a memorial to us, and also a memorial before God. ''Is not this Thy Son's body?'' ''Are not we the people whom You brought out of Egypt?'' So Christ remembers us (''Jesus, remember me . . .'') and before God says, ''Are not these the children whom Thou hast given Me?'' (cp. John ch. 17).

In this context our prayers to God are described as a memorial before God. So in Acts 10:4, the angel says to Cornelius, ''Your prayers and your alms are come up for a memorial (*eis mnemosunon*) before God''. This may reflect the priestly ministry of vicarious prayer when we bear the burdens and needs of others on our hearts before God, as the earthly counterpart of our heavenly High Priest's intercessions which are our Memorial before God. The background of this concept of prayer may again be the liturgical prayers of the high priest in old Israel presenting the prayers of Israel before God (Exod. 28:12, 29; 39:7). As a royal priesthood, bearing the needs of the world on our heart, are we not called in the name of Christ to constitute ourselves before God as a living memorial to the Father, calling upon the Father to remember all His creatures?

(c) Clearly then we do not remember an absent Christ. But the Christ whom we remember is the Christ who is present to bring the things we celebrate to our remembrance in an act of communion. This is why, as Bonhoeffer has reminded us in his *Christology,* the "*Who-question*" is the central one for us in our understanding, not only of the Eucharist, but of all Christology, not the What? or the How? The Reformed world after the Marburg Colloquy was torn asunder by the How-question: "How is Christ present in the sacrament?" This still divides the Lutheran and Reformed communions, both of which in their different ways are concerned to do justice to the presence of the whole Christ at His Table. Had Protestant theologians been more concerned to ask the Who-question there may have been a much greater common understanding of what we mean by the eucharistic sacrifice. Who is the Christ whom we set forth in the act of *anamnesis,* and who is so truly present and on whose humanity we feed? (Or should the question be asked in the form of the Pauline prayer, "Who art Thou, Lord?") Then the answer would take the form of a confession of faith. He is the One in whose representative humanity our broken humanity was assumed and judged. He is the One in whose self-consecration and self-offering we were consecrated and healed. He is the One in whose death we died, in whose body we were raised, and in whose continuing humanity our humanity is presented by our Great High Priest to the Father. *Who* is the Christ who lifts up our hearts and minds in the *sursum corda* and who makes us participants of the new humanity in Him? He is the One by whose eternal Spirit we are given by grace to share in the substitutionary self-presentation of Christ in the Holy of Holies. *Who* is the One who is so truly present in the eucharistic *parousia*? He is the One who is also absent (ascension)—*quodammodo praesens et quodammodo absens*—whom we await in the apocalyptic *parousia* (till He come!). *Who* is the One who draws us into such wonderful communion? He is the whole Christ, the God-Man in whom and through whom God and Man are reconciled, for God and man are one in the God-Man. *Who* is the One who so freely gives Himself to us and who makes such costly claims upon us? He is the One in whom all men have been reconciled to God and to one another, and who sends us out in mission to be ambassadors of this Gospel to the ends of the earth and to the end of the age.

In this way, the question about the place of Jesus Christ in worship assumes perhaps its most crucial form in the question about the place of Jesus Christ in the sacraments. But by seeking to answer the question in the form of the Who-question, do we not hold the past, the present and the future (*anamnesis* and communion and eschatological hope) together, in a way in which they can fall apart when we ask primarily the How-question? The Christ whom we remember is the Christ who lifts up into His life of communion with the Father, and whom we shall see when we become like Him in the apocalyptic *parousia*.

Again the *Who-question* is the imprtant one when we ask the question about the relationship between liturgy and mission, or between the Church and the world. When we withdraw from the world and on behalf of the world worship the Father in the name of Christ, we are not making some pietist escape from the world and the needs and claims of the world. The Christ in whose name we worship is the Christ by whose Cross the world is judged, and at the same time the Christ in whose Representative Humanity our humanity is raised and given the promise of redemption. The Risen Lord is the first fruits of the New Creation, the New Humanity. So we call upon the world to participate with us in our participation in the death and resurrection of Christ, to participate with us in our participation in the New Humanity, and to look with us beyond death to the fulfilment of God's purposes for all creation in resurrection. *Who* then is the Christ whom we worship? He is the Head of all creation, the Man in whom all things have been reconciled to God. He is not only the propitiation for our sins but also for the sins of the whole world. To remind ourselves constantly of the Who-question is to remind ourselves of the integral relation between liturgy and mission. The One whom we worship is the One who comes to us as our Apostle and High Priest and says, "As the Father hath sent me, so send I you." So likewise, as we engage in mission and face the world and address the world in the name of Christ, in the market place, and speak of the things of Christ in this world's language, *Who* is the Christ whom we proclaim to all nations? He is the One who calls all nations to the worship of God, the One in whom all are called to be renewed in the image of God and in the worship of God. So we call upon men to repent and to be baptised—baptised as a sign of participation in the New Humanity of Christ and in the worshipping Body of Christ. The prime question in mission is not, *What* do we proclaim? nor *How* do we proclaim? but *Whom* do we proclaim?

(*d*) The Holy Spirit, through whom we participate in the Person and Ministry of Christ, exercises a two-fold ministry, corresponding to the twofold priestly ministry of Christ—namely, of *representing God to man* and of *representing man to God*. It is in this double sense we are to interpret the work of the Spirit in taking of the things of Christ and ministering them to us. (*a*) Through the Holy Spirit *God comes* to meet us in worship, in the ministry of Word and Sacrament, and summons us to respond in faith and obedience and thanksgiving, in offering ourselves as a living sacrifice to God, which is our reasonable service. This is the one side of the dialogue, the communion, which is worship. (*b*) In our human—frail, broken, unworthy—response the Spirit helps us in our infirmities, lifting us up to Christ who in His ascended *humanity* is our God-given Response, the Leader of our Worship, the Pioneer of our Faith, our Advocate and High Priest, who through the eternal Spirit presents Himself for us to the Father. So in and through the mediatorial ministry of the Spirit, we worship the Father in the name of Christ. "For we know not what we should pray for as we ought; but the Spirit Himself maketh intercession for us with groanings which cannot be uttered. And he that searcheth the hearts knoweth what is the mind of the Spirit, because He maketh intercession for the saints according to the will of God" (Romans ch. 8:22–27). Is this not part of the significance of the *filioque* clause, that the Spirit comes from the Father and from the Son? It seems to me that this latter point is of great importance, because it is all too possible for us so to stress (*a*) that we neglect (*b*). We so stress that God comes to us as God to address us through His Word, that we short-circuit the real humanity of Christ, the role of the continuing Priesthood of Christ in representing men to God, and have a one-sided view of the work of the Spirit. We can then so obtrude our own response to the Word that we obscure or forget the God-given Response made for us in Jesus Christ. We so obtrude our own offering of praise, that we lose sight of the One True Offering made for us. Is this why we have so lost sight of the earlier Reformed understanding of the Lord's Supper which we find in Calvin, Knox and Robert Bruce? It can also mean that we lose much of the comfort of the Gospel. For God does not *throw us back upon ourselves* to make our response to His Word. But graciously He helps our infirmities by giving us Jesus Christ and the Holy Spirit to make the appropriate response *for us* and *in us*.

Can we adapt Gal. 2:20 and say, "We pray, and yet it is not we who pray, but Christ who prays for us and in us; and the prayers which we now offer in the flesh, we offer by the faithfulness of One who loved us and offered Himself for us?''

HIS WORSHIP IS OUR WORSHIP—THROUGH A WONDERFUL EXCHANGE

The Christian Gospel is a Gospel of Reconciliation, and reconcil-iation (atonement) is enshrined at the heart of all true worship. God in His grace lifts us up into a life of wonderful communion by effecting a wonderful exchange. This is in large part the literal meaning of the passage in 2 Cor. ch. 5:18–21: ''God was in Christ reconciling the world to Himself''—effecting at-one-ment. And how does He do it? ''Christ was innocent of sin, and yet for our sake God made Him one with the sinfulness of men, so that we might be made one with the goodness of God Himself'' (N.E.B.)—effecting atonement. Our Anglo-Saxon word ''atone-ment'' is a useful translation of the Greek, precisely because it holds these two moments together in the one work of reconcil-iation.

Now as Calvin argued in Book 4 of the *Institutes,* this is the heart of our theology of the sacraments, particularly of the Last Supper which so enshrines the *mirifica commutatio*—the wonder-ful exchange, that Christ took what was ours that He might give us what was His. He takes our broken, sinful humanity and cleanses it by His self-sanctifying life of obedience, death and resurrection—in the One True Offering to God of our humanity—and now comes back to us in the power of the Spirit to give Himself to us in an act where He gives us back our humanity (now cleansed) saying, ''Take, eat, this is my body which is broken for you''. Our recep-tion of Christ is thus the counterpart of the wonderful exchange. The Body on which we feed is that body which He assumed for our sakes, that in our worship of God we might be sanctified once and for all by the self-offering of Christ. In the communion of the Spirit, in virtue of this exchange, we know that His Humanity is our humanity (so graciously assumed), His Death our death (which we shew forth), His Life our life (till He come), His Self-Offering our offering, His Communion with the Father our communion, into which He lifts us by His Spirit. So the Last Supper enshrines so vividly the inner meaning of the Gospel.

Calvin is here spelling out, not only the meaning of the Evangel, but also the meaning of the Greek word for reconciliation. The

Greek word *katallasso* with the noun *katallage* (deriving from *allos*—other) means quite literally "to buy" something or someone, "to change one thing for another", "to effect an exchange". So Jesus says, "What shall it profit a man if he gain the whole world and lose his own soul, or what shall a man give in exchange for his soul?" That is, it is a bad deal for a man to sell his soul even if he gains the whole world in exchange (cf. also Romans ch. 1, where the Apostle speaks about those who exchange the glory of God in their worship for an image made like corruptible beasts). So the word comes to mean, to reconcile, to exchange friendship for enmity, love and peace for hatred. That, says the Apostle, is what God has done for us in Christ. Jesus became our brother man, took the form of a servant, went all the way to the Cross. Why? That He might take our hatred and give us His love, take our sins that He might give us His righteousness, take our death that He might give us His eternal life, that we might humbly and joyfully receive Him, clothed with all His benefits. And why does He effect this wonderful exchange? To bring us into His wonderful communion with the Father.

What does this mean for us in practice? When we come to the Lord's Table to worship on a Communion Sunday, we come to offer ourselves to the Lord. It may be that we feel utterly unworthy to be there. Our lives are so broken and sinful. What can we render to the Lord? But then the bread and wine are brought in and set before our eyes, and *consecrated*—NOT as a sign of our self-offering to the Lord, but as a memorial that 1900 years ago Jesus assumed my life, my body, my mind and my spirit, sinful though they are, sanctified them and in my name made that offering to God which I could never make. Indeed for a moment my self-offering is set aside that I may look at that great Offering made for me. But the service does not end there. That same Christ, who is our eternal offering in the heavens, now comes to me in an act of self-giving and says, "Take, eat, this is my body which is broken for you", and draws me with my self-offering of praise and thanksgiving into *communion* with Himself. He gives back my life to me, converted and regenerated in Him. Is it not for these evangelical reasons that communion follows consecration? If we might again adapt Galatians 2:20, we might say at the Lord's Table, "We offer ourselves to the Lord and yet it is not we who offer, but Christ who has offered Himself for us and who is our Offering, and the offering which we now make in the flesh we make by the faith of Him who loved us and gave Himself for us".

"We offer . . . and yet it is not our offering. It is Christ". This, it seems to me, is what (in intention at least) Rome seeks to say in the Mass. "It is bread . . . and yet suddenly we know it is not bread. It is Christ!" There is an evangelical intention, but she says it in the wrong way. She makes the moment of *conversio* what takes place in the elements, in the act of consecration—no doubt as the act of God in the action of the priest. But this obscures—in too Pelagian a fashion—the heart of the Gospel of grace, that the real *conversio* of our humanity took place in the substitutionary self-consecration of Jesus, in His life, death and resurrection, in the once and for all action of our High Priest. (Calvin and Robert Bruce could also speak of "conversion" in the use of the elements in their being set apart from all common use to this holy use, but not in the sense of a change in the elements themselves.) Our subjective conversion (our *mortificatio* and *vivificatio,* as Calvin expounded it in Book Three of the *Institutes*) takes place in our participation through the Spirit in that *Conversio*—the *palingenesia* in Christ.

In not too dissimilar fashion, evangelical Protestantism today can sometimes so emphasise the moment of subjective conversion, that that too becomes in Pelagian fashion the real moment of salvation, in a way that can obscure the Real Moment, the Conversion of our humanity in Christ. Our conversion through the Spirit takes place when by grace we are given to participate in the mighty acts of God done once and for all in Christ.

WHAT THEN IS CHRISTIAN WORSHIP?

Following J. J. von Allmen in his magnificent recent work (*Worship, its Theology and Practice,* Lutterworth, 1965), we can say three things.*

(1) In her worship, the Church recapitulates the History of Salvation.

In her worship the Church sets forth by word and action that perfect life of Worship which we see in Jesus Christ. As her response to the Worship and Ministry of Christ, she sets forth objectively in her liturgical life what God has done for her and for the world. In worship we sum up, we recapitulate, we echo the Offering, the Prayers, the Praises of Him who is our *Leitourgos,* in

*I am deeply indebted to this work for much in this article.

our self-offering, prayers and praises uniting with the whole company in heaven and on earth who worship God and "the Lamb upon the Throne". So Hebrews calls the angels worshipping spirits (*leitourgika pneumata*). Thus our worship has the character of witness—liturgical witness to grace, according to the divinely given ordinances of grace. We preach and pray and celebrate the sacraments, as our Lord commanded, not to bear witness to ourselves, not as a form of self expression but as a witness to Christ and what the world is in Christ and shall become through Christ.

Worship is thus human action, and yet it is that human action which is evoked by Christ, through the Spirit, in such a way that He is the One who acts in us and through us, so that our worship becomes real worship in Spirit and in Truth. So we can say it is not we who represent Christ, but Christ who re-*presents* Himself through the Spirit.

In this way, for example, all that we do in the Christian Year, in Advent, from Palm Sunday to Easter, Ascension, Whitsun, etc., all that we do in preaching, all that we do in Baptism and the Lord's Supper, we do as an act of *anamnesis* in the manner described above, setting forth, not just the past, but also the present and the future, believing that in and through our words and acts Christ makes us participants in His Person and Saving acts.

Clearly, however, worship as such must be from the heart. It must be real worship. Although it always has the character of objective witness to Christ, our participation in Christ must be the real participation of inner life and not only of outward words and actions. There must be the real counterpart of life, prayer, self-denial, praise, gratitude, ministry of love, faithful stewardship.

(2) *Worship is the Epiphany of the Church.*

The Church is the Church in her worship. Worship is not an optional extra, but is of the very life and essence of the Church. Nor is it a false grovelling in the dust of the religiously minded. Man is never more truly man than when he worships God. He rises to all the heights of human dignity when he worships God, and all God's purposes in Creation and in Redemption are fulfilled in us as together in worship we are renewed in and through Christ, and in the name of Christ we glorify God. So by the grace of God we seek to voice for all creatures the praises of God and realise our God-given destiny to be the priests of creation under Christ our Great High Priest.

Thus we must never stress mission at the expense of liturgy, not liturgy at the expense of mission. Both are forms of witness to Jesus Christ and are of the essence of the Church in the world. They must be carefully distinguished, but never separated. Both have as their end the concern that all creatures should glorify God, and in glorifying God realise their creaturely glory.

The Church, in bearing witness to Christ in her worship, is thus also bearing witness to what she has herself become in Christ. She makes visible in her worship what she knows she is in Christ, a redeemed community renewed in love, reconciled to God and one another. So she is called to be a visible fellowship of love. Just as truly as we are summoned unconditionally to make visible to the world the righteousness and unity which we have by grace in Christ, so are we summoned to be in ourselves what we are in the Person of Christ our Head, a worshipping people. To fail to take seriously her calling to be a worshipping community is to be guilty of antinomianism, to continue in sin that grace may abound.

(3) The Church in her worship foreshadows the Judgment and the Renewal of the world.

The Church in her witness bears witness to the Kingdom which has come in Christ, and which is present in the world, like seed growing secretly, or like leaven hidden in a lump. But the end is ''not yet''. What we already are *in Christ* we have yet to become in ourselves *through Christ* . . . So we await the apocalyptic *Parousia* when we shall be in ourselves what we are now in Christ, when we shall see Him whom we love and be like Him.

Therefore in her worship the Church bears witness to Him in whom we have been judged as well as to Him in whom we have been renewed, and participates by death and resurrection (baptism) in that judgment and renewal, waiting for the Last Judgment and the Renewal (*palingenesia*) of all things. She shows forth the Lord's death ''till He come''. The sacraments thus, as Calvin used to say, bear witness to the fact that Christ is in a manner present and yet in a manner absent. But when Christ is finally present in the *Parousia* we shall no longer need sacraments—although we shall still worship.

In this way the Church in her worship is a sign in the world of the Judgment of the world and is a threat to the self-righteousness and self-sufficiency of the world, and is doubtless rejected by the world. But at the same time in her worship she is a sign of the hope of the world, bearing witness in a proleptic way to the fulfilment of all God's purposes for the world.

Clearly then there are right ways and wrong ways of distinguishing the Church and the world. The Church lives in the world bearing witness to the fact that this world is God's world by right of Creation and Redemption. But she also bears witness to the fact that the world is not yet the Kingdom of God. We worship in the Spirit on the Lord's Day to bear witness to the fact that every day is the Lord's day. But we also worship on the first day of the week to bear witness to the fact that the secular city is not the celestial city, that there remains a rest for the people of God.

The Church on earth is thus that community within the world which in her worship anticipates the perfect community of the Kingdom, waiting for the marriage feast of the Lamb. But she is also that community which in the name of Christ goes out to fulfil a diaconal function in the world, knowing that this is the world that God loves and for which Christ died, and which shall yet realise her destiny in the good purposes of God. So she takes the form of a servant in the world, and seeks not to be ministered unto by the world but to minister. Like her Lord she must be willing to make herself of no reputation in the world (i.e. give up all talk about her own 'image' in the eyes of the world), for she lives *not* by the justification of men, but by the justification of Christ.

There is continuity and discontinuity between the Church and the world, as truly as the death and resurrection of our Lord means that there is both continuity and discontinuity between the Christ who died and the Christ who rose from the dead. The sign of that continuity and discontinuity is *baptism*. So the Church in her public worship is a sign in the world of the death and Resurrection of Christ and calls upon the world to participate in her worship in an act of death and resurrection. For worship is the function of the baptised, and baptism is as such the sign of the frontier between the Church and the world. The Church must never apologise for this frontier. Baptism is a witness to the freeness of grace and the costliness of grace. It is free for all men, and offered to all who come. But it is costly grace and lays costly claims upon all who do come. To stress free grace at the expense of the costly claims of grace is to turn free grace into cheap grace (indiscriminate baptism) and to make the Church a pedlar of cheap grace. It is to use the Church and her worship to sacralise the status quo. But to stress the costly claims of grace at the expense of the freeness of grace is to turn grace into conditional grace, which is not grace. It is to fail to bear witness to the Christ who lived and died for all men.

*   *   *   *   *

In the light of the foregoing account of the meaning and content of worship, may I suggest some weaknesses and dangers in much contemporary worship as I see it.

(1) The danger of making worship a two-dimensional thing and of short-circuiting the role of the humanity of Christ

It is possible to regard worship as a two-way encounter in which God comes to meet us now in personal encounter in the present moment, summoning us to respond in faith and obedience, where *no place* is given (or only lip service paid) to the God-given Response, and Offering and Intercessions of Jesus Christ as our High Priest. This would clearly undermine and destroy the sacraments.

For example, in baptism we would then bring our babies directly to God and ask God to bless them. But where is the One Baptism of Christ? Does not our baptism as a sacrament set forth the *Baptisma* of Him in whom we and our children have already been baptised in the Person of our Head, in the waters of Jordan and the blood of the Cross, and by whom we are given the promise of the Spirit at Pentecost?

Again, we might interpret the bread and the wine on the Lord's Table as the sign of our offering of ourselves to God (material elements being signs, it might be alleged, of the whole life and industry of man), an offering which we ask God to bless. But this again is to destroy the sacrament and turn the communion service into a glorified harvest thanksgiving. But where is the One True Offering of Christ?

Again it is possible for evangelical Protestants so to tumble over themselves backwards to avoid anything savouring of a Roman Pelagian sacrificial Mass, that they argue that the only sacrifice is that of our praise and our thanksgiving. But this can again destroy the sacrament, because it is possible so to obtrude *our* sacrifice of praise that we lose sight of the One True Sacrifice, and have no doctrine of a eucharistic sacrifice as we find it in Calvin or the sermons of Robert Bruce in our older Scottish tradition.

To reduce worship simply to this kind of two-dimensional thing, is to imply that God *throws us back on ourselves to make our response,* without giving us in the Man Jesus that Response which alone is acceptable to Him. Is this not to lose the comfort and peace of the Gospel as well as the secret of true Christian prayer?

(2) The danger of so emphasising the presence of the divine Christ that we lose sight of the human Christ

It is possible again to say that in all Christian worship Christ is present speaking to us, challenging us, exhorting us to be co-workers with Him in His mission to the world, that again no true place is given to the High Priestly ministry of Jesus as our Brother Man, who not only represents God to man, but also man to God.

This is the danger of certain Protestant emphases on the primacy of the *Word.* God comes to meet us and speak to us as the Living Word in Christ, and we respond in faith and obedience. This, it is maintained, is the Reformed emphasis on the role of the preaching of the word. But again as in the first danger, we lose sight of the fact that the Good News of the Gospel is that God has not only spoken a Word to us in Christ, but in Jesus of Nazareth given us one who from the human side has made the one true response to that Word, and submitted for us to the Judgments of that Word, and received for us the grace of that Word. This kind of emphasis on the primacy of the word was *not* that of Calvin or Knox or of any of the reformers. They always protested against a *nudus Christus,* but proclaimed that the Christ whom we preach is a whole Christ, Christ clothed with the Gospel, Christ clothed with His promises. Christ comes to us not only as God from the side of God. He comes to us as our brother man to do for us what we cannot do. In similar fashion this kind of Word-theology likewise destroys the sacramental relation and drives a false wedge between word and sacrament for this very reason. The whole Christ con-veys Himself to us in both word and sacrament, and certain con-temporary discussions as to which is more important can become beside the point.

I believe that this is also important in evangelism where the emphasis can become one where Christ as God challenges us and we "decide for Christ", as though *the* saving moment becomes the moment of *our* decision, rather than the Moment of the Life, Death and Resurrection of our Saviour for us. Surely it is *this* Saviour who summons us to decision where our amen is our response in the Spirit to His Amen for us.

(3) It is possible in worship to emphasise the Work of Christ (in an event theology) which loses sight of the Role of the Person of Jesus Christ, as our High Priest

We often isolate out the Cross of Christ, and the saving events which God has done for us in Christ, and stress the fact that worship is our response to these mighty acts. But if not interpreted carefully this can again mean that we fail to see the place of the humanity of Jesus Christ as the one who leads our worship, bears our sorrows on His heart and intercedes for us. We can become interested in the *blessings* of the Gospel which accrue to us from the *Work* of Christ, and so separate both the blessings and the Work from Jesus Christ Himself. This is the main burden of Bonhoeffer's plea that the Who-question be the primary one, rather than the What and the How. Lutheranism perhaps particularly has been susceptible to this weakness, as in Melanchthon's famous dictum, *Hoc est Christum cognoscere, beneficia eius cognoscere.*

At the Last Supper Jesus said, "This do in remembrance of *Me*"—not just of my death. Of course the Christ whom we remember is the Christ who died.

(4) Worship and the language of worship are not simply expressive of ourselves

It can never be too strongly stressed that worship is our response to Objective realities, to Jesus Christ and all that He has done for us. In worship we open our hearts to God and Jesus Christ, and set forth the one true Ministry and Worship of Christ. The Spirit does not speak of Himself. He takes of the things of Christ. He glorifies Christ. He brings Christ to our remembrance. This is the Holy Spirit who opens up our hearts in worship, praise, confession and intercession. Real prayer, like a good hymn, sets Christ, the work of Christ and the intercessions of Christ before our eyes. Is there not a real danger that much of our worship today is so subjectively controlled that while seeking to be expressive of the self, it falls short of being truly Christian worship? It can become romantic, pietist, or sentimental, but less than a true response to Jesus Christ our Lord.

The language of worship—doubtless like most language—should have a three-fold reference.

(1) An objective, factual denotative reference, setting forth Jesus Christ, and in intention directing the worshipper to

God, Father, Son and Holy Spirit. This is primary and must control everything else.

(2) A formal, coherent, connotative, syntactical reference, as when we are concerned about choice of words, the language we use, the formal structure of worship where we contrast and compare different liturgical rites and practices.

(3) A subjective, existential reference where our worship expresses the feelings of the heart and the mind of the church.

(2) and (3) must be controlled by (1), not least in a day when we can too readily stress (2) and (3) at the expense of (1). Only in this way can we worship the Father in spirit and in truth through Him who only is our *Leitourgos*.

13

THOMAS F. TORRANCE

Come, Creator Spirit, for the Renewal of Worship and Witness[1]

WHAT DO WE MEAN BY THE PRAYER, *Come, Creator Spirit?* IT cannot mean that the Holy Spirit should come and act as in the original creation of the world or in its creative preservation, and yet it is a prayer for his creative power. It is a prayer for the Holy Spirit in accordance with his new coming and acting as on the day of Pentecost. On that day the Holy Spirit came into the world and entered into the experience of men in a way that had never happened before. Certainly the Spirit continued to operate in the world and to be at work among men as he had been from the beginning, but at Pentecost something quite new happened, as new and distinct and indeed as unique at the Incarnation itself. Along with the birth, life, death, resurrection and ascension of Christ the pouring out of his Spirit at Pentecost belongs to the series of God's mighty acts which brought salvation to mankind and inaugurated the new age. They are acts which cannot be repeated and cannot be undone, for they have entirely altered the relation of the world to God. From that point all history presses relentlessly forward to its consummation when Christ will come again to judge the quick and the dead and make all things new. We live on this side of Pentecost and are on our way to meet the advent Christ. We live, therefore, after the new thing has happened, within the new age in which the Creator Spirit of God is abroad among men and actively at work among them in a new and distinctive way, in addition to his origi-

---

1. Address delivered to the World Alliance of Reformed Churches, Frankfurt, 5th August, 1964. I wish to acknowledge my indebtedness in this essay to the teaching of the Scottish divines from Knox, Craig and Boyd to Milligan, Wotherspoon and Manson.

From Thomas F. Torrance, *Theology in Reconstruction,* pp. 240–258. © SCM Press, England, 1965; William B. Eerdmans Publishing Company, Grand Rapids, 1966. Used by permission of the Publishers.

nal and continuing operation in the world. *Come, Creator Spirit* is a prayer of participation in this new happening, a prayer in which we allow it to overtake us; it is a prayer in which we ask that the new mode of the Spirit's entry into the lives of men at Pentecost may not be obstructed in our own experience.

How, then, are we to understand this distinctively new mode of the Holy Spirit's activity in the experience of men?

The meaning of Pentecost is determined by the great evangelical facts that lie behind it, for they made possible this new mode of the Spirit's activity. It is in the *Incarnation* and the *Atonement* that we learn the secret of Pentecost. With the Incarnation, God the eternal Son became Man, without ceasing to be God and without breaking the communion of the Holy Trinity within which God lives his own divine life. In the birth and life of Jesus on earth human nature and divine nature were inseparably united in the eternal Person of God the Son. Therefore in him the closed circle of the inner life of God was made to overlap with human life, and human nature was taken up to share in the eternal communion of the Father and the Son in the Holy Spirit. In this one Man the divine life and love overflowed into creaturely and human being, so that Jesus, Man on earth, received the Spirit of God without measure, for the fulness of the Godhead dwelt in him bodily. Jesus became the Bearer of the Holy Spirit among men.

But who was Jesus? He was very Man, our Brother. In him the Holy Son of God was grafted on to the stock of our fallen human existence, and in him our mortal and corrupt human nature was assumed into union with the Holy Son of God, so that in Jesus, in his birth and sinless life, in his death and resurrection, there took place a holy and awful judgment on our flesh of sin, and an atoning sanctification of our unholy human existence. It was only through such atonement that God in all his Godness and holiness came to dwell in the midst of mortal, sinful man. Because that took place in Jesus who made our flesh of sin his very own and who wrought out in himself peace and reconciliation between man and God, he became not only the Bearer but the Mediator of the Holy Spirit to men.

Now we may understand the distinctively new mode of the Spirit's coming into the experience of men. The inner life of the Holy Trinity which is private to God alone is extended to include human nature in and through Jesus. This is possible because of the atonement that took place in him, for now that the enmity between God and man has been abolished, God the Holy Spirit may dwell in the midst of mortal sinful man. This is the way that the divine love has taken to redeem man, by making him share in the holy power in which God lives his own divine life. The pouring out of that power from on high took place at Pentecost, with the entry of the Holy Spirit in his new mode of presence and activity into the experience of mortal men. On our lips the prayer, *Come, Creator Spirit,* is a prayer of commitment to what God has already done in Jesus Christ, and a prayer of participation in the divine nature, in the faith that it is only the power of God which can redeem fallen man, and that nothing short of the very life and breath of God himself can renew the life of his people. Hence for the Church to worship God is to draw into itself the holy breath of the life of God, and to live out that divine life on earth is to live a life of praise and witness to his glory.

That is the Church's belief in the Holy Spirit which it confessed in the Nicene Creed: 'And I believe in the Holy Spirit, the Lord and Giver of Life, who proceeds from the Father and the Son, who with the Father and the Son together is worshipped and glorified, who spoke by the prophets.' It is worth noting that it is in the Nicene (Constantinopolitan) Creed which is essentially a doxological act, in which worship and witness combine inseparably together, that the Church's faith in the Holy Spirit first came into clear articulation. By his very nature the Holy Spirit not only proceeds from the Father but lifts up to the Father; he is not only the Spirit sent by Christ but the Spirit of response to Christ, the Spirit in whom and by whom and with whom we worship and glorify the Father and the Son. Not only is he God the Holy Spirit descending to us, the Spirit by whom God bears witness to himself, but God the Holy Spirit lifting up all creation in praise and rejoicing in God, himself the Spirit of worship and witness by whom the Church lives and fulfils its mission to the glory of God.

THE NEW COMING OF THE HOLY SPIRIT AT PENTECOST WAS A COMING IN THE UTTER GODNESS OF GOD

We have become accustomed to think of the coming of the Holy Spirit far too much as the interiorizing in our hearts of divine salvation, with the result that the presence of the Spirit is so often identified with inward moral and religious states. Creator Spirit and our own creative spirituality tend to become confused. This way of thinking arose early in the history of the Church, gathered momentum in monastic piety and broke out again in Protestant pietism in its emphasis upon religious *inwardness* and *immediacy,* but all this has been greatly accentuated by modern habits in psychological and personalistic thinking. Certainly the Holy Spirit is sent into our hearts where he begets enlightenment and conviction, and bears witness with our spirit that we are the children of God, but the psychologizing and subjectivizing of this is entirely, or almost entirely, absent from the New Testament. The emphasis of the Apostolic Church was placed elsewhere. Pentecost meant the living presence of God among men in all his transcendent power and holiness as very God, for only God can give God and lift men up to himself. Hence the descent of the Holy Spirit upon the Apostolic Church lifted it out of itself and made it participate in the undiluted acts of Almighty God and in the uncreated life of the Holy Trinity. The emphasis is not upon man receiving but upon God giving, for man receives only as he falls under the transcendent power of the Creator Spirit who is not limited by man's lack of capacity, for he gives himself and presents himself to man even when he has no power to receive so that man's reception of the Holy Spirit is itself a creative work of God.

At this point let me plead for a reconsideration by the Reformed Church of what the Greek fathers called *theosis.* This is usually unfortunately translated *deification,* but it has nothing to do with the *divinization* of man any more than the Incarnation has to do with the humanization of God. *Theosis* was the term the Fathers used to emphasize the fact that through the Spirit we have to do with God in his utter sublimity, his sheer Godness or holiness; creatures though we are, men on earth, in the Spirit we are made to participate in saving acts that are abruptly and absolutely divine, election, adoption, regeneration or sanctification, and we participate in them by grace alone. *Theosis* describes man's involvement in such a mighty act of God upon him that he is raised up to find the true centre of his existence not in himself but in Holy God, where he lives and moves and has his being in the uncreated but creative energy of the Holy Spirit. By *theosis* the Greek fathers wished to express the fact that in the new coming of the Holy Spirit we are up against *God* in the most absolute sense, God in his ultimate holiness or Godness.[2]

As I understand it, this is the antithesis of the nineteenth-century notion of 'the divine in man' which imprisons him in the depth of his own being, or of the man-centred emphasis of so many modern

2. See the essays of Nissiotis and Philippou in *The Orthodox Ethos,* ed. A. J. Philippou, 1964.

Protestants upon their own existential decisions or their own creative spirituality. Let us not quarrel about the word *theosis,* offensive though it may be to us, but follow its intention, not to allege any divinization of man but to speak of the fact that man in the weakness and lowliness of creaturely human being is by God made free for God through the power of the Creator Spirit who is not and will not be limited in his acts by man's weakness or creaturehood or his lack of capacity. *Theosis* is an attempt to express the staggering significance of Pentecost as the coming from on high, from outside of us and beyond us, of divine power, or rather as the coming of Almighty God, the Maker of heaven and earth, to dwell with sinful mortal man, and therefore as the emancipation of man from imprisonment in himself and the lifting of him up to partake of the living presence and saving acts of God the Creator and Redeemer. Is there anything we need to regain more than this faith in the utter Godness of God the Holy Spirit?

Let us apply this to the Church. And here let us ask a double question. Does Pentecost mean that the Church is endowed with the Spirit as a gift for its possession and as the animating principle of its development? Or does it mean that through the coming of the Spirit the Church in its earthly and historical pilgrimage is made to participate in a perfected reality so that it lives out of a fulness above and beyond itself? Put bluntly and crudely: Does the Church possess the Spirit or is the Church possessed by the Spirit?

If we take the first alternative, then we have a doctrine of the Church as the extending of the Incarnation, a Church that is still evolving and is yet to reach its completeness and will do so only when it brings to its completion the redemptive work of Christ, a Church which through Christ's testamentary disposition to it of the Spirit is so invested with authority and endowed with grace that it fulfils its mission in history as the divine society authoritatively administering grace to all who will own obedience to its ways, and a Church which develops its worship and theology as the manifestations of its own rich vitality and the self-expression of its own individuality and tradition. You may think I have been describing the Roman Church, but actually I have been trying to speak of the whole Western Church which everywhere has the same basic tendencies. They certainly assume distinctively Roman forms, but these all have their recognizably Protestant counterparts. For example, where more than in the Protestant West do we get the notion of the Church as the community instinct with the Spirit of Christ which develops from age to age forms of life and worship in which it manifests its own rich and manifold vitality, and where more than in the Protestant multitudes do men believe in bringing in the Kingdom of God through co-redemption? Foolish Protestants, having begun in the Spirit we now think we are made perfect by the works of the flesh.

At the back of all this there lies deep down a confusion between the Creator Spirit of Holy God and the creative spirituality of Christian man, and therefore we think we can develop out of ourselves ways and means of translating the new coming of the Spirit and the new creation he brings into the forms of our own natural vitality. The terminology of Romans and Protestants may differ: what Romans call 'created grace' Protestants call 'the Christian spirit', but in both the supernatural energy and life of the Creator Spirit falls under the disposal of man. In Romanism and Protestantism alike the Church has domesticated the grace and Spirit of God in its own spiritual subjectivity instead of being the sphere of the divine freedom where the Lord the Giver of Life is at work as Creator Spirit. Protestantism may not have a legal centre and an articulated *magisterium* like Romanism, but it perpetuates in its own ways the same basic error, and therefore like the Roman Church is more and more imprisoned in its own developments.

If our worship and witness are conspicuous for their lack of Holy Spirit, it is surely because we Protestants, whatever we may confess in our creeds, have diminished belief in the transcendent power and utter Godness of the Creator Spirit, and have become engrossed in our own subjectivities and the development of our own inherent potentialities. Hence the first thing that must happen to us is a glad subjection to the lordly freedom and majesty of God the Holy Spirit, and a humble readiness for miraculous divine acts that transcend all human possibilities and break through the limitations of anything we can conceive. *Come, Creator Spirit,* is a prayer of open surrender to the absolute creativity of God.

IN HIS NEW COMING THE HOLY SPIRIT IS MEDIATED BY CHRIST AND AT THE SAME TIME MEDIATES CHRIST TO US

It is in grasping this mutual relation between the work of Christ and the work of the Spirit that we may understand what worship and its renewal really mean.

What, then, are the determining facts about this mutuality between Christ and the Spirit?

(*a*) The Holy Spirit in his new coming is mediated to us through

Christ in his divine and human natures. It behoved Christ to be God that he might give his Spirit to men, for only God can give God. It behoved Christ also to be Man that he might receive the Spirit of God in our human nature and mediate it to his brethren through himself. We are concerned here not primarily with the continuing presence and operation of the Spirit in the world which have been since the beginning of creation, but with the new coming of the Spirit in the profounder and more intimate mode of presence made possible by the Incarnation, and which the world cannot know or receive apart from Jesus Christ and what happened to our human nature in him.

Jesus Christ was born of the Virgin Mary into our human nature through the power of the Spirit; at his Baptism the Holy Spirit descended upon him and anointed him as the Christ. He was never without the Spirit, for as the eternal Son he ever remained in the unity of the Spirit and of the Father, but as the Incarnate Son on earth he was given the Spirit without measure and consecrated in his human nature for his mission as the vicarious Servant. He came through the temptations in the wilderness clothed with the power of the Spirit and went forth to bring in the Kingdom of God by meeting and defeating the powers of darkness entrenched in human flesh. He struggled and prayed in the Spirit with unspeakable cries of agony, and bore in his Spirit the full burden of human evil and woe. Through the eternal Spirit he offered himself without spot to the Father in sacrifice for sin; according to the Spirit of Holiness he was raised from the dead, and ascended to the right hand of the Father to receive all power in heaven and earth. There he attained the ground from which he could pour out the Spirit of God upon all flesh. As Lamb of God and Priest of our human nature he sent down from the throne of the Most High the gift of the Holy Spirit upon his Church that through the same Spirit the Father and the Son might dwell with men.

Jesus Christ, true God and true Man, is thus the Mediator of the Holy Spirit. Since he is himself both the God who gives and the Man who receives in one Person he is in a position to transfer in a profound and intimate way what belongs to us in our human nature to himself and to transfer what is his to our human nature in him. That applies above all to the gift of the Holy Spirit whom he received fully and completely in his human nature for us. Hence in the union of divine and human natures in the Son the eternal Spirit of the living God has composed himself, as it were, to dwell with human nature, and human nature has been adapted and become accustomed to receive and bear that same Holy Spirit. In his new coming, therefore, the Spirit came not simply as the one Spirit who proceeds eternally from the Father but as the Spirit mediated through the human nature and experience of the Incarnate Son. He came as the Spirit of Jesus, in whom the Son sent by the Father lived out his divine life in a human form, in whom the Son of Man lived out his human life on earth in perfect union with the Father above. He came as the Spirit who in Jesus has penetrated into a new intimacy with our human nature, for he came as the Spirit in whom Jesus lived through our human life from end to end, from birth to death, and beyond into the resurrection. And therefore he came not as isolated and naked Spirit, but as Spirit charged with all the experience of Jesus as he shared to the full our mortal nature and weakness, and endured its temptation and grief and suffering and death, and with the experience of Jesus as he struggled and prayed, and worshipped and obeyed, and poured out his life in compassion for mankind. It is still in the Name of Jesus Christ that the Holy Spirit comes to us, and in no other name.

(*b*) The Holy Spirit is mediated to us only through the glorification of Christ. Jesus Christ was himself the Bearer in our human nature of the fulness of the Spirit, but the Spirit in this his new mode of presence and activity could not be transmitted to others when they were yet in their sins or be received by others until atonement for sin was completed and the Mediator took his place on the throne of God in his consecrated and glorified Humanity.

It was only at infinite cost that Jesus Christ gained for us the gift of the Holy Spirit, receiving him in all his consuming holiness into the human nature which he took from our fallen and alienated condition. We shall never fathom the depth of the humiliation and passion that were his or the indescribable tension into which he entered for our sakes. In himself, in his Incarnate Person, he was both God the Judge and Man under God's judgment. Atonement had to be worked out within the union of his divine and human natures, in the inner determination of his Being in life and in death, in the fulfilling of judgment, in the expiation of guilt, in the perfection of obedience, and in the effecting of peace and reconciliation with God. Until he had sanctified himself and perfected in our human nature his one offering for all men, until he had made once and for all the sacrifice to take away sin, until he had vanquished the powers of darkness and overcome the sharpness of death, until he had ascended to present himself in propitiation before the Father, the Kingdom of Heaven could not be opened to believers and the blessing of the divine Spirit could not be poured out upon human flesh or be received by sinful mortal men. Only with the enthronement of the Lamb, only with the presence of our Surety and the continual intercession of our High Priest before the face of the Father, only with the taking up of the glorified Humanity of Christ our Brother into the unity of the Blessed Trinity, could the Holy Spirit be released in all his sanctifying and renewing agency to dwell with man. Then he came down freely upon the Body that had been prepared, the Church purchased by the blood of Christ, and lifted it up, unhindered by guilt and sin or the divine judgment, to participate freely in the very life of God.

There is one Mediator between God and Man, the Man Christ Jesus. The Holy Spirit comes to us only through him as the Spirit of Holiness, the Spirit of Redemption, and the Spirit of Glory. He comes to us from the inner life of Jesus as the Spirit in which he gained the victory over sin and temptation, as the Spirit in which he brought the divine holiness to bear upon our flesh of sin, sanctifying and perfecting in himself the very nature which he took from us, and therefore he comes in all the richness of the divine-human holiness of Christ. He comes to us from the triumphant obedience and victory of Christ in his Cross and Resurrection, as the Spirit clothed with mighty, redemptive acts transmitting the energy of Christ's risen and glorified Humanity, and as the Spirit of him who has entered into the new life and inherited all the promises of God, and therefore he comes in all the transforming power of the Saviour and Redeemer of men. He comes to us from the whole life of Christ constituted in death and resurrection as the one, all-sufficient and eternal oblation of mankind, as the Spirit in which Christ lifted up our human nature in worship and prayer and adoration to God, in which at last he presented himself in spotless sacrifice to the Father as the Head of Humanity and through this one offering presented us to him as those whom he had perfected in himself. And therefore the Spirit comes as the Spirit of a Manhood wholly offered to God in perpetual glorification and worship and praise.

What do we learn from this about the renewal of the Church's worship?

The Holy Spirit is God in his freedom not only to give being to the creation but through his presence in it to bring its relations with himself to their end and perfection. He is the Spirit who goes forth from God and returns to God. This answers to the twofold work of the Son when he came down for us and for our salvation and was made Man, and when he ascended again to the Father, presenting to him the humanity which he had sanctified and redeemed in the atoning oblation of himself. It is the same twofold work which took place at Pentecost in the man-ward and in the God-ward movement of the Holy Spirit, supervening upon the Church and lifting it upward in its faith and rejoicing in God.

It was through the power of the Spirit that Christ himself was born among us, lived his life of holy obedience and worship, gave himself in sacrifice for the sin of the world, rose again and ascended to the Father to be for ever the one offering and prayer that prevails for all mankind. It is through the power of the same Spirit who came down at Pentecost that we are united to Christ in his identification with us, and joined to him in his self-consecration and self-offering for us once and for all on earth and eternally prevalent in heaven. Jesus Christ who took our nature upon him has given to God an account for us, making atonement in our place, and in our name has yielded himself in sacrifice and worship and praise and thanksgiving to the Father. We have no other answer to the will of God, no other offering, no other response or worship, for without Christ we can do nothing. Jesus Christ is our worship, the essence of it and the whole of it, and we may worship God in Spirit and in Truth only as we are made partakers in his worship. The Spirit which Christ breathes upon us then becomes the Spirit of our response to him and through him to the Father.

We may express this in another way. The Holy Spirit was first given to Christ, and only transmitted from him to us through his intercession. He prayed the Father for the gift of the Paraclete upon those whom he loved, that they might be with him where he was, they in him and he in them, and he was heard in his prayer. He prayed with his life, and prayed with his death; to the supplication of his lips with strong crying and tears he added the pleading of his awful passion, and offered himself up in expiatory intercession in order to gain for us also the gift of the Holy Spirit. Pentecost was the counterpart on earth to wonderful things done within the veil, for Jesus Christ prevailed with God and the Spirit was poured out on human flesh. And the Holy Spirit continues to be given because the Lamb of God who bore away the sin of the world is for ever enthroned above, because the Atonement he made once for all is eternally valid with the Father, because Jesus Christ our High Priest ever lives to make intercession for us.

In coming upon the Church the Holy Spirit constitutes it the Body of Christ on earth in union with its Head, the risen and ascended Lord. But he comes upon it and dwells in it as the other Paraclete answering to the Paraclete above, as the Spirit of all prayer echoing in us the continual intercession of Christ. We do not know how to pray as we ought but the Holy Spirit intervenes in our stammering and weakness, and with groanings that cannot be uttered makes the prayer of heaven to resound on earth. All our prayer and praise and worship are sinful and unworthy but through the Holy Spirit breathed upon us they are cleansed in the sacrifice of Christ and absorbed into intercession and praise and worship within the veil. Indeed the Holy Spirit so unites earth to heaven and heaven to earth that in his coming Christ himself returns to take up his dwelling in the Church, and he it is who intercedes in its midst, who stands among us as our prayer and worship and praise, offering and presenting himself in our place to the Father, so that it is in him and through him and by him, in his name alone, that we appear before the Face of God with the one offering of his beloved Son in whom he is well pleased.

All true worship is therefore both *epiclesis* and *paraclesis,* i.e. the invocation of the Paraclete Spirit and the coming of the Paraclete to help us. We come with empty hands and empty mouth, and he puts into our grasp the Cross of Christ and into our mouth the prayer of the Lord. He assimilates us into the one all-sufficient worship of Christ, and the Father looks upon us only as we are found in him, consecrated through his self-sanctification and self-offering for us. The Holy Spirit is not to be thought of as acting in the place of, as if in the absence of, the exalted Lord, for in his coming and presence Christ himself is with us, acting for us not only from the side of God toward man but acting in us from the side of man toward God. It is through the agency of the Spirit that this takes place. Thus in our worship the Holy Spirit comes forth from God, uniting us to the response and obedience and faith and prayer of Jesus, and returns to God, raising us up in Jesus to participate in the worship of heaven and in the eternal communion of the Holy Trinity.

If the Holy Spirit is himself the immediate Agent of our worship, he is also the immediate Agent of its renewal, he who realizes in us the re-creative power of the risen and glorified Humanity of Christ. Now it cannot be emphasized sufficiently that it is through Atonement that we are renewed, through the obedience of the Holy One in our flesh and through the Blood of Christ shed for us; and that it is only after the completion of Christ's sacrifice for sin, his self-presentation before the Father and the pouring out of the Holy Spirit upon us, that the Atonement became effective for the remission of our sins and the cleansing of our conscience. From beginning to end it is through the *holiness* of Jesus that we are redeemed and regenerated. Therefore when the Holy Spirit comes to us as the Agent of our renewal he comes not only as the Holy Spirit of the one eternal God but as the Spirit mediated through Christ Jesus and charged with his divine-human holiness. He renews us by drawing us within the self-consecration of Christ made on our behalf and by assimilating us into his holiness. The Holy Spirit renews only through sanctification. If Jesus himself was raised from the dead according to the Spirit of Holiness, it cannot be otherwise with us.

It cannot be otherwise with our worship: renewal may come only through holiness, regeneration only through sanctification. What else can renewed worship be but that which through the Spirit is united to Christ's oblation of himself and is assimilated to his self-sanctification in the Truth? We worship God in drawing near to him by the new and living way which Jesus has consecrated for us, the way of his flesh, for he who sanctifies and we who are sanctified are all of one, Christ in us and we in him through one and the same Holy Spirit. We pray in the Name of Christ and he prays in our place, displacing our acts of devotion by his own self-offering, covering them with his holiness and absorbing them into his own intercession. Who then can disentangle our prayer from the prayer of Christ, for our worship is Christ's own presentation of himself and of us in him before the Father?

If this is the way of divine worship through our great High Priest, then conformity to the holiness and humanity of Jesus Christ is the test that must be applied to all our forms of worship. Are they really expressions of the holy mind and will of God incarnate in Jesus, or are they after all but forms of our own self-expression? Is our worship a constant participation in the holiness of Christ, in his own inner victory over sin and temptation, in his perfect oneness in mind and will with God? Is it the lifting up of our hearts through the Son in the Spirit to the Father? Is it a holding up of Christ in his finished work before Heaven as our only offering and prayer? Or is it the manifestation of our own piety adapted to the pattern of this present world in forms of our own choosing? Have we not obtruded upon God will-worship of our own which is little more in the last analysis than the worship of self or the holding up of our own spirituality? And is not the deepest reason for this that we have lost touch with the Spirit of Holiness? Surely degeneration in worship springs from a weakening in our sense of the utter holiness and majesty of the Most High and an estrangement from the creative source of holiness among men, the sanctified and sanctifying Humanity of Jesus.

IN HIS NEW COMING THE HOLY SPIRIT FOCUSSES ATTENTION UPON JESUS CHRIST, AND ENABLES US TO BELIEVE IN HIM AND BEAR FAITHFUL WITNESS TO HIM AS SAVIOUR OF THE WORLD

If the vicarious life and mediatorial work of Christ led to the supreme gift of the Holy Spirit, the function of the Spirit was not to bear witness to himself but to bear witness to Christ as God and Saviour, and through his glorification to gather all who believe in him into the unity and communion of Father, Son and Holy Spirit.

The Holy Spirit is not knowable independently in himself, but he is known through the one Word or self-revelation of God in Jesus Christ.

In himself the Spirit hides himself from us by his very mode of Being as Spirit, and effaces himself in his very mode of Activity as Spirit, throwing his eternal Light upon the Father through the Son and upon the Son in the Father. We know who he is because he creates in us beyond all creaturely or human capacities the ability to know the Unknowable, and therein reveals himself as Creator Spirit of the living God. The Spirit does not utter himself but utters the Word. He does not incarnate himself but incarnates the Son. He does not show his own Face, but shows us the Father in the Face of the Son. Yet as he comes to us from the Father and from the Son, he confronts us in himself with all the ultimate Godness of the Godhead, before whom we can only bow in worship and adoration and with all the reverence and obedience of our mind. We know him as no less Lord God, the Creator, than the Father and the Son, for he is the limitless power of all creation and re-creation, God the Holy Spirit in all the freedom and majesty of the eternal Being.

Such is the Spirit who bears witness to Christ, for Christ is not known and believed on the ground of human testimony but only on the ground of testimony that comes from God himself. He is not only the Spirit who comes forth from God and returns to God, but the Spirit sent to us by Christ and who directs us back to Christ, the Spirit of Testimony and the Spirit of Truth. It was through his agency that the Word of God was uttered in the Incarnation, by him that Christ was anointed to preach the Gospel, and in his power that the whole work of divine revelation and redemption was fulfilled. But so long as the Holy Spirit was not yet abroad among men, even the disciples were dull of hearing and slow in their understanding, and could not grasp the bewildering miracle of Jesus, for they stumbled and groped like men blinded by light. The Spirit was not yet because Christ was not yet glorified, for until the consummation of Atonement the Holy Spirit could not come upon them and they could not receive him without being consumed. Until Atonement was made and the Spirit was poured out they were incapable of becoming the habitation of the Holy One, and Christ could not open up their minds to grasp him for he could not be in them.

But the promise of the Paraclete was given: the Spirit of Truth would be sent to them and then they would know. What Christ said to them when he was yet present with them would not be lost, even if they did not understand it yet, for the Paraclete would teach them all things and bring to their remembrance all that Christ had said to them. He had still much more to say but they could not bear it yet. However, when the Spirit of Truth would come he would guide them into all the Truth. He would not speak from himself but speak what he heard and make known to them things that were still to take place. He would glorify Christ, for everything that he would make known he would receive from Christ himself. All that belonged to the Father belonged to Christ, and therefore what the Spirit of Truth would show them would be from Christ even when it was of the Father.

And the promise was fulfilled, in the gift of the Holy Spirit. They had to wait for the coming of the Spirit, continuing in prayer and in unity with one another and in obedience to such teaching of Christ as they had been able to follow. But when the Spirit came upon them they received power, for the Spirit both testified to them of Christ, creating in them understanding and faith, and made them witnesses themselves to Christ before the world, creating in them the sphere where Christ continues to be heard and to be believed. Thus through the coming of the Spirit God brings his self-revelation to its fulfilment, for the Spirit is the creative Subject of God's revelation to us and the creative Subject in our reception and understanding of that revelation. The Holy Spirit does not do this by continuing a work begun by Christ and now left off by him, as if we now passed from the economy of the Son into the economy of the Spirit. On the contrary, through the Spirit, in and with his coming, Christ himself returns to be present among us, living and speaking and operating in the Church which through the Spirit is constituted his Body on earth and in history. The presence of the Holy Spirit in the Church means that it is the living Lord himself who is here in his redeeming and sanctifying activity. The office of the Holy Spirit in the Church is not to call attention to himself apart from Christ but to focus all attention on Christ, to glorify him, to bear witness to his deity, to testify to his mind and will, and in him and through him to lead us to the Father. He is God the Spirit by whom we know God, for he is God the Spirit by whom God bears witness to himself. Transparence and self-effacement thus belong to the very nature and office of the Holy Spirit, as the Spirit of the Father and the Spirit of the Son, who is known only as the Father is known through the Son and the Son is known in the Father, and who together with the Father and the Son is worshipped and glorified as himself very God.

On earth there is no Kingdom of the Spirit, and no Body of the Spirit, but only a Kingdom of Christ and a Body of Christ through the Spirit, for the Spirit is present and at work among us in his transparent and self-effacing nature. It is his office constantly to call the Church out of the world and to create it as the sphere within which he realizes and perpetuates among men God's own witness to himself. In the Church, as we have seen, the Holy Spirit exercises a God-ward ministry as he acts from the side of men uplifting their worship in Christ to the heavenly Father, but in the Church he also exercises that God-ward ministry in that he creates and empowers from the side of men a witness to Christ as God and Saviour of mankind, and so constitutes the corporate witness of the whole Church as the mode of God's own witness to himself among men. This does not mean that the Church now takes the place of Christ in his absence, continuing or extending the work which he began to do when he was with us in the flesh, but that the Church is chosen to be the locus of his presence among men and that he himself the risen Lord is at work in and through it, yet transcending it in the freedom and power of his Spirit, for in spite of the constant failure and inadequacy of the Church Christ fulfils through it his one ministry as prophet, priest and king, on earth as in heaven.

In order to see the bearing of this upon the renewal of the Church's witness, we must consider further the *creativity* and the *transparency* of the Holy Spirit, for in his regenerative and recreative work the Holy Spirit remains the Creative Agent of all God's ways and works, and the uncreated transparent light of his self-revelation.

With the coming of the Holy Spirit at Pentecost God's redemptive and his creative acts merged together. It was a movement of recreation through atoning sanctification, for through the *Holy* Spirit the full creative impact of the divine Word broke in upon the apostolic Church constituting it a new creation in Christ, fulfilling in it the sanctifying and regenerating of our human nature that had already taken place in Christ, and so bringing it into a new state of being in which it was renewed after the image of God. The Holy Spirit was the quickening breath of this new creation, breathed out by God upon the Church and breathed in by the Church as it came to life under his power. He was the Spirit speaking the Word of God to the Church and creating within it faithful hearing and understanding of the Word, the Spirit testifying to the mighty acts of God in Christ and the Spirit of response to Christ in the Church forming it unto the obedience of faith in him. Not only did he act creatively upon the Church in the giving of life and the distributing of his manifold gifts but he brought his creative work to its completion or end in the establishment of the Church as the Body of Christ, the new sphere of existence in him. He was the Creator Spirit acting always both from the side of God toward man and from the side of man toward God.

What does it mean for us to come up against the creative activity of the Spirit in this way? What does it mean for our witness in the Church that the Creator Spirit should dwell with fallen man and recreate him in his knowledge and understanding of God? Fallen man is described in the Scriptures as man attempting to emancipate himself from the Creator, man snatching the very freedom God has given him in order to make himself and reproduce his own image, and therefore as man who even imposes the images of his own devising and fashioning upon God. In this way he changes the truth of God into a lie and worships and serves the creature more than the Creator, for he changes the glory of the uncorruptible God into an image made like to corruptible man. That is to say, man carries the sin whereby he fell into his continuing relations with God, and substitutes his own creativity for that of the Creator Spirit even in the realm of the knowledge and worship of God. Indeed it is in religion that man is most tempted to do this, so that religious forms can become the supreme expression of his sin.

Now the coming of the Creator Spirit as at Pentecost is the point where man's own sinful creativity has to be broken, where man in his Adamic existence, man as he created himself, is stripped of his own image and come to an end, for in the coming of the Spirit fallen man is brought up against the final power of the Creator himself. At that point he is either re-created and emancipated from himself for genuine faith in God, or he lapses back in conflict with the Spirit into his own self-willed existence and becomes even more securely imprisoned within his own inventions. Then the light that is in him is darkness indeed.

Is that not the story of the recalcitrant Jews face to face with Jesus? Out of their own distinctive piety and attitude to existence they had forged their own conception of the Messiah. They even bent the oracles and ordinances of grace to serve their end, and projected their own man-made traditions upon the Word of God, making it of none effect. And so they strove to become masters of their own destiny. Then when at last the Messiah actually came the conflict between their own image of God and that mediated by the Messiah was so intense that instead of surrendering to the creative impact of his Spirit upon them, they crucified the Messiah, and in a desperate attempt to force the hand of God they even resisted his Holy Spirit. Was that not the verdict of the martyr Stephen? 'Ye do always resist the Holy Spirit: as your fathers did, so do you.' And they stoned him to death.

Must we not ask whether this is not also the story of the Christian Church, even in modern times? Have we also not been at work forging our own image of God out of our own vaunted prior understanding or out of the depth of our own being, out of our own existential decisions and our own creative spirituality? Have we not also constructed our own conceptions of Christ to suit our own self-willed attitude to existence in the twentieth century? And then have we not been trying to justify ourselves by projecting this way of thinking back upon the Apostolic Church, alleging that its image of Christ is little more than the product of its own creative spirituality or the expression of its attitude to existence? And so have we not been busy crucifying again the Christ of the apostolic witness and resisting the Creator Spirit of Pentecost, substituting the creativity of men in place of the Holy Creativity of God?

The supreme questions must be asked once again. Do we really believe in the Holy Spirit? Do we believe that at Pentecost he came upon the apostolic witnesses as the Creator Spirit and, in spite of the distorting preconceptions of the human heart and the creative projections of the human spirit, transformed their understanding to receive God's own witness to himself in Jesus Christ and so empowered them to become faithful witnesses to Christ themselves? Do we believe the *kerygma* of Jesus Christ to be the creation of God's Spirit or the outgrowth of man's own religious consciousness? In short, do we really believe in Jesus Christ as God and Saviour?

Surely the New Testament makes it abundantly clear that the Holy Spirit is given to those who believe in Jesus and that we grow in the grace and knowledge of Christ as we surrender to the creative impact of the Holy Spirit upon us but that unbelief grieves the presence of the Spirit and quenches his power among us. What else is unbelief but resistance to the Holy Spirit, and what can obstruct the renewal of the Church and destroy its witness more than just unbelief? Let it be said quite bluntly that what we need urgently is a renewal of faith: of belief in Jesus Christ as in reality God himself incarnate among men, of belief in the Cross as indeed the objective intervention of God in human existence for the salvation of mankind, and of belief in the resurrection of Jesus Christ from the dead in body as the first-fruits of the new creation. The renewal of our witness will only come as we surrender ourselves to the miraculous divine power of the Creator Spirit, and commit ourselves to faith in Jesus Christ as God and Saviour.

Now if this faith is to be strong and our witness is to be clear we must guard against the impurities that arise when we seek to perfect the operation of the Spirit by our own works and so obtrude ourselves into the evangelical message. This is where the transparency of the Spirit comes in, for to be genuine our witness must be shot through and through with the uncreated light of God's self-revelation. Then alone can it be the means of God's own witness to himself among men.

In all our knowledge and proclamation of God in worship and witness we make use of human and earthly forms of thought and speech, cognitive, linguistic or liturgical forms, but in themselves these forms are quite opaque as far as their reference to God himself is concerned. In themselves they are merely expressions of human and earthly activity and reveal not God but man. If they are really to serve their purpose they must be made to point beyond themselves to the divine realities they are meant to signify. That can happen only through the power of the Holy Spirit as he himself testifies of God in and through them, for he alone can make the forms of faith and witness transparent by making the Reality of God shine through them. Only through the sanctifying presence of the Holy Spirit emancipating us from ourselves is Jesus Christ the Incarnate Word allowed to sound through to us and to take control of our proclamation, and therefore to confront men directly and personally through our witness.

Consider, for example, the Holy Scripture or the Sacrament of Baptism. The Scriptures are human documents written by men of earth and history, expressing the attitudes and thoughts and limitations of their writers, and can therefore be interpreted in their human reference. But they are much more than that, for they have been adapted by God under the impact of his Spirit for his own self-testimony, and therefore they are interpreted aright only as we allow the living Word of God himself to sound through them to us, and as through the Holy Spirit the Reality of God in Christ shines through to us—that is what our Reformers called the *perspicuity* of the Scriptures. Or take the Sacrament of Baptism, which is certainly a rite to be performed by men in visible, historical acts. But if we interpret Baptism by looking for its meaning in the rite itself or in its human celebration, then it becomes quite opaque. However, the meaning of Baptism does not lie in the external rite or simply its performance but solely in Jesus Christ himself, for Baptism directs us and our children to the saving act of God's love which he has already fulfilled for us in Jesus Christ. Therefore we interpret Baptism not by looking at what we do but by looking through the rite to Christ and his Gospel and by allowing Christ and his Gospel through the power of the Spirit to break through to us. Without sacramental transparence Baptism becomes blind and meaningless.

We recall too that this transparence comes from the Holy Spirit, from his own self-effacing nature and office in hiding himself, as it were, behind the Face of the Father in the Son and behind the Heart of the Son in the Father, yet revealing the one Triune God by letting his eternal light shine through himself to us. It is in his light alone that we see light, and through that light that we are confronted with the ultimate Being of God before whom the very cherubim veil their faces. It is the same Holy Spirit who is present and active in the *witness* of the Church testifying to Christ in fulfilment of the Lord's own promise. But if we turn our attention to the Spirit independently instead of turning our attention with the Spirit to Christ, or try to make the Spirit visible through perfecting his operation by our own works, then we violate the holiness of the Spirit by resisting him in his self-effacing office and confusing him with our own spirits. Thus everything becomes opaque, for we fail to distinguish him in whom we believe from our own believing, and in our proclamation we confound the earthen vessel with the heavenly treasure. We mix up ourselves with Christ and so darken witness and obscure vision of the Saviour.

Renewal of witness will come surely through the holiness of Jesus and renewal of our worship in him, that is, through the sanctifying and recreating power of the Holy Spirit lifting us again out of ourselves in Christ to worship the Father. Only the Spirit of Holiness can purge us from the falsification of the Good News by mixing up with it our own subjectivities and unrealities. Only the Creator Spirit begetting in us the simplicity of faith can make us free from ourselves and the distortion in our understanding of the

Gospel through our own preconceptions and inventions. Yet it is against the Holy Spirit that we have sinned, in substituting our own creativity for his, and in resisting his truth in the apostolic witness. We need to be cleansed anew by the Blood of Christ and receive afresh the Spirit he mediates to us through his atonement. Without the transparence of the Spirit we cannot exercise the kind of witness in which God in Christ bears witness to himself, but it is only when God's own self-witness is heard that the world will believe.

THE ORDERING AND EQUIPPING OF THE CHURCH FOR MINISTRY

14

THOMAS F. TORRANCE

The Ministry

THE MEANING OF ORDER[1]

ORDER IS THE CO-ORDINATING OF THE LIFE OF THE CHURCH IN ITS
fellowship, worship, and mission in the service of the glory of
God. The order of the Church's ministry is the ordering of its life
and work through participation in the obedience of Christ. Let us
elucidate that in a number of paragraphs.

(1) In the biblical revelation the whole concept of order is
viewed over against disorder and chaos. Apart from the ordering of
God's creative Word the world is without form or void, but into
the ordered cosmos there has broken the disorder of sin. It belongs
to the very nature of sin to divide, to disrupt, to be anarchic—sin is
lawlessness, *anomia*. The opposite of all that is order, harmony,
communion. When God made the world He made it in order and
everything was set in its due proportion. But through the lawlessness of sin the world fell out of proportion, out of order, and was
threatened with sheer chaos. Were it not for the persistent fact of
God's purpose of love the world would destroy itself; but in His
Covenant mercy God holds the world together in spite of its chaos,
and to that end He has promulgated His law which restrains and
contains disorder and chaos, and reduces it to a measure of proportion, even while it is in the grip of *anomia*, or lawlessness. But
God's Covenant contains the promise of a new order, of a new
creation when all things will be restored to their obedience and

1. Reprinted from *The Church Quarterly Review*, vol. CLX, Jan. 1959,
pp. 21–36; French text in *Revue d'Histoire et de Philosophie Religieuses*,
No. 2, pp. 129–142.

From Thomas F. Torrance, *Conflict and Agreement in the Church*, Volume
Two, The Ministry and the Sacraments of the Gospel, pp. 13–57. ©
Lutterworth Press, London, 1960. Used by permission of the Publisher.

perfection in the divine Will. Meantime wherever there is *anomia* it is met by the divine *nomos,* and there is conflict between disorder and order.

(2) The biblical revelation does not work with a concept of natural law, that is, of an order immanent in natural processes capable of being brought to its self-expression. There is an order of creation (*ordo creationis*) but that is not discernible by observing the creation (*cursus naturae*) but only by observing the creative Will of God. This creative Will of God will restore to creation its lost order, and restore to creation its true form and harmony in the Word of God. That is shadowed forth in the divine law promulgated in the Old Testament, the revealed law of God, but as yet that law set over against the lawlessness of the world is revealed mainly in its negative aspect of judgment upon disorder, and of restraint upon lawlessness. It is through the judgment of disorder that order is maintained, and laws are formed to make life in the disordered world possible at all. But the ultimate function of that law is to point beyond itself to the new law, the new order of the new Covenant. Under the old Covenant there was a divine form of administration or economy given in the law of Moses; but that points ahead to the new Covenant when the Covenant Will of God will bring and manifest a new form of administration or economy. This will be inserted into the world and written into its inner being—the new law to be inscribed upon the heart through the Spirit. As such it is a new order that comes from without and is planted within.

(3) That new order, the new economy, or rather the eternal Economy of God for His creation, came into the world in Jesus Christ. In the Incarnation the Word of God entered into His own disordered world; the Light shone into the darkness; the divine economy entered within historical and creaturely existence. In other words, the Covenant Will of God broke into our world and is completely fulfilled in Jesus Christ both from the side of God and from the side of man. That is the economy of which St. Paul speaks, when he describes its work as that of gathering up all things into Christ the Head, things visible and invisible, and their ordering in the eternal purpose of the divine love and fellowship. *OIKONOMIA* describes literally the ordering of a house, household administration. God is the great Householder who has come to take control of His own house and family and order it according to His Love. He does that in and through the Incarnation, in which His *OIKONOMIA* is not imposed upon the world from without but enters into it and operates from within it. *OIKONOMIA* represents

the great condescension of the divine Will to work out His purpose of love without violence within the alienated will of man, to work out His divine economy within the disordered existence of the world. Now the *mode of that economic condescension* is the way of Jesus Christ the Servant, the way of obedience even to the death of the Cross, and it is through that mode of economic condescension that He is exalted to be the Head of all things, and especially the Head of the Church, His Body.

(4) In Jesus Christ, therefore, in His Incarnation and in the whole course of His obedience, there has taken place in the divine economy a restoration of alienated man to fellowship with God, a conversion of rebellious humanity to the obedience and love of God. In other words, in the whole human life of Jesus the order of creation has been restored; in the midst of our disordered, sin-disrupted existence, there has been lived a human life in perfect order and proportion to the Will of God. The Covenant purpose of God in creation has been fulfilled and more than fulfilled. Here we have the divine economy entering into our creaturely and human existence and ordering it from within *against* our human nature, that is, against the consequences of sin in all its disorder, chaos, and lawlessness entrenched in fallen human nature. This is the order of redemption which reaches back to the original order of creation and far transcends it in the amazing purpose of the divine love, as the order, of the new creation. Here in the new Humanity in Jesus Christ nothing is out of order, or out of proportion. Everything has its proper order, proper time, proper place, proper sequence, and proper end. From beginning to end the whole life of Jesus in obedience to the Father is directed to His praise and glory, so that the new order of creation established and revealed in the Humanity of Christ can be spoken of as the praise of creation for the Creator.

(5) Order in the new creation is to be regarded as a third dimension. We are not concerned here simply with the Will of God and the obedience of man, with the Law of God, and the conformity of man to that divine law, but with a *third dimension,* with a divinely provided fulfilment of the divine Law. In the Old Testament we have a situation in which God gathers His children into Covenant relation with Himself, and within that Covenant He declares: "I will be your God, and you will be my children. . . . I am holy, therefore be ye holy. I am God, walk before me and be perfect." But God knows that His children are unable to be holy or obedient or perfect before Him; they are unable to fulfil the requirements of His Covenant Will, so that within the Covenant and as part of its Covenant mercies He graciously provides a way of response to His

Will, a way of obedient conformity to His Covenant which He is pleased to accept as from His people in the Covenant. That was provided in Israel's Cult or *leitourgia*. But that cultic pattern of response had to be acted out in obedience, while it pointed beyond itself to God's promise of a way of obedient fulfilment of it in the actual existence and life of His people. That was the theme in the Servant Songs, which was fulfilled at last in Jesus Christ, who in His obedient Humanity is our God-given way of response to the divine Will. God's Covenant Will is fulfilled for us, on our behalf, and in our stead, and through our participation in the obedient Humanity of Christ we are given to share in the fulfilled economy of the new Covenant, indeed of the new creation. That then is the third dimension. We are not simply concerned even in the Christian Church with the Will of God in love and grace, and then with the obedience of man in love and fellowship. We are concerned with these two, but with the two as fulfilled and completed in Jesus Christ in the obedient ordering and perfection of His human life as an oblation of all praise and thanksgiving to God the Creator and Father, and therefore of our sharing in His obedience through the power of the Spirit. Thus *order* in the New Testament refers to the concrete ordering of our human life and being in the obedient Humanity of Jesus Christ. All order in the Christian Church is a participation in His obedient Humanity—whether that order be an ordering of its daily life, daily worship, or daily fellowship, or daily mission. The whole of the Church's life is ordered through participation in the ordered life of Jesus Christ, the New Adam, the Head of the New Creation.

(6) The form which this re-ordering in Jesus Christ takes is the form of a Servant. It was through His obedience within our disobedient humanity that He restored us to order and peace in God. But in that He the obedient Servant is given to be the Head of all creation, all creation is now re-ordered in obedience to Him, for He gives it to share in His obedience to God. Because Christ is the Head of creation, chaotic, lawless creation is restored to order in Him, and because He restored order through obedience to the Father, He restores order to the creation through bringing creation into obedience to Himself, by granting it through the Spirit to share in His own obedience. Thus as Jesus was obedient in the Father, who sent Him to fulfil His Will, so the Church is ordered in its obedience to Christ who sent it to fulfil His Will. The obedience of the Church to Christ is not simply an imitation of His obedience but a fulfilling of God's Will through participation in Christ's obedience.

(7) It is through the Spirit that the Church is given to share in

Christ's obedience, and so to be ordered in and by and through His obedient Humanity. Christ is the Law of the Church's life, the Law according to which its life and work are to be ordered, but that Law is fulfilled not simply by external obedience and conformity but by inner and outer sharing in His Life, so that *through the SPIRIT* the Church is in-the-law to Christ (*ennomos Christou*), conformable to Him through communion with Him. It is the Spirit who is the Law of the Church's ordered life; not the Spirit as a new law of nature, not the Spirit as the soul of the Church, not the Spirit as a new immanent norm in the development of the Church through history, but the Spirit who gives the Church to share in the obedience of Christ the Head of the Body and who is other than the Church, its Lord and King but who in economic condecension has come to be obedient to the Father from within the Church, that the Church may share in an obedience not its own, and in an order that is new to it, indeed against its own nature; an order from beyond the Church's own being but in which it is given to participate by the Spirit.

(8) This being so, *actual order* as we see and have it in the historical Church on earth is essentially ambiguous. Its basic order is the obedient new humanity in Christ. The Church shares in that through the Spirit, so that its life is ordered through the Communion of the Spirit. But the Church that shares in that order of the New Creation is the Church that is sent by Christ out into history, to live its life in the physical and temporal existence that awaits redemption in the second advent of Christ. The Church in the midst of the old creation and all its disorder shares in the new creation and its new order. By sheer participation in the empirical life of this fallen world which comes under the divine judgment, and therefore the divine law, the Church participates in worldly forms and laws and cannot escape from them. It is sent to have its mission right there under law, but under law to share in the new order in-the-law to Christ through the Spirit. Just as the Son of God Himself condescended to be made under the law and through obedience to fulfil the Will of God, and as such was exalted above all, so the Church which is given to share through the Spirit in the new Humanity of Christ is sent into history to live out its new life in the form of a servant under the law—not to be fettered by the law, not to be schematized according to the forms and patterns of this age, that is, not to be legalized in its life, but to use the patterns and forms of the law of this age in the service of its new life in the risen and ascended Lord. Thus all order in the historical Church is essentially ambiguous because it is order in the overlap

of the two ages, this present age that passes away and the new age which through the Spirit already overlaps it in Christ.

Another way of putting that is to say that all order in the historical Church is essentially eschatological. By "eschatological" here two things are meant: (a) that order carries within it the tension between the new and the old; and (b) the tension between the present (including the past) and the future. True order in the Church of Christ is order that points above and beyond its historical forms to its new order in the risen Christ, and points beyond its present forms to the future manifestation of its order in the new creation. All order in the Church is thus ambivalent and provisional: it is order that visibly reflects its life hid with Christ in God, and order that exercises a provisional service in time, until Christ comes again. The outward order is like the scaffolding of a building which is to be torn down and cast away when the building itself is complete. In history God has given the Church its historical order and structure which participates in the forms of this passing world, but when the building of the Church as an habitation of God is complete, and its new order is revealed in the advent of Christ, the historical forms of order and structure will be cast away. Or to put it another way: all order is at once juridical and spiritual. It is at once participant in *nomos* and participant in *Pneuma,* that is, in Christ through the *Pneuma.* The validity of orders in the Church partakes of that ambivalence. Validity is at once a juridical term relative to the particular nomistic structure of a Church, relative to the law of a Church, but validity is also a spiritual term referring to the sharing of the Church in the authority of Christ through His Spirit, a sharing in the *exousia* of the Son of Man. It is that essential ambiguity in validity that makes it such a difficult term, and forgetfulness of it that causes persistent confusion.

Now in the light of all these eight paragraphs we have to think of the *order* of the Church's ministry with reference to its actual life in the space and time of this world. The ordering of the Church's life through sharing in, and therefore according to, the obedient Humanity of Christ, is an ordering within the physical and temporal life of this world. Order has therefore to be thought out in terms of *space* and *time.*

(1) Order in regard to Space

Because the Church is the Body of Christ, it has a physical and spiritual life in which the physical and the spiritual are not to be separated, though they may be distinguished, from one another. The Church as Body of Christ in history has therefore space. It has its place in this world, the place which it has been given by Christ, and into which He has sent it. It is in its place in the physical world that its life is to be ordered. Let us look at that in this way. Jesus Christ, the Man Jesus, is the place in this physical world where God and man meet and where they have communion with one another. The Temple in the Old Testament was the place where God put His Name, where He kept tryst with His covenanted people, and where they kept covenant with Him. Jesus Christ is that Temple on earth and among men where God has put His Name, and where He has appointed us to meet Him. It is the place where heaven and earth meet, the place of reconciliation. Jesus Christ is Himself God's mercy-seat, God's place in this world where He is really present to us in our place. But Jesus Christ ascended and He is in heaven—that is, He has a heavenly place far beyond anything that we can understand and far beyond our reach, but Jesus Christ through His Spirit has also bestowed His presence upon us in the Church, so that the Church on earth is the place of Christ.

The place of the Church in history is the place where Christ's presence is to be found. That is His real presence. It is of course above all in the Sacrament of the Lord's Supper, in the midst of the Church on earth, that we are given the real presence of Christ. That is the place of Christ in the place of the Church on earth. That is the place where heaven bends down to earth, and where man on earth is made to sit in heavenly places in Christ. Here we are concerned with two places, as it were: the heavenly place of Christ and the spatial place of the Church. The place of the Church is to be defined with regard to that heavenly place of real presence of Christ on the one hand, and with regard to its participation in the spatial context of the physical world on the other. The Church's life, worship, fellowship, and ministry are all ordered in regard to that twofold place, heavenly and earthly place. No adequate understanding of the order of the Church can neglect that twofold involvement in space enshrined so clearly in the Sacrament. Order will concern the indicating or defining of the place on earth where the heavenly place of Christ makes contact with it, but that earthly place cannot be so delimited and defined as thereby to define and delimit also the heavenly place of Christ. Christ the risen and ascended Lord is in a place that is beyond definition and delimitation. It is through the Sovereign Spirit that He graciously condescends to be really present in the appointed space of the Church and to make that His place on earth. But He does not thereby bind Himself to that place on earth; rather does He bind us through that place to His own real Presence, to His heavenly place, and so from that appointed place on earth He exalts us to sit with Him in heavenly places. All this means that the Church's *order* in space is concerned with the ordering of its physical fellowship and worship in the Spirit. Order serves the proclamation of the Word and the Eucharistic fellowship on earth, but orders it in such a way that it makes room in it all, makes a place in it all, for the Sovereign presence of the Spirit, for the heavenly place of Christ—that is, for His real presence. The Christian Church as the Body of Christ on earth knows nothing of a spaceless ordering of its life.

(2) *Order in regard to Time*

Because the Church is the Body of Christ, it has a temporal and eternal life in which the temporal and the eternal are not to be separated, although they may be distinguished from one another. The Church as the Body of Christ in history therefore has time as an essential ingredient of its reality. It has its time in this world, the time which it has been given by Christ, and into which He has sent it. It is in the time-form of this world, in historical existence that its life is to be ordered—to be ordered as Christ's Body in time. Now Jesus Christ in His historical life is the area in the time of this creaturely world where God and man, eternity and time, meet and have communion with each other. Israel through its history was the area within world-history into which God intervened with His redeeming purpose, in order to work into our time and from within our time toward that area in the fullness of time when God would become man and gather man into the life of God, when the Eternal would come into the passage of time, and gather time into union with the eternal. In Israel God bound our time into Covenant-relation with Himself, but all that is completely fulfilled in Jesus Christ where time is not only the sphere of the eternal event, but time is sanctified, redeemed, reconciled, and given new reality in union with Eternity, once and for all.

In Jesus Christ, therefore, the Eternal Son of God has lived His life within our time; He became time, and has in Himself elevated time into abiding communion with the eternal God. In Jesus Christ God has recreated time, redeemed it from its vanity, from its guilt and irreversibility, its decay and corruption, and given it a new reality in the new Humanity of the incarnate Son. But Jesus Christ has ascended and He is in heaven, in Eternity—that is, He has an eternal time far beyond anything that we can understand, or can measure by the kind of time we have in this passing age. It is not a timeless time, or a timeless eternity, but eternal time in which our time, redeemed new time, is eternally real in union with Eternity itself. That is the new time of the Kingdom manifested in the forty days of the risen Jesus Christ upon the earth, and within the lapses of our temporal history; but now that Jesus Christ has ascended, He has withdrawn that new time of His New Humanity from sight, from the visible succession of passing time on the plane of history.

And yet Jesus Christ bestows Himself upon us in time, and in such a way that our faith and worship are not timeless, any more than they are spaceless. It is within our passing time that He has time for us, that He makes time for us, makes time for communion, for faith, for worship, for growth, for development, for advance. It is in the Church in history that Christ has time for us, for by the very act of His ascension He waits for us and makes time for us, in which we can hear the Gospel, time in which we can repent, time for decision and faith, time in which we can preach the Gospel to all nations.

This was a frequent element in the teaching of the historical Jesus, in His parables of the householder or the king who went into the far country and waited till the right time to return, but in that period of waiting he gave his servants time, and then returned to call them to account for the time he had given them—the word sometimes used to describe that is *chronizein,* but it has also associated with it the word *chorein,* to make room, that is room for freedom to believe, freedom to decide, and freedom to be obedient (within time) until the return of the householder or king. It is in that light that we are to understand Christ's ascension, and the fact that by the very act of ascension, and His heavenly waiting until the right time for Him to return, Jesus Christ establishes the Church in history with temporal form within the passage of time where it has time to work, and time to obey Him. It is in that time that the Church has time to exist and carry out its mission, within the succession of history where there is time between revelation and decision, time between decision and act, time between present and future, time for the Gospel. Thus the existence of the Church as bound up with its mission is inseparable from time. The Church as the Body of Christ in history is the area within the time-form of this world where God and man meet in the Gospel, and where man is reconciled to God and united to Him in Jesus Christ.

But it is *IN Jesus Christ* that God gives the Church that time, and that place in time—and that means in the historical Jesus, and in the risen and ascended Jesus. Just as Jesus Christ is the place where heaven and earth meet, and God and man are reconciled, and the only place where that takes place, so Jesus Christ is the one place within time and the only place within time where God has provided time for the reconciliation of man, and man finds time for forgiveness and cedemption. Jesus Christ is Himself the fullness of time. Therefore the order of the Church in time means the ordering of the Church's life and mission in relation to the time of Jesus Christ, the historical Christ, and the risen and ascended Christ. In all Church order we are concerned with *the time of Jesus on earth* when God's Son condescended to enter within our fallen time in order to redeem it, but also with *the time of Jesus ascended into Eternity* who yet bestows Himself upon us in time through His Spirit. The time of the Church will therefore be defined by the relation of the Church in history to the historical Jesus Christ, and to the ascended and advent Jesus Christ; the Church's life, worship, fellowship, and ministry are all ordered with regard to that twofold time, heavenly and earthly, historical and eternal time. No adequate understanding of the order of the Church can overlook that twofold involvement in time.

Look at it like this. On the one hand, Christ by His ascension has withdrawn Himself from the visible passage of time on the plane of this earth in order to send us back to the one time in all history where in the fullness of time the Son of God became incarnate—that is the time of the whole historical life of Jesus, culminating in the "hour" of His death and breaking out into the new time of the resurrection. The Church is for ever bound to the historical Jesus, for the Truth and the Life of God have become historical fact in Jesus and are now historically communicated and transmitted. The Church exists in that history stemming from the historical Jesus, and lives by the Word historically communicated through the apostles. Therefore all the life and ministry of the Church has to be ordered in time, according to the nature of that divine event in time, the time of the historical Jesus. By withdrawing Himself from the visible succession of history, and by refusing to abrogate our existence in time by sheer immediacy, Jesus Christ gives us time, enables us to take time with the historical Jesus and the historical Word communicated by and from Jesus. Thus, far from abrogating our existence in the on-going time of this world, by His ascension Jesus Christ sends us into the time of this empirical world, and commands us within it to focus our attention on the time of the historical Jesus, to be bound by it, and to be obedient to it; for it is by that time and through it that Jesus continues to rule the Church and order it according to His Word in actual history. Hence throughout all its life on earth, throughout all its continuity in history, the Church lives its life in historical attachment to the fullness of time in Jesus, and in historical continuity with it. It is out of that one time in Jesus that the Church lives from age to age, and from it that the Church derives its own time in history. It cannot in any circumstances detach itself from the historical Jesus, or depreciate its historical attachment to Him in the fullness of time, for it is precisely by its being bound and obedient to the historical Jesus Christ in the tradition of the apostolic Church that Christ continues to rule over the Church by His Word and Spirit, making it His own Body and Servant in history.

Church order is therefore the ordering of the Church's life in history in relation to that one time in all history, the time of Jesus; for that is the only place in time where eternity and time have really met, and where they are for ever joined, and it is in and through that union of eternity and time in Jesus that the Church lives its life on the plane of history. On the other hand it is in that time of the historical Jesus that the Church, from age to age, still meets with the eternal God and is gathered up "into" eternal time. It is only within the time of the historical Jesus that the new time of the risen Jesus breaks in upon the Church in history, and gives it to share and abide in the new time of the new creation. It is in the historical Jesus that the new time overlaps with the old time in our history, and only there, so that it is as the Church lives there in that overlap of the two times, that it is given to share in new time above and beyond the time of this passing age on the mere plane of earthly history. The Church continues to live within the time of this on-going world, but it finds its life above and beyond it in the risen and ascended Lord, not in some timeless eternity, but in One who has Himself descended into our time, redeemed it and gathered it up in Himself into union with Eternity. The Church is therefore bound to the succession of time by relation to the historical Jesus, but it is precisely in the historical Jesus that it knows its true life to be hid with Christ in God, and to be found beyond the passing and successive forms of this age. This does not mean the abrogation of the Church's historical existence, but it does mean that the historical existence of the Church, its continuity within the succession of time on earth, is determined by relation to the new time of the risen Lord. Hence the Church within the succession of time on earth is given a new orientation within the limitations of time; so that instead of being fettered by the bonds of time, bound by the sheer irreversibility of time that is laden with guilt, instead of being determined by the temporal processes of this world, the Church within time has freedom to meet with eternity, to rise above its past and to live a new life from age to age in Christ.

It may help us to understand that by thinking a little naively of the "two times" of the Church, as *horizontal time* on the plane of history in which it is bound to, and ordered in relation to, the time of the historical Jesus, and as *vertical time* in the Spirit in which the Church shares with Christ the time of His new Humanity. If the Church had only horizontal time, then the Church would only be a construct of historical succession, having only its temporal origin in Jesus but actually being fettered and determined by its place within the temporal process. Then the Church would not be free to have real meeting with the risen Lord; it would be enslaved to history, enslaved to its own past and all the errors and sins of its past; it would not be free from all the limitations and determinisms of history. But the Church within history is the Church of Jesus Christ in whom the Eternal has broken into our sin-determined and guilt-fettered time, and brought freedom and redemption from bondage. Jesus Christ is the area in our fallen time where the Eternal has broken through the limitations of this passing age to which we are in bondage, and where God acts freely upon men through His Word and Spirit, confronting them with His own Person and enabling them to respond freely in spite of all the downward drag of sin, in spite of all the piled-up determinisms of our guilty past, in spite of our bondage in the time of this world. The Church is therefore the place within time where that free meeting with the Eternal is possible, where within time men are delivered from the tyrant forces of bondage and are made free for God, so that real meeting in faith and love is not only possible but actual.

In the light of all that, then, the order of the Church's ministry in time is to be regarded as the ordering of its life within the on-going time of history and its succession which makes time for meeting with the risen and ascended Lord. It is an ordering of the historical and temporal life of the Church that binds it to that one place in history and time in the historical Jesus, but because in Jesus the Eternal breaks into our history and time giving us, through the Spirit, freedom to meet with the living God within time and history, it is also an ordering that will not allow the life of the Church to be tied down to the temporal framework of mere succession on the stage of this world. The ordering of the Church's life and ministry in time means giving it such a new orientation within on-going time and all its limitations, that the time-forms of the

Church's historical existence become the signs of the new divine order that already breaks in upon the Church in history. Thus for example the historical succession in the ordering of the ministry, far from involving the Church in bondage to the past, attests the binding of the Church to the historical Jesus and so becomes the sign of the new ordering of the Church's life in Jesus Christ. Historical succession does not secure or guarantee the binding of the Church in Christ, for He, the risen and ascended Lord, is not bound by the forms of fallen time; for by His resurrection He has triumphed over them. Historical succession, however, binds the Church to that one time within our fallen history where the risen and ascended Lord keeps tryst with us as the Lord of all time and history, and where alone we may freely meet Him. It attests the fact that, through relation to the historical Jesus, Christ binds us to Himself on the ground of the historical incarnation, atonement and resurrection, and declares that we cannot find any life or salvation in detachment from the historical Jesus.

All this is wonderfully enshrined in the Lord's Supper. "This do in remembrance of Me. As often as ye do this, ye do proclaim the Lord's death till He come." In the Supper the Church's life and ministry is so ordered that it is bound to the historical Jesus, to His death on the Cross, but at that very point in time the Church is given to have communion with the risen and ascended Lord and to share in His New Humanity, and from the Supper it is sent out to proclaim that until He comes again. Thus the ordering of the Church's life and ministry should follow the pattern enshrined in the Lord's Supper. "For I have received that which I also delivered unto you. . . ." It is celebrated in that succession or tradition, and it is ordered within that continuity, but within that continuity it is the risen Christ, the Lord of the Supper, who comes through closed doors, through all the limitations of our fallen time and sinful history, and gives us to eat and drink with Him in the new time of the Kingdom of God. While the Supper is to be ordered therefore within the historical continuity of the Church, it is such an ordering that room is left within it for the new time of the Kingdom, and in the presence of that new time all the historical time-forms of the Church are relativized and given new orientation—they are taken under the command of the risen and ascended Lord, are made obedient to His real presence, so that instead of being mere limitations to the Church's life and ministry they are the signs pointing beyond to the reality of the new time of the new creation. In so doing they are themselves transcended, and made subordinate to communion with Christ in the time of His New Humanity.

(3) Order in regard to Space and Time

Space and time cannot be separated in the Church. The Church on earth and in history is inescapably involved in space and time and in all the machinery of physical existence, for it is sent out to minister the Gospel in space and time. It is in that involvement with space and time that lies the significance of its order. The Church's very bodily and historical existence and mission require spatial and temporal order if it is to perform its divine purpose in space and time, but it can only live its life and fulfil its work in space and time, if its place on earth is ordered in obedience to its share in Christ's heavenly place, and if its time on earth is made obedient to its share in Christ's heavenly time. Church order concerns the ordering of the Church's life and ministry in the meeting of heaven and earth in the place of the Church, and in the intersection of historical continuity and immediate unity with the risen and ascended Christ. The place that the Church has in the space-time form of this world is not abrogated, but in that place the Church is given to share in the real presence of the New Man and real time of the New Creation. Until Christ comes again to change the space-time form of this fallen world (not to eliminate it but to change and renew it) the Church shares in the real presence of the New Man and the real time of the New Creation, under the form of space and time as we know it in this on-going world, as under a veil, as in a mystery. The actual space of the Church, its physical place in this world, has to be regarded as the trysting place of Christ on earth; and the time of the Church, its historical actuality, has to be regarded as the time appointed by Christ for meeting with Him. This space and this time have to be used therefore in obedience to His appointment, in subordination to the space and the time of the historical Jesus, that is, the actual founding of the Church upon the rock of the apostles, and to the actual tradition of the historical Jesus which we have received from the apostles, for it is in that obedience within the space-time form of the Church on earth to the historical Jesus that the Church goes into history as His servant, the obedient Body of which He is the Head. Only as that Body is it His Church. Therefore the ordering of the Church in space and time is concerned with its obedience to Christ, to the risen Lord in the space and time of the historical Jesus alone. Then it is, however, that through the Spirit Christ keeps tryst with His Church in history and bestows upon it His real presence, so that the time and place of the Church become Christ's own time and place among men. Then it is that the Church lives and works as the earthly and historical form of Christ's Body (as Karl Barth has called it), obedient to Him, its risen Head and Lord, and as such it is the instrument He is pleased to use to proclaim His Word to all nations and to manifest Himself to all who believe.

In all this the Church looks upon itself as covenanted with Christ, and as gathered into union and communion with Him as His covenant-partner. Just as its historical succession in time and space does not secure or guarantee its unity with Christ, but only serves to attest its binding to Him in the time and space of the historical Jesus, so the Church's obedience to the time and space of its foundation in the apostles and to the apostolic tradition does not secure or guarantee that it is the Body of Christ. Throughout all its succession in the relativities and contingencies of our sinful history, throughout all its life of faith and obedience, in which the Church cannot but acknowledge its unfaithfulness and disobedience, the Church relies upon the New Covenant which Christ has made with it in His Body and Blood. It is only in that Covenant undergirding all its historical relativity and all its unfaithfulness that the Church's security rests. In obedience the Church relies not upon its own obedience but upon the obedience of Christ, and acknowledges that it is given a ground of faith and reliance beyond all the changes and chances of this passing world and all its own unworthiness. The Church can never justify itself, therefore, by claiming historical succession or doctrinal faithfulness, by reference to its own place and time on earth and in history, but must cast itself upon the justification of Christ's grace alone, and rely upon His covenant-mercies who promised that the gates of hell would not prevail against His Church, and that He would be in its midst until the end of the world. The ordering of the Church can never be allowed to assume a role of independence and authority as if the duly ordered Church, even in its obedience to Christ, could be anything more than an unprofitable servant. Order must always be maintained in ever renewed amazement at the grace of God, and in ever renewed thankfulness for His undeserved grace and justification.

To sum up. The Church is ordered in its life and ministry on earth:

(a) By being obedient to the historical Jesus Christ in space and time in the tradition of the apostolic Church, in which He, the risen and ascended Christ, comes to rule and order the Church by His Word and Spirit, making it His Body and Servant in history;

(b) By sharing in the obedience of Jesus Christ in space and time through the communion of the Spirit in which He, the New Man, gives it to share in His New humanity as He, the Lord, undergirds it in all its frailty and weakness by His New Covenant, so that already it is given to abide in the life and time and order of the New Creation;

(c) By looking beyond the historical and institutional forms of its ordering in space and time to the fullness of its life in Christ, who comes to meet it in mercy and judgment, and who at His Parousia will unveil the full reality of the Church in the glory of the Son of Man.

In this threefold way the Church looks upon its ordering in the space and time of this on-going world as the required form of its obedience to Christ or the attestation of its reliance upon the new Covenant founded for ever in the historical Jesus, as the sign that points to the new divine order of the Church's life communicated to it even now through Word and Sacrament in the Spirit, and as the provisional form given to it, until the redemption of the body, of the order of the new creation which will be revealed only at the final advent of Christ.

CONSECRATION AND ORDINATION[2]

In order to understand the New Testament teaching about consecration and ordination we have to examine the rites and language of the Old Testament tradition. The rites were not carried over as such into the Christian Church, for they were fulfilled in Christ and abrogated; but the New Testament does use the language of the rites to speak both of Christ and His Church, and it does adapt some of the Old Testament rites for its own use, but with entire freedom and with quite new significance. The basic line we have to consider is the consecration of the priest, and king, and prophet in the Old Testament, and see how they are fulfilled in Christ, and then see how *in this Christ* the New Testament thinks of the ministry as consecrated and ordained.

2. Prepared for the use of the *Aids to Devotion Committee* of the Church of Scotland, November, 1957, and reprinted from *Scottish Journal of Theology*, vol. 11/3, 1958, pp. 225 ff.

The Consecration and Ordination of the Priest

The main passages that concern us are Exod. 28 and 29; Lev. 6, 7, 8, 9; and Num. 8. It is worth remembering right away that the Leviticus passages fell in the Jewish Lectionary for the Passover week, and are clearly reflected in the Gospels, especially in John 13–17.

To get the proper perspective we have to remember that Israel was consecrated in the Covenant to be a holy people, a kingdom of priests to God (Exod. 19:6; Lev. 20:26; Deut. 7:6; 14:21; 26:19; 28:9; cf. Is. 62:12). As such, too, Israel was God's "first-born son"; that is, it occupied among the human family the part of "the head of the house" (the *ben-bayith,* the householder or steward of God's holy purposes, reflected in several of Jesus' parables). Within Israel it would appear that the primitive priests were the first-born sons, the heads of the house which is preserved in the Passover rite where the ceremony is conducted by the head of the house. But the first-born were "redeemed back" for life among the people and their place was taken by the tribe of Levi (Num. 3:12 f., etc.). Thus within Israel as a priestly nation, one tribe is set aside for priestly functions instead of the first-born, and within the tribe of Levi the "sons of Aaron" are set apart for special functions as liturgical priests. The Old Testament priesthood has thus an interim institutional character, and its importance lies in its functions and in obedience to the divine ordinances. It was the business of the Levites and priests to teach the Law to Israel, and so they lived scattered through the twelve Tribes. The sons of Aaron came to be divided into twenty-four courses, twelve functioning in the Temple and twelve in Israel, although all twenty-four came up to Jerusalem for the great festivals.

How then were *the priests* consecrated and ordained? This is very fully described. The whole congregation (*ekklesia*) assembled at the door of the Tabernacle where they were addressed by Moses and told they were about to act in accordance with God's ordinance. Then he "brought forward" or "brought near" or "presented" Aaron and his sons. They were solemnly washed at the Laver, and clothed with priestly garments. Aaron was anointed with oil by pouring, but his sons were only sprinkled with his anointing oil. Aaron only was called "the anointed", the *christos*. Then there followed sacrifices, the most significant of which was the "consecration offering" or "fill-offering". Some of this along with unleavened bread was offered for the consecration of Aaron and his sons, some of it was broken up into portions, and portions of flesh and bread were put into the hands of Aaron and his sons who offered them as "peace-offerings". Then Aaron and his sons repaired to the door of the Tabernacle and in the presence of the congregation partook of a sacred meal of what remained of the flesh of the fill-offering and bread of the consecration offering— that was called "a sacrifice of praise and thanksgiving". This was repeated for seven days, during which they stayed within the Tabernacle.

It is to be noted that in this rite the chief and proper subject is Aaron the high priest, although his sons are consecrated through association with him, and have their hands filled too and share with him in the sacred meal of consecration. But Aaron alone is the *christos*. (In an extended sense of cause all Israel is spoken of as *messiah* = anointed, Ps. 84:9; Hab. 3:13; Ps. 89:38, 51.) That act takes place only once and does not need to be repeated. The *Minḥah* that Aaron offers avails for himself and the sons of his house. On his death, his eldest son was clothed with his high-priestly garments and was consecrated with his priests in the same way—but the anointing was apparently not repeated, except to recover a break in the priestly line (2 Chron. 13:9). It has also to be noted that although the priests were consecrated only once, every time they went in and out of the Tabernacle or Temple they renewed their consecration through washing their hands and feet, while the high priest renewed his consecration through solemn and total baptismal ablution once a year in preparation for the renewal of the Covenant on the Day of Atonement. It should also be noted that the consecration of Aaron and the sons of his house to the priesthood was called "*the covenant of salt*".

What about *the Levites*? In Num. 8 we are told that all the Levites were cleansed and "separated" within Israel, cleansed by the sprinkling of the water of expiation (used at circumcision and in cleansing the leper to restore him to membership in the priestly race) and then they were "presented" to God with the same offerings as Aaron and his sons; but in addition all the Levites *had hands laid on them* by the Children of Israel (doubtless acting through their elders) gathered at the door of the Tabernacle, who offered them up to their holy use as their representatives. Then Aaron took the Levites and offered them before the Lord as an oblation on behalf of the people that they might do the service of the Lord. Here the laying on of hands indicates the representative part played by the Levites, but as such they are offered unto God. Thus in their case ordination is twofold: laying on of hands and commissioning by the whole priestly people, and offering to God as consecration for His service.

What about *Moses* in all this? As Augustine pointed out long ago, Moses stands above all this without any ceremonial consecration. It is he who offers the sacrifices for Aaron and his sons, offers them to the Lord, and consecrates them. He himself had no other consecration than that of his supreme relation to the Word of God alone. Moses did not therefore pass on a consecration he had himself received; he acted only as "the servant of the Lord", and the entire validity of the consecration of the priesthood depended on God's command and grace alone—not on any "priestly grace". The priesthood is represented as God's "gift" (Num. 18:7) and rests on its "givenness". Hence the Hebrew word to give, *nathan*, is frequently employed for ordaining to the priesthood; it is an appointment of grace.

The Language of Consecration and Ordination in the Old Testament

The general term used for consecration and/or ordination in the Septuagint is *hagiazo*, meaning "sanctify" or make holy. The emphasis here is always upon the fundamental fact that God will be sanctified or hallowed in the midst of His people (Exod. 31:13; Lev. 20:8—cf. also the incident of Nadab and Abihu in Lev. 10:1, 2, etc.). All consecration or hallowing is a sharing in God's hallowing of Himself in the midst of His people, and has its significance only within the Covenant in which He is Holy and requires His people to be holy too.

Three distinctive terms are used, however, to describe this sanctification or consecration of the priest in holy things:

(a) To clothe with priestly garments—"to put on" (including baptismal ablution, etc.);

(b) To anoint with holy oil (the preparation of which was a secret) given along with sprinkling of blood;

(c) "to fill the hands", which was accompanied by a special sacrifice of consecration.

Of these three it is the third that is the distinctive term for consecration or ordination—the priest has his hands filled: *mille' yadh* (מִלֵּא יָד; Exod. 28:41; 29:29; 35:35; Lev. 8:33; 16:32; 21:10; Num. 3:3; Judges 17:5, 12; 1 Kings 13:33; 2 Chron. 13:9; cf. 2 Chron. 29:31; Is. 43:26). The offering of consecration was called "filling" (*millu'im*).

What "filling the hands" means exactly is not clear. Generally it means that the priest has the priesthood committed to him; he receives it as a gift. Specifically it means that the act of consecration is brought to its fulfilment or completion when his hands are filled with the holy oblations. It can also be applied in an extended sense to the consecration of the altar through having the oblations laid on it. Its meaning is thus twofold, which comes out very well in the Greek of the LXX in its twofold translation of *mille' yadh*:

(a) *pleroun tas cheiras* (πληροῦν τὰς χεῖρας). Cf. Lev. 7:29; Exod. 32:29.

(b) *teleioun tas cheiras* (τελειοῦν τὰς χεῖρας) or simply *teleious* as applied to the priest as object or in the passive with the priest as subject. It is almost equivalent to *hagiazein*. Cf. Exod. 28:41; 29:33.

These words are used, then, to describe the act of the consecration of the high priest in whose self-consecration the sons of his house are also consecrated; that consecration is brought to its completion in the filling of the hands with the oblations and in the sacrificial meal of flesh and bread, "the sacrifice of praise and thanksgiving".

The Language of Consecration in the New Testament

Although in the Old Testament "to fill the hands" was the more technical term, it does not make very good Greek when translated literally. It is natural therefore that in the Greek the word *teleioun* should be preferred to *pleroun tas cheiras*. The latter expression is, perhaps, to be detected lying behind John 3:35, which has reference to Christ's baptismal consecration in the Jordan and His anointing of the Spirit. If so, the underlying Aramaic has been turned into smooth Greek, and the "filling of the hands" is not very recognizable except to one familiar with the Old Testament rite. Along with this should be compared John 17:2–4; cf. also John 4:34; 5:36. Possibly the Pauline *pleroma* hints of this too sometimes, cf. Eph. 1:23 ff.; 3:19.

It is, however, the word *teleioun* that is prominent in the New Testament, especially in the Fourth Gospel and in the Epistle to the Hebrews. The verb *teleioun* is of course often used in the New Testament with no relation to the conception of priestly consecration, but when it is found in John 17, Christ's high-priestly prayer, which clearly reflects the reading of Lev. 7–8, we must see it in a different light. The evangelist also uses the other word *hagiazein*, e.g. 17:17–19: "Sanctify them in the truth. Thy Word is truth. As thou hast sent me into the world, even so have I sent them into the world, and for their sakes I sanctify myself, that they also might be sanctified through the truth." Then in verse 23 Jesus prays that the disciples might be consecrated in one (*teteleiomenoi eis hen*).

When we turn to the Epistle to the Hebrews there are several instances of *teleioun* which refer to the consecration of the high priest, while the word *hagiazein* is used in a sense parallel to the usage, both in the Old Testament and in John 17. Thus Heb. 2:11: "For both he who sanctifies (or consecrates) and those who are sanctified are all of one, for which cause he is not ashamed to call them brethren." In Heb. 7:28 and 9:9 the other word, *teleioun,* is used of the consecration of Christ the High Priest. In the tenth chapter the writer uses both terms, *hagiazein* and *teleioun,* to describe the fact that through Christ's own self-offering once and for all we are consecrated. By consecration the author of this epistle meant what Paul meant by justification through the blood of Christ and sanctification through His Spirit. It is Christ's own consecration of Himself on our behalf which both justifies us and sanctifies us as His holy servants, giving us to share in His consecration in such a way that through Jesus Christ our High Priest we all, with our bodies washed with clean water and with our consciences sprinkled with His blood, draw near to worship God, that is as priests in the House of God. It is interesting also to note that in this Epistle the institutional priesthood of Aaron is set aside because fulfilled and abrogated in Christ, and that He is High Priest as God's First-Born Son, and therefore we are all first-born sons in Him, while the Church is the Church of the first-born. That is to say, here where the institutional priesthood is done away all God's children are priests after the fashion of the first-born in Israel. Just as we are given to share in Christ's Sonship, so we are given to share in His Priesthood. In Christ sonship and priesthood are the same.

The Consecration of the King

The classical passage about this is found in 2 Kings 11:12, 17 which describes the consecration of the king by Jehoiada, and which reposes upon Deuteronomy 17:18-20. It is also based on the rites formed under King David and carried out with regard to Solomon (1 Kings 1:33 ff.; 1 Chron. 29:22 f.; cf. 2 Chron. 6:42). The main elements here are as follows:

(a) Anointing, possibly along with washing in the Gihon. David and Saul were the first to be anointed, and the anointing was accompanied by the gift of the Spirit (1 Sam. 10:1; 16:13; cf. 1 Sam. 26:11; Ps. 2:2 (Acts 4:26)). David himself was anointed three times. (Cf. 2 Sam. 2:4; 5:3. This was regarded in the Old Testament as indicative of the Messiah; cf. Ps. 45:7 and Hab. 3:13.)

(b) The kings were enthroned and crowned—the royal insignia of David were apparently used in later times.

(c) The putting of the "Testimony" into the hands of the king. According to Deuteronomy the king had to copy out the book of the Law with his own hand, so as to remember it and rule by it.

(d) A covenant was made between the king, God and the people. In the case of God's covenant with David it was known as "a covenant of salt", like the covenant made by God with the house of Aaron. In the case of Solomon's consecration we know that there was also prayer and sacrifice—see 1 Chron. 29:22 f.

Here, then, in the consecration of the king the fundamental pattern of consecration was similar to that of the consecration of the priest, involving: anointing, filling of the hands, and affirmation of the covenant relation. The difference lies chiefly in that to which the king is consecrated, kingship, not sacrifice, and that the king's hands are filled therefore not with oblations but with the Law. He is crowned and enthroned, which does not apply to the priests.

The Consecration of the Prophet

We have even less information about this, but a clear instance of the consecration of Elisha by Elijah is given in 1 Kings 19:16. It was by anointing followed later by investment with the prophet's mantle. In Ps. 105:15 "the anointed" and the prophets are synonymous. The anointing of both Saul and David gave them prophetic gifts, and presumably that meant that the anointing of kings was an extension of the anointing of prophets through whose Word proclaimed and enunciated God ruled as King.

In Is. 61:1 the Servant of the Lord speaks of himself as anointed to preach the Gospel, which Christ claimed to be fulfilled in Himself, Luke 4:18; John 10:36.

In addition to this Old Testament tradition, it should be noted that in the Judaean Scrolls the Anointed of the Lord, the Messiah, is regarded apparently as deriving both from the House of David and from the House of Aaron—the anointed priest-king. The members of the community initiated into the new covenant are spoken of as "anointed ones" and as forming a holy and "priestly" messianic community. That may have some influence on the New Testament, e.g. on 1 Peter.

Summary of the New Testament Teaching

Jesus Christ is the fulfilment of the threefold consecration to the office of priest, king, and prophet in the Old Testament. We have seen something of the fulfilment of priestly consecration in Christ, but kingly and prophetic consecration was also fulfilled in Him (Luke 4:18; Acts 4:26; 10:38; Heb. 1:9). This was all fulfilled in His anointing by the Spirit, which no doubt referred to His birth of the Spirit as well as to His anointing at His Baptism in the Jordan; it was as the Anointed Son of the Father that He gathered up and fulfilled the threefold anointing of Prophet, Priest, and King. The Church which He has made His own was anointed with Christ's Spirit at Pentecost by the Baptism of the Spirit, so that through Baptism all who come to Christ are not only given the right to be sons of God but are anointed with His anointing, receive the *chrism* of the Spirit (1 John 2:20, 27; 2 Cor. 1:21), or are given the *seal* of the Spirit, as St. Paul puts it.

Here, then, in Christ the First-Born Son of God and our High Priest, we are restored to the priestly Kingdom, for He has washed us from our sins in His own blood and made us kings and priests unto God. Every one who is a Son of God through Christ the Son belongs to this royal priesthood, and shares in Christ's self-consecration on our behalf. Christ alone is the *Christos,* the Anointed and Consecrated One (John 10:36), but we who follow Him in Baptism are given to share in it, putting off the old impurity and putting on Christ as our priestly garment, clothed with His righteousness, His consecration, and His holiness. Here there is no institutional priesthood like that of the Aaronic priesthood. That was an imperfect interim-measure only, necessarily done away when the true priesthood of sonship, the priesthood of the first-born, was restored in Christ. Here priesthood and sonship are the same, but when this is so, it is Baptism, through which we are consecrated as sons of God, which is our consecration to priesthood in Christ.

Consecration and Ordination of the Ministry in the New Testament

When we turn to the consecration and ordination of a special ministry as Christ's gift to His Church we find that this has its place only within the consecration of the whole membership of Christ's Body, and therefore within the ministry of the whole Body, which it has through sharing in Christ's vicarious Self-consecration. But within that there is something else. There are in fact two things: (1) The special consecration of the apostles in Christ's Self-consecration; and (2) the apostolic ordination of others through the laying on of hands and prayer.

(1) *The special consecration of the apostles in Christ.* The accounts of Christ's appointment of the apostles, His "making" of them, of His drawing them into a very private and close relation to Himself and to His teaching and His passion, and above all His special purpose for them in the Last Supper, as reflected in the Fourth Gospel as well as the Synoptics, are of special importance.

Although the Lord's Supper belongs to the whole Church, its first enactment belonged peculiarly to the apostles, who were at that point given a special place in the New Covenant and in the Kingdom of Christ, appointed to sit upon twelve thrones judging the twelve tribes of Israel, as the patriarchs of the New Israel, the Foundation of the Church. Jesus' solemn washing of their feet and His deliberate actions at the Supper clearly designed for the disciples peculiarly, and His high-priestly prayer of consecration in which He prayed above all for the disciples, make it clear that He regarded Himself, in going forth to the Cross, as the High Priest in whose Self-oblation and Self-consecration He was giving the disciples to share in a most intimate way as "the sons of His house". His Self-consecration as the *Christos,* His action as the High Priest on the Great Day of Atonement, was fulfilled once and for all, and can never be repeated. Just as when Aaron acted all Israel acted in him and through him, for he acted for all Israel, but at the same time the sons of his house had a special place in it, being sprinkled with the blood of sacrifice and with the oil of anointing, so when Christ went forth to the Cross all His people were given to share in it, for He acted on their behalf and in their stead; and yet in a special way the Twelve were given to be related to it. They alone went forth to the events of His passion after having shared with Him the consecration meal of the bread and wine of the Last Supper, and they alone, as it were, were sprinkled with His blood in Gethsemane where they were taken to watch and pray with Him in His awful agony; and they alone when He returned from His sacrifice had breathed upon them His Spirit in the Upper Room and so were anointed with His anointing. As such the apostles belonged to the once-and-for-all events of the Founding of the New Covenant in the Body and Blood of Christ; they remain for ever the authoritative witnesses of the New Covenant, the Pillars of the Church, in whom and through whom Jesus Christ made an everlasting Covenant of Salt with His Church, making it a royal priesthood in Himself.

The apostle-disciples were appointed to their ministry like Moses directly through the Word, and were given to sit, as it were, in Moses' seat, or rather in Christ's seat, inasmuch as they mediated His Word to the Church and in Christ's Name were appointed to rule and order His Church; but, like the sons of Aaron, the apostles shared peculiarly in the Self-consecration and anointing of their High Priest. All that is something that cannot be repeated, and therefore cannot be extended. The apostleship can have no successors, for the apostles remain under Christ as the permanent authorities over the Church, the foundation upon which all other ministry within the Church depends. And so they were sent out by Christ with His Commission to engage in the mission of reconciliation. It was in the fulfilment of that commission and mission that they came to ordain others to the ministry, giving the sign of the laying on of hands to attest that they were sent to fulfil their ministry within the one Commission of Christ given to His apostles, and within the once and for all Consecration of His Church upon the foundation of the apostles. But in taking an entirely different method of ordination from that which they had received the apostles showed unmistakably that they were in no sense extending their office to others, but ordaining a ministry in dependence upon their unique ministry in Christ.

(2) *The apostolic ordination of others through the laying on of hands and prayer*[3] (Acts 6:6; 13:3; 1 Tim. 4:14; 5:22; 2 Tim. 1:6; cf. Acts 14:23; 2 Cor. 8:19). The laying on of hands is the only ceremony that is taken over from the Old Testament by the New Testament Church for the consecration and ordination of its ministry. The consecration of the Church and of its ministry in the apostles had of course already taken place, and taken place once for all, so that whenever in the history of the Church there is an ordination to the ministry that ordination is grounded upon the once and for all consecration of the Church and its apostolic ministry in Christ; it shares in it, takes place only within it, and is the means whereby that consecration is through prayer related directly and particularly to those set apart for the ministry within the sphere of the apostolic commission and mission.

It does not appear that the early Church took over the rite of laying on of hands from Judaism so much as from the Old Testament. The elders in the Sanhedrin were instituted apparently only by enthronement in Moses' seat, but later on ordination by laying on of hands took the place of this. This rite may have had earlier

3. In this section I am indebted to the discussion of A. Ehrhardt, *The Apostolic Ministry, Scottish Journal of Theology Occasional Paper* no. 7, ch. II.

usage in Judaism which influenced the New Testament Church, but the evidence on the whole suggests that the apostles went back directly to the Old Testament itself for their guidance.

In a recent work (*The New Testament and Rabbinic Judaism,* pp. 224 f.) Professor Daube has pointed out that three different words are used in the Old Testament for a rite of blessing or ordination with hands. (1) *Nasa* to describe the priestly blessing when hands are lifted up, e.g. in the Aaronic benediction. This was an act of prayer and blessing in which the Name of God was put upon the people—the act used by Jesus in blessing His disciples at His ascension. (2) *Sim* or *shith* which describes the act of placing hands upon someone for blessing, as in the patriarchal blessing of Joseph's sons by Jacob. It was possibly this act that was used by Jesus in healing, and perhaps by the early Church at Baptism. (3) *Samakh* which describes the solemn act of laying (literally ''leaning'') on of hands as applied to sacrifices when sins are symbolically transferred to a victim, or used where the transference of guilt or association in responsibility is indicated, e.g. in stoning a blasphemer or in instituting someone to responsible office. (I cannot agree with Professor Daube's psychological interpretation of *samakh* as ''the pouring of personality'' from one person to another.) There is no evidence that Jesus ever used this. In Judaism the laying on of hands was not used for the ordaining of ''the seven of a city'' or local ''elders'', although their appointment to the local presbytery required the authorization of the Presbytery of the People or the Sanhedrin in Jerusalem. In the second century (and possibly in the first) rabbis were ordained by *samakh,* the solemn laying on of hands, called ''the laying on of hands of the elders''.

There are two instances of laying on of hands in the Old Testament important for the Christian precedent. (1) The laying on of hands through which the Levites were ordained to their office. This was an act carried out by the people, presumably through their elders, and was a lay-act in which the Levites were inducted into responsible representation of the people, appointed to stand for the first-born of the people in their ministry at the Tabernacle. The act of laying on of hands was completed when they were offered to God by the priests. (2) The other instance is the act of Moses in ordaining Joshua as his successor in the leadership of the people. In doing so Moses was commanded to ''put of his honour upon Joshua'' (Num. 27:18, 23; Deut. 34:9). With this act God bestowed upon Joshua His Spirit to enable him to fulfil his appointed task. Joshua was not of course ordained to take Moses' place either as a priest or as the mediator of the Word of God, but simply in civil and military leadership of the people. He was a lay-governor under the Kingship of God. This was in a different sense an act of *lay ordination*.

Laying On of Hands in the New Testament

The first case of laying on of hands was that of the seven elder-deacons in Acts 6. Here, as we have noted, hands were laid on the seven by the congregation, not by the apostles (except according to Codex Bezae), but they were set before the apostles, to indicate that the apostles had part in the act. It was, however, an act of lay ordination like that of the Levites in the Old Testament. At the same time the language used in the Old Testament of Joshua's ordination is reflected in Acts, in the choice of seven men in whom there was the Spirit. But again the language also seems to reflect the appointment of the seventy elders in Numbers 11:16, when, without any laying on of hands, God put His Spirit upon them to enable them to fulfil their office on appointment to the Presbytery of Israel. The laying on of hands upon the seven elder-deacons in Acts was accompanied by prayer, and these ordained were given the Spirit in fulfilment of their ministry. The fact that the apostles did not lay hands on them suggests that they were not being appointed as their deputies, but only as their assistants (i.e. as Levites!).

The instance of the separation of Paul and Barnabas by the command of the Spirit and their ordination at the hands of a group of prophets and teachers to which they belonged at Antioch seems to be (as Professor Daube suggests) a case of ordination for special embassage, in which they were commissioned to carry out a particular task on behalf of the rest. They were not ordained as "Rabbinic" pupils or disciples, but rather sent out as "apostles" of the community on a limited mission. The language used here, e.g., "separate me Paul and Barnabas", also suggests that used of the Levites in Num. 8:6f. It does not seem to refer to ordination in the proper sense. This sort of thing was a common Rabbinic practice in the second century, but may well have been used earlier.

The most important instance of ordination by laying on of hands in the New Testament is that of Timothy, described in two verses, 1 Tim. 4:14 and 2 Tim. 1:6, which have to be taken together with the other passages in Timothy and Titus regarding the appointment and ordination of other ministers.

In 1 Timothy 4:14 we read: "Neglect not the gift that is in thee which was given thee by *prophecy* with the laying on of hands of the presbytery." In 2 Tim. 1:6, we read: "Stir up the gift of God which is in thee through the laying on of hands." Putting these together, as I think we must, I make the meaning to be as follows: Timothy has been carefully instructed in the faith and trained in the *didaskalia* which he exercises; in that training it was clear that he was called to the ministry, that God had imparted to him a gift for its fulfilment; at the same time that gift is looked on as imparted formally through the act of laying on of hands, authorizing him as an accredited teacher and minister, but used by God as the means of imparting to him a *charisma* for the ministry. The act of laying on of hands has been carried out by Timothy's teacher Paul, and by the presbytery acting together. It is possible, as Professor Daube suggests, that the laying on of hands of the presbytery (*epithesis ton cheiron tou presbyteriou*) is simply a Rabbinic term for "the ordination of elders" (*semikhath zeqenim, Bab. San.* 13 b). But it seems more likely that it means that the presbytery as a whole laid on hands, while Paul acted along with them and doubtless presided over them in the act of ordination. The fact that Timothy, who is put in charge of missionary churches by Paul and commanded to appoint elders in them, is not to lay hands suddenly on people, indicates that he would himself be the chief minister in ordaining presbyters in that area under his supervision, but that he should only do it after due and careful training. According to Rabbinic rules a man was not to be ordained to teach until he had reached the age of forty. It may be with that in mind that Paul exhorts Timothy not to let anyone despise his youth, for, young as he is, he is fully authorized by Paul and the presbytery to undertake his ministry.

This instance is of fundamental importance for a number of reasons:

(a) It provides us with a clear case of what even Professor Daube (who sees it, however, as parallel to Rabbinic ordination) calls "apostolic succession". Timothy is not appointed to be an apostle, but he has the full authorization of Paul the Apostle to do the office of a minister, and indeed of a bishop; and as such he is to fulfil the same office in ordaining others as Paul fulfilled in ordaining him.

(b) But this ordination is a corporate act of the presbytery. It was the presbytery that was the repository of authorization at the local level, although the presbytery had also to be acting within the sphere of the apostolic commission and mission, a link that was supplied by St. Paul. It is not suggested that it was the local presbytery that joined with Paul in ordaining Timothy. At any rate it is clear that the presbytery is the medium of ordination although

Paul has a special part in it, and Timothy afterwards takes a similar place in the ordination of others. Presumably, however, he would not act apart from the presbytery, except perhaps in founding a new church and appointing and ordaining new presbyters, in which instance he would be the authorized person acting within the apostolic commission to undertake that; but once established the presbytery would act as a body with Timothy. Here both "presbyterian" and "episcopalian" elements are clearly held together.

Now in interpreting what the New Testament has to say about ordination and its adaptation of Old Testament rites, we have to remember that nowhere does the New Testament take over an Old Testament rite and develop it as such. What it always does is to lay several images or rites together, elements of which are then used in the freedom of the apostolic Church for its own purposes in forming a new image or a new rite which derives its significance not from the Old Testament ceremonies or images as such but from Christ and from what the apostolic Church makes of it. How then are we to interpret the New Testament concept of ordination?

(1) The first thing to note is that by selecting this rite of laying on of hands, which was essentially a *lay rite* both in the Old Testament and in Judaism, the Christian Church made it decisively clear that the Christian ministry was not to be interpreted in the sense of the priesthood of the Old Testament. That had been fulfilled in Christ who alone is Priest. But because all that was fulfilled in Christ, permanent elements of significance in it might well be transferred from Christ to the interpretation of the Christian rite. That is what happened.

(2) The main element in the laying on of hands seems undoubtedly to be the commissioning of ministers of the Word to proclaim the *kerygma* and teach the *didache* in obedience to the apostolic witness to Christ and in following their example and ordinances. Ordination is for those who labour in the Word and carries with it acknowledged authorization to do so, authorization that derives from the apostolic commission as an attestation of the tradition of the apostolic teaching and preaching of the Gospel. Here we recall the old rites of consecrating the king by filling his hands with "the testimony", and the consecrating of the prophet through whose Word it is God who acts and rules.

(3) But this ordination has other elements associated with it; the gift of the Spirit, the bestowal of a special *charisma* for the ministry; and it is performed with prayer. It is difficult to resist the conclusion that, while in the Old Testament three different sets of expressions are used to describe three different forms of laying on

or lifting up of hands, the New Testament seems to blend elements of all three together. That was certainly done immediately after New Testament times. Thus in addition to the strict concept of *samakh,* commissioning with authority to minister the Word, ordination also draws into its orbit the concept of blessing the one ordained through prayer, and calling upon him the gift of the Spirit, who brings a special *charisma* to the one ordained for the fulfilment of his ministry. But also the other idea found in the practice of *samakh* in the Old Testament is not absent: that of offering or presenting the one upon whom hands are laid before God, symbolized by the presentation of the seven before the apostles, as Joshua was presented before Eleazar by Moses when he ordained him, or the Levites were presented before the Tabernacle and then offered to God. That is a concept which Paul applies to his missionary congregations; he offers them to God as an oblation. According to Calvin this element is a powerful ingredient in ordination, for the ordinand after the analogy of the Old Testament sacrifices is through laying on of hands offered to God for His service and so consecrated. This act of ordination takes place in the Name of Christ the King and Head of the Church, so that all the ordinand does when ordained is to be done in the Name of Christ. That Name is his sole authority; nothing is to be done apart from it. But to ordain in the Name of Christ, and to act in the Name of Christ, is to act within the Self-consecration of Christ on our behalf, as the language of the Name of God declared by Christ to the apostles in John 17 indicates.

(4) Ordination thus means ordination in the sphere where we are all consecrated through participation in Christ's Self-consecration on our behalf. We recall that the disciples were specially related to the Self-consecration of Christ at the Last Supper, for in His solemn prayer of consecration they were associated by Christ with Himself as those who would take His Word to others so that others would believe through their word and be drawn into the unity of the one Church of Christ. We cannot dissociate ordination in the Name of Christ from that fact. Those ordained are to be regarded as drawn in a special way within the sphere of Christ's Self-consecration so that it is only as they share in His Self-consecration that they can minister the Word to others in His Name. It is in this connexion then that we have to see the relation of ordination to participation in the Lord's Supper, and see the Lord's Supper as the New Testament counterpart to the meal of consecration in which Aaron and his sons participated at their consecration, "a meal of thanksgiving and praise". That expression is reflected in

an important passage in Hebrews 13 which speaks of the ministry in several injunctions and adds: "Through him then let us offer up a sacrifice of praise to God continually, that is the fruit of the lips which make confession to his name continually." It was not unnatural therefore that in very early times, as in the *Apostolic Constitutions,* the rite of ordination to the ministry was looked upon as being brought to its completion when the one ordained first celebrated the Lord's Supper, for it was when the gifts of bread and wine were put into his hands that the Lord Himself fulfilled the act of consecrating His servant to His ministry, as He consecrated the apostle-disciples at the Last Supper. It is significant therefore that all the earliest consecrations and ordinations known to us took place in a Eucharistic context. This is a practice that should still be followed. The act of the presbytery in ordination should be followed by the celebration of Holy Communion in which the newly ordained person should dispense the Sacrament for the first time. The early Church of Scotland practice of "fasting" at ordination seems to have been derived from the old rite of the consecration of the priests with its seven days of separation.

The Doctrine of Ordination

In gathering up our discussion to present a doctrine of ordination we must consider it from three aspects:

(1) The source of ordination: its derivation from Christ through the ministry of the Church.

(2) The end of ordination: that to which a man is ordained determines the nature of ordination.

(3) What the act of ordination means and how it is carried out.

(1) *The source of ordination.* Who is it who ordains a man to the ministry? In answer to that question we have to give the unambiguous answer: Jesus Christ Himself. Ordination is His act. It is His authority that stands behind it, and therefore it can be done only in His Name. But Christ ordains within His Church which He founded upon the apostles and it is through that Church that He acts. Here we are confronted with a fundamental duality, but it is also the fundamental duality of Revelation. Revelation is the act of Christ which is brought to bear upon us directly through His Spirit, but it is Revelation which He communicates to us through the Word historically mediated in the Holy Scriptures. The risen and ascended Lord has bestowed His Spirit upon the Church, but the Spirit utters to us what Christ has already said: He does not speak of Himself and does not teach us anything new, but takes what

Christ has already revealed and leads us fully into its Truth. The Church is thus bound to the New Testament Scriptures, but in and through the New Testament Scriptures the risen and ascended Lord communicates Himself directly to His Church in the communion of the Spirit. So it is with ordination. It is the risen and ascended Lord who acts directly through His Spirit ordaining His servant to the ministry, but He does that in and through the Church which He has once and for all established in the apostles and bound to the Revelation which He has committed to the Church through the apostles.

The Church is bound to act in obedience to the apostolic teaching and commands, and through them it is bound to the historical Jesus Christ. When the Church from age to age ordains men to the ministry in the Name of Christ, it does that only within that obedience to the apostolic teaching and ordinances, and only within the sphere of the apostolic commission and mission given by Christ in founding the Church. That duality is apparent already in the New Testament Church. It is the risen and ascended Lord who bestows gifts upon the Church through the Spirit, but these gifts are bestowed for exercise within the one Church founded upon the apostles and within the sphere of their commission by Christ. The apostles appointed the rite of the laying on of hands to mark out and delimit the sphere of their commission, and to attest the propriety of a ministry within that sphere. That laying on of hands cannot be regarded as determining or delimiting the sphere of the operation of the Holy Spirit, for although Christ has bound the Church to its foundation in the apostles, He is Himself sovereignly free over the apostles as the risen and ascended Lord. The laying on of hands cannot be understood therefore as securing or guaranteeing the presence or the operation of the Holy Spirit, but as the apostolically given sign witnessing to the presence of the Spirit, attesting the obedience of the Church to its apostolic origins and binding its continuance, and the continuance of its ministry, within the sphere of the apostolic commission and authority. It is Christ, not the apostles, not the Church, who bestows upon the ordained minister the Spirit and the gifts of the Spirit for the exercise of his office; nevertheless it is clear that the laying on of hands was given by the apostles with the promise of Christ to impart spiritual gifts for the fulfilment of the ministry.

Ordinarily and normatively we are to understand the laying on of hands as the apostolically appointed sign and instrument used by the Spirit in bestowing the *charisma* for the ministry. Its necessity is one of obedience to the apostolic ordinance, and it attests that the ordination of the ministry derives from the historical Jesus and His historically communicated authority to the apostles. But the historical Jesus is risen and ascended, and it is He who from generation to generation continues to bestow His Spirit upon the Church and continues to bestow the grace-gifts for the ministry of Word and Sacrament within the Church. Therefore it is Christ the living Lord who is the actual Ordainer in ordination, although He makes use of the ministers who have been sent by Him already to carry out the ordinance within the Church on earth. It is only in this togetherness of "the Risen Lord" and "the historical Jesus" who is one Lord Jesus Christ, the King and Head of the Church, that we must think of ordination. The risen Lord sends us back to the historical Jesus and sends us back always to the commission He gave to the apostles, so that ordination is through the historical communication of the apostolic Word and the apostolic commission. The historical Jesus still commissions His ministers through that external and historical succession, and therefore the historical mediation or communication of ordination is of fundamental importance as attesting the binding of the Church to the historical Jesus and the historical Revelation.

The Church which separates itself from the historical Jesus ceases thereby to be Christ's Church, for it cuts itself off from its historical rooting and grounding in the historical Revelation and Incarnation. But within that historical communication it is the risen Lord Himself who ever comes to His Church acting obediently in His Name and Himself ordains. He Himself is really present where we meet in His name to obey His command, and He fulfils what He promises, and His presence in grace and in the power of His Spirit undergirds all our actions. We rely in all ordination therefore not upon the faithfulness of the Church, nor upon the unbroken nature of the historical succession, for these are all involved in the relativities and contingencies of this fallen world; but upon the faithfulness of Christ who remains with His Church that lives and acts in His Name. It is His covenant faithfulness undergirding our weakness and faltering faithfulness, and renewing our participation in Him, that is the ground of our reliance in every act of ordination.

It is this same fundamental duality in ordination that gives the concept of the so-called "validity of orders" its elusive ambiguity. Validity must refer absolutely to the fact that it is Christ the Lord who ordains, and ordains to ministry in the Church of God. He it is who honours that ministry as His own gift to the Church and makes it efficacious through His Spirit. But validity also refers to the responsible transmission of authorization from generation to generation, attesting the obedience of the Church in all its ordinations to the apostolic teaching and ordinances. Because this involves historical communication and responsible action it involves a duly intended and orderly act of ordination. It cannot be given in abstraction from the ordering of a Church's life, from its discipline and polity. Thus validity has also a juridical aspect, in which the term is relative to the legal structure of a Church in history. It refers to the responsible authorization of a Church in history, which orders its life and discipline in obedience to the apostolic Church and therefore is bound up with the canonical way of administering life and discipline in that Church.

In the Church of Scotland we ordain a man to the ministry of the Word and Sacraments in the Church of God, because we believe it is Christ Himself who ordains, but in ordination the Church (through its authorized ministers) commits to him due authorization to minister the Word and Sacraments within the discipline of the Church of Scotland within which he also promises at ordination to be subject to the Church. But the Church of Scotland does not thereby claim that, in that sense of authorization, it has authorized its ministers to administer the Word and Sacraments in every other Church. It does not necessarily acknowledge the authorization of those ordained in other Churches as giving them authority to administer the Word and Sacraments in the Church of Scotland, but it does not for that reason question the validity of their orders in the sense that their ordination is an act of Christ and is honoured by Him in making their ministry efficacious. The Church of Scotland does claim, however, that in obedience to the teaching and ordinance of the apostles "the laying on of hands of the presbytery" is the proper and responsible way of ordaining the ministry and of transmitting in the historical communication of the Church due authorization for the ministry of Word and Sacraments within the sphere of the apostolic commission and mission. While it acknowledges that authorization for the ministry of the Word and Sacraments is inescapably bound up with the discipline of the Church of Scotland and is therefore relative to its own structure and law, it claims that its careful and orderly transmission of ordination from generation to generation is in full conformity to the apostolic ordinance and teaching, and therefore reaches beyond what is merely relative to the particular legal institutions of the Church of Scotland itself to what is valid in the Church of God.

(2) *The end of ordination*. Ordination means ordination to the ministry of Word and Sacraments, that is to dispensing Word and

Sacraments. Strictly, therefore, "ordination" should be used only for the order of those who dispense the Word and Sacraments. It is using "ordination" in a somewhat loose sense to speak of ordaining deacons or deaconesses or ordaining elders, for they are not ordained to dispense the Word and Sacraments but are set apart or consecrated to assist in that ministry, even though a rite of laying on of hands may be used. A rite of laying on of hands is used also in some baptismal rites or in confirmations, but it does not therefore mean that those who have hands laid on them are ordained— what determines ordination is the end to which ordination is directed and intended by the Church. This involves two important points.

(a) That which a man is ordained to minister, the Word and Sacraments, is more important than ordination. Ordination is in order to minister the Word and Sacraments, and therefore ordination is subordinate to the Word and Sacraments which it serves. In other words, the ministering of Word and Sacraments is subservient to the Word and Sacraments themselves. The ministry is but an earthen vessel, as St. Paul put it, but it contains the heavenly treasure, and must never be confounded with the heavenly treasure. Therefore in the ministering of the Word and Sacraments, the mysteries of God, the ministering itself must be dependent upon that which is ministered and can never exalt itself over it. Ordination does not give the minister authority over the Word and Sacrament, but sets him in a servant-relation to them. They are always transcendent to the ministry and their efficacy cannot be tied to the ministry or only be relative to the worth of the ministers. The very authority which a minister has for ministering Word and Sacraments lies in the Word and Sacraments and not in himself—that is another way of saying that the ministry is at every point dependent upon the apostolic Word and Ordinances, for it is through the apostles that we have committed to us the Word and Sacraments and it is only in obedience to the apostolic ordering of the ministry that we administer them.

(b) There can in the nature of the case be no higher ministry than that of the ministry of Word and Sacraments, for that would be to suppose that there was a higher authority than that of the Word and a higher sanction than that of the Seals of the Word directly instituted and given by Jesus Christ. If ordination is defined by its end in the ministry of Word and Sacrament, and Word and Sacrament are more important than the ministering of them, it follows that there is only one order of the ministry in the proper sense; that of the minister dispensing Word and Sacraments. The order of the presbyteral ministry is not only the highest order, but in the strict sense the only order of the ministry. Other so-called orders are either for the assistance of this order or for the convenience of maintaining unity and concord and discipline among those so ordained. The fact that there is only one order of the ministry in the strict sense is the meaning of the so-called parity of ministers in a Presbyterian Church, but this does not preclude distinctions in jurisdiction either in the Church Courts to which presbyters are subject or among presbyters themselves. Thus, as Calvin says, "The political distinction of ranks [i.e. distinctions in Church polity, not 'politics'] is not to be repudiated, for natural reason itself dictates this in order to take away confusion; but that which shall leave this object in view, will be so arranged that it may neither obscure Christ's glory nor minister to ambition or tyranny, nor prevent all ministers from cultivating mutual fraternity with each other, with equal rights and liberties."[4]

There can therefore be no doctrinal grounds for any distinction between a presbyter and a bishop or a presbyter-bishop, nor any ground at all for a distinction in order, though there may well be ecclesiastical or historical grounds for making a distinction in function and therefore for adding some measure of jurisdiction to one presbyter to enable him responsibly to fulfil that extra function. But such a distinction in function could not make a bishop more of a minister or give him a higher ministry in relation to Word and Sacrament than that of any other presbyter. The doctrine of parity of ministers must not therefore be confused with differences in function or relative distinctions in jurisdiction. Thus in the Reformed Church we acknowledge that some presbyters are set apart and are acknowledged to have a special *charisma* for teaching doctrine and for keeping a "watching brief" over the purity of the Church's proclamation and doctrine in obedience to the teaching of the apostles. These are the "doctors" of the Church, and they are responsibly commissioned to exercise their functions with appropriate jurisdiction, not in their case in Church or pastoral government, and so they are not given ecclesiastical jurisdiction of any kind but in the teaching and training of the ministry and in doctrine. That does not in any way do away with "the parity of ministers" in the sense that the doctors have a higher ministry or a superior order to other presbyters. The same would apply to the "bishop-in-presbytery", although in that case where his special function would be concerned with pastoral discipline he would

4. *Comm. on Num.* 3:5.

naturally be set apart for that in the appropriate way by the Presbytery, in "the laying on of hands by the Presbytery", so keeping him under its own authority but commissioning him to act responsibly for it in the ways the Church would lay down. Here the nature of "the laying on of hands" would be determined by the end intended and determined by the Church. In this instance it would not be determined simply by the Word and Sacraments, but by something else: a function to act as spiritual counsellor and guide to his fellow-ministers, and to act in a presidential capacity or even a representative capacity for the presbytery in its solemn acts and deliberations. But because the bishop-in-presbytery could be given no higher relation to the Word and Sacrament—that is in the nature of the case impossible—he could have no higher order than that of his fellow-presbyters.

(3) *What ordination is and how it is carried out.* Ordination is the solemn setting apart to the ministry of Word and Sacraments of a man who has been called to that ministry. It is an act in which the whole Church concurs, although the act of ordination itself is carried through by those who have already been ordained, for they only are the proper instruments for "regular" association of others with the commission they have received and which they in obedience to the apostolic ordinance devolve upon others. It is not that they thus transmit "grace", or the Holy Spirit, nor that they transmit divine authority; but in so doing they attest that it is Christ alone who acts, and they make evident that they are acting only in obedience to Christ's own commissioned apostles. But, as we have already noted, the act of ordination is also the lawful act in the discipline of the Church where responsibility in office is devolved in an orderly or canonical way upon others in succession to their fathers in the same office. It is an act that takes place in space and time: in the space or place of the Church where Christ has put His Name on earth, the visible Church, and in the time or historical continuity of the Church which Christ has sent out into history to proclaim the Gospel of His Kingdom until He comes again. Thus the physical, visible, and temporal action in ordination attests the binding of the Church to the physical, visible, and temporal incarnation and the Church once and for all founded by the incarnate Son on the apostles and prophets. Just as the Church's life and worship is neither timeless nor spaceless, but in the historical and risen Jesus Christ, so the act of ordination is not a spaceless and timeless act in which the visible and temporal element is of no importance.

On the other hand, the act of ordination is not a Sacrament in the proper sense—although Calvin himself was not averse to calling it a sacrament. It is certainly not a "Sacrament of the Gospel", that is a sign and seal of a saving ordinance through which salvation is bestowed in the unity of Word and appointed Sign; but because ordination is the appointed ordinance with its accompanying and appropriate sign for the ordering of the ministry of the Word and Sacraments, it necessarily partakes of the sacramental character of the Word and Sacraments and is rightly performed only within the Church as the Body of Christ, within the Covenant-signs-and-seals of the Church's incorporation into Christ. No unbaptized person can ordain or be ordained, for no uncovenanted person can be commissioned within the ministry of the New Covenant; and no one who is not himself a communicant member of the Church can ordain or be ordained, for no one who has not himself shared in the communion of the New Covenant and in the Self-consecration of Christ, sealed upon His own at the Holy Supper, can be a consecrated minister of the New Covenant. Just because ordination has this setting within the Church's incorporation into Christ in Word and Sacrament, it must take place in the context of Word and Sacrament as well as in the context of the Church's solemn judicial action in a Sacral Court.

This dual aspect of the rite of ordination reflects its dual character. It takes place in and through an act of the Presbytery met and constituted as a Sacral Court of the Church. Ordination is not properly and validly enacted by any association of presbyters, but by an association of presbyters duly convened within and according to the discipline and constitution of the Church by a resolution of the appropriate court as a whole; for it must be an act in which the whole Church concurs and which therefore has the acknowledged authority of the Church. That is the judicial aspect of ordination, which has its appropriate ceremonies such as the interrogation and response, the taking of vows and the signing of the formula in the Church's roll, and the solemn act of laying on of hands, which in part is an essential legal act attesting the lawful and responsible bestowal of a commission or the canonical conferring of authority to minister the Word and Sacraments within the bounds of the Church and its mission. This judicial part of ordination is not carried out in and by itself apart, but only within the whole spiritual action of ordination, though it is particularly in the laying on of hands that the overlap between the judicial and the spiritual aspects of ordination is most apparent.

Ordination is primarily a spiritual act within the Church in which Christ Himself is the Principal Agent, and in which the ordained ministers (those preaching presbyters to whom it belongs to act thus in Christ's Name) act as servants of Christ and only in obedience to His commands. The whole act of ordination is therefore dependent upon the Word of God as mediated through the apostolic tradition. If ordination is by Christ in accordance with His Word, then it is carried out only in "sacramental" dependence upon His Word—it is the Word which commissions to the ministry, and the Word which is the sole repository of divine authority in the Church and which bestows that authority as the Church acts in obedience to it. The Word is the sceptre through which Christ the risen and ascended Lord continues to govern and rule His Church and continues to call men into His ministry and to command them in His service. Ordination takes place therefore in accordance with the apostolic Warrant, in solemn declaration of the Word, and in the context of the Church meeting to wait upon that Word in its proclamation through the heralds sent by Christ to the Church. Only when the royal proclamation of the Word of the King has been made does the Church through its ministers act in obedience to it in the ceremony of ordination.

The other parts of this ceremony are prayer and the laying on of hands. The *Westminster Form of Church Government* puts the laying on of hands first, but the *Second Book of Discipline,* following the order of the *First Book of Discipline* and the teaching of Knox and Calvin, puts prayer first. That indicates that the primary element in ordination is the *epiclesis,* the response of the Church to God's Word made in the prayer calling for the bestowal of the Spirit upon him being set apart to the ministry. It is Christ Himself who ordains through the sending of His Spirit, and it is entirely the divine intention and act that determines the nature of the ordinance and its effect. The emphasis upon the act of prayer as an *epiclesis* also makes clear that the formal act of laying on of hands, necessary and important as it is juridically, is not to be regarded mainly as a legal act, but as the apostolically appointed sign attesting that it is Christ who ordains, that it is the Spirit who acts, and that the rite of ordination has its root and ground beyond in the Self-consecration of Christ in His own prayerful Self-oblation on our behalf. Within that act of prayer the laying on of hands has its essential and indispensable place. But when it is taken within that act of prayer we must say with Augustine: "*Quid aliud est manuum impositio quam oratio super hominem?*" The imposition of hands is primarily the lifting up of hands in prayer, so that actual tactual laying on of hands is really secondary. On the ground of biblical teaching, however, in which it is clear that the act of *samakh* was the main ceremonial act, we lay stress upon tactual imposition as well as the laying on or lifting up of hands in blessing; for in the biblical teaching tactual imposition itself is recognized as an act offering and presenting the one who is the object of laying on of hands to God in dedication and consecration for His service. It is because of this extremely close relation between laying on of hands in prayerful offering and the lifting up of hands in prayer in blessing that many of the earliest books of Church Order omit its actual mention, for the stress was laid upon the act of prayer and was considered to be implied in it. That was the attitude of John Knox in 1560, although in 1572 (if not actually earlier) the imposition of hands was restored in detailed action and has ever since been regarded as indispensable in the Church of Scotland.

Accompanying and preceding the act of ordination there are other rites which have their proper place and are designed to attest the fact that the person ordained is acknowledged as one who has himself received a divine call to the Holy Ministry, that his own private recognition of that call is confirmed by the Church acting through its duly constituted Courts, and confirmed by the congregation which has called him to be its minister in the Name of Christ. The act of ordination thus requires the *imprimatur* of the Church as a whole and the acclaim and acquiescence of the local congregation, who also take vows in support of the minister and in obedient acknowledgment of the fact that their minister has been *sent* to them by Christ Himself. The minister himself takes vows which bind him to the continuity of the Church's obedience to the apostles in doctrines and ordinances, and in which he solemnly promises to fulfil His ministry with devotion to Christ as His servant, and, without lording it over the flock, to seek their good in the Lord. At the same time he acknowledges that the government of the Church is agreeable to the Word of God, promises to be subject to its discipline, to take his due part in its affairs, and to seek the unity and peace of the Church. But in his undertaking these vows, as in the administration of ordination to him, the Church makes it clear that the minister acts not on his own charges or on his own resources, but only on the *command* and therefore only in reliance upon the *promise* of Jesus Christ who remains the same yesterday, to-day, and for ever, and who never fails to keep His Word.

15

ENCOUNTER

*Christ's Ministry Through His Whole Church and Its Ministers**

GOD DOES NOT SPEND THE MAJOR PART OF HIS TIME IN CHURCH. His first and last acts are the creation and recapitulation of all things. Even in carrying out his purpose of salvation he works not only through his church but also through other agents. This wider scope in the action of the triune God must be kept in mind when one studies the ministry of the church and the place and function of its ministers.[1]

We speak about Christ when we speak of the ministry, about what *he* does through his church in and for the world. (I) He joins in baptism new members to himself, letting them share in his ministry. (II) He appointed the aspostles to be the pioneers of his church, and his continuing presence draws the whole church into the apostolic ministry. (III) He gives grace to all the baptized, assigning to them their particular authority and function in his ministry. (IV) He lets the whole church share in his suffering, calling each member to be spent in his ministry in love and obedience to God and in love and service to men.

Only in the context of this total ministry of Christ through his

1. In this paper the term "ministers" refers to members of the church who have been entrusted with a special function, or office in the life and mission of the Church. The term "ministry" refers to what Christ does through the total membership of the church. We thereby reject the common equation of the term "ministry" with the ministers and their work. But at the same time, for the purpose of this paper, we do not use the term "the ministry of the laity" as it is identical with "the ministry of the Church."

*A contribution of the Department on the Laity to the Section on "The Redemptive Work of Christ and the Ministry of his Church" of the Fourth World Conference on Faith and Order held at Montreal in July 1963.

From *Encounter,* Vol. 25, no. 1 (Winter, 1964), pp. 105–129. Permission granted by Christian Theological Seminary.

Church in and for the world can the question about the authority and function of ministers within the church be answered. The structure of each of the following chapters is therefore as follows: (1) After a comparison between Christ's ministry and ours, (2) the ministry of Christ through the whole church is described; (3) Christ's service through ministers of the church is discussed, and (4) some questions are raised which need further clarification.

Some of the official preparatory documents for the Fourth World Conference on Faith and Order held at Montreal in July 1963 have been extensively quoted. By doing this we want to reaffirm these Faith and Order documents and sometimes expand or qualify certain statements. It is not wholly justified to say that "in the present ecumenical discussion on the understanding of the church, in so far as it happens under the auspices and direction of 'Faith and Order,' it is striking to find that 'Faith and Order,' quite rightly demanding a renewed attempt at an ecumenical understanding of the ministry of the Church, evidently thinks only about Ministry in terms of the Clergy or the body of ordained Ministers. It is striking, because it seems as if the Department of Faith and Order is unaware of the thinking and searching which is going on in its sister department in the World Council of Churches, the Department on the Laity."[2] To a great extent this was indeed the case in former Faith and Order studies, but the situation has fortunately changed.[3]

We are aware of the fact that the following treatment and division of the subject is too schematic and by no means exhaustive. We have singled out baptism and the apostolic, charismatic, and sacrificial ministry of the church, because these seem to be central in the present discussion on the ministry both within the Department on the Laity and the Commission on Faith and Order. Each chapter deals with the same Christ, the same church and the same ministers of the church. No opposition must be seen between the apostolic and the charismatic element or between ministry and sacrifice. What is truly apostolic is also charismatic and vice versa, what is true service and ministry is indeed also sacrifice. If we concentrate on what *Christ* does through the ministry of the whole church and through ministers, it must be clearly understood that

2. Hendrik Kraemer, *A Theology of the Laity* (London: Lutterworth Press, 1958), p. 10.
3. For a short review of the emergence of the concern for the ministry of the laity in the thinking of the Faith and Order movement, see *The Layman in Christian History,* ed. Stephen C. Neill and Hans-Ruedi Weber (London: S.C.M. Press; Philadelphia: Westminster Press, 1963), chapter 16.

we speak about the second person of the *Trinity*. God the Father
sent Christ, and they work now through the Spirit.

I. A PEOPLE BAPTIZED FOR SERVICE

1. *Christ's baptism and ours*

Through his baptism Christ was initiated into the ministry which
led him to the cross and resurrection. By seeking the baptism of
John, Jesus himself interpreted his baptism as a "baptism into
solidarity with sinners and the initiation of redemptive action,
baptism into obedience to the Father and love for the lost, a step-
ping into the unknown." Thus "the baptism of Jesus was consecration to his vocation as the Messiah who was the Servant of the
Lord . . . His baptism anticipated, so to speak, his entire life, from
the moment of baptism right on to death . . . It was also the way to
resurrection and exaltation."[4]

Similarly through our baptism Christ incorporates us and ordains us for participation in his ministry. "The outpouring of the
Spirit at Pentecost is the counterpart of what happened to Jesus at
his baptism . . . The same Spirit who remained on Jesus for his
messianic ministry has ever since Pentecost dwelt in the church,
which is the temple of his body." "For Jesus baptism meant that
he was consecrated as Messiah. For us baptism means that we are
consecrated as members of the messianic people . . ." "The life of
which baptism is the starting point is a life 'in Christ' . . ." "So
our baptism anticipates our entire life," and therefore "Paul's
ethics are essentially 'the ethics of baptism.' The one business of
our life is to realize, to give effect to, what was given to us in our
baptism . . ." "What happens in baptism is that my little life is
taken up into God's plan of salvation, the mighty movement of
salvation history whereby it is carried along towards its eschatological fulfilment at the '*parousia*' (the second coming) of Christ."[5]

2. *The ministry of all the baptized*

According to this understanding of baptism, to be baptized means
immediately to be called to the life of a servant. The Faith and
Order Report on Baptism states this clearly:

4. Faith and Order Report on "The Meaning of Baptism," in *One Lord,
One Baptism* (London: S.C.M. Press, 1960), pp. 53 ff.
5. *Ibid.*, pp. 54 ff.

a) *To be baptized is to live in and for Christ.* The "natural" thing in human life is to live simply for oneself. But the selfish, godless life is subject to the powers of corruption, the tyranny of sin and death. Man cannot live simply for himself without ruining both his own and other people's lives. It was in order to deliver us from this that Jesus Christ gave himself up to death, the one righteous for the many sinners. "One has died for for all; therefore all have died" (II Cor. 5:14). Christ died on the cross; by baptism we are united with him and made participant in his death; through baptism we have died with him. Baptism means that Christ draws us into his work of salvation. By nature we are members of "the body of sin" (Rom. 6:6) and "the body of death" (Rom. 7:24); by baptism we are grafted, so to speak, into "the body of Christ," of which we are made members. This means that we no longer belong to ourselves but to him. Hence the passage quoted from II Corinthians 5 continues as follows: "He died for all, that those who live might no longer live for themselves but for him who for their sake died and was raised" (v. 15). The fruit of baptism is obedient service. To be baptized is to have a new Lord and to be in the service of Christ. But to serve the Lord is also to serve his church and to serve the world.

b) *To be baptized is to live in and for the church.* By baptism we are incorporated into Christ, made members of the body of Christ. But the body of Christ is his church. The baptized person is no longer simply an individual person, but a member of the church. By baptism one living stone after another is built into the temple of the Lord, one member after another into the body of Christ. All these members have a direct relation to Christ, who is the head. From him the whole body draws its increase and growth (Eph. 4:16). But in relation to one another and to the whole body, each member has its own special function of service and support to fulfil. All the baptized are called to engage in a life of worship and prayer and in a work of service (*"ergon diakonias"*), in the church, "for the building-up of the body of Christ" (Eph. 4:12). By the quality of their service and the contributions they make, the growth of the body may be promoted or retarded. "For the whole body is joined and knit together through that which every member supplies, according to the working in due measure of each part" (Eph. 4:16).

c) *To be baptized is to live in and for the world.* To be baptized means to be delivered from the powers of the world and to have a place as a member in the body of Christ. The baptized has his citizenship in heaven (Phil. 3:20), and is therefore exhorted to set his mind on what is above, not on what is on earth (Col. 3:1 ff.). This has often been interpreted in the church as meaning that the Christian ought to be unconcerned with earthly affairs, having as little as possible to do with the world, and that the church ought to separate itself from the world as much as possible. Baptism declares on the contrary that the work of Christ has to do with the world, and the kingship of Christ, which the Father has given him, has to do with the world. Since all power in heaven and on earth has been given to him, his command is, ''Go ye therefore''—out into the world, the whole world. This is his charge to the church and his charge to every baptized person. The place of the baptized is wherever in the world there is room for service, for the baptized, like his Lord, is a servant. Baptism proclaims that, as the Christian has been called out of the world, so he returns to the world as its servant; or only in his union with the world's redeemer is he free to participate creatively and fully in its common life. It is part of this service that he should praise God by the way in which he lives his life; by the worship in which he exercises the priesthood of all believers; by the manifesting of Christ's love through a compassionate concern for the world of men; and by taking his place as a responsible participant in the world's life.[6]

It must be acknowledged, however, that in most churches and for most Christians baptism does not play this decisive role. In the understanding and experience of most church members it is neither a real incorporation into the community of the committed nor an ordination for full participation in Christ's ministry. This devaluation comes mainly from the separation of baptism and faith. The remedy is not necessarily believers' baptism. Has baptism immediately to be related to the faith of the baptized or can it initially be administered on the basis of the corporate faith of the church? While this question may remain open, there is no doubt that under no circumstances may baptism and faith be separated. Where the faith of the parents or the local church is obviously lacking children's baptism is an equally irresponsible act as the baptism of unbelievers. Only the recovery of the full meaning of baptism can save our talk about the ministry from irrelevance.

3. The basic ordination of baptism and the special ordination of ministers of the church

Baptism is the ordination into the apostolic, charismatic and sacrificial ministry of the church. What this means and what it implies

6. *Ibid.*, pp. 68 ff.

for all who are baptized will be spelled out in the next three sections. Here we want only to insist on the fact that this ordination of baptism is basic for the whole study on the ministry.

One may understand and interpret any subsequent special ordination within the church quite differently, but this basic, once for all and life-long ordination of baptism remains valid. Every specially ordained minister of the church is and remains first of all a baptized member of the church. He or she continues to belong to the laity, if this term is derived from the biblical use of the word "*laikos,*" to belong to God's "*laos,*" to God's people.[7] It is therefore wrong to define the laity over against especially ordained ministers and vice versa.

However, the basic ordination of baptism does not exclude subsequent ordinations for special tasks. It is indeed possible and necessary to distinguish within the total baptized membership of the church persons who have been "set apart" through a special ordination for a special task.

The term "set apart" ("*aphorizein*") is often used and equally often criticized in this connection. It is a dangerous term: "To be set apart" translated into Aramaic means "a Pharisee"; whoever uses this term is in danger of Pharisaism. Nevertheless it is indeed one of the several biblical terms used for designating the action by which God singles out something or somebody for a definite purpose.[8] However, the term is by no means used only for especially ordained ministers of the church. In the New Testament it occurs in connection with the following three main acts.

a) In the last judgment the Son of Man will set apart men into two groups, as a shepherd sets the sheep apart from the goats (Matt. 25:31; *cf.* also Matt. 13:49). This ultimate setting apart does not happen in baptism. The church is not identical with all those who "enter and possess the kingdom" (Matt. 25:34). Baptized members of the church can never with pride and self-assurance look down on the outsiders. "Not only is the Church as a solidarity composed of sinners, bound up with the solidarity of all men, but through its solidarity with Jesus Christ, it is identified with sinners

7. This theologically significant and generally accepted derivation is etymologically probably wrong. In the ancient church the term "laity" was most probably derived from the general use of the word "*laikos,*" or belonging to the "plebs," the common non-consecrated profane people. See Ignace de la Potterie, "L'origine et le sens primitif due mot 'laic,' " *Nouvelle Revue Théologique,* LXXX (Sept.-Oct. 1958), 840–853.

8. Together with "*aphorizein*" other terms must be studied in this connection, such as, to call ("*kalein*"), to choose ("*eklegesthai*"), to appoint ("*tassein*"), to entrust ("*pisteuein*"), to lay on hands ("*cheirotonein*").

under divine judgment, and with the solidarity of mankind in suffering and guilt.''[9]

b) Nevertheless the church is set apart from the world. "You shall be holy to me; for I the Lord am holy, and have set you apart from the peoples, that you should be mine" (Lev. 20:24). This setting apart happens in a manifold way: when in the synagogue of Ephesus some Jews proved obdurate, "speaking evil of the new way before the whole congregation, he [the Apostle Paul] left them, setting apart his converts" (Acts 19:9). On the one hand, the world sets the church apart ("Blessed are you when men hate you, when they set you apart . . . on account of the Son of Man," Luke 6:22). On the other hand, Christians must set themselves apart ("Come away and be set apart from them, says the Lord," II Cor. 6:17; see the Pharisaic perversion of this by Peter in Gal. 2:15!). In the Bible this second setting apart is not directly related to baptism, but especially in a missionary situation it is at baptism where this visibly happens. "Baptism . . . marks the frontier of the Church as it faces the world in witness to Christ, in its renunciation of all evil.''[10] After baptism we find ourselves in a dialectic relationship to the world. "In calling the Church to live in, with and for the world, Christ leads the Church into conflict with the 'world.' Since Christ and the Spirit are uniquely present in the Church, the Church is not dissolved into the world. It is not absorbed in the sinful world to which it is sent as mission, but is engaged in continual struggle with it in the fulfilment of its mission to redeem. Yet the Church does not preserve its self-identity by arrogant assertion of itself as over against the world, or by protective isolation from the world. It is most surely separate from the sinful world when it most fully embodies and most humbly expresses the Servant-form of the incarnate Lord, and becomes the Servant suffering for the world, bearing in its body the dying of Christ for men, and thus demonstrating in action its willingness to make the world's suffering its own. Conversely, the church is most surely absorbed in the sinful world when it is afraid to spend its life for the world and seeks rather to save itself, when it becomes self-defensive and trusts in its own wisdom or strength, and when in spiritual pride it holds aloof from the world or in pride of power seeks to control the world for its own ends.''[11]

9. *Report on Christ and the Church* ("Faith and Order Paper," No. 38; Geneva: W.C.C., 1963), p. 60.

10. *Ibid.,* p. 45.

11. *Ibid.,* p. 24. (The term "world" is placed in quotation marks when it indicates the fallen world of sin and death under the rule of Satan in N.T. language.)

c) Within this set apart people there are certain persons set apart for a special ministry or task. "Paul, the servant of Christ Jesus, apostle by God's call, set apart for the service of the Gospel" (Rom. 1:1; *cf.* Gal. 1:15). Such a special setting apart happens also for specific tasks which need not necessarily imply a life-long ministry. Thus the Holy Spirit said to the congregation in Antioch, "Set Barnabas and Saul apart for me, to do the work to which I called them" (Acts 13:2). Here the purpose of our being set apart becomes clear: both God's people as a whole and certain persons within it are set apart for a service and mission according to the call of God. Setting apart then means to "delegate," to "commission." It is not so much a setting apart *from* as a setting apart *within* and *for*. There are no set apart, ordained, apostolic, charismatic, and sacrificial ministers within a people which would not share all these attributes and functions. There are only set apart ministers within a set apart people, specially ordained ministers within the people which has received the general ordination of baptism, special apostolic and charismatic ministries within the apostolic-charismatic church and special sacrificial functions within the sacrificial people.

Alas, the same is true with regard to this special ordination as we saw in the case of the basic ordination of baptism: the empirical reality does not demonstrate the true meaning of the act. Special ordination means too often not setting apart *within* and *for* the ordained people of the baptized, but setting *over above* and apart *from* the laity.

Ministers of the church are wrongly set *over above* the people. To lead, to have the oversight and therefore to exhort, does indeed belong to their genuine functions, as will be shown later. But this never means to "lord over" or to set the pattern. It is significant that the New Testament writers never created and used the term "*hypertage.*" On the contrary, they introduced the term "*hypotage,*" mutual submission. However, popular misconceptions of special ordination tend to make ministers the accepted Christian type: "They serve the Lord full-time!" "They are God's men!" This has led to a subtle clericalization not only of the church but of theology, of the concepts of mission, service and unity, and even of the person of Christ.

It is wrong for ministers of the church to be set *apart from* the people. Especially in the West, when a man is ordained, he takes up a distinctive *office* in the church and at the same time enters upon an *occupation* by which he earns his living. The important distinction between "office" and "occupation" is very often blurred in Faith and Order discussion on the ministry, disregarding the fact that in many Eastern churches and in economically poor churches this silent and often unconscious equation of office and occupation is by no means the norm. Even in the West the "Western pattern" no longer everywhere corresponds with reality (many professional nonordained church workers in economically rich churches, worker priests). Moreover, such an unconscious equation of office and occupation is dangerous and confusing. The fact of occupation is an immensely powerful thing. For most of us, our "job" determines where we live, the people we associate with, the skills we possess and, in subtle ways, contributes to our moral judgments, our interests and our whole mental and physical make-up. "Clericalism" (with its reaction in "anticlericalism") stems less from particular theories of orders than from clerical professionalism. That serves to explain why the churches of the Reformation, which in some measure owe their separate existence to a reaction against previous clerical abuses, so quickly succumbed to an equally stubborn clericalism. Each ordination for an office which at the same time becomes an occupation tends to set apart and isolate from, instead of becoming a commission within and for the people. We welcome therefore the emphasis laid on *A Tent-Making Ministry*[12] by the Division of World Mission and Evangelism. There will always be offices which because of the service involved must also be full-time salaried occupations. We plead, however, that in the discussions on the ministry the Western pattern be not uncritically accepted and that, for clarity's sake, the distinction between office and occupation be clearly made.

4. Questions to be studied

a) In most churches the incorporation aspect of baptism has—at least in theory—been maintained while the ordination aspect has to a great extent been lost. How can it be recovered? Should the total meaning of baptism be restored, including the renunciation of the devil, the immersion and the chrismation (anointing) as we know it from the baptismal liturgy of Hippolytus.[13] Or should one rather seek for a new interpretation of confirmation?[14]

12. *A Tent-Making Ministry: Towards a More Flexible Form of Ministry"* (Division of World Mission and Evangelism, WCC, 1962). A more extensive research pamphlet on the same theme will be published in 1963 by the same division.
13. Quoted for instance in Lukas Vischer, "Ye Are Baptized" (Department on the Laity, WCC, 1961), pp. 8–10.
14. *Cf.* Max Thurian, *Confirmation: consécration des laics* (Neuchâtel et Paris, 1957).

b) In the life of most baptized there is a tension between joining Christ's service in and for the church and joining his service in and for the world. Of course, the church is in the world and the baptized are the church, whether they are gathered for worship and any other manifestation of the church or whether they are in the midst of their daily work and "secular" leisure time activities. But time spent in our secular jobs cannot be spent also for church work in the narrow sense of the word, and vice versa. The question then is this, how much time and energy should members of the church spend in and for church gatherings and church activities in order to be most effective in Christ's service? How many or how few gatherings and activities should an obedient church have?

c) If baptism is the basic ordination of each Christian, what does special ordination add? What does it do that baptism does not? Thus: what is a minister that a layman is not?

d) The Western assumption that ordination for an office in the church is naturally to be combined with taking up a church occupation is neither biblical nor congruent with the experience of the church throughout the centuries and today. What, then, are the right criteria for judging where and when an office should or should not become also an occupation?

e) In most churches today, one can distinguish besides the normal membership three "ministerial" groups which often overlap: (1) Persons who through a special ordination have been entrusted with the office of the administration of the sacraments, the teaching and preaching of the gospel and pastoral oversight; usually this is a life-long charge and often (but not necessarily) combined with a church occupation. (2) Persons who are employed full-time by the church for various services; they may or may not be specially ordained for these services. (3) Persons who on a voluntary basis fulfill for a shorter or longer period ministries in the church without being ordained or paid. Is this an abnormal situation which should be corrected? What are the criteria for judging who should be ordained?

II. AN APOSTOLIC LIFE

1. Christ, his apostles and the church

"When the term was completed, God sent (*'apostellein'*) his own Son . . . to purchase freedom for the subjects of the law, in order that we might attain the status of sons. To prove that you are sons, God has sent (*'apostellein'*) into our hearts the Spirit of his Son"

(Gal. 4:4–6). God's apostolate through his Son is now continued through God's apostolate through the Spirit in the apostolic church. This apostleship is first of all a *mission,* a fact almost ignored in former Faith and Order discussions which were centred only on the question of the how of apostolic succession. To *what* do we succeed? It is this mission of reconciliation in and to the world into which we are called by becoming disciples and agents of Christ. The apostolic mission begins with prayer and worship ("God has sent into our hearts the Spirit of his Son, crying, 'Abba! Father'," Gal. 4:6). It is continued in a life of obedience and service which witnesses to the servant Lord whom the Father has sent.

Thus the apostle Christ lets the whole church share in his apostolic ministry. However, as an indispensable link between Christ and his church stand the Twelve, the personally mandated eye-witnesses of the Lord, the pioneers of the church. It was to them that Christ spoke, "As the Father has sent me, so I send you" (John 17:18). "God's sending of Jesus has its counterpart, and in a sense its continuation, in the commissioning of the apostles (Matt. 10:40; 28:18–19; John 20:21; Acts 9:17; 10:29). In their initial calling the Twelve were given a double function. They are the nucleus of the reformed Israel, and at the same time they have a mission to Israel (Mark 3:14; 6:7)."[15] In one sense the ministry of the Twelve was unique and untransmissible. They laid the foundation. The document of their unique ministry is the New Testament: "In its most definite sense the term 'apostolic' refers to the Holy Scriptures as the source and norm of the Church's existence throughout history. The Church lives by the New Testament, as the canon of its life and faith, and is begotten from age to age in this apostolic tradition through the gospel which they handed on, as it continues to be built up through the exegetical study of the Holy Scriptures."[16] Yet in another sense, the ministry of the apostles is continued from generation to generation. It is continued in its double function mentioned earlier: (1) The apostles were the nucleus and first fruit of the church; through the basic apostolic succession in which the whole church stands this pioneering ministry of being the church sent into the world is continued in the worship and daily life of all the baptized. (2) The apostles received also a mission to the church; through the special apostolic succession the ministers of the church continue that other apostolic task in their intercession and work for the church.

15. *Christ and the Church,* p. 57.
16. *Ibid.,* p. 54.

Three of the tasks most commonly attributed to the apostolic ministry are (a) the act of representation, (b) the authoritative teaching and disciplining, and (c) the pastoral oversight of the church so that it may worship and serve in unity. In the following we will show how these three tasks are being continued both by the whole church which stands in the basic apostolic succession and by the ministers of the church who stand in the special apostolic succession.

2. *The apostolic ministry of the church*

"It is the continuity of the redeemed life of the church in Christ which is the heart of the apostolic succession, or continuity in the apostolically founded church. Hence all members through baptism partake in the apostolic succession, all share in the one apostolic mission and are called to take part in the ministry of the Gospel."[17]

This is a new emphasis in Faith and Order Reports. When the conferences at Lausanne in 1927 and Edinburgh in 1937 discussed the apostolicity of the church, they not only ignored the primary mission emphasis in the apostolicity but also dealt with the subject of the apostolic succession exclusively from the point of view of the especially ordained ministers of the church. This was still the main emphasis at the Faith and Order Conference at Lund in 1952, although the Lund Report contains the following paragraph: "All agreed not only upon the continuity assured by the constant action of the risen Lord through the Holy Spirit, but also upon the value of some form of continuity in history, assured by some means under the action of the Holy Spirit. All would emphasize the apostolic continuity of Christian life within the Christian community of men and women, redeemed by the one Cross of Christ, seeking to follow the example and teaching of the same Master and inspired by the continuing presence of the same living Lord. Most would also regard the preaching of the Gospel and the administration of the sacraments as essential means of continuity."[18]

This rediscovery of the basic apostolic succession in which the total church stands by virtue of baptism is intimately related to the rediscovery of the role of the laity. It is not by chance that in all major confessions one speaks today about the *lay apostolate*.

This basic apostolic succession leads those who are baptized into Christian worship and a Christian way of life in the midst of

17. *Ibid.*
18. *Report of "The Third World Conference on Faith and Order, Lund 1952"* (London: S.C.M. Press, 1953), p. 25.

the everyday world. They have to continue what those who were first baptized did, who "met constantly to hear the apostles teach, and to share the common life, to break bread, and to pray" (Acts 2:42). This succession of discipleship draws all the baptized immediately into the succession of mission: "Go ye therefore and make disciples of all nations" (Matt. 28:19), a mission which happens not only and not primarily through organized evangelism campaigns, but through the quality of a Christian life in the everyday world which evokes astonished or irritated questions (I Peter 3:15).

a) The apostles were representatives of Christ and the church; they acted as a *"pars pro toto,"* as a representative part for the whole. By virtue of the basic apostolic succession groups of baptized and even individual members can become full representatives of the church. The worship service of a congregation, a saint's life in the midst of the secular world, a charisma suddenly manifesting itself in an everyday situation, a Samaritan healing wounded men somewhere on a highroad; all these are spontaneous representations of Christ and the whole church no less important than the official representations through the words and acts of especially ordained ministers in the fulfilment of their office.

b) The apostles were the authorized teachers and preachers of the gospel. By virtue of the basic apostolic succession all baptized Christians who persevere in the apostles' teaching (*i.e.* who let the gospel shape their life by prayerful study of the Bible, by using the means of grace given to us in the sacraments and by the discipline of Christian fellowship) have authority to teach and discipline. The power of the keys was given not only to Peter (Matt. 16:19), but also to the whole congregation (Matt. 18:17 ff.), because ultimately it is Christ's power and Christ's presence which authorizes any disciplinary action. The same is true of teaching. Even Paul's and Silas' sermons had to undergo the scrutiny of ordinary Christians in Beroea who were "studying the Scriptures every day to see whether it was as they said" (Acts 17:11). Indeed, Paul himself continually exhorted the congregations to use their spiritual discernment (I Thess. 5:21; I John 4:1). When there was flagrant sin, doctrinal error or schisms in a congregation, the local church as a whole and not only the ministers of this church or the sinners and schismatics were held responsible for the state of affairs (I and II Corinthians, the letters to the seven churches in Rev. 2-3). At present, however, doctrine is formulated almost exclusively by professional theologians and church leaders shape the discipline. The present reality is far estranged from what a recent Faith and

Order Report sees as the proper theological task: "Theology is not primarily a function of individuals but of the Church, in which Christians are called to think together and learn from one another..." "This search for the mind of Christ is a corporate task; it belongs to the Church to maintain doctrinal purity and to assimilate its thinking to the mind of Christ, so that it may in all things grow up into the head, and stand before the world as witness to the truth."[19] Indeed, the authority of the technical knowledge of the Bible which professional theologians draw upon must be complemented by the authority of that knowledge of God's person and work which men and women gain as they seek to be obedient in concrete secular situations.

c) Through their pastoral oversight of the local churches the apostles had a ministry of unity. By virtue of their basic apostolic succession all baptized Christians are entrusted with this concern for unity. A unity which includes only unity in doctrine, sacraments, and special ordination without the unity of Christians in the social structures of their daily life and work is still-born. This unity at the frontier is the main concern of all the baptized. Their basic apostolic succession commissions them to seek and manifest it. However, even in the most recent Faith and Order Reports the unity at the frontier is not given the weight and decisive importance it really has. The thinking on the unity of the church remains focussed on the unity possible in the light of those acts over which the ministers of the church have authority, *e.g.* the sacraments. Many baptized Christians have found and have manifested a deep unity among members of different confessions at their place of work or in their fulfilment of tasks in the church (*e.g.* the group of international civil servants in Brussels, many ecumenical youth movements, the predominantly lay committee of the Scottish Kirk Week). But this unity is on the whole not given any authority. It is restricted and judged at the table of holy communion by the official position of the church which has been substantially determined by the doctrine concerning the ministers of the church.

Because the basic ordination of baptism has been devaluated, the basic apostolic succession has also been weakened. The above description of the apostolic ministry of the whole church is a statement of faith rather than an account of empirical realities. A consumer church cannot be apostolic and thus missionary. Neither an other-worldly church nor a world-conforming church has that apostolic way of life which aroused the astonished or irritated

19. *Christ and the Church,* p. 50.

questions of men of other faiths or no faith. Immature Christians cannot truly represent Christ and his church. Biblical illiterates have no authority to frame doctrine and discipline. Neither confessional relativists nor parochial confessionalists can have the concern for unity at the frontier.

3. Apostolic ministers of the apostolic church

Throughout the centuries the second function of the apostles, namely their mission to the church, was continued through the work of the ministers of the church. Since very early in church history the continuity of this function has by many been related to episcopal ordination. Such episcopal ordination throughout the centuries is indeed a valuable sign for the continuance of the second apostolic function, but it does not guarantee either the basic apostolic succession of the whole church or the special apostolic succession of the ministers of the church. Only Christ, his presence, and his ministry, can guarantee continuance.

What is the function of these apostolic ministers within and for the apostolic church? How do they relate to the whole church's act of representation, its authority to frame doctrine and discipline and its concern for unity?

a) Like the apostles the apostolic ministers are called to be pioneers.[20] They have first of all a missionary character and task. They are called to cross frontiers, to go as representatives of the church into new areas and eras. In Western Christendom and its theologies the ministers of the church have been considered far too exclusively as pastors and church leaders at the expense of their function as pioneers, missionaries and forerunners of the church.

b) As soon as the apostolic presence and witness of pioneer ministers begins to result in the gathering of God's people in a given new area or time, the pioneer ministers receive the additional task of strengthening the nascent church. As Peter and Paul were appointed "to lend strength" ("*sterizein*") to the church (Luke 22:32; Acts 18:23), so all ministers are called to do. This strengthening function includes many things. It begins with the continuous intercession for the church. Paul wrote to the Christians in Rome, "Continually I make mention of you in my prayers," and when his converts in Galatia were in danger of falling out of grace, he was again in travail with them, first of all in the struggle

20. *Cf.* Anthony T. Hanson's most stimulating study on *The Pioneer Ministry* (London: S.C.M. Press, 1961).

of intercession. The strengthening includes then also all that Paul mentioned in Colossians 2:28-29: "Christ it is we proclaim. We admonish everyone without distinction, we instruct everyone in all the ways of wisdom, so as to present each one of you as a mature member of Christ's body. To this end I am toiling strenuously with all the energy and power of Christ at work in me." Certainly also the administration of the sacraments belongs to this strengthening function of the ministers of the church, although in the New Testament it is never explicitly said that only especially ordained ministers should administer the sacraments.

c) Like the apostles the ministers of the church are entrusted with the concern for unity. They are used by Christ for the "*oikodomē*," the building-up of his church. This building-up process began with Peter (Matt. 16:18), and Paul devoted his whole life to it. According to Ephesians 4:10-16, the ministers are given to the church in order "to mend the nets," "to adjust," "to put in order," "to equip for the fight" (all these belong to the original meaning of the term "*katartismos*" used in v. 12). The outcome of this is not only that the "saints" (*i.e.* all the baptized Christians) can now fulfil their work of ministry, but also that the church is being built up into maturity and full unity.

When the ministers serve the church in this pioneering, strengthening and unifying way, the whole church will manifestly live an apostolic life. Without the basic apostolic succession the specific apostolic succession is nothing. Yet without the service of those given men and women who stand in the specific apostolic succession the apostolicity of the whole church is in danger of withering away. The ministers must really serve, however, not domineer or manipulate, both of which would keep the church immature. The ministers are the helpers of the church and not vice versa. The tragedy of a great part of church life in all continents and confessions is, however, that this essential relationship has been reversed. Ministers have become the accepted Christian type who sets the pattern. They "mobilize the laity" in order to "use" them as their helpers, whereas it is their calling to be themselves the forerunners and helpers of the laity, so that the total church begins to cross frontiers, becomes mature and united for its ministry.

4. *Questions to be studied*

a) How can the apostolic church recover its primary missionary character, so that succession means first of all a succession in mission, in being the church sent into the world for the ministry of reconciliation? Static, introverted structures of the church and static, self-sufficient patterns of ministry hinder the rediscovery of this full apostolicity of the church. We welcome therefore the ecumenical studies on "the missionary structure of the congregation"[21] and on "flexible and missionary forms of ministry."[22] What do these two studies contribute to the Faith and Order study on the ministry?

b) To be representatives of Christ and the church, the baptized must be both near to God and near to the world of today. Their spirituality must be a holy worldliness. What are the marks of this lay spirituality and how can its growth be fostered?

c) To be forerunners and pioneers of the church the ministers must not be estranged from the everyday world. However, both the present theological training and the fact that most of them are professional church workers tend to alienate them from the workaday world. What is the remedy for this?

d) If all the baptized have to exercise their authority to teach and discipline and if theology is thus to become a corporate task of the church, theological training can no longer be restricted to ministers only, but must envisage the whole membership of the church. What does this imply for Christian education programs, the nature of sermons, the role of theological colleges?

e) If a main task of ministers is to strengthen all the baptized in the growth of maturity, their relationship to the membership of the church must become that of a partner in a conversation and not that of a prima donna before an audience. How can the prima donna image of the minister be shattered both in the minds of ordinary church members and in the minds of ministers?

f) The conversation between theological specialists and those who come to learn God's person and work mainly as they seek to be obedient to God in concrete secular situations must begin in the Commission on Faith and Order itself. Its present membership includes almost no persons of the above-mentioned second type.[23] Does this mean that the constitution (and language!) of the Faith

21. A study undertaken by the W.C.C. Department on Studies in Evangelism. See the periodical "Concept" (Geneva: W.C.C.), which reports about the progress of this study.

22. A study undertaken by the W.C.C. Division on World Mission and Evangelism. See note 12 and subsequent publications.

23. The present Commission on Faith and Order has 120 members, of which there are 111 ordained ministers having studied theology, 5 professional lay theologians, only 3 people in secular occupations and only one woman.

and Order Commission must be radically changed? Or does it rather mean that in the planning and the carrying through of all Faith and Order studies the Commission should constantly consult with *ad hoc* local groups of Christians who earn their living in a secular job and have specialized knowledge in other fields than theology? (N.B. What is needed is not in the first place a popularization of the results which Faith and Order commissions of professional theologians have reached, but consultation with theologically alert representatives of the whole membership of the church, especially also in the beginning stage of a study!)

g) What is the theological significance of the unity at the frontier which many baptized find today? Are matters of unity only to be decided on questions of ministerial order, and is the Lord's table to be only within the prerogative of the ministers? If not, how can the authority of all the baptized in the concern for unity be reestablished: through revolutionary (prophetic?) action against the advice of ministers, or how else?

III. A CHARISMATIC LIFE

1. Christ, the fountain of grace, and the charismata

"The grace of the Lord Jesus Christ and the love of God and the fellowship of the Holy Spirit be with you all." For centuries the Church everywhere in the world has been sent out for its work of ministry with these words of benediction. The grace of Jesus Christ accompanies the church. It gives its true state of life, its growth into fulness, and its dynamic ministry.

The apostle Paul introduced into the Christian vocabulary the term *"charisma"* for indicating that the church lives solely by grace and the power of the Spirit. He spoke on the one hand about *charismata* which are such specific gifts of the Spirit as those mentioned in Romans 12:6–8 and I Corinthians 12:8–10, 28–30. These can be quite ordinary and unspectacular things, such as the gift of administration or humble service and unexpected things which take the church by surprise, such as prophecy and the speaking in tongues. On the other hand, Paul called *charisma* all that God did for us in the history of salvation (Romans 5:15 f.; 11:29) or in our personal life, such as the event when God rescued Paul in a dangerous situation (II Corinthians 1:8–11). Later, in the time of the Pastoral Letters, the *charismata* were especially linked with the special ordination of ministers of the church (I Tim. 4:14; II Tim.

1:6). It would be wrong, however, to want to separate neatly these three meanings of the term *charisma*. It is a dynamic and open concept. Instead of setting up lists or classifications of *charismata* one does better to study the biblical criteria how to discern a *charisma: Charismata* are those gifts or events whose source is God's grace, whose purpose is a concrete service and whose nature is a manifestation of the power of the Holy Spirit (see the affinity of the terms *"charisma," "diakonia"* and *"pneumatika"* or *"energēma"* in I Cor. 12:1-6). *Charismata* lead to the confession that Jesus is Lord, they build up the Body of Christ and they result in the harvest of the Spirit whose first fruit is love (I Cor. 12:3; 12:7; 13).

How then does this given grace through the power of the Spirit affect the ministry of the church and its ministers? (a) It characterizes their particular state of life, (b) it lets the church and its ministers grow into the fulness of God's manifold grace, and (c) it assigns to each one his or her particular place and form of ministry.

2. The charismatic life of the church

a) The basic ordination of baptism initiates into a new state of life. Those who are baptized live by grace and no more by self-justification. The signs and premises of this charismatic state of life are the *charismata* which everyone in the church receives and whose steward (not owner!) everyone is called to be (I Cor. 7:7; I Peter 4:10). In this sense the church is a continuous Pentecost, a body of people who every day anew receive the new life in Christ through the Spirit. This charismatic state fills with wonder, not with pride. Wherever Christians begin to look down on men of other faiths or no faith, they lose their true state and herewith their church membership, beginning to live by merit and self-assurance instead of grace. *Charismata* set their stewards apart within and for the human community, they do not alienate men from their environment. *Charismata* make truly human, because they lead into a responsible dependence on God, into God's sonship.

b) This charismatic state is the condition for growth into the fulness of God's manifold grace. How does this growth happen? Firstly, grace creates personality and community at the same time: it is never given in general, but always to me or to you as a specific *charisma* (Rom. 12:3, 6). Therefore every baptized person is irreplaceable and indispensable. Yet all the great *charismata* texts lead up to the image of Christ's body. The same grace which gives individuality also incorporates. Therefore no member can live alone, merely edify himself, and forego the mutual edification in the body. Secondly, grace assigns each baptized person his God-given place and limits, and at the same time gives him power to grow beyond his natural place and limits. Grace disciplines the Promethean drive in man and gives the humility to accept a limited work of service. Yet each *charisma* is a manifestation of the renewing power of the Spirit, so that the very acceptance of the God-given limitation becomes the beginning of growth through the power of the Spirit.

· c) The charismatic state and growth lead the church to its charismatic ministry in worship and daily life, where all the given *charismata* are used for service. This manifests itself in manifold spontaneous services in the Christian community (Rom. 12:6-8). Most often, however, the charismatic ministry does not mean that something extra is done or planned. The church's ministry consists in the first place in its charismatic state and growth, in what the church is and becomes and not in what it does and plans. Christian work is not so much something special done besides our ordinary work, but it is ordinary work done with grace (Rom. 12:9-13:10).

Again we have described the church not as we see it but as Christ sees it and calls it to become. In fact, a church can "fall out of grace" (Gal. 5:4) into world-conformity or self-righteous religious activity. Therefore, God gives his church again and again a most important gift of grace, namely charismatic ministers, in order to maintain and strengthen the whole church in its charismatic life.

3. *Charismatic ministers of the charismatic church*

"Strikingly enough, the most extended exposition of ministry in the New Testament (Eph. 4:7 ff.) sets out from the dictum, 'Each one of us has been given his gift, his due portion of Christ's bounty.' The ministries of apostles, prophets, evangelists, pastors, teachers, are said to have been given to 'equip God's people for work in his service,' that by the conjoint ministry of the whole Church in dependence on its Head, all the members might attain to mature manhood, 'measured by nothing less than the full stature of Christ' (see Eph. 4:13-16). A more powerful statement could hardly be framed to indicate the importance both of the special ministries set within the Body of Christ and those given to the members generally, as well as the dependence of both on the one Lord. He maintains the unity of the Body and its ministries and enables the growth of all in himself. The nature of the Church as the people of the Spirit sets both the goal and the bounds of the labours of the special ministries."[24]

a) The particular state and authority of a minister do not reside only in the *charismata* whose steward this minister happens to be. For the inward and outward growth of the church, and in view of the fulfilment of its ministry, certain things have to be done continuously: pioneer work in areas where there is as yet no church, the teaching of the gospel, the administration of the sacraments, the pastoral oversight. A member of the church may be equipped with the most needed *charismata* for fulfilling one or several of these necessary functions in the church. He may therefore be called by the church to fulfil officially the appropriate function and, through a special ordination, be set apart within the church for serving the church in this way. However, not everybody who has received the *charismata* most needed for teaching, pastoral care, or leadership can thereby assert himself as a teacher, pastor, or leader in the church. He may be called to teach mathematics, to become a personnel officer in industry or a political leader. In this sense the state and authority of ministers are not based on *charismata,* but on the calling of the church which has discerned these ministers as men and women given by Christ to help the church. Nevertheless, there is an intimate connection between the state and authority of a minister and the *charismata* he must "rekindle" and "not neglect" (I Tim. 4:14; II Tim. 1:6). Often persons have to be called by the church who are not equipped with the *charismata* most needed for the work to be done. In these cases both those who call and the one who accepts the call have in prayer earnestly to seek for the *charismata* needed. The *charismata* may then follow the call instead of preceding it. However this sequence may be, for the full state and authority of a minister both the call (usually confirmed through special ordination) and the *charismata* corresponding to the given task are needed.

b) The *charismata* give diversity to the church and thus help it grow into the fullness of grace. "Having gifts that differ according to the grace given to us, let us use them." As there are "varieties of gifts" so there are also "varieties of ministry" (Rom. 12:6; I Cor. 12:4 f.). This is not only true for the whole church, but also for the ministers. A pattern which concentrates all functions within the church upon one man despises God's richness of grace. Only through a diversity of ministers working together in many different functions can the rich diversity of grace given to the whole church be evoked and be brought to flourish. God gives his church always

24. *Christ and the Church,* p. 56.

those *charismata* it needs for the fulfilment of its ministry in a given time and place. He may withhold well-known *charismata* and give quite new ones. Accordingly the pattern not only of the ministry of the whole church but also of the functions fulfilled by ministers is never static but changes. The church must have the courage to give place to new *charismata* and thus to new ministerial patterns. The sclerosis of the church's life consists to a great extent of patterns which were created by formerly necessary *charismata* whose time has now passed but whose patterns of service are not allowed burial. The renewal of the church's life, on the other hand, consists to a great extent of the new *charismata* being given the freedom to manifest themselves in new patterns of ministry.

c) Ministers in the church share the basic charismatic state, growth and ministry of all the baptized as described above. They are called to be pioneers of a life by grace in a world which wants to live by merit. Yet being the ministers of this charismatic church they are also called to special tasks. First of all, they have to follow Paul who wrote to the Corinthians, "I give thanks to God always for you because of the grace of God which was given you in Christ Jesus, that in every way you were enriched by him . . . so that you are not lacking in any *charisma*" (I Cor. 1:4 ff.). Only in this spirit of continuous thanksgiving can ministers believe that all the baptized have indeed received *charismata*. Without this belief everything goes wrong: ministers begin to consider themselves as the only charismatics, they begin to set the pattern of everything in the church, then they mobilize the laity for their own plans, teach them their own clericalized image of Christ and the church and thus "quench the Spirit" (I Thess. 5:19). Exactly this has happened over and over again in the course of church history. To be a minister of the charismatic church means, however, something quite different. While giving thanks for the charismatic church the ministers have to look out for the varied *charismata* given to the church here and now. They have to help these *charismata* in their flourishing (instead of being afraid of them). They have to direct all *charismata* to service in church and world. And as the manifoldness tends to lead to chaos they have to harmonize ("*harmologizein*") the *charismata* so that they serve in peace.

4. Questions to be studied

a) What is the relation between the *charismata* and ordinary natural gifts or events? Can one say (as the above suggested dynamic conception of the term *charisma* and the criteria of its discernment suggest) that each natural gift or event can become or cease to be a *charisma* according to the use made of it?

b) Most biblical passages seem to indicate that the *charismata* were mainly given for the up-building of the inner life of the church. Does this mean that what Christians do in secular jobs, in their families and citizenship, has nothing to do with the *charismata*? Or can one say that the *charismata* are given also for service in the world as the above exposition suggests?

c) The New Testament seems to suggest that *charismata* are only given to those who believe in Christ Jesus and have received the basic ordination of baptism; but many people outside the church live and serve in an obviously charismatic way. What does this imply for our conception of the church, its limits and its mission?

d) Does the Catholic pattern of ministers (bishop, priest, deacon) or any other traditional set pattern do justice to the manifold and changing *charismata*? If not, how can a flexible pattern of ministration within the church be found which is nevertheless a true manifestation of the Apostolic and Catholic Church?

e) Which forms of structure, budget and activities of a local and regional church do not stifle the given *charismata*, but examine and then either discipline or develop them?

IV. A SACRIFICIAL LIFE

1. Christ's suffering and ours

In the only two passages according to which Jesus spoke about his baptism, he related it to his suffering (Mark 10:38; Luke 12:50). "The baptism of Jesus, like his whole messianic work, was 'accomplished' through his death on the Cross."[25] Baptism is the beginning of the way of the cross, which is the specifically Christian way to victory. Christ the Servant became the Highpriest, offering himself as the Victim, and thus becoming the Victor. This is the pattern which characterizes also the church and gives depth to its ministry. There is a cheap "ministry" or "service," in which one serves without being spent. Service then becomes self-justification and self-glorification. However, in the Bible service is always costly. It includes suffering, self-giving, and sacrifice. The church and its members cannot fulfil their ministry and remain the same.

25. *One Lord, One Baptism*, p. 53.

According to the Gospels Christ never gave either to himself or to his disciples the title "priest." He spoke about his suffering and the suffering of his followers which is inevitably related to the willing submission to the will of the Father and to the fulfilment of the ministry. Theologians have perhaps been too preoccupied with Christ as Priest and have tried to define the ministry of all the baptized too exclusively in terms of the priesthood of all believers—a symptom of the clericalization of current theological thinking. When the author of the letter to the Hebrews painted Jesus as the Highpriest, he did so in order to show that Christ's whole obedience supersedes all existing sacrificial ritual and priestly service. The emphasis lies on Christ as the victim, the passover lamb that has once for all been sacrificed for us (*cf.* the words of institution of the Last Supper; I Cor. 5:7; Eph. 5:2; Rev. 5:6). The texts where the New Testament speaks about the church as a royal priesthood (I Peter 2:4–10; Rev. 1:5–6; 20:6) must be seen in this context of the self-sacrifice of Christ as passover lamb. "The high-priestly work of Christ consists in his complete oblation of himself in obedience and love to God and in love and service of men. That work, decisively done on the Cross, is continued by Christ in the Church. The priesthood of believers means that they are permitted and enabled to share in the continuing highpriestly work of Christ by offering themselves in love and obedience to God and in love and service of men."[26]

2. The church: a living sacrifice

The church fulfils priestly functions when it is gathered for worship: "Through Jesus, then, let us continually offer up to God the sacrifice of praise, that is, the tribute of lips which acknowledge his name . . ." (Hebrews 13:15). The church is a "holy priesthood, to offer spiritual sacrifices acceptable to God through Jesus Christ" (I Peter 2:5). This is certainly done most clearly when the church gathers in the presence of the Lord who has offered himself as the passover lamb, *i.e.* during the celebration of the eucharist. However, it would be wrong to think mainly or even exclusively of the eucharist and the church assembled for worship when speaking about sacrifice. The above quoted text from Hebrews continues, ". . . and never forget to show kindness and to share what you have with others; for such are the sacrifices which God approves" (*cf.* also Phil. 4:18). The text in I Peter 2 continues, "But you are

26. T. W. Manson, *Ministry and Priesthood: Christ's and Ours* (London: The Epworth Press, 1958), p. 70.

... a royal priesthood ..., to proclaim the triumph of him who has called you out of darkness into his marvellous light,'' and then the letter refers mainly to the suffering which Christians will have to endure for the sake of Christ in their everyday life. It is significant that Paul introduced quite secular terms for describing the worship acts and worship gatherings of the church, while he used often cultic and sacrificial terms for describing the everyday life of those who are baptized. "By boldly utilizing cultic terms to speak of aspects of its life which were in no sense cultic the early Church reflects its own understanding of the radical new context in which its worship in any sense must be understood."[27] Baptism is a *"mimesis,"* *i.e.* a dramatic presentation of what has to be worked out in a daily dying and rising with Christ. So every worship act must gather up and point to the basic worship of daily life, about which Paul wrote to the Christians in Rome, "I implore you by God's mercy to offer your very selves to him: a living sacrifice, dedicated and fit for his acceptance, the worship offered by mind and heart" (Rom. 12:1).

This is the deepest and most meaningful description of the ministry of the church and its members: a living sacrifice. Indeed, through the self-offering of Christ for us, those who are taken into this sacrifice can now be "holy," "blameless," "irreproachable," "acceptable," and "well-pleasing" (all terms which were used for describing a sacrifice). The church is now a "sacrifice" (Rom. 12:1; 15:16; Phil. 2:17) "presented" to God. The term "to present" has also the technical meaning of "bringing a sacrifice up to the altar" and this is possibly its meaning in Rom. 6:13 ff.; 12:1; II Cor. 4:4; Eph. 5:27; Col. 1:22, 28, and II Tim. 2:15. As such Christians are the *"pars pro toto"* for all nations, the "first fruits of humanity" (Rev. 14:4; James 1:18, and several times in the Pauline letters). Again, as Christ through his sacrifice became "the first-born," so through Christ's atonement the whole church becomes "the assembly of the first-born citizens of heaven" (Heb. 12:23). These are dangerous terms which inevitably mislead to the worst kind of religious pride as soon as they are taken out of the sacrificial context. The church is first fruit and first-born, because Christ associates it with his suffering. "We are God's heirs and Christ's fellow-heirs, if we share his sufferings now in order to share his splendour hereafter" (Rom. 8:17). These sufferings of Christ in his church are intimately connected with the sufferings of

27. *Report on Worship* ("Faith and Order Paper," No. 39 [Geneva: W.C.C., 1963]), p. 55.

the whole created universe which "groans in all its parts as if in the pangs of childbirth" (Rom. 8:22). The church fulfils its ministry only if it becomes the focus for the need of the world. All doubts, all sins, all sufferings must be remembered there. Instead of defending God against doubts and attacks Christians are called to open their hearts and their fellowship for the agony of the world, continuously struggling in intercession followed by the question, "What shall we do?" All the activities of corporate worship lead into the worship of everyday life where all the baptized are called to be spent as a living sacrifice.

Through Christ, its head, the church is now in fact this sacrificial community. Through the sin of its members, however, the church has continuously attempted to preserve its own life, its worldly privileges, powers and status. Here, too, the church has still to become what it is. Therefore Christ has given it ministers to be its forerunners and helpers in its sacrificial life.

3. Ministers, disciplined by suffering

The most vivid pictures about what a minister is and does have been painted by Paul in I Corinthians 3:18–4:13; II Corinthians 4:1–15 and 5:14–6:10. "Christ's underlings," "stewards of the secrets of God," "like men condemned to death in the arena," "a spectacle to the whole universe," "fools for Christ's sake," "weak," "in disgrace," "hungry and thirsty and in rags," "roughly handled," "disciplined by suffering:" this is only the beginning of a long list which speaks—just as the difficult text in Col. 1:24—about suffering with Christ for the sake of the church and the world. The astonishing thing is that the life of the ministers on the one hand reproduces in the church the life of Christ, and that on the other hand nothing is said of the ministers that could not be said of the church as a whole, even of any individual Christian. The ministers must carry out Christ's ministry of humble service and suffering, so that the whole church may be drawn into the same ministry and suffering which is for the sake of the whole world.[28]

In the light of this it is not astonishing that Paul sometimes used sacrificial language to describe his life and service. According to the pattern laid down by Christ he knows himself first of all to be a victim: "Captives in Christ's triumphal procession, God uses us everywhere to reveal and spread abroad the fragrance of the

28. *Cf.* Anthony T. Hanson, *op. cit.,* pp. 57–88.

knowledge of himself! We are indeed the incense offered by Christ to God'' (II Cor. 2:14 f.). Here, Paul used the sacrificial terminology in a figurative way, but he knew that the *"martyria"* (*i.e.* the witness) of Christ could lead to martyrdom in the literal sense of this word. "Yes, if I am poured out as a libation upon that sacrifice which is the offering up of your faith, I am glad of it, and I share my gladness with you all'' (Phil. 2:17). Only in this context does Paul also use priestly terms in order to describe his service: his whole life-work serves "to present (!) each one of you as a mature member of Christ's body'' (Col. 1:28). "My priestly service is the preaching of the Gospel of God, and it falls to me to offer the Gentiles to him as an acceptable sacrifice, consecrated by the Holy Spirit'' (Rom. 15:16).

The great temptation of ministers consists in seeking "to escape persecution for the cross of Christ'' (Gal. 6:12) and to become lords instead of servants disciplined by suffering.

4. Questions to be studied

a) What is the relationship and difference between Christ's suffering and ours? Biblical texts seem to suggest an intimate connection while much systematic theology makes a neat distinction between the two, insisting so much on Christ's unique compensatory and expiatory sacrifice, that the sacrificial dimension in Christian life tends to be forgotten. Can one say that Christ's sacrifice at the cross was a unique, once for all sacrifice of atonement, that in his church Christ continues, however, to offer sacrifices of praise to the Father and that he continues to suffer in the missionary and pastoral labor of the church and its ministers?

b) What is the theological significance of the fact that Paul used secular terms for designating the meeting for worship and often sacrificial terms to designate the everyday life of the baptized?

c) If every act of worship must gather up and point to the basic worship of daily life, what implications does this have for our forms of worship? What is the role of the total congregation and of its ministers in worshipping assemblies? What is the role of worship acts and assemblies for everyday life?

d) If ministers are to be forerunners and helpers of the church in its sacrificial life, how can they fulfill this function if they are in the relatively safe position of professional church workers?

e) What are the criteria for discerning the difference between the ecclesiastical baggage which the church must give up and the iron ration which the pilgrim people needs?

EPILOGUE: SURPRISED BY JOY

This paper as a whole, and especially its last section, has emphasized the aspect of suffering in Christ's ministry through his church and its ministers. This is a biblical emphasis and, we think, a necessary reminder today. However, it is not the whole of the biblical message. We are baptized into the death of Christ with a view to *the new life*. This new life is a reality more certain than all realities of this world. It is first of all a life of expectancy, for God has given us a "new birth into a living hope by the resurrection of Jesus Christ from the dead" (I Peter 1:3). "We *shall* also be one with him in a resurrection like his" (Rom. 6:5). Through the power of the Spirit the glorious future now already becomes present fact: "In baptism you *were* raised to life with him [Christ] through your faith in the active power of God who raised him from the dead" (Col. 2:12).

The firstfruits in this harvest of the Spirit are love and *joy* (Gal. 5:22). The term joy occurs often in the letters of Paul, who at the same time has spoken so profoundly about the suffering of Christ, his church and its ministers. "If my lifeblood is to crown that sacrifice which is the offering up of your faith, I am glad of it, and I share my gladness with you all. Rejoice, you no less than I, and let us share our joy" (Phil. 2:17 f.).

Indeed, the church is sent as the army of victorious victims under Christ the Victor. Christians know therefore that the sufferings of this time are no sufferings unto death, but *"ôdines," i.e.* birth pangs of the coming kingdom (Matt. 24:8; Rom. 8:22). Just as a woman in travail cannot escape into the past or the future because of the very real pains and yet in this present crisis concentrates all her thoughts and longings upon the coming joyful event, so Christians live in this world. Again and again in their labour they are "surprised by joy" (C. S. Lewis). Where there is no joy in the ministry of the church and the work of its ministers the most human and gracious element of all ministering is lacking.

16

HANS KÜNG

The Continuing Charismatic Structure

2. THE CHURCH OF THE SPIRIT

Freedom is demanded of the church precisely because freedom has been given to the Church. The indicative precedes and makes possible the imperative: ultimately it is not because freedom has to be struggled for and won that it is granted, but it is because it has been granted that it can and must be lived. True freedom is not rooted in man's existence, but comes to him from outside.

Freedom is a gift, a gift of God. The basis and origin of man's freedom lie not in man himself but in the freedom of God, in the freedom of his grace which freed us in Christ. "For freedom Christ has set us free" (Gal. 5:1)—Christ lived a life of service to others and of obedience to God's will which included his death, and he was then freed and glorified by God. How does this freedom come to men? Through the call of the Gospel: "For you were called to freedom" (Gal. 5:13). It is also the work of the *Spirit,* who takes possession of us in word and sacrament and awakens his freedom in us: "where the Spirit of the Lord is, there is freedom" (II Cor. 3:17). The *Spirit* gives the believer this threefold freedom from sin, law and death: "For the law of the Spirit of life in Christ Jesus has set me free from the law of sin and death. . . . To set the mind on the flesh is death, but to set the mind on the Spirit is life and peace. . . . But you are not in the flesh, you are in the Spirit, if the Spirit of God really dwells in you. Anyone who does not have the Spirit of Christ does not belong to him. But if Christ is in you, although your bodies are dead because of sin, your spirits are alive because of righteousness. If the Spirit of him who raised Jesus from the dead dwells in you, he who raised Christ Jesus from the dead will give life to your mortal bodies also through his Spirit which dwells in you'' (Rom. 8:2–11). Freedom is given to us when we accept the spirit which supports us, the Spirit of God, the Spirit of Christ. Man is flesh in his state of slavery to the world, but ''we have received not the spirit of the world, but the Spirit which is from God, that we should understand the gifts bestowed on us by God'' (I Cor. 2:12). The Spirit of God turns man away from the world and himself and places him under God's grace. The reign of the world is finished, the true reign of Christ begins. The Spirit of the Lord takes possession of us, and opens to us intransient things, life and the future. He gives us a re-created childhood: a new freedom from sin, law and death in peace, joy and life. But the Spirit is only given to the individual through being given to the community, the Church. What significance does this have for the Church? What is the significance of this Spirit which has been given to it?[14]

(a) *The Spirit as an eschatological gift.* In the messianic time of salvation, according to the prophetic expectation of salvation, not only individual prophets and wise men, warriors, singers and kings, were to be filled by the spirit of God, by God's creating power and strength of life; it was to be given to the whole people.

''For I will pour water on thirsty land, and streams on the dry ground; I will pour my Spirit upon your descendants and my

14. For the biblical idea of the Holy Spirit, see the dictionary articles by H. Kleinknecht, F. Baumgarten, W. Bieder, E. Sjöberg and especially E. Schweizer in ThW VI, 330–453 (Lit.); E. Käsemann in RGG II, 1272–1279; F. Mussner in LThK VIII, 572–576; among the theologies of the New Testament see in particular R. Bultmann; as well as the older works by H. Bertram, F. Buchsel, E. Fuchs, H. Gunkel, H. Leisegang, W. Reinhard, P. Volz, N. A. Waanink. The following more recent monographs are important: C. K. Barrett, *The Holy Spirit and the Gospel Tradition,* London-New York 1947; E. Schweizer, *Geist und Gemeinde im NT,* Munich 1952; S. Zedda, *L'adozione a figli di Dio e lo Spirito Santo,* Rome 1952; H. von Campenhausen, *Kirchliches Amt und geistliche Vollmacht in den ersten drei Jahrhunderten,* Tübingen 1953; N. Q. Hamilton, *The Holy Spirit and Eschatology in Paul,* London 1957; R. Schnackenburg, *The Church in the NT,* London-New York-Freiburg 1965; I. Hermann, *Kyrios und Pneuma. Studien zur Christologie der paulinischen Hauptbriefe,* Munich 1961; K. Stalder, *Das Werk des Geistes in der Heiligung bei Paulus,* Zurich 1961; L. Cerfaux, *The Church in the Theology of St. Paul,* London-New York-Freiburg 1959; also cf. the commentaries on Acts and the Pauline letters. For the literature on charisms see C II, 3.

blessing on your offspring" (Is. 44:3; cf. 63:14). "And I will put my spirit within you, and cause you to walk in my statutes and be careful to observe my ordinances" (Ez. 36:27; cf. Zech. 4:6).

The early Christian communities, the Pauline communities as well as that in Jerusalem, saw the expectation of the prophets as having been fulfilled in reality. The pouring out of the Spirit is the signal for the beginning of the eschatological event—the pouring out of the Spirit upon *all* mankind; on sons and on daughters, on old men and young men, on menservants and maidservants, as well as on their masters (Joel 2:28 f.). Spirit in this context, in the Old and New Testament alike, is not used, as the word often was, in the sense of breath, or angel or demon (or ghost or spirit of the departed), nor in the sense of soul or source of life, nor in the sense of the seat of knowledge and volition, the living ego of a man. No, in this context the Spirit of *God* is referred to, the *Holy* Spirit; its holiness separates it distinctly from the spirit of man and of the world. This Spirit is not some magical, mysteriously supernatural aura of a dynamistic kind, nor a magical being of an animistic kind, but God himself in his especially personal and self-giving aspect: as a power which gives itself to man, but cannot be controlled by man, as a power which creates life. The Spirit is God himself, a merciful power establishing his reign over man's heart, over the whole of man, inwardly present to man and apparent in his workings to man's human spirit.

It is not the place here to go into the discrepancies in the interpretation of the idea of the Spirit which are apparent in the New Testament. We can sum them up briefly as follows: the *Judaic Old Testament* tradition starts more from "animistic" conceptions: spirit is imagined as a self-contained person-like subject, which can take possession of a man and enable him to carry out particular feats of strength; the workings of the Spirit are here rather thought of in terms of particular situations and actions rather than in terms of a permanent situation. The *hellenistic* conception, on the other hand, starts from a more "dynamistic" viewpoint: spirit is imagined as an impersonal power or divine substance, which fills men with a kind of aura, not temporally but permanently.

But these differences are not crucial, for: (1) the two conceptions are not mutually exclusive, but complementary; there are traces at least of animistic conceptions in the hellenistic tradition, and dynamistic conceptions in the Old Testament; (2) in the New Testament a clear distinction between the two traditions is impossible, for they are never contrasted; on the contrary, we very often find them used by one and the same writer; (3) in the New Testament any kind of magic naturalism is generally avoided, and where it seems to be invoked, it is always with a view to expressing the power and effect of the spirit in man in his totality; (4) in the New Testament, despite the difference between the origins of the two traditions, there is a significant uniformity in basic conceptions: (a) Pneuma in the New Testament is not opposed in a platonic or idealistic way to the body or to nature, but is the miraculous divine power as opposed to all things human; (b) Pneuma in the whole of the New Testament is seen as an eschatological gift, albeit in different ways.

The Spirit is God's eschatological gift with which the community, and the individual who is incorporated into the community through baptism, is blessed in the last days. In Mark and Matthew we find relatively few sayings about the Spirit, mostly christological ones; they are concerned not to present Jesus as the first pneumatic of the community, which they might well have done, but rather to express Jesus' unique eschatological position, namely that God himself is uniquely present in Jesus. Only John the Baptist speaks of a more general eschatological outpouring of the Spirit: "I have baptized you with water; but he will baptize you with the Holy Spirit" (Mk. 1:8). Not until after Jesus' resurrection did the community experience the sending of the Spirit, God's sign which sealed them as the eschatological community.

Whereas in Mark and Matthew the coming of the Spirit is generally regarded, as in the Old Testament, as something exceptional, the hellenistic Luke, who is concerned less with the parousia of Christ than with the missionary history of the Church, sees the Spirit as given permanently to all members of the community. The gift of the Spirit is often seen as a natural consequence of believing, or of baptism (Acts 2:38 f.; 9:17; 10:44; 19:6). The basis for Luke's widely ranging narrative of Pentecost, to which several historical objections have been raised, is a decisive experience of the sending of the Spirit in the early Church, evidently connected with the ecstatic speeches of the disciples: "they were all filled with the Holy Spirit" in order to "tell of the mighty works of God" (Acts 2:4, 11). According to rabbinic teaching the Spirit had disappeared with the last Old Testament prophets; the apocalyptics concealed their pneumatic gifts under pseudonyms, and there were only a few isolated prophets among the Zealots. But the Acts of the Apostles proclaims the outpouring of the Spirit on the whole community. The ecstatic praises of God in which the eschatological

Spirit finds utterance, reveals the community of the disciples as the eschatological community of salvation, in whom the prophecy of Joel about the eschatological outpouring of the Spirit has been fulfilled (Acts 2:14–21; cf. Joel 3:1–5). Even for Luke, of course, Pentecost is not the moment of the Church's birth: that is Easter, and for Luke too the community of Jesus Christ existed before Pentecost (Acts 1:15). And according to the fourth gospel, which, like the other gospels and Paul's writings, makes no mention of a pentecostal event *after* Easter, the Spirit was already given at the time of Easter (Jn. 20:22). But through the giving of the Holy Spirit the community recognized itself and testified to itself as the eschatological community. Thus the time of the Church, for Luke an essentially missionary Church, is the time of the Spirit. The Spirit bestows power, authority and legitimacy. The Spirit as divine authority links communities to the one Church and gives continuity; he guides the early Church and its missionaries, gives offices (Acts 20:28), sends out ecclesiastical decrees through the Church (15:28), is connected with the laying-on of hands (6:6; 13:2 f.) and legitimizes the testimony of the Church (5:32). Numerous miracles further strengthen the Church and the legitimacy of its messengers.

By contrast with the Acts of the Apostles, Paul makes it clear that the Spirit is not just a special gift for a special external action, but that he determines fundamentally the existence of the believer. In Acts the Spirit is given to the faithful; in Paul's writings prayer itself is an act of the Spirit; for Paul there can be no new eschatological existence at all without the Spirit. If there is no Spirit, it does not mean that the community lacks its missionary commission, but that there is no community at all. "For all who are led by the Spirit of God are sons of God. For you did not receive the spirit of slavery to fall back into fear, but you have received the spirit of sonship. When we cry 'Abba! Father!' it is the Spirit himself bearing witness with our spirit that we are children of God, and if children, then heirs, heirs of God and fellow heirs with Christ, provided we suffer with him in order that we may also be glorified with him" (Rom. 8:14–17). So the Spirit is in a much profounder way the eschatological saving gift of God (cf., among the writings which draw on Paul, Heb. 6:4 f.; I Pet. 1:2).

How does Paul come to add this dimension of profundity to his conception of the Spirit? He thinks of the Spirit wholly in the light of the decisive saving event, the great eschatological turning point: the death and resurrection of Christ. The giving of the Spirit is linked to this eschatological event, in which God himself acted in Jesus Christ. So for him the Spirit is no obscure and nameless power such as it was for hellenistic gnosticism, but is, being the Spirit of God acting in *Christ,* the Spirit of Christ (Rom. 8:9), the Spirit of Jesus Christ (Phil. 1:19), of the Son (Gal. 4:6), of the Lord (II Cor. 3:18). By his resurrection Jesus became the glorified Kyrios, with power over the Spirit and the freedom to impart that Spirit. The Pneuma is so much his own, that he too can be seen as Pneuma, and phrases such as "in the Spirit" and "in Christ", or "the Spirit" and "Christ in us", are parallel ones. Christ himself is called "the spiritual rock" (I Cor. 10:4 A.V.). It is the resurrection of Christ which has fundamentally altered the situation, for through it Christ became a "life-giving spirit" (I Cor. 15:45), indeed "the Lord is the Spirit" (II Cor. 3:17). Paul does not mean here the absolute identity of two personal entities, but rather that the Kyrios appears in the mode of existence of the Pneuma. The Kyrios is identical with the Pneuma as soon as he is seen not in isolation but in his actions both with regard to the community and the individual. This explains why the Kyrios and the Pneuma can at the same time be put on the same level, and the Pneuma seen as subordinate to the Kyrios (II Cor. 3:17 f.). The encounter between the believer and "Theos", "Kyrios" and "Pneuma" is ultimately one and the same encounter: "The grace of the Lord Jesus Christ and the love of God and the fellowship of the Holy Spirit be with you all" (II Cor. 13:14; cf. I Cor. 12:4-6; Gal. 4:4-6; Rom. 5:1-5). In each case it is the action of the one God.

The Spirit is thus the earthly presence of the glorified Lord. In the Spirit Christ becomes Lord of his Church, and in the Spirit the resurrected Lord acts both in the community and in the individual. The power of his resurrection is more than a power of ecstasy and miracle; it produces a new creation. The Spirit opens up for the believer the way to the saving action of God in Christ. He does this not as a magic power which man cannot resist; he creates the possibility of man's replying with a responsible and conscious affirmative. He gives him, through the knowledge of the crucified Christ, the realization that in Jesus Christ God acted for him. The Spirit gives faith in the cross and resurrection of Christ and gives the power to live a life of faith. He is the "spirit of faith" (II Cor. 4:13; cf. II Cor. 5:5, 7). The Spirit is not man's own potential, but entirely the gift, the power and strength of God. The Holy Spirit, as *God's* Spirit, must be distinguished from *man's* own spirit, his human self; he should not be confused with man's spirit, since he is the *Holy* Spirit, free from all sin. The Holy Spirit is always entirely God's Spirit and is not absorbed into the individual spirit of man (cf. Rom. 8:16; I Cor. 2:10 f.). At the same time, God's Spirit can win power and dominion over man, so that he becomes man's inner self, so that a man no longer lives by his own strength, but by God's (cf. Rom. 8:9-15, 26 f.). In this way God's Spirit does not work, as in the gnostic view, as an automatically divinizing substance. The Spirit is the power which creates faith, and the norm according to which the believer is constantly summoned to live: "If we live by the Spirit, let us also walk by the Spirit" (Gal. 5:25; cf. 6:8). The pneumatic existence of the believer is lived in the dialectic between an indicative and an imperative.

The Spirit makes the believer a part of Christ's body. It is he who creates the unity of this body, which consists of many members, with different gifts of the Spirit (cf. I Cor. 12). By becoming a part of Christ through the Spirit, the believer guarantees his pneumatic existence. Not only does God assure the believer, through his Spirit working in the risen Christ, of eternal life in the *present*—since the resurrection of the crucified Christ means a final victory over death; but also God will, through the same life-giving Spirit, give him eternal life in the *future* too: "If the Spirit of him who raised Jesus from the dead dwells in you, he who raised Christ Jesus from the dead will give life to your mortal bodies also through his Spirit which dwells in you" (Rom. 8:11). The Spirit is the power of future life. The work of the Spirit of God in Christ will be perfected—again a difference from the gnostic view—in the future, in the redemption of our bodies (Rom. 8:23), so that at the end all things are put in subjection under Christ and the Father (cf. I Cor. 15:27 f.).

So the Spirit of God, given to the Church and the individual, the Spirit of the risen Lord, is the sign that the last days have begun and have been fulfilled, but have not been finished and consummated. Since the resurrection of Jesus the community of believers can regard the resurrection of all men at the end of time not as an uncertain hope, but as a firm certainty. The reality of the present Spirit guarantees the reality of future glory. By contrast with the Qumran community, which also speaks of an outpouring of the Spirit in the present, the Christian community sees the Spirit as a guarantee and seal of that perfection which is to come but which has already begun: God has "put his seal upon us and given his Spirit in our hearts as a guarantee" (II Cor. 1:22; cf. 5:5). "We ourselves, who have the firstfruits of the Spirit, groan inwardly as we wait for adoption as sons, the redemption of our bodies" (Rom. 8:23). "In him you also, who have heard the word of truth, the gospel of your salvation, and have believed in him, were sealed with the promised Holy Spirit, which is the guarantee of our inheritance until we acquire possession of it, to the praise of his glory"

(Eph. 1:13 f.). "And do not grieve the Holy Spirit of God, in whom you were sealed for the day of redemption" (4:30; cf. Tit. 3:6 f.).

The ecclesia is the eschatological people of God, the people of God of the last days: we have been looking at this fact from an entirely new perspective. God has not called and gathered his people simply as an alien being, an outsider. He has not made a new covenant, with his people as a distant party to an agreement, completely uncommitted in his personal existence. No, God has revealed himself in his entire living power, and it is through his self-giving power that he makes his claim to reign over his people. He himself is, through his Spirit which is at the same time the Spirit of Jesus Christ, present and efficient in the ecclesia. There are no limits to his self-giving power, which has been revealed to his people and has transformed its whole existence, indeed recreated it anew. His power sustains it and leads it towards its goal. The young communities of the Church, as we can see not only in the Acts but in Pauline and Johannine writings as well, were consoled and strengthened in joy and hope by their *experience* of God's power in his Spirit, whatever historically explicable differences there may have been in the actual phenomena of these experiences. This, as they recognized, was the essential difference between them and other religious groups in Judaism (the apocalyptic sects and the Qumran community) and in the hellenistic world (gnosticism and the mystery religions): only the community of Jesus Christ had received through their glorified Lord the Spirit of God as the guarantee and firstfruits of salvation. Only they could therefore make "demonstration of the Spirit and power" (I Cor. 2:4; cf. I Thess. 1:5).

This then is the biblical background to what Vatican II had to say about the Spirit which sanctifies the Church: "When the work which the Father had given the Son to do on earth (cf. Jn. 17:4) was accomplished, the Holy Spirit was sent on the day of Pentecost in order that He might forever sanctify the Church, and thus all believers would have access to the Father through Christ in the one Spirit (cf. Eph. 2:18). He is the Spirit of life, a fountain of water springing up to life eternal (cf. Jn. 4:14; 7:38 f.). Through Him the Father gives life to men who are dead from sin, till at last He revives in Christ even their mortal bodies (cf. Rom. 8:10 f.). The Spirit dwells in the Church and in the hearts of the faithful as in a temple (cf. I Cor. 3:16; 6:19). In them He prays and bears witness to the fact that they are adopted sons (cf.

Gal. 4:6; Rom. 8:15 f., 26). The Spirit guides the Church into the fullness of truth (cf. Jn. 16:13) and gives her a unity of fellowship and service. He furnishes and directs her with various gifts, both hierarchical and charismatic, and adorns her with the fruits of His grace (cf. Eph. 4:11 f.; I Cor. 12:4; Gal. 5:22). By the power of the Gospel He makes the Church grow, perpetually renews her, and leads her to perfect union with her Spouse. The Spirit and the Bride both say to the Lord Jesus, 'Come!' (cf. Rev. 22:17). Thus, the Church shines forth as 'a people made one with the unity of the Father, the Son and the Holy Spirit' (St. Cyprian, St. Augustine and St. John of Damascus)'' (CE 4). This text also contains some ideas which must be examined further, again in the light of the New Testament.

(b) *The Church as the temple of the Spirit:* The Church is the work and the tool, a sign and a witness of the Spirit of God which fills it. It is, to use the scriptural image, a temple, a building filled and reigned over by the Spirit: *a building of the Spirit.* How are we to understand this scriptural image of the Church? The idea of the Church as a temple built by God, by Christ or by the Holy Spirit, is one we find at various points in the New Testament (cf. Mt. 16:18; Mk. 14:58; Jn. 2:19; Heb. 3:2-6; 10:21; Rev. 21:22). Three classic texts give us important perspectives for the link of this particular image with the Spirit.

1. The *individual community* is built by the Spirit (I Cor. 3:16 f.). The image of the temple is not an idealized picture of an ideal Church. This is made clear by the fact that its first use in the New Testament shows it being applied to an individual community, to the community in Corinth in fact, about which we know a good deal. We know in particular that the "saints" in Corinth had, as Paul's two letters reveal, only too often acted in an unsaintly manner. It is this community of unsaintly saints which Paul addresses—by way of an admonition—as a temple of the Spirit: "Do you not know that you are God's temple and that God's Spirit dwells in you?" (I Cor. 3:16).

To refer to the Church as a temple, therefore, does not mean referring to the Church in a spiritualized sense. These people, this community with all its evident human failings, is the temple of God. Although it must be admonished to live according to the Spirit, this Church is nonetheless in the Spirit, or rather, the Spirit dwells in it: God's moulding power and life-giving strength has through Christ taken possession of it, has overwhelmed and penetrated it in its entire existence. In the Spirit, God himself and the

Kyrios are effectively present in the community of believers despite all their human weaknesses. The Church is the place of God's special presence on earth. Just as God was once thought of as dwelling in a stone temple, both in the Jewish and Gentile religions, he now lives in the community of Christ. It no longer needs a stone temple, it is itself the new spiritual temple. For this very reason the community has the responsibility of maintaining the temple in brotherly unity. "If anyone destroys God's temple, God will destroy him. For God's temple is holy, and that temple you are" (I Cor. 3:17). Any Church which like the Corinthians destroys the unity of the community by making factions drives out the Spirit. Anyone who drives out the Spirit destroys the temple, destroys the community and ultimately destroys himself. The fact that the Church, the community, is a building of the Spirit, implies a charge upon the members of the community: since they are spiritual, they must lead spiritual lives.

2. The whole Church is a building of the Spirit (Eph. 2:17–22). In these verses from Ephesians[15] the remarks quoted above from I Corinthians are extended to cover the whole Church, in accordance with the total salvation-historical conception of the letter, and with special reference to the Jews and the Gentiles, those who are "far off" and those who are "near": "And he came and preached peace to you who were far off and peace to those who were near; for through him we both have access in one Spirit to the Father. So then you are no longer strangers and sojourners, but you are fellow citizens with the saints and members of the household of God, built upon the foundation of the apostles and prophets, Christ Jesus himself being the chief cornerstone, in whom the whole structure is joined together and grows into a holy temple in the Lord; in whom you are also built into it for a dwelling-place of God in the Spirit."

Here we have a more detailed description of the inner structure of the building of the Spirit. The "foundation" of this spiritual building is the "apostles and prophets", that is, the prophets of the New Testament, of whom Paul often speaks, as do also Acts, Revelation and the Didache; the directly commissioned apostolic authorities, and the charismatic prophetic authorities—all those who had the word directly from Christ (who elsewhere is himself described as the foundation of the Church, cf. I Cor. 3:11). The "stones" are the members of the Church, all those who believe in

15. Among the more recent commentaries on Ephesians cf. especially H. Schlier, *Der Brief an die Epheser,* Düsseldorf ²1958, 118–145.

Christ; not only Jews, but Gentiles too, who were previously strangers and sojourners but are now citizens and members of the household of God, all are "built in" to the dwelling-place of God in the Spirit. The "cornerstone" is "Christ Jesus", or rather, he is the "keystone", as most modern exegetes prefer to read, by contrast with I Cor. 3:10 f.; the keystone which rounds off and holds together the whole arch. The temple as a whole is "a holy temple in the Lord" or "a dwelling-place of God in the Spirit", which means the same thing; "in the Lord" and "in the Spirit" are parallel phrases. The "Lord" holds the building together, gives it a basis and a purpose; the "Spirit" gives the power and strength by which the building exists. The Church is a building which exists in the Spirit and through the Spirit and by virtue of the Spirit of the Lord. The glorified Lord sends his Spirit and turns his fellowship of disciples into a Church. It is through the Spirit that the reconciliation effected by Christ between Jews and Gentiles becomes effective and fruitful. In *one* Spirit and in *one* body they all have access to the one God. The Spirit therefore makes the Church a completely pneumatic reality. For "dwelling-place, temple, building in the pneuma" we could also read "pneumatic temple, building, house". And it is the "pneumatic house" to which the third classic text refers.

3. The faithful are *built up* and *themselves build* the building of the Spirit (I Pet. 2:4–7). The image of the cornerstone, even more than that of the keystone, emphasizes the fundamental importance of the risen Lord for the Church as a building of the Spirit or, as it is called here, a "spiritual house": "Come to him, to that living stone, rejected by men but in God's sight chosen and precious; and like living stones be yourselves built into a spiritual house, to be a holy priesthood, to offer spiritual sacrifices acceptable to God through Jesus Christ. For it stands in scripture: 'Behold, I am laying in Zion a stone, a cornerstone chosen and precious, and he who believes in him will not be put to shame.' To you therefore who believe, he is precious" (I Pet. 2:4–7).[16] Here again the indicative precedes the imperative: the Church is God's house, a spiritual house. Christ is the cornerstone, as the quotation from Isaiah makes clear, the stone at the corner which supports the whole house: a living stone, since Christ, rejected and crucified, is now the risen and living Christ. Only through the living Christ are Christians living stones, freed from death. The Church is built up

---

16. Among the more recent commentaries on I Pet. see esp. K. H. Schelkle, *Die Petrusbriefe,* Freiburg-Basle-Vienna 1951, 57–63.

of believers on the foundation-stone of Christ—as a *spiritual* house; not a material earthly temple, nor yet a completely spiritualized temple, but as a pneumatic temple which lives by the Pneuma and of which all the members are filled and vivified by the Pneuma.

Because we are living stones, we must *let ourselves be built up*; whether the original Greek form is indicative or imperative, the meaning at all events is imperative. Not that Christians as pious people can build up the house by themselves; another builds with them. They must in faith put themselves at the builder's disposal; as believers they must serve the house. How? The image of the spiritual house, the spiritual temple is transposed into that of the temple-priesthood: the believers must offer sacrifices to God. But here again the writer is not thinking of material earthly offerings, animals, meats and incense, but pneumatic offerings: prayer, praise and thanks, penitence, fruits of faith and love. These sacrifices are not to be offered by the believers, but by the High Priest, Christ; then they will be well pleasing to God and their acceptance is certain. Then the believers will become a true "holy priesthood".

Vatican II has this to say about the image of the building of the Spirit: "The Church has more often been called the edifice of God (I Cor. 3:9). Even the Lord likened Himself to the stone which the builders rejected, but which became the corner stone (Mt. 21:42 par.; cf. Acts 4:11; I Pet. 2:7; Ps. 117:22). On this foundation the Church is built by the apostles (cf. I Cor. 3:11), and from it the Church receives durability and solidity. This edifice is adorned by various names: the house of God (I Tim. 3:15) in which dwells His family; the household of God in the Spirit (Eph. 2:19–22); the dwelling-place of God among men (Rev. 21:3); and, especially, the holy temple. This temple, symbolized by places of worship built out of stone, is praised by the holy Fathers and, not without reason, is compared in the liturgy to the Holy City, the New Jerusalem. As living stones we here on earth are being built up along with this City (I Pet. 2:5). John contemplates this Holy City, coming down out of heaven from God when the world will be made anew, and prepared like a bride adorned for her husband (Rev. 21:1 f.)." (CE 6)

The Spirit of God communicated through the glorified Lord is thus seen to be, in various ways, the basis of the Church's existence, its source of life and controlling power. The Church is filled and vivified, sustained and guided by this Spirit, the power and strength of God. The Church owes to the Spirit its origin, existence and continued life, and in this sense the Church is a *creation of the spirit*. But this expression does not only suggest a *unity* of Spirit and Church, a unity which seems explicitly emphasized in the images of the spiritual building; to refer to the Church as a creation of the Spirit also emphasizes a distinction which is taken for granted in Scripture and on occasions referred to explicitly. It is important in the Church today, especially as regards Church unity, to stress this distinction.[17]

(c) *The Church under the reign of the Spirit.* The distinction between Spirit and Church has its basis in the divine nature of God's Spirit or, as we can also put it, in its freedom. Spirit and Church, however closely linked, are not on the same plane; the Church is subordinate to the Spirit of God. This distinction of freedom can be summed up in four sentences:

1. The Spirit is *not* the Church. It would be dangerous to try to identify the Church and the Holy Spirit; for the Holy Spirit is the Spirit of God, not of the Church; hence the fundamental *freedom* of the Holy Spirit. Just as the Holy Spirit, although he dwells in a Christian, is not identical with the Christian's spirit, so the Spirit is not the Spirit of the Church but of God. There is no mention in the New Testament of the Holy Spirit as the "Spirit of the church", only as the "Spirit of God", as the "Spirit of Jesus Christ". This Spirit proceeds not from the Church nor from an individual Christian, but from God. He is not the possession or property of the Church, nor its power and strength, but God's. Through him God

17. In addition to the general systematic works on the idea of the Church (see A II, 2) and the relevant sections in the dogmatics (esp. K. Barth, *Church Dogmatics,* Edinburgh-Naperville, Illinois 1956, IV/I, 643–650) there are the more recent monographs on the relationship Spirit–Church: A. Vonier, *The Spirit and the Bride* (Coll. Works, II. London 1952); Westminster, Md., 1952; P. Nautin, *Je crois à l'Esprit Saint dans la Sainte Eglise,* Paris 1947; R. Prenter, *Le Saint-Esprit et le renouveau de l'Eglise,* Neuchâtel-Paris 1949; K. Rahner, *The Dynamic Element in the Church,* London-New York 1964; J. G. Davies, *Der Heilige Geist, die Kirche und die Sakramente,* Stuttgart 1958; S. Tromp, *Corpus Christi quod est ecclesia,* vol. I–III, Rome 1957 ff.; O. Ertis. *Die Erneuerung der Gemeinde durch den Geist,* Kassel 1960; H. Volk, *Gott alles in allem,* Mainz 1961, 86–112; P. Brunner, *Pro Ecclesia,* Berlin-Hamburg 1962, I, 213–224; W. Mühlen, *Der Heilige Geist als Person,* Münster 1963; *Una mystica persona. Die Kirche als das Mysterium der Identität des Hl. Geistes in Christus und den Christen,* Munich-Paderborn-Vienna 1964.

acts *in* the Church, reveals himself and comes *to* the Church, provides a foundation *for* the Church and sustains it. He governs the Church, but never becomes the Church's own spirit, nor merges with it. He remains God's own Spirit and for this reason is and remains the *free* Spirit.

We are the Church, we the fellowship of men who believe in Christ. We, the Church, are a human structure. But the Holy Spirit is divine, not human. For all the links between them there is no identity, but rather a fundamental distinction between the Spirit of God and the human structure of the Church. This difference is not merely a general and abstract one, the ontic difference between the divine and the human. The real Church, of which we are speaking, is not only a Church composed of people, but of sinful people. The real Church is not only human, but also sinful. We are the Church, justified but sinful men, we, the fellowship of the righteous who are yet constantly dependent on forgiveness: *communio sanctorum* indeed, but also regrettably always the *communio peccatorum*. So the Church is sinful. The Spirit of God on the other hand is not sinful, but the Holy, the completely Holy, Spirit. Hence the Spirit is in this very much deeper sense also the *free* Spirit, truly free from sin, guilt and death.

This free Spirit of God is essential for our understanding of the Church, as well as for our understanding of the believer as a man made free by God's Spirit. But the free Spirit of God in no sense belongs to the Church and must in no way be confused with it.

To avoid confusing the Spirit and the Church, it would be better not to speak of the Church as a "divine" reality. The individual believer, after all, does not become a "divine" reality because he is filled with and governed by the Spirit. It would also be better not to speak of an organic development of the Church and its spirit. The romantic and idealistic view of Church history overlooks the fundamental difference between the perfect Spirit of God and an imperfect Church. It is because of the distinction between the Spirit and the Church that its development often includes developments in the wrong direction, and progress often includes retrogression. Finally, to avoid confusing the Spirit and the Church, it would be better not to speak of the "sense of the faithful" (*sensus fidelium*) in the Church as though it were a revelation of the Holy Spirit. The Church's sense of the faith can never be a source and a norm of the revelations of the Spirit. On the contrary: revelations of the

Holy Spirit provide the source and norm of the Church's sense of the faith. These concrete examples show that the Holy Spirit in the Church is and remains a free Spirit.

It is obvious how important this distinction is. The Church does not *per se* and in each case represent the Holy Spirit; the Church has to prove its holiness in action. Only by accepting the distinction can we truly face up to the all too human aspect of the Church, its failures and shortcomings, its sin and guilt, in a proper liberating way. A Church which identifies itself with the Holy Spirit cannot say the *Confiteor*. It cannot, may not, confess that it has sinned in thought, word and deed, through its fault, through its most grievous fault. It will be forced into unsound theological prevarications and apologetics which convince no one. In short, it will fall prey to an idealistic and triumphalist conception of the Church which is full of illusions. And it will therefore not be a *free* Church.

Only by drawing this distinction can we really listen to God's word in the Holy Spirit and be obedient to the Holy Spirit, in a truly liberating way. A Church which identifies itself with the Holy Spirit has no need to listen, to believe, to obey. It turns itself into a revelation, it knows and does everything. It needs only to listen to itself, to obey itself and believe in itself, and urge others outside the Church to listen, believe and obey. In short, it will fall prey to a self-glorifying and egocentric conception of the Church, and again it will be anything but a *free* Church.

But a Church which distinguishes between itself and the Holy Spirit can face up to sin and failure in the Church soberly and humbly, but also with the liberating hope of those already justified that they will be forgiven anew. A Church which draws this distinction will believe, obey and hope without putting its trust in itself, but precisely in God's Holy Spirit. A Church which proudly identifies itself with the free Spirit of God is a Church which for all its vaunted strength is ultimately weak, for all its imagined freedom is ultimately unfree. But the Church which humbly distinguishes itself from the free Spirit of God is for all its undeniable weakness strong, and for all its apparent unfreedom ultimately free.

So it is that we believe *in* the Holy Spirit (*credo* in *Spirito Sancto*); by contrast we believe *the* holy Church (*credo sanctam ecclesiam*). We do not believe *in* the Church, in the final analysis we never believe in ourselves. We, the Church, believe in the Holy Spirit just as we believe in God, from whom the Holy Spirit cannot be distinguished. In this faith in the Holy Spirit the holy Church is best taken care of.[18]

2. The Spirit *precedes* the Church. The Holy Spirit is not an external extra to the Church, as though the Church could exist without the Holy Spirit, although perhaps only in an imperfect and unvital way. When Scripture refers to the Church as a spiritual house, as a temple of the Holy Spirit, it does not mean that the Church is the outward form or framework into which the Spirit, the living content, then entered. The Church is not something which competent and clever ecclesiastical organizers, administrators and big business men can work out and set up, *after* which the Holy Spirit can find in it a centre of operations or even a resting-place.

The Spirit of God comes first; and through the Spirit God in his freedom *creates* the Church, and constantly creates it anew from those who believe: "No one can say 'Jesus is Lord' except by the Holy Spirit" (I Cor. 12:3). Through the operation of the Spirit the Church is created and created afresh each day: *emitte spiritum tuum—et creabuntur*! There is no Christian existence which is not created and must constantly be created; and none is created without the operation of the Spirit. There is no Church which is not created and must constantly be created; and none is created without the operation of the Spirit. Of course, there is no Church without the decision of believers and their free gathering together. But the believers who congregate in the Church do not summon themselves. They do not even summon themselves to faith. God himself calls them through the word of Christ in the power of the Holy Spirit to faith and hence to the Church as the fellowship of the faithful. God in the Holy Spirit acts in perfect freedom. The beginning is his, as is the continuation and the end. Everything is his, who in the freedom of his power and strength remains the sovereign Lord of the Church.

3. The Spirit works *where* he wills. The Spirit of God cannot be restricted in his operation by the Church; he is at work not only in the offices of the Church, but where he wills: in the whole people of God. He is at work not only in the "holy city", but where he wills: in all the churches of the one Church. He is at work not only in the Catholic Church, but where he wills: in Christianity as a whole. And finally he is at work not only in Christianity, but where he wills: in the whole world.

The power of the Spirit of God can pass through *all* walls, even church walls. It is true that the Holy Spirit has his dwelling and his

18. Cf. A II, 2.

temple in the Church, which he fills and which he governs. Here his power is especially revealed, since in the Church and through the Church the word of God is preached and his sacraments are administered. But the Spirit of God, if domiciled in the Church, is not domesticated in it. He is and remains the free Spirit of the free Lord not only of the "holy city", not only of Church offices, not only of the Catholic Church, not only of Christians, but of the whole world.

Certain questions arise here. Might *Christians* not be more cautious, more open and just in their judgments and attitudes towards the great non-Christian religions of the world if they were completely convinced of the fact that the Holy Spirit, who is revealed in and through the Church, is the free Spirit of the Lord of the whole world, who is at work where he wills? Might *Catholics* not be more restrained, more open and friendly in their judgments and attitudes towards the other Christian Churches if they were completely convinced that the Holy Spirit, in whom as Catholics they put, or ought to put, their whole trust, is also the hope and strength of the whole of Christendom and desires in freedom to be so? Might *Church leaders* not be more modest, more open and humble in their judgments and attitudes towards other Christians if they were completely convinced that the Holy Spirit, who is certainly promised to those who hold office in the Church, is not a Spirit of office reserved for the privileged few, but is the Spirit of God, who has been poured out in the hearts of all who believe and love and who acts and desires to act freely in all hearts and minds? The free Spirit is at work where *he* wills.

4. The Spirit is at work *when* he wills. The Spirit of God is not, of course, a Spirit of arbitrariness or apparent freedom, but of real freedom; he is a Spirit of order, not chaos; peace, not contradictions, in the Church as well as in the world. This is what Paul had to remind the Corinthians, who, proud of their spiritual gifts, had neglected order in the Church: "God is not a God of confusion but of peace" (I Cor. 14:33). Arbitrariness, disorder and chaos in the Church cannot be the work of the Holy Spirit.

At the same time, God's Spirit does not blow when he *must,* but only when he *wills.* No decrees of the Church, in doctrine or practice, can force him to act or not to act at a given time. True, God is absolutely free, and is thus free even with regard to his freedom. He is so overwhelmingly free, that he can bind himself, as he does indeed in word and sacrament. But by being bound to word and sacrament he affirms not his limitations or unfreedom, but his all-powerful, abundant freedom.

God's Spirit knows no law but that of his own freedom, no authority but that of his own grace, no power but that of his own faithfulness. God's Spirit is at all events not bound by the laws or authority or power of the *Church*. God's Spirit is not ruled by ecclesiastical laws or authority or power. He himself reigns and rules sovereign over them. Anyone in the Church who supposes he can dictate to the Spirit on the basis of law, authority or power must necessarily fail. The Church cannot take over the Spirit, or in any real sense "possess" him, control or limit, direct or dominate him.

The Church cannot do any of these things, either through its word or its sacraments. God binds himself in the Spirit to word and sacrament, not on the basis of the Church's law, but on the basis of his own freedom; not on the basis of the Church's authority, but on the basis of his free grace; not on the basis of the Church's power, but on the basis of his faithfulness. The fact that God binds himself to word and sacrament of the Church, lays an obligation not on him but on us. We do not demand something of him, he demands something of us: our unconditional *faith*. Neither word nor sacrament works automatically; where there is no faith, they are not operative. Anyone who thinks that the Spirit can be compelled with word or sacrament, or with law and authority, power or order, is leaving out of account precisely that faith which the Spirit demands of him: faith not in his or the Church's law, authority, power or order, but in God's free grace and faithfulness. It is true therefore of the Church too that the Spirit blows not when he must, but when he wills.

Here again certain questions arise. Might not Catholic doctrine on the sacraments be more discriminating and more accurate in its theory of *opus operatum* if it took as its starting-point the fact that even the *opus operatum* cannot compel the *Spiritus operans*, but must be subject to him in faith? Might not Catholic canon law manipulate all its canons and tenets more restrainedly (for example, in its view of the sacraments), if it constantly realized that its canons and tenets, provided they are meaningful and appropriate, can be seen as the concrete presentation of God's demands upon us, but can never be seen as demands of the Church upon the Holy Spirit, as though to compel him to act at a certain time in a certain manner? Might Catholic judgments with regard to the preaching and sacraments of other Christian Churches (for example, with regard to the validity or invalidity of marriage rites, ordination or Eucharist) be more cautious, if their starting-point were the freedom of the Holy Spirit, who blows when and where he wills, that freedom which in nearly all cases would make a definite *negative* judgment impossible?

The Church cannot dictate to the Spirit or regiment it. It can only pray and beg: *Veni*! God's Spirit may dwell in the spiritual house of the Church, and remain with the Church and work through it. But he dwells and remains and works there not on the basis of a law, because he must, but on the basis of his faithfulness, because he wills. "He who calls you is faithful, and he will do it" (I Thess. 5:24).

We, who are the Church, must never forget that we are sinners, albeit justified, and must constantly be aware of the fact; we live therefore in contradiction to God's Spirit, we "grieve" him and can, from our viewpoint at least, lose him. We must not forget that our faith, though it may give us certainty, is constantly threatened and challenged; we can only trust in God's faithfulness and grace. It is by no means automatic that the Spirit should remain with us, the Church. All we can do is to pray penitently, not only "*veni sancte Spiritus*" but also "*mane sancte Spiritus*", remain with us, despite our faithlessness, because of your faithfulness. The Church, despite its constant failures, has never lost the free Spirit of God in all its members; this is not something to be taken for granted, it is the miracle of God's faithfulness, which we can never take for granted but must constantly believe and pray for anew.

But the work of the Holy Spirit is not only to be seen in these general terms. It is true that the Spirit is given to the *community*. But the community is composed of individual believers, received into it through baptism. The operation of God in the Spirit is directed towards these individuals in the Church, it is something concrete and individual. This becomes clear when we describe the pneumatic reality of the Church in terms of what may be called its charismatic structure.

3. THE CONTINUING CHARISMATIC STRUCTURE

There seem to be two reasons why for such a long time Catholic theology and the Church overlooked the importance, both in theory and practice, of the charismatic structure of the Church.

First a certain clericalism and legalism, which in recent times has been much criticized within the Catholic Church itself. A clericalistic attitude can only recognize real and decisive activity and initiative in the Church if it comes from the clergy rather than from other members of the people of God. Juridical thinking is deeply mistrustful of any movements of the free Spirit of God, the Spirit which is operative in the Church where and when he wills, which cannot be regimented.

Secondly, the fact that the ecclesiology of Catholic textbooks was exclusively based on the ecclesiology of the pastoral epistles (and of Acts), and largely overlooked the specifically Pauline ecclesiology of the letters which were undoubtedly written by Paul, although it often formally cited Pauline texts. The variety and the inner tensions of the New Testament were ignored or harmonized in an unreliable way. But, as we have already seen, the various differences that there are in conceptions of the Church, of the Spirit, of the charisms, are undeniable. Here it is helpful to examine how the word "charisma" is used.

The oldest New Testament document—earlier even than Mark or Matthew—is, along with the two letters to the Thessalonians, the first letter to the Corinthians. No other New Testament writing gives such original and detailed information about the external and internal ordering of a Church. This first letter to the Corinthians, which like all uncontested Pauline letters speaks neither of "elders" or "bishops" (with the sole late exception of the reference to "bishops and deacons", Phil. 1:1), nor of ordination or the laying-on of hands, repeatedly refers to the "charismata" or "pneumatika" which, according to Paul, are bestowed on each Christian according to the measure of his faith; the letter also contains long chapters about the charismatic structure of the Church, which is a presupposition of Paul's other letters and occasionally may be glimpsed in them. By contrast, in the pastoral letters, which are among the latest New Testament writings, the Pauline view that each Christian has received the Spirit and his gifts is overlaid by a strongly emphasized theology of Church office. The Spirit is given in ordination. Despite the obvious references to Paul, the pastoral letters, significantly enough, do not use the Pauline word πνευματικός at all, nor does it appear in Luke's Acts of the Apostles, which chronologically comes between the Pauline and the pastoral letters. Moreover, the word "charisma", which does not appear in Acts either, is used only twice in the pastoral letters (I Tim. 4:14; II Tim. 1:6), in each case, we may note, in connection with ordination. This is one of the numerous and weighty differences between the Pauline and the pastoral letters, which have caused even Catholic exegetes to doubt the Pauline authorship of the pastoral letters—a question to which, as is well known, there can only be historical, not dogmatic answers.

Although Catholic theologians are convinced that the pastoral letters, along with other "early Catholic" writings, were not included by the early Church in the canon of the New Testament without good reason, they may not draw from this the same conclusions as several Protestant theologians have done: namely that the pastoral letters can best be seen as a "contrast" to the real "gospel" as it was preached by Jesus and interpreted by Paul at his most profound. Catholic hermeneutics demand that the New Testament καθ' ὅλου, as a *whole,* in all its writings should be taken seriously, and that the whole truth of the New Testament should be accepted as it stands. Thus the "early Catholic" writings, as much as Acts and the pastoral letters, demand scholarly and positive study. Any exegesis must, of course, take note of the fact that the Pauline letters have a primacy of originality, not only because of the authenticity of the apostolic author and his temporal closeness to the Gospel of Jesus, but also because of his thematic closeness to the Gospel. The Acts of the Apostles, on the other hand, and the pastoral letters, both of which are often based on Paul, are evidently *secondary* testimonies. But precisely as such they should be seriously and positively examined, which should not be difficult for the theologian who thinks historically.[19]

This hermeneutic introduction makes it abundantly clear why an ecclesiology based primarily on Acts and the pastoral letters, which merely acknowledged the Pauline texts or used them to support arguments drawn from elsewhere, necessarily neglected the charismata of all Christians, and why only the "hierarchical" rather than the pneumatic and charismatic structure of the Church was examined. The rediscovery of the charisms is a rediscovery of specifically Pauline ecclesiology, the importance of which for the problems of Catholicism and ecumenism cannot be overestimated. Rigorous theological investigation is needed to show how fruitful Pauline ecclesiology could be in the contemporary situation; in the present context it will help us to throw light on the continuing charismatic structure of the Church. Before examining charisms in detail, three recurring misconceptions about them must be discussed.[20]

---

19. Cf. A I, 3.
20. In addition to the literature cited in C II, 2 and the articles on charisms and the Spirit in the dictionaries of the Bible and of theology, cf. esp. F. Grau, *Der neutestamentliche Begriff. Seine Geschichte und seine Theologie,* Diss. Tübingen 1946; J. Brosch, *Charismen und Ämter in der*

(a) *Exceptional or everyday phenomena*? It is a misconception to think of charisms as principally exceptional, miraculous or sensational phenomena. The prototypical charism in that event—apart from the driving out of demons, healings, acts of power, miracles—would be glossolalia, which is often quoted in this connection; speaking ἐν γλώσσῃ or ἐν γλώσσαις (I Cor. 12-14; Acts 10:46; 19:6; Mk. 16:17), the ecstatic language of the Spirit which may be unintelligible, unarticulated sounds (I Cor. 14:6-11, 23) and which is uttered in praying or singing, praising or giving thanks (I Cor. 14:15 f.; cf. Eph. 5:19; Col. 3:16).

What is Paul's attitude to these exceptional charisms, such as were also found in mystery religions outside the Church? Speaking with tongues was a feature of hellenistic ecstatic mysticism, as for example the Delphic Pythia and the Sibyls, who murmured ominous phrases in their mantic trances.

It would be wrong to suppose that Paul rejected or even mistrusted these exceptional gifts on principle. He welcomes all gifts of the Spirit, and he himself is apparently specially gifted in speaking with tongues (I Cor. 14:18). But he emphatically reduces in importance this sensational gift, by insisting that it is nothing compared with the charism of interpretation; it is not of itself edifying for the community, nor does it clarify the understanding of the man who prays. It is thus less valuable than prophecy and is to be used in the community only within certain limitations (I Cor. 14). In the list of charisms (I Cor. 12:28) it takes last place. In his letter to the Romans, probably written in Corinth, Paul in a list of charisms does not mention it at all (Rom. 12:6-8).

In addition to minimizing the importance of such charisms of enthusiasm, Paul criticizes the miraculous hellenistic "pneumatika", the powers of ecstasy and wonders and, instead of the

---

Urkirche, Bonn 1951; E. Lohse, *Die Ordination im Spätjudentum und im NT*, Berlin 1951; H. von Campenhausen, *Kirchliches Amt und geistliche Vollmacht in den ersten 3 Jahrhunderten*, Tübingen 1953; K. Rahner, *The Dynamic Element in the Church*, London-New York-Freiburg 1964; E. Schweizer, *Gemeinde und Gemeindeordnung im NT*, Zurich 1959; R. Bultmann, *Theology of the New Testament*, London [3]1965; E. Käsemann, *Ministry and Community in the NT*, in *Essays on NT Themes*, London-Naperville, Illinois 1964, 63-94; G. Eichholz, *Was heisst charismatische Gemeinde? I Cor 12*, Munich 1960; O. Perels, *Charisma im NT*, in Fuldaier Hefte 15, Berlin 1964, 39-45; H. Schürmann, *Die geistliche Gnadegaben*, in *De Ecclesia. Beiträge zur Konstitution "Über die Kirche" des* 2. *Vatikanischen Konzils*, ed. by G. Barauna. Freiburg-Frankfurt a.M. 1966, 494-519. The details which follow are drawn from my article, "The Charismatic Structure of the Church", *Concilium* 4/1, April 1965.

very common hellenistic expression, he usually substitutes, on purpose we may suppose, the word "charisms". When he uses the word "pneumatika" (I Cor. 12:1; 14:1) he points out their distinctive Christian features. Demons and dumb idols may also because of their power have an irresistible attraction for people (I Cor. 12:2), signs and wonders can also occur outside the Church, and can be done by Antichrist. There are lying prophets and lying apostles as well as true ones. The obvious conclusion to be drawn from this is that the signs and wonders are not unequivocally signs of the Holy Spirit, of the real charism.

Since there are different spirits and spiritual phenomena, it is essential that there should always be "the ability to distinguish between spirits" (I Cor. 12:10). Paul establishes two principal criteria for recognizing the Spirit which comes from God. The first is stated at the beginning of his detailed discussion of charisms (I Cor. 12:2 f.): the Spirit which comes from God enables a man to affirm that Jesus is the Lord. Only "in the Holy Spirit" can a man assert that "Jesus is Kyrios". The Spirit which comes from God binds men to Jesus and to his reign. Jesus Christ is the centre of all preaching and all actions of the community. This is how Paul distinguishes the specifically Christian element: Where Jesus, rather than any person or power of this world, is the Lord, the Spirit is from God (cf. I Jn. 4:2 f.).

The second criterion is the element of service attached to the charism. The true charism is not simply a miracle; it is something in the service of the community, giving a sense of responsibility towards the community and the desire to edify and benefit it. Charism is directly connected with the community. "To each is given the manifestation of the Spirit for the common good" (I Cor. 12:7). Paul also mentions less striking charisms, such as exhortation and acts of mercy (Rom. 12:8), service (Rom. 12:7), teaching (Rom. 12:7; I Cor. 12:28 f.), the utterance of wisdom and knowledge (I Cor. 12:8), faith (I Cor. 12:9), discernment of Spirits (I Cor. 12:10), helping and administration (I Cor. 12:28), and so forth.

Charisms are by no means only exceptional things, they are everyday phenomena in the life of the Church. Christians should desire earnestly the higher charisms, and these are not striking ones like speaking with tongues, but everyday ones. "But earnestly desire the higher gifts. And I will show you a still more excellent way", says Paul at the conclusion of his list of charisms (I Cor. 12:31). And this "more excellent way", the best and greatest of the charisms, is the least sensational, the most everyday of gifts: love. Without love, speaking with tongues and prophecy, even faith or the renunciation of all property or martyrdom, is nothing: "If I speak in the tongues of men and of angels, but have not love, I am a noisy gong or a clanging cymbal. And if I have prophetic powers, and understand all mysteries and all knowledge, and if I have all faith, so as to remove mountains, but have not love, I am nothing. If I give away all I have, and if I deliver my body to be burned, but have not love, I gain nothing" (I Cor. 13:1-3). This charism which is above all others, and regulates all others, is revealed unobtrusively in the thousand very unsensational situations of everyday life, and effects what man of his own nature can never hope to achieve: "Love is patient and kind; love is not jealous or boastful; it is not arrogant or rude. Love does not insist on its own way; it is not irritable or resentful; it does not rejoice at wrong, but rejoices in the right. Love bears all things, believes all things, hopes all things, endures all things. Love never ends" (I Cor. 13:4-8).

The Constitution "On the Church" of Vatican II refers explicitly to "charismatic gifts, whether they be the most outstanding or the more simple and widely diffused", and adds the warning: "Still, extraordinary gifts are not to be rashly sought after, nor are the fruits of apostolic labour to be presumptuously expected from them". At the same time it is stressed that true charismatic gifts "are exceedingly suitable and useful for the needs of the Church" (CE 12).

The everyday nature of charisms will become clearer when we examine the various kinds of charismatic gifts.

(*b*) *Uniformity or diversity*? A second misunderstanding of the charism would be to suppose that there is only one particular kind of gift, for example, that connected with some kind of ordination. The only charism mentioned in the pastoral letters, and mentioned with emphasis, is "the gift of God that is within you through the laying on of hands" (II Tim. 1:6), "the gift you have, which was given you by prophetic utterance when the elders laid their hands upon you" (I Tim. 4:14). If this were the only real charism of the Spirit, we should have to assume that charisms were exclusively "sacramental" or institutionalized in some way or another, rather than being a manifold variety of gifts of the Spirit designed for diverse services.

That this is not the case is revealed by the fact that those letters of Paul in which the charism plays an extremely important part contain no references to ordination at all. Nothing could have been further from his mind than to sacramentalize or make uniform the charism, and hence the workings of the Spirit. On the contrary, the workings of grace and of the Spirit of God are characterized for him by richness, variety, exuberance: "in every way you were enriched in him . . . so that you are not lacking in any spiritual gift . . ." (I Cor. 1:5, 7); "as you excel in everything" (II Cor. 8:7); "God is able to provide you with every blessing in abundance, so that you may always have enough of everything" (II Cor. 9:3).

A glance at the lists of charisms which Paul gives in various places (especially I Cor. 12:28-31; Rom. 12:6-8; Eph. 4:11 f.) is enough to show how diversified they are. Apart from the gifts of speaking with tongues, of miraculous healing and exorcism, there are the following groups of gifts:[21]

(1) Charisms of *preaching*: these include the functions of apostles, prophets, teachers, evangelists and exhorters;

(2) Charisms of *service*: these include the functions of deacons and deaconesses, of those who give alms and tend the sick, and of the widows who are in the service of the community;

(3) Charisms of *leadership*: "first converts", elders, bishops, pastors.

But this is not the sum of the charisms, by any means. Even though the word itself may not be used in the immediate context, it is clear that Paul regards suffering as a charism (II Cor. 4:7-12; cf. Col. 1:24). Ultimately *every* "*vocation*" is an "*assigning*" (cf. I Cor. 7:17) of the charism (cf. Rom. 12:3, 6): "Each has his own *special gift* from God, one of one kind and one of another . . .; let everyone lead the life which the Lord has *assigned* to him, and in which God has *called* him" (I Cor. 7:7, 17). Charism is different from a gift for music or mathematics, for example, which one either "has" or does not have. Charism is bestowed, assigned, distributed not on one's own behalf, but on behalf of others; it is not a natural talent, but a call of grace, a call to service. In this sense, of course, even natural talents can become charisms; indeed Paul seems even to regard one's state of life—being married or unmarried (I Cor. 7:7), circumcised or uncircumcised (I Cor. 7:18-20), being a free man or a slave (I Cor. 7:20-24)—as a potential charism: as a call to service. From this viewpoint we can see why Paul can so easily transfer from talking about the apostolate and public functions in the community to talking about private

21. Cf. E. Käsemann, *op. cit.,* 68-70.

virtues when he is listing various charisms (cf. I Cor. 12:28-30; Rom. 12:6-8). Charisms are potentialities which are appealed to, aroused and created by the Spirit of God.

Any gift of the Spirit, any vocation is therefore a charism. Even eating and drinking can become charisms—not of themselves, but when they are done "in the Lord" and "for the Lord"; eating or fasting out of obedience to or love of the Lord, keeping or not keeping certain regulations, living or dying (cf. Rom. 14)—the same is true of everything, provided it is done in faith, in conscience (Rom. 14:22 f.). So the *whole* man with all his human gifts is enlisted in the Lord's service; new gifts are given to him by the Spirit of God, and his life is given a goal.

The Constitution "On the Church" emphasizes that charisms are assigned to Christians according to the free will of God in his grace: "allotting his gifts 'to everyone as he will' (I Cor. 12:11)." The charisms thus prepare us to discharge the *variety* of services which the community has need of: through his gifts the Holy Spirit "makes them [the faithful] fit and ready to undertake the various tasks or offices advantageous for the renewal and upbuilding of the Church". Charisms are explicitly distinguished from sacraments (which include ordination).

Since charisms take such varied forms, they are necessarily spread generally throughout the Church.

(*c*) *Charisms: for the few or for all*? A third misunderstanding of the nature of the charism is to suppose that charisms are limited to a small group of people, that there is a special rank or class of charismatics. But it is far from the case that the great variety of charismatic gifts is concentrated and centralized in a few individuals, the leaders of the community, for example (elders, bishops, elder-bishops).

Charisms, as has been made clear above, are a general rather than a specific phenomenon in the Church. Since they are so various, and everyday, they must be general.

On the evidence of the New Testament it would be impossible to limit charisms to those who hold office in the Church. For a start, Paul gives a very different answer to the question of order and rank in the "hierarchy" than we would usually give today. Carefully numbering them, he lists as follows: "God has appointed in the Church first *apostles,* second *prophets,* third *teachers,* then workers of miracles, then healers, helpers, administrators, speakers in various kinds of tongues. . . . But earnestly desire the higher gifts" (I Cor. 12:28, 31).

In this charismatic order of preference the *apostles* come first, which for Paul include more than the original twelve (cf. Rom. 16:7; I Cor. 9:5); they are the original witnesses of the risen Lord, sent out by him and authorized to preach in his name. Second the *prophets* who are mentioned elsewhere (Eph. 2:20) together with the apostles as the foundation of the Church; they light up the road of the individual and the community, in present and in future, by the freedom of their Spirit-inspired proclamations; they too have been chosen and authorized by God. Third come the *teachers,* who hand on and interpret the message of Christ, shedding light on the tenets of faith and the commandments of that message, and interpreting the Old Testament according to the ideas of the young Church. Like the prophets, they derive their message from the original testimony of the apostles, and direct the present and the future of the community, but instead of intuitive proclamations their work is rather the systematic and theological development of ideas.

But the Church which receives these charisms is in the interim situation between "not yet" and "but already". No member of the community has a plenitude of all charisms. In making his lists Paul is concerned to show that no one can be all things to the community, even though he knows that in individual cases one person might have a number of special gifts, as was true of Paul himself. The nature of these gifts means that the community can never be a one-man band, since charisms are variously distributed: "Are all apostles? Are all prophets? Are all teachers? Do all work miracles? Do all possess gifts of healing? Do all speak with tongues? Do all interpret?" (I Cor. 12:29 f.).

The fact that no one person can do everything is particularly true for Christians with the function of leadership. We may notice that the gift of leadership (κυβερνήσεις, the art of the steersman, of the guide) is not mentioned first, but next to last, together with the helpers, in Paul's list. It is difficult to determine what functions are involved here. Paul urges the Corinthians to be subject to "first converts" (the "first converts in Achaia", I Cor. 16:15 f.; cf. the "first convert in Asia", Rom. 16:5). In the first verse of Philippians, probably one of his last letters, Paul sends a greeting to "bishops and deacons", but we know nothing of their rôle in the community. Much earlier, Paul speaks of those holding authority in the Church (cf. I Thess. 5:12; Rom. 12:8), who are to be recognized and revered: "But we beseech you, brethren, to respect those who labour among you and are over you in the Lord and admonish you, and to esteem them very highly in love because of their work" (I Thess. 5:12 f.).

The charisms of leadership in the Pauline Churches did not at all events produce a "ruling class", an aristocracy of those endowed with the Spirit who separated themselves from the community and rose above it in order to rule over it. The entire New Testament carefully avoids using secular terms of office to describe functions in the community (ἀρχή, τιμή, τέλος), because all of them express a relationship of rulers and ruled. Instead, and by direct contrast, the New Testament speaks of "service" (διαχονία). Still more inclusive, for Paul, is precisely the concept of charism (cf. Rom. 12:6-8), which, as we shall see, describes with theological precision all the services and functions in the Church. The charism cannot be subsumed under the heading of ecclesiastical office, but all Church offices can be subsumed under the charism.[22]

This makes it clear that charisms are not limited to a particular set of persons but are given to each and every Christian. Each Christian has *his* charism. Each Christian is a charismatic. *"Each* has his own special gift from God, one of one kind and one of another" (I Cor. 7:7); "To *each* is given the manifestation of the Spirit for the common good" (I Cor. 12:7); "as *each* has received a gift, employ it for one another, as good stewards of God's varied grace" (I Pet. 4:10).

According to Acts, chapter 2, the Spirit has been poured out "on all flesh". And whoever has a share in the Spirit has a share in the gifts of the Spirit. So charisms are not special marks of distinction belonging to a chosen few, whether on account of their enthusiasm or of their office in the Church, but a distinguishing mark of the whole Church, of the fellowship of all believers. In a Church or community where only ecclesiastical officials rather than all the members of the community are active, there is grave reason to wonder whether the Spirit has not been sacrificed along with the spiritual gifts.

The Constitution "On the Church" emphasizes the general distribution of charismatic gifts: "Allotting his gifts 'to everyone according as he will" (I Cor. 12:11), He (the Holy Spirit) distributes special graces *among the faithful of every rank"*. Here again the text is quoted: "To each is given the manifestation of the Spirit for the common good" (I Cor. 12:7). However, the sentence which the Constitution seeks to apply to those "who preside over the Church" is spoken by Paul, as the

22. See under Chap. E.

text shows beyond any doubt, to the whole community and hence to each individual Christian: "Do not quench the Spirit . . . but test everything; hold fast what is good" (I Thess. 5:19-21).

(d) *The charismatic community*. We have seen that charisms are everyday rather than fundamentally exceptional phenomena, that they are various rather than uniform in kind, and that they are found throughout the Church rather than being restricted to a particular group of people. These conclusions lead to others; that they are phenomena not exclusive to the early Church, but present and contemporary ones; and not peripheral phenomena, but central and essential elements in the Church. Hence one can speak of a *charismatic structure of the Church,* which *includes but goes far beyond the hierarchical* structure of the Church. The theological and practical implications of this are evident.

The prime importance of the idea of charism for Pauline ecclesiology is underlined by the fact that it is, as no other so definitely is, a *specifically Pauline idea.*[23] The Greek word has no Hebrew equivalents, and is difficult to trace, though it may have existed in pre-Christian times. The word was used, outside the Pauline tradition and in no way as a technical term, for a present or a mark of favour; but Paul, so far as we know, was the first to give a technical sense to this rare word and introduce it into theology.

On the basis of all the foregoing evidence we can attempt a theological description of what charism means; in its widest sense it signifies *the call of God, addressed to an individual, to a particular ministry in the community, which brings with it the ability to fulfil that ministry.* We have seen how interconnected charism, vocation and service are; terminologically they seem to merge together; thus "charisms" can alternate with "services" (I Cor. 12:4-6), or with "vocation" (Rom. 11:29; I Cor. 7:7). Prerequisites for "services" are "charisms" and "vocation".

Taking charism in this widest sense, rather than seeing it as a strange, exceptional and miraculous power, we can translate the word simply as "gift of grace" (in secular language there is often an overlap between the ideas of a "gift" for something and a "vocation" for something). But charism as a "gift of grace" must never be seen as something autonomous, as distinct from the giver. All charisms are expressions of God's grace and power, in the Spirit. They all point to the one great charism of God, the new life

23. Cf. E. Käsemann, *op. cit.,* 63-64.

which has been given to us in Christ Jesus; "The charism of God is eternal life in Christ Jesus our Lord" (Rom. 6:23; cf. Rom 5:15 f.). In the fullness of Christ's grace the riches of spiritual gifts are revealed to us (cf. I Cor. 12:4–6; Eph. 4:8, 11; Jn. 1:16). Whether a man is an apostle, a prophet, teacher, evangelist, a bishop or a deacon, whether he consoles, exhorts, forgives, loves—all these things are gifts in Jesus Christ and point to him who is and does all these things in his own person. Charisms are the revelations, in concrete and individual form, of the charis, the power of God's grace, which takes hold of us, leads us to our appointed service and gives us an individual share in the reign of Christ. And to the extent that we have a present share in the grace and the reign of Christ in the Spirit, our charisms are expressions of power (ἐνερ-γήματα), "the manifestation of the Spirit" (I Cor. 12:6 f.): "All these are inspired by one and the same Spirit, who apportions to each one individually as he wills" (I Cor. 12:11). Charisms are pure gifts of the Spirit, and yet the Christian can and must "earnestly desire" the higher charisms (I Cor. 12:31), can and must pray for them (cf. I Cor. 14:13).

In this way we have found an answer to the question: how, given the tremendous variety of charisms which fills the Church, can there be unity; and how, given the freedom of the Spirit, can there be order? The fundamental answer is that the Spirit creates unity and order: "There are varieties of gifts, but the same Spirit . . . to each is given the manifestation of the Spirit for the common good" (I Cor. 12:4, 7).

Unity and order are not created, for the men who have these charisms, by levelling out their variety. It is important for the unity and order of the community that each person has *his* charism. *To each his own*: that is a fundamental principle of the charismatic ordering of the Church. No individual can set himself above others and attempt to seize or subjugate everything; by taking rather than leaving to each his own, he will create not order but disorder (I Cor. 12:12–30). At the same time each one has his charism not for himself but for his fellows. *With one another for one another*: this is a second principle of the charismatic ordering of the Church. More than the "fruits of the Spirit" (Gal. 5:22), which are rather directed towards the sanctification of the individual (love, joy, peace, patience, kindness, goodness, faithfulness, gentleness, self-control), the charisms exist for the "edification of the Church" (I Cor. 14:12; cf. Eph. 4:12 f.). The Christian is not to use his charism as a weapon with which he can seize power and position in the Church, but as a gift for the service of others and of the whole community. Hence the first fruit of the Spirit (Gal. 5:22) and the greatest of the charisms is love (I Cor. 13); charism summons us to follow the way of the cross, the way of service and love. *Obedience to the Lord*: this is a third principle of the charismatic ordering of the Church—we recall the criterion for the discernment of spirits. Order in the Church means for the individual Christian living in one spirit with his individual charism, living a life of love and mutual service, obedience to the one Lord.[24] All charisms have their origin in one and the same giver: God himself through Christ in the Spirit. All charisms are subject to one and the same "law", the law of love. All charisms have one and the same goal: the edification of the community.

The charismatically orientated ordering of the Church does not therefore mean either enthusiasm, which ends in anarchy and disorder, nor legality, which petrifies into mediocrity and uniformity; neither anarchy nor uniformity, neither too much order nor too little, but order in freedom: "where the Spirit of the Lord is, there is freedom" (II Cor. 3:17). Even evidence of hierarchical structures in the early Church—the appointing of elders (an idea borrowed from the Jewish synagogue structure in the Palestinian tradition), which appears to have occurred early on in the Pauline communities (cf. the elder-bishops in Acts, and the indications in Philippians 1:1), and to have solved the problem of the succession to the apostles—even this must be seen not as the beginnings of a clerical ruling system, but against the background of the fundamentally charismatic structure of the Church.[25]

But even this fundamental charismatic structure is only a temporary thing, part of the "not yet" of the eschatological period. It belongs to the "imperfect" things of this interim period and will be replaced by the fullness of perfection: "When the perfect comes, the imperfect will pass away" (I Cor. 13:10).

On this basis of New Testament understanding, we can now appreciate and understand in its complete context the principal text of Vatican II (there are countless other references) on the charisms: "It is not only through the sacraments and Church ministries that the same Holy Spirit sanctifies and leads the People of God and enriches it with virtues. Allotting His gifts 'to everyone according as he will' (I Cor. 12:11), He distributes special graces among the faithful, whatever their position. By

24. Cf. E. Käsemann, *op. cit.*, 76–78.
25. See Chap. E.

these gifts He makes them fit and ready to undertake the various tasks or offices advantageous for the renewal and building up of the Church, according to the words of the Apostle: 'The manifestation of the Spirit is given to everyone for profit' (I Cor. 12:7). These charismatic gifts, whether they be the most outstanding or the more simple and widely diffused, are to be received with thanksgiving and consolation, for they are exceedingly suitable and useful for the needs of the Church. Nonetheless, extraordinary gifts are not to be rashly sought after, nor are the fruits of apostolic labour to be presumptuously expected from them. In any case, judgment as to their genuineness and proper use belongs to those who preside over the Church, and to whose special competence it belongs, not indeed to extinguish the Spirit, but to test all things and hold fast to that which is good" (cf. I Thess. 5:12, 19–21) (CE 12).[26]

If the charisms of individual Christians were discovered and furthered and developed, what dynamic power, what life and movement there would be in such a community, such a Church! "Do not quench the Spirit, do not despise prophesying" (I Thess. 5:19 f.). But Paul's next sentence indicates that these workings of the Spirit and of men filled with the Spirit can lead to tensions and difficulties: "But test everything; hold fast what is good, abstain from every form of evil" (5:21 f.). . . .

26. Cf. Card. L. Suenens, "The charismatic dimension of the Church," in *Council Speeches of Vatican II*, ed. by Y. Congar, H. Küng, D. O'Hanlon, London-New York 1964, 18–21.

Part Four:

THE CHURCH'S MINISTRY TO THE WORLD ON BEHALF OF JESUS

Editor's Introduction

IT IS A FUNDAMENTAL POSTULATE OF A THEOLOGY OF THE church in mission that all ecclesiology is determined Christologically. It has been the endeavor of the first three parts to demonstrate this and draw forth certain implications. God is known in his acts, and through these acts, which occur in the drama of salvation history, a theology is created which, grounded in the mission of God in Christ, points forward to the mission of the Church in the Spirit and power of Christ.

The nature of this ministry is, therefore, also Christologically determined. However, this does not imply a mere theory of ministry, but rather it demands an engagement in ministry which at its very core is theologically determined. In this concluding part, the nature of Christian ministry is explored as first of all *incarnational,* then *kerygmatic,* and finally *diakonal.*

God exists for the world, Barth tells us (Chapter 17), and thus the Church which exists for him must also exist for the world. In Christ, God exists in the flesh for the world. This incarnation of God as both the one who summons the creature into response and as the one who makes that response in his own humanity, determines the orientation, meaning, and purpose of the Church. The sending of God's Son into the world does not cease with the sending of the Church into the world. The Church is formed under the imperative of the incarnation—to know the world as it really is and to reveal the world to the world as it exists under judgment and as the object of reconciliation.

The incarnational Church must experience solidarity with the world, Barth continues, visibly and exoterically, not invisibly and esoterically. In the Church's ministry there is no subtle line drawn which permits the Church to maintain a certain security by drawing back at the last moment for the sake of its own identity. In being conformed to Christ, the Church does not become identical to the

493

world in its solidarity with the world. The radical distinction between Church and world can exist because it is a distinction which carries the full weight of the incarnation itself—Jesus in his solidarity with humanity does not lose his identity as the divine Son of God.

The practical effect of this solidarity is a responsibility for the world, says Barth. The Church is under obligation to the world, for Christ has obliged himself to the world for the sake of its reconciliation. This obligation does not arise out of ethical principles, as though the Church is obliged to share what it possesses itself; nor does the obligation arise out of humanitarian principles, as though human need constitutes a demand upon divine mercy. No, the obligation is a dogmatic postulate which arises out of the theological determination of the Church as the predication of Christ in the world as reconciling love. One could say that the Church needs the world for the sake of its own identity as much as the world needs the Church. It is this obligation to the world which pushes the Church in its ministry beyond that which is owed to either ethics or pity.

In a section which is among the most powerful and provocative that Dietrich Bonhoeffer ever wrote, this obligation is discussed with penetrating and relentless logic (Chapter 18). The proper ethical question in regard to the mission of the Church is not "How can it be good?" but "What is the will of Christ?" The reality of God includes the reality of the world, as that which is affirmed and reconciled in Jesus Christ. Thus, says Bonhoeffer, the old distinction between the sphere of the Church and the sphere of the world has been dissolved. The Church does not deprive the world of "space" for its own existence. Only in the midst of the world can Christ be Christ. The world is taken up in the body of Christ at the incarnation.

It follows, says Bonhoeffer, that the responsibility which the Church has toward the world is concrete and always concerns "my neighbor." This responsibility involves the acceptance of guilt—we members of the Church can no longer maintain our "innocence," for we are accomplices in the sins of the world for the sake of its reconciliation to God.

This is an unnerving, though powerful, idea. It demands to be taken seriously, but also to be carefully critiqued. In Chapter 19, I suggest a view of Bonhoeffer's concept of the body of Christ which seems more in line with the biblical data, and yet which preserves the thrust of his basic concern. The incarnational Church does share in the *kenotic* function of solidarity and acceptance of guilt, but, as Bonhoeffer himself points out, this is Christ's guilt, not our own. It is the guilt and sin which Christ himself bore and which must be continually borne in order that the world may be brought under both judgment and hope. There is an evangelical dimension to the Church's ministry, in this incarnational solidarity, which preserves the radical difference without breaking the solidarity and dissolving the obligation to the world. It needs to be said that the church which is merely different no longer makes a difference in the world. Merely to appear distinct from the world is for a church to abandon the world to its hopelessness and also to lose vital connection with Christ.

In his book, *Freedom Made Flesh,* Ignacia Ellacuría speaks, out of the concern of liberation theology, of this same incarnational imperative for the Church. The section from his book which has been included as Chapter 20 focuses on the Latin American situation, but the ecclesiastical focus and theological framework are pertinent to a much broader picture.

Salvation history is also salvation *in* history, argues Ellacuría, and thus the gospel deals with human social structures and relations. That is, salvation is intrinsically political. The theme of liberation is rooted in the Exodus motif, and is taken to be a universal and cosmic aspect of divine revelation. "The risen Christ," says Ellacuría, "is to be fashioned by the continuing historical incarnation of his redemptive action as Lord of history." Ellacuría goes on to say that Christ will not attain his full measure as Savior until all the different kinds of salvation needed are integrated into him. The charism of a Church is never abstract, but concrete, in terms of meeting specific human need. Sin is social as well as personal, structural as well as ethical. The death/resurrection motif points not only to personal conversion, but to the conversion of social structures, effecting actual liberation from oppression and bondage. As a sign of transcendence, the Church must be present in the world as a liberating force. Thus, the Church points beyond itself as a "sign" to the fulfillment of this redemptive and incarnational hope within history.

The inclusion of this selection is not meant to be an endorsement of all of the assumptions in liberation theology, but to demonstrate a contemporary attempt to take seriously the incarnational nature of ministry. In hearing this plea, we are at least called back to the implications of the incarnation itself as a mission of God in the world by which divine hope is made flesh and the oppressive structures of sin are broken and destroyed.

The second subsection on the *kerygmatic* nature of ministry calls our attention to the act of proclamation as foundational for the reconciliation of the world. In Chapters 21 and 22, Helmut Thielicke and Karl Barth point to the act and content of proclamation. Thielicke is concerned for the transcendent character of the *kerygma* of the Church. It is a representation of God's presence in the world as the eternal one. God continues to address the world as one who stands within but not contained by world-views or first principles. Proclamation does not call man out of history into existential faith, but existentially grasps him as a historical being and calls him into the new being which is Christ.

Barth reminds us that proclamation involves judgment upon the world, but it is not a judgment which the world can pronounce, nor even bear. Jesus Christ is the "judge judged in our place." Thus the content of proclamation is rooted in salvation history. This history is to be narrated in the act of proclamation; that is, told as a story of his history which determines ours. It is not he that needs proclamation, says Barth, but proclamation that needs him.

The theological foundations for the ministry of preaching are here clearly laid out for us. Preaching must be done artfully, but it is more than an art. It must be done cogently and skillfully, but it is more than rational discourse and technique. In the "narrating" of the event of salvation history, the act of proclamation re-enacts the Word-Event of God's presence to the world, for the sake of reconciliation.

Kornelis Miskotte, who served for 25 years as a parish minister as well as Professor of Dogmatics and Ethics at Leyden University, is sympathetic to Karl Barth's "theology of the Word" and contributes an interesting discussion on the nature of preaching (Chapter 23). Miskotte tells us that the Word of God reveals to us the eternal silence of the "gods." The acts of God in history constitute the hermeneutical horizon for the being of God and produce faith as the conclusion and response to these acts. Thus, proclamation as narration of this redemptive history causes the original creative Word to break forth as a revealing and reconciling Word. God is the original questioner, and proclamation reopens the question for which faith is the only appropriate response. Miskotte argues that this proclamation is the true source of renewal in the Church, not innovative methods or techniques. He calls into question the contemporary mood which disparages preaching as "mere words" which hinder communication, and he counters with the claim that in the "spoken Word" the letter becomes Spirit and there is a recovery of the prophetic communication through which both judgment and hope produce healing and wholeness.

As a concluding note to this discussion of the *kerygmatic* nature of ministry, Barth sets in sharp relief the "aweful" task of the preacher (Chapter 24). It is not a matter of *how* one should preach, says Barth, but a question of whether one *can* preach the Word of God! For human words to take up the task of becoming God's Word to man is at first impossible, but is then made possible and necessary by God's own presence in the act of proclamation. The preacher becomes the servant of the event which takes place when the Word is proclaimed. And finally, Barth reminds us, mission alone legitimates preaching.

We are thus brought to the third aspect of the Church's ministry to the world on behalf of Christ—the *diakonal* ministry. In a brief section (Chapter 25), Karl Barth again sets forth the fundamental "law of service" which constrains the Church as the community of Christ. This service cannot be narrowed down to the diaconate, but must be the total life of the Church expressed through each office and function. No person is exempt and no sphere is excluded.

T. F. Torrance then proceeds to disclose the nature of this service in an essay which expounds the content of Jesus Christ as the true *diakonos*—the servant of God. It is this service which provides the norm and content for Christian service. Jesus takes upon himself the sins and weaknesses of those whom he serves. He "hazards" his own existence. He assimilates his disciples into his own *diakonia* and founds the Church as the on-going manifestation of his own service.

The Church must avoid two temptations, says Torrance: first, the temptation to use temporal power to fulfill this service and thus insure success, and secondly, the temptation to leave the corporate aspect of this service to the state and restrict its ministry to forgiveness. Instead, the Church must present Christ "clothed with his gospel" and Christ "clothed with the needs of men." Intercession, witness, and reconciliation characterize this service as the manner of the Church's conformity to Christ.

In an attempt to work out the theological implications of the *diakonal* nature of the Church's ministry, Karn Griffen discusses the role of the Church as a "therapeutic community" which offers the service of healing and growth through counseling and caring (Chapter 27). The Christian counselor, says Griffen, is "cloaked in the covenant community" so that the counselor is united in a common humanity with the incarnate Jesus as well as the other person. The implications of this for the counseling ministry of the Church are thought-provoking and far-reaching. Counseling cannot be considered to be an adjunct to the central act of the Church in its own existence, but rather is the "enfleshed" ministry of Jesus himself who provides the resources of his own body and blood, of his own wholeness and faith, to those who are paralyzed and immobilized by fears within and without.

The epilogue to this entire discussion of ministry properly belongs to T. F. Torrance, who, as much as any other contemporary theologian, is both a churchman and a prophetic voice, summoning the Church to its true calling. The Church must re-examine the prosecution of its mission, says Torrance, for there can be found within it a certain self-inflicted obsolescence due to preoccupation with relevance to current forms of self-expression. Furthermore, there can be found a "moral inversion" through which material purposes and ideological causes become the focus of a "homeless" moral passion. This inversion exposes a lack of the Holy Spirit as the source of the Church's Christological sense and direction of mission. Lacking this root and direction, the Church is helplessly caught in the cross currents of various pressure groups, socio-moral movements, and anxiety-induced innovations from within.

Torrance calls for a renewal of the Church's worship through a new understanding of the humanity of Christ which gives an objective basis for our own approach to God. He suggests that new conceptual structures of reality need to be worked out which scientifically expose the mind of the world to the rationality of God's own mind, producing *metanoia* which leads to more openness of mind and heart to the creative Spirit of God.

In returning to the theological foundations for ministry, we are not seeking a reinstatement of an "old conservatism" which mistakes ancient tradition for the original Word. It is the original Word of reconciliation, historically given, incarnated, proclaimed, and re-presented in living structures of liberation and expectation, that we are invoking on behalf of a world that will not be comforted with a stone, when the cry is for bread. "This is the bread which came down from heaven, not such as the fathers ate and died; he who eats this bread will live forever. . . . 'Lord, give us this bread always'" (John 6:58,34).

17

KARL BARTH

The Community for the World

THE COMMUNITY OF JESUS CHRIST IS FOR THE WORLD, I.E., FOR each and every man, for the man of every age and place who finds the totality of earthly creation the setting, object and instrument and yet also the frontier of his life and work. The community of Jesus Christ is itself creature and therefore world. Hence, as it exists for men and the world, it also exists for itself. But it is the human creature which is ordained by nature to exist for the other human creatures distinct from it. It is what it is, and exists for itself, only in fulfilment of this ordination. Even within the world to which it belongs, it does not exist ecstatically or eccentrically with reference to itself, but wholly with reference to them, to the world around. It saves and maintains its own life as it interposes and gives itself for all other human creatures.

In this way it also exists for God, for the Creator and Lord of the world, for the fulfilment of His purpose and will for and to all human creatures. First and supremely it is God who exists for the world. And since the community of Jesus Christ exists first and supremely for God, it has no option but in its own manner and place to exist for the world. How else could it exist for God? The centre around which it moves eccentrically is not, then, simply the world as such, but the world for which God is. For God is who He is, not *in abstracto* nor without relationship, but as God for the world. The community of Jesus Christ is the human creature whose existence as existence for God has the meaning and purpose of being, on behalf of God and in the service and discipleship of His existence, an existence for the world and men.

That it exists for the world because for God, follows simply and directly from the fact that it is the community of Jesus Christ and

From Karl Barth, *Church Dogmatics*, IV/3, pp. 762-764, 768-795. © T. & T. Clark Ltd., Edinburgh. Used by permission of the Publisher.

has the basis of its being and nature in Him. He calls, gathers and upbuilds it. He rules it as its Lord and Shepherd. He constitutes it ever afresh in the event of His presence and by the enlightening power of His Holy Spirit. He is the centre around which it moves eccentrically. In Him and by Him it is won for God and claimed for His discipleship and service. For in Him God is not for Himself but for the world. In Him God has given Himself to and for the world to reconcile it to Himself. In Him God, supremely and truly God, has become man. This decides the orientation, meaning and purpose of His community. As the people created by Jesus Christ and obedient to Him, it is not subsequently or incidentally but originally, essentially and *per definitionem* summoned and impelled to exist for God and therefore for the world and men. In this way but only in this way, as the human creature thus orientated, can it and will it also exist for itself, in correspondence with the fact that the God who acts and speaks in Jesus Christ expresses His own true divinity precisely in His true humanity.

The disciples as a whole, namely, as the body of disciples or Christendom, are the "salt of the earth" (Mt. 5:13), the "light of the world" (Mt. 5:14), and, as "sons of the kingdom," the good seed sown in the field which is the world (Mt. 13:38). It is to be noted that we are not told that it is proper to them, or required of them, to be this, or that they are to become salt, light and seed in extension or completion of some very different determination of their existence. As they are disciples of Jesus, ordained to be with Him, it belongs originally and essentially to their existence that "he might send them forth" (Mk. 3:14). Paul, too, writes indicatively and not imperatively that "ye shine as lights in the world" (Phil. 2:15). As a city on a hill they cannot be hid from the world around, nor be of no significance to it (Mt. 5:14). Τὸ φῶς ὑμῶν, the light which they have and are, which as such is not put under a bushel but naturally on a candlestick, actually shines among men. To be sure, there is a powerful element of exhortation in the λαμψάτω: they are to become what they are. But how can this fail to happen? They would necessarily be something very different, and not the disciples of Jesus, if they were not salt, light and seed. Their sending forth, first to Israel (Mt. 10:5f.), then to the nations (Mt. 28:19f.), simply explains their being and nature. As the disciples of Jesus, from the very outset they do not exist for themselves, or they do so only as they exist for the world according to the tenor of these images.

To be sure, the community is the people which is called out of the nations by the Word of God, which is separated from the world, which is separately constituted within it and which is thus set over against it. To be sure, it is in this distinction that its particular glory is displayed as the glory of the firstborn to whom is entrusted what is to the world the absolutely new thing of the self-declaration and knowledge of the omnipotent mercy of God. To be sure, it acquires and has, with all its members, its own full share in this good thing. How could it be light without itself being bright, or seed without itself being living? It is in the community first, and in the life of the men called to it and gathered in it, that salvation, reconciliation, the covenant, the justification of man before God and his sanctification for Him, can and should be expressed *de facto,* that the peace of God which passeth understanding should be experienced, tasted and felt as an event. As it exists for the world, neither it nor its members who belong to it and also exist for the world can or will go away empty. But this is true only as and to the extent that it is for the world, i.e., only in the sphere and power of the determination in virtue of which, transcending itself, it is what it is. Called out of the world, the community is genuinely called into it. And the reality of its calling out depends upon there being no gap between it and the calling which ineluctably follows, upon the separation from and the turning to the world taking place in a single movement.

The true community of Jesus Christ is the community which God has sent out into the world in and with its foundation. As such it exists for the world. It does so not in virtue of any dignity, authority or power immanent to its creaturely nature as one people among others, but in virtue of the plenary power with which it is invested, and which is thus proper to it, in and with its particular foundation as this people. No creature as such can exist for others. Even the Church is a creature. How, then, can it exist for the world, for the totality of creatures, for all men? To the extent that it can, it is not "of the world" even though it is "in the world" and itself a creature (Jn. 17:11), just as the One who sends it forth with plenary divine power is not "of the world" (Jn. 17:16). And the fact that it can exist for the world is the plenary power with which it is invested by Him and with its foundation and as He sends it forth. It is invested with it in the context of His divine sending and in correspondence with the plenary divine power proper to Him. We can and must speak of it as strongly as this, but not more strongly. Its sending is not a repetition, extension or continuation. His own sending does not cease as He sends it. It does not disappear in its sending. It remains its free and independent presupposition. Its sending is simply ordered on its own lower level in relation to His. The power with which it is invested is comparable with His as is necessarily the case since He Himself gave it, but neither quantitatively nor qualitatively is it equal. He is sent to precede it on the way into the world. It is sent to follow Him on the same way. These are two things. But the two sendings are comparable because they have the same origin. The one God who sends Him as the Father also sends them through Him the Son. Again, they are comparable because they have the same goal. He and they are both sent into the world, which means very generally that they are directed to the world and exist for it.

At this point we naturally have in mind Jn. 20:21: "As my Father hath sent me (ἀπέσταλκεν), even so send I you (πέμπω)"; and also Jn. 17:18: "As thou hast sent me into the world (ἀπέστειλας), even so have I also sent them (ἀπέστειλα) into the world." The adverb καθώς used in both verses indicates the interconnexion, parallel, analogy and comparable nature of the two processes. The emphatic κἀγώ at the beginning of the second statement in both cases underlines, of course, the fact that Jesus is conscious that He with His sending is to be ranged alongside the Father who sends Him. He sends them in execution of His own sending. If the two processes are put in the perfect and present in Jn. 20 and the aorist in Jn. 17, the different nuances required by the contexts simply serve to emphasise their character as a historically interconnected event. In Jn. 20 the use of the two verbs ἀποστέλλειν and πέμπειν, which in any case are hard to distinguish in Johannine terminology, enables a distinction to be made between the sending of Jesus Himself and that of His disciples. In both cases, however, "sending" means to be invested with δόξα, to participate in the dignity, authority and power given to the one commissioned to go to a third party for the discharge of his mission. Hence we note the point, which is important in the present context, that it is twice emphasised in Jn. 17 that the goal of the sending both of Jesus and of His disciples is the cosmos. The world is the third party to which they are sent, Jesus by the Father and the community by Jesus. Both His and their fully accredited embassy is to the world.

In the third sub-section we shall have to speak of the mission to the world which the community has to accomplish as sent by Jesus

Christ. It is not idly, but as it performs this, that the community exists for the world. This action, however, has a hidden yet not unrecognisable preliminary form in which it may be concretely described. It has as it were a living root in which it does not seem to be action, nor to take place for the world, but in which already there does take place something decisive for its empowering and actualisation. There, not in the inactivity but in the quietness of this basis, there begins the obedience of the community to its commission. What does not begin there will either not be action at all or only disobedient and therefore powerless and unfruitful action. If the community sent into the world is active towards the world at all, not like a fire of straw which suddenly flares up and as quickly dies down again, but rather like a constantly kindling, shining, warming and even consuming flame, then it is from the quietness of this basis where the movement is prepared and intimated, from which it derives its impulse, direction and law and by which it will be continually renewed, corrected and transcended. In this second sub-section we must now indicate the more essential elements concerning this basis of the active execution of the commission linked with its sending into the world.

We may begin by stating that the true community of Jesus Christ is (1) the fellowship in which it is given to men to know the world as it is. The world does not know itself. It does not know God, nor man, nor the relationship and covenant between God and man. Hence it does not know its own origin, state nor goal. It does not know what divides nor what unites. It does not know either its life and salvation or its death and destruction. It is blind to its own reality. Its existence is a groping in the dark. The community of Jesus Christ exists for and is sent into the world in the first basic sense that it is given to it, in its knowledge of God and man and the covenant set up between them, to know the world as it is. We may well say that, itself belonging also to the world, it is the point in the world where its eyes are opened to itself and an end is put to its ignorance about itself. It is the point in the world where the world may know itself in truth and reality. From this basic sense in which the community exists for and is sent into the world there necessarily proceeds what it may do on its behalf. If it did not have this knowledge, how could it do anything for it, or how could it do the right thing for it? But to know it, because to know God and man and the covenant between them, is given to it from the very outset in and with its founding, gathering and upbuilding, seeing that it has its origin in the prophecy of Jesus Christ and is created by the revelation and in the knowledge of the divine act of reconciliation accomplished in Him. The revelation and knowledge of this divine act is at the same time the revelation and knowledge of the world as it really is, as ordered, reformed and renewed by this divine act, of its origin, state and goal, of its possibilities and limitations, of its nature and perversion, of its need and promise. It is first and basically in the knowledge thus grounded that the community confronts the world, or rather assists it as itself belonging to it.

But to know the world means concretely to know man, to see with free and untrammelled eyes who, what, where and how men exist. It thus means to be constantly aware, both as a whole and in detail, both inwardly and outwardly, of what is involved in man's existence and situation as determined by the good creation of God, by the disruptive factor of his own intervening transgression and its consequences, and decisively and predominantly by the grace of God. To know man is to see together all these conditions of all human life, to see each of them only in its positive and negative relations to the others, and therefore to see each individual man, or each natural or historical group of men, on the basis of the fact that God's good creation, man's own sin and the reconciling grace of God may all determine his being and nature, its action and inaction. To know men is respectfully to weigh their great and little, collective and individual achievements and works in their positive significance, neither dramatising nor underestimating their limitation and corruption, their aberration and cruelty, but quietly and yet firmly seeing them in the limits of their guilt and therefore as intolerably evil, and above all knowing both human good and human bad in its limitation by what God is and has done for them all. To know man is to see and understand, how in fact all men, the strong and the weak, the clever and the foolish, the able and the needy, the leaders and their willing or unwilling followers, the indolent and the industrious, the religious and the irreligious, the apparently or genuinely law-abiding and the crude or refined transgressors, the Western and Eastern orators, newspaper men and liars, the men whose interests and orientation are academic, technical, aesthetic, political, or ecclesiastical, and the men who have no interests or orientation at all—it is to see and understand how all of them are both impelled and restricted. To see and understand men is to perceive, that is, how all of them are impelled by some normal or abnormal faith in a life which is thought to be meaningful for them and by the more or less justifiable or at least understandable concern that they should seek to do this or lest they might miss it; and yet how all of them are restricted by the limitations of the *condition humaine,* by the brevity of their day, by the contingence of their environment and their own potentialities, by the relationships imposed upon them or more or less fashioned by themselves, and by their various distinctive or unknown personal rivals and opponents. Nor should it be forgotten that all these men who are impelled and restricted are also active to impel and restrict. Yet to know man is not merely to see and understand all this. It is to see and understand above all that God is the God of all these men, that His omnipotent mercy rules over all without exception, over both their heights and their depths, their glory and their misery, that no matter how lost they are they are not lost to Him, that no matter how hard they fight against Him they cannot break free from Him, that as they are created so they are also guided and upheld by His hand. To know men is to see and understand that, as surely as Jesus Christ died and rose again for all, the grace of God has reference and is promised and addressed to all. To know men, to be aware of them, in this critical and comprehensive way is to know the world as it is. For the world as seen in all its distinctions, antitheses and inner contradictions and yet as seen in relation to Jesus Christ and therefore originally and definitely with God, is the world as it really is. The world as seen and understood in any other way is not the world as it is; it is a mere picture of the world projected idealistically, positivistically, or existentially, scientifically or mythologically, with or without a moral purpose, pessimistically or lightheartedly, yet always with an unhealthy naivety and one-sidedness. The world thinks that it knows itself when it draws and contemplates a book of such pictures, whereas in truth, or rather in the most radical untruth, it misses its own reality and is simply groping in the dark as it turns the various pages. In these pictures men and the world are not seen nor understood. For how can they be when, as in these pictures, they are played off against each other in terms of their different ways and conditions instead of being generously seen together from every angle? But how can we acquire the generosity of this common view unless originally and definitively we see them together with God? And how can we do this both critically and comprehensively, with any real cogency or clarity, unless we do so on the sure basis and ground of God's covenant with man, with all men, concluded in Jesus Christ? As the world is neither able nor willing for this, so it is in no position to know itself in its true reality.

The community is the place in the world where man and therefore the world may be known as they are with the free and untrammelled and universal gaze, with the critical and yet comprehensive generosity, which we have just described. But are man and the world really known as they are in this place? The gift of this knowledge implies the question of its realisation. Is the task thereby set perceived and tackled? In other words, do we have the true community of Jesus Christ? It may well be affirmed that we have to do here with a true *nota ecclesiae,* with an external sign by which the true community of Jesus Christ may be infallibly known. In this as in every other respect the true community of Jesus Christ does not exist esoterically and invisibly but visibly and exoterically, so that it may be noted by the world around. To be sure, those around cannot see that it is the enlightening power of the Holy Spirit, the constraining love of Jesus Christ, which enables them to know the world as it is. But even the community and its members cannot see this; they can know it to be true and actual only in faith. On the other hand, the knowledge which has this hidden basis, if it is not merely given to men but realised by them, must and will be noticeable even to those without in the manner in which the community comes to them, acts towards them, thinks of them and speaks to and concerning them, and finally in the manner in which it discharges its commission to them. It necessarily emerges in the being and activity of the community, whatever their attitude to it. It necessarily impresses itself upon them, causing them to consider that in the community it has to do with a society of men who are at least honestly attempting, and are also able, to see and understand them in their own place and manner, in their worldliness. They cannot possibly be seen and judged and addressed and treated by the true community of Jesus Christ as strangers by strangers, but rather as those who are well acquainted. If the basis of the critical and comprehensive generosity with which they are approached by the Christian community, if God Himself as the secret, origin and goal of the community's view of them, is hidden from them, yet they cannot fail to note this generous view as such, puzzling though it may be. This can and should be accepted as a criterion, and indeed as a fundamental criterion, whether all is well with the Church to which we belong and for which we are in part responsible, and with ourselves as responsible members of this Church. Where the freedom, the openness, the universality and the generosity of this knowledge of the world as it is cannot be seen, noted and detected without, where the community does not give those around something to think about in this regard, where the impression is rather given that they are not really known but are merely preached at in ignorance, this may well be a bad and supremely alarming sign that something is decisively wrong in the inward relation of the community to its own basis of existence and that under the cover of sacred zeal there is a process of defection from its Lord. Everything is perhaps lacking to the community, and all that has still to be said about its existence for the world is perhaps built on sand or in the air, if there is a deficiency or failure at this central point, and if in its surrender to a picture of the world in place of the reality it ranges itself with the world in its groping.

We continue our description of the basis and origin of the obedience of the community to its task by stating that the true community of Jesus Christ is (2) the society in which it is given to men to know and practise their solidarity with the world. Not their conformity to it! The community cannot be conformed to the world; the salt is not to lose its savour (Mt. 5:13). On the contrary, it is very unlike the world inasmuch as in distinction from it its eyes are open—opened by Jesus Christ, by the enlightening power of the Holy Spirit—to the light of the life given in Jesus Christ as this also shines in Him. But as it may see this light, it must see and express its own solidarity with the world. What shines for it, and illumines it when it is given to it to see it, is the love (Jn. 3:16) with which God has loved the world to such a degree and in such a way that He has given His only Son for it. If it is to share this love, where can it find itself set, or try to set itself, but at the side and indeed in the midst of this world which God has loved? It necessarily closes its eyes again to the light which it may see in distinction from the world, and therefore conforms again to the world, if it tries to ignore or to deny in practice the fact that it belongs to the world, thus attempting not to be in solidarity with it. It necessarily flees the love of God if it tries to flee the world and not to be worldly within it. In this attempt it necessarily becomes unfaithful to its sending, not to a place alongside or above the world, but to the world itself, before it has even taken the very first step. Solidarity with the world means full commitment to it, unreserved participation in its situation, in the promise given it by creation, in its responsibility for the arrogance, sloth and falsehood which reign within it, in its suffering under the resultant distress, but primarily and supremely in the free grace of God demonstrated and addressed to it in Jesus Christ, and therefore in its hope. How can there be any question of a generous view and understanding apart from this participation? The community which knows the world is necessarily the community which is committed to it. This brings us to the second basic sense in which it exists for the world. Of what value would be all it might do for it if it were done with no share, or with only a reserved and partial share, in its existence, if it were only done to it externally and from a distance? If the community acts, and acts meaningfully, then it does so as it sees and finds its own cause in that of the world, and that of the world in its own.

Here, too, our concern is with men. Now there can be no doubt that in the discharge of its mission to them the community has in a sense to keep its distance, and even to contradict and oppose them. Without saying No it cannot really say Yes to them. But of what value would be all its well-founded and solemn withdrawal, or its well-meaning and justifiable contradiction and opposition, if it did not proceed from the profoundest commitment to the whole of humanity and each individual man?

The No of the Pharisees to those around was undoubtedly sincere, but it could not be significant nor fruitful because, as their name indicates, it was the No of separatists, of those who separated themselves and were separate from the rest of men by the fact that they did not think that they had any share in their transgressions and corruption and the impending wrath of God, that they were not prepared to accept any responsibility for the actions and impulses of this *'am ha'aretz,* that they would not share the consequences of its folly and wickedness, and therefore refused to participate, of course, in the hope which dawned precisely for this *'am ha'aretz,* this *profanum vulgus.*

What is telling and important from the standpoint of the community is not the true or false principles or the lack of principle which confront it in men, but the man himself who is controlled or not controlled by these principles and of whom it knows that as such he belongs to God. What is telling and important is the indestructible destiny of this man, his aberrations and confusions, and the universally applicable Word of his justification and sanctification accomplished in Jesus Christ. From this man it cannot separate itself. It belongs to him. It must share unreservedly in his existence. ''When he saw the multitudes, he was moved with compassion'' (Mt. 9:36). And the fact that He was moved with compassion means originally that He could not and would not close His mind to the existence and situation of the multitude, nor hold Himself aloof from it, but that it affected Him, that it went right to His heart, that He made it His own, that He could not but identify Himself with them. Only He could do this with the breadth with which He did so. But His community cannot follow any other line. Solidarity with the world means that those who are genuinely pious approach the children of the world as such, that those who are genuinely righteous are not ashamed to sit down with the unrighteous as friends, that those who are genuinely wise do not hesitate to seem to be fools among fools, and that those who are genuinely holy are not too good or irreproachable to go down "into hell" in a very secular fashion.

Les saints vont en enfer (G. Cesbron). The solidarity of the community with the world means to give as little offence as possible to Jews and Greeks as well as fellow-Christians (I Cor. 10:32). Even more strongly, it means to be as a Jew to Jews and as without law to those who are without law (I Cor. 9:20). Or to put it more strongly still, it means to be all things to all men (I Cor. 9:22).

The solidarity of the community with the world consists quite simply in the active recognition that it, too, since Jesus Christ is the Saviour of the world, can exist in worldly fashion, not unwillingly nor with a bad conscience, but willingly and with a good conscience. It consists in the recognition that its members also bear in themselves and in some way actualise all human possibilities. Hence it does not consist in a cunning masquerade, but rather in an unmasking in which it makes itself known to others as akin to them, rejoicing with them that do rejoice and weeping with them that weep (Rom. 12:15), not confirming and strengthening them in evil nor betraying and surrendering them for its own good, but confessing for its own good, and thereby contending against the evil of others, by accepting the fact that it must be honestly and unreservedly among them and with them, on the same level and footing, in the same boat and within the same limits as any or all of them. How can it boast of and rejoice in the Saviour of the world and men, or how can it win them—to use another Pauline expression—to know Him and to believe in Him, if it is not prepared first to be human and worldly like them and with them?

It manifests a remarkable conformity to the world if concern for its purity and reputation forbid it to compromise itself with it. The world only too easily sees itself in a community which has no care but for its own life and rights and manner and which thus tries to separate itself from those around. The world itself constantly divides into individual cliques, interested groups, cultural movements, nations, religions, parties and sects of all kinds, each of which is sure of the goodness of its own cause and each anxious within its limits to maintain and assert itself in face of all the rest. The world will not accept the inward interconnexion of its whole striving, activity and suffering, but seems naively or with conscious superiority to assume that it should not think or speak or act or conduct itself in terms of universality and solidarity. To be sure, there is no lack of philosophical, moral, political and even religious insights which clearly point in this direction in principle, nor of the corresponding well-meant reminders and admonitions. Quite obviously, however, there is no basic impulse necessarily driving in this direction. And it can quietly acquiesce in this lack and find justification for its sectarianism if it discovers that the community of Jesus Christ finally suffers from the same deficiency, that it takes the form only of another and perhaps even more radical separation, that it does not accept the solidarity of its particular humanity with all other good or bad human manifestations, that it is not, in contrast to the world, determined and controlled in practice by a basic impulse irresistibly driving it to the breadth of that great interconnexion. As distinct from all other circles and groups, the community of Jesus Christ cannot possibly allow itself to exist in this pharisaical conformity to the world. Coming from the table of the Lord, it cannot fail to follow His example and to sit down at table with the rest, with all sinners.

What we said concerning the *nota ecclesiae* which is to be affirmed in this context must now be developed and deepened. The community is the noteworthy point in the world at which the latter not only sees and understands itself as it is but at which, in spite of its inner distinctions and contradictions, it is permitted and commanded in a way which is exemplary to achieve inward peace and unity. What are all the internal antitheses of the world compared with that in which the community as the people of Jesus Christ confronts the world in its totality? Yet that which separates the community from the world also binds it to it, and that with a strength which has no peer in the various alliances, brotherhoods and unions known also to the world. For in it there rules the One who, verily distinct from the whole world as the eternal Son of the eternal Father, unreservedly gives Himself to it to reconcile it in His person to God, making common cause with it, not avoiding its sin but bearing it and making it His own. How can the particularity of the human fellowship established and ruled by Him fail to manifest itself in the fact that, without being able to do for it what He has done, it follows Him in this attitude of His to the world? By the enlightening power of His Holy Spirit it is not led out of the world but into the world. Its singularity cannot express or declare itself in separation from the world but only in the most genuine attachment to it. This means, however, that precisely in the spirituality of its existence, in its whole being and action, it can only approach the world in a sincerely worldly character, making it obvious that in good and ill alike it belongs to it. What it has to do in the world saves it from being lost in the world even though it is worldly. But only as it does this in truly worldly fashion, does it do so as the true community of Jesus Christ. The world cannot see, of course, in whose service it stands or whom it follows and obeys in its worldly being and action in the world. But it can and should see the community as the place where it is given to men to do in an exemplary way that of which it is not itself capable in its internal contradictions, not tearing down bridges but building and traversing them, being with others and like them for all their singularity, sharing and bearing as their own all the hopes and burdens in the existence, situation and constitution of others. And again, if the community is neither able nor willing to do this, we are faced by the menacing question whether it is really adapted to perform that which it has been commanded to do in the world in and with its mission. Might it not be that, if it holds back at this point, being like the world instead of unlike it in an exemplary way, it basically lacks no less than everything for the discharge of its task?

In description of the basis on which the community executes its commission, it must be said finally and decisively that as the true community of Jesus Christ it is (3) the society in which it is given to men to be under obligation to the world. As they know it, and are united in solidarity with it, they are made jointly responsible for it, for its future, for what is to become of it. Jesus Christ their Lord, when He was in the world, suffered with it and for it, and acted for it and to it. And the prophetic Word of this work of His, as the Word of truth about its new reality established in Him, is the Word of renewal which here and now applies to the world and affects it. Hence His community cannot be content contemplatively to know the world in all its heights and depths. The God who acts in Jesus Christ does not Himself confront it in this way, merely as an omniscient spectator. Nor can it be content to participate only passively in its being and corruption, its nature and degeneration, its history and destiny. God Himself has not associated with it in this way, in idle co-existence. To be sure, the community as the people of God in world-occurrence is not burdened with the commitment and responsibility which God has assumed and carries towards it. It has neither created the world nor reconciled it to God. Itself a creature among others, it belongs to the world. Hence it cannot be its task to rule it as does the God who reconciled it to Himself in Jesus Christ and who will finally do so as the coming Redeemer in the last revelation of Jesus Christ. Nevertheless, it is called and appointed to the active service of this God. Within the limits of its creaturely capacity and ability it is ordained and summoned to co-operate with Him in His work. And since His work is on and in the world, in its own place and manner it, too, is pledged to the world and made responsible for what is to become of it. Different though its action may be from His, in its own definite function and within the appointed limits it, too, is summoned and freed and commissioned for action in and towards the world. Hence in the course and movement of the world, in its rises and falls, in its progressions, retrogressions and pauses, it cannot possibly be neutral or passive, nor withdraw into itself, into its profounder knowledge of it, or into a sincere but inactive participation in its situation. It is sent to the world to play its own part in its own way, not merely knowing it better in its good and evil, its greatness and misery, nor merely hoping and suffering with it, but also waiting with it for its future and with it hastening towards this future. To the basic sense in which it exists for the world there belongs as a third and as it were culminating element the consciousness, which excludes any possible quietism, that it is committed to it, i.e., that it is sent in order that it may zealously do for it that which is required and possible in the light of this future.

In the world it has to do with men. It could perhaps ignore and pass by as non-essential both the world and what takes place in it if it were not that in the world, whether in small things or in great, we are always concerned with the existence, enterprises and experiences, the acts of commission and omission, the triumphs and defeats, the joys and sorrows, the short life and bitter death of men. It is because this is so, because the call comes to it from the man whom God has elected and loved, that the community of Jesus Christ and the men united in it are bound to the world and everywhere summoned to action in relation to it. For God's active intervention for man, His eternal election of all men in the One, His giving of this One for all, His Word which goes out to all in this One, is the basis of its own being and existence. Whether it knows and values and accepts and confirms the fact or not, the brothers of this One, those who in Him are justified before God and sanctified for Him, are all fellowmen with the men united in the community. Hence an inactive or neutral faith in relation to them could not possibly be faith in the God who has done this for all in that One. It is thus impossible that the community which believes in this God should pass by those who are without as the priest and Levite passed by the man who had fallen among thieves.

All those who are without are waiting not only for the understanding and solidarity and participation, but for the helping action of the Christian community, for that which it alone in the whole world can do for them. Whether they are aware of it or not, their whole being and striving and existence utters the cry of the Macedonian: "Come over... and help us" (Ac. 16:9). To be sure, they do not realise that they await and need what the community of Jesus Christ can do and is called to do for them if God acknowledges its activity. If they did, why should they look around for so many different means with which they think they can help themselves? Yet this does not alter the objective fact that they do actually need and lack and seek and expect to find the one thing which the Christian community of all creatures is called to do for them. In spite of every appearance or subjective experience to the contrary, this is true of every man, since none can evade what God is and has done for him in Jesus Christ and what it is appointed that he, too, should know in His Word. Therefore: "Behold, I say unto you, Lift up your eyes, and look on the fields; for they are white already [not in four months but already] to harvest" (Jn. 4:35). This is why the community is under obligation to the world. It cannot possibly refrain from meeting, within the framework of its task and ability, the actual and existing request of humanity. It cannot leave it in the lurch, nor to its own devices. It has no option but to follow the saying of Jesus to His disciples in Mk. 6:37: "Give ye them to eat," and therefore to give hungry men that which they need and in spite of every appearance to the contrary demand. It is true, of course, that they cannot do this without first allowing Him to fill their own hands that they may give. How could they do it if it were not really given them to do it, and therefore if they themselves had not to ask for that which is necessary thereto? Only the *ecclesia orans* can and will be the *ecclesia efficaciter laborans,* the community which really corresponds to its responsibility. It is also true that when what is given to it passes through its hands it does not go hungry but is itself fed. Yet when it asks for it, it is given in order that it should pass through its hands to men, and that it should thus do and accomplish what it is sent into the world to do.

Again the community would be guilty of too close conformity to the world if it were to exist within it for its own sake, refusing the active assistance which it ought to give. The world indeed thinks that it can and should nourish and sustain itself as each and all satisfy themselves, playing the role of their own neighbours, assistants and helpers. It is a profoundly hungry world just because the way of the priest and Levite is only too characteristically its own. What it needs is not to be confirmed and strengthened by another variation of its own way, but to be pointed beyond it in unambiguous practice. It waits for a Good Samaritan to appear within it who will not act for himself, who will not be his own neighbour, assistant and helper, who will relieve it of the burden of being left to itself and having to save and preserve itself. A community alive and interested and active only in and for itself, and inactive towards those around, might well be familiar in its conformity to the world, and to that extent acceptable, but in the long run it could only prove a source of disillusionment. The Christian community cannot encounter the world in this conformity. To be sure, it is not itself the Good Samaritan who has come into the world as the Saviour, active not for Himself but only for it in the manner and the power of God. And it is well advised not to try to play this role. But it is gathered and upbuilt by this Good Samaritan for active service on His behalf, and it is actually sent out into the world in this service. If it cannot do what He does, and it should not pretend it can, it may and should follow Him in what He does. It may and should be obedient to His command. It exists to do this, and therefore to set up in the world a new sign which is radically dissimilar to its own manner and which contradicts it in a way which is full of promise. In all its creaturely impotence and human corruption, it is required to do this. It is indeed made responsible for doing it, and therefore, for all the modesty incumbent upon it, it must not fail to do it.

We are thus given a fuller and sharper understanding still of the *nota ecclesiae* visible in this context. The true community of Jesus Christ does not rest in itself. It does not merely contemplate the striving of the world with its better knowledge. It does not refrain from active participation. It exists as it actively reaches beyond itself into the world. It acts and works within it. Not by a long way does all its supposed or ostensible ecclesiastical outreach into the world validate it as the real community of Jesus Christ, as the true Church. It might well reach beyond itself in denial or falsification of its task, or with shortsightedness, ignorance or arrogance. In its undertaking, as in that of the builder or the king of Lk. 14:28f., the question might seriously arise whether it has sufficient to finish. It is not a matter of any activity in the world, but of that which is required, of that which corresponds to its commission, of that for which it is empowered by the One who gives it. In no circumstances, however, may it or should it try to evade this task. In discharging it, it will always need the forgiveness of the sins which it commits, and therefore correction, and therefore constant self-criticism. But even the most stringent self-criticism must never be a reason or occasion for prudently doing nothing. Better something doubtful or over bold, and therefore in need of correction and forgiveness, than nothing at all! If even in the most holy reserve and modesty and prudence it prefers to fold its hands and therefore to rest in itself, it is certainly not the true Church. The true Church may sometimes engage in tactical withdrawal, but never in strategic. It can never cease wholly or basically from activity in the world. It does not exist intermittently, nor does it ever exist only partially, as the sent community, but always and in all its functions it is either leaping out or on the point of leaping out to those to whom it is sent. In every respect, even in what seems to be purely inner activity like prayer and the liturgy and the cure of souls and biblical exegesis and theology, its activity is always *ad extra*. It is always directed *extra muros* to those who are not, or not yet, within, and visibly perhaps never will be. It exists in this venture which is no more than the simple and unassuming venture of its obedience. It is recognised as the true Church by the fact that it is engaged in this venture of obedience. Self-criticism in the Church is meaningful and fruitful only if it does not arrest it in this venture but stimulates and impels it afresh and as never before. And only as it makes this venture can it be sure of the forgiveness of its sins. The world exists in self-orientation; the Church in visible contrast cannot do so.

The true community of Jesus Christ is the society in which it is given to men to see and understand the world as it is, to accept solidarity with it, and to be pledged and committed to it. We have made these statements in development of the proposition that the Church as the true community exists essentially for the world and may thereby be known as the true Church. But the presupposition that it is the society in which these things are given to men requires certain elucidations, and above all it needs a solid foundation.

We may begin with three elucidations. We are dealing (1) with men to whom it is *given* in their adherence to the fellowship of the Church to exist in the way described, i.e., as those who know the world, who accept solidarity with it, and who are committed to it. It is not self-evident, nor does it belong to their human nature, that they should have either the commission, the will or the power for this. But they have not ascribed or arrogated to themselves the commission to exist in this way for the world. Nor have they conceived of themselves the resolve to execute it. Nor do they set to work in an immanent power. The freedom to exist for the world is given to these men. As they exercise it, they enjoy a gift which is made to them. Their liberation is the reality of a grace which is not proper to them, which they have not won, but which is shown to them.

We are dealing (2) with a society or *fellowship* in which men are freed to exist for the world, and therefore not with certain isolated individuals who exist alone, but with those who are called by the same Lord, who enjoy the same knowledge, who share in the same promise and who stand in the same order. It is in fulfilment of the promise which applies in common to all, and in expressions of obedience to the order which is equally binding on all, that it is given to them to exist for the world as described. To be sure, the freedom to see and understand the world, to accept solidarity with it and to be committed to it, is a freedom which is given to them personally and which has to be expressed in personal responsibilities and decisions. It is not given to them, however, as a freedom for their personal enrichment and adornment, to be used according to their personal judgment in accordance with their individual standards and goals. It is as members of the community, and to empower them for participation in its work, that they are given it as a freedom which each is to exercise in accordance with the promise which applies equally to all and the order which equally determines all. It is in order that each in his own place and manner, but all in the same sphere and therefore in unity and concord, may represent the society as such and act on its behalf, that they are thus endowed to exist for the world.

With intentional restraint, we have said (3) that it is given to *men* in this society to exist as described in this way for the world. At this point we must be rather more explicit. The gift or endowment or grace of liberation for this knowledge of the world, this solidarity with it and this responsibility for it, are ascribed and allotted and promised to the Christian community. The Christian community as such and all its members exist under the promise of this grace. The fulfilment of this promise, however, may not be flatly equated with the existence of the Christian community; we cannot simply say that the grace of this liberation belongs to all its members in virtue of their obedience to this collective and without their needing specifically to request, receive and exercise it. Even within the framework of their membership in the people of God, the dealings of God with men are always free. God unites with men but He is not bound to them. And the union of men with God, as the purpose of their history with Him, has always to be specifically and personally realised by each of them. This is not less true in relation to the fulfilment of the promise made to the community as such and to all its members in respect of its existence for the world, i.e., the promise of the grace which liberates and capacitates it for this existence. Hence our formula could not be to the effect that the Christian community is the society in which it is given to all men, in virtue of their membership, to exist for the world in the sense described. This would imply that the fulfilment of the promise might be understood as an automatically created state which leaves no room either for the freedom of divine grace or for that of its human recipients. And in this case there would be need neither of a special divine giving nor a special human receiving of this gift, neither of a special human requesting of it nor a special divine hearing of the request. This is not the way of things between God and man even in the sphere of membership of His people and even in respect of man's enablement as a member of this people to exist for the world. On the contrary, the liberation for this takes place in the history of this people, which is also the history of the dealings of God with the individuals gathered in it. In practice, therefore, the fulfilment of the promise does not take place either contemporaneously or in equal measure in the being and action of all these men, but always in a specific measure and manner in the being and action of some of them, many perhaps in some cases and few in others. Hence our formula must be that it is given to *men* in this society to exist for the world as described. Since the promise of this grace applies to the Christian community as such and to all its members, it is evident that none is debarred from receiving it and therefore that none may regard himself as not adapted to and therefore dispensed from participation in its sending to the world. How can a man be gathered to this people if he thinks he has no share in its mission, if he does not refer to himself the promise of the grace of liberation, if he does not pray for the fulfilment of this promise in himself? Yet, since the fulfilment of this promise is a matter of the free dealings of God with him and *vice versa,* it is no less evident that there will always be difference in the participation of individual Christians in the sending of the community. In the one community participant in that promise and existing under the order established by it, there will always be Christians who are temporarily, provisionally and transitorily more advanced and those who are temporarily, provisionally and transitorily more retarded in respect of their knowledge of the world, their solidarity with it and their responsibility for it. This does not mean that there are two ranks: on the one side an institutionally and once-for-all privileged circle which is responsible for the whole and represents it; and on the other a class which is finally deprived of this privilege and can and should leave it to the other group to act responsibly and representatively in matters of the community's mission. What it does mean is that there is a fluid distinction between those to whom it is given here and now in a specific way to exist for the world in the sense described, and those to whom it is not given here and now in this specific way, who have thus to look forward, or rather eagerly and humbly to move forward, to the hour of their own particular equipment for it. In this respect all are directed to the work of the enlightening power of the Holy Spirit, to the free grace of God, to their own prayer for it and to their own willingness in relation to it. And we may be confident that the power of the Holy Spirit will see to it that the distinction is really fluid, that those who were last to-day may be first to-day or to-morrow, and that those who were first yesterday may be last to-day or to-morrow. Fulfilled in this history, however, the existence of the community for the world will always be realised with this fluid distinction or differentiation between those who have a more direct and those who have a more indirect part in its mission.

In relation to this third point it may be noted historically that the older Protestant theology was concerned about a distinction between different members of the Church, describing the Church as a *corpus mixtum* which in its visible form is composed of true and serious believers on the one side and unfruitful and hypocritical believers associated with them on the other, the former being understood in Calvinistic circles as the elect of God and the latter as the reprobate who may also be found in the Church. What gave rise to this distinction was the problematical aspect which even the renewed Christianity of the 16th century presented and which was bound to cause deep concern and to occasion the most serious misgivings. It is to be found already in the *Augustana* (VIII), and in view of it the definition of the Church as the *congregatio sanctorum* in which the Gospel is purely preached and the sacraments are rightly administered (VII) acquires almost a purely formal and technical character. Yet the Church is the *congregatio sanctorum*. And we have seen how a fuller concept of these *sancti,* i.e., that those united in the Church are the *membra Christi* who truly believe in Him and truly obey Him, was brought to the forefront by Melanchthon in the *Apology* and the *Aug. variata,* and became the decisive element in the conception of the Church advanced by Calvin and the Reformed. If, then, the more mixed and questionable aspect of the men united in the Church could not be overlooked, and if it was still desired to maintain the distinction between believers and unbelievers, the elect and the reprobate, within it, then in explanation of the implied contradiction there was no option but to make the further distinction that the true *sancti,* i.e., those who truly believe and obey, the elect, constitute the true but invisible Church, whereas in the visible Church they are ad-mixed with the others who are quite different inwardly but can-not yet be differentiated outwardly.

Neither individually nor in combination can these distinctions be called a particularly fortunate element in Reformation and post-Reformation doctrine. On the basis of the one Lord and the calling of His one community we could never arrive either at the distinction between the believing and unbelieving or the elect and reprobate among its members, or at the distinction between an invisible Church comprised only of believers and a visible comprised of both believers and unbelievers. We become en-tangled in these distinctions only if in our definition of the Church we look abstractly at the men assembled in the commu-nity rather than at the Lord and His action. But who tells us to do this? And if we do, what right or competence have we either to make the first distinction, dividing the community into two groups, and then to go on to identify the first group as the real Church which is invisible and the second as the mixed and improper Church which is visible. On the basis of the one Lord, the one calling of His community and the one promise and order which He has given it, we can only see and understand all those united in it as elected by Him and therefore as summoned and ordained to faith and obedience, but also as participant in the forgiveness of sin in all its forms, and therefore as those who deny faith and withhold obedience, as those who in some way are all both generally and individually recalcitrant in relation to the One who calls them. Again, on this basis, i.e., of what they are in and by Jesus Christ, we can only describe all of them as the invisible Church, i.e., the Church which in its reality is directly visible only to God and to its own members only in faith, but also—in respect of the warfare of the spirit against the flesh and the flesh against the spirit in which they are all involved—as the visible Church which both they and the world may know. With all men generally each of those assembled in the community is in Jesus Christ a *justified* and *sanctified* sin-ner, yet also a justified and sanctified *sinner*. The only point is that as a Christian, as a member of the community in distinction from the rest, each is both these things in the particular sense that he may know that he is a man of whom both these things are true, yet not in equilibrium, but in a definite order of superiority and inferiority. This is the positive fact which makes the older Protestant distinctions impossible.

We, too, have made a distinction within the one community of Jesus Christ in our third elucidation of the concept of a society in which it is given to men to exist for the world in the sense described. We have not made it in relation to the men gathered in it as such, but in relation to the work of the Lord which takes place in their society. We have referred to all the promise of the grace which capacitates these men to participate in the sending of the community to the world. Hence we have not presumed to differentiate between believers and unbelievers, the elect and the reprobate, within the community, as though we could and should do this in the light of what they all are in and by Jesus Christ. Nor have we had any cause to differentiate between a pure, invisible Church embracing qualified Christians on the one side, and a mixed, visible Church embracing both qualified and unqualified Christians on the other. The distinction which we have made is not to be equated, therefore, with the distinctions made in the older Protestant theology. On the other hand, there remains the *tertium comparationis,* and the resultant element of truth in the older distinctions, namely, that we cannot see and understand the community of Jesus Christ as a monolithic block, as a collective of which the individual elements, as mere parts of the whole, are all equally and in the same way blessed, endowed and determined contemporaneously and to the same degree. The One who gives to it the grace, endowment and determination for its existence for the world is its living Lord, and it for its part, as the recipient of His grace and endowment and determination, is His living community. It exists in His history with it, and it with Him. And this history takes place in a series of free fulfilments of the promise given to it and all its members, and therefore in a fluid and not a static distinction between persons who participate more directly or more indirectly in its mission. There is no cleavage of the community into qualified and unqualified members. We are all qualified and all unqualified. In the ongoing common history of the community, there may have arisen yesterday, and there may arise to-day, a juxtaposition of those who participate more directly and those who participate more indirectly in its mission, but this may also reverse itself and become very different to-morrow. All members participate in the mission of the community. A distinction arises, however, in the different times and forms in which there is a realisation of this participation in specific men. It is for this reason that we must exercise restraint and describe the community, not as the society in which it is given to all men, but rather as that in which it will be given to men, i.e., to some men, to exist for the world.

Having made these elucidations, we now turn to the question of the basis of our presupposition that the Christian community really is the society which exists for the world as it is given to some of those united in it practically to fulfil this existence. Where do we derive this assumption? How far is it possible, because necessary and responsible, to count on it that we may start with the fact, and continually return to it in what we say concerning the sending of the Christian community, that this endowment and therefore the execution of its mission actually take place? How do we ourselves know that when we begin with the statement that the Christian community exists for the world we are not just idealising its reality, or announcing a programme, but realistically describing the historical actuality of the one Church which is at one and the same time both invisible and visible?

We may begin with the general assertion that this is a statement of faith. This does not mean—for otherwise it would be a strange statement of faith—that we make it only on the basis of a postulate, of a more or less probable assumption, or at least of a conceivable speculation, and therefore with some degree of uncertainty. Hence we must be careful not to say that, as distinct from statements grounded in some kind of *a priori* or empirical knowledge, it is "only" a statement of faith. Precisely as a statement of faith it is a statement of certain knowledge established with a force which cannot be excelled or even equalled. When the Christian community believes that it exists for the world, it knows what it believes. What it says in this regard, therefore, can be said only with unconditional, assured and joyous certainty if it is really made as a statement of faith. That it is a statement of faith means that like all such statements, in the context of and in relation to all the rest, it speaks of a particular form of God's action towards man and in and on the world for the world's salvation and His own glory. That the community exists for the world is true in the same sense in which it is true—to mention just a few examples—that God has loved the world from eternity, that He has created it as the world thus loved by Him, that in His Son He has given Himself to it and for it, that Jesus Christ in His death has reconciled it to Himself, justifying man before God and sanctifying him for Him, that He as the Servant of God is Lord over all men and all things. That the Christian community exists for the world is one element in the one comprehensive truth of this divine activity. And the statement which expresses this aspect, like other statements expressing different aspects and in indissoluble connexion with them, is one of the true human answers to the true Word in which the God who acts for the salvation of the world and His own glory has declared and revealed Himself, both making Himself known and continuing to do so. This statement, too, cannot be fashioned or uttered otherwise than in hearing this divine Word, i.e., otherwise than in the knowledge of faith awakened by this divine Word and obedient to it. But fashioned and uttered in this hearing and obedience, it has a genuine and supreme content of knowledge, and is established with a force that cannot be surpassed or even equalled. We must now consider the basis which its particular declaration has in the Word of God.

That the community of Jesus Christ really exists for the world is something which as hearers of the divine Word and therefore with the sure knowledge of faith, we affirm at the very same moment at which we also affirm that God lives, or concretely that Jesus Christ is risen again from the dead. As surely as God lives, and lives indeed as the Creator, Reconciler and Redeemer of the world made by Him, and for the man to whom He has turned as His covenant-partner; as surely as Jesus Christ lives, the One who has fulfilled His will and been raised by Him from the dead, and lives indeed for the world which has been reconciled by Him but is still moving to its consummation; as surely as this is not a mere opinion or hypothesis or arbitrary theory but God's revelation of the reality of His action and therefore the truth, so surely does the community of Jesus Christ really exist for the world. As God exists for it in His divine way, and Jesus Christ in His divine-human, so the Christian community exists for it in its own purely human. All ecclesiology is grounded, critically limited, but also positively determined by Christology; and this applies in respect of the particular statement which here concerns us, namely, that the Church exists for the world. The community neither can nor should believe in itself. Even in this particular respect, there can be no *credo in ecclesiam*. Yet as it believes in God the Father, the Son and the Holy Ghost, it can and should believe and confess its own reality: *credo ecclesiam,* and therefore the reality rather than the mere ideal that it exists for the world. In what follows we shall seek to develop this knowledge of the basis of our presupposition from the most important standpoints which claim our attention.

The Christian community knows (1) that it owes its origin and continuation to a very definite power, to the constant working of which it is totally directed for its own future. The power of its own human and creaturely being and action, which it also has, is not to be recognised in this basic power, nor in any other power which it might even partially control. It can only acknowledge, recognise and confess it as the free power of God which does in fact establish and direct it in superiority from without. But it recognises it as the free power whose operation is its own freedom to be exercised by it. For what it sees to be the working of this power is not that it is mastered, naturally or mechanically moved, and as an object pushed and forced and driven by it, but rather that it is placed by it in the freedom of a definite, genuinely human and spontaneous thought, volition, decision and activity in which it is created, nourished and sustained by it as an active subject. The operation of this power is that it finds itself summoned to give its own corresponding, and to that extent appropriate, and to that extent obedient answer to the Word of God spoken to and reasonably received by it. The power which establishes, directs and upholds it is the power of this divine Word. This Word makes it what it is as a creature among creatures. To it, it owes both the fact and the manner of its existence. For the Word spoken to and received by it has and exercises the power to give it this freedom. We refer to the powerful operation of the Holy Spirit. If it knows itself, it knows itself in its existence on this basis.

The Word of God, by whose Holy Spirit, i.e., by whose free and liberating power the community is established and continually sustained, is, however, the Word of joy, omnipotence and mercy by which God has made heaven and earth or the world as His own possession. It is the Word of Him who has loved, loves and will love the world. As the light of this God and His love, the Word shines into the world, causes men to receive it, awakens them to hearing and obedience, calls them together and mirrors itself in the being of their fellowship. The community as the gathering of these men finds itself illumined by the eternal light of this God and His love, being itself set alongside His light in the world as a created and indirect light wholly dependent upon and nourished by Him, yet nevertheless a true light. By this God and His love it is liberated for its distinctive being, for its common human thought, volition, decision and activity according to His mind and will and along the lines indicated by His love. This means, however, that it can see and understand itself, its own existence in this basic sense, only in the light of the illumining and therefore constitutive power of the Holy Spirit as the power of the Word of God, and therefore only in relation to the world created and actively loved by this God. Hence it is not the case that its task to be a light in the world is only an immediate or more distant deduction from the gift of its being and existence. On the contrary, in and with the gift of its specific being, and therefore in and with its creation, it receives, not from itself but from its Creator, this determination and task. In this sense it is originally and essentially light, i.e., the light which by the power of God and therefore of the Holy Spirit may reflect His eternal light in the world. In this sense, it has fundamentally no option but to exist for the world as it reflects the light of God and is itself light. It necessarily understands itself otherwise than in faith, otherwise than in the light of the Word of God which establishes it, and therefore in a radical self-misunderstanding in which it tries to ascribe to itself a being in contradiction, if it seeks to ascribe to itself any other existence than that in which it actualises the gift of this existence, and therefore fulfils this determination and task. If and to the extent that it does this, in great and little things alike it is constantly opposed by its own reality.

The Christian community knows (2) that what it can do and effect and accomplish of itself in its human and creaturely spontaneity, as empowered by the power of the Holy Spirit, can consist only in its confession of Jesus Christ. To confess Him is its business. This includes many things in many different forms. The one thing which includes the many and by which it is established and nourished is the simple fact that it exists as the assembly of those who commonly confess Jesus Christ. It does, of course, know other good and evil lords and helpers and powers and forces. It exists in their sphere. It wrestles with them, either joyfully and thankfully on the one side or with alarm and repugnance on the other. But it cannot wrestle with Jesus Christ. It exists as He exists. It belongs basically and from the very outset to Him. He is its being at its very root. He is the Word in which God addresses it, gives Himself to be known by it and causes Himself to be received by it. He is the self-proclamation of His creative, reconciling and redeeming act. And because it cannot look past Him or go behind Him to compare Him with others and to choose between them, He alone is its being with the singularity of God Himself and the power of His Spirit. It has not chosen Him as this One; He as this One has chosen it. All vindications of its exclusive attachment to Him can consist only in the assertion and description of this fact that He as this One has chosen and established it. It stands or falls with Him. If it were possible, it would prefer to fall with Him rather than to stand without Him. For without Him, it could only exist, if not necessarily as a collection of atheists in the technical sense, yet factually and practically "without God in the world" (Eph. 2:12), i.e., without the One who by His action shows Himself to be the only true God. It can stand only as it stands by Jesus Christ. It is not accidentally or incidentally that it bears His name; His name is the revelation of its basis. Again it would have to ascribe to itself an existence in contradiction with itself if it were ashamed of this basis and were not prepared to confess that it is the community which bears this name and this name alone. It cannot possibly disguise the fact that not only much or most of what it has to represent, but everything, has its specific weight and meaning and power in the fact that originally and properly it has Him in view, recalls Him, points to Him and proclaims Him. Hence it does not merely confess in themselves and as such various Christian truths such as the love of God, the love which man must then show to God and neighbour, grace and its triumph, forgiveness, sanctification, the life of the future world. It confesses the truth of the person of Jesus Christ in His work, and the truth of His work in His person, as the substance in which all these truths are truth but without which they are only empty religious ideas and principles, not to say mere rhetorical flourishes. It confesses reconciliation as it has taken place in Him, the covenant as it has been concluded in Him, Him as peace and hope, Him as the Way, Him as the Lord. It is sent to do this. As it does it, it lives by its root, existing and knowing itself in its reality.

But the Jesus Christ whom it confesses, thus living by its root, is in His person as very God and very man, and in His work as the Mediator of the covenant, the God who acts in and for the world and reveals Himself to it. And in this One God is not merely the Brother of some but of each and all men, having taken their part and bound Himself to them for blessing and cursing, for life and death. The living Lord who acts and reveals Himself in this One is thus the God who is absolutely interested in the world, who in spite of all the theoretical and practical godlessness of men is never without man, but always was and is and will be with him and for him. Hence the community called and built up by this One can confess Him only as it confesses to the world, to men, and to all men without distinction, that He is the One in whom God is their God. This is what differentiates its confession from an accidental, arbitrary or optional action. This is what makes its confession of

Jesus Christ imperatively necessary on the basis of its being. Might it not be content to exist of Him and by Him and with Him only for itself, to understand His name only as the sum and His action only as the origin and guarantee of the salvation experienced in Him, and His Word only as the ever necessary direction to be assured and worthy of its salvation in Him? We recall the classical definition of the Church according to which it might actually be content with this. Why does this definition need to be completed and corrected? Why does the community have to be the confessing community, confessing Jesus Christ, not only *intra muros* but to all men without distinction (Mt. 10:32)? Why is it set under the unmistakeable threat that otherwise He as the one true Son of the one true God will not confess it as His community before His Father in heaven and therefore in the final and supreme decision? To this question there is obviously only one answer, namely, that it must confess Him before men because the Father in heaven, as whose Son He founds and gathers and upbuilds it, is the God of all men and therefore of others beside itself, because He causes His sun to shine on the good and the bad and His rain to fall on the righteous and the unrighteous (Mt. 5:45), because His community can know Him only as the Son of this Father, because it cannot possibly keep to itself or suppress or not confess the fact that it knows Him thus, because it would *ipso facto* deny the One whom it knows as the Son of this Father if it did not confess Him as such, because, to be His community, it has no option but to reach out beyond its own circle and to confess Him to all men. Its most inward being has an irresistible impulse towards that which is without, its most proper being towards that which is alien. In its very exclusiveness its knowledge demands universal confession. Precisely the name revealed to it, as the name which is above every other name, demands proclamation as such. It exists as it is pledged to the one Jesus Christ and therefore basically and without reservation to the world. It would not exist in the reality established by Him if it were not prepared to exist in this commitment to the world. Nor would it know itself if it were unwilling to see its reality in its existence in this commitment, or to try to exist as in any sense a non-confessing community.

The Christian community knows (3) that its confession of Jesus Christ as the distinctive action for which it is empowered by the Holy Spirit can only be, in all its human and natural spontaneity, a grateful response to the fact that first and supremely Jesus Christ has confessed it, does confess it, and will continually do so. It is its own free action, yet not an arbitrary but an obedient action. It is a venture of the first order, yet not an independent or unauthorised venture, if among all the many lords in question it confesses Him as the Lord of all lords, if substantially and decisively it chooses to remember and vindicate and proclaim Him alone. As we have seen, it chooses Him as the community chosen by Him which cannot but choose Him. It is the people personally and therefore supremely preferred by Him, and as such it must give to confession of Him preference over all other possible actions. It is personally and supremely preferred by Him, however, in the sense that He wills to be specifically present with it, to dwell within it, and to speak and act by it, i.e., by its ministry, and in the sense that He actually does these things, not in any external and contingent relationship, but in an intimate and necessary connexion in which He is its Lord and it is the body inspired and directed by Him. He Himself, risen from the dead, does not only exist eternally in heaven at the right hand of the Father as Head, but also in His prophetic office, as the living Word of God, in the power of the Holy Spirit, as the Head of His body, and therefore historically on earth within world-occurrence. As the One He was and is and will be, He Himself goes through the twilight and obscurity of this lingering time with the humanity reconciled to God in Him but not yet redeemed. He did not merely live once; He also lives to-day with us and like us. He does not merely live, speak and act, the Son of God, as the Lord over time; He also lives, speaks and acts, the Son of Man, in time and therefore as participant in what takes place as our history in time. Now He certainly does this in other forms as well as in the existence and history of His community. He is not bound to it as it is bound to Him. We fail to see His lordship if we do not reckon with the fact that in His self-proclamation He, the living One, may go other ways than those indicated by the human and creaturely limits of His community conditioned by its constant obduracy. Yet this does not alter the fact that His community, and alone so far as we can see it, has the promise, and may and should live by the truth of the promise, that it is the body of Jesus Christ which in the power of the Holy Spirit He as its Lord has personally called into existence and directs and sustains, so that in its existence it is the earthly-historical form and representation of His own.

"Where two or three συνηγμένοι (are gathered, or constituted a synagogue) εἰς τὸ ἐμὸν ὄνομα (in the sphere of the revelation and knowledge and therefore the confession of His name, in the act of salvation which has taken place in His person and work, and in the revelation of salvation present in Him), there am I in the midst of them" (Mt. 18:20). The rather more restrained form in which the saying is handed down in Codex D and other manuscripts is worth noting, but it does not seem to imply any real weakening of content: "Two or three cannot be gathered in my name, except I am there in the midst of them." In neither version, of course, is it meant that because they have come together in His name He comes into the midst as a Third or Fourth, but conversely that they are gathered by Him in and with the fact that He is in the midst of them.

He is the primary and proper Subject acting in and with the community. It is constituted by His confession made not only in heaven but also with power on earth. Its confession of Him gratefully follows His confession of it.

Now the One who constitutes the community by confessing it, this primarily and properly acting Subject in its history, is the One who, in that as very God He became and was very man, did not will to withdraw or to hold aloof from, or to be alien to, either the world as His creation or humanity as the world of His fellows, but who rather willed to intervene and give Himself personally for it in its totality, taking to Himself and therefore away from it the whole burden of its folly and corruption and misery and suffering, and in His person justifying every man against every accusation and sanctifying every man to every good work. Nor is He merely the One who willed all these things, but the One who totally and not just in part accomplished them. Moreover, He is the One who continually attests and reveals and makes Himself known as He who has done such things for its reformation and renewal, so that He is not idle or dumb, but actively with it on the way as the authentic Prophet of its new reality. This is the One who has called the community into being and maintains it in being. This is its Head. His Holy Spirit is the power by whose distinctive activity it is enabled to confess Him. What does this signify for it as His body, as His earthly-historical form of existence? What can be the meaning and *telos* of its own existence as the predicate of this Subject? In the light of Jesus Christ as the basis of its existence, obviously it cannot be its own meaning and *telos,* nor can it rest content with its own being as such. In the light of its basis in Him, it is sent in the same direction as He is, i.e., into the world, in order that it may exist, not for itself, but for the world as He did. What He gives to the twos and threes, and to the hundreds and thousands, who, as He is in the midst, are assembled in His name into His circle of light to confess Him, and what they receive from Him, can only correspond to what He Himself is and does in the time which hastens to its end but is still left to the world. It can thus consist only in the fact that He gives it to them to take a ministering part in His prophetic work, claiming them for this service and equipping and directing them in its discharge. The intimate and necessary connexion between Him as the Head and the community as His body would obviously snap if it tried to exist otherwise than in this imitative and ministering participation in His mission to the world. As the community has its basis in Him, and knows in Him its Head, with all its being it can try to actualise only this connexion with Him, and in all its work only this participation in His mission, in His prophetic work. It would completely mistake its one basis in Him, and therefore itself, if it tried to substitute for the way on which He precedes a circular course in which its concern were only for its own confirmation and expression. On the way on which He precedes, however well or badly it can only belong to men and the world, and seek to exist for them, in the strength imparted to it if also in its own impotence.

The Christian community can and should understand itself (4) in the full New Testament sense of the term as a likeness. As such it is a subsequent and provisional representation of the divine-human reality distinct from itself. As this both precedes and follows its own being, the community can only indicate, reflect and represent it subsequently and provisionally. It can only portray and denote it imperfectly and inadequately in a way which obscures as well as enlightens, achieving similar but not the same colours and contours. It can only be its duplicate. Yet as it is essentially proper to it to derive from it and to move towards it, in all its imperfection it has a genuine share in that which it denotes and portrays. The Chirstian community can and should understand itself as a likeness in this specific sense. The reality distinct from itself which it denotes and portrays as this likeness is the kingdom of God which commences and is already particularly revealed in the resurrection of Jesus Christ as the *terminus a quo* of its own specific history, and which will be definitively and universally manifested in the final appearing of Jesus Christ as the *terminus ad quem* of its own history. And the kingdom of God is the establishment of the exclusive, all-penetrating, all-determinative lordship of God and His Word and Spirit in the whole sphere of His creation. Jesus Himself is this kingdom in all its perfection. In Him this divine lordship is inaugurated. For in Him, this human creature, the Creator and Lord dwells and acts and speaks directly and without restriction in the rest of His creation. In Him the calling of all humanity and indeed of all creation to the service of God, and therefore the unity of all the forms and forces and works of the creature, is already a completed event with a perfection which cannot be transcended. The community has its origin in His revelation, and therefore in the calling which has gone out universally in Him, and therefore in the established divine lordship of the kingdom in the seed form of the Easter event. And it moves towards His manifestation, and therefore the manifestation of the kingdom, in the full visibility of the tree (Mt. 13:32) with birds nesting in the branches. It recognises that this is so, that it has its origin in the one and moves towards the other, as it has its basis of existence, in the manner described under our three heads, in the impelling power of the Holy Spirit, in its empowering for the confession of Jesus Christ, in which it recognises that it is to His confession of it that it may gratefully respond with its confession of Him. And encircled by this origin and future, it resembles Him, and the lordship of God set up in Him, and the calling of all humanity and all creatures to the service of God as it has gone forth in Him. Neither it nor anyone else can or should ascribe to it more than a resemblance to this first and final reality, and to its revelation as it has already taken place and has still to take place. It is not identical with it. It has and maintains in face of it its own reality which is neither divine nor divine-human but a specific form of creaturely and human reality. Yet as the body, as the earthly-historical form of existence, of Jesus Christ, it is His likeness, and may and should recognise that this is so. We need not waste words on the obscurity and confusion with which in its existence it reflects Him and the kingdom of God as revealed already in its commencement but still to be revealed in its consummation. It need not doubt, nor can it be contested, that He reflects Himself in it, that it is created and ordained to be His likeness. As it beholds Him "with open face" (2 Cor. 3:18), it is changed, not into an *alter Christus,* but necessarily into an image of the unrepeatably one Christ. It receives from the Lord, who is the Spirit, a glory which, if it is not the same as His own, corresponds and is analogous and similar to it—the glory of His own image. Hence, although it does not belong to it to set up the kingdom of God in the creation of God, as though it were not already set up, and although it cannot belong to it to manifest this kingdom, as though it had any power of manifestation and as though its manifestation were not the work of the One in whom it is set up, yet it can and should indicate the kingdom and its revelation in its existence. The purpose of its existence is the

subsequent and provisional representation of the calling of all humanity and all creatures to the service of God as it has gone forth in
Jesus Christ. The origin and goal of the ways of God, which took
place initially but perfectly in the resurrection of Jesus Christ, and
which will take place definitively and no less perfectly in His final
appearing, is the calling of every man and indeed of all creation to
the service of God. The function of the community is to follow and
yet at the same time to precede His universal call.

"Make a joyful noise unto the Lord, all ye lands. Serve the
Lord with gladness: come before his presence with singing.
Know ye that the Lord he is God" (Ps. 100:1f.)—this is the
Alpha and Omega of the call of Jesus Christ Himself. It is to this
that there corresponds the very imperfect but quite unmistakeable calling of the Christian community between the origin and
the goal, in the time between the times. To it first among all
creatures the call of God has gone forth, and gone forth effectively, as its existence shows. It could and can hear it. In it, it is
recognised by at least some among the great masses of men and
nations, invincibly if only from afar and with considerable
obscurity, that the Lord alone is God. In it, some men, even
though they are weary and heavy-laden because blind and deaf
and lame, do come into His presence with real singing, if only in
the form of sighs and croaks. In it, even though under the severe
pressure of human corruption and always on the edge of the
abyss of the Christian and therefore the worst possible deception, and yet always restrained and called back to reality by His
call, the attempt is at least made to serve the Lord, and to serve
Him in the only way possible, i.e., with joy and therefore without murmuring or complaint. In it, even though from the depths
and with many a discord, yet continually lifted out of the depths
and brought into an obvious final harmony, creatures are
gathered out of every land and speech and natural and cultural
sphere, and for all their difference and antagonisms united with
one another in this joyous praise.

For all its weak and doubtful character, therefore, there takes
place in it a subsequent and provisional fulfilment of the prophecy
of Jesus Christ which takes up the Easter message and anticipates
the "Behold, I make all things new" (Rev. 21:5) of the last day,
not with the perfection with which Jesus Christ Himself, risen
from the dead, was once its fulfilment, nor with the perfection with
which He will be at His coming again to judgment, but, in virtue of

His presence and action in the Holy Spirit by which it is constituted in this time between the times, as a reflection and replica of the glory which is His alone, in participation in it, and therefore with its own glory as the representation, indication and likeness of His prophecy.

As the community perceives itself to be this likeness, however, it can and should see and understand—and this brings us to the same goal by a fourth path—that it exists for the world. As a likeness of the prophecy of Jesus Christ, it obviously has itself a prophetic character. And in its prophetic character it cannot possibly be an end in itself. According to the purpose and power of the one who fashions and uses it, a likeness points beyond itself to what he intends to indicate and represent in using it. What the One who fashions and uses His community as a likeness of His own existence indicates and represents by it is His own prophecy in its full sweep, namely, the calling of the world to the service of God which He has inaugurated and will consummate but which in this time between the inauguration and the consummation proceeds in the power of His Holy Spirit and therefore with the same perfection which characterises it in its origin and its goal. The ongoing of this calling of the world to the service of God takes place in the likeness of the community founded, maintained and guided by the power of His Holy Spirit, between the *terminus a quo* of its history and its *terminus ad quem,* here and now, in every hour of our time which is the time between the times. This time is not, therefore, a vacuum between the other two. It is the time of the *parousia* of Jesus Christ in its second and middle form, in the power of His Holy Spirit; and therefore it is especially the time of the community (*C.D.,* IV, I, § 62, 3). This time is given the community in order that it may be to the world an indication, representation and likeness of its calling in Jesus Christ to the service of God as it proceeds in this time between. In this sense it is given it for its own supreme joy, which is not, however, its joy in itself, but can only be its joy in this ongoing calling of the world, and therefore in the progress of the mission of its Lord and hence of its own mission to the world, namely, joy in the fact that it may be in and to the world a likeness of the kingdom of God which has come but is still to come, and therefore that in this sense it may exist for the world.

In retrospect, our concern in the four trains of thought just concluded has been to show the basis of the presupposition that the Christian community is the society to which it is given to exist for the world. In relation to this by no means self-evident statement of faith, our concern has been with the *intellectus fidei,* i.e., with the theological establishment of the truth of its content. We could do this only by theological reflection. That is to say, since our concern is genuinely with a statement of faith, or with a specific form of the general statement of faith: *credo ecclesiam,* we could establish it only as along four different lines we dealt with the work and Word of God in the context in which it is also the basis of the reality of the Church and of its orientation to the world. Beginning with its basis in the power of the Holy Spirit, we considered the work for which the Church is thereby empowered, namely, the confession of Jesus Christ, then tried to see that this can only be an answer to His confession of it, and finally sought to interpret its existence as the subsequent and provisional likeness of the prophecy of Jesus Christ described under the first three heads. All four lines of thought, however, have finally brought us to a recognition of the reality of the Church in its address to the world, and therefore to a recognition of its existence for the world, and to this extent, therefore, to an illumination of the basis of the presupposition with which we started and in terms of which we have now to continue. This is what had to be shown, *quod erat demonstrandum,* in this second sub-section.

18

DIETRICH BONHOEFFER

Christ, the Church, and the World

THE CONCEPT OF REALITY

WHOEVER WISHES TO TAKE UP THE PROBLEM OF A CHRISTIAN ethic must be confronted at once with a demand which is quite without parallel. He must from the outset discard as irrelevant the two questions which alone impel him to concern himself with the problem of ethics, 'How can I be good?' and 'How can I do good?', and instead of these he must ask the utterly and totally different question 'What is the will of God?' This requirement is so immensely far-reaching because it presupposes a decision with regard to the ultimate reality; it presupposes a decision of faith. If the ethical problem presents itself essentially in the form of enquiries about one's own being good and doing good, this means that it has already been decided that it is the self and the world which are the ultimate reality. The aim of all ethical reflection is, then, that I myself shall be good and that the world shall become good through my action. But the problem of ethics at once assumes a new aspect if it becomes apparent that these realities, myself and the world, themselves lie embedded in a quite different ultimate reality, namely, the reality of God, the Creator, Reconciler and Redeemer. What is of ultimate importance is now no longer that I should become good, or that the condition of the world should be made better by my action, but that the reality of God should show itself everywhere to be the ultimate reality. Where there is faith in God as the ultimate reality, all concern with ethics will have as its starting-point that God shows Himself to be good, even if this involves the risk that I myself and the world are not good but thoroughly bad. All things appear distorted if they are not seen and

From Dietrich Bonhoeffer, *Ethics*, Part 1, ch. II, pp. 55–72; VI, pp. 194–216. Copyright © 1955 by Macmillan Publishing Co., Inc. © SCM Press Ltd. 1955. Reprinted by permission of Macmillan and SCM Press.

recognized in God. All so-called data, all laws and standards, are mere abstractions so long as there is no belief in God as the ultimate reality. But when we say that God is the ultimate reality, this is not an idea, through which the world as we have it is to be sublimated. It is not the religious rounding-off of a profane conception of the universe. It is the acceptance in faith of God's showing forth of Himself, the acceptance of His revelation. If God were merely a religious idea there would be nothing to prevent us from discerning, behind this allegedly 'ultimate' reality, a still more final reality, the twilight of the gods and the death of the gods. The claim of this ultimate reality is satisfied only in so far as it is revelation, that is to say, the self-witness of the living God. When this is so, the relation to this reality determines the whole of life. The apprehension of this reality is not merely a gradual advance towards the discovery of ever more profound realities; it is the crucial turning-point in the apprehension of reality as a whole. The ultimate reality now shows itself to be at the same time the initial reality, the first and last, alpha and omega. Any perception or apprehension of things or laws without Him is now abstraction, detachment from the origin and goal. Any enquiry about one's own goodness, or the goodness of the world, is now impossible unless enquiry has first been made about the goodness of God. For without God what meaning could there be in a goodness of man and a goodness of the world? But God as the ultimate reality is no other than He who shows forth, manifests and reveals Himself, that is to say, God in Jesus Christ, and from this it follows that the question of good can find its answer only in Christ.

The point of departure for Christian ethics is not the reality of one's own self, or the reality of the world; nor is it the reality of standards and values. It is the reality of God as He reveals Himself in Jesus Christ. It is fair to begin by demanding assent to this proposition of anyone who wishes to concern himself with the problem of a Christian ethic. It poses the ultimate and crucial question of the reality which we mean to reckon with in our lives, whether it is to be the reality of the revelational word of God or earthly imperfections, whether it is to be resurrection or death. No man can decide this question by himself, by his own choice, without deciding it wrongly, for it presupposes the answer given, namely that, whatever our decision may be, God has already spoken His word of revelation, and even in the false reality we cannot live otherwise than through the true reality of the word of God. Thus when we ask about the ultimate reality we are thereby at once inescapably bound by the answers to our question. For the question conveys us into the midst of its origin, the reality of the revelation of God in Jesus Christ.

The problem of Christian ethics is the realization among God's creatures of the revelational reality of God in Christ, just as the problem of dogmatics is the truth of the revelational reality of God in Christ. The place which in all other ethics is occupied by the antithesis of 'should be' and 'is', idea and accomplishment, motive and performance, is occupied in Christian ethics by the relation of reality and realization, past and present, history and event (faith), or, to replace the equivocal concept by the unambiguous name, the relation of Jesus Christ and the Holy Spirit. The question of good becomes the question of participation in the divine reality which is revealed in Christ. Good is now no longer a valuation of what is, a valuation, for example, of my own being, my outlook or my actions, or of some condition or state in the world. It is no longer a predicate that is assigned to something which is in itself in being. Good is the real itself. It is not the real in the abstract, the real which is detached from the reality of God, but the real which possesses reality only in God. There is no good without the real, for the good is not a general formula, and the real is impossible without the good. The wish to be good consists solely in the longing for what is real in God. A desire to be good for its own sake, as an end in itself, so to speak, or as a vocation in life, falls victim to the irony of unreality. The genuine striving for good now becomes the self-assertiveness of the prig. Good is not in itself an independent theme for life; if it were so it would be the craziest kind of quixotry. Only if we share in reality can we share in good.

It is a fundamentally mistaken formulation of the question that gives rise to the old dispute about whether it is only the will, the mental act or the person that can be good, or whether goodness may also be predicated of performance, achievement or success, and, if so, which of these two precedes the other and which is more important. This dispute has found its way even into theology, and there, as elsewhere, it has been the source of serious errors. It tears asunder what by its origin and essence forms a unity, namely, the good and the real, man and his work. To object that Christ, too, had this distinction between person and work in view in His saying about the good tree that brings forth good fruit (Matt. 7:17) is to distort the meaning of this saying of Jesus into its exact opposite. What is meant by this saying is not that first the person and then the work is good, but that only the two together are good or bad, in other words that the two together are to be understood as a single unit. The same holds true of the distinction which has been drawn by Reinhold Niebuhr, the American philosopher of religion, in his use of the two concepts 'moral man' and 'immoral society'. The distinction which is intended here between individual and society is a purely abstract one, just as is that between the person and work. In such a case one is tearing asunder things which are inseparable and examining separately parts which in isolation from each other are dead. The consequence is that complete ethical aporia which nowadays goes by the name of 'social ethics'. Naturally, if good is supposed to lie in the conformity of something that is with something that should be, then the relatively more massive resistance which is offered by society to that which should be must necessarily lead to an ethical favouring of the individual at the expense of society. (And conversely it is precisely this circumstance which suggests that this concept of the ethical has its sociological origin in the age of individualism.) The question of good must not be reduced to an examination of the motives or consequences of actions by applying to them some ready-made ethical yardstick. An ethic of motives or of mental attitudes is as superficial as an ethic of practical consequences. For what right have we to stop short at the immediate motive and to regard this as the ultimate ethical phenomenon, refusing to take into account the fact that a 'good' motive may spring from a very dark background of human consciousness and unconsciousness and that a 'good attitude' may often be the source of the worst of actions? And just as the question of the motivation of action is in the end lost in the inextricable complexities of the past, so, too, does the question of its consequences finally disappear from view in the mists of the future. On both sides there are no fixed frontiers and nothing justifies us in calling a halt at some point which we ourselves have arbitrarily determined so that we may at last form a definite judgement. Whether one pursues the line of the ethic of motives or that of the ethic of consequences, it is a matter of sheer expediency, dependent on the conjunctures of the times, that in practice one always ends with some such arbitrary setting of limits. In principle neither of these has anything to commend it in preference to the other, for in both of them the question of good is posed in abstract terms and in isolation from reality. Good is not the correspondence between a criterion which is placed at our disposal by nature or grace and whatever entity I may designate as reality. Good is reality itself, reality seen and recognized in God. The question of good embraces man with his motives and purposes, with his fellow-men and with the entire creation around him; it embraces reality as a whole, as it is held in being by God. The divine words 'Behold, it was very good' (Gen. 1:31) refer to the whole of creation. The good demands the whole, not only the whole of a man's outlook but his whole work, the whole man, together with the fellow-men who are given to him. What sense would it have if only a part were to be called good, a motive perhaps, while the action is bad, or if the reverse were the case? Man is an indivisible whole, not only as an individual in his person and work but also as a member of the community of men and creatures in which he stands. This indivisible whole, this reality which is founded on God and apprehended in Him, is what the question of good has in view. With respect to its origin this indivisible whole is called 'creation'. With respect to its goal it is called the 'kingdom of God'. Both of these are equally remote from us and equally close to us, for God's creation and God's kingdom are present with us solely in God's self-revelation in Jesus Christ.

Participation in the indivisible whole of the divine reality—this is the sense and the purpose of the Christian enquiry concerning good. For the sake of avoiding a misunderstanding, there is need at this point of some further clarification of what is meant here by reality.

There is a way of basing ethics upon the concept of reality which differs entirely from the Christian way. This is the positive and empirical approach, which aims at the entire elimination from ethics of the concept of norms and standards because it regards this concept as being merely the idealization of factual and practically expedient attitudes. Fundamentally, according to this view, the good is no more than what is expedient, useful and advantageous to reality. From this it follows that there is no universal good but only an infinitely varying good which is determined in each case on the basis of 'reality'. This conception is undoubtedly superior to the idealist conception in that it is 'closer to reality'. Good does not consist here in an impossible 'realization' of what is unreal, the realization of ethical ideas. It is reality itself that teaches what is good. The only question is whether the reality that is intended here is capable of satisfying this demand. It now transpires that the concept of reality which underlies the positivistic ethic is the meretricious concept of the empirically verifiable, which implies denial of the origin of this reality in the ultimate reality, in God. Reality, understood in this inadequate sense, cannot be the source of good, because all it demands is complete surrender to the contingent, the casual, the adventitious and the momentarily expedient, because it fails to recognize the ultimate reality and because in this way it destroys and abandons the unity of good.

The Christian ethic speaks in a quite different sense of the reality which is the origin of good, for it speaks of the reality of God as the ultimate reality without and within everything that is. It speaks of the reality of the world as it is, which possesses reality solely through the reality of God. Christian belief deduces that the reality of God is not in itself merely an idea from the fact that this reality of God has manifested and revealed itself in the midst of the real world. In Jesus Christ the reality of God entered into the reality of this world. The place where the answer is given, both to the question concerning the reality of God and to the question concerning the reality of the world, is designated solely and alone by the name Jesus Christ. God and the world are comprised in this name. In Him all things consist (Col. 1:17). Henceforward one can speak neither of God nor of the world without speaking of Jesus Christ. All concepts of reality which do not take account of Him are abstractions. When good has become reality in Jesus Christ, there is no more force in any discussion of good which plays off what should be against what is and what is against what should be. Jesus Christ cannot be identified either with an ideal or standard or with things as they are. The hostility of the ideal towards things as they are, the fanatical putting into effect of an idea in the face of a resisting actuality, may be as remote from good as is the sacrifice of what should be to what is expedient. Both what should be and what is expedient acquire in Christ an entirely new meaning. The irreconcilable conflict between what is and what should be is reconciled in Christ, that is to say, in the ultimate reality. Participation in this reality is the true sense and purpose of the enquiry concerning good.

In Christ we are offered the possibility of partaking in the reality of God and in the reality of the world, but not in the one without the other. The reality of God discloses itself only by setting me entirely in the reality of the world, and when I encounter the reality of the world it is always already sustained, accepted and reconciled in the reality of God. This is the inner meaning of the revelation of God in the man Jesus Christ. Christian ethics enquires about the realization in our world of this divine and cosmic reality which is given in Christ. This does not mean that 'our world' is something outside the divine and cosmic reality which is in Christ, or that it is not already part of the world which is sustained, accepted and reconciled in Him. It does not mean that one must still begin by applying some kind of 'principle' to our situation and our time.

The enquiry is directed rather towards the way in which the reality in Christ, which for a long time already has comprised us and our world within itself, is taking effect as something now present, and towards the way in which life may be conducted in this reality. Its purpose is, therefore, participation in the reality of God and of the world in Jesus Christ today, and this participation must be such that I never experience the reality of God without the reality of the world or the reality of the world without the reality of God.

THINKING IN TERMS OF TWO SPHERES

As soon as we try to advance along this path, our way is blocked by the colossal obstacle of a large part of traditional Christian ethical thought. Since the beginnings of Christian ethics after the times of the New Testament the main underlying conception in ethical thought, and the one which consciously or unconsciously has determined its whole course, has been the conception of a juxtaposition and conflict of two spheres, the one divine, holy, supernatural and Christian, and the other worldly, profane, natural and un-Christian. This view becomes dominant for the first time in the Middle Ages, and for the second time in the pseudo-Protestant thought of the period after the Reformation. Reality as a whole now falls into two parts, and the concern of ethics is with the proper relation of these two parts to each other. In the scholastic scheme of things the realm of the natural is made subordinate to the realm of grace; in the pseudo-Lutheran scheme the autonomy of the orders of this world is proclaimed in opposition to the law of Christ, and in the scheme of the Enthusiasts the congregation of the Elect takes up the struggle with a hostile world for the establishment of God's kingdom on earth. In all these schemes the cause of Christ becomes a partial and provincial matter within the limits of reality. It is assumed that there are realities which lie outside the reality that is in Christ. It follows that these realities are accessible by some way of their own, and otherwise than through Christ. However great the importance which is attached to the reality in Christ, it still always remains a partial reality amid other realities. The division of the total reality into a sacred and a profane sphere, a Christian and a secular sphere, creates the possibility of existence in a single one of these spheres, a spiritual existence which has no part in secular existence, and a secular existence which can claim autonomy for itself and can exercise this right of autonomy in its dealings with the spiritual sphere. The monk and the nineteenth-century Protestant secularist typify these two possibilities. The whole of medieval history is centred upon the theme of the predominance of the spiritual sphere over the secular sphere, the predominance of the *regnum gratiae* over the *regnum naturae;* and the modern age is characterized by an ever increasing independence of the secular in its relations with the spiritual. So long as Christ and the world are conceived as two opposing and mutually repellent spheres, man will be left in the following dilemma: he abandons reality as a whole, and places himself in one or other of the two spheres. He seeks Christ without the world, or he seeks the world without Christ. In either case he is deceiving himself. Or else he tries to stand in both spaces at once and thereby becomes the man of eternal conflict, the kind of man who emerged in the period after the Reformation and who has repeatedly set himself up as representing the only form of Christian existence which is in accord with reality.

It may be difficult to break the spell of this thinking in terms of two spheres, but it is nevertheless quite certain that it is in profound contradiction to the thought of the Bible and to the thought of the Reformation, and that consequently it aims wide of reality. There are not two realities, but only one reality, and that is the reality of God, which has become manifest in Christ in the reality of the world. Sharing in Christ we stand at once in both the reality of God and the reality of the world. The reality of Christ comprises the reality of the world within itself. The world has no reality of its own, independently of the revelation of God in Christ. One is denying the revelation of God in Jesus Christ if one tries to be 'Christian' without seeing and recognizing the world in Christ. There are, therefore, not two spheres, but only the one sphere of the realization of Christ, in which the reality of God and the reality of the world are united. Thus the theme of the two spheres, which has repeatedly become the dominant factor in the history of the Church, is foreign to the New Testament. The New Testament is concerned solely with the manner in which the reality of Christ assumes reality in the present world, which it has already encompassed, seized and possessed. There are not two spheres, standing side by side, competing with each other and attacking each other's frontiers. If that were so, this frontier dispute would always be the decisive problem of history. But the whole reality of the world is already drawn in into Christ and bound together in Him, and the movement of history consists solely in divergence and convergence in relation to this centre.

Thought which is conducted in terms of two spheres regards

such pairs of concepts as secular and Christian, natural and super-natural, profane and sacred, and rational and revelational, as though they were ultimate static antitheses, serving to designate certain mutually exclusive entities. It fails to recognize the original unity of these opposites in the reality of Christ, and in the place of this true unity it sets the forced unity of some sacred or profane system in which these contradictory concepts are combined. In such a system the static antagonism persists. But these things assume quite a different form with the recognition of the divine and cosmic reality in Christ. The world, the natural, the profane and reason are now all taken up into God from the outset. They do not exist 'in themselves' and 'on their own account'. They have their reality nowhere save in the reality of God, in Christ. It is now essential to the real concept of the secular that it shall always be seen in the movement of being accepted and becoming accepted by God in Christ. Just as in Christ the reality of God entered into the reality of the world, so, too, is that which is Christian to be found only in that which is of the world, the 'supernatural' only in the natural, the holy only in the profane, and the revelational only in the rational. The unity of the reality of God and of the world, which has been accomplished in Christ, is repeated, or, more exactly, is realized, ever afresh in the life of men. And yet what is Christian is not identical with what is of the world. The natural is not identical with the supernatural or the revelational with the rational. But between the two there is in each case a unity which derives solely from the reality of Christ, that is to say solely from faith in this ultimate reality. This unity is seen in the way in which the secular and the Christian elements prevent one another from assuming any kind of static independence in their mutual relations. They adopt a polemical attitude towards each other and bear wit-ness precisely in this to their shared reality and to their unity in the reality which is in Christ. Just as Luther engaged in polemics on behalf of the secular authority against the extension of ecclesiasti-cal power by the Roman Church, so, too, must there be a Christian or 'spiritual' polemical reply to the secular element when there is a danger that this element may make itself independent, as was the case soon after the Reformation and especially in nineteenth-century German secularist Protestantism. In both of these polemi-cal protests the process is the same: men's attention is called to the divine and cosmic reality—Jesus Christ. Luther was protesting against a Christianity which was striving for independence and detaching itself from the reality in Christ. He protested with the help of the secular and in the name of a better Christianity. So, too, today, when Christianity is employed as a polemical weapon against the secular, this must be done in the name of a better secularity and above all it must not lead back to a static predominance of the spiritual sphere as an end in itself. It is only in this sense, as a polemical unity, that Luther's doctrine of the two kingdoms is to be accepted, and it was no doubt in this sense that it was originally intended.

To think in terms of spheres is to think statically and is therefore, theologically speaking, to think in terms of laws. That is easy to demonstrate. If the secular becomes an independent realm by itself, then the fact of the world having been taken up into Christ is denied. It is denied that the reality of the world has its basis in the reality of the revelation, and this in turn implies denial of the gospel which is addressed to the whole world. The world is not apprehended as being reconciled by God in Christ, but rather it is seen either as a region which is still entirely subject to the claims of the Christian sector or else as one which opposes the law of Christ with a law of its own. If the Christian sector presents itself as an independent entity, then the world is denied that fellowship into which God entered with the world in Jesus Christ. A Christian law is established which condemns the law of the world and is maintained in an irreconcilable struggle against the world which God has reconciled with Himself. Law always engenders lawlessness; nomism leads to antinomism; perfectionism to libertinism. The present case is no exception. A world which stands by itself, in isolation from the law of Christ, falls victim to licence and self-will. A Christianity which withdraws from the world falls victim to the unnatural and the irrational, to presumption and self-will.

Ethical thinking in terms of spheres, then, is invalidated by faith in the revelation of the ultimate reality in Jesus Christ, and this means that there is no real possibility of being a Christian outside the reality of the world and that there is no real worldly existence outside the reality of Jesus Christ. There is no place to which the Christian can withdraw from the world, whether it be outwardly or in the sphere of the inner life. Any attempt to escape from the world must sooner or later be paid for with a sinful surrender to the world. It is after all a matter of experience that when the gross sins of sex have been overcome they are succeeded by covetousness and avarice, which are equally gross sins even though the world may treat them less severely. The cultivation of a Christian inner life, untouched by the world, will generally present a somewhat tragicomical appearance to the worldly observer. For the sharp-sighted world recognizes itself most distinctly at the very point where the Christian inner life deceives itself in the belief that the world is most remote. Whoever professes to believe in the reality of Jesus Christ, as the revelation of God, must in the same breath profess his faith in both the reality of God and the reality of the world; for in Christ he finds God and the world reconciled. And for just this reason the Christian is no longer the man of eternal conflict, but, just as the reality in Christ is one, so he, too, since he shares in this reality in Christ, is himself an undivided whole. His worldliness does not divide him from Christ, and his Christianity does not divide him from the world. Belonging wholly to Christ, he stands at the same time wholly in the world.

Even when we have appealed to the reality in Christ in order to overcome this thinking in terms of spheres, we are still confronted with another important question. Are there really no ultimate static contraries, no spaces which are separated from one another once and for all? Is not the Church of Jesus Christ such a space, a space which is cut off from the world? And, finally, is not the kingdom of the devil a space of this kind, and one which will never enter into the kingdom of Christ?

Undoubtedly the New Testament contains statements about the Church which fit in with the conception of a space. One may think, for example, of the representation of the Church as a temple, a building, a house, and even as a body. And one may conclude from this that, when it is a question of describing the Church as the visible congregation of God on earth, it is impossible to avoid the notion of space. The Church does indeed occupy a definite space in the world, a space which is delimited by her public worship, her organizations and her parish life,[1] and it is this fact that has given rise to the whole of the thinking in terms of spheres. It would be very dangerous to overlook this, to deny the visible nature of the Church, and to reduce her to the status of a purely spiritual force. For this would be to render ineffective the fact of the revelation of God in the world, and to transform Christ Himself into a spirit. It is essential to the revelation of God in Jesus Christ that it occupies space within the world. But, of course, it would be entirely wrong to interpret this space in a purely empirical sense. If God in Jesus Chirst claims space in the world, even though it be only a stable 'because there was no room in the inn' (Luke 2:7), then in this narrow space He comprises together the whole reality of the world at once and reveals the ultimate basis of this reality. And so, too, the Church of Jesus Christ is the place, in other words the space in

1. *Cf*. Bonhoeffer, *The Cost of Discipleship*.

the world, at which the reign of Jesus Christ over the whole world is evidenced and proclaimed. This space of the Church, then, is not something which exists on its own account. It is from the outset something which reaches out far beyond itself, for indeed it is not the space of some kind of cultural association such as would have to fight for its own survival in the world, but it is the place where testimony is given to the foundation of all reality in Jesus Christ. The Church is the place where testimony and serious thought are given to God's reconciliation of the world with Himself in Christ, to His having so loved the world that He gave His Son for its sake. The space of the Church is not there in order to try to deprive the world of a piece of its territory, but precisely in order to prove to the world that it is still the world, the world which is loved by God and reconciled with Him. The Church has neither the wish nor the obligation to extend her space to cover the space of the world. She asks for no more space than she needs for the purpose of serving the world by bearing witness to Jesus Christ and to the reconciliation of the world with God through Him. The only way in which the Church can defend her own territory is by fighting not for it but for the salvation of the world. Otherwise the Church becomes a 'religious society' which fights in its own interest and thereby ceases at once to be the Church of God and of the world. And so the first demand which is made of those who belong to God's Church is not that they should be something in themselves, not that they should, for example, set up some religious organization or that they should lead lives of piety, but that they shall be witnesses to Jesus Christ before the world. It is for this task that the Holy Spirit equips those to whom He gives Himself. It is, of course, to be assumed that this testimony before the world can be delivered in the right way only if it springs from a hallowed life in the congregation of God. But a genuine hallowed life in the congregation of God differs from any pious imitation of it in that it at the same time impels a man to testify before the world. If this testimony ceases to be given, that is a sign of the inner corruption of the congregation, just as the absence of fruit is the sign of the decay of the tree.

If one wishes to speak, then, of the space or sphere of the Church, one must bear in mind that the confines of this space are at every moment being overrun and broken down by the testimony of the Church to Jesus Christ. And this means that all mistaken thinking in terms of spheres must be excluded, since it is deleterious to the proper understanding of the Church.

So far we have been speaking of the world only in the sense of the world which is reconciled with God in Christ. We have spoken of reality always in the sense of the reality which is taken up, maintained and reconciled in God. And it is in this sense that we have had to reject all thinking that is conducted in terms of two spheres. But this still leaves open the question whether the 'world', if by this we understand the 'disordered' world which has fallen under the power of the devil, and whether sinful reality ought perhaps to be conceived as a space or realm which is established in opposition to the Church, or to the kingdom of Christ. Is perhaps the final static antinomy which justifies this thinking in terms of two spheres the antinomy of the kingdom of Christ and the kingdom of the devil? At first sight this question appears to demand an affirmative answer, yet when it is examined more closely it is in itself by no means conclusive. Christ and His adversary, the devil, are mutually exclusive contraries; yet the devil must serve Christ even against his will; he desires evil, but over and over again he is compelled to do good; so that the realm or space of the devil is always only beneath the feet of Jesus Christ. But if the kingdom of the devil is taken to mean that world which 'lies in disorder', the world which has fallen under the devil's authority, then here, especially, there is a limit to the possibility of thinking in terms of spheres. For it is precisely this 'disordered' world that in Christ is reconciled with God and that now possesses its final and true reality not in the devil but in Christ. The world is not divided between Christ and the devil, but, whether it recognizes it or not, it is solely and entirely the world of Christ. The world is to be called to this, its reality in Christ, and in this way the false reality will be destroyed which it believes that it possesses in itself as in the devil. The dark and evil world must not be abandoned to the devil. It must be claimed for Him who has won it by His incarnation, His death and His resurrection. Christ gives up nothing of what He has won. He holds it fast in His hands. It is Christ, therefore, who renders inadmissible the dichotomy of a bedevilled and a Christian world. Any static delimitation of a region which belongs to the devil and a region which belongs to Christ is a denial of the reality of God's having reconciled the whole world with Himself in Christ.

That God loved the world and reconciled it with Himself in Christ is the central message proclaimed in the New Testament. It is assumed there that the world stands in need of reconciliation with God but that it is not capable of achieving it by itself. The acceptance of the world by God is a miracle of the divine compassion. For this reason the relation of the Church to the world is determined entirely by the relation of God to the world. There is a love for the world which is enmity towards God (Jas. 4:4) because it springs from the nature of the world as such and not from the love of God for the world. The world 'as such' is the world as it understands itself, the world which resists and even rejects the reality of the love of God which is bestowed upon it in Jesus Christ. This world has fallen under the sentence which God passes on all enmity to Christ. It is engaged in a life-and-death struggle with the Church. And yet it is the task and the essential character of the Church that she shall impart to precisely this world its reconciliation with God and that she shall open its eyes to the reality of the love of God, against which it is blindly raging. In this way it is also, and indeed especially, the lost and sentenced world that is incessantly drawn in into the event of Christ.

It is hard to abandon a picture which one has grown accustomed to using for the ordering of one's ideas and concepts. And yet we must leave behind us the picture of the two spheres, and the question now is whether we can replace it with another picture which is equally simple and obvious.

We shall need above all to direct our gaze to the picture of the body of Christ Himself, who became man, was crucified and rose again. In the body of Jesus Christ God is united with humanity, the whole of humanity is accepted by God, and the world is reconciled with God. In the body of Jesus Christ God took upon himself the sin of the whole world and bore it. There is no part of the world, be it never so forlorn and never so godless, which is not accepted by God and reconciled with God in Jesus Christ. Whoever sets eyes on the body of Jesus Christ in faith can never again speak of the world as though it were lost, as though it were separated from Christ; he can never again with clerical arrogance set himself apart from the world. The world belongs to Christ, and it is only in Christ that the world is what it is. It has need, therefore, of nothing less than Christ Himself. Everything would be ruined if one were to try to reserve Christ for the Church and to allow the world only some kind of law, even if it were a Christian law. Christ died for the world, and it is only in the midst of the world that Christ is Christ. Only unbelief can wish to give the world something less than Christ. Certainly it may have well-intentioned pedagogical motives for this course, but these motives always have a certain flavour of clerical exclusiveness. Such a course implies failure to take seriously the incarnation, the crucifixion and the bodily resurrection. It is a denial of the body of Christ.

If we now follow the New Testament in applying to the Church the concept of the body of Christ, this is not by any means intended primarily as representing the separation of the Church from the world. On the contrary, it is implicit in the New Testament statement concerning the incarnation of God in Christ that all men are taken up, enclosed and borne within the body of Christ and that this is just what the congregation of the faithful are to make known to the world by their words and by their lives. What is intended here is not separation from the world but the summoning of the world into the fellowship of this body of Christ, to which in truth it already belongs. This testimony of the Church is foreign to the world; the Church herself, in bearing this testimony, finds herself to be foreign to the world. Yet even this is always only an ever-renewed consequence of that fellowship with the world which is given in the body of Christ. The Church is divided from the world solely by the fact that she affirms in faith the reality of God's acceptance of man, a reality which is the property of the whole world. By allowing this reality to take effect within herself, she testifies that it is effectual for the whole world.

The body of Jesus Christ, especially as it appears to us on the cross, shows to the eyes of faith the world in its sin, and how it is loved by God, no less than it shows the Church, as the congregation of those who acknowledge their sin and submit to the love of God.

God and the world are thus at one in Christ in a way which means that although the Church and the world are different from each other, yet there cannot be a static, spatial borderline between them. The question now is how one is to conceive this distinction between Church and world without relapsing into these spatial terms. Here one must go to the Bible itself for advice, and the Bible has its answer ready.

DEPUTYSHIP

The fact that responsibility is fundamentally a matter of deputyship is demonstrated most clearly in those circumstances in which a man is directly obliged to act in the place of other men, for example as a father, as a statesman or as a teacher. The father acts for the children, working for them, caring for them, interceding, fighting and suffering for them. Thus in a real sense he is their deputy. He is not an isolated individual, but he combines in himself the selves of a number of human beings. Any attempt to live as though he were alone is a denial of the actual fact of his responsibility. He cannot evade the responsibility which is laid on him with his paternity. This reality shatters the fiction that the subject, the performer, of all ethical conduct is the isolated individual. Not the individual in isolation but the responsible man is the subject, the agent, with whom ethical reflexion must concern itself. This principle is not affected by the extent of the responsibility assumed, whether it be for a single human being, for a community or for whole groups of communities. No man can altogether escape responsibility, and this means that no man can avoid deputyship. Even the solitary lives as a deputy, and indeed quite especially so, for his life is lived in deputyship for man as man, for mankind as a whole. And, in fact, the concept of responsibility for oneself possesses a meaning only in so far as it refers to the responsibility which I bear with respect to myself as a man, that is to say, because I am a man. Responsibility for oneself is in truth responsibility with respect to the man, and that means responsibility with respect to mankind. The fact that Jesus lived without the special responsibility of a marriage, of a family or of a profession, does not by any means set Him outside the field of responsibility; on the contrary, it makes all the clearer His responsibility and His deputyship for all men. Here we come already to the underlying basis of everything that has been said so far. Jesus, life, our life, lived in deputyship for us as the incarnate Son of God, and that is why through Him all human life is in essence a life of deputyship. Jesus was not the individual, desiring to achieve a perfection of his own, but He lived only as the one who has taken up into Himself and who bears within Himself the selves of all men. All His living, His action and His dying was deputyship. In Him there is fulfilled what the living, the action and the suffering of men ought to be. In this real deputyship which constitutes His human existence He is the responsible person *par excellence*. Because He is life all life is determined by Him to be deputyship. Whether or not life resists, it is now always deputyship, for life or for death, just as the father is always a father, for good or for evil.

Deputyship, and therefore also responsibility, lies only in the complete surrender of one's own life to the other man. Only the selfless man lives responsibly, and this means that only the selfless man *lives*. Wherever the divine 'yes' and 'no' become one in man, there is responsible living. Selflessness in responsibility is so complete that here we may find the fulfilment of Goethe's saying about the man of action being always without conscience. The life of deputyship is open to two abuses; one may set up one's own ego as an absolute, or one may set up the other man as an absolute. In the first case the relation of responsibility leads to forcible exploitation and tyranny; this springs from a failure to recognize that only the selfless man can act responsibly. In the second case what is made absolute is the welfare of the other man, the man towards whom I am responsible, and all other responsibilities are neglected. From this there arises arbitrary action which makes mock of the responsibility to God who in Jesus Christ is the God of all men. In both these cases there is a denial of the origin, the essence and the goal of responsible life in Jesus Christ, and responsibility itself is set up as a self-made abstract idol.

Responsibility, as life and action in deputyship, is essentially a relation of man to man. Christ became man, and He thereby bore responsibility and deputyship for men. There is also a responsibility for things, conditions and values, but only in conjunction with the strict observance of the original, essential and purposive determination of all things, conditions, and values through Christ (John 1:3), the incarnate God. Through Christ the world of things and of values is once more directed towards mankind as it was in the Creation. It is only within these limits that there is a legitimate sense in speaking, as is often done, about responsibility for a thing or for a cause. Beyond these limits it is dangerous, for it serves to reverse the whole order of life, making things the masters of men. There is a devotion to the cause of truth, goodness, justice and beauty which would be profaned if one were to ask what is the moral of it, and which indeed itself makes it abundantly clear that the highest values must be subservient to man. But there is also a deification of all these values which has no connexion at all with responsibility; it springs from a demoniacal possession which destroys the man in sacrificing him to the idol. 'Responsibility for a thing' does not mean its utilization for man and consequently the abuse of its essential nature, but it means the essential directing of it towards man. Thus that narrow pragmatism is entirely excluded which, in Schiller's words, 'makes a milch-cow of the goddess' when that which has value in itself is in a direct and short-sighted manner subordinated to human utility. The world of things attains to its full liberty and depth only when it is grasped in its original, essential and purposive relevance to the world of persons; for, as St. Paul expresses it, the earnest expectation of the creature waits for the manifestation of the glory of the children of God; and indeed the creature itself shall be delivered from the bondage of corruption (which also consists in its own false self-deification) into the glorious liberty of the children of God (Rom. 8:19–21).

CORRESPONDENCE WITH REALITY

The responsible man is dependent on the man who is concretely his neighbour in his concrete possibility. His conduct is not established in advance, once and for all, that is to say, as a matter of principle, but it arises with the given situation. He has no principle at his disposal which possesses absolute validity and which he has to put into effect fanatically, overcoming all the resistance which is offered to it by reality, but he sees in the given situation what is necessary and what is 'right' for him to grasp and to do. For the responsible man the given situation is not simply the material on which he is to impress his idea or his programme by force, but this situation is itself drawn in into the action and shares in giving form to the deed. It is not an 'absolute good' that is to be realized; but on the contrary it is part of the self-direction of the responsible agent that he prefers what is relatively better to what is relatively worse and that he perceives that the 'absolute good' may sometimes be the very worst. The responsible man does not have to impose upon reality a law which is alien to it, but his action is in the true sense 'in accordance with reality'.

This concept of correspondence to reality certainly needs to be defined more exactly. It would be a complete and a dangerous misunderstanding if it were to be taken in the sense of that 'servile conviction in the face of the fact' that Nietzsche speaks of, a conviction which yields to every powerful pressure, which on principle justifies success, and which on every occasion chooses what is opportune as 'corresponding to reality'. 'Correspondence with reality' in this sense would be the contrary of responsibility; it would be irresponsibility. But the true meaning of correspondence with reality lies neither in this servility towards the factual nor yet in a principle of opposition to the factual, a principle of revolt against the factual in the name of some higher reality. Both extremes alike are very far removed from the essence of the matter. In action which is genuinely in accordance with reality there is an indissoluble link between the acknowledgement and the contradiction of the factual. The reason for this is that reality is first and last not lifeless; but it is the real man, the incarnate God. It is from the real man, whose name is Jesus Christ, that all factual reality derives its ultimate foundation and its ultimate annulment, its justification and its ultimate contradiction, its ultimate affirmation and its ultimate negation. To attempt to understand reality without the real man[2] is to live in an abstraction to which the responsible man must never fall victim; it is to fail to make contact with reality in life; it is to vacillate endlessly between the extremes of servility and revolt in relation to the factual. God became man; He accepted man in the body and thereby reconciled the world of man with God. The affirmation of man and of his reality took place upon the foundation of the acceptance, and not the acceptance upon the foundation of the affirmation. It was not because man and his reality were worthy of the divine affirmation that God accepted them and that God became man, but it was because man and his reality were worthy of divine being that God accepted man and affirmed him by Himself becoming man in the body and thereby taking upon Himself and suffering the curse of the divine 'no' to the human character. It is from this action of God, from the real man, from Jesus Christ, that reality now receives its 'yes' and its 'no', its right and its limitations. Affirmation and contradiction are now conjoined in the concrete action of him who has recognized the real man. Neither the affirmation nor the contradiction now comes from a world which is alien to reality, from a systematic opportunism or idealism; but they come from the reality of the reconciliation of the world with God which has taken place in Jesus Christ. In Jesus Christ, the real man, the whole of reality is taken up and comprised together; in Him it has its origin, its essence and its goal. For that reason it is only in Him, and with Him as the point of departure, that there can be an action which is in accordance with reality. The origin of action which accords with reality is not the pseudo-Lutheran Christ who exists solely for the purpose of sanctioning the facts as they are, nor the Christ of radical enthusiasm whose function is to bless every revolution, but it is the incarnate God Jesus who has accepted man and who has loved, condemned and reconciled man and with him the world.

Our conclusion from this must be that action which is in accordance with Christ is action which is in accordance with reality. This proposition is not an ideal demand, but it is an assertion which springs from the knowledge of reality itself. Jesus Christ

2. In the first picture of his Dance of Death, which represents the Creation, Hans Holbein personifies the sun, the moon and the wind. In this way he gives expression in a naive form to the fact that reality consists ultimately in the personal. In this respect there is an element of truth in primitive animism.

does not confront reality as one who is alien to it, but it is He who alone has borne and experienced the essence of the real in His own body, who has spoken from the standpoint of reality as no man on earth can do, who alone has fallen victim to no ideology, but who is the truly real one, who has borne within Himself and fulfilled the essence of history, and in whom the law of the life of history is embodied. He is the real one, the origin, essence and goal of all that is real, and for that reason He is Himself the Lord and the Law of the real. Consequently the word of Jesus Christ is the interpretation of His existence, and it is therefore the interpretation of that reality in which history attains to its fulfilment. The words of Jesus are the divine commandment for responsible action in history in so far as this history is the reality of history as it is fulfilled in Christ, the responsibility for man as it is fulfilled in Christ alone. They are not intended to serve the ends of an abstract ethic; for an abstract ethic they are entirely incomprehensible and they lead to conflicts which can never be resolved, but they take effect in the reality of history, for it is from there that they originate. Any attempt to detach them from this origin distorts them into a feeble ideology and robs them of the power which they possess in their attachment to their origin, of witnessing to reality.

Action which is in accordance with Christ is in accordance with reality because it allows the world to be the world; it reckons with the world as the world; and yet it never forgets that in Jesus Christ the world is loved, condemned and reconciled by God. This does not mean that a 'secular principle' and a 'Christian principle' are set up in opposition to one another. On the contrary, any such attempt to achieve some sort of commensurability between Christ and the world at least in the form of a general principle, any such attempt to provide a theoretical basis for Christian action in the world, leads, in the form of secularism or the theory of the autonomy of the various domains of life, or else in the form of enthusiasm, to the ruin and destruction of the world which in Christ is reconciled with God; it leads to those eternal conflicts which constitute the underlying material of all tragedy and which precisely in this destroy the totally untragic unity of Christian life and action. When a secular and a Christian principle are opposed, the ultimate reality is taken to be the law, or more exactly a multiplicity of irreconcilably contradictory laws. It is the essence of Greek tragedy that a man's downfall is brought about by the conflict of incompatible laws. Creon and Antigone, Jason and Medea, Agamemnon and Clytemnestra, all are subject to the claim of these eternal laws which cannot be reconciled in one and the same life; obedience is rendered to the one law at the price of guilt in respect of the other law. The meaning of all genuine tragedies is not that one man is right and the other wrong, but that both incur guilt towards life itself; the structure of their life is an incurring of guilt in respect of the laws of the gods. This is the most profound experience of classical antiquity. Especially since the Renaissance it has exercised a decisive influence over western thought; in the early periods of the Church and in the Middle Ages there were no tragedies, but in modern times it has only very rarely been perceived that this tragic experience has been overcome by the message of Christ. Even the modern Protestant ethic invokes the pathos of tragedy in its representation of the irreconcilable conflict of the Christian in the world, and claims that in this it is expressing an ultimate reality. All this unconsciously lies entirely under the spell of the heritage of antiquity; it is not Luther, but it is Aeschylus, Sophocles and Euripides who have invested human life with this tragic aspect. The seriousness of Luther is quite different from the seriousness of the classical tragedians. For the Bible and for Luther what ultimately requires to be considered in earnest is not the disunion of the gods in the form of their laws, but it is the unity of God and the reconciliation of the world with God in Jesus Christ; it is not the inescapability of guilt, but it is the simplicity of the life which follows from the reconciliation; it is not fate, but the gospel as the ultimate reality of life; it is not the cruel triumph of the gods over falling man, but it is the election of man to be man as the child of God in the world which is reconciled through grace.

To contrast a secular and a Christian principle as the ultimate reality is to fall back from Christian reality into the reality of antiquity, but it is equally wrong to regard the Christian and the secular as in principle forming a unity. The reconciliation which is accomplished in Christ between God and the world consists simply and solely in the person of Jesus Christ; it consists in Him as the one who acts in the responsibility of deputyship, as the God who for love of man has become man. From Him alone there proceeds human action which is not worn away and wasted in conflicts of principle but which springs from the accomplishment of the reconciliation of the world with God, an action which soberly and simply performs what is in accordance with reality, an action of responsibility in deputyship. It is now no longer established in advance what is 'Christian' and what is 'secular'; both of these are recognized, with their special qualities and with their unity, only in the concrete responsibility of action which springs from the reconciliation that has been effected in Jesus Christ.

We have just said that for action which corresponds with reality the world remains the world, but in the light of our whole discussion so far it is clear that this cannot now mean that the world is in principle isolated or that it is declared to be autonomous. If the world remains the world, that must be because all reality is founded upon Jesus Christ Himself. The world remains the world because it is the world which is loved, condemned and reconciled in Christ. No man has the mission to overleap the world and to make it into the kingdom of God. Nor, on the other hand, does this give support to that pious indolence which abandons the wicked world to its fate and seeks only to rescue its own virtue. Man is appointed to the concrete and therefore limited responsibility which knows the world as being created, loved, condemned and reconciled by God and which acts within the world in accordance with this knowledge. The 'world' is thus the sphere of concrete responsibility which is given to us in and through Jesus Christ. It is not some general concept from which it is possible to derive a self-contained system. A man's attitude to the world does not correspond with reality if he sees in the world a good or an evil which is good or evil in itself, or if he sees in it a principle which is compounded of both good and evil and if he acts in accordance with this view; his attitude accords with reality only if he lives and acts in limited responsibility and thereby allows the world ever anew to disclose its essential character to him.

Action which is in accordance with reality is limited by our creatureliness. We do not ourselves create the conditions of our action, but we find ourselves placed in these conditions from the outset. Our action is limited by definite boundaries in the forward but never in the backward direction, and these boundaries cannot be overstepped. Our responsibility is not infinite; it is limited, even though within these limits it embrace the whole of reality. It is concerned not only with the good will but also with the good outcome of the action, not only with the motive but also with the object; it seeks to attain knowledge of the given totality of the real in its origin, its essence and its goal; it discerns it as subject to the divine 'yes' and 'no'. Since we are not concerned with the realization of an unrestricted principle, it is necessary in the given situation to observe, to weigh up, to assess and to decide, always within the limitations of human knowledge in general. One must risk looking into the immediate future; one must devote earnest thought to the consequences of one's action; and one must endeavour to examine one's own motives and one's own heart. One's task is not to turn the world upside-down, but to do what is necessary at the given place and with a due consideration of reality. At the same time one must ask what are the actual possibilities; it is not always feasible to take the final step at once. Responsible action must not try to be blind. And all this must be so because in Christ God became *man*, because He said 'yes' to mankind and because it is only we ourselves, as men and in human restriction of judgement and of knowledge in relation to God and to our neighbour, who possess the right and the obligation to live and to act. But because it was *God* who became man, it follows that responsible action, in the consciousness of the human character of its decision, can never itself anticipate the judgement as to whether it is in conformity with its origin, its essence and its goal, but this judgement must be left entirely to God. All ideological action carries its own justification within itself from the outset in its guiding principle, but responsible action does not lay claim to knowledge of its own ultimate righteousness. When the deed is performed with a responsible weighing up of all the personal and objective circumstances and in the awareness that God has become *man* and that it is *God* who has become man, then this deed is delivered up solely to God at the moment of its performance. Ultimate ignorance of one's own good and evil, and with it a complete reliance upon grace, is an essential property of responsible historical action. The man who acts ideologically sees himself justified in his idea; the responsible man commits his action into the hands of God and lives by God's grace and favour.

A further consequence of this limitedness of responsible life and action is that it takes into account the responsibility of the other man who confronts it. Responsibility differs from violence and exploitation precisely in the fact that it recognizes the other man as a responsible agent and indeed that it enables him to become conscious of his responsibility. The responsibility of the father or of the statesman is limited by the responsibility of the child and of the citizen, and indeed the responsibility of the father and of the statesman consists precisely in rendering conscious and in strengthening the responsibility of those who are committed to their care. There can, therefore, never be an absolute responsibility, a responsibility which is not essentially limited by the responsibility of the other man.

We have now seen that the limit of responsible action lies in the fact that the deed ends in the grace and judgement of God and is bounded by the responsibility of our neighbours, and at the same time it becomes evident that it is precisely this limit which makes the action a responsible one. God and our neighbour, as they confront us in Jesus Christ, are not only the limit, but, as we have already perceived, they are also the origin of responsible action. Irresponsible action may be defined precisely by saying that it disregards this limit, God and our neighbour. Responsible action derives its unity, and ultimately also its certainty, from the fact that it is limited in this way by God and by our neighbour. It is precisely because it is not its own master, because it is not unlimited and arrogant but creaturely and humble, that it can be sustained by an ultimate joy and confidence and that it can know that it is secure in its origin, its essence and its goal, in Christ.

THE WORLD OF
THINGS—PERTINENCE—STATECRAFT

On the basis of our knowledge that responsibility is always a relation between persons which has its foundation in the responsibility of Jesus Christ for men, on the basis of our knowledge that the origin, essence and goal of all reality is the real, that is to say, God in Jesus Christ, we are now enabled and obliged to say something also about the relation of the responsible man to the domain of things. We will call this relation pertinence. That has two implications.

The first is that that attitude to things is pertinent which keeps steadily in view their original, essential and purposive relation to God and to men. This relation does not corrupt them in their character as things, but it purifies this character; it does not extinguish the ardour of devotion to a cause, but it refines and intensifies it. The greater the purity of the service to a cause or to a thing, and the more completely this service is free from personal subsidiary aims, the more thoroughly the thing itself will recover its original relation to God and to man, and the more completely it will set man free from himself. The thing for the sake of which the ultimate personal sacrifice is made must serve man precisely in this. If, for example, an attempt is made to render a science useful to men in an illegitimately direct manner for demagogic, pedagogic or moralistic purposes, then it is not only the man but also the science which is ruined. If, on the other hand, in this science man exclusively and unreservedly serves the cause of truth, then in the selfless surrender of all his own wishes he finds himself, and the thing for the sake of which he has rendered this selfless service must in the end serve him. Thus it is essential to the pertinence of the action, to the correspondence of the action with the thing, that one should never overlook this relation of the thing or the cause to the person. It is true that we know this relation only in a thoroughly imperfect form. Either the thing makes itself independent of the person or the person makes himself independent of the thing, or else the two stand side by side completely unrelated. What is needful is the restoration of the original relation on the basis of the responsibility which has its foundation in Jesus Christ.

The second implication is that from its origin there is inherent in every thing its own law of being, no matter whether this thing is a natural object or a product of the human mind, and no matter whether it is a material or an ideal entity. We take the word 'thing' in this sense as meaning any datum in which there is inherent an essential law of this kind, no matter whether or to what extent it is a neutral or rather a personal entity. This definition will include the axioms of mathematics and of logic as well as the state or the family, a factory or a commercial company; in every case it is necessary to discover the particular inherent law by virtue of which this entity exists. The more intense the connexion between the thing and the existence of man, the more difficult it becomes to define the law of its being. The laws of logical thought are more easily defined than, for example, the law of the state; and again it is easier to detect the law of a joint-stock company than the law of an organic growth, of the family or of a people. The correspondence of responsible action with reality also involves the detection and pursuit of these laws. The law appears in the first place as a formal technique which requires to be mastered; but the more closely the particular thing with which we are concerned is connected with human existence, the clearer it will become that the law of its being does not consist entirely in a formal technique, but rather that this law renders all technical treatment questionable. The problem of a technique of statecraft is the best example of this, while a technique of radio manufacture is relatively unproblematic. There can be no doubt that statecraft, political science, also has its technical side; there is a technique of administration and a technique of diplomacy; in its widest sense this technical side of statecraft includes all positive legislation, all positive treaties and agreements, and even all those rules and conventions of internal and international political coexistence which are not legally defined but which are sanctioned by history. Finally, it even includes all the generally accepted moral principles of the life of the state. No statesman can disregard any one of these laws and conventions with impunity. Arrogant disdain for them or violation of them denotes a failure to appreciate reality which sooner or later has to be paid for. Pertinent action will conform with these laws and conventions; its observance of them will not be merely hypocritical, but it will regard them as an essential element in all order; it will acknowledge and turn to advantage the wisdom of these conventions which has been achieved through the experience of many generations.[3] Precisely at this point pertinent action will be incontrovertibly compelled to recognize that the essential law of the state comprises something more than these rules and conventions of statecraft. Indeed, precisely because the state is indissolubly bound up with human existence, its essential law extends ultimately far beyond the range of anything that can be expressed in terms of rules. And it is precisely at this point that the full depth of responsible action is achieved.

In the course of historical life there comes a point where the exact observance of the formal law of a state, of a commercial undertaking, of a family, or for that matter of a scientific discovery, suddenly finds itself in violent conflict with the ineluctable necessities of the lives of men; at this point responsible and pertinent action leaves behind it the domain of principle and convention, the domain of the normal and regular, and is confronted by the extraordinary situation of ultimate necessities, a situation which no law can control. It was for this situation that Machiavelli in his political theory coined the term *necessità*. In the field of politics this means that the technique of statecraft has now been supplanted by the necessity of state. There can be no doubt that such necessities exist; to deny their existence is to abandon the attempt to act in accordance with reality. But it is equally certain that these necessities are a primary fact of life itself and cannot, therefore, be governed by any law or themselves constitute a law. They appeal directly to the free responsibility of the agent, a responsibility which is bound by no law. They create a situation which is extraordinary; they are by nature peripheral and abnormal events. They no longer leave a multiplicity of courses open to human reason but they confront it with the question of the *ultima ratio*. In the political field this *ultima ratio* is war, but it can also be deception and the breaking of treaties for the sake of one's own

3. Pertinent action is not by any means necessarily dependent on specialist training, as was all too long supposed in Germany. In England pertinent action on a large scale is entrusted not to the specialist but to the amateur. Sociologically speaking, pertinent action will be most effectively ensured by a sound balance of specialism and dilettantism. *Translator's note: sachgemäss* ('pertinent') may bear various meanings within the range 'expedient-appropriate-realistic'.

vital needs. In the economic field it is the destruction of human livelihoods in the interest of the necessities of business. The *ultima ratio* lies beyond the laws of reason, it is irrational action. The true order is completely reversed if the *ultima ratio* itself is converted into a rational law, if the peripheral case is treated as the normal, and if *necessità* is made a technique. Baldwin was right when he said that there was only one greater evil than violence and that this was violence as a principle, as a law and a standard. He did not mean by this the extraordinary and abnormal necessity of the use of violence as the *ultima ratio*; if he had meant that he would have been a mere enthusiast and not a statesman; above all he did not wish to see the extraordinary and peripheral case confused with the normal case, with the law. He wished to preserve the relative order which is secured through the pertinent observance of law and convention, when to abandon this order for the sake of a peripheral event would mean chaos.

The extraordinary necessity appeals to the freedom of the men who are responsible. There is now no law behind which the responsible man can seek cover, and there is, therefore, also no law which can compel the responsible man to take any particular decision in the face of such necessities. In this situation there can only be a complete renuniciation of every law, together with the knowledge that here one must make one's decision as a free venture, together also with the open admission that here the law is being infringed and violated and that necessity obeys no commandment. Precisely in this breaking of the law the validity of the law is acknowleged, and in this renunciation of all law, and in this alone, one's own decision and deed are entrusted unreservedly to the divine governance of history.

There can be no theoretical answer to the question whether in historical action the ultimate goal is the eternal law or free responsibility in the face of all law but before God. Great nations are opposed in this in an insurmountable and ultimate antinomy. The greatness of British statesmen, and I am thinking here, for example, of Gladstone, is that they acknowledge the law as the ultimate authority; and the greatness of German statesmen—I am thinking now of Bismarck—is that they come before God in free responsibility. In this neither can claim to be superior to the other. The ultimate question remains open and must be kept open, for in either case man becomes guilty and in either case he can live only by the grace of God and by forgiveness. Each of these men, the one who is bound by the law and the one who acts in free responsibility, must hear and bow before the accusation of the other. Neither can be the judge of the other. It is always for God to judge.

THE ACCEPTANCE OF GUILT

From what has just been said it emerges that the structure of responsible action includes both readiness to accept guilt and freedom.

When we once more turn our attention to the origin of all responsibility it becomes clear to us what we are to understand by acceptance of guilt. Jesus is not concerned with the proclamation and realization of new ethical ideals; He is not concerned with Himself being good (Matt. 19:17); He is concerned solely with love for the real man, and for that reason He is able to enter into the fellowship of the guilt of men and to take the burden of their guilt upon Himself. Jesus does not desire to be regarded as the only perfect one at the expense of men: He does not desire to look down on mankind as the only guiltless one while mankind goes to its ruin under the weight of its guilt; He does not wish that some idea of a new man should triumph amid the wreckage of a humanity whose guilt has destroyed it. He does not wish to acquit Himself of the guilt under which men die. A love which left man alone in his guilt would not be love for the real man. As one who acts responsibly in the historical existence of men Jesus becomes guilty. It must be emphasized that it is solely His love which makes Him incur guilt. From His selfless love, from His freedom from sin, Jesus enters into the guilt of men and takes this guilt upon Himself. Freedom from sin and the question of guilt are inseparable in Him. It is as the one who is without sin that Jesus takes upon Himself the guilt of His brothers, and it is under the burden of this guilt that He shows Himself to be without sin. In this Jesus Christ, who is guilty without sin, lies the origin of every action of responsible deputyship. If it is responsible action, if it is action which is concerned solely and entirely with the other man, if it arises from selfless love for the real man who is our brother, then, precisely because this is so, it cannot wish to shun the fellowship of human guilt. Jesus took upon Himself the guilt of all men, and for that reason every man who acts responsibly becomes guilty. If any man tries to escape guilt in responsibility he detaches himself from the ultimate reality of human existence, and what is more he cuts himself off from the redeeming mystery of Christ's bearing guilt without sin and he has no share in the divine justification which lies upon this event. He sets his own personal innocence above his responsibility for men, and he is blind to the more irredeemable guilt which he incurs precisely in this; he is blind also to the fact that real innocence shows itself precisely in a man's entering into the fellowship of guilt for the sake of other men. Through Jesus Christ it becomes an essential part of responsible action that the man who is without sin loves selflessly and for that reason incurs guilt.

CONSCIENCE

There is a reply to all this which undeniably commands respect. It comes from the high authority of conscience; for conscience is unwilling to sacrifice its integrity to any other value, and it therefore refuses to incur guilt for the sake of another man. Responsibility for our neighbour is cut short by the inviolable call of conscience. A responsibility which would oblige a man to act against his conscience would carry within it its own condemnation. In what respects is this true and in what respects is it false?

It is true that it can never be advisable to act against one's own conscience. All Christian ethics is agreed in this. But what does that mean? Conscience comes from a depth which lies beyond a man's own will and his own reason and it makes itself heard as the call of human existence to unity with itself. Conscience comes as an indictment of the loss of this unity and as a warning against the loss of one's self. Primarily it is directed not towards a particular kind of doing but towards a particular mode of being. It protests against a doing which imperils the unity of this being with itself.

So long as conscience can be formally defined in these terms it is extremely inadvisable to act against its authority; disregard for the call of conscience will necessarily entail the destruction of one's own being, not even a purposeful surrender of it; it will bring about the decline and collapse of a human existence. Action against one's own conscience runs parallel with suicidal action against one's own life, and it is not by chance that the two often go together. Responsible action which did violence to conscience in this formal sense would indeed be reprehensible.

But that is not by any means the end of the question. The call of conscience arises from the imperilling of a man's unity with himself, and it is therefore now necessary to ask what constitutes this unity. The first constituent is the man's own ego in its claim to be 'like God', *sicut deus,* in the knowledge of good and evil. The call of conscience in natural man is the attempt on the part of the ego to justify itself in its knowledge of good and evil before God, before men and before itself, and to secure its own continuance in this self-justification. Finding no firm support in its own contingent individuality the ego traces its own derivation back to a universal law of good and seeks to achieve unity with itself in conformity with this law. Thus the call of conscience has its origin and its goal in the autonomy of a man's own ego. A man's purpose in obeying this call is on each occasion anew that he should himself once more realize this autonomy which has its origin beyond his own will and knowledge 'in Adam'. Thus in his conscience he continues to be bound by a law of his own finding, a law which may assume different concrete forms but which he can transgress only at the price of losing his own self.

We can now understand that the great change takes place at the moment when the unity of human existence ceases to consist in its autonomy and is found, through the miracle of faith, beyond the man's own ego and its law, in Jesus Christ. The form of this change in the point of unity has an exact analogy in the secular sphere. When the national socialist says 'My conscience is Adolf Hitler' that, too, is an attempt to find a foundation for the unity of his own ego somewhere beyond himself. The consequence of this is the surrender of one's autonomy for the sake of an unconditional heteronomy, and this in turn is possible only if the other man, the man to whom I look for the unity of my life, fulfils the function of a redeemer for me. This, then, provides an extremely direct and significant parallel to the Christian truth, and at the same time an extremely direct and significant contrast with it.

When Christ, true God and true man, has become the point of unity of my existence, conscience will indeed still formally be the call of my actual being to unity with myself, but this unity cannot now be realized by means of a return to the autonomy which I derive from the law; it must be realized in fellowship with Jesus Christ. Natural conscience, no matter how strict and rigorous it may be, is now seen to be the most ungodly self-justification, and it is overcome by the conscience which is set free in Jesus Christ and which summons me to unity with myself in Jesus Christ. Jesus Christ has become my conscience. This means that I can now find unity with myself only in the surrender of my ego to God and to men. The origin and the goal of my conscience is not a law but it is the living God and the living man as he confronts me in Jesus Christ. For the sake of God and of men Jesus became a breaker of the law. He broke the law of the Sabbath in order to keep it holy in love for God and for men. He forsook His parents in order to dwell in the house of His Father and thereby to purify His obedience towards His parents. He sat at table with sinners and outcasts; and for the love of men He came to be forsaken by God in His last hour. As the one who loved without sin, He became guilty; He wished to share in the fellowship of human guilt; He rejected the devil's accusation which was intended to divert Him from this course. Thus it is Jesus Christ who sets conscience free for the service of God and of our neighbour; He sets conscience free even and especially when man enters into the fellowship of human guilt. The conscience which has been set free from the law will not be afraid to enter into the guilt of another man for the other man's sake, and indeed precisely in doing this it will show itself in its purity. The conscience which has been set free is not timid like the conscience which is bound by the law, but it stands wide open for our neighbour and for his concrete distress. And so conscience joins with the responsibility which has its foundation in Christ in bearing guilt for the sake of our neighbour. Human action is poisoned in a way which differs from essential original sin, yet as responsible action, in contrast to any self-righteously high-principled action, it nevertheless indirectly has a part in the action of Jesus Christ. For responsible action, therefore, there is a kind of relative freedom from sin, and this shows itself precisely in the responsible acceptance of the guilt of others.

From the principle of truthfulness Kant draws the grotesque conclusion that I must even return an honest 'yes' to the enquiry of the murderer who breaks into my house and asks whether my friend whom he is pursuing has taken refuge there; in such a case self-righteousness of conscience has become outrageous presumption and blocks the path of responsible action. Responsibility is the total and realistic response of man to the claim of God and of our neighbour; but this example shows in its true light how the response of a conscience which is bound by principles is only a partial one. If I refuse to incur guilt against the principle of truthfulness for the sake of my friend, if I refuse to tell a robust lie for the sake of my friend (for it is only the self-righteously law-abiding conscience which will pretend that, in fact, no lie is involved), if, in other words, I refuse to bear guilt for charity's sake, then my action is in contradiction to my responsibility which has its foundation in reality. Here again it is precisely in the responsible acceptance of guilt that a conscience which is bound solely to Christ will best prove its innocence.

It is astonishing how close Goethe came to these ideas with a purely profane knowledge of reality. In the dialogue in which Pylades tries to persuade Iphigenia to overcome the inner law and to act responsibly we read:

Pylades
An over-strict demand is secret pride.

Iphigenia

The spotless heart alone is satisfied.[4]

Pylades

Here in the temple you no doubt were so;
And yet life teaches us to be less strict
With others and ourselves; you too will learn.
This human kind is intricately wrought
With knots and ties so manifold that none
Within himself or with the rest can keep
Himself quite disentangled and quite pure.
We are not competent to judge ourselves;
Man's first and foremost duty is to go
Forward and think about his future course:
For he can seldom know what he has done,
And what he now is doing even less . . .
One sees that you have rarely suffered loss;
For if that were not so you would not now
Refuse this one false word to escape this evil.

Iphigenia

Would my heart like a man's could be resolved
And then be deaf to any other voice!

However greatly responsibility and the conscience which is set free in Christ may desire to be united, they nevertheless continue to confront one another in a relation of irreducible tension. Conscience imposes two kinds of limit upon that bearing of guilt which from time to time becomes necessary in responsible action.

In the first place, the conscience which is set free in Christ is still essentially the summons to unity with myself. The acceptance of a responsibility must not destroy this unity. The surrender of the ego in selfless service must never be confused with the destruction and annihilation of this ego; for then indeed this ego would no longer be capable of assuming responsibility. The extent of the guilt which may be accepted in the pursuit of responsible action is on each occasion concretely limited by the requirement of the man's unity with himself, that is to say, by his carrying power. There are responsibilities which I cannot carry without breaking down under their weight; it may be a declaration of war, the violation of a political treaty, a revolution or merely the discharge of a single employee who thereby loses the means of supporting his family; or it may be simply a piece of advice in connexion with

---

4. (More exactly: . . . has enjoyment of itself.) The introduction of the characteristic concept of 'enjoyment' is also to be noted here.

some personal decisions in life. Certainly the strength to bear responsible decisions can and should grow; certainly any failure to fulfil a responsibility is in itself a responsible decision; and yet in the concrete instance the summons of conscience to unity with oneself in Jesus Christ remains irresistible, and it is this which explains the infinite multiplicity of responsible decisions.

Secondly, even when it is set free in Jesus Christ conscience still confronts responsible action with the law, through obedience to which man is preserved in that unity with himself which has its foundation in Jesus Christ. Disregard for this law can give rise only to irresponsibility. This is the law of love for God and for our neighbour as it is explained in the decalogue, in the sermon on the mount and in the apostolic parenesis. It has been correctly observed that in the contents of its law natural conscience is in strikingly close agreement with that of the conscience which has been set free in Christ. This is due to the fact that it is upon conscience that the continuance of life itself depends; conscience, therefore, contains fundamental features of the law of life, even though these features may be distorted in detail and perverted in principle. The liberated conscience is still what it was as the natural conscience, namely the warner against transgression of the law of life. But the law is no longer the last thing; there is still Jesus Christ; for that reason, in the contest between conscience and concrete responsibility, the free decision must be given for Christ. This does not mean an everlasting conflict, but the winning of ultimate unity; for indeed the foundation, the essence and the goal of concrete responsibility is the same Jesus Christ who is the Lord of conscience. Thus responsibility is bound by conscience, but conscience is set free by responsibility. It is now clear that it is the same thing if we say that the responsible man becomes guilty without sin or if we say that only the man with a free conscience can bear responsibility.

When a man takes guilt upon himself in responsibility, and no responsible man can avoid this, he imputes this guilt to himself and to no one else; he answers for it; he accepts responsibility for it. He does not do this in the insolent presumptuousness of his own power, but he does it in the knowledge that this liberty is forced upon him and that in this liberty he is dependent on grace. Before other men the man of free responsibility is justified by necessity; before himself he is acquitted by his conscience; but before God he hopes only for mercy.

19

RAY S. ANDERSON
Living in the World

1 'THE INCARNATIONAL CHRISTIAN'

> Long ago there lived a Man who was crucified for being too loving and too lovable.
>
> And strange to relate I met him thrice yesterday.
>
> The first time He was asking a policeman not to take a prostitute to prison; the second time He was drinking wine with an outcast; and the third time He was having a fistfight with a promoter inside a church.[1]

IF THERE ARE TWO SIDES TO HUMANITY, CHRIST WILL BE FOUND on the wrong side. This has never been acceptable to man, but it is the way of God. And it was the way of Christ. He was not a religious man in the way that men think of the religious 'side of life'. He did not have access into the privileged sanctuaries of the priests. In the midst of a religious culture that prized appearance and cultivated form, he appeared among men clothed simply in grace and truth. He refused to recognize as spiritual that which was artificial and affected. He valued the truth of being and doing over right-sounding words and beautiful prayers. He stated divine realities in terms of human experience. His life-style was that of a man who lived among men; where distinctions were made between the sacred and the profane which tended to be inhuman, he openly 'profaned' the sanctity of even the law to give dignity to man (Luke 6:6–11). He appeared in the world, as Bonhoeffer said,

1. K. Gibran, *Sand and Foam,* Alfred A. Knopf, New York, 1926, p. 40.

From Ray S. Anderson, *Historical Transcendence and the Reality of God,* pp. 252–276. © Geoffrey Chapman Publisher, London, 1975; William B. Eerdmans Publishing Company, Grand Rapids, 1975. Used by permission of the Publishers.

'incognito as a beggar among beggars, as an outcast among the outcast, despairing among the despairing, dying among the dying'.[2] This incomprehensible solidarity with the destiny of all flesh, leading him to accept in obedience the death of a sinner—a refugee from God—caused his own disciple to protest, and brought forth a rebuke upon all human ways of thinking which seek to deny that solidarity: ' . . . you are not on the side of God, but of men.'[3]

This solidarity of God with all humanity through the life of the Incarnate Logos, revealed the kenotic form of divine transcendence and constitutes the kenotic community of lived transcendence in the Spirit. There now appear to be two distinct dimensions to this lived transcendence: the way of God coming to man, and the way of man coming to God. These two dimensions correspond to the kenotic community and the ek-static community of life in the Spirit. Instead, then, of three separate, but related implications of historical transcendence in terms of lived transcendence, it would now appear that there is but one implication: lived transcendence is a community of life in the Spirit which is both kenotic and ek-static. The two-foldness of the implication was explored in the previous chapter [of *Historical Transcendence*]. What will now be taken up in this chapter for further consideration is but one aspect of the kenotic community as it relates to the problem of how we should understand the relation of the kenotic community to the world. This was raised, and then left for further explication in this chapter, as the problem of how one can make a distinction between a member of the kenotic community and the world when the single 'qualifying' principle is to share the common humanity of Jesus Christ.[4] This will leave the second dimension of lived transcendence—the ek-static community—to be further explored in the final chapter [of *Historical Transcendence*].

There does exist a tension between Christ and the world expressed as an irreconcilable contradiction between good and evil, love and hate, and light as opposed to darkness (John 3:19-20); there is a corresponding tension, it appears, between the kenotic community and the world: 'I am praying for them; I am not praying for the world. . . . They are not of the world, even as I am not of the world . . . the world has not known thee, but I have known

2. *Christology*, p. 11.
3. Matthew 16:23.
4. See *Historical Transcendence and the Word of God*, p. 236.

thee; . . .'[5] World history exists as an antithesis to God's thesis, that is, his creative purpose and will. When man seeks through religion a common denominator to these irreconcilable 'worlds', the essential solidarity between God and man is obscured in the religious movement which originates in man himself.[6] The conception of religion as a synthesis which resolves the antithesis (human contradiction) and the thesis (divine will) either dissolves the reality of God into the self-consciousness of the human subject, or volatilizes the reality of the human into a supra-human transcendence which takes the form of mysticism. In either case, the solidarity of God with man *in* his contradiction is lost. When the eternal Logos entered into the world and 'became flesh', a solidarity was established between God and man at the level of *actual* humanity, not idealized humanity. It is in this sense that one can say that Jesus is on the 'wrong side', if one makes any distinction at all within man as such, which, of course, is untenable in view of the Incarnation itself. The particular tension between Jesus and the world was not between judge and lawbreaker, but it was a tension created by the 'yes' uttered through his life of obedience from the side of the lawbreaker himself. 'I did not come to judge the world but to save the world', said Jesus.[7] As such he lived in the world as the 'new man', who was also at the same time 'one body' with estranged man.

It is in this sense, then, that the kenotic community exists in tension with the world. Not the tension of condemnation, making a distinction by separation from, but the tension which results from penetration of the world—the tension which is produced by the reconciling act itself. The Christian also bears the irreconcilable contradiction in the 'one body'—the kenotic community. But not so as to dissolve the contradiction so that there is a religious synthesis. But the Christian is the 'new man' even as Christ was the 'new thing' of God's grace.[8] The conformity, then, of the Christian is to the Incarnate Son of God and not to the world,[9] but this conformity involves a solidarity with humanity—solidarity with the world—which can be expressed as the incarnational aspect of kenotic community.

5. John 17:9, 16, 25.
6. This is a theme established by Karl Barth. Cf. *Church Dogmatics,* IV/3, pp. 708-709.
7. John 12:47.
8. Ephesians 2:15.
9. John 17:14-16; Romans 12:1-2.

> Solidarity with the world means full commitment to it, unre-
> served participation in its situation, in the promise given it by
> creation, in its responsibility for the arrogrance, sloth and
> falsehood which reign within it, in its suffering under the
> resultant distress, but primarily and supremely in the free
> grace of God demonstrated and addressed to it in Jesus Christ,
> and therefore in its hope . . . the community which knows the
> world is necessarily the community which is committed to
> it.[10]

The kenotic community does not merely penetrate the world as a privileged community which maintains its own distinctive bound-aries and identity—a form of 'spiritual colonialism'—but the penetration can only be one which bears the 'incognito' of the Incarnation itself; not in a 'cunning masquerade', as Barth again reminds us, but

> in an unmasking in which it makes itself known to others as
> akin to them, rejoicing with them that do rejoice and weeping
> with them that weep, not confirming and strengthening them
> in evil nor betraying and surrendering them for its own
> good; . . . by accepting the fact that it must be honestly and
> unreservedly among them and with them, on the same level
> and footing, in the same boat and with the same limits as any
> or all of them.[11]

Now if this is taken seriously, as it must be if the kenotic community follows out its own intrinsic character, the Christian dare not break the 'incognito' by setting the sacred over against the secular and the supernatural over against the natural. This would itself be a conforming to the world rather than conforming to the Incarnate Son of God. This was the distortion of the Pharisees in Jesus' own day—they represented God to the world in precisely the way in which the world expected it and in such a way that the world could securely embrace it without being confronted and shattered by it. The miracles of Jesus were far easier to live with than his own words. By his miracles he could be put in the cate-gory of a 'holy man' and allowed to remain within the society which had a place for the religious man. But his words—'if you háve seen me you have seen the Father'—had no form of accom-modation because they were spoken 'man to man', out of the same secular, human context and existence in which his contemporaries

10. Karl Barth, *Church Dogmatics*, IV/3, p. 773.
11. *Ibid.*, pp. 774–775.

lived. The transcendence of God in its kenotic form means precisely this. That the reality of God enters into an absolute relation with the world in its own forms. The transcendence of the eternal Logos was not demonstrated by the supernatural over against the natural, nor by the miraculous breaking into the historical, but through a solidarity of relation in which the total 'otherness' of God is actually there in confrontation. The attributing of miracles to Jesus, therefore, did not break this 'incognito' of kenotic transcendence, for the category of miracle belongs to the created world, not to God; but neither did the miracles attest to his transcendence in an unambiguous way, for the authority behind miracle was as often taken to be demonic.[12]

Now we have seen that the characteristic of kenotic community is solidarity, not separation. Conformity to the Incarnate Son of God entails solidarity with humanity, which shares a common nature with Jesus Christ. Therefore, we can conclude that the kenotic community does not exist as an entity in time and space distinct from the community of man as such.[13] This is the conclusion to which Bonhoeffer was forced after making an attempt, first of all, to identify Christ with community and then to locate that community as entity within the world. We have already shown how, in Bonhoeffer's earlier works, the sociological aspect dominated his thinking in terms which gave shape and space to the community of Christ. This thinking can still be found in his Christology lectures of 1933 where he says: 'What does it mean that Christ as *Word* is also community? It means that the Logos of God has extension in space and time in and as the community.'[14] But even as this concept of the church was put at the disposal of the

12. 'The miracles are no breaching of the incognito. The ancient religious world is full of miracle workers and healers. Jesus is not alone in this. The realm of miracles is not identical with the realm of God. True, the miracles may exceed normal everyday happenings, but they are only on another level within the created world. The concept which goes with miracle is not that of God, but that of magic. Magic remains within the world. If Jesus does miracles, he preserves his incognito within the magical picture of the world. It is not miracle which accredits him as the Son of God in the New Testament. On the contrary, his authority is taken to be demonic.' D. Bonhoeffer, *Christology*, p. 115. It is this ambiguous quality of miracle which makes it unsuitable for an evidence of the transcendence of God in and of itself. A miracle has no ontic value in terms of divine transcendence while the humanity of Christ does.

13. We are moving towards the point where 'kenotic community' will have a more specialized meaning. See *Historical Transcendence*, p. 259.

14. *Ibid.*, p. 60.

Confessing Church during the war in order to make an absolute distinction between the true community of Christ and the Nazi-controlled State Church, Bonhoeffer was already creating a non-spatial concept of the community of Christ through an emphasis on Christ as the transcendent 'person' who was concretized, not by the spatial form of the community, but through a life of discipleship and obedience.[15] And so, by the time Bonhoeffer took up the writing of his lectures which were published posthumously as *Ethics,* he was to criticize the restriction of love to the 'closed circle of the devout', and suggested that we must leave behind the picture of 'two spheres', that of the church and the world, each with its own space.[16] And so he is led to make his strongest statement with regard to the relation of the church to the world:

> If we now follow the New Testament in applying to the Church the concept of the body of Christ, this is not by any means intended primarily as representing the separation of the Church from the world. On the contrary, it is implicit in the New Testament statement concerning the Incarnation of God in Christ that all men are taken up, enclosed and borne within the body of Christ and that this is just what the congregation of the faithful are to make known to the world by their words and by their lives. What is intended here is not separation from the world but the summoning of the world into the fellowship of this body of Christ, to which in truth it already belongs.[17]

What continued to plague Bonhoeffer was the way in which the 'congregation of the faithful' could preserve its own identity if all men were assumed to belong to the body of Christ by virtue of their common humanity with the Incarnate Son of God. As we have seen, his concept of the 'secret discipline' was one such attempt to define the church in its dynamic life of the Spirit within the total body of Christ.

The matter with which we are concerned here, however, is the identification of the body of Christ with the total community of

---

15. Cf. John A. Phillips, *The Form of Christ in the World,* pp. 74–76. Out of this period came Bonhoeffer's two books: *Life Together,* SCM Press Ltd., London, 1970, first published under the title *Gemeinsames Leben,* Chr. Kaiser Verlag, Munich, 1949; and *The Cost of Discipleship,* SCM Press Ltd., London, 1969, first published as *Nachfolge,* Chr. Kaiser Verlag, Munich, 1937.
16. *Ethics,* pp. 129, 205.
17. *Ibid.,* p. 206.

man. 'Everything would be ruined if one were to try to reserve Christ for the Church', says Bonhoeffer, 'and to allow the world only some kind of law, even if it were a Christian law. Christ died for the world, and it is only in the midst of the world that Christ is Christ.'[18] The language which Bonhoeffer uses here seems to state quite explicitly the situation as we have already done in terms of the kenotic community. In a kenotic sense, the body of Christ is co-extensive with all humanity, and this is the principle to which Bonhoeffer appeals as being intrinsic to the Incarnation. But is this in accordance with the New Testament's use of the expression 'body of Christ'?

The use of the figurative expression 'body of Christ', or its shortened form 'body', is restricted to those letters generally attributed to Paul.[19] It is obviously an expression and concept which is uniquely Pauline, and only a brief study is needed to see that he generally uses the expression as either an organic or a spatial metaphor to represent the redeemed fellowship of those who are baptized by the Spirit into Christ through faith. A passage which is typical of such an intended significance is found at the beginning of a long exposition on the nature of this fellowship:

> For just as the body is one and has many members, and all the members of the body, though many, are one body, so it is with Christ. For by one Spirit we were all baptized into one body—Jews or Greeks, slaves or free—and all were made to drink of one Spirit.[20]

In a passage with eucharistic overtones, where a strong ethical demand is considered to arise as an implicit condition of participation in the body of Christ, Paul draws the lines of fellowship around the body of Christ as it is defined by those who all 'partake of the one bread'.[21] Those who worship idols cannot participate in this fellowship because they are not of the *same body*. We are forced to the inescapable conclusion that Paul intended by the expression 'body of Christ' to include only those who have received the Spirit and thus constitute the fellowship of the redeemed, as distinct from the total community of man.

Now what do we say to this? First of all, it may be that it was

18. *Ibid.*, pp. 205–206.
19. The relevant passages are: Romans 12:4–5; I Corinthians 10:16; 11:29; 12:12–27; Ephesians 1:23; 3:6; 4:4; 4:12; 4:16; 5:30; Colossians 1:18; 1:24; 3:15.
20. I Corinthians 12:12–13.
21. I Corinthians 10:17.

574   RAY S. ANDERSON

unfortunate that Paul chose to use the very powerful and illuminating metaphor of the body to designate those who were participants
in Christ by receiving the Spirit as opposed to those who only share
a common humanity with Christ. I say unfortunate, because the
phrase is thus pre-empted from use in the kenotic sense of signifying that the Incarnation has incorporated humanity into a catholicity of covenant response. It is this idea that Bonhoeffer has in mind
when he says that it is 'implicit in the New Testament statement
concerning the Incarnation of God in Christ that all men are taken
up, enclosed and borne within the body of Christ'.[22] The expression 'body of Christ' has genuine incarnational significance when
referred to the fact that all men are 'brothers' of Christ through the
flesh. The use of the expression by Paul in a restrictive sense to
those who are baptized into fellowship with Christ through the
Spirit tends to restrict Christ to the redeemed fellowship as defined
in either ethical or spatial terms (and usually both). This has the
further effect of obscuring the kenotic community in its relation to
all men and has the danger of placing an obstacle between the
world and its solidarity with God—an obstacle which the Incarnation itself removed once and for all.

I think that we also need to say that Paul certainly did not intend
to restrict the Incarnation in its effects to the body of Christ as he
defined it. 'God was in Christ', says Paul in another place, 'reconciling the world to himself, not counting their trespasses against
them, and entrusting to us the message of reconciliation.'[23] While
it is true that Paul's correspondence was directed to the church,
and thus his Christology tended to be shaped by the ecclesiastical
problems with which he was dealing, he did at least recognize that
those who were on the fringes of the church, if not indeed outside
the body of Christ, were 'brothers for whom Christ died'.[24] In his
personal ministry with men in the world, Paul became 'all things to
all men' including becoming a man 'outside the law', because he
was 'under the law of Christ'.[25] This would at least seem to be an
implicit assertion that the ground for all men's relation to Christ is
the same, and that the 'law of Christ' is in fact a governing principle which superseded distinctions made on any other basis. But
perhaps the strongest testimony to the incarnational truth that those
not considered as belonging to the church are nonetheless 'brothers
of Christ' comes from Christ himself, who encouraged the visiting

22. *Ethics,* p. 206.
23. II Corinthians 5:19.
24. I Corinthians 8:11; Romans 5:6; 14:15.
25. I Corinthians 9:19-23.

of the sick and those in prison, the clothing of the naked and the feeding of the hungry as equivalent to that which is either denied or done to Christ (Matthew 25:31–46).

Because it is doubtful that one can follow Bonhoeffer in attempting to re-interpret the expression 'body of Christ' and give it a more universal significance as representing the place which all men have in Christ by virtue of a common humanity, I would prefer to use the metaphor in the commonly accepted biblical sense, as long as it is clearly understood that it refers to but one aspect of Christ's relation to the world, and thus cannot be taken as a definitive distinction between the kenotic community and human society in general. Accordingly, I intend to signify by the expression 'kenotic community', that incarnational solidarity which the Christian has with all humanity, a solidarity which permits of no distinction made between the Christian and the world by limiting the Incarnation to a community of human fellowship within human society. Up to this point, kenotic community has been used in a general sense of solidarity with the world, with its general implication being that it includes all that is meant by the term 'church' as well. From this point on, the expression 'kenotic community' will take on a more specialized meaning, as it refers quite specifically to the solidarity which the church has with man in the world.

However, it must immediately be added that solidarity with the world does not constitute identity with the world. The solidarity with humanity which resulted from the 'Word becoming flesh', did not make Jesus 'identical' with the world, nor did it make him 'identical' with every other man in the sense that, as man, he had an existential existence independent of the divine Logos.[26] The distinction between Christ and man was absolute while at the same time there was a solidarity with man which is permanent. This is the implication of the *kenosis* when considered as the historical transcendence of God through the Incarnate Logos. The kenotic community, therefore, cannot be distinguished from the world by splitting the solidarity of all humanity in Christ, and thus cannot take the form of one entity within humanity set against another. That is, the distinction cannot be either an organic or a spatial one in terms of the church as entity. The kenotic community, considered incarnationally, is the foundation of all human community, and the church can never deny its common participation in this

26. The question of how we are to understand Jesus as a 'real man', and yet not identical to all men, is explained with lucidity and keen insight into the historical problems by Lewis B. Smedes, *The Incarnation: Trends in Modern Anglican Thought,* J. H. Kok N. V., Kampen, 1953, pp. 147ff.

community without denying Christ himself. This, of course, does not yet say what 'church' is, but it says what 'church' cannot be—namely, an entity which distinguishes itself from the world by breaking solidarity with humanity. At the very least, this seems to be an imperative of the Incarnation which calls into question every implication that Christ can be contained within a specific organism which exists as an entity within the world. It calls into question the implication that absolute distinctions are to be made at the *boundaries* of the church which lie within humanity. But it also raises the question of how *any* distinction can be made within the solidarity of kenotic community.

Here again we must allow the implications of historical transcendence to be traced out patiently into the life of lived transcendence. We have seen that the solidarity of the divine Logos with humanity did not obliterate the distinction between God and man, but rather, clarified it in such a way that an intimate relation with God is now possible through the Incarnate Son of God. Historical transcendence taught us that Logos is not intrinsically alien to flesh, and that *kenosis* is not a renunciation of transcendence. The issue involved in the question of the divinity of Christ is that of the transcendence of God. Divine transcendence is not a quality of being which is defined by abstracting from a non-divine creation or nature. Transcendence is difference in solidarity, and as such, it is the extrinsic, rather than the intrinsic reality of Being. Or, one could say, it is *par-ousia* rather than *ousia*. Through the Incarnation we see exposed the *par-ousia* of God which is the 'presence' of God as three-in-one. But we also discover that the creation of God, and thus his creature, exists in the same form of 'presence' which is expressed as difference within solidarity. The image of God is rooted in the transcendence of God, which means that man is capable of experiencing absolute difference in solidarity. The kenotic community is the ground for the solidarity, within which the 'difference' can be experienced as transcendence without destroying the solidarity. The 'metaphysic' for grasping this lies in the very structure of the Trinity itself as the 'presence' (*par-ousia*) of God given in the Incarnation.

When we speak, therefore, of the incarnational Christian, it is much more than a certain 'style of life' which is exemplified in the life of Jesus to be used as a model of kenotic living. The incarnational Christian bears witness to the 'presence' (*par-ousia*) of Christ within the solidarity of kenotic community. It is impossible for the body of Christ as an organism which exists as an entity within the world to be this 'presence' without obliterating the very distinctives which give it the status of an entity. Why is this? Precisely because man is already entity by virtue of his solidarity with humanity. Each man bears the totality of humanity in himself and thus is the hypostasis of humanity. Two or three, or more men, cannot be 'hypostatized' into an entity distinct from other men and thereby have a particular ontological relation to the humanity of Christ which is different from that of each man's hypostasis of humanity. 'Where two or three are gathered in my name', said Christ, 'there am I in the midst of them.'[27] But what really is the *difference* between that 'gathering' and any other gathering on the part of any other two or three men as viewed from the perspective of the solidarity of man? There is none at all. The 'presence' of Christ in the two or three can only be known when the boundary between them and others is obliterated so that the difference can become 'presence' at the level of human solidarity. The moment the 'two or three' attempt to embody the 'difference' in any form or structure which separates them from other men, a boundary has been drawn which will place Christ either on one side or the other. It should be clear from the Gospel accounts of Jesus' life and ministry that he recognized no such boundaries. Therefore, I have asserted that it is impossible for the body of Christ to exist as an entity in the world in such a way that *its* distinctiveness represents the difference, or that its boundaries represent the transcendence of God as the 'presence' of Christ. This does not mean that the body of Christ as a fellowship of Christians does not have a significant life of its own within the kenotic community, but that is not the point under discussion here. The point is, the 'difference', or the transcendence of God, can only be expressed in solidarity with humanity. To this extent, when the church sets itself out to be 'different' from the world, it no longer makes a 'difference' to men in the world.

It remains, therefore, to state precisely how the difference or the transcendence of Christ within the kenotic community has its true expression. The subtitle of this chapter holds the clue. The 'incarnational Christian', not the incarnational church, is the point at which to begin. There is a sense in which the church too is incarnational, but only through the incarnational life of its members. Lived transcendence is an incarnational life which involves complete solidarity with an absolute difference. Only in 'man to man' relations can this occur. This is not simply a 'philosophy of personalism' where the I-Thou relation is seen as an ontological link

27. Matthew 18:20.

with divine transcendence. I say 'man to man' only because I wish
to emphasize that solidarity is involved with our being human
'entities' where one person's humanity is qualitatively the same as
that of another. 'Man to man' does not mean 'individual to individual', but person to person in the sense that there is a catholicity
of humanity which locates the core of our personhood in the humanity which God has taken to himself. The capacity for I-Thou
relations, of course, does mean that there is capacity for transcendence, that is, a difference within solidarity. But considered
from the standpoint of divine transcendence, the human I-Thou
relation fundamentally belongs to the kenotic community—it does
not constitute the 'difference'.

Spirit and Word constitute the possibility of solidarity with a
difference. It was through the Spirit that the Incarnate Word
existed in solidarity with man and yet brought 'difference' to bear
in an absolute sense—Jesus is God. The 'difference' was expressed 'man to man', that is, at the level that he was, yet God's
'presence' was there in an absolute sense. But it was the 'presence'
(*par-ousia*) of God himself in Christ by the Spirit which constituted the difference as well as the unity. There was a 'oneness'
with God which was particularly expressed from a relation of
solidarity with man. This is the truth captured by the language of
the prayer of Jesus: 'The glory which thou hast given me I have
given to them, that they may be one even as we are one, I in them
and thou in me, that they may become perfectly one, so that the
world may know that thou hast sent me and hast loved them as
thou hast loved me.'[28] The prayer that those who believe in Jesus
are 'to be one', is not simply a prayer for a communal type of life.
A communal group as 'entity' does not impress the world with the
reality of God, nor with the love of God, because the very boundary which creates the entity of communal life breaks solidarity
with the world. No, the oneness must be incarnational. That is, it
is first of all the oneness which Jesus experienced with the Father
which is to be the same oneness which the Christian experiences
with God in Christ.

While Jesus made it perfectly clear that he was not the Father,
he did not hesitate to claim that he was standing 'as the Father'
among men. 'He who has seen me has seen the Father . . .'[29] Jesus
did not merely stand as the representative of the Father, point away

28. John 17:22–23.
29. John 14:9.

from himself as if to say: don't look to me, I am not the Father, look away from me to the Father and then you will see God. But he clearly said that the Father was *there* in him, and that to know him was to know the Father. There was a transparency, as it were, not in a docetic sense, where the humanity of Christ only seemed to be real, but in the sense that truth is transparent and undivided. The distinction between Father and Son did not involve a separation in terms of 'presence' (*par-ousia*). The 'presence' is, therefore, the 'oneness' in the sense that 'presence' is the ek-stasis of divine being in communion. When we say that God is 'there' in Christ, we do not mean present to man as an entity among other entities, but God is 'present to himself' in Christ. The humanity of Christ is the horizon of divine existence which at the same time becomes the horizon of human personhood. This means that solidarity with humanity gives an ek-static dimension to humanity through the oneness of Christ with the Father. Christ, therefore, is not related in a 'one-to-one' relation with man as individual, abetted by the Holy Spirit as another 'individual'; rather, Christ is 'present' to humanity in its catholicity, which each person bears in its totality as one aspect of personhood. But this 'presence' of Christ is itself personhood as the ek-static movement of being into communion. Through the Holy Spirit, then, *each* person shares in the 'oneness' of personhood—'as we are one . . . that they may be one.' Therefore, the Holy Spirit cannot be said to 'individuate' Christ by relating him 'person by person', but as the Spirit brings man from his 'individuated' existence to completion of personhood in oneness with the life of God, this 'oneness' is oneness with 'presence', so that Christ is 'present' to the world through the horizon of his own humanity, which each person bears in its totality.

Now if we take this 'as we are one' to be the kind of thing signified by 'that they may be one', it becomes clear just what it means to express lived transcendence in terms of being an incarnational Christian. The Christian is enabled to express the same transparency within his solidarity with man and thus stand 'as Christ' in the world. Thus, instead of pointing away from himself, from his own humanity, to Christ, the Christian must say: to become involved with me is to come up against Jesus Christ who is 'present' to our humanity through the reality of the Holy Spirit who completes my life in the personhood of divine communion. While it is true that one cannot speak as another (or the same) Incarnation of Christ, one should live and speak incarnation*ally* so that Christ again has hands to reach out into the world to give, feet to walk the roads of life with men, and arms to embrace the lonely and hold close the estranged.[30] Here then is the closing of the circle of transcendence towards which we have been moving for a considerable time. The solidarity of the Christian with the world is not simply a fact of his existence in kenotic community with Christ in the humanity of all men, but it is the 'place' where God transcends the world in love. For God's transcendence is the *difference* which love makes in solidarity. Again, it is not that the world needs the Christian, and thus is incomplete without that love (though that is true), but it is that the Christian is incomplete without the world, without closing the circle of transcendence by loving the world that God loves (John 3:16). This is why I have shown that the kenotic community is not just the church assuming a posture of humility and poverty, nor is it just the world; it is Christ in solidarity with the world, but in such a way that there is tension also.

The kenotic community is also the ek-static community, but there no boundary can be drawn, though not all believe and receive the Spirit. But what the world receives, it receives by 'looking to' the Christian, who 'gives' the transcendence in which he himself lives. When Peter and John were confronted by the 'world' at the door of the temple, they interrupted their prayers and said to the man: 'Look at us. . . . I give you what I have; in the name of Jesus Christ of Nazareth, walk' (Acts 3:1-6). Through the Holy Spirit,

30. Karl Barth would not agree that the Christian 'stands as Christ' in the world, for his concept of being incarnationally related to the world is heavily weighted by an eschatological emphasis: 'In the community it takes place that Jesus Christ Himself, the living Word of God, is present and revealed to certain men together in world-occurrence as the One He is above in the height and hiddenness of God. . . . These men in their own time and place here find themselves commonly ruled and determined by the fact that in speech and action He always comes to their time and place.' *Church Dogmatics,* IV/3, pp. 756-757. What Barth wants to preserve is the hiddenness, the 'grace' of the church, in its world occurrence. It is only when Christ 'comes to their time and place' that the community of Christ becomes Christ. I feel that there is an important eschatological dimension to a life of lived transcendence, and I will deal with this in the final chapter [of *Historical Transcendence*], but to emphasize the eschatological at the expense of the incarnational aspect of the Christian's life is to introduce an unnecessary dialectic between eternity and time. I would like to feel that by understanding 'presence' as the presence of God to himself by the life of the Spirit in the solidarity of man with Christ, this 'presence' is *not* made the predicate of human existence (which is what Barth warns against), while at the same time taking seriously the temporal and historical aspect of 'presence' as lived transcendence in the solidarity of kenotic community.

God is present to himself in the Christian. This is the ek-static dimension of the kenotic community which has its primary focal point in the believer and only secondarily in the church as a functioning entity within the world. This does not mean that the Christian is an 'individual', who only has a subsequent relation to the community of Christ, for his believing, as we have asserted earlier, is conditioned at its source by his belonging.

The Spirit has no historical transcendence of his own, but has the historical life of Christ as transcendent grounds in history. Thus, when the Spirit of God assumes concrete form in the world, he re-forms man in the image of the Incarnate Son of God, which is the true image of God for man. We also said that the Spirit forms Christ in the concrete life of the *other* person in the kenotic community, not in one's own life. This makes it possible for one to have a real relation to Christ in the Spirit without denying one's actual existence. We can now see that this is rather an artificial way of stating the case. For, obviously, when I receive the Spirit of God as a gift, I am re-formed in the image of Christ *for* the other person, even as another is *for* me. In thinking now specifically of the way in which Christ is 'present' in the kenotic community in such a way that there is a 'difference' within the solidarity, one must assume that there is a 'difference' between the one who has received the Spirit of Christ as a gift of faith, and so belongs to the 'body of Christ', as Paul says, and the one who, though he is in the same kenotic community, has not rightly received the gift of faith and thus is not living a life of lived transcendence in the Spirit.

I wonder if one would want to go so far as Bonhoeffer and say that the one who has not professed faith in Christ is a Christian nonetheless, because he is in the kenotic community (the body of Christ for Bonhoeffer), and that the only difference is that the believer *knows* that he is a Christian while the unbeliever does not?[31] I think that I can understand why Bonhoeffer wants to say that, because he is anxious to avoid any implication that the church or Christian 'possesses' Christ in some way that the world does not, or even that Christ possesses the church in a way that he does not the world. And I would agree that one would want to eliminate the static 'spaces' and 'boundaries' which separate the church from the world by conferring distinctiveness upon the church as an entity within society.[32] But I think Bonhoeffer is closer to the truth when he speaks of the 'foreignness' and strangeness which enters

31. *Ethics*, p. 143.
32. *Ibid.*, p. 201.

in when the Christian testifies to the world's belonging to the kenotic community through Christ;[33] however, I would think that this 'foreignness' points to an *absolute* difference *within* the solidarity of the kenotic community which has its source in the transcendence of Spirit who re-forms particular entities of humanity into the image of Christ by making them one with the community of God's own life. And I would think that if the term 'Christian' is to have any significance at all it should have a transcendent significance, not a relative one. I would prefer, myself, to make a transcendent distinction between Christian and non-Christian, while at the same time preserving the solidarity.

But the transcendent significance cannot be determined by the boundaries of the body of Christ as entity, but only through the life of the Spirit where solidarity with humanity is ontologically united with the humanity of Christ. If we seem to have lost a great deal in relativizing the boundaries of the church, we have gained even more in now being able to absolutize the difference between belief and unbelief in terms of life in the Spirit, without splitting the solidarity of Christ with man. The 'difference', we can now say, is not institutional, or even sacramental, but evangelical. In fact, only an evangelical Christian can affirm the complete solidarity of humanity in Christ and at the same time testify to the absolute difference.

If one seeks to establish the transcendence of God (the difference) as sacramental or institutional, either the solidarity of Christ with humanity is ruptured in order to make the distinction, or what is basically implied in such a concept of transcendence leads (ultimately) to an explicit assertion—namely, that there is really no absolute distinction between the body of Christ and the world. In this case, the kenotic community is taken to be identical with the church and the boundaries are obliterated without retaining the centre. It would appear, then, that one cannot be an incarnational Christian without also being an evangelical Christian.[34]

33. *Ibid.*, p. 206.
34. I think it would be fair to say that this is, in substance, the conclusion reached by Lewis B. Smedes in his study of modern Anglican thought, and the way in which the church is identified organically and incarnationally with the humanity of Christ. A speculative view of the Incarnation, says Smedes, which seeks its extension in the church and its completion in the Eucharist, separates the work of Christ from the person. 'If Anglican theologians would, at the beginning of their theological reflection, take their stance in the redemptive-historical situation of the Bible, they would be led into more biblical thinking about Christ and the believer's relation-

The boundaries can only be erased if there is a centre. But what we must explore further is the question: How does an evangelical Christian know where the centre is?

2 'THE EVANGELICAL CHRISTIAN'

> If therefore the divine style chooses the foolish, the shallow, the ignoble, to put to shame the strength and ingenuity of all profane writers, there certainly is need of the illuminated, enthused and eager eyes of a friend, and intimate, a lover, in order to discern through such a disguise the beams of heavenly glory. *Dei dialectus soloecismus* ... ['God speaks bad grammar'].[35]

Not a few of J. G. Hamann's contemporaries (Immanuel Kant included) were certain that he had taken leave of his senses after a conversion experience in London upon reading the Bible through twice while living alone in his small flat. What Hamann saw with 'the eager eyes of a lover' was a language strange to the master of transcendental empiricism.[36] For what Hamann had received was the gift of faith, and in that gift, the reality of God's love and grace for him. Hamann's faith was evangelical—he received Jesus Christ as his Lord and Saviour through a direct response to the Word in the power of the Spirit.[37] It was also incarnational—for he

---

ship to Him.' *The Incarnation,* p. 178. I am assuming that what Smedes is referring to here is that which I would call an evangelical relationship to Christ, that is, through the gift and in the power of the Spirit, one is united to the whole person of Christ and thereby participates in his life of obedience to the Father. I think that I am saying a bit more than Smedes, in suggesting that the evangelical Christian also exists incarnationally in solidarity with the kneotic community, and that if his Christianity leads him to deny this solidarity he is in effect denying Christ. This, of course, is a much different concept of an incarnational relation to Christ than that of the Anglican Church (as presented by certain theologians) which Smedes is criticizing.

35. J. G. Hamann, *J. G. Hamann—A Study in Christian Experience,* R. G. Smith, Collins, London, 1960, p. 186. Smith's brackets.

36. On one occasion, as Gregor Smith records it, Kant besought Hamann to write 'in human language. Poor son of earth that I am, I am not organised to understand the divine language of the intuitive reason.' *Ibid.,* p. 47.

37. Hamann, in writing of his own conversion, says: 'My son, give me thy heart!—Here it is, my God! Thou hast demanded it, blind, hard, flinty,

lived a life of utter solidarity with man in his weakness and human-ity.

> One must give oneself with just as much confidence to the stream of circumstances as to the stream of the passions when God is with us and our life is hidden in him ... If you see your friend on the list of tax-gatherers [a reference to the possible post at the excise office], do not be annoyed ... I will remain on the farthest shore, or begin to serve from below, as low as ever I can.[38]

In many ways, Hamann is a model of the man who can live an incarnational life because he has an evangelical faith. Because his life was totally centred in God, he needed no boundaries at which to reinforce his life in distinction from, or before, others. He prized neither success nor power, and avoided the semblance of even those religious postures which ordinarily accompanied the way of the Christian in the world. His rule was to have none. He revealed Christ in the world, not by representing himself as a saint, but by driving the truth deep into the centre of his life and forcing his weakness and untruth to be exposed outwardly in such a way that he was transparent in his very concealment.

> A strict morality seems to me to be more contemptible and shallower than the most wilful scoffing and mockery. To drive the good deep inside, to drive the evil to the outside, to seem worse than one really is, to be really better than one seems: this I consider to be both a duty and an art.[39]

Thus avoiding the 'kaleidoscope of the inward life', he sought always to exist in relation to God and so needed no boundaries between himself and the world. Perhaps this is expressed most clearly in his 'marriage of conscience' to Anna Regina Schumacher. This relationship lasted for all of his life, and while some might interpret his unwillingness to go through the motions of a legal ceremony as an arbitrary and antisocial gesture, it is more likely that in his 'marriage' Hamann was 'expressing the

---

astray, unrepentant though it was. Purify it, make it new, and let it be the workshop of thy good Spirit. It has deceived me so often when it was in my hands that I no longer wish to acknowledge it as mine. It is a leviathan that thou alone canst tame—through thy indwelling it will enjoy rest and com-fort and blessedness.' *Ibid.*, p. 155.

38. J. G. Hamann, letter to J. G. Linder in Riga, *ibid.*, p. 62.
39. J. G. Hamann, *ibid.*, p. 109.

immense weight which he gives to faith as the ground of his whole existence.'[40] Hamann himself spoke of the arrangement as being aimed at not 'lessening her happiness', and adds:

> This ongoing romance of my life, which has now been running for seventeen years . . . is for me a true sign and miracle of the ineffable and incomprehensible plan of a higher, invisible hand.[41]

The particular character of that which I have termed an evangelical faith is the reality of its centre resting totally on the act of God in Jesus Christ as the sole source of one's existence in the world. It was the reality of this centre to his life which marks both Hamann's remarkable consistency of faith as well as his unusual lack of concern for boundaries. Because the two are not usually found in what we have come to regard as evangelical Christianity, I want to explore this further in hopes of exposing the way in which a lived transcendence can be understood as solidarity with the world within which there exists an absolute difference.

C. H. Dodd makes the interesting suggestion that, while the centre of the new people of God is clear enough—Jesus Christ— the boundaries are not drawn at all.[42] One could show how this is true at several levels. For Christ, the boundary of the Logos was human flesh itself. Nothing marked him off from other men. He wore no halo, held no office, and recognized no boundary between his life and other men. His transcendent difference was totally contained in the centre of his human existence as the divine Logos. Again, while he became the centre of a group of followers and disciples, the boundaries were never clear. Judas the disciple proved to be a betrayer, while Nicodemus the Pharisee was revealed as a friend.

In contrast to the religious distinctives of Judaism, which was a 'boundary' religion, the 'new people of God' who received the Spirit and thus were recognized as 'belonging' to God, operated with no fixed boundaries. For example, in the days during which the early church was experiencing its own formative shape and style, Peter was prepared in a vision, which taught him that God makes no distinction between that which was formerly designated as clean and unclean from a religious and ceremonial standpoint, to proclaim the gospel of Jesus Christ to a gathering of Gentiles in

---

40. This is Gregor Smith's appraisal, *ibid.*, p. 61.
41. *Ibid.*, p. 61.
42. *The Founder of Christianity*, Collins, London, 1971, p. 92.

Caesarea (Acts 10). When the Holy Spirit came upon the gathering, causing them to praise God, Peter responded by saying: 'Can any one forbid water for baptizing these people who have received the Holy Spirit just as we have?'[43] Clearly, a boundary was being erased between Jew and Gentile with no other boundary put in its place, with only the authority of the Spirit left at the centre. Nor was the boundary which was removed merely a racial distinctive, for in the writing of the gospel of Mark (was Peter one of the sources for Mark?), when Jesus' words concerning the defilement which comes, not from that which enters a man, but that which is expressed from his heart, were recorded, an editorial insertion immediately follows: 'Thus he declared all foods clean.'[44]

It would perhaps be an oversimplification to say that religion tends to reinforce its authenticity and power through the boundaries which are drawn between the sacred and the profane, while faith lives only before God in a world with no boundaries. For it must be admitted that the religious life of Israel was circumscribed with boundaries which God himself had drawn rather severely between their life and that of the Gentiles, down to the calculation of the last hour of the Sabbath and the smallest plant of the garden. And yet, the operative principle of their life was faith—a life before God which exposed them to all the weaknesses and helplessness of a people *without* a powerful boundary. The character of their life was established in Abraham, the father of the faithful, says Paul, and not Moses, the giver of the Law.[45] Yet, it is unmistakably clear that with Jesus Christ the boundaries were totally removed in the form of religious distinctives and replaced by the boundary which is Christ himself: 'Now that faith has come', says Paul, 'we are no longer under a custodian; for in Jesus Christ you are all sons of God, through faith.'[46]

This is at the heart of what it means to speak of an evangelical Christian. It is not merely that man has been liberated from religious boundaries in order to take up residence as a citizen of a secular, desacralized world. Rather, the evangelical Christian lives in the reality of Christ as both the boundary and centre of his existence. But, henceforth, to say that Christ is the boundary of man's existence is not to be able to define that boundary in any way that draws a line between men which will serve to 'contain' Christ. Here the evangelical Christian has often failed to under-

43. Acts 10:47.
44. Mark 7:19.
45. Galatians 3:14-18.
46. Galatians 3:25, 26.

stand the true imperative of the Incarnation and the true significance of historical transcendence, for the boundary of Christ includes all humanity, both Jew and Gentile, both male and
female;[47] the kenotic community of Christ places all men within
the boundary of that community by virtue of a common humanity
shared with Christ. This is the solidarity which belongs to historical transcendence which the church as the body of Christ must not
violate by the placing of boundaries between itself and the world.
But here also is where we must learn from historical transcendence
that solidarity of God with man is precisely the *place* where the
absolute difference is experienced in the form of the 'presence'
(*par-ousia*) of the oneness of God. Thus, while kenotic community
is a way of expressing the solidarity of God with man in an incarnational way, it is also a way of pointing to the reality of transcendence, for it is the place where faith lives in utter dependence
upon the life which God gives.

I have said that only the evangelical Christian can be an incarnational Christian. This is but another way of saying that lived transcendence is only possible because of historical transcendence.
This life of faith is not simply the way in which man now comes to
authentic self-understanding by taking a strictly eschatological
view of his historical existence. Nor is it simply a life of the Spirit
where Spirit assumes the form of one's own faith-existence, be it
ethical, ideological or religious in form. The evangelical Christian
can dare to be incarnational and affirm solidarity with the world
without running into the error of spiritual solipsism at the centre or
historical relativism at the boundary of his life. The reason for this
is that *both* the boundary and the centre, both the solidarity and the
difference, are rooted in the transcendence of God as historically
given in the life of Jesus Christ.

It will now become clear why it was so important in Chapter VI
of *Historical Transcendence* to show how the historical transcendence of God comes to us as a revelation contained in Scripture. It also becomes clear why, if Scripture is severed from its
transcendent authority as it refers to the historical reality of the
person and life of Jesus Christ, the transcendent grounds for an
incarnational life collapse in the ruins of either an existentialist or a
rationalist theology. The distinguishing mark of the evangelical
Christian is, therefore, the historical transcendence of the reality of
God which serves as the noetic and normative impulse for a life of
faith. Apart from Scripture, which admittedly can be rationalized

47. Galatians 3:28.

into a dead letter without the movement of Spirit to quicken belief, one is cut off from the historical transcendence of God as it has been uniquely given to man in the life of Jesus Christ. But if this is true, then it also means that Scripture itself, despite (or even because of) its place in the ambiguity of all that is historical, has a transcendence of its own which stands over and against the epistemological and hermeneutical canons which (rightly) are brought to bear from the standpoint of man's contemporary place in history. It is this transcendence which the Evangelical discovers in Scripture which, rather than enslaving him to the supposed narrow boundaries of a deadly orthodoxy, actually frees him to take radically and seriously the Incarnation as an imperative which both draws the authentic boundary to the human situation and reveals its true centre.

The great temptation which lurks in the drawing of boundaries, is the power which it gives man to predicate the reality of his own existence. Because the motivation behind this quest for power arises out of man's basic insecurity and 'powerlessness' in the face of the threats to existence, the boundaries are usually drawn at the places where one's existence can be defined with the greatest precision. While most boundaries give the appearance of embodying the points at which man asserts his greatest strength, they are actually the points of greatest vulnerability. For this reason, they are defended with an almost irrational passion when someone challenges their existence. The boundaries which God placed around Israel, fencing her off from the rest of the world, were designed to show the radical difference which life entails when God is at the centre. When these boundaries became the points of Israel's strength, as predications of her own place of privilege and power in the world, rather than evidences of God's radical claim upon life, the boundaries become barriers behind which the ego entrenched itself in opposition to God himself. In this sense, all boundaries which separate man from man, and man from God, are 'semitical circles' which seek to contain and confirm man's identity within a particular horizon which he invests with something of an absolute quality.

There is a form of incarnationalism which is, strictly speaking, a 'semitical circle' of humanism. The Incarnation is abstracted into an ideological boundary within which the 'divinity' of man himself can be asserted. A transcendent God who invades this sphere and seeks to drain off all divinity for himself *has* to be denied the right of existence. Therefore, that which passes as a radical theology of incarnation is actually a radical ideological humanism, and, of course, it must assert the 'death of God'. For in this case, God's solidarity with man must not be allowed to destroy the boundary of absolute humanism, with its own intrinsic laws which govern the nature and destiny of existence.

So then, the boundaries which man asserts are inherently 'positivistic'; that is, the boundary actually does define the laws by which man interprets and orders his existence. There is, therefore, a common denominator running through the positivisms of the rational man, be they empirical, logical or historical; and of the psychical man, be they behavioural or Freudian; and of the spiritual man, be they idealist, existentialist or fundamentalist. All of these boundaries can be termed 'semitical circles' because they are of the type which transpose a limitation of creaturehood, which is meant to signify man's dependence upon God as the centre of his existence, into a law by which man predicates the power of his own creaturely existence. When evangelical faith adopts a 'boundary mentality', it becomes fundamentalist, which is simply a variant form of the positivism which is inherent in all attempts to seek the laws of truth and reality within boundaries which man can control. When fundamentalism and liberalism attack each other in the name of the truth of God, the struggle is over *where* the boundaries are to be drawn. The true antithesis, on the other hand, is between the historical transcendence of God and *all* boundaries which seek to contain God or identify God through the laws of creaturehood, whether they are defined in religious, ethical or rational terms.

When the Incarnation is seen to provide, not only a solidarity of God with man, but a centre of transcendence within that solidarity, all of the laws of creaturehood, including all that is human, can be affirmed as real in that they point to the transcendence of the Creature-Redeemer. But here, as we have seen, it is not simply that the creature points to the Creator, the Creator meets himself in the creature in such a way that historical transcendence is *this* meeting of God with God, and not simply the creature's recognition of the Creator in historical clothing. This is the content and the core of evangelical faith, and this is why the Scriptures are a normative and thus transcendent source for this content. The *centre* which the evangelical Christian knows in faith within his solidarity with the world is neither the Word alone as a noetic source of revelation, nor the Spirit alone as an existential source of revelation, but both together. There is a danger of a 'positivism of Spirit' in the form of a charismatic experience, as we have seen, in which the kenotic community is introverted, and thus ultimately divided and fragmented. But there is also a danger of a 'positivism of the Word' by which faith becomes a purely rational assent to the dead letter of Scripture. Here, too, there is introversion, and the boundaries drawn along the lines of a particular 'doctrine' of Scripture simply reproduce the 'semitical circle' of the orthodox Jews in Jesus' own day.

If then we are to follow this imperative of the Incarnation into some practical form for the church existing in the world as both the kenotic and ek-static community, what are the implications? Certainly, one would not want to confuse a boundary in the sense that it has been understood with the practical forms by which any organism functions in human society. By that I mean, institutional forms of a Christian community are not necessarily its boundaries. The so-called non-institutional forms of the church miss the point completely, it seems to me, and in attempting to direct their energies totally to the formation of an organism without any form or structure in the world, they may be judged to have failed. The failure may not be seen as any lack of a spiritual motivation, but in failing to be a truly kenotic community. The non-institutional church which attempts to function as an organism of personal relationship may even have more rigid boundaries than the institutional church itself. Nor is a compromise any better, where one makes a dichotomy between the church as an historical institution and the *Ekklesia* as a community of personal fellowship, while attempting to operate with both as valid and necessary.[48] The concept of kenotic community is not that of the formation of an organism as opposed to an institution, but that of solidarity with the world as one pole of the existence of the church. The kenotic

48. This was the attempt made by Emil Brunner, most clearly set forth in his book *The Misunderstanding of the Church*, where he sought to establish the fact that the *Ekklesia* was considered originally to be a brotherhood of called people, living in mutual love. Thus, it was essentially personal and not legal or institutional. It comes into existence as a result of the *Kerygma* and the reception of the Holy Spirit, and is structured by the gifts of grace (*charismata*) and ministries (*diakoniai*) rather than by legal or moral laws. Therefore, the *Ekklesia* can never become the church as an institution in society (pp. 107ff.). See also *The Christian Doctrine of the Church, Faith and the Consummation,* Dogmatics, Vol. III, pp. 32, 41, 45, 47. Because Brunner held that the *Ekklesia* as a personal organism was never intended to become an institutional entity within society, he did not set out to replace the church as an institution with *Ekklesia*, but saw it (the church) as the I-It dimension of man's experience within which the I-Thou relation took place through personal encounter. This, of course, reflects his reliance upon Buber for his basic categories for understanding faith. Not only does Brun-

community as an imperative which the Incarnation demands permits no distinction between the Christian and the non-Christian which resides intrinsically in the Christian (or the church) *as such*. When one 'defines' the church or the Christian, then, the distinctive must be solely in the 'difference' which has its source in the historical transcendence of God. The 'difference' is Christ, not that redemption is set over against creation, but so that man is liberated to participate in Christ's ek-static fulfilment of all creaturehood through the life of the Spirit. The 'difference' is the centre (Christ) and not in distinctions drawn between men, or between the church and the world as entities. I do not see that the institutional forms of the church are intrinsically inimical to kenotic community, as long as the institutional form is governed by a faith which is both incarnational and evangelical.

There is a certain 'integrity' intrinsic to both the incarnational and evangelical aspect of the church. This integrity has its roots in the historical transcendence of God in Christ, and so too is without boundaries. Such an integrity can only take the form of fellowship which lives out of a centre. But in this case, the centre—Christ— demands that one live a life of solidarity with one's fellow-man in the world. To turn aside from one in the world, to show love only towards a fellow believer, is a violation of the integrity of Christ himself.[49] It is a violation of kenotic community. The church which denies its solidarity with the world becomes an 'untruthful' church and no longer has the 'incarnational credibility' that is the mark of Christ himself.[50] But there is also the demand of evangelical integrity, in which the true distinctive of Word and Spirit as

---

ner's *Ekklesia* slip dangerously close to becoming merely a 'brotherhood' of co-humanity, but he is unable to give it any real ontological relation to the historical transcendence of God in Christ. Brunner's 'event' language cannot adequately account for the existence of kenotic community as the incarnational dimension of *Ekklesia*.

49. Cf. Galatians 2:11-12, where this is established in principle by Paul's rebuke to Peter. Cf. also the teaching of Jesus concerning loving those who are one's enemies, and those who cannot repay: Matthew 5:43-48; 25:31-46.

50. 'Is the church then credible?', asks Hans Küng, 'does she help men to be truthfully christian, to be truthfully human?' *Truthfulness: The Future of the Church*, Sheed and Ward, London, 1968, p. 126. A truthful church, for Küng, is a church that is *provisional*, that is, not an end in herself; *unassuming*, that is, to be constantly in need of grace rather than dispensing it; *ministering*, that is, to take the way of the cross rather than the way of triumphal procession; *conscious of guilt*, that is, to exist 'in grace' and not

known in a life of union with Christ is to be preserved from untruth. Where evangelical integrity is violated through that which compromises the transcendence of Scripture in the sense that it is normative for the content of historical transcendence, the incarnational aspect of Christian faith is reduced to an ideal of ethical or social existence.

The outline which begins to emerge is that of a dynamic and evangelical faith which has its centre in historical transcendence and its circumference in kenotic community. The solidarity of kenotic community acts as a living context in which the Christian closes the circle of transcendence by living 'as Christ' in the world. The church, then, or body of Christ, as Paul likes to speak of it, does not have the centre in itself. As though, either as an organism or as an institution, it embodies the *ultimate* reality of Christ. The church exists, rather, as the penultimate along with the world, and cannot close the circle of transcendence, that is, cannot express the truth of Christ apart from its *ultimate* relation to the world. The removal of the boundaries from the church means, at least, that it is de-ultimatized in terms of its own existence apart from the world, and in this way can find its oneness (in an ecumenical sense) if it has the mind of Christ.

Again, in practical terms, as well as in the most profoundly theological sense, the form of such an incarnational, evangelical existence in the world can best be expressed as *diakonia,* a transcendence of service. Thus, more important than the *form* of the church in the world, is the *mode* of the church's existence in the world. *Diakonia* refers to function rather than status, and, as such, expresses first of all the life of the Incarnate Logos as the mode of his freedom to be for man in the expression of his life of divine

---

'in righteousness'; and finally, *obedient,* that is, to remain free from all claims except the radical will of God as revealed in Jesus Christ (pp. 51ff.). Therefore, Küng suggests, it is not more 'truthful' to leave the church as an historical institution than to stay within it (p. 141). The evidences of truthfulness seem to be those which arise out of what I have called the kenotic community: 'Wherever, among individuals or groups, there is a truthful church, there occurs a necessary demythologising and de-demonising, a deepening and humanising of the world and of man; there dawns something of that complete justice, that eternal life, that cosmic peace, that true freedom and that final reconciliation of mankind with God, which one day God's consummated kingdom will bring.' p. 215. My difficulty with Küng comes with his starting point. He takes as the basic question: What did Jesus want? (p. 48). While it seems to me that the true starting point is in the question: Who was Jesus?

Sonship with the Father eternally. As T. F. Torrance so well expresses it:

> Thus through the Incarnation it is revealed to us that God in His own Being is not closed to us, for He has come to share with us the deepest movement of His divine heart, and so to participate in our human nature that the heart of God beats within it. We know that in the springs of His own eternal life God is ever open and ready and eager to share the weakness and sorrow and affliction of others and to spend Himself in going to their relief and in saving them.[51]

In *diakonia,* therefore, we are dealing with the essential character of kenotic community itself. For the service which the Christian renders is not the giving of something which he possesses to those who do not possess it, nor is it the case of the rich or the advantaged sharing with the poor and disadvantaged. It is Christ himself who has taken *our* weaknesses upon himself, who has borne our sorrows and our sins, who has absorbed our pain and tasted our death. He is the *diakonos,* the servant who provided in his own person the ground and the source of all such service. As members of the kenotic community, we are made rich through his poverty (II Corinthians 8:9). Apart from this transcendence of *diakonia* which creates the kenotic community out of all humanity through the suffering love and divine obedience of the Son of God in the flesh, the Christian's service to his fellow man assumes the proportions of an offensive and self-ingratiating prostitution of love. The church is not and cannot become the 'servant to the world' and thus distinguish herself as incarnational. For the church is also the kenotic community, and only *knows* that Christ's *diakonia* takes all human weaknesses and needs upon himself. But the world does not know this until the Christian closes the circle of transcendence through *diakonia* in fellowship with Christ and gives material and physical substance to the spiritual reality of this grace. The church is the place where Christ, clothed with his gospel, meets the Christ clothed with the desperate needs and the human hopes of the world.[52]

51. 'Service in Jesus Christ', *Service in Christ,* Essays Presented to Karl Barth on his 80th birthday, edited by James I. McCord and T. H. L. Parker, Epworth Press, London, 1966, pp. 4, 5. Readers of this essay will note how indebted I am to Professor Torrance for his exposition of the concept of *diakonia* with respect to the Incarnation.
52. 'The Church cannot be in Christ without being in Him as He is proclaimed to men in their need and without being in Him as He encounters us

The church, therefore, does not heal and help the physical and social needs of man as a kindly physician or a benevolent case worker, but struggles as the kenotic community to bind its own members into the body of Christ, sharing the battle against the forces of evil and exposing itself to the pain and anguish of emotional as well as physical suffering. This mark of service as the kenotic community is itself ek-static, for creaturehood finds itself lifted to fellowship in hope with the life of the Creator through the eternal Sonship of Christ, the Incarnate Word. The gospel is not simply clothed with physical and material dress to make it creditable to man, *diakonia* is the gospel, for it is lived transcendence. The evangelical and incarnational dimensions coincide in the same way as the Word has his mode of being in the flesh. The service of the Word brings to man a transcendent power of liberation from bondage and participation in the life of God. But this Word is itself the response, and thus the service of response has its ground in the historical transcendence of the divine Word made flesh.

How then can the church have its own 'space' in the world, or its own 'form'? How then could there exist boundaries around Christ which were smaller than the world itself? These are rhetorical questions, and meant only to confirm the truth of lived transcendence as a life of solidarity with man in which there is expressed an absolute difference. The difference is God. But with God the difference does not constitute division, or, ultimately, separation. Lived transcendence, then, is not only a life in the world, but a life in God. For, while the kenotic community has its heart on earth, it has its head in heaven. If through historical transcendence we have discovered the 'lost lane-end into heaven', then we have found more than there is in this life.

---

in and behind the existence of every man in his need. Nor can the Church be recognized as His except in that meeting of Christ with Himself in the depth of human misery, where Christ clothed with His gospel meets with Christ clothed with the desperate need and plight of men.' T. F. Torrance, *ibid.*, p. 9.

20

IGNACIO ELLACURÍA

Liberation: Mission and Charism

TALK OF LIBERATION IS IN THE AIR ALL OVER THE WORLD TODAY, particularly in those regions which feel they are shackled by oppression. People talk about political liberation, social liberation, economic liberation, and so forth. The varied uses of the word suggest the wealth and depth of the term, but they also hinder its elaboration in any unified or unitary sense. Too many branches have sprouted on the tree of liberation, and their profusion now threatens the healthy growth of the trunk itself.

My purpose here is not to prune the tree by excising the superfluous branches. My purpose here is to explore and clarify the term insofar as that is possible by considering the vocation of the Latin American Church in present-day history. I shall suggest that the specific mission and charism of the Latin American Church can be tied up integrally with the basic concept of liberation. To say this is to explore the deeper recesses of the concept of liberation and to call for the radicalization of the Church's activity.

The linking of these two tasks lies at the very heart of this study. Liberation is both a political concept and a religious concept. At the very least it is certainly a Christian concept. We should not be frightened by the fact that it possesses both these features. Rather, we should be stimulated. Today the Church is clearly and openly turning its gaze to the world. At such a moment we cannot view the mission of the Church as something outside the boundaries of the political realm. The fact is that the world of humanity, as a formal totality, cannot help but be political. Hence the Church has only two alternatives. Either it does not turn fully to the world or else it must incarnate herself in the political realm. The reason for choosing the latter alternative is not that the political realm is a part of the overall social reality and hence deserves attention also. It is that the political realm, more than ever before, is an all-encompassing dimension which embraces what human beings are forced to put up with rather than what they can actively do. It is not simply that the political element touches upon every other dimension. Even more to the point is the fact that everything which is done or not done has some impact on the configuration of the political realm. And in turn the political realm—note that I am distinguishing ''the political realm'' from ''politics'' here—gives singular configuration to the shape of man's personal life. It is a grave mistake to think that one can lead a personal life outside the bounds of the political realm.

It is this link between the political realm and the totality of man—or man as a totality at least—that justifies the relating of Christianity to the political realm. And by Christianity I am referring to a whole way of living. In what specific way does Christianity, as opposed to other religions, view its relationship to the political realm? That is a question which deserves detailed consideration, but here I simply want to note the fact that the political realm and Christianity are necessarily related to each other. It would be an exaggeration to maintain that all theology, insofar as it is intellectual reflection on Christian faith and action, must be specifically political theology based on eschatology, the future, and hope.[1] But it is quite correct to maintain that theology and Christianity cannot be everything they are supposed to be unless they are willing to confront the totality embodied in the political realm.

These and other theoretical reasons justify the kind of reflection we are undertaking here. But the most potent justification is the concrete situation of Latin America and its peoples. The fundamental task incumbent on Latin Americans today vis-à-vis the political realm seems clear enough, however much people may dispute the most suitable ways to carry out this task in the con-

---

1. See *Diskussion zur ''politische Theologie,''* edited by Helmut Peukert (Mainz: Grunewald-Kaiser, 1969). The theology of liberation can find support in a preliminary analysis of what we are to understand by ''political theology,'' but it does not depend on the latter. It is being worked out in terms of Latin America, and it is independent of political theology as the term is often used. Furthermore, it should be remembered that political theology owes its impetus to the Third World.

crete. The real question here is this: What can Christianity and the Christian contribute to the carrying out of this political task? Are there two distinct tasks here, one incumbent on the Latin American as a Christian and the other incumbent on the Latin American as such? What are we to say about this involvement in politics on the part of Christians and the Church, which is regarded as meddling by many? Is it correct to say that Christians, insofar as they constitute a Church, are improperly meddling when they concern themselves with the political situation? Is involvement in the political realm the same thing as involvement in politics?

Besides these questions, there are other things to consider. Some lay people and priests have felt obliged by their ecclesial vocation to become highly politicized. In some cases they seem to have gone to excess, impoverishing the Christian message on the one hand or relying on politics too much as a tool on the other. Neither in theory nor in practice do they seem to have managed to unify their action so that it is both fully Christian and fully political. The Latin American Church evinces a "guilty conscience" in this area. Those Christians who have undertaken political commitments feel obliged to do so out of respect for their Christian vocation; yet they cannot seem to figure out or establish the intrinsic relationship between their Christian mission and their worldly activity. But the same "guilty conscience" is evident in those who reject political commitment and involvement, because they cannot help but see links between Christianity and the exigencies of societal reality.

The road towards solving this whole problem complex would seem to lie in a thorough analysis of the mission and charism of the Latin American Church insofar as it is a living and distinct segment of the universal Church, and in a thorough Christian analysis of the concept of liberation. This concept seems at first glance to be political, and it is certainly used in different senses by different political groups. Has the Church acted here as it has often done in the past, maintaining allegiance to a political concept in vogue in order to bolster its power rather than to carry out its mission? What is the intrinsic relationship, if any, between the Church's mission and liberation? What sort of liberation can be viewed as a contemporary and pertinent embodiment of the Church's salvific mission? Can the concept of liberation offer a sound and adequate synthesis of what the secular activity and the Christian activity of Latin Americans should be?

These questions may help us to spell out a well-rounded concept of liberation and to give a sound orientation to the pastoral activity of the Church in the specifically Latin American situation. But if we are to answer these questions satisfactorily, we must first consider in what sense it is possible to talk about a charism and mission peculiar to the Latin American Church. Having done that, we should be able to show that a sound concept of liberation gives adequate expression to that charism and mission today. The historicity of salvation demands that the Church in Latin America be Latin American. If it turns its attention and energy to the Latin American situation, it should be able to figure out what its mission and charism is in the light of the gospel message. In the remaining pages of this chapter, I shall devote two sections to the historicity of salvation and its implications and two sections to the specific mission and charism of the Latin American Church.

SALVATION HISTORY AND HISTORICAL SALVATION

There would be no need to start so far back if the thinking of many segments of the Latin American Church were not dominated by a prejudice that causes the Church itself to remain in a state of alienation. This prejudice, which is very operative but not necessarily formulated in explicit terms, might be expressed as follows: The Church has always been the same, and it will continue to be exactly the same in the present and the future; moreover, it should be one and the same everywhere. Underlying this prejudice is the assumption that social realities are hard-and-fast realities rather than realities in history. Nature is regarded as a substance, and any change or mutation is regarded as something fortuitous and accidental. This overall outlook is clearly evident in the talking and thinking of many ecclesiastics. Its seriousness can scarcely be overestimated because its impact extends from the structuring of the hierarchy to the Church's understanding of its mission and the ordering of ecclesial activities.

Faced with the prejudice, we must remind ourselves that not even natural realities themselves should be conceived exclusively in terms of substance. In particular, historical realities cannot retain their basic identity unless they continually undergo profound changes; for change and transformation are essential to every historical reality. What this change entails exactly may be open to debate. Some may agree with Hegel that it involves the negation of every present moment; some may agree with Bergson that it is a perduring evolutionary search for ever new and more perfect forms; some may agree with Zubiri that it involves a permanent process of creation in which unforeseen possibilities are fleshed out in reality. It is not easy to spell out the essence of historical reality, and people may well debate the whole matter. But one can scarcely deny that there are historical realities, that the Church is a reality in history, and that change is an essential component of all historical realities. Here "essential" does not just mean "necessary." It also means that change takes place in historical realities on a deep and important level which involves both their totality and their basic unity. As Zubiri puts it in another context, the Church must always be the same and yet never quite the same.

One should not assume that this jeopardizes the unity or identity of the Church. Fear has caused theologians and ecclesiastics to forget the historical character of the Church and of its salvific mission. Theologians have forgotten the profoundly historical character of the biblical message and have focused their thinking around concepts such as nature and substance that were inherited from Greek thought. Ecclesiastical leaders have identified the unity of the Church with an imperial form of organization that was more concerned about structure than about interpersonal communion.

Today people commonly talk about salvation history, and about Christianity as salvation history. Some people, to be sure, do wonder whether Christianity really is a religion of salvation purely and simply. They feel that the peculiar character of Christianity lies in the fact that it has gone beyond the classic framework of salvation peculiar to most religions; that it is to be viewed more in terms of "deification."[2] Leaving that whole question aside, we can certainly say that the category of salvation does have an important place in the Christian message and in Christian activity. There certainly is a salvation history, and Vatican II based its dogmatic thinking on this theme to a large extent. But if we accept the importance of salvation history, then obviously we must accept the fact that Christian salvation is a historical salvation. Let us consider these two points in a bit more detail.

God's word to man is a historical Word of salvation. It is certainly a word concerning salvation throughout its history; but when this revealed word reaches its culmination in the Word, then it takes on a very specific name, i.e., Jesus the Savior. The name of God for us, his being-with-us and his being-for-us, is embodied in

2. It is Zubiri who objects to calling Christianity a salvation religion. He sees man's deification as the essential and formal element of Christianity.

the name of Jesus; and its purport and function is embodied in the word "Savior." Christianity affirms that man is in need of salvation, and that the salvation needed by man cannot be attained apart from Jesus. At this point we are not yet going to try to spell out the thrust and import of this salvation offered by the Father in and through his Son. But in the very fact of saying that the salvation of mankind is to be found only in the incarnate God, we are already offering an interpretation of man and alluding to something that transcends man. This transcending, however, does not imply separation; instead it implies the shouldering of the totality that man is. At this point we glimpse the necessity of interpreting this salvation in dialectical terms; for while it is the salvation of man, it is not from man. In other words, this salvation subjectivizes the work of salvation in a locus that is superior to man; at the same time, however, it incorporates everything that man is as an object of salvation and draws it into the overall process, so that it can truly be the salvation of a person.

This supreme Word of salvation is historical, not only as salvation but also as word. It is not simply a natural word, a word that is deduced from the natural essence of the world and existing things. This view would strip time of the personal and theological dimensions of revelation. In fact, however, the historical singularity of Jesus as the Word of God uncovers the ultimate meaning of every prior divine word and definitively sets in motion the essential historicity of the whole process. By so doing, it allows for a truly metahistorical dimension in which the transcendence of both the natural and the personal realm is rendered present. Thus the message and promise of Christianity cannot be deduced *a priori* from the nature of man or the world; it must be related to an irruption that is both free and historical.

The Word of salvation is historical in another sense as well. Jesus, the Christ, is a word for all human beings; but he is also a word for each individual human being. He is the word for all time, but he is also the word for here and now. He is the latter, not because each individual assimilates what is meant for all or because the here and now is simply a moment in a process that remains ever the same, but because he is a Word that is a person and because his Word is a personal one. It is a personal Word because this word is spoken to a given individual. All other voices are voices crying in the wilderness. Jesus the Word and the words of Jesus have not been spoken or heard once for all time and all people. They are heard and nurtured and fulfilled in a journey through history that is shaped by the historical situation. Rather than talking about history of dogmas, we should talk about a history of revelation—although the two terms cannot be used in the same way. The human being who hears the word is always a distinct and different human being; and the personal word that he or she hears personally is not something that is simply received but rather something that is shared between two persons. Because of its profoundly historical character, then, revelation always gives more and more of itself—to paraphrase the happy expression of Zubiri.

Now if that is the case, then the fundamental question to ask in any attempt to discover the mission and charism of the Latin American Church would be this: What will Christian revelation offer when it issues its summons to the Latin American as someone distinct from the European and the North American? What will this revelation say to the Latin American? What will it say in the Latin American? Our answer to these questions will determine the ability of Christianity to face up to the Latin American situation and say something worthwhile. It will also specify the Christian identity of the Latin American.

But it is not just that there is a salvation history. There is also the fact that salvation must be historical. This implies two things: 1) Salvation will differ with the time and place in which it is fleshed out; 2) it must be fleshed out in history, in human beings who live in history. Salvation cannot be defined in univocal terms. Nor can it be defined as if man were a spirit without history, a spirit who is not incarnated in history. Nor can it be defined as if salvation in the "hereafter" were not supposed to be signified and signalized in the "here and now."

The historicity of salvation could be deduced from the historicity of revelation itself. If revelation has a history and if salvation has been proclaimed in a historical way, that is due to the fact that man himself is historical and it is his salvation that is being sought. It seems preferable, however, not to focus on a deductive process when one is trying to pay heed to the biblical message. Here I do not intend to present all the data of the Bible in order to prove the historicity of salvation. But I do want to highlight some of the more noteworthy points in order to lead into a discussion of the historical character of salvation.

Israel comprehended its salvation on the basis of its own liberation in history. The revelation of God's word was embodied in its own history as a people, a people with concrete problems of a predominantly political cast. It was the salvation of a people, rather than of isolated individuals. This salvation had much to do with liberation from the nation's political enemies. They were the enemies of Yahweh because they were the enemies of his people. At this stage of salvation history people moved from political experience to religious experience. They hoped and expected that religion would interpret and resolve political problems—that is, problems which were those of the nation as a public totality. The individual belonged to the people of Israel, the people being the overall object of salvation. Through membership in this people, the individual could hope for his or her own salvation in the here and now situation. To be sure, there were religious projections associated with this notion of salvation; and on the whole they were imperfect and ambiguous. Indeed, as we shall see, mere aping of these same projections would be tantamount to denying salvation history itself.

Personal problems did not lie outside this process of salvation. Salvation was liberation from one's personal sorrows, one's personal sins, and—to some extent—from death itself. All this was seen in the light of the relationship between man and God, but it had immediate repercussions of a profane and public nature. Israel needed the categories of guilt and sin in order to interpret the reality surrounding it. But even though sin suggested an immediate reference to God, it was also a category that evaluated the human world on every level—private and public, personal and structural. As we shall see later, it was a category that transformed the interpretation of history and of political activity.

So political was salvation in the eyes of the Israelite nation that in the early stages it was not able to differentiate the religious realm and the political realm satisfactorily. Israel thought that its salvation would be attained historically by virtue of its historical relationship to Yahweh as his special people. If it remained faithful to the covenant in the course of history, its reward would be complete political triumph over other nations; and this would pave the way for a definitive material well-being for all.

The level of interpretation rises with the advent of the prophets. The nation's religious thinking is purified and deepened by a more religious idea of God and a more personal conception of the God-man relationship. But this continues to have real repercussions on the politico-religious interpretation of Israel's history and salvation. There certainly is a surpassing of earlier religious experience, but this surpassing does not entail erasing the note of politicization or forgetting the relationship between the religious and moral deportment of the nation on the one hand and its destiny in history on the other. Even Jeremiah, whose early chapters seem to focus mainly on the more religious sin of idolatry, never ceases to be a political prophet. He threatens the nation with political punishments for their sins, and he also puts much stress on those sins which we today would call social sins. These sins, and Jeremiah's denunciation of them, clearly have political import.

To indicate the shift of the prophets towards the more spiritualistic interpretation of the New Testament, one can look to a singular text in Jeremiah for support:

> *The days are now coming, says the Lord,*
> *when I will make a righteous Branch*
> *spring from David's line,*
> *a king who shall rule wisely,*
> *maintaining law and justice in the land.*
> *In his days Judah shall be kept safe,*
> *and Israel shall live undisturbed.*
> *This is the name to be given to him:*
> *The Lord is our Righteousness.*
>
> (Jer 23:5-6)

It is an important passage because it reiterates the classic scheme: the need for salvation, since uprightness and justice are not practiced and hence there is no security or peace; the hope of a historical salvation for a historical people; the promise of a savior whose name is "The Lord is our Righteousness." This saving Lord will bring justice to the earth, and his presence among men must be viewed as the presence of God and of righteousness. Only then will there be peace and security among human individuals and nations.

The term "righteousness" (or "justice") is extraordinarily complex in the prophetic tradition. In essence, however, it is the opposite of the injustice that is committed against human beings—particularly against the weak and powerless. This notion gradually paves the way for the New Testament conception of justification. We cannot show here how there is clearly no justification without justice or righteousness, so I shall simply mention the fact that in its use it can be illegitimately restricted in two ways. It can be interpreted in such a way that the religious dimension is reduced to a purely interior and spiritualistic one of direct relationship to God, and to a purely individual dimension in which salvation and condemnation apply solely to the individual as an isolated entity.

Granting that the word "spiritualization" itself is ambiguous and does not adequately describe the underlying reality, we still cannot deny that the religiosity of the Old Testament is somehow "spiritualized" in the faith of the New Testament. Nor can we deny that this was due in part to the fact that Israel suffered political downfall, so that the religious realm was "depoliticized" to some extent. In some sense one can talk about a negation of the Jewish religious experience. But in fact this negation is not an abolition of that experience; it is rather a surpassing of it. The Jewish religious experience was not reduced to nothingness by the Christian faith; instead it was preserved and surpassed. The Jewish religious experience did not avoid the danger of using God for the sake of temporal welfare and political domination. It hardly managed to get beyond a purely social and political realization. While it related the temporal realm to Yahweh, it did so in an inadequate and purely extrinsic way. Hence it could be denied and annulled "atheistically," and it deserved to be. And that applies as well to God's causal intervention as it was interpreted by popular Judaism.

Does this mean that the New Testament proposes that individuals are to be religious while the political realm is to be atheistic? Is there no relationship between the political realm and the Christian realm? Or is the only proper relationship between them to be found in a theocratic State?

An affirmative answer to these questions would seem to be implied in Marx's theses on Feuerbach. While we may disagree with him, his remarks can help us to figure out the proper relationship between the political realm and the Christian realm; and this is a basic problem in trying to determine the mission and charism of the Latin American Church.

In his first thesis Marx accuses Feuerbach of regarding the theoretical approach, the purely contemplative and interior approach, as the authentically human approach. According to Marx, Feuerbach retreats back towards purely contemplative interiorization because he views praxis solely in terms of its "sordid manifestation in Judaism." Marx recognizes that Jewish religiosity is a political praxis, but he sees it as a shabby form of political praxis. To that extent Feuerbach is right in rejecting it. But Feuerbach is wrong in thinking that anthropological purification is to be attained by abandoning praxis in every form. Jewish praxis is to be rejected because it was not transforming in itself, because it left transformation directly to God in terms of reward or punishment for man's religious or moral acts which did not effect the transformation of social reality. Jewish praxis led to an alienated praxis. Man should not flee from praxis, however. Instead human beings must rehabilitate praxis in terms of its own immanent essence. They should abandon all transcendent reference to God and live out the immanent praxis that will transform nature and history. True human fulfillment is to be found in fashioning a truly human society, a societal humanity.

Here some questions are very much in order. Is Feuerbach's interpretation of Jewish praxis correct? Is it correct to interpret Christianity as a process of interiorization? Is no other praxis possible except the completely immanent praxis proposed by Marx? It is certainly true that Marx made certain truths clear. Man must not confine himself to interpreting and contemplating the world; he must go on to the important task of transforming it. The principal ethical mission of man does lie in this effort of transformation. The inescapable goal of human action is indeed to fashion a truly human society, a humanity that will live as a social community. If man does not flesh out this new humanity, no one else is going to do it for him. And man's salvation or condemnation does lie in the success or failure of his effort to fashion this new humanity. But just as Marx sees an alternative to Jewish praxis on the one hand and Feuerbach's Christian interiorization on the other, so today's Christian is entitled and even obliged to look for a fourth alternative—one that gets beyond Jewish politicization, purely contemplative interiorization, *and* the purely immanent praxis envisioned by Marx.

The Christian must admit that the social version of Jewish religiosity and the religious version of its political activity are primitive. The Christian must assert that the presence of the divine in the reality of nature and society is not that of a demiurge who miraculously rewards or punishes the religious behavior of human beings and nations. The Christian must realize that activity which transforms the world and society and which is rooted in Christian inspiration is the essential and constitutive sign which alone makes man's salvation and divinization real and present. Christians have tended to view the spiritualizing of the Old Testament as a process of Platonizing, and the process of supernaturalizing as a process of extra-naturalizing. Thus they have tended to disregard two basic and central tenets of Christianity: 1) Only in the humanity of Christ are we to find access to the Father; only thus does the Father reveal himself to human beings and only thus can people be brothers and sisters, children of God. 2) The risen Christ is to be fashioned by the continuing historical incarnation of his redemptive action as Lord of history.

To get beyond the other alternatives cited above, we must look to the deeply Christian category of "sign." The humanity of

Christ is the sign of his superhumanness, the worldly aspect of the Church is the sign of its otherworldliness. As the bearer of salvation, the Church must be the sign that makes salvation present and effective in a historical way. The sign leads us beyond itself, but without the sign there is no beyond for us. The sign both is and is not what it signifies. And in our present context the sign cannot be something arbitrary or whimsical. By its very nature it should lead us towards that which it claims to signify, as is evident from the historical example of Christ himself. The sign enables and obliges us to transform the worldly realm because it is only in this realm that we can find the sign at all. It obliges us to look for that sign which will truly call our attention to that which God has revealed in Jesus Christ. It obliges us not to rest content within the sign itself; for if it truly is the sign established by Christ in his historical revelation, it will drive us beyond itself. If Christian acitivity is framed in terms of a sign, then we will be able to get beyond naturalism and extra-naturalism, secularism and mere pietism. Indeed we will be able to get beyond all sorts of schizophrenia and contradictory significations that now mar the witness of Christians in the world.

A LATIN AMERICAN CHURCH IN LATIN AMERICA

We have noted that Christianity is a salvation history, that salvation is meant to be historical, that the Church is the bearer of this historical salvation, and that the Church must flesh out its sign function in history even as its founder became incarnate in history. Now if all that is true, then the Church in Latin America must necessarily be Latin American.[3] The Church must operate in history and in a historical way. It must, in other words, communicate the presence and summons of God's historical word to each and every human being in a real-life way. This process of historicization means that the Church must be incarnated in time and place, and in the set of conditions which each place exerts on a given time. By that I mean that not all of us who live in the same age necessarily live in the same time frame.

It might seem that there is no need to stress the importance of

3. Here we take for granted as a basic socio-historical presupposition the fact that Latin America is a differentiated and yet unified reality. Obviously many different cultures coexist in Latin America. The context should make clear which Latin America I am talking about here.

localization and temporalization since Vatican II and Pope Paul VI have urgently recommended these two approaches. But the actual reality of this incarnation in the liturgical, theological, and administrative realms of the Church prevents us from entertaining any illusions about the matter. There is no profound acceptance of the historicity of salvation. Nor is there any real acceptance of its most direct and immediate corollary, namely, the differences in mission and charism to be attributed to different local and regional churches. Hence we are compelled to emphasize certain ideas which justify the distinctive incarnation of the Church in Latin America and which provide a basis for determining what the exact nature of that distinctive incarnation might be.

If faith were merely the acceptance of a fixed deposit of dogma by some universal human being, then the only accommodation or adaptation required would consist in the correct translation of certain texts whose distinctive history and language had somehow been forgotten in the past. But that is not what faith is. There is no universal human being; nor is the deposit of dogma formed by items of intellectual content which are learned, accepted, and then simply transmitted. Faith is a personal relationship, which takes its start from a personal God and is personally addressed to a person who is conditioned by his time and place, his people, and his history. The original communication took place at a specific point in history, but this communication continues on as a living, personal reality through the mediation of the Church.

In and through this faith, salvation is communicated. The divine word accepted by faith is what saves; but it saves insofar as it is received and accepted, not by mankind in general, but by this specific human being. God's word saves only insofar as it has been historicized; and it can be historicized and brought to its fulfillment only in the concrete reality of the living human individual. The universality of salvation and God's word should not be taken to mean that it touches only that which is common to all human beings. It is not universal by a process of abstraction; it is universal by a process of concretization. Its full totality becomes real only in the salvation of the whole human being and of all human beings. The authentic universality of salvation will be achieved only when it fully takes in all the historical variation and variety of concrete human lives.

It is up to the Church to perpetuate this universal salvation in a way that fits in with this authentic universality. The Church may not entertain the notion that the catholic universality of its mission consists in the ahistorical repetition of the same salvific scheme over and over again to all the human beings who exist and live in history. To do so would be to disown the historical character of salvation and the salvific character of the Church. To paraphrase a classic dictum of theology, one can say that outside the Church there is no salvation, but only what has been taken up by the Church can be saved within it.

The fulness of salvation that is proper to the Church requires a full-fledged incarnation in the radical historical variety that is lived by human populations. By the same token, the Church will attain its salvific plenitude only when every human being is saved in his or her totality. It is this totality, in the twofold sense of universality and plenitude, that will offer the Church the means for its full-fledged growth. It is not a matter of quantity or numbers, of the saved being few or many. It is a matter of plenitude, of a plenitude that is qualitatively historical and qualitative in an historical way. The distinct and different modes of human existence must be assumed and saved by that which carries on the salvation of Jesus Christ, i.e., by the Church. Christ himself will not attain his full measure as Savior until all the different kinds of salvation needed by human beings and their historically different situations are integrated into him. Until this happens, Christ's incarnation, redemption, and resurrection will not attain their full measure.

On this journey towards the qualitative plenitude of salvation in the Church, full-fledged Christian incarnation in specific privileged locales will challenge and contradict spurious forms of incarnation that are not in line with the gospel message. The Church is ever in danger of being turned into a worldling, of distorting the obligation of incarnation in such a way that it ends up aping the sinfulness and alienation evident in the world's mode of existence. Within the Church we must recognize and accept the diversity of its members, the charisms of different individuals, and the diversity of the local churches. By virtue of their distinctive forms of incarnation in specific situations, these local churches are called upon to live the plenitude of the gospel message in distinct ways. We see some acknowledgement of this fact insofar as the distinct vocations of various religious orders are recognized; but this recognition must be broadened to cover all the sectors of the Church that live Christianity in their own distinctive ways.

Such would be the case with the ecclesial sector which we call Latin American. It is Latin American, not only because it lives in Latin America, but also because it seeks to respond wholeheartedly to the distinctive sociological reality of Latin America. It makes perfect sense to ask what is the peculiar mission and charism of the Latin American Church as opposed to that of the Church in other areas of the world.

CHARISM OF THE LATIN AMERICAN CHURCH

In this section I shall try to describe Latin America as a salvific category, that is to say, as a distinctive reality which must be saved in a distinctive and specific way by the gospel message and which can contribute to the plenitude of Christian salvation in its own qualitative way. It is not just a geographic reality. Proper use of the term cannot be based solely on the fact that one belongs to a designated geographical region. Geographic location is one condition, but it is not the thing that gives formal identity to the reality called Latin America. It is no easy matter to provide a sound sociological description of the Latin American reality, but a solid theological interpretation of Latin America depends on such a description. So I shall attempt it, knowing full well that I am not telling the whole story but rather speaking from a specific point of view.

From that viewpoint it must be said that Latin America should not be viewed as a shadowy imitation of the Western world, but rather as an integral part of the Third World. Quite obviously Latin America's mode of existence in the Third World is not the same as that of other areas such as India or Vietnam; and life in South America is not exactly the same as life in Central America. What is more, basic elements of occidental culture do seem to form part of the culture of Latin America itself. That does not invalidate our basic assumption here, however, because the historical individuality of Latin America is clear enough and is still in the process of formation.

This fact permits us to posit a definite future as an element that gives configuration to the Latin American present. That future cannot be mere imitation of the developed countries, of the United States in particular. It must be Latin America's own future, shaped by Latin Americans and by the proper available means. If our tools are mere imitations, then our future will be a mere imitation also; this holds true particularly in the field of education. And if we do not have a clear idea of our own distinctive future, we will not be capable of fashioning suitable tools of our own.

Operating from an ecclesial viewpoint we can indicate some characteristics of this future, mainly because the impact of Christianity continues to be significant with respect to the sociological reality of Latin America. At the very least we can talk about a Christian predisposition in Latin America, although we must also admit that Latin American Christianity must be purified in many ways if it is to play a profound role in shaping the future of Latin America.

A reconversion of the Church to the Third World, to those features of the Third World that are clearly evident in Latin America, would simultaneously help to purify the Church and make a significant contribution to the future of Latin America. Much of the intraecclesial tension evident in Latin America today is due to the resistance of ecclesial structures to the notion that we must fashion a Church here which will correspond and respond to the social reality in which the Church lives its life. This resistance prompts even greater insistence from others that the Church become a Church of the poor, a Church of the Third World, with all the consequences that option would entail.

The fact is that the reality of Latin America demands some such effort at conversion if the Church is to be an effective aid in the creation and realization of the future of Latin America. From the standpoint of the gospel message it is indisputable that a turning towards the poor would purify the Church. And it would be easy to show that a purified Church is absolutely necessary if it is to provide the full measure of salvation that is properly its own, and if it is to fully carry out its mission in giving shape to the future of Latin America.

The Church has a universal vocation of salvation, but its most proper locale is the world of the poor. This does not mean that there must be poor people for the Church to exist or to be holy—a thesis which is shared by certain Marxists and certain lackeys of capital (more than capitalism) including some Christians. But if there are poor people around, then the Church cannot be holy or salvific unless it lives in, with, and for the poor. But the poor are not just the mission of the Church. They are also its salvation and the locus of Christ the Savior's presence. By the same token, it is true both in terms of past history and the present day that those who stand at the other end of the spectrum represent the locus of the Church's perdition. Only by incarnating itself in the reality of the Third World and serving the most needy can the Church hope to purify itself, renew its life, and recover the true impulse of the gospel message. If it does this, it will immediately turn into a sign of contradiction and suffer persecution; and this will prove that the

Church is the authentic bearer of the word and promise of its founder.

Is it not true that this decisive turning towards the poor is the mission of the Church in Latin America, and of the Latin American Church within the universal Church? In Latin America "the poor" are not a fringe group, they are the majority. In a real sense they define what Latin America is: poor in health, poor in education, poor in living standard, poor in having a say in their own destiny. By virtue of the universal vocation of the Gospel and by virtue of the historical summons specific to the region in which the Latin American Church lives, it must be the Church of the poor. If it were to be that in truth, then it would give impetus to a new historical form of Christianity that should be transmitted to the universal Church. And this new form will be transmitted, if it acquires the necessary drive and tension.

The fundamental, specific charism of a given Church cannot be determined in the abstract. We should not be surprised that local churches have their own specific charisms when we realize that localization is essential to the Church. The determination of a community's specific charism cannot be made in the abstract; it must be figured out on the basis of real-life experience and history. This follows from the fact that the Church itself is historical, as is the salvation proclaimed by it and realized in it. But if localization is not to turn the Church into a worldling, if its real-life awareness is to remain authentically Christian, then it must meet a prior condition; it must first turn towards the poor. The perennial message of the Gospel must be heard and heeded in its natural locale, that is, in a Church incarnated in the world of the poor. That world is lit up by the gospel message, and the good news becomes light and life from within the context of that world. If this is realized adequately, then there will inevitably appear charisms of a more individual character, charisms that are prophetic, or hierarchical, or theological, or whatever.

Such charisms are already finding their voice in Latin America on all these levels. The reason is to be found in the fact that Latin America, as a member of the Third World, is speaking out on problems that are very much related to the specific nature and thrust of the Christian message. These problems have to do with such issues as the oppressive power of money, the greedy quest for profit, the desire to possess money and enjoy its benefits, the disparagement of the human person, and the existence of inhumane living conditions. What Latin America seems to need most is the very thing that is the most authentic strain in the gospel message: the denunciation of wealth and greed, the liberation of the oppressed from injustice in all its forms, respect for the human person as a child of God, the formation of a worldwide community of human beings, and the transcending of human history.

Thus Latin America represents a historic challenge to the possibilities of Christianity. Why? Because the seed of the Christian faith has been sown there, because it offers the best opportunity for calling attention to Christian values, and because it obliges the Church to be what it truly is or else to stop posing as the word of salvation. The full and integral salvation of the Third World, of the world of the poor, is a great historical challenge. Responding to this challenge should be regarded as the fundamental charism of the Latin American Church. The Johannine writer centered God's commandment around this point: "To give our allegiance to his Son Jesus Christ and love one another as he commanded" (1 Jn 3:23). This commandment must be carried out in history, and it is peculiarly incumbent on the Latin American Church. There are two inseparable aspects to this commandment. Faith alone is not enough; love and the works of love alone are not enough. Urged on by the social reality in which it lives and in which it should incarnate herself, the Latin American Church is at a point in history where it can and must respond to the charism that is truly its own and that exists here and now.

CHURCH MISSION AND LATIN AMERICAN TASKS

For obvious historical reasons the Latin American Church is faced with the obligation and possibility of giving a total incarnation to the Christian message of salvation. As we noted earlier, this total incarnation cannot help but present itself in secular and political terms. The question is not whether the Church should be a political force or not, whether it should clash with other political forces; for the Church should never go out in search of political power. What is involved here is the Church's fidelity to its own mission. It must foster the full, integral salvation of man—and that entails a political dimension. Precisely because the Church is the bearer of Christian salvation, it cannot fail to offer its service to the task that confronts Latin America.

But that raises certain questions. The Church in Latin America has a specific mission, and Latin America itself faces an urgent task. Are the two things distinct and different from one another? Will the people of the Church find themselves left on the sidelines as Latin America undertakes its task of radical transformation?

The answer to these questions is to be found, I think, in the concept of liberation, which is both political and Christian at the same time. All complete liberation is political, and all authentic liberation is Christian. In the following reflection I shall try to show the dual political and Christian character of liberation, and to indicate how they can be brought together.[4] It is not a matter of discussing the question in abstract terms, because the problem itself is certainly not abstract and because these reflections were not intended to represent a theoretical discussion but rather to provide a program of action.[5]

Liberation differs from other possible alternatives in its radical nature. Radicalized Christians latch on to the concept of liberation while other Christians shun it or try to soften its impact. Politicians in power tend to prefer other terms—"development," for example—while opposition politicians lean towards "liberation" or equivalent terms. (It all depends, of course, on the relationship that exists between the party in power and the party out of power. Sometimes the opposition is the "loyal" opposition.)

Is there a sound theoretical and theological basis for the radicality of the concept of liberation? Leaving aside the whole area of social theory, we can certainly say that there is a solid basis for its radicality from the standpoint of Christian theology. Why? Because any Christian judgment about the prevailing situation in Latin America must be guided and dominated by the category of sin, and because the redemption of sin in Christianity is governed by a distinctive schema involving death and redemptive bloodshed. But before I examine the negative, critical aspect of liberation and its positive, constructive aspect, I think we must consider the specific and peculiar sinful character of the structure that now prevails in Latin America.

The judgments made by the Medellín Conference and other

4. The theology of liberation is now in the process of formation. It is focusing attention on, and raising questions about, many major theological concepts: collective sin, redemption, resurrection, salvation, the Third World as the Servant of Yahweh, secularization, nature and person, eschatological hope, sign and transcendence, politics and Christianity, prophetic denunciation, revolution and violence, the new man and the new earth and so forth.

5. The reflections in this book were prepared for a conference on joint pastoral action.

authoritative sources are quite clearcut. While the precise sinful character of the Latin American situation may have to be worked out more fully, the basic Christian evaluation cannot be other than it is. The existing situation does not allow the base majority to exist as full-fledged persons or to live as human beings. They are crushed by the weight of basic needs that cry out for alleviation. An institutionalized system of injustice actively impedes the establishment of fellowship among human beings. Modelled on the consumer society of the capitalist world, it poses obstacles to solidarity and Christian transcendence. The world and society, which are supposed to serve as the medium of God's presence among human beings, deny the very essence of God as love and as the touchstone for every other reality. Instead of making visible the incarnated image of Christ, the existing situation is a permanent denial of that image. From a Christian standpoint there is only one word for such a situation: It is sin.

Some people will claim that some of these negative features are not due to the specific will of persons as such; that they should be regarded as natural deficiencies which can be cured by integral development rather than as sin which must be redeemed by liberation. This viewpoint is not valid, however. It is valid insofar as it exculpates individuals as such from guilt. It is not valid insofar as it denies the character of sin that applies to the structure as such. The existing structure negates and denies the Christian way of life. It is not just that it does not signify in a visible way what Christianity is as God's presence among men; it positively and actively makes it impossible for people to lead a Christian life. Historically speaking, we cannot simply talk about defects or deficiencies; we must regard the situation as one of sin. To do otherwise would be to wallow in abstractions that would lead us into serious mistakes in trying to formulate solutions. Moreover, if we forget the important place of the category of sin in any Christian interpretation of personal and societal reality, we will greatly impoverish the Christian message and relativize man and society. It is said that we have lost our consciousness of sin, but the problem goes deeper than that. We have also lost our knowledge of what sin is to begin with. We must get beyond the partial notion of sin as a merely individual violation of some law. We must recover the social dimension of sin as the annulment of God's presence among human beings and the domination of evil which prohibits the freedom of God's children.

Once we have recovered our knowledge of what sin really is, we must heighten people's awareness of it and promote Christian confrontation with everything that is sin. This confrontation operates in the dialectic of death and resurrection. Only those who die will live; only those who deny themselves can follow Christ. There is no way to Christian resurrection except through the redemption that finds expression in death on the cross. If people reject the label of sin, the reason is that they are trying to evade the necessary consequences of a recognition of the reality of sin. They are trying to evade the necessity of dying to the present situation in order to fashion a new, more authentically Christian situation. They are looking for placebos so that they will not have to face the harsh reality of Christian solutions. We should not forget that the negative, dialectical philosophy transmitted to Marx by Hegel is comprehended by the German theologian in terms of the New Testament dialectic which maintains that only negation leads one to a higher, surpassing affirmation. Insofar as this negation has been interpreted in purely individual and ascetic terms, in terms of intention rather than incarnate implementation, it is clearly an impoverishment of the Christian message. And this impoverishment has forced people to work out a political secularism outside the boundaries of Christian life.

Liberation takes the historical signification of Jesus of Nazareth with full and radical seriousness. It accepts the archetypal idea of death and resurrection with all its implications. It accepts the presupposition that salvation must necessarily take the form of incarnation, granting the presence of sin in history. But it does not rest content with this archetypal idea, which might just as well be inferred from a philosophical analysis of historical reality. It also turns its attention to the concrete image of Christ in the concrete circumstances of his earthly life in history. Its aim, of course, is not mere imitation but rather an authentic following of Christ; but this does not prevent it from giving transcendent value to his individual figure in history in the whole matter of determining what integral salvation is meant to be. It does not presume that one can know God and his plans for history apart from the one who is the Word of God. Instead it believes that this Word, for whom all things were created, had to be an incarnate Word so that what was originally nature could move through death and resurrection towards personal plenitude.

In this Christian vision of liberation we must have both features: death and resurrection. The latter presupposes the former. But if the former is truly Christian, it is sustained and guided by the hope of a resurrection that has already begun here and now. There is no resurrection without death. Without the sorrow-laden disappearance of the existing structure of sin, we cannot enter a new earth as new human beings. And since this whole treatment here is aimed at praxis, I should like to highlight some possible ways of dying to sin and of rising to new life. For both the negative and the positive aspect must be operative in a spiraling process that leads us further and further on.

The first question that the Latin American Church must ask itself is this: What are the sins that must be eradicated from Latin America? There can be no salvation without the eradication of sin; and if it is to be pardoned, sin must be wiped out. Like Christ, the Church is here to take away the sin of the world, not just certain individual sins. The Latin American Church, in its unity and its diversity, must engage in a profound and ongoing examination of conscience on the local, regional, and continental level. It will not be able to do this unless it first makes an earnest effort to bring back before its eyes the full image and message of its founder; unless it first commits itself wholeheartedly and primarily to the service of the world of the poor. To abet this examination of conscience in Central America, one can propose certain basic and critical topics that surface when one observes our concrete situation from the standpoint of basic Christian categories.

It is not easy to provide a systematic presentation of the sins evident in Latin America, to focus on one radical sin from which all the others flow. Any such attempt would require a wealth of studies—sociological, psychological, historical, philosophical, and theological—which lie far beyond the scope of my treatment here. So I shall content myself with an ordered enumeration of the more blatant problems.

From a biblical perspective it may well be that the root sin is to be found in an overall way of life, a civilization, that is grounded on the twin notions of profit and private property. It is not that wealth and private property are evil in themselves. They are necessary to some extent, given the imperfect state of the world and human beings right now. But the very fact that our way of life is grounded on, and conditioned by, the quest for profit and for more and more private property represents a serious form of idolatry. It produces a whole series of pernicious consequences that give shape to consumer society. Perhaps never before in history has it been so easy to appreciate the full import and perduring value of the Bible's persistent denunciation of riches and greed for riches. The very existence of the Third World, which is an obvious corollary of the existence of the other two worlds, and the different standards of living to be found in any particular nation are decisive proof that a national or international society based on the notion of profit represents a negation of both God and man. It might seem that I am making too much of a concession to Marxism in stressing the role of private property in the unjust configuration of society. But I would reject that accusation for several reasons. First, I am not talking solely about private property; I am also talking about the greedy quest for profit. Second, my judgment against them is based on the fact that they are fundamental items in the present structuring of society. Third, wealth is one of the central concerns of the Bible itself when it tries to pass judgment on human beings and society itself. Fourth, the reality of Latin America itself offers sufficient proof of the radical nature of this sin insofar as it is subject to internal pressure from the powerful and external pressure from foreign economic interests. Fifth, Marxism itself has come to rest in a form of private property; though it might claim to be a national form of ownership, it is no less private and restricted vis-à-vis other nations.

One consequence of this basic sin, at least to some extent, is the situation of objective injustice and institutionalized violence. This situation has been highlighted and stressed often enough. Its existence is scarcely denied by anyone, except perhaps by selfish interests. It need hardly be pointed out that the Bible sees it as one of the most serious sins of all, one which greatly inflames the wrath of God. Under this heading we would have to list the innumerable forms of oppression suffered by the vast majority of the Latin American people. A small minority holds the reins of economic power, and uses this to expropriate for itself all the other forms of power. The conditions of life are inhumane; most people suffer from hunger, insecurity, poverty, and lack of education. It is not simply that we have an unjust situation marked by inequities in the distribution and sharing of goods that should belong to all; it is that this situation is actively fostered or, at the very least, allowed to continue without any effort being made to change it.

To make sure that this basic situation does not change in character, the communications media are manipulated. They are used primarily to give the people a false image of reality, to inculcate a set of values that will prop up the consumer society that has generated the existing state of dehumanization. The communications media represent the hypocritical conscience of the ruling class in society, obscuring or deforming the real state of affairs. How much oppression is embodied in what the communications media say or keep silent about! How oppressive they are when they are kept in the hands of those who hold power in a consumer society!

And then there are the excesses evident in the holding and use of political power. Power is kept out of the hands of the people. The main goal is to defend the established order, and even torture is permissible to achieve that goal. Pressure from other nations and from external interest groups also helps to keep most people from developing maturity, personal awareness, and the autonomy implied in true personal liberty.

The list could go on and on. There is no room for hope or for a transcendent vision. The materialism of consumerism and the oppressive weight of life's basic necessities make it impossible for people to get beyond mere immanence. Human beings are forced to live on something less than a truly human level by the weight of artificially created needs (consumerism) or by the weight of real societal needs that go unfulfilled. The same basic framework continues to operate, proving that the oppression resulting from unfulfilled basic needs is due in large measure to the multiplication of artificial consumerist needs.

These are some of the sins of the world in which the Church lives. But we cannot overlook the sins of the Church itself, which is supposed to save the world from its sin. Just as the world and society are supposed to serve as the mediating channel of God, so the Church is supposed to be the supreme sign of Christ's redemptive presence among human beings. The sin of the world resides in the fact that it, the supposed medium of God, distorts his presence. The sin of the Church resides in the fact that it does not adequately carry out its irreplaceable mission as the sign of Christ, the sign that is supposed to make his presence real and effective. At the insistence of Deschamps, Vatican I affirmed that the Church is a sign by its very nature; that it bears indisputable witness to the divine mission of Jesus Christ and is supposed to prove its credibility. It is time for us to spell out the import of that teaching, to stress the fact that the presence of the Church should offer a natural and ready motive for drawing closer to the divinity of Christ. Our stress today should be on testimony rather than on apologetics. We should spell out why the Church must make itself truly present in the world of the poor in order to carry out its sign function and to follow Jesus of Nazareth. In a visible and real-life way, he served as the sign of his own divine sonship.

The Church can never cease to be an efficacious sign of Jesus' divinity. For that very reason, however, everything within it that obscures its fundamental mission and denigrates its basic vocation takes on the formal character of sin. Does the Latin American Church fully measure up to that mission, particularly with regard to the poor and the oppressed? Not always, and in some places it does the job less satisfactorily than in other places. It is here that our collective examination of conscience takes on greatest urgency. It is in this connection that we must give careful consideration to two basic aspects that are directly related to the liberative mission of the Church: 1) its real and authentic self-awareness and self-understanding; 2) its understanding of its mission.

The Church in Latin America sees itself as a locus of salvation, as it must. But the notion of salvation that underlies the thinking of most people in the Church is that of the eternal salvation of the individual, which is guaranteed and to a certain extent effected by the ecclesiastical organization. To be sure, the polar opposite of this view is also to be found in the same Church. Some people see salvation in purely temporal terms and deny any role to the organizational Church as such. But the very existence of this view proves the prevalence and weight of the prevailing individualistic view.

Without going into a detailed study of the consequences of the prevailing view, we can readily see some of the more important consequences of such a view of salvation. There is an almost exclusive emphasis on internal, individual sins, and an almost total neglect of the social dimension of historical sins which politically condition the behavior of individuals and the transcendent import of their actions. The authentic following of Christ is devalued and stress is laid on sacramental grace. As a result, people completely lose sight of the historical visibility of grace and the visible configuration of one's life in accordance with the historical life of Jesus of Nazareth. The Christian dimension of temporal activity is not explored. There is greater concern for the organizational setup of the Church, for its institutional and sociological form, than for persons and interpersonal community.

Insofar as the Church's understanding of its mission is concerned, dedication to the poor does not stand out as the principal task; nor can it be said that the Church articulates its mission as that of liberating human beings from every form of oppression. The Church in Latin America has been, and continues to be, excessively concerned with wealth and power and overly caught up in service to the privileged sectors of society. This cannot help but have grave consequences for its function as a sign of Christ, and for its evangelical liberty and effectiveness. It is not just that the Latin American Church runs the risk of turning into a worldling, of becoming salt without savor and leaven that does not uplift the mass. The bad thing is that this approach may be viewed as an inescapable means for carrying out the task of evangelization; that the Church may feel it has to use power, wealth, and pressure tactics in order to come out triumphant in the task of evangelization. That the Church finds it necessary to get involved in secular tasks, particularly in education, is scarcely a new phenomenon. But secular tasks have their own inner dynamic, and this dynamic is conditioned by the dynamism of the world that was so strongly condemned in the New Testament. Hence it has often happened that the secular dynamism has won out over the dynamism of the gospel message. Today another secular and political task is proposed in connection with the mission of the Church. This time, however, it must be guided and motivated by a non-worldly dynamism, by the Christian dynamism of poverty, service, and liberation rather than by the worldly dynamism of wealth, power, and oppression. As I have already suggested, the whole dynamic of the Third World must be interwoven with the dynamic of Christianity. This does not mean that they are to be equated outright, but it does mean that they are parallel. They can give impetus to each other, and they can even be brought together in the dialectical synthesis of sign and signified.

It is the category of sin that provides us with the key for justifying the activity of the Church in the secular realm. In its overall orientation today, the secular realm as a political totality can be clearly diagnosed in evangelical terms as sin. The mission of the Church is to take away the sin of the world. The Church must call things what they are and propose pathways to redemption. And the Church must do the same with respect to itself.

But it is not enough for the Church to dedicate itself to taking away the sin of the world. Christian salvation does not consist in the absence of sin but rather in the fulness of life. The Latin American Church must work to promote the creation of a new man on a new earth as the eschatological sign of something that is yet to come but is already present and operative. The Church must not rest content with prophetic and apocalyptic denunciation. Admittedly it can never give up this work of denunciation. It must always adopt a critical attitude towards any human achievement, precisely because it sees the character of any achievement as a sign and medium of something that is not merely and purely human. The Church can never forget that it must contribute to the destruction of the objective structures of sin, to the destruction of objectified sin. But the Church is also obliged to help fashion the new man and the new structures which will make his existence possible. It is not the Church's specific job to create the actual technical models. Its task is rather to work out the true meaning and import of their creation and utilization. The Church is not the mass, but the leaven in the mass.

What might this meaning be in terms of the reality of Latin America? It can be expressed in terms of liberation and liberty.

Liberation must be preached and turned into a reality because it is, in the last analysis, a liberation from sin. It must be proclaimed insofar as the sinful character of certain structures and behavior patterns becomes evident. But liberation must also be turned into a reality. The Church, itself a sign, must work for the full liberty of human beings as the sign that foreshadows and makes possible the liberty of the children of God. First of all, this liberation must be from every form of injustice and from everything that can be regarded as unjust oppression that demeans man's dignity and fulfillment. It must also be liberation from the pangs of basic human needs. It must be liberation from the objective shackles of hunger, sickness, ignorance, and helplessness, and from the artificially created subjective shackles of a consumer society. In short, it must be liberation from nature that is designed to further the creation of the human person.

Given the existing situation, there can be no liberty without liberation. But the Church must work for liberation with its gaze focused on liberty. In other words, its work on behalf of the elimination of dire needs and oppression will serve as a backdrop for its struggle to affirm the values of human fulfillment and personal community as signs of man's full control over himself. It is to this end that the Church's efforts on behalf of the humanization and personalization of man are directed. In the last analysis it is liberty that defines the being of the human person, even though it may not serve as a complete or formal definition. On a different plane, it also defines the essence of the Christian. The Christian is one who is free from the law, which oppresses man from without; the Christian is one who is free from the concupiscence that oppresses man from within. And the Christian is one who is free from the total and permanent oppression of death. Only in this way does the Christian achieve full liberation from sin in a new divinization which makes total liberty possible.

In this work of liberation there is no doubt that the Latin American Church can to some extent be in accord with various movements that have similar aims. This fact may create confusion for some people, even for people of good will. But if people consider the most positive aspect of the problem—that is, the liberty that one is trying to make possible—no confusion is really possible, at least for people of good will. Two features of the

Church's commitment can be highlighted as differentiating ones: its attention to the strictly personal dimension of liberty, and its attention to the transcendent dimension of the Christian's activity in the world.

In its work of salvation the Church has frequently exaggerated the individual dimension, the element of personal responsibility regardless of what structures or circumstances prevailed. That was one of the reasons why the Church did not see why it ought to interfere with structures themselves. It did not see them as a direct object of its salvific activity. All it asked of them was that they allow it to act freely upon individuals or that they facilitate its efforts with human souls. Only slowly and belatedly did the Church come to pay close theological and sociological attention to the importance of structures. It began to pay sociological attention to them when it noted the importance of structures in giving shape and configuration to the personal life of the individual. It began to pay theological attention to them when it realized that structures serve as a sign medium which either abet or hinder what we might call the "presentability" of God.

This new awareness of the role of structures helped the Church to realize that it must work for the transformation of structures. But this awareness has not caused the Church to forget the indispensable role of persons and interpersonal community in this same process of social change. It has learned the importance of structures. But it continues to teach the point that structural changes, without a corresponding conversion in individuals, cannot really facilitate the rise of the new man whom we are seeking. There is no sense debating here which should come first, for the two types of transformation are obviously tied together. The point is that individual persons, too, must undergo conversion. Through the process of death and resurrection they are supposed to attain the liberty proclaimed in the Sermon on the Mount, so that the new world can come into existence. Human persons are the ones who are meant to find their fulfillment in God so that they do not fall back into the molds of the old man as they attempt to fashion new structures. It is the human person who is supposed to attain conversion, salvation, and fulfillment in and with structures. One of the great dangers facing the renewed Church is that it forget this.

The second differentiating feature mentioned above is the transcendent dimension of secular activity. Once again we find that the Church has only gradually come to its present view of the matter, and that is no accident. For a long time it has worked exclusively on behalf of the transcendent dimension. It has paid attention to the temporal thrust of the spiritual realm and to the importance of the whole man, but only in terms of the hereafter. The Church has not devoted sufficient attention to the necessity of fleshing out salvation here and now and embodying the hereafter in the here-and-now sign. The Church is now growing more and more acutely aware of the necessity of mediating and signifying the totality of salvation in the sign-bearing visibility of activity in this world. The Church is the one who most truly possesses and implements a particular kind of knowledge. It knows that reality is not exhausted by its temporal, worldly dimension; that human activity does not terminate in the immanence of this world and history. The liberty which the Church tries to procure by its efforts does not terminate in the here and now; it is fleshed out here and now so that its full measure may be attained in the hereafter. In some transcendent way the eschatological future is already present in our activity today; it makes room for the here-and-now presence of the risen Christ among men, and he is the ultimate exemplar and pillar of the hope that underlies our activity.

The Church will not carry out this mission on behalf of liberty if it does not promote the fullness of liberty within itself. It must be clearly evident in the Church itself that liberty is possible for human beings. The Church must begin to liberate itself so that it will be obvious that it is free of all worldliness; free of the trappings of wealth, honor, and power; free of avarice, fear, and servile attitudes; free of structures that configure its hierarchy and its methods of government along the lines of the most dictatorial States. The Church must encourage within its own boundaries the fullest measure of liberty possible, since that is what the New Testament sought to proclaim. The Church must foster and encourage a maturity motivated by love and liberty rather than by fear. It must promote a maximum of personal relationships and a minimum of institutional relationships. It must always place the value and worth of the person above that of the institution.

Today the phenomemon of secularization in all its various forms is of grave concern to all the churches. One typical form of the phenomenon in Latin America is political. People in the church feel more and more obliged by the critical societal situation to become political. This has its dangers, but in all likelihood it represents a historical necessity and a historic opportunity. As a prophetic community and an eschatological sign, the Church is essentially political. Why? Because the objectified character of the public community is nothing else but the social and political body of human beings united together. As such, this body expresses and signifies the fulness of man as a being with others even as it structures and conditions the personal behavior patterns and the total development of the individual. What is more, Christian salvation is proffered in the framework of the people of God. This framework of a people necessarily possesses a public and political character. It is a kingdom in the world even though it is not of this world.

More and more it is becoming clear that secular activity is an obligatory praxis for Christian faith. Once liberation is viewed as Christian liberation, it seems that there is no real difficulty in establishing a link between the obligation to live the Christian faith and the obligation to live a life of activity in the world. Christian liberation, which is a redemptive liberation, is an interpretation and a praxis that is both fully secular and fully Christian. And it is this in a singular way within the context of the reality of Latin America. To see it in this light seems to be the particular charism of the Latin American Church. To carry out this liberation in a fully Christian sense seems to be the particular mission of the Latin American Church. For its own good and the good of the universal Church, the Church in Latin America must be truly Latin American with all the consequences that entails.

21

HELMUT THIELICKE

Outline of the Task of Proclamation

THE VALUE OF A DOGMATICS DEPENDS ON WHETHER IT CAN BE preached. We have been implicitly discussing this in all the previous chapters, especially the last. We have had to do so because we have defined theology as a process of reflection which arises out of faith, i.e., out of proclamation already heard. It is thus subordinate to proclamation and yet also continually related to it.

This abiding relation between theology and proclamation has determined our guiding question, namely, what it means to talk of God in a historical phase of self-conscious secularity, and what it means to understand this phase in relation to God.

We now know the framework within which what we can say about God must be put. It must be put in a dialectic which is determined by two statements at opposite poles.

The first is that God condescends to the world. His Word is an addressed Word. To talk of God is to speak of this relation.

The second is that God transcends the world. He is not a cipher for purely immanent occurrence. He cannot be exchanged, as a cipher might be, for some other concept. Prayer is for this reason something more than reflection on the world.

While it is right to ask where God is to be found in life, and while sheer and aloof transcendence is to be rejected, God can never be reduced to his presence in the world. The term "God" can never mean something other than God himself. If it could be a cipher for something else, e.g., fellow-humanity, this would imply the death, not of God, but of this concept of God. The cause of death would be interchangeability. What is interchangeable can be replaced. What can be replaced does not have the quality of

From Helmut Thielicke, *The Evangelical Faith,* Vol. I, pp. 378–385. ©
William B. Eerdmans Publishing Company, Grand Rapids, 1974. Used by
permission of the Publisher.

uniqueness and certainly cannot be the basis, goal, and meaning of all being.

Within this dialectic we shall now try to indicate with the help of examples some themes of proclamation that arise against this background. Our use of models means that we can give only aphoristic pointers. (For a more systematic treatment cf. ThE.) In the form of proclamation, which carries with it a relation to the world, we shall be offering an interpretation of the totality of human reality from the standpoint of eternity, or, better, in the light of the Word of God.

What does this mean?

Obviously it does not mean that we shall be attempting to formulate a Christian world-view that will enable us to present, with the help of Christian norms and a claim to binding truth, a total view of reality that will place at our disposal a closed and eternally valid and hence irreformable interpretation of all the phenomena of nature and history. Attempts of this kind would contradict what redemption means for the emancipation of reason, namely, that it can relate materially and openly to a reality which has been dedivinized and robbed of its numinous force. This opening up of reason means its liberation from prejudice. It is no longer tied to specific premises as under the dominion of medieval Aristotelianism. Hence it is not tied to the implications of these premises. Christian premises which might lead to the erection of a closed nexus of life and meaning would have the character of an intellectual theocracy. They would contest the adulthood and openness of reason. They would thus involve a fundamental self-contradiction. Instead of opening up reason they would put it in ideological cement. Christianity, too, can be ideologized.

(1) Our first point, then, is that Christianity, unlike Marxism, Idealism, etc., does not carry with it a world-view which subsumes all conceivable phenomena under Christian axioms and assigns a fixed place to all natural and historical processes. God can never be understood as the first principle (whether as cause or substance) from which all phenomena can be deduced (as effects or accidents).

God is certainly the basis, goal, and meaning of being and occurrence. But this meaning is not to be regarded and formulated as a principle. It is a believed meaning. Hence we cannot see it. We cannot pursue it in its manifestations. Thus we believe that God is righteous, that he is love, that he wills salvation. But we do not see the relation of manifested reality to this theme of righteousness, love, and salvation.[1] We believe in the one whose thoughts are higher than ours but we cannot think these thoughts after him. Our reality does not make these thoughts clear. What we see has no meaning; we believe, however, that there is meaning to it. We believe in the theme without seeing the relation between it and its execution. This execution is hidden under the veil of the cross. God appears to us in the form of his opposite. There are two quite different reasons for this.

(a) God does not correspond to our image of him. He is not, for example, the God of Job during Job's affliction. He is not a cipher for the correspondence between guilt and punishment or merit and reward. (b) God in love has assumed the form of lowliness, the "non-divinity" of the cross. If he cannot be demonstrated or presented ontically and historically, this is not for philosophical reasons, e.g., that transcendence cannot be objectified or that the ground of reality does not have the form of reality. No, the reason why he cannot be demonstrated or seen is that in loving condescension he takes another form, and that in virtue of his solidarity with man he seems only too human, whether as a psychological phenomenon (Feuerbach) or as a phenomenon of religious history which like the incarnation is embedded in many analogies.

Because God, as meaning, cannot be grasped as a principle to which all phenomena can be related or from which they can be derived; because he is the one in whose higher thoughts we believe even though we cannot see them in their execution, a closed interpretation of the world is impossible. We are confronted by the openness of venture and by constant surprise. Every unexpected turn in knowledge, every experience which overtakes us and which apparently does not belong in the domain of faith, shatters the supposedly Christian systems which have been built up secretly in our heads and hearts.

The question of theodicy lurks everywhere at all times. The question why God permits this or does that, or whether he exists at all, shows that faith thrusts us out into open country. It challenges the definitiveness of secretly constructed principles. It rebels against their rule.

Hence we have always to confess with Job: "Yet will I trust in him" (Job 13:15). Faith bears witness here that God cannot be imprisoned in a world-view in which everything is easy. We can only believe in him whose thoughts are higher than ours; we can-

1. Cf. A. Flew in *New Essays in Philosophical Theology,* pp. 96-99.

not put these thoughts into systems. We are thus liberated from all systems. We are not imprisoned in a Christian world-view or in Christian ideologies. We are summoned to openness and to ventures of a higher order.

This is why there can be no Christian philosophy of history. God is the Lord of history. He has disclosed his purposes for mankind. This has led some people to speculate on the possibility of a Christian interpretation of history.[2] A mark of what faith says about history, however, is that it is never about history as a whole, just as a mark of what it says about creation is that it is not about the whole universe. Statements of this kind deal with details rather than the whole. They refer to the highly personal encounter of faith with the Thou of God.

It is thus very much to the point that Luther in his exposition of the first article of the Creed does not say that God created the world at large and then me among other things. He first says that God created me. The development of Israel's belief in God takes a similar course. Yahweh is first known in detail, in a small segment of life, as the God who brought Israel out of Egypt. Only then does the certainty arise that he is the Lord of the nations and the cosmos. He is first known in the immediacy of faith as the God of the covenant, our God. Only then is the implied insight that he is the Lord of the world and of history made explicit. The God of all eternity is first the God of David's house and people in the thanksgiving prayer of 2 Samuel 7:17ff. The eschatological expectation linked to the fulfilment of universal history, namely, that all the nations will come up to Mount Zion (Matthew 8:11), arises out of the certainty of personal faith that Christ is risen, that he is risen for me.

This point that statements about the whole are always explications of a reality of faith experienced in detail has important implications for proclamation.

We can see that the secular way of putting questions of faith is to ask first about the totality. The question is always a general one: What is the meaning of history? How can God allow evil? What about predestination and free will or the omnipotence of God and opposition to him? How can the statistical fact that some are predestined and others are not be harmonized with the righteousness of God? The problem of pedagogical method which this poses is

2. Cf. K. G. Steck, *Die Idee der Heilsgeschichte* (1959); M. Kähler, *Geschichte der protestantischen Dogmatik im 19. Jahrhundert* (1962), pp. 103ff.

that speculatively illuminating answers cannot be given to such questions. For these broad questions focus on relations with which we are legitimately confronted only in the details of the personal experience of faith.

Luther drew attention to this in model fashion in his introduction to Romans (WA Bibel, 7, 2–27). We must not fly too high. We do this if in the matter of predestination we raise the general statistical question. This leads to confusion, cowardice, or libertinism. Like Paul in Romans, we should make Christ and the gospel our first concern so that we may know our sin and his grace. We must turn to the details of faith. Then the question of predestination arises, not as a speculative statistical problem, but as wonder at the fact that with no obvious merits I am justified out of free grace. No one can adequately handle the broad problem of predestination and free will or predestination and the righteousness of God. We must first be brought to the point of our own faith-encounter with the free grace of God if we are to approach this problem legitimately. Such problems, then, are not for beginners who have not yet come to the point of detailed experience. This wine is too heady for infants. Each doctrine has its own measure, time, and age.

The implied problem of proclamation arises when the church writes memoranda on general questions such as industrial relations.[3] These studies of great economic, political, or historical matters may be very objective. They may make effective use of statistics. They may embody information contributed by experts. But they do not stop at objective argument. The argument focuses on a point which has to do with the faith, the personal faith, of those who are here confessing in the medium of argument. For this is what they are doing.

If this element is not noted or the faith shared, such documents cannot be understood even though their arguments are accepted. If, however, an objective statement is in the last resort proclamation, then in spite of the armor of argument it shares the defenselessness of proclamation. It is defenseless because the faith which it proclaims cannot be demonstrated. It depends on the sovereignty of the inner witness of the Spirit. Hence even this way of tackling the great questions of history from the standpoint of faith reaches a point where argument ends and the issue is whether the one who is addressed in the arguments is ready to come, or is called, to the place of belief which is also the source of the arguments.

---

3. This does not apply to papal encyclicals, since they appeal in large part to natural law.

In exactly the same sense the believer can reason with interested parties about the relation between predestination and free will. He can use arguments, and his arguments may even leave an impression of intellectual cogency. In the last resort, however, the validity of what he says will demonstrate itself, not in the fact that he proves his point, but rather in the fact that he issues a summons to personal faith and makes it plain that only in the light of this do his arguments have a justifiable basis and goal.

(2) Interpretation of the world from the standpoint of eternity does not start, then, with the fixities of a world-view. At the same time it does have a criterion by which a hierarchy of values may be set up, even though this hierarchy is so general that it leaves plenty of room for modifications in detail. This criterion is the primacy of man over things and over the world of the material in general. Man is summoned by the Creator to subdue the world (Genesis 1:28). Hence even the world's orders are not ends in themselves. They are to serve man and to be the structure of his fellow-humanity (cf. the Sabbath in Mark 2:27).

The basis of the fact that man is not to be reduced to the functional or degraded into a mere means to an end lies in a quality of the human which transcends man's being in the world. Man has an alien dignity. This consists in the fact that he has been loved and visited by God, that he has been bought with a price (1 Corinthians 6:20; 7:23), and that Christ died for him (Romans 14:15; 1 Corinthians 8:11). Hence a proclamation which relates to the orders of life, to social structures, to the role of sex, to economic relations, etc., must use the primacy of man as a criterion.

A proclamation of this type will not be afraid of being concrete. It will discuss given social structures. It will introduce biological data as arguments in the sphere of sex. But these concrete elements will not be ends in themselves. They will serve as illustrations of the criterion whether the alien dignity of man is being respected in the structures. Thus sex will be understood purely as a biological medium for the human relation between two sexual beings (cf. ThE, III, § 2020ff.). In the way in which the primacy of man is established, e.g., by alien dignity and not by immanent functional worth, proclamation will seek to show that God is present in the world even though he is more than this presence.

(3) Interpretation of the world from the standpoint of eternity teaches us to be objective and bold. If in opposition to the mythical view of the world it robs the world of its numinous force, in opposition to secularism it de-ideologizes the world and shatters the many pseudo-absolutes which are constantly being set up. To

be soberly objective does not mean being ordered to the world of things. As the previous section has shown, it can only mean perceiving the true order of rank which is established under the primacy of man's alien dignity. Hence the new objectivity is the objectivity of love and not a purely secular rationality (1 Corinthians 10:23). I receive the objectivity of love, however, only as I find in man something that transcends him and that I cannot "see" but only believe. Only that which transcends the world lets us be truly worldly, i.e., lets us turn to the world boldly and without reserve.

(4) Interpretation from the standpoint of eternity does not treat man as an abstract bearer of humanity or, as one would say today, of existence. It treats him as concrete man in the web of secular relations. The fact that theology, and especially Theology A, usually overlooks this axiom of Christian proclamation has given rise to a new form of the ancient heresy of Docetism.

In early church history[4] Docetism denoted a heretical version of Christology. On this view Christ's body was regarded as a mere appearance and the substance of the message of the incarnation was thus impaired. Christ was called exclusively the Son of God. The related divine predicates did not seem to permit us to ascribe to him such features of humanity as limitation, finitude, and the possibility of temptation or suffering. The result of such theological ideas was a more or less shadowy and unreal heavenly being lacking any solidarity of existence with other men.

Docetism recurs today in a modified but no less momentous form. The only thing is that it now arises at another place. It has as it were slipped over from Christology into anthropology. Now it is man who is spoken of in an abstractly general and shadowy way.

G. Ebeling has rightly pointed out[5] that the concept of reality is, ironically, one of the most abstract in human thought. The earnest statement that God is not an idea but a reality is misleading inasmuch as it makes God a potential abstraction by trying to do the very opposite.

The same is true when we speak about man, who does not really exist as this nominalistic concept. Yet the concept is bandied about both in the pulpit and on the rostrum. The result is that the word of proclamation loses the constitutive and integral element of ad-

---

4. A. von Harnack, *Dogmengeschichte,* 5th ed. (1931), I, pp. 212ff.; E.T. *History of Dogma* (1961), I, pp. 253ff.

5. *Wort und Glaube,* 3rd ed. (1967), p. 201; E.T. *Word and Faith* (1963), pp. 199f.

dress. The one who is addressed does not see that it is he who is meant and affected. He feels no compulsion to undertake the task that is left to him, namely, that of subsuming himself as an individual under the master-concept "man."

More precisely, this docetic misunderstanding of man means that he is dissected out of the reality of history which surrounds and engulfs him and isolated as a being apart. As Bultmann puts it,[6] the NT sees the monstrous power of this sphere, the world. It sees that its cares and desires distract man from authentic concern for himself, from the questions of God and the world to come. It sees that man, imprisoned by the world, worries about things that are subject to corruption. It thus sees that the world is passing away. Man is entangled in it, not to his salvation, but to his destruction. Now this is all true. Nevertheless, it is only part of the story. Is it not also true that the freedom of man is attested in this world of his? Is not the world shown to be the place where God wills to encounter him both in his works and in his fellow-men, his neighbors? Is it not the place of his gifts and tasks—a place which is opened up to him by the fact that he is called out of it and then sent back into it? Is not the world the sphere which God has loved and for which he gave his only begotten Son? Can we really understand the world, then, merely as the power which imprisons man?

If we do understand it thus, then real man is brought to light only when he is isolated from this alien power and seen in himself apart from this world which heteronomizes him. But then he becomes a mere appearance, a worldless abstraction. For this aeon is not just an "accident" of his being which can be abstracted away without loss of the substance, the result being the human as such. This world is part of the essence of man. He "is" his world. The structure of this world with its laws of constriction, its autonomous trends, and its pitiless severity is only a macrocosmic reflection of his heart. Conversely, the heart is only a microcosmic expression of this world of his. Babylon can only try to be as great and immoderate as our Babylonian heart (Francis Thompson, "The Heart," Sonnet II in *Poems* [1937], p. 320; on the relation between the world and man cf. ThE, I, § 2144ff. and *Geschichte und Existenz*, 2nd ed. [1964], pp. 66ff.). Man is man in his world and not man apart from his world. He is the one who qualifies this world of his and who objectifies himself in its structures. If he detaches himself from this context, the human is reduced to unreality.

6. GV, II (1952), pp. 59ff., esp. p. 68.

This anthropological Docetism has come into theology by the way of existentialism. Existentialism views the external world as hostile and its movement as restrictive.[7] The world involves man in self-alienation. It heteronomizes and "fixes" him.[8] It is simply there (Heidegger). It is the sphere of the technically useful. Strictly, it can be spoken of only as a meaningless reality.[9] No sphere of life, whether animal, vegetable, or cultural, has any meaning. In face of the unconditional radiance of authentic existence the whole world becomes a background without meaning.[10] It becomes the dark foil which sets in relief the burning light of existence. The focus on this unconditional radiance of authentic existence is what allows entry to Docetism. It leads us to speak of man in the abstract and hence introduces the supposedly authentic man who is detached from the world and whom it can no longer "fix."

When this idea of abstract man is adopted in theology it takes from the gospel message its legitimate recipient and thereby changes it essentially. The change may be seen in its effect. Its form is found to be dull and insipid. The hearer does not see its relevance. Preached in this way, the gospel does not reach him. It does not speak to the reality which concerns him. This reality is what gives rise to the ultimate questions, e.g., the question of possible freedom in the impulsion of autonomous processes, or the question of meaning in the perfection of actualized goals and the self-perfecting means of actualization, or the question of the possibility of love and fellow-humanity in an increasingly organized world which separates the I and the Thou from one another by its impersonal structures, or the question of the possibility of being oneself in the midst of social categorization, or the question of the possibility of faith in the closed and immanent functional nexus of all things and processes. What can it mean in this world of forces that man with his alien dignity has immediacy to God, that in virtue of this immediacy he is not enmeshed in this world of forces, that he is detached from it, that he encounters it, and that in the name of his commitment to the ultimate he is no longer subject to the penultimate?

If redemption does not relate to man in this connection of his with the world, then it does not relate to him at all.

Yet man is aware that he is more than his secular functions. He

7. O. F. Bollnow, "Existenzphilosophie," *Systematische Philosophie* (1942), p. 349.
8. J. P. Sartre, *L'Etre et le Néant* (1943).
9. Bollnow, *op. cit.,* p. 356.
10. *Loc. cit.*

is the being which transcends itself. Beyond all the immanent goals that he might attain man asks about the meaning which he has possibly missed in so doing (cf. the question of the rich young ruler in Mark 10:17). He asks about the design of creation which he has discarded and the prescribed identity which he has failed to win.

Since these are relevant questions for man, not least for modern man, the gospel is also relevant when, in contrast to the law, it comes as a liberating word which seeks man in the midst of his relations and blesses him with the royal freedom of the children of God. Conversely, when the word of redemption bears no correlation to the hopeless self-interpretation of man which persuades him that he has been betrayed and sold out to the structures of immanence, then this word seems irrelevant to those who are hopeless and oppressed; it is like an alien visitor from remote antiquity and both Redeemer and those who are invited to redemption are docetic shades.

The message of redemption is secular or it is nothing. It represents God in the world or it is sound and smoke. But to present God in the world does not mean equating him with the world. For—if we may repeat the decisive statement which we have tried to develop in this book—only that which transcends the world can make us worldly. Or, even more directly, only he who did not think it robbery to be equal with God (Philippians 2:6) and who left his eternity can direct us to time. And only to him who overcomes the world in his name is the world given back as an inheritance in which he is to keep the faith and to prove his freedom.

22

KARL BARTH

The Proclamation of Jesus Christ

EVEN MORE INCISIVELY, IT IS NOT JUST ANY JUDGMENT WHICH He exercises and executes, but the judgment of God. And as we have already said, it is for this reason the ultimate judgment. It is the judgment against which there can be no appeal to a higher court. Nor is this merely because the world is in the power of this Judge and has no means to refuse or escape Him. It is decisively because this Judge is the measure of all righteousness, because any right which man might seek apart from Him or set up and assert side by side with Him could only be wrong, because conversely any right being or action on the part of man can consist only in His bowing before the judgment of this Judge and recognising and accepting His sentence as just whatever it may be.

This fact that God has here come amongst us in the person of His Son, and that as a man with us He exercises judgment, reveals the full seriousness of the human situation. In this judgment God obviously has something to say to man which apart from this direct confrontation with God he is unwilling to say to himself, and caught in this unwillingness he cannot say to himself. Man has obviously given himself quite a different account of himself than that which he is now given by God. It obviously was and is something strange to him that he, for his part, can be in the right and do right only in subjection to the judgment of God. Obviously the righteousness of God is something strange to him as the measure of all righteousness, and therefore God Himself is a stranger. Obviously he for his part is estranged from God; although as the creature, the human creature of God, he is appointed to know God, although he is as near, no, nearer to God, than he is to himself, and therefore can and must be truly acquainted with Him. Obviously

From Karl Barth, *Church Dogmatics,* IV/1, pp. 219–228. © T. & T. Clark Ltd., Edinburgh. Used by permission of the Publisher.

he does that which in the knowledge of God he could never do: he sets up his own right against God; he measures himself by this right; he thinks that measuring himself by this right he can pronounce himself free and righteous. He wants to be his own judge, and he makes himself his own judge. All sin has its being and origin in the fact that man wants to be his own judge. And in wanting to be that, and thinking and acting accordingly, he and his whole world is in conflict with God. It is an unreconciled world, and therefore a suffering world, a world given up to destruction.

It is for this reason—the fault and evil are evidently great and deep enough to make it necessary—it is for this reason that God Himself encounters man in the flesh and therefore face to face in the person of His Son, in order that He may pass on the one who feels and accepts himself as his own judge the real judgment which he has merited. This judgment sets him in the wrong as the one who maintains his own right against God instead of bowing to God's right. We will have to explain this when we come to speak of sin as such. For the moment it is enough to maintain that because it is a matter of the appearance and work of the true Judge amongst those who think they can and should judge and therefore exalt themselves, therefore the abasement of the Son to our status, the obedience which He rendered in humility as our brother, is the divine accusation against every man and the divine condemnation of every man. The whole world finds its supreme unity and determination against God in looking for justification from itself and not from God. And as a world hostile to God it is distinguished by the fact that in this way it repeats the very sin of which it acquits itself. In this way that which is flesh is flesh. And for this reason the incarnation of the Word means the judgment, the judgment of rejection and condemnation, which is passed on all flesh. Not all men commit all sins, but all men commit this sin which is the essence and root of all other sins. There is not one who can boast that he does not commit it. And this is what is revealed and rejected and condemned as an act of wrong-doing by the coming of the Son of God. This is what makes His coming a coming to judgment, and His office as Saviour His office as our Judge.

But those who are judged and rejected and condemned by God as wrong-doers are lost and condemned to perish, indeed they are already perishing. They stand on the left hand of God, under the divine No, in the sphere of that which God does not will, but rejects, and therefore in the sphere of that which is not, in the darkness in which there is no light, in the affliction in which there is no help, in the need from which there is no redemption. The power of God still rules over them, but as the power which holds and imprisons them, the power of His condemnation. The love of God burns where they are, but as the fire of His wrath which consumes and destroys them. God lives for them, but the life of God can only mean death for those who are His enemies. That is how the men exist who will be their own judges, who will acquit themselves, who in so doing commit all sins *in nuce,* and who are therefore judged and rejected and condemned by God as wrong-doers. And because all men are determinedly against God in this, this is how every man necessarily exists—in a lost state as one who is lost. God would not be God if there could be any altering the universality and logic and completeness of what is necessarily done here, if there could be any escaping this sequence of sin and destruction. It means eternal perdition to have God against us. But if we will what God does not will, we do have God against us, and therefore we hurry and run and stumble and fall into eternal perdition.

But again God would not be God if His reaction to wrong-doers could be compared to a mechanism which functions, as it were, independently of His free ruling and disposing. That is not how it is on His right hand, where He says Yes to the creature, where He frees his powers and blesses his love and gives him life which is life indeed. God is the Lord in all His rule, even in that of His wrath and the destruction and perdition which it brings. He Himself determines the course and direction and meaning of it: not some necessity immanent to its occurrence; not a force to which man when he sins against God becomes subject absolutely, i.e., otherwise than in conformity to the sovereign will and disposing of God which obtains even in His rule on the left hand. How God will fulfil the sentence to which man has fallen inescapably victim is a matter for Him to decide. He can fulfil it—in all its strictness—in such a way that in fulfilling it there is attained that which man in his perversity tried and never could secure for himself—his pardon. Without relaxing or mitigating the sentence, let alone as a judge who is unjust by reason of his laxity, He can exercise grace even with His judgment and in execution of it. He can be so much in earnest against sinful man that He is for him. He can bring on him all that must come on him as a wrong-doer at the left hand of God and under His No, in order to set him at His right hand, in order finally to say Yes to him, in order to address and treat him as one who does right and not wrong. God is free to judge in this way. He is not obliged to do so. There is no inner compulsion forcing Him to exercise this strange judgment. Even less is there any right or claim on the part of man on the ground of which he can expect this strange judgment. Everything is against any such judgment being even conceivable: a serious judgment of God's enemies the result of which is grace, liberation, redemption proceeding out of captivity, love out of wrath, life out of death; a judgment which in the event makes the enemies of God His friends; a judgment in which this does not happen arbitrarily but in a fixed order, not in a wild divine inconsequence but with a clear purpose and according to a firm plan; and therefore a judgment beside and after and beyond which there need be no further fear of judgment; a judgment which concludes once and for all with the redemption and salvation of the man who had been rightly accused and condemned and had fallen a helpless victim to destruction. Everything is against the possibility of a judgment like that. But we cannot encroach on the freedom of God. We cannot, therefore, say that it could not please God in His grace, out of sheer faithfulness and mercy to us men, to be our Judge in this strange fashion.

But in the last resort there is only one thing which tells us that this is in fact possible—that in Jesus Christ His Son our Lord He has acted in this and no other way as our Judge and the Judge of all men. We now return to our question: Why did the Son of God become man, one of us, our brother, our fellow in the human situation? The answer is: In order to judge the world. But in the light of what God has actually done we must add at once: In order to judge it in the exercise of His kingly freedom to show His grace in the execution of His judgment, to pronounce us free in passing sentence, to free us by imprisoning us, to ground our life on our death, to redeem and save us by our destruction. That is how God has actually judged in Jesus Christ. And that is why He humbled Himself. That is why He went into the far country as the obedient Son of the Father. That is why He did not abandon us, but came amongst us as our brother. That is why the Father sent Him. That was the eternal will of God and its fulfilment in time—the execution of this strange judgment. If this strange judgment had not taken place, there would be only a lost world and lost men. Since it has taken place, we can only recognise and believe and proclaim to the whole world and all men: Not lost. And since it did take place, what does it matter what may be said against the possibility of it?

But what did take place? At this point we can and must make the decisive statement: What took place is that the Son of God fulfilled the righteous judgment on us men by Himself taking our place as man and in our place undergoing the judgment under which we had passed. That is why He came and was amongst us. In this way, in this "for us," He was our Judge against us. That is what happened when the divine accusation was, as it were, embodied in His presence in the flesh. That is what happened when the divine condemnation had, as it were, visibly to fall on this our fellow-man. And that is what happened when by reason of our accusation and condemnation it had to come to the point of our perishing, our destruction, our fall into nothingness, our death. Everything happened to us exactly as it had to happen, but because God willed to execute His judgment on us in His Son it all happened in His person, as His accusation and condemnation and destruction. He judged, and it was the Judge who was judged, who let Himself be judged. Because He was a man like us, He was able to be judged like us. Because He was the Son of God and Himself God, He had the competence and power to allow this to happen to Him. Because He was the divine Judge come amongst us, He had the authority in this way—by this giving up of Himself to judgment in our place—to exercise the divine justice of grace, to pronounce us righteous on the ground of what happened to Him, to free us therefore from the accusation and condemnation and punishment, to save us from the impending loss and destruction. And because in divine freedom He was on the way of obedience, He did not refuse to accept the will of the Father as His will in this self-giving. In His doing this for us, in His taking to Himself—to fulfil all righteousness—our accusation and condemnation and punishment, in His suffering in our place and for us, there came to pass our reconciliation with God. *Cur Deus homo?* In order that God as man might do and accomplish and achieve and complete all this for us wrong-doers, in order that in this way there might be brought about by Him our reconciliation with Him and conversion to Him.

It came to pass, we have just said; as we do when we tell the story of something that happened in the world at a definite place and a definite point of time. To think the matter out further and to understand it in detail, all that remains actually for us to do is simply to recount it in the manner of a story which has come to pass (which it is), to bring it before ourselves as something which has objectively happened. There and then, in the existence of the man Jesus of Nazareth, who was the Son of God, this event came to pass in the kingly freedom of the God who is holy and righteous in His faithfulness and mercy. There and then there took place the strange judgment which meant the pardon and redemption of man the wrong-doer, the making possible of that which seemed to be contrary to every possibility. It was made possible as it was done. And it was done as God became man in Jesus Christ, in order to do that in our place and for us. It took place in Him, in the one man, and therefore there and then, *illic et tunc,* and in significance *hic et nunc,* for us in our modern here and now. To be known and explained and proclaimed with this significance it cannot and must not be ignored or dissolved in favour of its significance, so that it disappears in it. Before there is any consideration of its significance, it can and must be taken as that which is significant in its significance, and therefore in and for itself as the history of Jesus Christ as it took place there and then, and as it can be and is recounted: That is how it happened for us. For upon the fact that it happened for us there depends the further fact that it has a significance for us as something which happened for us. Upon the fact that it confronts us as something that happened there depends the further fact that it can be seen by us to have this significance. Where there is nothing significant, and seen to be significant, there can be no significance or recognition of it. But the significant thing is what happened in Him, in Jesus Christ, in this one man. It is His history as such. It alone is the basis of faith. Its proclamation alone is the summons to faith—faith in this strange judgment, and the invitation and constraint to submit to it. Jesus Christ for us as a supremely objective happening is the word of reconciliation on the basis of which there is a ministry of reconciliation.

The New Testament distinguishes this happening in relation to its significance by an ἅπαξ or ἐφάπαξ. This marks it off as an event which has to be considered in its uniqueness and particularity, which cannot be dissolved, or merely commemorated *sotto voce* for the sake of completeness. Jesus Christ died for sin once, is the highly compressed form in which it is stated in Rom. 6:10. And it is from this that in v. 11 there is derived the necessity to reckon ourselves dead indeed unto sin. According to Rom. 5:6f. it happened at a particular time (κατὰ καιρόν). It was indeed when we were still without strength, sinners (v. 8), even enemies (v. 10), that He died for us (ὑπὲρ ἡμῶν, v. 8), that we were reconciled to God by the death of His Son (v. 10). Christ died once for our sins, the just for the unjust, to bring us to God (I Pet. 3:18). And especially in the Epistle to the Hebrews: Not with a daily repetition like the High Priests of the Old Testament, but once only did Christ offer sacrifice with the offering of Himself (7:27). Again in contradistinction to the sacrificial ministry of the Old Testament, He entered once into the holy place by His own blood and made (in that way) an eternal redemption (αἰωνία λύτρωσις) for us. Just as man dies once, so He is once revealed at the end of the age to take away sin by His sacrifice (9:26f.). And all that has still to be done, according to this passage, is that He should finally appear in correspondence to the judgment which awaits man after death. In that He fulfilled the will of God we are sanctified once and for all by the sacrificial offering of His body (10:10, 14), again in contradistinction to the Old Testament order, within which there can be no question of a cleansing of man once and for all (10:2).

In order to see and grasp this event as such, and therefore in its uniqueness and distinction in relation to its significance, we must try to find some way of making the accustomed unaccustomed again, the well-known unknown and the old new: that is, the outline of the evangelical history with which we are so familiar and the stimulating singularity of which we may so easily overlook, especially in the form in which it is presented in the synoptic Gospels. It is obvious that in these Gospels there is relatively little express mention of the significance of the Christ event which took place then and there. For that reason, up to our own day they have often been estimated less highly (even by Luther) in comparison with Paul and John as mere "history," although, of course, on the other hand, they have sometimes been given a no less dubious preference. But now let us consider this history carefully once more: how radically puzzling and therefore significant it is just as it stands, factually and without any great attempt to draw attention to it, in its simple character as history. What do we find in this history?

In a first and larger part we have a picture of the sayings and acts of Jesus Christ in His entry into and life in Galilee within the wider and narrower circle of His disciples, the multitudes, and the spiritual and (on the margin) the political leaders of the people. Jesus over against and in the midst of His disciples stands out in marked contrast to this whole world of men. He belongs to it, and He intensively addresses Himself to it, but He is a stranger within it. His indications of the kingdom of God coming on earth, both spoken and confirmed in signs and wonders; the imperatives spoken by Him as a summons to recognise and acknowledge this kingdom: all these are seen again and again to be in practical and theoretical antithesis to the whole being and thinking and willing of these men. He brings, and in His whole existence He is, the evangel, good news for all of them. But what comes of it? What can and will the crowds finally make of it? What comes of it in the ears and hearts of the scribes and Pharisees? What does it mean for a Herod? We hear of the poor and sick and publicans and sinners who seem to receive it gladly and willingly as Jesus believes they can and will. But where are they at the last? What has become of them and the Gospel they heard? When Jesus goes to Jerusalem, they remain anonymously in Galilee, and none of the Evangelists thinks it worth while even to mention them again. We hear of the disciples and women who followed Him, and that Jesus counted those blessed who did so. Among them is Peter, who was honoured (Mt. 16:15f.) with that revelation of the Father concerning the Son, who became the first confessor and who was described by Jesus as the rock on which He would build His Church. But immediately after Peter is rebuked as Satan because he will not and cannot think as God but only as man. And later Peter will deny Him thrice. Among them too is Judas, who will betray Him. And finally all the disciples will forsake Him and flee, just flee. What has really happened? According to this presentation there has passed through the midst of all these men One who is absolutely superior to them, exalted above them, and fearfully alone. And He has finally gone from them after confirming and for the first time revealing their corruption, after showing and revealing them to be, in His light and confronted by Him, blind and deaf and lame, driven and controlled by all kinds of demons, even dead. The Lord has been among them. And in the course, and as the result of His being among them, in fulfilment of His proclamation and work, and as its conse-quence, the Lord has shown Himself their Judge, the One for whom not one of them was a match, on whom they were all broken to pieces, in face of whom they all showed themselves once more and this time finally to be sinful and lost Israel, sinful and lost humanity and—we have to see and say it—an in-adequate and also a sinful and lost band of disciples.

Certainly from the very first the Evangelists do indicate one or two strands which point in another direction, which soften this hard picture of the contrast, the picture of the judgment that falls on all flesh with the coming of the kingdom, which plainly give us to understand that in this picture we have the first, but not the final, word. But these are either obvious reminiscences of sayings and acts which the disciples did not then understand on the first stage of the way of Jesus, prophecies the meaning of which they only perceived and introduced into their accounts in the light of their fulfilment—or else (and there are passages in which this is palpable) *vaticinia ex eventu,* an expression of the instruction which the community itself had later to undergo in face of the event in which that strange progress of the Lord through their midst came to its inconceivable climax. It is often difficult to decide whether we are dealing with the one group or the other when we come across these strands. But the main strand gives us the picture offered by the first main section of the evangelical records, and impartially considered and estimated, it undoubtedly confirms the hard picture which John the Baptist had and drew of the One who was to come: the picture of the man with the fan in His hand, of the judgment of God which would fall in His existence, of the One at whose coming the Baptist saw the axe laid at the root of the trees. It has to be added that we go far beyond this picture, for at the end of this first part of the evangelical record there are no good trees left to stand. The formulation in which Paul gathered together the results of the first part of the Epistle to Romans is not too stringent to fit here: that every mouth will be stopped, and the whole world guilty before God. By the works of the Law—even the Gospel Law as proclaimed by Jesus of Nazareth—no flesh will be pronounced righteous before God (Rom. 3:19f.).

But now there comes the great surprise of the second part of the history. In the Synoptic tradition it overlaps a good deal with the first. The sections from the record of the entry into Jerusalem up to and including the last supper can be regarded as belonging to the first or the second part, or as the transition from the one to the other. But from the description of the scene in Gethsemane at any rate the second part forms a self-contained whole. It is essentially shorter than the first, but it obviously presents the—strange—end towards which the earlier narratives hasten. Yet it cannot fail to be noticed formally by the unity of its subject-matter, and by the unbroken sequence of the events reported in it (which are substantially the same in all the Evangelists). And in substance it stands out by reason of the fact that we have now very few sayings of Jesus and no actions at all, although more than once there seems to have been a temptation to act (the twelve legions of angels in Mt. 26:53, and that He should "come down from the cross" in Mt. 27:42). Jesus no longer seems to be the subject but the object of what happens. His speech is almost exclusively that of silence and His work that of suffering.

What these chapters bring before us is an arrest, a hearing and prosecution in various courts, a torturing, and then an execution and burial. They are, of course, a logical consequence of the first part as seen in the light of the result of what it has to tell us and of the initial preaching of John the Baptist. It is only to be expected that Jesus of Nazareth will try the world which has so shamefully rejected Him, will try Israel and even the band of disciples. It is not difficult to postulate that there will now take place the destruction of Jerusalem and the temple, and that the presentation of it will form the continuation and a suitable complement to the first part. In the last larger collection of sayings before the transition to the second part, the Synoptic apocalypse, this later event already emerges in its main outlines. And Jesus has a saying about His destruction and re-erection of the temple which, whether it was understood or misunderstood, played a particular role in the hearing before the high priest in Mk. 14:58, and then again in the taunting of the Crucified in Mk. 15:29. To the same context belongs quite naturally the saying to the daughters of Jerusalem in Lk. 23:28, when He tells them not to weep for Him but for themselves and their children. But all that is still future. And—however obvious—it is not in the events of A.D. 70 that the Gospels and the rest of the New Testament find the decisive divine answer to Israel's rejection of its Christ. Even in the Synoptic apocalypse this forms only, as it were, the next horizon of the final events there depicted, with no autonomous significance in relation to the true centre. And although in the real second part of the Gospels we have the description of a judgment which falls on Israel, the surprising thing is that it is not a judgment which falls directly on the guilty—as formerly on Samaria and Jerusalem. The One who is prosecuted according to this story, the One whose passion is enacted in all its stages, is the only innocent One, the One who has indeed divine authority to accuse in the midst of sinful Israel the "King of the Jews." There is, in fact, a complete reversal, an exchange of roles. Those who are to be judged are given space and freedom and power to judge. The Judge allows Himself to be judged. That is why He came to Jerusalem, entering it as a King. He is, in fact, judged . The content of the second part of the Gospel story gives us, therefore, a second and a difficult picture: difficult because of the oppression, anguish and execution of the one man who stands silent and suffering in the midst; difficult because the accusation, condemnation and punishment to which it refers all fall on the very One on whom they ought to fall least of all, and not at all on those on whom they ought to fall. The most forceful expression of this scandalous contrast is the Barabbas episode (Mk. 15:6–15) in which a murderer is in every respect acquitted instead of Jesus, and Jesus is condemned to be crucified in his place. It is only under compulsion that Simon of Cyrene (Lk. 23:26) carries his cross after Him. And those who are—unwillingly—crucified with Him are both robbers (Mk. 15:27f.) whose fellowship with Him shows that He is not dying a hero's death, but the death of a criminal—"He was numbered with the transgressors" (Is. 53:12), He, the King and the Judge of Israel. Those who taunted Him on the cross (Mk. 15:29) were quite right: instead of the destruction of the temple—this! the man who had seemed to threaten it hanging in shame and agony and helplessness on a Roman gallows. That is what we are told in the second part of the Gospel story.

It is content simply to tell the story—this is how it was, this is how it happened. There is interpretation only in the lightest and sometimes rather alien strokes, of which we have to say much the same as we did of what we called the softenings occasionally found in the first part. The real commentary on this first part and the whole is, of course, the Easter story, which we can describe as the third and shortest part of the Gospel history. This tells us that God acknowledged this Jesus of Nazareth, the strange Judge who allowed Himself to be judged, by raising Him from the dead. It tells us of the forty days in which this same One— whose history this was and had to be—was again in the midst of His disciples, differently, but still actually in time and space, talking with them, eating and drinking with them, beginning with them a new Gospel history, the time of His community, the time of the Gospel as the goods news about the Judge who allowed Himself to be judged, the time of the proclamation of this event. He Himself was and is this event, the origin, the authority, the power, the object of the proclamation laid on the community. He Himself, He alone: He who was alone and superior and majestic in Galilee; He who was again alone but beaten and humiliated in Jerusalem in the very midst of Israel. He, the Judge who allowed Himself to be judged, lives and rules and speaks and works. He is Himself the word which is to be proclaimed to all creatures as the Word of God. That is what the Easter narrative tells us. It gathers together the sum of all that has been told before. Or, rather, it tells us how the sum which God Himself had already gathered together in all that had gone before was revealed as such to the disciples—again by Jesus Himself. The Easter story is the Gospel story in its unity and completeness as the revealed story of redemption. The Easter story is the record of how it became what it was (in all its curious structure a history of redemption) for the disciples—not by their own discovery but by the act of God in the word and work of Jesus Himself. It tells us, therefore, that this history, Jesus Christ Himself as He exists in this history, is significant in and by itself. It tells us that all the significance which Jesus Christ as the subject and subject-matter of this history can acquire for individual men by means and as a result of proclamation (which has Him as its origin and object), has its basis and truth and practical and theoretical power in the fact that He is significant in and by Himself—even as He exists in this history. What is significant in itself has the power to become significant and will in fact become significant. But only that can become significant which is already significant, and in such a way that this being is the power of the corresponding becoming.

The Gospel story in its unity and completeness, Jesus Christ Himself who was the Judge and who allowed Himself to be judged in execution of His judgment, is the being which is the power of the corresponding becoming, the significant thing which can and will acquire significance for many individual men. It is of Him that we can and must speak, His story that we must recount, in Him as the One who existed in this story that we can and must believe. That this should happen is the meaning and purpose of the time of the community which begins with the Easter story. But He does not need first to be spoken of. Existing in that history, living and ruling and speaking and working as the One who exists in that history. He speaks for Himself whenever He is spoken of and His story is told and heard. It is not He that needs proclamation but proclamation that needs Him. He demands it. He makes it possible. He makes Himself its origin and object. He is its basis and truth and power. Our need of proclamation is another matter, but we need the proclamation which has its centre not in itself but outside itself in Him, in His history. Again, He does not need our faith, but our faith needs Him. He awakens and nourishes and maintains it by making Himself its origin and object, by allowing man to believe in Him. It is, of course, true that we need faith, but only the faith in which we look beyond ourselves, not to something that cannot be passed on to us, but to Him, considering and apprehending Him in the history in which He has His existence. Again, He does not feel a fulfilment in our life, the life of believers. But if there is to be a fulfilment, if faith is not to be a mere acceptance of the truth of an old story, but the determination of our actual life in time, there is again a need of Him, of the fact that in virtue of the Easter story by which it happened, in the power of the sum which God has gathered in it, His history is itself not an old and past history, but a history which is the new history for every man, the presence and action of Jesus Christ Himself, true in the sense of being actuality for us, to be accepted as true because it proves itself to be actuality by its own power. We need this proof, this fulfilment in life— but only the proof and fulfilment which He gives, the actuality which does not need first to be brought about in us, but which is proper to Him, to His history and the telling of His history in itself, so that from Him and by Him it can become actuality for us. Jesus Christ as He exists in this history cannot, therefore, be merged into all the significances which do, in fact, come to Him, or disappear in them. He cannot, therefore, be identified with them or forgotten by reason of them or shamefacedly relegated to the sphere of a purely historical beginning and cause of the thing which really matters, proclamation, faith, fulfilment (and, if possible, the Church and sacraments). He Himself is the thing which really matters. He is always the Lord over and in everything that has its beginning and cause in Him. It all comes from Him, or better: He comes when it comes. It all lives by Him. It cannot be without Him. It looks back to Him. It also looks forward to the future as His future. It has to be guided by Him. It has to be interpreted by Him, and not *vice versa*. He Himself and His history as it took place then and there is identical with the Word of God, not with that which may result from the Word of God in the way of proclamation and faith and fulfilment in and through and from us men who hear it. The relationship between the significant thing which He is in Himself and the significances which He may acquire for us is an irreversible relationship.

On this basis and in this sense we say and must say, as when we tell a story: It came to pass that Jesus Christ, the Son of God, as man, took our place in order to judge us in this place by allowing Himself to be judged for us. In saying this, and saying it in this way, we keep to the Easter story as the commentary on the Gospel story in the unity and completeness of its first two parts: to the affirmation made in the event of Easter that in and for itself, in and through the existence of the One who acts and suffers in it, and therefore objectively for us, this Gospel story is the story of redemption.

23

KORNELIS H. MISKOTTE

Preaching as the Narrating of the Acts of God

HEAVEN AND EARTH

THERE IS A REFUGE OF DEFENCE AGAINST THE NIHILISTIC FEELING
about life, a religious, a Christian refuge of defence which is
imagined to be stormproof because of the unassailable mystery of
nature. Who can resist the charm of being at home in the world, as
we find it, say, in the work of Ernst Wiechert?[20] Despite the fact
that we have been impregnated by the Bible, we still imagine that
we are meeting this same at-homeness in the world in what the
Scriptures mean by the phrase 'heaven and earth.' But even though
it be true that this term stands for the realm in which God does his
work and that hence potentially 'everything' can be hallowed and
'everything' can be counted as acceptable, the structural difference
between this term and terms like 'cosmos' and 'universe' is striking, and to neglect it will lead only to misinterpretations. Immediately significant is the addition to 'heaven and earth' of 'the
sea, and all that is in them' (Ps. 146:6), the 'naive enumeration of
the incidental phenomena' as in Psalm 104, but also statements
such as that 'heaven and earth' are rolled up together (Isa. 34:4),
that 'in their duality they are nevertheless one in their transiency,'
that they 'flee' (Ps. 114:3), that they are summoned to listen and to
be witnesses of that which happens between God and man. The
earth quakes, the heavens drip, even the foundations of the
heavens tremble (Judg. 5:4; Deut. 32:1; II Sam. 22:8; Ps. 68:8;

20. For example, in *Missa sine nomine;* Eng. *Tidings,* tr. Marie
Heynemann and Margery B. Ledward (New York: Macmillan, 1959).

From Kornelis H. Miskotte, *When the Gods are Silent,* pp. 187–207,
319–340. Translated by John W. Doberstein. English translation copyright
© 1967 by William Collins Sons & Co., Ltd. By permission of Harper &
Row, Publishers, Inc.

Isa. 51:6; Rev. 20:11). And, to conclude this sketch of the structural difference of the Old Testament, it speaks of a new heaven and a new earth (Isa. 65:17, 66:22).

We, who are by nature pagans, look for the reality of God in that which is the first and the ultimate ground of experience, in the world, in the unshakable durability of things, the inexhaustible coherence of cosmic forces. Therefore the witness and the interpretation will have no power if they do not follow the direction given by the sacred texts and begin to get away from this way of thinking—not in order to surpass it with a higher, broader conception of the world, but rather to fit oneself into what looks like the far narrower framework of the relationship between YHWH and his people, his help for the wretched, his signs, which, erected on this earth, are in every respect—intellectual, moral and material—poor.

In the New Testament precisely this line is continued: 'nature' is a hardly noted background of the saving events; the night is rent by the light of the proclaiming angel and the singing of the multitude of the heavenly host; the sun is darkened when the Son of man yields his spirit into the Father's hands; the lilies of the field and the birds of heaven are not celebrated for their beauty, but rather function as emblems, as examples of God's care for his own; the stars stand above us to perform the service of shining upon the doings of men and are destined to fall from the heavens; the clouds pass across the face of the sky, called in due time to encompass the coming in glory like a dazzling escort that will strike terror into the hearts of men. Nature as such is speechless. Thus one of the main lines of the Old Testament is carried through and maintained in the New, namely, that faith in the Creator is a conclusion from the acts of God which have been manifested on the basis of the covenant. It can also be called an extrapolation, but in this case it is a valid and necessary one. In the last analysis the New Testament persists on this main line, which is the complete opposite of the ancient mythological conception, according to which even towns and temples and other sacral things are represented as 'created'[21]—precisely where the cosmos itself is seldom thought of as being created.

Now, when we ask what is the function of the Old Testament in preaching and direct our attention to those points which the New Testament passes over, we discover still other lines of testimony, a remainder of wider experience, an approach to a broader praise of

21. Cf. Th. C. Vriezen, *An Outline of Old Testament Theology*, p. 217.

God, a torso of different knowledge, a reference to creation, its depth and breadth, its peculiar beauty and terror, its more independent speech, and its hidden intimation of the last things. All this should still have its place in the church's preaching and instruction. That which was in the first instance necessarily ignored comes back into the picture, is rediscovered as being a surplus, a hidden spring of wider ranging promises. But everything goes awry again the moment we forget how greatly dependent the power of all this is upon the Name; even heaven and earth have only a flashing and flickering career as an accompaniment to the history of salvation which is enacted in and upon the nomadic life of those who are called. When we keep a secure hold on this, the 'naive' world picture of the Old Testament begins to show its peculiar superiority.

In so-called 'nature Psalms' (8, 19, 24, 104), in the testimony of the prophets concerning the creation, that primal act which was the ground of all the later acts of God in history (Amos 4:13, 5:8; Isa. 17:12ff., 51:9ff.; Jer. 5:22, 31:35; Hab. 3:10), there lives a future that is full of peace, and what the *chokmah* contains takes on a new radiance from the revelation, the time, the presence of Immanuel, the God who is with us.

Retrospectively, the preaching of the church appropriates all of these words, and particularly the creation accounts in Genesis 1 and 2. And when we do this, we are not only testifying that this is not a theogony, that God is not the demiurge, etc., but rather we understand that *holid* ('begetting') and *qana* ('creating') and *'asah* ('doing,' 'bringing forth') and *vatsar* ('forming') are very closely connected and that they support and accompany the basic word *bara'* (creation exclusively by God), in order to describe the miracle,[22] the incomparably new thing, which in a certain sense looked at from the point of view of the time of revelation, assures us beforehand of the consummation of all of God's works in proleptic perfection. This is now plain to be seen; therefore it must be newly understood.

Notwithstanding the prophecy which has set the stamp of judgment and alienation from God upon the world (Amos 7:4; Jer. 4:23ff.; Zeph. 1:2ff.; Isa. 51:6) and in spite of the inescapable

[22. The term used here, *das Entrückte,* is from Martin Buber's translation of the Old Testament. 'Miracle' may be misleading, but I despair of finding an English equivalent. The term means that which is 'removed from understanding,' incomprehensible, strange, paradoxical, On Buber's concept of 'miracle,' see Maurice Freedman, *Martin Buber: The Life of Dialogue* (New York: Harper Torchbook, 1960), pp. 234f., 243ff.—Tr.]

apocalyptic destruction which is to come, the gaze of the Old Testament remains fixed upon a new universe (a new 'heaven and earth'), a new reality in which righteousness will dwell even though it too will remain the dwelling place of men (Isa. 11:1-9, 9:6, 25:6f., 65:25).

If we remember, however, that this new reality burst forth in the resurrection of Christ as the hidden glory of YHWH's definitive redemptive action, then here too the enclosure of the Old Testament leaves room for its disclosure; in other words, then there is room in preaching and instruction for the creation, for the joy of light and harvest, for the song of the furrows, ridges, and meadows settling and softening, shouting and singing beneath the showers from 'the river of God' (Ps. 65). Then there must be room in preaching and instruction for the resounding or the whispered proclamation of the fact that the creation is good, that it is very good, that this 'beginning' is the beginning of an End but also the beginning of the Beginning, the prelude to the inbreaking of the Messianic time[23] and the eternal destination of all things.

It is a strange thing how the doubt of some Old Testament scholars whether the Old Testament writings ever speak of a creation at all, whether their prevailing conception is not that of an endless, continuing passing of time, with no *creatio ex nihilo* and no 'new heaven and new earth,' can, in all its soberness, be of service to preaching. Not if we flatter and reduce eternity to endless time,[24] but rather when we see time as being gathered up into the purpose and work of YHWH, so that we cannot for a moment think of a 'beginning' of the world (which, after all, is humanly inconceivable) apart from him who is the Originator of the world as well as his people, who is the voluntary partner of general history as well as redemptive history, from him who by his nature is eternally the Creator, who calls into being the things that do not yet exist, just as he called into being the things that did not exist.

This preaching of the depth and breadth of creation is an effective preventive of a kind of spiritualism and dualism which could, with some reason, be read out of some (isolated) New Testament, especially Pauline, testimony. Correction on the basis of the 'surplus' of the Old Testament often proves to be an urgently necessary operation in order to get away from the compulsive

23. 'Perhaps in his first word *bere'shith* [Gen. 1:1] there was already in the author's mind a far distant goal of the course of the world, the *acharith hayyamim,* the end of days.' W. Eichrodt, *Theologie des Alten Testaments,* II, 53. Cf. O. Procksch, *Die Genesis* (1924), p. 441.

24. Oscar Cullmann, *Christ and Time,* pp. 62ff., 92f.

temptation of falling back into a religion, a biblical, pneumatic religion. The soteriological cannot be derived from the cosmic, but even less dare it be isolated. Salvation embraces the creation; it is inclusive, not exclusive; but in order to arrive at this perception one must travel the right road.

The voice of the Old Testament, however, also prevents us from thinking of the presence of God in the world as being evident and demonstrable. Creation, no less than redemption, is a work of eternal love; but as such it is also no less hidden than the redemption. Only in the Word is it perceivably present to faith through the working of the Holy Spirit. Therefore preaching is concerned to bear witness to the Word, which, as Guido Gezelle said, 'plunged so deep' and is 'so sweet'—sweet, because it radiates God's good pleasure (Pss. 145:9, 15f.; 147:7ff.; 148:3ff.)

The depth dimension to which the New Testament points ('All things were created through him and for him. He is before all things and in him all things hold together,' Col. 1:16–17), the depth dimension that reveals itself only as we understand the creation in the light of that other affirmation (which according to Genesis antedates our perception), namely, that 'he is the head of the body, the church' (v. 18)—this depth dimension dare be preached and testified on the basis of the whole breadth of the created world as the Old Testament does. The creation, the created world is good; it sings a song of praise out of the pure creation (we should not speak of a 'fallen creation'!) in the midst of our present time. This work of God, like the work of atonement, knows no past. And precisely in our age of epidemic melancholy, preaching must bear witness to the healing and salvation that lies in 'mere existence' itself, because and in so far as the Lord our God is and was and will be the Creator of it. 'Joy is indeed the first word and the last word of the whole gospel. . . .Joy and truth are the same thing, and where there is the most joy there also is the most truth. What this joy is I will not tell you; you have only to follow the counsel of the psalm and open your mouth: ''Open your mouth wide and I will fill it'' [Ps. 81:10].[25]

THE DEEDS OF YAHWEH

Teaching, sacred instruction, is never so much obscured as it is by the insistent endeavour to reason everything out to the end, to be

25. Paul Claudel, *Positions et Propositions,* II.

logically consistent. It hardly needs to be said that in itself this inherent tendency of the human mind constitutes a great gift, though even on the level of the natural and immediate it is threatened at once because of its lack of a binding rule and a meaningful purpose, and therefore often turns out to be sterile. However this may be, in trying to understand the Word we must not be unrestrictedly logical, attempting to be absolutely consistent. Nor can we do this with impunity. Translated into the language of exegesis and philosophy, this simply expressed precept means that every word, every concept stands within a 'hermeneutical horizon,' in its own characteristic milieu, in the context of the whole from which it receives its signification, its formative power, its tone. For example, anybody who uses the word 'omnipotence' cannot reason out the content of this word to its conclusion without ending up with the idea of an empty, monstrous tyranny. And so it is with all the 'attributes' of God in the Old Testament. The 'layman' is now having to bear the consequences of a rationalistic theology which has estranged itself from the mystery of language in general and the language of the Message in particular. What the spokesmen and self-acknowledged leaders of intellectual life have permitted themselves to perpetrate in the way of asserted logical 'conclusions' and caricatures of the Message is often enough to be traced back to a fault of theology itself. Theology has largely ignored what Johann Georg Hamann had to say to it; later on, phenomenology passed it by, and the modern Jewish philosophy of language has as yet hardly caught up with it. Here the thinking of Eugen Rosenstock can be instructive to us. All this must be incorporated into the practice of preaching and teaching. We need to know the function of the basic words of the Old Testament. The basic words are the core of the Message. The structure of the whole, which is not directly given as such, continues to be determined by these basic words.

One of the most important of these basic words is the word *ma'aseh*. It is in most cases translated as 'work' (in thirty-seven of the thirty-nine places in which it appears in the Psalms, the Septuagint renders it as *erga* and the Vulgate translates it in all thirty-nine instances as *opera*).[26] This makes it clear that the being of God is assumed to be a *nunc stans*[27] to which the 'attributes' are attached as appendages; this reduces the 'works' of creation and

26. Fr. Breukelman, 'Die Kirchliche Dogmatik Karl Barths als Hermeneutik' (unpubl.).

[27. The One who is 'standing now,' in the traditional conception of the eternity of God.—Tr.]

the 'deeds' of history to the same level and defines them throughout in terms of the former. In the use of the word *opus* the emphasis is upon the constant performance of a particular work and
thus the word signifies what is to be done, what has been done,
what has been performed. But in the Vulgate the word *mela'kah*
('work') and also in many places the word *'abodah* ('service') are
translated as *opus*. Nothing but 'works'! The differences and
nuances must be more sharply defined. Here it is sufficient to state
that in no case dare we reduce the *ma'asim* of God to a common
denominator. What we are dealing with here is a—albeit
'primitive'—perception of the God who always manifests himself
in a completely concrete situation in an act which has a definite
purpose (with respect to man) and in which his 'virtues' are made
known. Anticipatively, we may say here that the 'deeds' must not
be interpreted on the basis of the 'works,' but rather the 'works'
must be seen in the light of the 'deeds.' This is highly important
for preaching and instruction today.

It is precisely the act-character of God's being that determines
the fact that God distinguishes himself *in* the world *from* the world.
It is the reverse side of the fact that he elevates himself above
Being. The fact that God's revelation can be called the revelation
of 'what is not' in the sense we attempted to set forth above, has its
counterpart in this act-character of revelation. The presupposition
of the witness which we owe to the world can be summarized in
the phrase 'the Being of God in act,' namely, the act of his love,
which we find in Karl Barth.[28] This is not a 'dogmatic statement'
but simply a transcription of the hermeneutical horizon which we
must take into account if we are to understand the Old Testament
and the whole of the Scriptures. It constitutes a great illumination
that comes out of the essence of the Bible and a great outreach for
the essential thing in the Bible. From God's deeds there grows the
knowledge of his 'virtues'[29] and in the knowledge of his virtues his
nature. 'The Lord, the Lord, *a God merciful and gracious, slow to
anger, and abounding in steadfast love and faithfulness,* keeping
steadfast love for thousands, forgiving iniquity and transgression
and sin.' This is at once the standing formula and the liturgical
doxology which holds together the Old Testament at its core
(Exod. 34:6f.; Num. 14:18; Pss. 103:8, 86:15, 145:8; Neh. 9:17;
Jonah 4:2). Here we must think through to the end and be

28. *Church Dogmatics,* Vol. II, pt. I, pp. 257ff.
29. K. H. Miskotte, *Bijbelsch ABC* (1941), pp. 83f., 95ff.

thoroughly consistent, but always within the given horizon, which is Being in act.

This opens up still another side of the act-character of revelation, namely, the unity between the 'inward' and the 'outward.' This is true in the Old Testament even with respect to men; we find there no experiences, feelings, or attitudes which can be separated from conduct, performance, action. 'Hearing' is 'doing,' not-doing is not-hearing (cf. Gen. 39:10, 22:16–18; Exod. 18:24, 24:7). Likewise God's *chesed* is not limited to an attitude; rather *chesed* bursts forth of itself as soon as he proceeds to act. He performs mercy (Exod. 20:6; Deut. 5:10). The whole sphere of human existence, the whole of man's life, the whole history of the people is conditioned by the fact that God is 'rich in mercy.' And this is to be perceived precisely in his acts, not behind them in his 'essence', not apart from them in the world, not in the everyday experience of events. The deeds are revelation of his being, which lies beyond what we call existence (*Dasein*) and which distinguishes itself *from* the world *in* the world. His revelation could never be distinguished from the facticity of the world if it coincided with the universe or were mingled with the totality of history. On the other hand, his revelation would not be open to men, it could not be grasped by man, if it did not actually and actively establish real encounters, going beyond the experiences of 'nature' and sometimes running contrary to them. In such meetings there is no sense in distinguishing between attitude and act; actually such a distinction would again nullify the only kind of knowledge that is appropriate when we are dealing with 'Being in act.'

This can also be demonstrated in the remarkable fact that the language of the Old Testament has no word for our term 'thinking'; *chasaab* and *machashabah* signify 'purposing to do something.' It has to do with the plans and imaginations of the heart, which are already the inception and beginning of the act and are discernible in the 'work of the hands.' A striking example—as it were, at the end of our conception of the sequence of attitude-act-result—is the use of the word 'fruit' (*peri*). It is the result of an action—as in the case of man, so also in that of God—in which 'Being in act' is already contained (Isa. 3:10; Jer. 6:19, 21:14; Mic. 7:13; Amos 6:12). In Jer. 32:19 'great in counsel' is parallel with 'mighty in realization' (Buber's translation); thus the inward goes into action in the outward —in an instant, one would say, if we think of their unity as being simultaneity in *time*. This is not the case, however. Rather the complete unity of attitude-act-result insists upon maintaining itself on the horizontal level of experience; it insists upon being felt, recognized, feared, and praised in history. 'The Lord said, "I will blot out man whom I have created from the face of the ground"' (Gen. 6:7), and when he says this, it is already accomplished, it is already *ma'aseh*; the act begins already in the declaration of the intention. And this action is to be understood as God's response to the imagination of the thoughts of the heart of the creatures who do not respond to him. Of them it is said, 'The wickedness of man was great in the earth and . . . every imagination of the thoughts of his heart was only wicked continually' (v. 5). This does not mean that they merely had wicked intentions, but rather that they were out for nothing else but evil and accordingly did nothing else but evil.

We see how this kind of thinking attacks and shakes our customary doctrine of God. But this is the very thing that can be a liberation for modern man, a liberation from his ordinary conceptions, say, of providence, which is still foremost in his mind (even though it be in the form of denial of it) and block the way of the Word to his mind and heart. The point of reference for his thinking is still the creation, the universe, nature, the great power of natural law, which he admires and almost worships, and the great demonic monster, which he fears and almost curses. If the Message is carried into this province of ancient ontology which has now lost its lustre, it becomes distorted beyond recognition, though less where it is radically rejected than where the attempt is made to take it seriously with the help of the apparatus which is customary in that ontology. Modern man has basically forgotten how to orientate himself upon history, how to think of himself as a recipient and doer of history. How then can he understand a special history in which God gives himself up to be his master and companion, his guide and partner? He cannot think in any terms except that of the triangle relationship of God-nature-man and he feels that God is in league with nature against him, instead of being his ally over against nature. And where he still has some notion of what history means, he also charges all the blows of fate, all the powers and dominions, to the account of this hostile or indifferent entity. All that remains for him is to resign himself to the world as it is or rebel against it (the divination of a new creation of the world by man is—as yet—almost completely ruled out for the European mind).

It is clear that rebellion is a last attempt to stand firm in history; it lives by the fact that in the hotchpotch of paganism and Christianity the latter at least contains an element of reminiscence of the acts of God and the corresponding acts of men. Resignation, however, is the actionless answer, a late offshoot of paganism. It means to 'answer silence with silence'[30]—utterly, dumbly, hopelessly.

But for the teaching of those who are on the brink of atheism in the church, for protection of their spiritual health (or even for the healing of their schizophrenia, which derives from the amalgamation of paganism and Christianity), the thinking of the Old Testament is indispensable.

We give another example of this: the references to the strife, the controversy of YHWH. True, the idea of judgment should really come into consideration first. The fact that YHWH is also the Judge, and is so in all his acts by reason of his nature, his virtues, would in itself include the fact that he is not on the side of the world; his 'wrath' is the majestic example of his rebellion against the powers and dominions, against the chaos, against unrighteousness. But this can all too easily be understood as a figurative expression for a 'principle.' Now, 'Being in act' is also 'being in fellowship,' and this is what kindles the strife, the battle of God. In the cosmic drama of his judgment God the helper fights the battle, the *rib*, the case of the downtrodden *tsaddiq* ('righteous'), the oppressed people. But this means that he is fighting his own *rib* against those who 'rise up against him' in order to topple him from his throne; but in doing this he is fighting against the persecutors of the afflicted. In this battle it becomes apparent that these oppressors are destroying the peace of his covenant, that they are actually his oppressors (cf. Matt. 25:40, 'As you did it to one of the least of these my brethren, you did it to me'; Acts 9:4, '. . . why do you persecute *me*?').

One could almost think that the controversy of YHWH embraces the whole life of the world, so that one would be dealing with an Israelite parallel of the ancient Greek wisdom that 'war is the father of all things.' The opposite is true, however; for the necessity and the passion with which the *rib* is constantly being fought among men originate in an all-controlling motive: it is fought for the sake of the covenant in which life as 'being in fellowship' is preserved from extermination. And it is primarily his faithfulness that makes God such a doer, such a warrior; he acts and strives in order to create a new peace in righteousness and constantly to launch the freedom of the *'aniyim* ('afflicted') against

---

30. Alfred de Vigny, quoted in Albert Camus's *The Rebel*, tr. Anthony Bower (London: Hamish Hamilton, 1953), p. 51.

their enemies (*tsarim;* cf. Gen. 13:7f.; I Sam. 2:1-10, 24:9-23; Isa. 50:1-9; Ps. 74; Ps. 98).

Thus in this matter of controversy it must be remembered that Being in act includes a Being in fellowship, that the life of God, like the life of man, is designed for relationship, meeting, and encounter. Therefore there is no partiality in God's action; therefore the controversy is waged equally, if not even more vigorously, against the people (*'am*) because of the privilege of election—and it is waged in deeds, in the history in which nature merely participates as a spectator. Listen to the language of the prophet Micah (6:1-3):

> *Hear what HE says,*
> *'Arise, declare the controversy before the mountains,*
> *that the hills may hear your voice.'*
> *Hear, you mountains, HIS controversy,*
> *and you primal ones, foundations of the earth;*
> *for HE has a controversy with his people,*
> *he contends with Israel.*
> *—My people, what have I done to you?*
> *And what have I refused you?*[31]
> *Answer me!*

In his deeds God distinguishes himself *in* the world *from* the world. In his deeds his perfections are manifest, in them his nature shines forth as it is. But how shall we distinguish the deeds of God from other events? By listening to the Word! What we mean is the Word that contains power, if you will, the magical, evocative Word, at least the dynamic, effectual Word, the Word that does not return empty (Isa. 55:11).[32] True, this Word is the perogative of YHWH, as when he 'calls the stars by name,' makes decisions with his 'deed-word' and 'word-deed,' establishes covenants, creates anew; but the prophetic word is joined to it as is a satellite to its planet. And just as every Word of God is independent and unique and cannot be placed in one category or relegated to one sphere, so the word of his servants always stands by itself. And it

31. Luther's translation: '. . . *und womit habe ich dich beleidigt*' ('in what have I injured you?'). [Here as throughout, I have followed the Revised Standard Version as far as practicable, but have translated the author's version literally, including capitalization and italics for emphasis. The author most frequently cites Buber's translation, but he does not always indicate this.—Tr.]

32. Cf. Gerhard von Rad, *Theologie des Alten Testaments,* II (1960), pp. 98ff.; Thorleif Boman, *Hebrew Thought Compared With Greek,* p. 58.

is precisely in this independence (in which at the outset we must leave it and not immediately look to see whether it has any cross-connections with other utterances and whether it discloses a general meaning-content) that the prophetic word shares the momentousness of the Word of God.

If we were to say that the prophetic word accompanies and illuminates the history, this would be to jump to a hasty conclusion; the continuity of history is hidden, the contingency is manifest—or better, there is no history at all in the ordinary sense in which we use the term. But then how are the acts of God to be remembered? In a uniquely appropriate kind of narration in which a special way of remembering is actualized. The narration is again Word, but in a derivative sense, a completely human word, not the 'act-word' of God himself, not prophetic utterance, which is raised to the level of functional identification with the Word of God, but rather the *Torah*, the instruction, which receives its light from the original acts of YHWH in order to present the contingent events in the continuum of the tradition, the memory, in the permanency of the teaching.

It must be understood that the narrative, just as it is, is implicitly teaching. We are not to seek for something behind it, we are not to hang a moral on it. We need not look for the original experiences of the persons involved in the story. What a pity it is that we have been so long accustomed and are still inclined to think of the narrative as a mere vestment of some higher content! And what a pity that later Judaism thought of it as an illustration of the Law and extended this conception to the whole of the Scriptures! But Psalm 78, for example, announces that it will present parables and dark sayings—and then presents no Law or *chokmah* at all, but rather enumerates the glorious deeds, the wonders of God's guidance:

> *Listen, my people, to my teaching,*
> *incline your ear to the words of my mouth.*
> *I will open my mouth in a parable,*
> *Dark sayings gush forth from of old.*
> *What we have heard, that we may know,*
> *and our fathers told,*
> *we do not hide from their sons*
> *in a late generation,*
> *telling HIS praises,*
> *his victorious power and his wonders*
> *which he performed.*

THE NARRATIVE

Israel thought of the creation as being the first act of holy history.[33] He who lives in it must tell about it. He must pass over from the naïveté of merely observing to the still deeper childlikeness of telling a story. For later generations than ours it will be almost incomprehensible that academic scholarship was capable of reducing the sacral narrative (not to speak of the preaching of the narrative and to say nothing of the Christian preaching of the narrative) to little stories which mean nothing whatsoever to us in our existence, which affect us less than the Greek or Teutonic myths and contain less wisdom than the Grimms' fairy tales. And even stranger will it be to those of a later generation (in so far as they again become conscious of their task as interpreters and witnesses) that the preachers allowed themselves to be cowed by this attitude. But already we are in the midst of a general awakening from this hypnosis and lethargy, which was a consequence of the habit of reducing the word-structure to its elements and tracing these back to their origin.[34] We have now discovered that the narrative as such is teaching and that the teaching comes *anōthen* ('from above'), from the order of divine truth. We are gradually being freed from the delusion, inherited from the nineteenth century, that (a) the narrative is 'only a story' and (b) that the teaching can be summed up in a few main ideas. It has dawned upon us that both orthodoxy and liberalism have strangulated the dimension of the Word in order to understand the words pseudohistorically, pseudologically, and pseudoethically. The 'historical,' measured by the standard of the Word, does not get at the history (*Geschichte*); the 'logical,' measured by the standard of the Word, does not extend to the truth; the 'ethical,' measured by the standard of the Word, remains beneath the level of the Commandment; and the 'religious' obscures the Word, as what has been said about 'Being in act' has demon-

---

33. Cf. O. Procksch, *Die Genesis;* W. Zimmerli, *I Mose 1-11.*
34. Cf. S. F. H. J. Berkelbach van der Sprenkel in *Handboek voor de Prediking,* I (1948), p. 37: 'What has happened with the Old Testament is like what happens when a man obsessed by historical interest tears an old building apart piece by piece until he is able to visualize each stone back in the quarry and the timbers as trees in the forest. Such knowledge may have increased our knowledge of wood and stones; what we are concerned with is the building, its style and its purpose.' This is, of course, somewhat sharply expressed, but it does convey rather strikingly what preaching and instruction have missed in the scientific treatment of the Old Testament data.

strated to us. It is the acts of God that count. They need to be narrated.

This other dimension is indicated by the form of the narrative. We are thrown off the track when we interpret the narrative as a myth which has formed around a 'historical' kernel, the livery of a universal truth, an illustration of an admonition.[35] The event, the truth, the Commandment are not to be enucleated from the time process in such a way that we recover rational or superrational data while the narratives remain as empty shells. The time pattern of the narrative always asserts itself in the quality and direction of the divine action and Commandment. We all have in our blood the religious notion of an eternal content in an accidental form; and it also seems to relieve us of many intellectual difficulties and emotional impediments. Nevertheless, such a reduction from the concrete to the abstract, from the accidental to the general, dare not be applied here. How are the Name and the acts of God related to each other (we have met this question before)? And how can the concrete be an enduring element of the true reality that surrounds us, that 'happens' to us? And how can man preserve and interpret the encounter with these acts of God? Bergson's well-known distinction between *memoire* and *souvenir,* between the image of past facts consciously and intentionally recalled to consciousness and the spontaneous encounter with the atmosphere, the purport, indeed, the 'essence' of past events, which cannot be achieved by any exertion of effort, can probably be helpful to us here. Buber's concept of a 'poetizing memory'[36] certainly contains an important indication. But in the last analysis there are no 'analogies' which would be adequate to make clear what happens when God's action becomes manifest as *ma'aseh,* as his acting in history, when in all history he distinguishes himself from history through what he does, when he is mighty in his 'virtues,' in his love, when he moves the world and thereby and therein and beyond this *is himself,* when his Name rises high like the face of the sun—which shines for all men—and when he makes his dwelling place with the lowly.

When we preach from the Old Testament we must speak of the acts of the Lord. From the very beginning the world was really created as the realm of a real covenant. The quickening *ruach*

35. Cf. Eduard Buess, *Die Geschichte des mythischen Erkennens* (1953), pp. 192ff.
[36. *Dichtende Gedächtnis,* cf. Maurice S. Freedman, *Martin Buber: The Life of Dialogue,* p. 234, where this is spoken of as 'mythicizing memory.'—Tr.]

descended upon the places which he had separated, upon the men whom he had chosen. Should we ever forget what liés in the phrase 'acts of the Lord,' we shall completely forget how to 'preach from the Old Testament'; for there can be no preaching from the Old Testament if we abandon the sphere of the story of God. It is true, of course, that preaching cannot be reduced merely to the telling of how things were, but it is certainly a telling of how things were in such a way that the hearer can understand how things are, how things stand now between God and man in 'ongoing history.' Hence, there is already something dubious about speaking of the righteous*ness,* the mercifulness of God; for actually the 'attributes' of God are really attributes of his action.[37] He causes to be told to us from mouth to mouth and from generation to generation what he has *done* (to this extent it is 'past') and what *he* has done (to this extent it is present). In both cases, however, the act-event is bound up with the narrative, because YHWH precedes us and is still ahead of us. This statement is inalienable; it rules out the kind of false subjectivism which would interpose an anthropology before the acts (which is wrong even philosophically), as is done in the following: 'The being of things depends upon our attitude toward them; things give themselves to us in the way in which we comport ourselves toward them. This also applies with respect to God. God gives himself to us according to our attitude toward him. The way in which we believe we know him is the way in which he is toward us, the way in which we too have him.'[38] No! Fortunately, honestly, in conformity with the narrative of his deeds, this is simply ruled out by the Word. And better things are provided for us. Never can our attitude be more than a response; anything that would be more would be less. Response is the only appropriate thing, for the narrative becomes an address which speaks to us here and now.

What we say about God, whatever of praise and prayer is laid upon our lips, is an answer to his glorious and fearful acts. Therefore the preacher is charged with the task of understanding and retelling the story. If there is any chance of getting away from the paltry talk, the dogmatic assertion, and the moral tyrannizing in preaching, it lies in the endeavour to discharge this task with a new reverence and joy. Even those on the fringes of the church will be

37. Cf. H. Cohen, *Religion der Vernunft,* pp. 109ff.; K. H. Miskotte, *Bijbelsch ABC* (1941), ch. VII, 'De Daden.'

38. Heinz Zahrnt, *Es begann mit Jesus von Nazareth* (1960), p. 160. [This passage is omitted from its context on p. 142 of the Eng. tr., *The Historical Jesus* (New York: Harper & Row, 1963).—Tr.]

served by this; and in a world of things, of overconscious reportage and talk, it will be felt as a blessing if the unconscious, the imagination is touched and awakened. This happens through the naming of real things (as opposed to emptying them of content)—the thing that happens, for example, in terse, lapidary, moving poetry. But along with the moving power of poetry there goes a kind of personal address, which modern man hardly knowns except in the form of propaganda. This address speaks to him, appeals to his freedom, not to his needs and wants, and he begins to breathe again, for he is hearing that he is really a part of the story. But the narrator and witness is glad that he simply has the privilege of telling it without guile and without any other motive.

If we take up the task in this way, we shall discover that we must be clothed with a new childlikeness. With us Western intellectuals this cannot happen except by way of reflection. But, thank God, it is not true that it is impossible to become more childlike through reflection and thinking things through to the end; the child, the artist, the people live in a direct, plastic, imaginative comprehension of life as having promise, in an unsophisticated acceptance of the wonders in which existence moves. Just as Christ was not a 'smasher' of things (*Kaputtmacher*), as Blumhardt said, so theology dare not carry to extremes the Western tendency to murder the child in us.

Telling the Story

The storyteller—and the preacher is also a storyteller, one might even say, essentially a storyteller—is not concerned to say how things 'actually were,' but rather how they actually took place.[39]

39. There are three tested means of convincing ourselves how thoroughly the older Biblical criticism—with its brilliance and quite apart from the unmistakable truth (or better, accuracy) of its content—was a prosy, Philistine affair, determined in every respect by a civilization which had cut itself off from any sense of culture as a totality: (a) the reading of a literary work which, though based upon nothing but 'scientific' data, probes the depths of pagan values themselves to discover their deep human core—I am thinking of Thomas Mann's *Joseph and His Brothers,* with its four parts, (1) The Tales of Jacob, (2) Young Joseph, (3) Joseph in Egypt, (4) Joseph the Provider; (b) an examination of the phenomenology of religion, in so far as it is presented by sympathetic minds—I am thinking of Rohde, Dilthey, Scheler, Otto, Kristensen, van der Leeuw; (c) an encounter with a self-interpretation of Judaism carried out with the assistance of a well-grounded hermeneutics of the Old Testament, such as that of B. Jacob, Martin Buber, and above all Franz Rosenzweig. In these three ways the

For the philosopher this popular conception resolves itself into something else, but this 'something else' is in the last analysis his own existence, that is, his own spontaneously conceived attitude toward reality; indeed, one can say that this 'something else' is his own self-realization in the unmoving timelessness of his mind. He is afraid of the *verbum scriptum,* the written Word, and the *ecclesia visibilia,* the visible church, because they are a threat to the 'pure presence and immediacy of experience.' So here we stand in the pulpit, facing people who come from a life which is more and more determined by the concrete and material, and as likely as not our heads are full of terms and concepts which come from an intellectual life that is increasingly split by controversy. The people and the concepts do not meet. Only a few have the gift

---

disintegration to which the Eastern texts have in many respects been subjected by the Western, formalistic intellect (which, indeed, has exercised only a temporary dominion) can be ended and replaced by a better and more congenial kind of understanding, in which the gains won by scientific analyses and deductions dare not be lost. On this general subject see Joachim Wach, *Das Verstehen,* 3 vols. (1926, 1929, 1933). Treasures of wisdom which make all vapid reduction look ridiculous are found in the works of Johann Georg Hamann. In another way they are to be found in a man like G. K. Chesterton, in his *Heretics* (1905), especially the chapter 'Science and the Savages,' and also *The New Jerusalem* (1920) and *The Everlasting Man* (1925). Paul Claudel should also be mentioned in this connection (*Figures et Paraboles,* etc.). We are thinking also of Stefan Zweig's drama *Jeremias,* Franz Werfel's Jeremiah-epic *Hearken Unto the Voice,* and Richard Beer-Hofmann's *Jacob's Dream* and *Der junge David.* The purpose of these references to literature is, naturally, not to advocate an esthetic approach to exegesis; we are talking about preparation for and initiation in the art of narration. And naturally, it is also not our purpose to say that this is to be learned preferably from literary works with biblical themes; the fact is, however, that we become more readily aware of the plasticity and graphic quality of the narration when art is devoted to these materials with which the interpreter and witness is dealing every day. It is urgently necessary to seek for an antidote to the modern reappearance of dryness in the orthodox as well as the 'dialectic' style of preaching (after all kinds of rank growth has been, quite rightly, pruned out). Even a few drops of imagination can work like a tonic. The fact that in many respects the nineteenth-century academic mind, even in the field of the social sciences, failed to recognize the legitimate place of intuition, of the vision and anticipation of a synthesis, has resulted, especially among such sober-minded people as the Dutch, in a dangerous impoverishment. Dry soberness without the counterweight of 'imagination'—which is to be distinguished from any kind of mere caprice—leads to a vulgarity which can hardly be compensated for by later instruction.

of giving blood and life to abstract ideas; but we shall not escape the danger by—even formally—striking the attitude that now one is going to talk about God with real power and liveliness, that is, present a really convincing argument.[40]

In our conviction the Bible is essentially a narrative, a story, which we must pass on by retelling it. And in this way it can come about that the story may 'happen'—so to speak, in an 'unbloody repetition'—to those who listen to us. Look!—this is the way God dealt with men back there; but because it is he, will he not also deal with you in the same way? Yes, as soon as you discover who this He is, your telling of the story will begin to run; if you are united with that other life outside and beyond your own, then your own drama of salvation will begin to unfold and show that it is already moving toward its solution—how, you yourself do not know.[41]

To tell a story well means to tell it in such a way that the centre, the beginning, and the end of all things become visible; every human life and human endeavour is related to Christ, to this particular Presence of God—and related to him, they are related to the beginning and the end. If among us men no story is worth the trouble of telling if it does not have love at its centre, from which we see at the beginning the mystery of birth and at the end the mystery of death, bleeding, shining, threatening on the horizon, then far less is the Bible story told biblically if the Centre, the Beginning, the End do not clearly appear as parts of the one

40. Cf. Martin Buber, 'Die Sprache der Botschaft,' in *Die Schrift und ihre Verdeutschung*, p. 56: 'For it would be a fundamental failure to understand the nature of the Bible if one were to assume that it always attaches to the message, in the way that bad parables have a "moral" attached to them.'
41. Franz Rosenzweig, 'Die Schrift und das Wort,' *Kleinere Schriften* (1937), pp. 134ff., reminds us that the Scriptures were intended to be read aloud in a narrative prose rhythm and states that the oral word (e.g., in the form of commentary) must not stand alongside of the written word, but rather that the Scripture itself must again be heard as spoken word, not as spoken poetry (which even as spoken word remains self-sufficient within itself) but rather as declarative, 'addressive' prose, nonlyrical, nonmagical. Rosenzweig closes with these words: 'Before and beyond it [i.e., poetry] there was prose, and it was nonpoetry; it was nonrhythmical, unbound but not disengaged speech, unmeasured but not extravagantly fulsome (*masslos übermässiges*) word. All poetry which has since come into being within the circle of its light is inspired by its prose spirit. *Since that time* in the dark silence that surrounded the beginnings of mankind the door which separates each from every other and all from the Outside and the Beyond *has been broken* and never again will it be altogether closed: the door of the Word.'

Presence. For the Presence is act, *actus purus,* which is directed to the future;[42] and we go to church or the church school or to a religious drama to listen to the telling of it, and we keep on going until it speaks to our own life here and now, and again and again—as the story of how life itself, and therefore our life, is judged and saved, 'God is present, and if he acts through messengers, they are not mere letter carriers who bring news of something that happened the day before yesterday and may perhaps already have been rendered obsolete by events; rather God is acting and speaking directly through them in this moment of *their* lives.'[43]

Thereon depends the power of *aletheia;* for truth is not located anywhere, truth happens, it comes to us, involves us in its process. Truth in its Old Testament meaning is neither a pure object of 'knowledge' nor a pure encounter with 'being'; truth is the act of God through which unfathomable human existence is drawn into the history which is at once his history and ours. Our past is his, his future is ours. His hand was in our past, our future is participation in his ultimate and penultimate acts.

Then comes the rich colour of Sunday, of the way to church, of the light that lightens our 'going up,' and the eager expectation that says: This is the day of salvation, of understanding, of coming back to the truth.

> *Warum ist Wahrheit fern und weit,*
> *Birgt sich hinab in tiefste Gründe?*
> *Niemand versteht zur rechten Zeit!*
> *Wenn man zur rechten Zeit verstünde,*
> *So wäre Wahrheit nah und breit*
> *Und wäre lieblich und gelinde.*
>
> *(Why is truth so far away,*
> *hiding itself in the deepest depths?*

42. O. Noordmans, *Herschepping* (1934), pp. 83f.: 'The creation has cosmic proportions; but we do not in pagan fashion carry the cosmic in the direction of the colossal, but rather toward the human dimension, toward the side of history. We do not fight shy of history; the Christian concept of God is not afraid of confinement; Jesus' ministry on earth is counted as extending over three years. Compared with the incarnations of the Buddha this is nothing at all. . . . Augustine rejected the idea of cosmic periods and opposed to it the "once-for-allness" of history. If we think of creation too much as a system of orders, this suggests repetition. Creation can be thought of in good critical terms only as we keep our eye on history. Thus "history with God" goes with history.'

43. Franz Rosenzweig, 'Die Schrift und das Wort,' p. 136.

Nobody understands at the right time!
If we understood at the right time,
then truth would be near
and kind and gentle). [44]

At the right time! Now is the acceptable time, now is the day of salvation. No religion can be transmitted by narration; but faith lives, today as always, by the telling of that which the Lord did then and in such and such a way on earth. And he himself, he who now speaks to me, is with us on earth. His Name is in the sanctuary, and it is glorious above the whole world.

The telling carries the truth on. Even the Law, even the revelation that came there and then, is a factor in the story of God which is now unfolding. 'Narrative philosophy' therefore often bewilders the systematician; sometimes the storyteller seems to him to be an artist, an actor, a lively juggler, an enthusiast, sometimes a one-sided bigot, then again a refined bungler, often a muddlehead and alarmist. All this is inaccessible to dogmatics, unless it is itself transposed into a way of thinking which is open to the acts of God, to the open arena of his benefactions and judgments. It then becomes apparent that right here is where objectivity and order prevail, the objectivity and order which lie in the course of the divine narrative itself.

We may believe that narrative preaching remains the most appropriate vehicle for the witnessing of the Name in our day. Much that generally annoys the systematician remains indispensable if one is to do even partial justice to the suprareligious character of preaching. So again and again it depends—humanly, instrumentally speaking—on the depth, the contours, the perspective, the transparency which are caught and evoked by the so much despised 'artist.'

I am thinking of the great example of the eminently graphic sermons of John Donne (preached between 1619 and 1629). In Holland, H. W. Creutzberg and H. J. de Groot in an earlier generation, and A. van Selms and M. A. Beek in more recent times have given us magnificent, refreshing examples of what 'ordinary' storytelling can do—though I must admit that such storytelling, if it is to remain pure, as it does in the case of the men mentioned above, (quite properly) presupposes some unspoken theological insights, which are often sadly lacking in popular tellers of the Bible story.

44. Goethe, *West-östlicher Divan, Hikmet Nameh (Buch der Sprüche)*.

Moreover, doctrine is already inherent in the form of the Biblical narrative itself. This becomes evident in the point of the story, the key words, the trend of the events, the accents and idioms, and above all in a 'dialogical element which stretches the narrative upon a framework of question and answer, dictum and counterdictum, statement and added statement.'

It requires no further demonstration that what has been said applies especially to the preaching of and instruction from the Old Testament. It would require too much space at this point to show that narration can in itself be pure exegesis in the full sense and thus can help us to perceive that we are being introduced into the uninterpreted world of living, ongoing time.

* * * * *

One can say—with reservations, because we cannot fathom the depths of unbelief in the soul of other times and places—that such an experience of the absence of God as that which we see today in the way of the Gentiles never existed before. In any case, the way of the Word presents itself more than ever before as a journey into a strange land, precisely because the Word is the only thing that launches out against the distress which has been brought about by the fact that the world has been stripped of its gods. The attestation, the interpretation, and the application of the Word in human words are in themselves subject to great weakness, and now their weakness becomes especially apparent as they enter into a strange land.

One may be tempted to reply that the depth dimensions of human existence always recrudesce in the questions man cannot help asking about the origin, the meaning, and the goal of life. It may be asserted that man's newly acquired 'maturity' (*Mundigkeit*) has not stopped this questioning. It least of all can indulge in the bliss of an unquestioning immediacy. The man who has 'come of age' cannot fend off the question of death; he simply cannot be indifferent to this radical reversal of existence into nothingness, this annihilation of his existence. Thus in a time when the gods are silent, the question would be intensified tenfold.

Often we find in the church a preconceived notion, born of love and perplexity, to the effect that 'the fields are white for harvest' (Jn. 4:35), because, after all, the people who no longer find any answer in science, philosophy, new religion, and pseudoreligion and have been largely left in the lurch by literature must surely find it impossible to close their minds to the Word. Hitherto the real need for decision has repeatedly been covered up and repressed in the face of the glamour and power of worldly wisdom, but now men who are in flight from this hellish emptiness must surely run straight into the arms of salvation. Godless men, we are told, are easier to reach than religious men! We suspect that here the strength of this questioning on the part of modern man is overestimated. The truth is that men's disillusionment and weariness have burrowed into and established themselves in the depths of the soul in the form of an infinite sadness.

But the most important thing has not yet been mentioned. The real and original questioner is God. God questions man, and man has to answer him, even if for the time being the answer is veiled in questioning words. In the precedence of his eternal priority God takes the initiative. He rules in freedom over the indeterminability of the liberating answer. Therefore a man, thus called into question by God, should stand up and face the question, even though he has shut himself up in ultimate sadness. But despite the fact that he has shut himself up, something has touched him, and the despair that is thus churned up in his life leads to the projection of fresh questions—questions which he has already dismissed and put behind him as hopeless. Then he begins again to set up a barrage of problems. And he does so because for him this is more tolerable than to be the one who is himself being questioned. In these questions he moves in the opposite direction from that he previously took. Once he sought God by way of religion; now he flees from him by way of claiming that he has 'come of age' in order to shake him off once and for all—and all because this God, this misunderstood, rejected, and by this very token sovereign, God has come too close to him.

When we say that because of this situation, the way of the witness takes on the character of a journey into a strange land, it may be objected that though it may be true that modern man's compulsive resort to his independent 'adulthood' is occurring in a gradually more serious form, it must nevertheless be regarded fundamentally as a process which has existed in the way of the Gentiles at all times. Then the strange land into which the witness must go today would have to be regarded only as a relatively greater, more radical, more closed and sinister strange land. But today the strangeness of the strange land has been intensified by its appearance in our common intellectual life, and as far as I can see, no parallel for this can be found in earlier times. But this fact is a threatening one only in so far as we start with the assumption of the necessity and the salutariness of words, thinking, speaking, preaching. This brings us up against something exceedingly practical. What we are referring to is the depreciation, the devaluation of human words. It is not necessary here to attempt an analysis of our time with special reference to this statement. We shall rather examine what the church has done and is doing in the 'mission territory of Europe' in order to face this phenomenon or to evade it and conclude from this examination the extent of its embarrassment. We shall do this, of course, always keeping in mind that we too share responsibility for the church's plans, endeavours, and experiments.

It should be noted that we barely mention the criticism of the 'preaching church' which is going on within the church, the insiders who are tired of preaching, the approaches toward liturgical renewal, the use of plays and drama to proclaim the message, etc., and concentrate upon those endeavours which proceed on the assumption and assertion that preaching can be dispensed with. We concentrate our attention at this point because here the attempt is made to show how universal is the ineffectiveness of words and how greatly preponderant among the disciples are the negative reactions to it—the utter boredom, the irritation, the reproach of *mauvaise foi*. How can this be remedied? We really cannot believe that here a fundamentally new procedure has to be introduced when up to this time speech as the creator of interhuman relationship has been a part of fundamental anthropology and when even a few decades ago the church was able to accommodate itself to a new armament by recognizing a philosophy of language as a universal basis of the knowledge of human existence. In the context of our consideration of the authority and the outgoing of the Word it is impossible to avoid dealing with this amazing position which is being put forward by certain pioneers and is meeting with a remarkable, hardly audible, but far-reaching response.

1. We encounter one line of thought in a rejection of preaching, based upon a depreciation of human speech, fostered by a group of ministers and young laymen who have discovered the epigonous character of our communication and oppose the 'eschatological' Christian to the 'Constantinian' Christian. They believe that we have lost the presuppositions of the Scriptures, and since it would be uncharitable and fruitless to initiate the multitude or even an elite into the procedures, the only way left is that of direct testimony, if indeed even this is not doomed to futility because preaching, the press, and propaganda have juggled away the substance and meaning of words. Somewhat after the fashion and the venture of the French worker-priests, but in this case with the

intellectuals and the younger generation in view, the idea is to submerge oneself, to make oneself unrecognizable, to dispense with verbal testimony and operate only through example, through one's existence (though even this way of putting it still sounds too deliberate). Fellow humanity, identification with one's fellow men should be left to speak for itself. In their judgment, words, clear, purposive, definite statements, indicative as well as imperative, are merely destructive of communication. Everything is 'talked to pieces'; only the ordinary, everyday speech that is used in our work and our leisure still has any function. Oddly enough, in these circles there is a new approach to the understanding of the Lord's Supper, which becomes an uninterpreted celebration where friends gather together for a daily meal, where warm inwardness irradiates the materiality of things. They would allow the church to go on its way, not without some amazement at its somnolence, doing what it has always done according to tradition and what in this post-bourgeois, 'post-Christian' age may for a time continue to be a help to an older, dying generation. For their part, however, it is time to keep silent. And this means that there is not even any place for the 'non-religious' proclamation of the Gospel. It is not religion as such, they would say, that produces alienation and ambiguity, but rather words, empty, divisive human words, which can be twisted and interpreted in a thousand different ways. This petrifact is regarded almost as a mythical enemy who blocks our way to the man who has been touched by nihilism or has already been brought back into line as a conformist, but is completely lonely. Speech, conversation remains, but it moves on the level of the profane; it has special, unexpected accents, it is a brotherly kind of pointing to an existence in brotherliness in the midst of the spiritual suffering of this age.

2. Still more radical is the sound of other voices that tell us that we still do not know what it means to live in an industrialized age. Not that they deplore industrialization or that they would wish to obstruct its sweeping power. On the contrary, they welcome it, if not with undivided joy, nevertheless calmly, in solidarity not only with the individuals who are threatened but also the world in its tremendous new advance. They say quite objectively, not laying down a norm but simply stating a fact: in the past man resorted to prayer in time of famine, but modern man proceeds (more or less adequately) to act. Men in past centuries regarded heaven as the place which would give ultimate meaning to life; the new man believes in the earth, the heritage which has been assigned to him. Former man was oriented toward God, modern man is oriented

toward his neighbour, his fellow man. Why?—because the man of the European centuries lived in the church, whereas the new man lives in society. In the process that led up to this and its present conclusion, the gods have fallen. The way of the Messiah was not in vain. Now the Name ('I am present as I will be present,' Exod. 3:14) has revealed itself as the guarantor of the real unity of mankind. Then it would be translated 'I happen' (*Ich geschehe*). Here there is nothing to explain or interpret. Even ethics becomes more and more self-evident. Readiness to serve, self-sacrifice, perseverance, confidence, courtesy are the virtues needed to endure the scrupulous exactitude of life together in a technical society. Word and prayer may be regarded as a luxury, but work and service are indispensable. Thus the simple, factual recognition that sociological changes have taken place becomes an impulse compared with which a special ethics is superfluous.

The horizon of the industrial age with its work and its 'spontaneous' ethics is the osmosis, the mutual inclusiveness, of all nations. This is our heaven, which came down as the kingdom of heaven when the heavens were rent—first in ancient Israel and conclusively in the Messiah Jesus—and which since then has accompanied the way of the Gentiles and, so to speak, absorbed its plans. Now we are with the Father when we are in the world with all our heart and strength. No other people in antiquity regarded the earth as the dwelling place of one united humanity. Israel in its prophecy and its songs (and its genealogical tables) extolled the land promised to it as a pledge of the future; one earth for the one mankind under the one heaven. This is the great love story which is called life. Long before Abraham lived, love had already driven men out of their ties to mother earth, their veneration of their many progenitors, their many fatherlands, each of which had its own ideological heaven. Christianity discovered these heavens and also the heaven that is revealed to faith and merged them all in the heaven of the universe, the heaven that belongs to the earth.

But wherever discoveries take place one must expect reactions from the object discovered. Our modern society is built upon a false idea of creation. 'Nature' must be subdued, and our work lacks effectiveness because it scorns the Sabbath which points beyond 'nature' as the object of science to the original Creation: No one can live without visions, and there are narrow visions, of which Communism is one. We men of the age of discoveries are compelled by our own discoveries to become believers, believers in what we have discovered, and to make this faith visible in what we do, which today means in our actual work in the world—in an age in which heaven has become objectively identified with the earth, but which still largely fails to give a modern response to the grace of such a common gift.

What further purpose can preaching, teaching, ethical guidance serve in such a situation? The salutary event of the industrial age is, so to speak, completely forensic. We have only the freedom to accept it, and the burden of the admonition is nothing but a warning not to allow ourselves to be diverted by what no longer obtains. The Christian has abandoned the church as a temporary makeshift in favour of society, in which, by God's will, the really important thing is happening, in which the one mankind is in process of being born and new virtues are ineluctably springing up from the cursed and blessed earth. We must learn to see that church and society have merely represented transitory spheres existing side by side, but which in principle and now in fact represent events in time, so that now 'society' has become the successor and takes the place of the church.

If the watchword of the first group was existence, simple, unobtrusive 'being there,' then here the marching order (given without emphasis) is presence, the kind of presence which wipes out its own tracks and loses itself in service. The striking thing about this is that the Old Testament is made to serve as a basis for this attitude. But more important than expressing our surprise at this is that we ponder the profound earnestness of this interpretation and beyond this our real situation. It is not difficult to recognize in what is here set forth certain lines which remind us of Rosenstock's *Soziologie*.

'In hard tasks God's daily preservation; we need no other revelation.' Today in the technical age this should read: 'In happy tasks practical preservation, by virtue of the ancient revelation.'

> *You shall know me.*
> *It will happen on that day—*
> *His utterance it is—*
> *I grant the heavens,*
> *And they grant the earth,*
> *And the earth grants the grain, the wine, the olive oil,*
> *And they grant to him-whom-God-sows.* (Hos. 2:20–22)

To put such vistas into words or even to think of them is highly exceptional, a gift and inspiration of the moment. Our proper and customary speech is our presence in the world; we ourselves must become wholly worldly, not merely under the guise of an incognito but in a genuine, unreserved sharing of the lot and fate of the world.

3.   A third—seemingly less radical—group is concerned to regain human wholeness. To this end they endeavour to establish educational centres where people, who are more or less active in evangelistic and apostolic ministry in specialized social areas, can study and practise methods by which the wholeness of man can be renewed and in some measure be given exemplary embodiment. But here too the central problem is the derogation of verbal communication—in two respects: first, because the world around us is conditioned to this derogation, and second, because it is believed that it also constitutes a definite obstacle to new initiative and enterprise. We look abroad—the people of Asia and Africa come into our purview, and near at hand the rootless rebels, juveniles and adults, demand our attention.

The *saeculum* in which we live is tremendous, and the secularization which has already occurred is accepted and affirmed by Christians (almost the same distinctions that Gogarten makes are employed). To the establishment of systems, the fixing of boundaries, the static authorities, which the reactionaries are again bringing to bear everywhere, this group opposes a metaphor of resurrection. The incarnation of the Son is interpreted as an archetype of the apotheosis of man. How can this be said and communicated to the man of our time? Preaching as such, no matter how it may be modernized, is feckless. For the Word is no longer effectual. In a certain sense we are deluding ourselves if we think it was any different in the past. It is forgotten that incarnation, becoming a human being, is a collective, communicative process, and this is true on a far broader front in the age of emancipation and maturity than it was in earlier times. For then one could still feel secure in a sacral community or retreat into the remnants of it. Even if one broke away from the existing order in search of new, as yet hardly surmised orders, one was at least a part of an active minority sustained by hope—and to one's own surprise one always found a certain continuity. So it was, for example, in the Benedictine monasteries and the Brethren of the Common Life. This circumstance still allowed one to trust that the speech which was common to all and even a certain bold experimentation with words would be understood with a considerable degree of unambiguousness and effect. Today, however, in the process of what Bouman has called the 'revolution of the solitary,' communication by means of words has been almost completely undermined. It does not follow that one should proceed to act without a pre-understanding. Naturally, the ultimate concern is action; but first we must search for an equivalent of words and the effect which was formerly inherent in words, even though these words were used and understood by minorities. It must not be forgotten, however, that becoming a man (*Menschwerdung*) is an unconscious process, but that words as vehicles of expression have been overshadowed, gnawed away, and almost devaluated by overemphasis upon verbal communication and the conscious mind. And here the qualities of the body offer themselves as forms of expression of a deeper, more direct, more unreserved, and genuine fellow humanity.

There is no reason whatsoever to suspect that there is something heathenish in this. The real concern here is with the biblical Christian message! But this message must be transmitted in a whole way, addressing the whole man. And today this is impossible without contact with the springs of the unconscious. Education is a process that goes on in the hidden levels of personality. The strongest dam against the climate of the technological age, against the tendencies and effects of movies and advertising, against 'the spiritual powers in the air' (Eph. 2:2), is the group, whose members find mutual understanding in dancing, in mimic presentations which express something held in common. This includes amateur plays, 'sociodrama,' and pantomime. In the group the individual recovers his wholeness and regains control of his lost mental and spiritual powers. Then speech too is gradually delivered from being merely a functional drill. The imagination is awakened and ordinary, everyday things are perceived as they speak the language of myth, and symbols, which have faded into allegory, again become representations. Man acquires ears that are open to the silent mystery which surrounds only the Word. What Karl Rahner says is true: 'To be able to be a Christian one must . . . have the capacity to hear and to understand the primal words of the heart, the words that reach not only the technical rationality of man and his disinterested pseudo-objectivity, that are not merely signals of an assertion of biological existence and the promptings of the herd instinct, but that are rather, as it were, *sacral*, indeed, *sacramental*, and thus convey and creatively implant in the primal centre of man what they signify.'[13]

We have spoken of these three groups and we have conveyed no more than a summary impression of the attempts which are being

13. 'Das Wort der Dichtung und der Christ,' *Schriften zur Theologie*, IV (1960), p. 445.

made to proceed apostolically into the strange land. Martin Buber said in a 'Reminiscence' written on the occasion of his eightieth birthday: 'In language as in all areas of human life today nothing can be asserted to have continuance, unless it be through sacrifice.'[14] But is it necessary, desirable, or even possible, not merely to perform a service of rigorous restraint, simplification, and renewal in the realm of speech, but to sacrifice the realm of speech itself? This seems to me impossible. No estrangement or antagonism, however overwhelming it may actually be, can furnish a norm and, as it were, force a sanctioning of this alienation. And nothing normative can be established if the human phenomena do not point to an ontic structure. It is true that the conditions of human existence are all determined by sin which is factually and potentially a depleting factor, but they cannot be thought of, even experimentally, as having been changed or even abolished in their structure. This is not to deny that in this realm the *nihil* can assert itself so powerfully that we yield to the temptation to regard this disorder in man as an independent structure and to adjust all his communication to its behaviour.

Existence, presence, wholeness—these find their crown, their efflorescence, their justification, their illumination, their real goodness in the Word and only in the Word. The constant witness to this among us in this very age is the emphasis upon 'dialogue.' 'Experimental poetry' has arisen in revolt against the excess of 'talk,' against the myriad ways in which it has been emptied of meaning. It is true that in this art of 'experimental poetry'—as well as in the earlier Expressionism—one can judge how great has been the pressure of the tyranny of the technological age, but one can also see in it the hope that many have only temporarily repressed the child within them. It is in sonship that poetry is authentically preserved and secured. The challenge of art continues. The nameless powers can be named and exorcised by words. 'If the world, the glorification of which has given to art its structure, has now been shattered, the question is where the creative artist can discover the authentic being which, though now latent, can only be brought to efflorescence through him.'[15] The speechless dark is a challenge. If, because of the devaluation of human speech, we do not answer the challenge with the appropriate medium, namely,

14. 'Erinnerung,' *Die Neue Rundschau* (1957), p. 576.
15. Karl Jaspers, *Man in the Modern Age,* tr. Eden and Cedar Paul (New York: Doubleday Anchor Books, 1957), p. 141. [Translation altered.—Tr.]

human words, then we who are committed to the biblical Word will, quite contrary to our intention, be again confronted with the mask of being from whose gorgon-stare it was precisely the Word that freed Israel and us. Today, when the silence of the gods is passing over into an imperialism of dumb facticity, the world is waiting—consciously or unconsciously—for the prophetic ministry to make its onslaught. To choose resignation, positivism, the disregard of the Word, means, in our opinion, that we do not understand the need of the hour and will fail to give the appropriate answer. The tendency toward monological thinking and living, which seems to be inherent in the West, will be immensely intensified in our social deviations, in the context of the 'lonely crowd,' if the Word is not addressed to man, the Word that makes him an individual again, that frees him to say 'thou' and to live as 'we' with his fellow man, and that shows him a future. In this situation we dare not be ashamed—precisely because all the effort expended to bear witness in a way that will speak to our time seems to put us to shame—to be confident that we have a new and really relevant ministry of the Word today and to say with Siegfried von der Trenck (even though the tone of his statement is somewhat pretentious, and the jingling sound of it may strike us as awkward):

Wir sind die Grübler der nordischen Welt,
wir brauchen die Sonne unmittelbar,
wir brauchen das Wort, schlicht, einfach und klar,
wie es sich einst vor uns hingestellt.
Und mag denn der Stein zum Eckstein werden
und mögen da Völker untergehn,
das Wort bleibt immer und ewig stehn—
das Wort überdauert Sonnen und Erden,

das Wort, vor dem es nicht Weise, nur Narren gibt,
nicht Frommen, nur Sünder,—ganz feindlich wir alle,
das Wort, das kündet mit lautem Schalle:
Also hat Gott die Welt geliebt.

(We are the brooders of the northern world,
we need the sun directly,
we need the Word, plain, simple, and clear,
as once it stood before us.
And though the stone become a cornerstone
and though the nations perish,
the Word remains eternally and forever,
standing—the Word outlasts the suns and earths,

the Word, in the presence of which there are no wise men,
*   only fools,*
no holy men, only sinners—enemies are we all,
the Word, that proclaims in mighty tones:
God so loved the world).

Sing it, O you who are perplexed, sing it as you wait for the morning, sing it softly into the ears of this sad world! Sing it upon your knees, sing it as under a veil, but out in the open, sing it as women sing in hope and as soldiers before a battle! Let it also be like a song one sings at his work, a song that surrounds our journey into the strange land with expectation far beyond all expectation! Our preaching should sometimes be pervaded with the note of the hymnic speech.

We shall also have to recognize afresh and bring to light not only the distinction but also the connection between this Word and 'speech in general,' its connection with the wordlike quality (*Worthaftigkeit*) of human existence, the fact that human existence is based upon words and speech. When we say with Luther, 'The Word they still shall let remain,' then in the threatening situation we face now when the use of words is met with extreme antagonism, this applies also to the word of man, to human speech. Word and love belong together. The 'devaluation' of speech goes hand in hand with the dying of love. Love has always been the field of the most widely propagated dilettantism. Now it appears to be close to radical impotence. Coldness preserves dying life. The last stages of the outgoing of the Word appear to be without any authority. But even to think such a thing is impossible if we know what this divine undertaking means. The Word 'outlasts suns and earths,' it creates and guides whole cultures, it visits and blesses individuals in their despair. The ministry of the Word of love dare not be allowed to remain void because of the isolation, the rebellion, and the hardening of the modern mind. 'God so loved the world'—with his heart, his act, his Word. There the Word becomes song, and as Rilke said, 'song is existence.'

PROPHECY TODAY

Thus our previous experience with preaching, with our mission, impresses upon us the necessity of seeking a new kind of prophetic proclamation. The extent to which it can or should be really new is uncertain. We shall attempt here merely to recall the equipment that we shall need today.

The aim of preaching and instruction will not be to understand the word of Scripture as a contribution to the enrichment of man's religious or quasi-religious experience. It may be that this enrichment of experience may come as a more or less generous extra gift, but to make this the real goal would be to distort the primary event toward which the prayer that the Word may be opened is directed. The purpose of it is that there may be a meeting of prophecy and history in this present hour. This applies, of course, primarily to personal life. There is no collective history, but there is a history of the church which is woven together by the life histories of its members. Here primarily is where the superreligious encounter which we seek takes place. Where the literal and historical is heard 'mythically,' where it proves its supertemporal meaning in a new time, or where the letter becomes prophecy, there we find a point of intersection with history. A new kind of listening is personal listening. And listening to the prophecy as a person is anything but merely listening as an individual; it means rather to be silent in the presence of the superpersonal, objective representation of the Name and to be drawn out of the exile of godlessness into the exodus of a long journey with our Pioneer and Covenant Lord.

'In a rationalistic age, in the midst of a frenzy of textual and historical investigation, after four centuries of default of heirs. . . someone was again found who no longer considered the Bible as merely an arsenal but rather a treasure, not as something to utilize but rather as something to eat . . . someone was found . . . to take God at his word, to surrender himself *wholly and artlessly to the Word* of God as it is delivered to us by the church, to love it, to repeat it as it is, and following the instruction given by the angel to the man of Patmos, to devour it, to allow it to pass entire into his entrails through the medium of teeth, tongue, and taste. The Word of God! Again there was someone to listen to it directly, to *prefer it just as it was to the fantasies of personal devotion*. There was found a new heart that embraced the holy enthusiasm which dictated the sublime Psalm CXVIII[= 119].'[16]

This is how the church is built and preserved. In the midst of its ever latent decay there is ultimately no power that can save and preserve it except the Scripture, the Word, the Name so understood. In the last resort, the church becomes a peculiar fellowship solely through this hearing of the Word; provided that the church clearly sees what has become perfectly clear, namely, that the

16. Paul Claudel, *Introduction au 'Livre de Ruth.'* [In the original this quotation is given in French.—Tr.]

authority and outgoing of the Word through prophecy (preaching) frees the Scripture from the self-estrangement which it suffered by having been treated as a book. Precisely when the book is removed from the mountain of tradition under which it is buried, from abstract speculation, from liturgical formalization, precisely when the book again becomes the independent, rude, verdant, symphonic thing that it is (not a catalogue of proof texts for dogmatics, not a daily calendar for pietists, and not a target for bourgeois critics and know-it-alls), precisely then does the power of the Word rise up from the rediscovered Book like a phoenix, the divine bird, the winged sun. 'This is why, along with the pelican in her piety and the roaring lion of Judah, the phoenix appears on the pediments of the cathedrals as a symbol of Christ' (Schmidt Degener). But it is even more a symbol of the constancy of the Scripture which had languished and died in its own nest. The living church is where the Scriptures, which have been wrongly relegated to the status of a book, rise to life and become speech, song, and poetry in which the Word takes wings and celebrates its triumph. Every time this occurs, there the church exists, there it is being built.

There is no conflict between this worship in the church and the fact that the peoples are to be fed and guided, that cultures are subjected by the Word to the true judgment and the right guidance. Indeed, the point is that these two things, the 'integral' devotion of the church and the wavering of the people who are to be integrated, must be kept together and constantly viewed together. Prophetic proclamation causes the individual to subject his private devotion to the passion of listening to the Word, but it also causes the church and the people to transform their distracted and only half-serious attention into a devoted worship in the cult which always has its eye upon the fact that we have been sent out into the world. The conclusion (the *ite missa est* of the Anthroposophists' service) is the *Menschenweihehandlung,* the service of the dedication of man. This way of putting it is a fair description of a good transition from cult to culture, from prophecy to politics in the broadest sense of the term.

Cult and prophecy. The sermon is an integrating, if not the central, element in the synagogal as well as the Christian cult; though from a historical point of view one must probably say that it is the central element. For people are moved and persuaded and their lives are formed essentially through preaching, namely, through preaching which regards itself and offers itself as that which confirms the fulfilment of the promise and which therefore establishes the basis for the 'courage to be' (Tillich) and the strength to work. The countermovements, the reactions, heretical and corrective, are also a part of this dominant,[17] which stimulates and modifies history, but which is always something more than merely the source of such effects. That is to say, it is the representation of the *eschaton,* which fills the heart of the individual and the church with adoration and expectation in the face of the world, the world in which they have been placed precisely in order to set an example of this kind of listening to God's Word.

'The cultic act is itself an element of the *Heilsgeschichte.*' [18] The hieratic constant creates a bed for the stream of power that flows from the emergent, contingent action of preaching. There is more correlation of meaning and function here than we can go into at this point. Preaching itself, even prophetic-reformatory or chiliastic-apocalyptic preaching, still retains the marks of an act of worship; it is cultic, and of all the cultic acts it impinges most strongly upon the history of man. We mean this in a purely formal sense here; for heresy, revolutionary movements, and the visions of fanatical enthusiasts are also determinative of history, and through history in many unseen ways, of our personal intellectual life. They are necessary countermovements, and more often they bear Israelitic rather than gnostic features. And when this is true they are well adapted to break through the smug proprietorship and the closed mind of the church which has become terribly secure and confident. An example of this is the neglect of the Old Testament in the Middle Ages and its consequence, the still widespread tendency among intellectuals in Roman Catholic countries either to regard the Old Testament Scriptures as a collection of Semitic stories or to deal with them in a very recondite way—covered, of course, by the highest authority in the church, which admonishes the faithful not to scorn allegorization. One could in large part explain the development of Rome by the fatality of an Old Testament which has either been radically ignored or completely dena-

17. I use the word 'dominant' here in the sense of Reinke's biological theory of dominants.
18. Rudolf Bultmann, 'Kirche und Lehre im Neuen Testament,' in *Zwischen den Zeiten* (1929), p. 19. Cf. Gerhard Friedrich's article 'kerysso,' TWNT, III, pp. 659ff., esp. 702f., where he points out that the act of proclamation itself is a realization of the salvation for which the prophets of the Old Testament were waiting, namely, YHWH's 'seizure of power.' This, however, is perhaps overstated, and at most one may identify the Word which the Messiah himself speaks with the event which is attested therein.

tured. It would appear that in modern intellectual life there are individuals who have some misgivings about how little the teaching in which they were reared squares with the structures of the Old Testament, and then—from a historical point of view, partially correctly, but in principle ultimately untenably—they discover that the liturgy is the norm of the proclamation. Among many others, Leon Bloy might be mentioned as an illustration. 'He who teaches the Scriptures will take care not to neglect the allegorical or analogical sense attached to certain words by the holy fathers, especially when this meaning springs naturally from the literal sense and is supported by a large number of authorities. Indeed, the church received from the Apostles this mode of interpretation and has approved it by its example, in the same way as this is apparent in the liturgy. Not that the fathers meant to prove the dogmas of faith by this method alone, but rather because in their own experience they found that this method was good for the nourishing of virtue and piety.'[19] A statement like this is the fruit of a sowing which has played a part in forming the face of the earth in Roman Catholic countries. On the other hand, the result of regular intercourse, through the medium of preaching, with a literally interpreted Old Testament in Calvinistic, particularly Anglo-Saxon, countries is clearly apparent even in political structure and the attitude of the people toward life. In this connection something should be said concerning the historical place and influence of the Dutch Reformed, the Remonstrants, and the Mennonites. These cannot be understood if one does not see the characteristic differences and agreements in their attitude toward the Old Testament. In these movements prophetism asserted itself—blazingly, smoulderingly, or quietly; hence their reserve with regard to the sacral, their refusal to have anything to do with the profane world, their acceptance of a theocratic order of life, the veiled Messianism of the direction of their life, their matter-of-course laicism which carried with it something of the priestly ministry, hence their high ethical standards and their sober combativeness, and hence also their respect for the potentialities of the ordinary man.[20] We merely allude to these things in order to remind every interpreter of

19. Cf. the encyclical *Providentissimus Deus* of Leo XIII (not in Denzinger); also *Enchiridion symbolorum,* No. 1941ff.
20. Cf. D. Heinemann in *Wending* (1951); Père Sertillanges, *Wending* (1952); Eugen Rosenstock, *Die europäischen Revolutionen* (1931), passim.

what a glorious and responsible task instruction on the basis of the Old Testament must be.[21] The question 'What do you think of the Christ?' and the question 'How do you read the Old Testament?' are closely related to each other. But just as Christ can be preached under a veil where we do not see it, so the power of the Old Testament witness communicates itself in words which appear to be very much uncircumcised. Be that as it may, history goes on revolving about the event of prophecy, and as long as it remains history (for when the apparatus of economic causality holds its autonomous sway or the consciously guiding hand of man does not operate, we can really no longer speak of 'history' at all), it is intellectually determined by what happens or does not happen on the margin of our 'post-Christian' world, namely, in the church. History—yes, it is determined by the Name, the Word, the testimony even where the stream of intellectual life turns away from this hidden bed to seek its own channel and even where events turn with overwhelming force against the salvation and the mysteries confessed and reverenced in the past. Ernst Jünger is doubtless correct when he says that Europe is a conspicuous example of the ingratitude of human nature. Even the deepest impulse of science operates only in a world from which (fortunately) the gods have been banished, a world in which the Logos sets out to serve and to govern—for the welfare of God-protected humanity. And yet this science is capable of emancipating itself to a large extent from this purpose and meaning in order finally to allow the salutary demythologization of the world to turn into an atheistic myth, the *mythos atheos* (Ziegler). This science is capable of again unleashing the powers which had been bound; it can take time, which was humanized through the Revelation, and again empty it of meaning by reducing it to a formal concept, which on top of this is loaded with the severest antinomies. Not everyone can see that it is actually the 'church' from which they are dissociating themselves,

21. John A. Mackay, *Heritage and Destiny*, pp. 101f.: 'The Book opened up to him [Robinson Crusoe] a strange, new world which transformed his life. The Bible, which has been traditionally unknown by the classes and masses of the Hispanic world, has been the supreme spiritual inwardness which, according the the heads of two Argentine universities, Ricardo Rojas and Juan B. Téran, and the greatest Spanish man of letters, Miguel de Unamuno, has been entirely lacking in the religious life of Hispanic American lands....In their view, the greatest single need of culture, of politics, and of religion in those great southern lands is a firsthand knowledge of the Book of books.'

even in this extreme alienation from it ('church' as a code word for the claim to be a surviving representation of the authority of God). One could, for example, take Mauthner's *History of Atheism in the West* or Ziegler's *The Changing Form of the Gods* and pursue the question whether there has ever been a movement, an idea, a world view, a theory which has stood on its own feet completely unrelated and indifferent to the salvation which once went out over the earth mediated through the testimony, binding the 'powers' and dethroning the 'gods.' If we were to do this, we would hardly find a single such movement, idea, world view, or theory. (The only place where we would find such a thing would be where all such ultimate questions have been barred, as in neopositivism and in dialectical materialism, where it should be remembered that only in the technical-national sense are these questions declared to be not worth discussing.) We cannot go into this, even though it is very definitely relevant to the theme of 'prophecy and history.' Precisely in this epoch we see an involuntary corroboration of the objective importance which proclamation and instruction, prophecy and witness have even in a dechurched society. In a city of empty churches, in a civilization that threatens to congeal in its aberrations because it has grown hard in its betrayal of its origin, we find such reminders of the presence of the Word. *Christus regnat in medio inimicorum* ('Christ reigns in the midst of his enemies'); he is always exalted, even where he is rejected. The one covenant, fulfilled in him, always remains, even where the ancient enmity of chaos flaunts its pride. And the Word remains nomadic, unfathomable in its ways as it walks the road of exodus, and compassionately near—so much so that the 'history of atheism' can become one of the partial, contrasting elements in the history of the Name of God on earth.

The Spoken Word

We need here to call attention to a point which appears to lie apart, namely, that even in this theme of 'prophecy and history' we must keep in mind the fact that the first of these elements, prophecy, is operative primarily through the spoken word and its written expression. It is remarkable that, not only in times when men were quite naturally (and also because of the illiteracy of the great majority) dependent upon the spoken word, but also in modern times, the spoken word (and its literary expression, which presents itself vocatively, pragmatically, existentially, not speculatively, theoretically, noncommittally) has proved to be the power that awakens, binds, and activates community. This applies to the French Revolution just as surely as it does to the Krishnamurti movement, to Bolshevism and Fascism as well as to—evangelism. This confronts us with a very important factor, important also for the question of what the interpreter and witness has to do in our time on a level above that of mere presence. Our inundation with an ever increasing mass of printed matter cannot proceed at this rate without evoking an enormous reaction, which will result partly in irresponsible experiments and partly in a renewed receptivity to the spoken word. This will mean not only the gaining of a formal acceptance and a new stillness, but will also diminish an essential danger that confronts the church and the synagogue, the danger of the 'literaturizing' of the message, the danger of turning it into literature. The Scriptures are not and never were intended to be a book for reading, but always a book to be read aloud to others and orally applied. We shall never be able fully to repair the damage which was done by the art of printing (despite its advantages) to the decisive importance of speech in its function as address, as encounter. It is perhaps not impertinent here to discuss this point in somewhat greater detail.

In order to characterize more sharply what is meant, we quote a few lines of the philosopher Louis Lavelle, which indicate a completely opposite tendency, as cannot be otherwise with such a consistent spiritualist. 'Scripture is a word which, instead of slipping away into time, remains *fixed in duration*. . . . Silence puts us in rapport with God as the word does with other men. . . . If the place where ideas abide is an immobile and inaccessible eternity which intervenes only in some sudden encounters, the property of the Scripture is to attach them to an object which renders them available and permits us to rediscover them. . . . It is the property of Scripture to *capture the eternal in the temporal*, that is to say, to oblige us to bring ourselves into time beyond time.' But Lavelle also says: 'The most serious danger of Scripture is that while it encloses the Word in the letter it may put the letter in the place of the Word.'[22]

In the spoken word, in oral teaching, which overcomes the harmfulness of 'writing,' the danger of 'literature,' the solitude of

22. Louis Lavelle, *La parole et l'écriture* (1947), pp. 159, 168, 171, 182. [In the original this quotation is given in French. The term 'spiritualist' applied to Lavelle is, of course, used in its philosophical sense.—Tr.]

'reading,'[23] man meets the 'power' of speech. In the midst of an explosive or a calm situation (though the latter too can have world-historical consequences) the Holy Scriptures are again being recognized as being speech which is actually and originally not a written word but rather essentially a spoken word. This characteristic is altogether clear in the Old Testament; there the accent of recitation is heard, there the 'gestural' rhythm and the 'colometric' form of the phrases leap to the eye.

What we have here is the simplest combination of speech and writing, the missive or letter. Here speech becomes something sent, something present; its aim is to 'make present'—more than this, it is a sign of a very particular presence. This is address, not poetry, this is prose that irrupts into the 'prosaic' world. This is another mystery, the inner side of the intellectual decisions of history (in so far as we still live in history), namely, that there is no other writing which is by its very nature word, *dabar,* speech from mouth to mouth, face to face, heart to heart.[24]

The habit of regarding 'Bible reading' as the really serious and fruitful thing and 'hearing' as a merely decorative addition has introduced a deterioration in our service of worship and threatens to kill the history-creating power of the spoken word. In the cultic act of preaching the Word is freed from the bonds of written form, in order that, thus freed, it may enter into a congregation, a people, a world. According to the Reformation insight, everything depends upon the letter rising up and becoming spirit,[25] the past event becoming a present event, the narrative becoming testimony,

23. Reading, speaking, preaching is everywhere—in the form of the 'quibbling' of the Talmud, the dialectics of scholasticism, and the lecture business of the modern university, but above all in the form of the Sunday sermon, the Bible hour, the spoken homily or meditation—'the salvation of man by reason of the simple fact that it is *oral*' (Rosenzweig).

24. Here reference should be made once more to the discoveries of the philosophy of language set forth earlier by Hamann and Herder and in our time by Jean Gebser and Eugen Rosenstock. The last-mentioned even demands of the university that for the sake of humanity it should learn to think in a different way, in the sense that scholarship and science should be pursued in communication with the neighbour and as such become an act of pastoral care (*Seelsorge*) for the neighbour and the community.

25. 'God is present, and when he acts through messengers, these are not mere letter carriers who bring news of something that happened the day before yesterday, something which may already be outdated by events, but rather, directly in this their moment, God acts by them and speaks through them.' Franz Rosenzweig, 'Die Schrift und das Wort,' *Kleinere Schriften* (1937), p. 136.

the testimony becoming the act of God. This rising up is actually a self-elevation. And this self-elevation appears as the mystery in even the most simple cult, and around its invisible altar the saints kneel and the aeons gather. It is—we retain the cultic simile—the self-elevation of the Name, the confirmation of the fathomless power of election: 'I will be with you as I will be with you' (Exod. 3:14). This needs to be spoken to a person; it is the ever-recurring springtime of the presence. The monstrance of the presence, the Word-which-is-Act—behold, God rises up above gods and cultures, for our welfare, in the moment when he is pleased to do so! And these moments are the junction points in the ongoing story of Immanuel. The light of that story shines through the window of our poor chamber to assure us that we are at home. The strong wind of the story blows through the inner courts of melancholy and sweeps away the hanging gloom. The depth of the story wells up and with gentle power floods our frozen brain. The movement of the story takes us with it into far regions where for a moment we find and possess eternal youth. The Name illumines the narrative; the purpose of the narrative is the amazingly new disclosure of the Name, its sublimity and its nearness. In the Name and through the Name the letter becomes spirit, the past event becomes present event, the narrative becomes testimony, the testimony becomes act, the act becomes the act of the presence.

The reader will certainly say that nothing is accomplished with these high-flown effusions, that they sound like empty vapourings. But however inadequately it may be expressed and despite the appearance of false portentousness, our purpose is not to prove a blustering assertion, but simply to state the real reason why we go to church. Anything that does not have in view this presence through the Word ultimately leads to stripping away the meaning of the service of worship as an event *sui generis*.

If it be asked whether such an expectation also applies to the Old Testament, we can only refer again to what was said earlier about the functional unity of the Testaments, about the Old Testament disclosing itself only as it is seen by itself, about the way it speaks 'for itself' precisely when it goes out and speaks to the Gentiles, about the way in which the 'expectation' participates in the 'fulfilment,' about the way in which the 'word world' of the time of expectation contains a 'surplus' over against the 'word world' of the time of remembrance.

The essential thing, however, remains the unutterable Name, which binds the Old Testament to the New, particularly by means of a very definite anthropomorphism. 'It is a matter of him who is present as God-with-us, as he wills to be present. It has to do with him whose deepest singular self is at the same time his revealed manifestation. It has to do with him who is nowhere more *Spirit* than he is in his *earthly* being, who deals with us humanly— humanly not despite his divinity but by virtue of his divinity.'

How wearisome and frustrating is the question 'How do we preach from the Old Testament, and when, and will it catch fire!' It will not catch fire if salvation has not kindled the hour. It will remain talk about these things, it will talk these things to pieces, it will be bourgeois or popular, religious or idealistic, it will be remote and increasingly remote from real life, if we regard preaching as being opposed to this anthropomorphic mystery. It remains, perhaps, to give some good advice, but it is difficult to find and is actually unobtainable where the testimony of the fathers and brethren given in the 'surplus' is still so grossly undervalued.

Rather than handing out advice, for example, about when in the church year it would be advisable to preach from the Old Testament, rather than stating themes which would be more timely and topical today, it would appear to me to be more important to urge that we avoid all theological speculation on the basis of the literary evidence and derive the real earnestness of the matter from the written form of the Old Testament itself. The high place and the practical, penetrative power of preaching can again become clear. Our calling as preachers is the calling of those who are subjected and dedicated to the letter, the letter which is in itself spirit—the calling of ministers of the Word, i.e., of an authority which by the grace of God helps men in their life through the expounding and interpreting of the Scriptures. If this is realized, vulgar popularity will fall away, the bourgeois mentality will be shattered, our embarrassment over the Old Testament will be put to shame, and our sense of responsibility will become a form of our election. What seems comprehensible will become obscure, and the incomprehensible in God will become light to a new comprehending reason.

24

KARL BARTH

The Need and Promise of Christian Preaching

ON SUNDAY MORNING WHEN THE BELLS RING TO CALL THE CON-gregation and minister to church, there is in the air an *expectancy* that something great, crucial, and even momentous is to *happen*. How strong this expectancy is in the people who are interested, or even whether there are any people whatever who consciously cherish it, is not our question now. Expectancy is inherent in the whole situation.

Here is an ancient and venerable *institution*, capable of change and yet constant, ancient and usually modern as well (though it does not like either word), often and severely attacked from out-side and still more often and more severely compromised from within, but possessed of an inexhaustible ability to live or at least to exist. Abundantly equal to the severest intellectual, political, social, and even religious shocks in the past, why should it not continue so in the future? Its existence is grounded upon a claim that seems to stand in grotesque contradiction to the facts, and yet there are actually only a few people—and very few important people—who dare loudly and unequivocally and wholly to deny its right to make such a claim. Here is a *building*, old or new, of which the very architecture, even apart from the symbols, paint-ings, and appointments which adorn it, betrays the fact that it is thought of as a place of extraordinary doings. Here are *people*, only two or three, perhaps, as sometimes happens in this country, or perhaps even a few hundred, who, impelled by a strange instinct or will, stream toward this building, where they seek—what? Satisfaction of an old habit? But whence came this old habit?

From Karl Barth, *The Word of God and the Word of Man*, pp. 104–135. Translated by Douglas Horton. Copyright 1928 by Sidney A. Weston. Copyright 1956, 1957 by Douglas Horton. By permission of Harper & Row, Publishers, Inc.

Entertainment and instruction? Very strange entertainment and instruction it is! Edification? So they say, but what is edification? Do they know? Do they really know at all why they are here? In any case here they are—even though they be shrunk in number to one little old woman—and their being here points to the event that is expected or appears to be expected, or at least, if the place be dead and deserted, was once expected here.

And here above all is a *man*, upon whom the expectation of the apparently imminent event seems to rest in a special way, not only because he has studied the technique of the event and is supposed to have mastered it, not only because he is paid and employed by the community or is tolerated almost without opposition in the function evidently associated with the event, but also because freedom is displayed here as well as law: the man himself chose this profession, God knows from what understanding or misunderstanding of it, and he has now for better or for worse wedded his short, his only life to the expectation of the event. And now before the congregation and for the congregation he will *pray*— you note: pray—to God! He will open the *Bible* and read from it words of infinite import, words that refer, all of them, to God. And then he will enter the pulpit and—here is daring!—*preach;* that is, he will add to what has been read from the Bible something from his own head and heart, "Biblical" ideas, it may be, according to his knowledge and conscience, or ideas which fly boldly or timidly beyond the Bible; yesterday one prepared a "fundamentalist" (positive), and another a "liberal" (liberale) sermon. But does it make so much difference which it was, when the subject is considered? Every one must apparently, perhaps *nolens volens,* speak of God. And then the man will have the congregation *sing* ancient songs full of weighty and weird memories, strange ghostly witnesses of the sufferings, struggles, and triumphs of the long departed fathers, all leading to the edge of an immeasurable event, all, whether the minister and people understand what they are singing or not, full of reminiscences of God, always of God. "God is present!" God *is* present. The whole situation witnesses, cries, simply shouts of it, even when in minister or people there arises questioning, wretchedness, or despair. Then perhaps it is witnessed to best of all—better than when the real problem is obscured or concealed by abundant human success.

* * * * *

But what does the situation mean? To what kind of event does the expectancy reflected in it point?

What does "God is present" mean? Evidently not quite the same in this connection as it does when we use it of a blossoming cherry tree, Beethoven's ninth symphony, the state, or even our own or others' honest daily work. Else why the superfluous appurtenances? Why the unique features here, if they do not point to a unique, specific, bolder meaning of "God is present?" Is it not true that when people come to church, they consciously or unconsciously leave *behind* them cherry tree, symphony, state, daily work, and other things, as possibilities somehow exhausted? The answer, God is present, which is doubtless given, in a way, in all of these things—the content of truth in them, their witness to a meaning in life—has evidently itself become a question, become the great riddle of existence. The impenetrable muteness of the so-called nature that surrounds us, the chance and shadowy existence of every single thing in time, the ill fortune and ill fate of nations and individuals, the basic evil, death—thoughts of these things come to us, disquiet us, and crowd out all that might assure us God is present. The question will no longer down, but breaks out in flame: *is it true*? Is it true, this sense of a unity in diversity, of a stationary pole amid changing appearances, of a righteousness not somewhere behind the stars but within the events which are our present life, of a heaven above the earth—not only *above* the earth, that is to say, but above the *earth*? Is it true, this talk of a loving and good God, who is more than one of the friendly idols whose rise is so easy to account for, and whose dominion is so brief? What the people want to find out and thoroughly understand is, *is it true*? And *so* they reach, not knowing what they do, toward the unprecedented possibility of praying, of reading the Bible, of speaking, hearing, and singing of God. *So* they come to us entering into the whole grotesque situation of Sunday morning, which is only the expression of this possibility raised to a high power.

They want to find out and thoroughly understand: they do not want to hear mere assertions and asseverations, however fervent and enthusiastic they may be. And they want to find out and thoroughly understand the answer to this one question, *Is it true*?—and not some other answer which beats about the bush. Let us not be surprised that this want of theirs seldom or never meets us openly with such urgency as I have indicated. People naturally do not shout it out, and least of all into the ears of us ministers. But let us not be deceived by their silence. Blood and tears, deepest despair and highest hope, a passionate longing to lay hold of *that* which, or rather of *him* who, overcomes the world because he is its Creator and Redeemer, its beginning and ending and Lord, a passionate longing to have the *word* spoken, *the* word which prom-

ises grace in *judgment,* life in *death,* and the beyond in the *here
and now, God's* word—this it is which animates our church-goers,
however lazy, bourgeois, or commonplace may be the manner in
which they express their want in so-called real life. There is no
wisdom in stopping at the next-to-the-last and the next-to-the-
next-to-the-last want of the people; and they will not thank us for
doing so. They expect us to understand them better than they
understand themselves, and to take them more seriously than they
take themselves. We are unfeeling, not when we probe deeply into
the wound which they carry when they come to us for healing, but
rather when we pass over it as if we did not know why they had
come. We are misled not when we assume that they are brought to
us by the last and profoundest questions, but rather when we think
that when they come to us they may really be put off with next-to-
the-last and less profound answers.

They are often put off, to be sure, for the time being; even when
they do not find what they are actually seeking, they are touched,
delighted, gratified by the forms of their worship (broadly religious, Christian, or Fundamentalist-Christian)—though they
might find better forms in other churches. Catholicism, for instance, illustrates on a grand scale how, if need be, people can
successfully be put off, lulled to sleep, and made to forget their
real want by being entertained in a manner both felicitous and, for
the time being, final. But let us not deceive ourselves: *we* are not
Catholic, nor are our congregations. With us, in spite of all appearances of retrogression, the situation has advanced to a point
where the dispensing of even the best chosen narcotics can only
partly, or only for a little time, succeed. Do not believe the kind-
hearted, who assure us that we have done our work well, even on
those occasions when we have shown skill only in avoiding the
true meaning of the situation! Do not hearken to the timid who
despairingly warn us not to let the situation become too serious,
not to change from our customary broadsides to sharpshooting! It
is *not* the voice of the church of God that speaks in them.

The serious meaning of the situation in our churches is that the
people want to hear the *word,* that is, the answer to the question by
which, whether they know it or not, they are actually animated, *Is
it true*? The situation on Sunday morning is related in the most
literal sense to the *end of history;* it is eschatological, even from
the viewpoint of the people, quite apart from the Bible. That is to
say, when this situation arises, history, further history, is done
with, and the *ultimate* desire of man, the desire for an *ultimate*
event, now becomes authoritative. If we do not understand this
ultimate desire, if we do *not* take the people seriously (I repeat it,

more seriously than they take themselves!) at the point of their life perplexity, we need not wonder if a majority of them, without becoming enemies of the church, gradually learn to leave the church to itself and us to the kind-hearted and timid. Is it psychologically strange that the more wide-awake sons of ministers and theologians continue to join this silent army of deserters? Do they not do so because they know from close observation that people will hardly find in our churches what they are really seeking? Am I not at least partly right when I say that people, educated and uneducated alike, are simply *disappointed* in us, unspeakably disappointed? Have they been too often—perhaps for centuries— *put off*? Has the church, in spite of its very best of intentions to meet their needs, too often indulged in secondary utterances?

And instead of continuing to make new plans for putting off the disappointed, out of alleged love for people, would it not be better for us to pay attention to the fact that the sole and simple reason for their staying in the church is that in the vast and ceaseless unrest of their lives they may be taken *seriously* and *understood*—taken *more* seriously and *better* understood than in the church (in contrast to Methodist, communistic, or anthroposophic meetings) they usually are? By allowing us at least to baptize, confirm, marry, and bury them, they still show that they place expectancy in us—and this is miraculous enough. It is miraculous enough that there are still so-called congregations and parishes. It would perhaps be better for us if there were none, in order that we might at least perceive that the hour had struck. At any rate, we should not depend upon the patience of God, which meets us frequently in the patience, not to say drowsiness, of our audience, to save us from the penitence which is the first need of our generation.

* * * * *

But this is only one side of the situation on Sunday morning. The other is still more important. Outwardly it is symbolized by the opening of the *Bible,* at least in our Protestant churches.

It is worth while to stop here a moment to see what immeasurable consequences follow upon the Reformers' proclamation that the word of God expressed in the Holy Scriptures is the foundation and final aim of the church. No one who has never bemoaned this act of the Reformers has a right to rejoice in it with Reformation joy; for by it—so far as we and our congregations are concerned—a door of conscience was bolted against the attempt to temporize with Reality.

How incomparably more securely, uninterruptedly, and confidently the other church goes its way, having wisely left this dangerous principle of the Word undiscovered! We have absolutely no occasion, however, to curl our lip at the sense of certainty displayed by Catholics. I think of what a Benedictine from Alsace once told me. It was during the war. One evening, being choirmaster of his monastery, he was chanting the Magnificat with his confrères, when suddenly a French shell crashed through the roof and exploded in the nave of the church. But the smoke thinned away and the Magnificat continued. I ask you whether a Protestant sermon would have been continued. At those times when the task of being *verbi divini ministri,* as we of the Reformed churches say, has worried and oppressed us, have we not all felt a yearning for the "rich services" (schönen Gottesdiensten) of Catholicism, and for the enviable rôle of the priest at the altar? When he elevates the Sanctissimum, with its full measure of that meaning and power which is enjoyed by the material symbol over the symbol of the human word as such, the double grace of the sacrificial death and the incarnation of the Son of God is not only preached in words but consummated under his hands, and he becomes a *creator Creatoris* before the people. I once heard it announced literally at a first mass, "*Le prêtre un autre Jésus Christ!*" If only we might be such too! Even at the mass the Bible is displayed; but how unimportant, how indifferent a matter is the delivery of the sermon based upon it—and yet, again, how completely the poorest of sermonettes is transfigured by the saving radiance of the eucharistic miracle! For the sake of this miracle people actually come alone to church. How evident, obvious, well-ordered, and possible is the way of God to man and of man to God which leads from this center—a way which the Catholic priest may daily walk himself, and indicate to others! How brilliantly the problem is solved there; the need of the people being perfectly understood, it is possible to put them off by a far-reaching and, for the time being, final act; the equilibrium of the soul and the world being seemingly disturbed with great violence, it is unnecessary to disturb it actually; and the final word of redemption is spoken!

We do not wish to cast a shadow on the Gospel content and effect of the Catholic altar sacrament by suggesting that *we* possibly have something better. Yet it is very clear that the Reformation wished to see something better substituted for the mass it abolished, and that it expected that that better thing would be—our preaching of the Word. The *verbum visibile,* the objectively clarified preaching of the Word, is the only sacrament left to us. The Reformers sternly took from us everything but the Bible.

Today we are apparently preparing to turn the clock backwards a bit—to the days before the Reformation at least. We refrain from quoting Question 80 of the Heidelberg Catechism, which boldly dubs the papal mass a "denial of the one sacrifice and passion of Jesus Christ and a cursed remnant of idolatry." Is this because of our increased tolerance and delicacy of feeling or because of the waning of our sense of mission? And what is indicated by our present-day efforts to *broaden* the narrow, fearfully narrow, basis of Protestant Christian preaching? Is it not simply a faint-hearted yearning for something that is not Protestantism? And what could more clearly prove the direction we are traveling than the positively facetious proposal to fill the aching void in the church of the *Word* by a so-called "sacrament of—*silence*?" And is not the deep impression made upon us by Heiler's oppressive book on prayer more remarkable than the book itself? And what is one to think when he hears serious men seriously speak of going back even *behind* Catholicism to introduce the dance into the church?

The perplexity out of which all this arises is only too easy to understand. The door the Reformation bolted against us is not easy to open; after four hundred years the situation has not changed and, though obscured by the incense smoke which diverse folk would like today to see again ascending, it actually can never change; the frontier that separates the land of Jehovah from the land of Baal, if not, as the *figura* indicates, hermetically closed, is none the less effectually closed; and the preaching of the Biblical word of God is laid upon us with the whole dead weight of a historical reality and cannot be shaken off. We are confronted by the difficulty that, instead of lingering in the bright light of the Middle Ages, such as shines from the close of the second part of Goethe's Faust, we are compelled to live in the dusky shadows of the Reformation, though only as Epigoni. This is indeed a difficulty, but no more a difficulty than that other, of which we were speaking a little while ago—that our hearers and erstwhile hearers expect to hear from us and from our church the Word, the answer to the question, *Is it true*? Scylla and Charybdis!—facing each other from opposite sides, between which we must find our way.

* * * * *

But we must look more closely at the side of the situation symbolized on pulpit and altar by the open Bible. What makes it so difficult for us to remain true to the scriptural principle of the Reformation? We must answer honestly. It is not the age of the

Bible, not its remoteness or strangeness (that is, the strangeness of its "philosophy"). It is not the rivalry of Goethe and Schiller, of Buddha and Nietzsche, which tempts us away from it. And as a rule it is not that the abundant flow of our own inspiration, if confined to the ideas of the Bible, would seem a little cramped. No, it is because the Bible has a somewhat uncanny way of bringing into the church situation its *own* new and tense and mighty (*mightier!*) *expectancy*. If the congregation brings to church the great *question* of human life and *seeks* an *answer* for it, the Bible contrariwise brings an *answer*, and *seeks* the *question* corresponding to this answer: it seeks questioning *people* who are eager to find and able to understand that its seeking of them is the very answer to their question. The thoughts of the Bible touch just those points where the negative factors in life preponderate, casting doubt over life's possibilities—the very points, that is, where on the human side we have the question arising, Is it true? The Bible, with uncanny singleness of interest, omits all the stages of human life where this crisis is not yet acute, where a man in unbroken naïveté can still take comfort in the presence of God in the cherry tree, the symphony, the state, or his daily work; but it does become concerned with him, and with weird intensity, at the stage—shall we call it the highest or the lowest?—where doubt has seized him. Even praise and thanksgiving and jubilation and certainty have their place in the Bible not on the hither but on the farther side of the point where man begins to seek, to ask, and to knock; where that last perplexed craving has seized him and leads him, let us say, to church.

To give only one typical illustration—notice where the Bible touches human life in the *Psalms*. Here it comes to men who are clearly conscious of guilt, who are sick, who are oppressed by enemies personal and national, who are aware of their remoteness from God and the things of God, who are in doubt and despair, and faced by vicissitude and death.

The Bible responds without ado to the man who has awakened to a consciousness of his condition and to whom certainty has everywhere begun to waver; and its way of answering him is to ask with him, in its own way,—think of the forty-second Psalm, think of Job—*Is it true?* Is it true that there is in all things a meaning, a goal, and a God?

In two respects the Bible's question differs from and alters that of the awakened man. In the first place, it gives *his* question its first real depth and meaning—and in a way that leads even the most frightened, the most humbled, and the most despairing man on to the edge of a worse abyss than he has dreamed of; in a way that makes gladness and grief, good and bad, light and darkness, Yes and No as we know them, the contradictory elements of our existence, suddenly draw very close together, and our most instant and urgent question seem trivial and die away; in a way that shows us that all our previous questioning has really been preparation and practice for the question of questions which now arises, Are we asking in dead *earnest*? Are we asking after *God*?

When the patient Job pours out his grief, he is thinking evidently of a grief which, humanly speaking, has no end. When Paul speaks of sin he means not the puppet sins with which we torment ourselves, but the sin of Adam in which we are begotten and with which we are born, the sin of which we shall not rid ourselves as long as time shall last. The darkness of this world to which the writings of John refer is not merely the darkness of a night in which and through which there are various friendly candles burning for every one except the most rabidly pessimistic; the reference is properly to that darkness in which the question whether one ought rather to be an optimist or a pessimist is quite beside the point. And when Jesus Christ dies on the cross he asks not simply, Is it true? but "My God, my God, why hast Thou forsaken me?" People have attempted to absolve Jesus from blame for this utterance by the argument, difficult to substantiate, that it was not an expression of real despair—and the fact has been quite overlooked that it was not less but *more* than doubt and despair: as our old dogmatists knew, it was *derelictio,* a being lost and abandoned. To suffer in the Bible means to suffer because of *God;* to sin, to sin against *God;* to doubt, to doubt of *God;* to perish, to perish at the hand of *God*. In other words, that painful awareness of the boundary of mortality which man acquires with more or less certainty in life's rise and fall becomes, in the Bible, the order of the God of holiness; it is the message of the *cross,* and from it, in this life, there is no escape. The cross is the demand of God that we ask about him, about God: it is his declaration that as long as we live, though all other questions may finally be answered, we may not tear ourselves loose and be free from *this* one. Clearly and ever more clearly through the Bible, through both the Old and the New Testaments, this message struggles for a hearing and becomes unambiguous and unmistakable in Jesus Christ. The Bible seeks people who can and will ask about God. It seeks those who are capable of letting their *little* questions—and which of them is *not* little in comparison?—merge in the *great* question about the cross, that is, about God. "Come unto me, all ye that labor and are heavy laden." For what purpose? To "take *my* yoke upon you." It is not obvious, even to the most awakened seekers, that they labor and are heavy laden to the end that they may take *his* yoke, *Christ's* yoke, upon them. Though we may have understood this a thousand times, it is still impossible to understand.

There is a second crucial change which the Bible makes in the awakened consciousness. Our questions about human life, even in their highest forms, are mere questions to which the answers sought are additional and must be matched to them. But as the *Bible* takes these questions, translating them into the unescapable question about God, one simply cannot ask or hear the "question" without hearing the *answer*. The person who says that the Bible leads us to where finally we hear only a great No or see a great void, proves only that he has not yet been led thither. *This* No is really Yes. *This* judgment is grace. *This* condemnation is forgiveness. *This* death is life. *This* hell is heaven. *This* fearful God is a loving father who takes the prodigal in his arms. The crucified is the one raised from the dead. And the explanation of the cross as such is eternal life. No other additional thing needs to be joined to the question. The question is the answer.

This equation is the essence of the whole Bible, but by what truth, what fact, can it be proved? I know no other than the reality of the living God, who *is* what he is, who is self-proved. The Bible disclaims all proofs of God. It witnesses to revelation: we beheld his glory and we beheld it as the answer in the *question*. How could we find out and understand the answer in any other way? But the *answer* is the essence of it. It would be no question if it were not the answer. It is only in order that it may really *be* an answer to man that it must meet him as a question. God is the Yes in its fullness: it is only in order that we may *understand* him as *God* that we must pass through his No. The strait gate leads to life; it is only because it is *this* gate that it must be so narrow. "I will give you rest." "My yoke is easy, and my burden is light." It is only in order that we may know this to be *true* that we must take the yoke and the burden upon us. "When ye shall *search* for me with all your heart, I will be *found* of you, saith the Lord." Only the *Lord* can speak so: only he can reduce seeking and finding, question and answer, to one. But the Bible is witness that he *does* so.

This is what the *other* side of the situation in the church comes to. Have I put it correctly? It is the *greater* expectancy that the *Bible* brings into the situation. It is expectant of people who *in* its question will recognize their own question as well as God's answer—a final answer, which redeems, re-creates, enlivens, and makes happy; an answer which casts the light of eternity upon time and upon all things in time; an answer which generates hope and obedience. It is expectant of people who have eyes to see what eye hath not seen, ears to hear what ear hath not heard, and hearts to understand what hath not entered into the heart of man—people who will and can receive the Holy Spirit as security for what has *not yet* appeared even to the children of God, and has *not yet* appeared to them *because* they are children of God—people who will and can believe in the *promise* in the midst of their need. *God* expects, *God* seeks, such people. In the Bible it is not *we* who seek answers to questions about *our* life, *our* affairs, *our* wants and wishes, but it is the *Lord* who seeks laborers in *his* vineyard. The expectancy brought to the situation by the *congregation,* intense as it may be, is in truth small and insignificant in comparison to that expectancy, as mute as the other but far more real, which comes from the side of the open *Bible.* If the awakening of the people in this situation is significant and striking, it is so only in the light of what God expects there. The reason the human expectancy is to be taken seriously, and cannot be taken seriously enough, is because it is an adumbration of the great expectancy with which God arrives first upon the scene. This is an uncanny situation; who would not recognize it? It is easy to understand why we should like to avoid it. But we cannot kick against the pricks; we are held fast from the very side from which the uncanny element comes originally into the situation, from the Bible side; *we* are held fast, I repeat, by what came over Christianity four hundred years ago.

*　*　*　*　*

The event toward which this expectancy is directed from both sides is Christian preaching. And the man who stands, perhaps not at the center but certainly in the foremost and most exposed position, is the Christian preacher, the minister. As the minister of the people who come or do not come to church on Sunday, he must be the first to give them the *answer*; and as the minister of the Bible he must be the first to be prepared to submit to God's *question* by asking the question about God, without which God's answer cannot be given. If he answers the *people's question* but answers it as a man who has himself been *questioned by God,* then he speaks— the word of God; and this is what the people seek in him and what God has commissioned him to speak. For being truly questioned by God and truly questioning about God, he will know God's answer and so be able to give it to the people, who with *their* question really want *God's* answer, even when they do not realize it. When he does do *that,* what event in the world is more momentous and decisive than Christian preaching?

The whole situation in the church suddenly becomes intelligible if it is seen to be the framework of *this* event; the existence of the minister is justified if he makes himself the servant of this event; and the very act which in Protestantism should form the crux of its service, the sermon as the exposition of Scripture, becomes fraught with meaning, when it is a preaching of the word of God. It is simply a truism that there is nothing more important, more urgent, more helpful, more redemptive, and more salutary, there is nothing, from the viewpoint of heaven or earth, more relevant to the real situation than the speaking and the hearing of the *Word* of God in the originative and regulative power of its truth, in its all-eradicating and all-reconciling earnestness, in the light that it casts not only upon *time* and time's confusions but also beyond, toward the brightness of *eternity,* revealing time and eternity *through* each other and *in* each other—the Word, the Logos, of the Living God. Let us ask ourselves—and, as we do so, think of Jesus Christ—whether the will of God does not drive us, and the plight of man, modern man, here in Germany in 1922, does not call us, toward this event?

What Christian preaching ours would be, if it *were* this event! And that it is, is the promise contained in it: if we do our full work as ministers we can but confirm this promise, for it is *implicit* in our taking seriously the situation in which we find ourselves between the congregation and the Bible. And taking it seriously can be nothing more nor less than seizing upon, believing and trusting in, and being obedient to God's promise, which lies behind it all.

But we must not stop here. *Speaking the word of God* is the *promise* of Christian preaching. Promise is not fulfillment. Promise means that fulfillment is guaranteed us. Promise does not do away with the necessity of believing but establishes it. Promise is *man's* part, fulfillment is *God's.* We can only believe that what is God's is also man's. "*We* have this treasure in *earthen* vessels." No confusing of God's part with man's, of the treasure with the earthen vessel! No one indeed seems to confuse these two so easily as we theologians and careless philosophers, the very ones who ought to know better! But it is clear that even we can speak God's word if we can only believe. The word of God on the lips of a man is an impossibility; it does not happen: no one will ever accomplish it or see it accomplished. The event toward which the expectancy of heaven and of earth is directed is none the less *God's* act.

Nothing else can satisfy the waiting people and nothing else can be the will of God than that he himself should be revealed in the event. But the word of God is and will and must be and remain the word of *God*. When it seems to be something else, however brilliant, however Christian, however Biblical that something else may be, it has ceased to be itself. A too early fulfillment robs us even of the promise.

* * * * *

And now mention must be made of the great *peril* which inheres in the situation of which we have been speaking. Is there not every likelihood that men will seem to have undertaken and—who knows?—accomplished the feat of taking God's word on their lips as their own? To be sure, the more we seem to have done so and the more threatening the actual peril is, the more complete and successful our sermons may appear—and the fuller our churches—and the better blessed and more satisfying our activity. But what does blessing mean? And what, in the ministry, is satisfaction? Do the prophets and apostles, not to speak of Jesus Christ, give us the impression of being people who have succeeded, who could at the end look back upon a blessed and satisfying life? Strange that we do so much better than they! What can it mean? It means above all that we should feel a fundamental alarm. What are you doing, you man, with the word of *God* upon *your* lips? Upon what grounds do you assume the role of mediator between heaven and earth? Who has authorized you to take your place there and to generate religious feeling? And, to crown all, to do so with results, with success? Did one ever hear of such overweening presumption, such Titanism, or—to speak less classically but more clearly—such brazenness! One does not with impunity cross the boundaries of mortality! One does not with impunity usurp the prerogative of God!

But does not the profession of the ministry inevitably involve both? *Is* not the whole situation in the church an illustration of man's chronic presumption, which is really worse here than in any other field? Can a minister be saved? I would answer that with men this is impossible; but with God all things *are* possible. *God* may pluck us as a brand out of the fire. But so far as *we* know, there is no one who deserves the wrath of God more abundantly than the ministers. We may as well acknowledge that *we* are under judgment—and I mean judgment not in any spiritual, religious, or otherwise innocuous sense but in the utmost realism; Moses and

Isaiah, Jeremiah and Jonah knew of a certainty why they did *not* want to enter into the preacher's situation. As a matter of fact, the church is really an impossibility. There can be no such thing as a minister. Who dares, who can, preach, knowing what preaching is? The situation of crisis in the church has not yet been impressed upon us with sufficient intensity. One wonders if it ever will be.

Is there any one of the many objections which today are raised against the church and against Christianity by their detractors, both educated and uneducated, which does not simmer down to the very objection which we should have to raise against ourselves if we were more clearly conscious of what as ministers we are daring to do? Whether the objections are fair or unfair, shrewd or silly, ought we not in a way to accept them, as David did the stone-throwing of Shimei the son of Gera, with the thought that there is a reason behind them—rather than to rush to defend ourselves against them in the armor of a subtle but questionable apologetic? Would it not be wiser to let certain storms which threaten quietly work out upon us their purifying strength than to meet them at once with an ecclesiastical counterstorm? Would it not be better for us, instead of reading ministerial, theological, and similar periodicals, to take up Feuerbach, for example, and to read him without trying continually to escape from his snares? If God has chosen us— miracles being *possible* with *him*—and if he will justify us *as* ministers even *in* the church situation, we may be certain that he will do so only *when* we come under *judgment*, when the church comes under judgment, and when our ministry comes under judgment. For it is not until then that we can obtain the promise, that we can believe.

It is ours to take upon ourselves the great question of God, the question which utterly humbles and even kills all flesh, and to do so not in a comfortable, expansive way as men in general might, but—since nobody is a man in general—in our very capacity as priests, as mediators. It is not until then that we shall be capable of being "priests" (Geistliche), that is, of hearing God's *answer* and then answering the question of *men*. Not until our preaching arises from need will our work become a *mission*. Mission alone can legitimize preaching.

There is a lesson for us in the sixteenth chapter of Leviticus: it was the law that on the great day of atonement the high priest should bring a bullock, kill it, and offer it as a sin offering to "make an atonement for *himself*, and for *his* house" *before* offering the goat as a sin offering for the people. Would it not be wise for us to offer up the bullock—and in the meanwhile at least to let the goat live? Have we not been refusing to admit that judgment must begin at the house of God? Have we not been refusing to acknowledge that we and our calling and our church belong where all flesh must belong? Ought this not to have been the point at which we always *began,* of which we always thought *first, from* which our work in the study and the pulpit took its departure? Have we not been wishing, secretly or openly, for worldly or for Christian reasons, to escape the utter disillusion this entailed? Ought we, taking our stand against the world, against unchristian views of life, and against the unreligious masses, to have been flinging out accusations which we had not first applied in their full weight to our own selves—and applied so forcibly as to have squeezed out of us what breath we had for condemning others? Ought we to have been speaking of the sin *Eritis sicut Dei,* without first having said each to himself: *Thou* art the man, thou *more* than all others? And if we ought not, how can we but *be* under the judgment from which only the word of God can extricate and save us, as it can extricate and save *all* flesh? Our refusal to examine ourselves first can mean only that we are *not* satisfied with the promise, that we will *not* believe. How then can we hear and speak the word of *God* or our congregations learn to know and live it? How can any one believe us? How can we preach the forgiveness of sins, the resurrection of the body, and the life everlasting—not merely in words but in reality?

We are *worthy* of being believed only as we aware of our unworthiness. There is no such thing as *convincing* utterance about God except as Christian preaching feels its *need,* takes up its *cross*, and asks the *question* which God demands in order to be able to answer it. From this need we may not hope to flee.

The charge that young Luther brought against the Catholicism of the Middle Ages was that it desired to be *free* from this need. Almost every page of his exposition of the Psalms and the Epistle to the Romans speaks of the sense of alarm which seized him when he made the discovery that what the Scholastics and the Mystics were cultivating, as he put it in the Heidelberg Disputation of 1518, was a *theologia gloriae,* a naïve religious will to be edified, a *flight* from the question which God demands in order to be able to give his answer. *Here* he entrenched himself; and his theology, which became that of the Reformation and which we claim as the basis of our own, he defined as a *theologia crucis*. This arises at the point where man has sacrificed his highest and best—*just* that,—where he has delivered it up to be judged and *so* has laid hold of the promise; and this he does on the strength of his faith and on the strength of his *faith alone,* because he himself has been laid hold of by the unsubstantiated, self-substantiated mercy of God, because *Christ* the *crucified* is, in his *derelictio,* the bearer of the promise. "It is he that hath made us and not we ourselves: we are his people and the sheep of his pasture." But how are the people to hear this in the Christian preaching of the church, if the church itself has not yet heard it?

* * * * *

Is our own basically a *theologia crucis*? This, it seems to me, is the question of destiny which our Protestant churches face today; and today, in bitter truth, we have occasion to observe what the cross is.

We need today ministers who take their work *seriously;* but this seriousness must concern itself for the *inwardness* of the church and in no sense for the church itself. The ministers who are concerned for the church are no longer equal to the almost infinite seriousness of our present condition. We need ministers who are *efficient,* but not necessarily efficient in *business*. Ministration of the word is not *ad*ministration, however smoothly it may go. Its efficiency will have to prove itself in situations into which in business only the inefficient are usually drawn—in failure and ineffectualness, in the most severe isolation, and in conclusions which seem forever negative. We need ministers who are *devout*—provided devotion means obedience to the call, Follow *me*, which may perhaps lead us away from everything that the conservative or the liberal call devotion.

What ought seriousness, efficiency, and devotion to mean in a basic *theologia crucis*? For us they must mean in any case a resolute leave-taking of everything that partakes of the nature of the Catholic altar sacrament. In this most ingenious symbol of its sovereignty, the church depicts its fancied *escape* from judgment, though its escape is actually from *grace;* it is not satisfied with the promise but must possess, enjoy, and experience the fulfillment— to *experience* it, as if the way to the experience of fulfillment did not lie through the death of all human sovereignty, and first of all that of the church! Under no circumstances and in no sense ought we to desire to be *creatores Creatoris*. Ours is not to give *birth* to God but to give *testimony* of him. Whatever is of the nature of the altar sacrament is a *flight* from the need of Christian preaching, and therefore a flight from its *promise*. Let us not deceive ourselves; there are many things of this nature which for some time have seemed not at all Catholic but very evangelical and even very modern. I leave it to you to consider whether something of this nature has not penetrated into our most ordinary homiletic and pastoral activities, into our *traditional* church forms, and even more into our *newer,* and most of all into our *newest* efforts in the realm of form—not to mention a penetration, a deep penetration, into our systematic and historical presentation of theology of all types. It enters everywhere that an asset appears which is not also a liability, everywhere that there is haste without waiting, giving without taking, possessing without dispensing, knowing without not-knowing, doing right without doing wrong, sitting still without rising up, or a present kingdom of heaven without the "poor in spirit." No one can really arrive by this means at certainty and victory. For God, from whom certainty and victory come, is one who dwells in a light which no one can approach unto, and he desires to be recognized and worshipped as such. This is the crisis of Christian preaching.

You will note that in speaking of this fatal tendency I make no direct charge against any one. The matter lends itself ill to the making of charges. For I am aware that much may be said and done which at first glance seems to come within a hairbreadth of this fatal tendency, but which none the less arises from the need and therefore shares the promise of Christian preaching. All praise to whatever possesses this character, be it said or done today by the Right or the Left, by low churchmen or high churchmen, by old or young! *Fiat, fiat*!

> *"One fate is not decreed for all.*
> *Let each man, on his separate way,*
> *Let each man labor as he may,*
> *And standing, guard him lest he fall."*

The matter cannot be settled by setting up, in opposition to this or that, a new affirmative, or even a negative. It can be settled only by allowing *thought* to enter into what is said and done—thought concerning the one thing needful and inescapable which confronts us pastors and theologians, and our churches with us, in greater reality today than ever before. And thought means *recollecting* the *meaning* of what we say and do. When thought enters in, perhaps this or that will cease to be said and done or begin to be said and done otherwise than heretofore. Perhaps the same thing will need to be said and done with another meaning than it has had. Thought means fundamentally neither affirmation nor negation, but only—a marginal note, a "pinch of spice." Thought, in any case, need not separate us from each other, even if its theoretical and practical results are not the same with all of us. I hold therefore that it must be fundamentally possible in the long last to come to an agreement in thought even with a Catholic theologian, and even over the subject of the altar sacrament—without any accompanying desire to take it from him. The need and promise of Christian preaching, the divine judgment and divine justification, are in the last analysis the life even of the church of the Council of Trent. There is so much of the Catholic in us Protestants that we cannot suppose that the ideals of the Reformation are totally dead in the other church. Little entitles us to suppose so. Supposing so only makes a *rapprochement* between us the more difficult. But that *rapprochement* is made no less difficult by our supposing that the ideals of the Reformation are somehow obvious in us and to us. They are obvious *neither* in us *nor* to us. One can *not* take it for granted that we know them and that they are alive in us. Today, tomorrow, and continually, they must be revivified in us. Reformation is truly no less possible and necessary today than it was four hundred years ago. Reformation takes place where thought takes place.

If today you feel the longing for reformation more as a bitter anxiety than as anything else, remember that it may not be otherwise. According to the eighth chapter of Romans, there is more hope when one sighs *Veni Creator Spiritus,* than when he exults as if the spirit were already his. You have been introduced to "my theology" if you have heard this sigh. If you have heard it and understood it—and understood it perhaps better than you cared to—then you will also understand why I should like to close with a confession of *hope*. It consists of a few sentences taken from Calvin's commentary on Micah 4:6 ("In that day, saith the Lord, will I assemble her that halteth, and I will gather her that is driven out, and her that I have afflicted"). "Although the church," Calvin comments, "is at the present time hardly to be distinguished from a dead or at best a sick man, there is no reason for despair, for the Lord raises up his own suddenly, as he waked the dead from the grave. This we must clearly remember, lest, when the church fails to shine forth, we conclude too quickly that her light has died utterly away. But the church in the world is so preserved that *she* rises *suddenly* from the dead. Her very preservation through the days is due to a succession of such miracles. Let us cling to the remembrance that she is not without her resurrection, or rather, not without her many resurrections. *"Tenendum est, ecclesiae vitam non esse absque resurrectione, imo absque multis resurrectionibus."*

25

KARL BARTH

The Law of Service

1. In the light of its basic law, the law to be sought and established and executed in the Christian community must always have the character and intention of a law of service. It must always be law within an order of ministry. The community of Jesus Christ, as the body of which He is the Head, exists as it serves Him. And its members, Christians, as members of this His body, exist as—united by the service which they render to their Lord— they serve one another. This first and decisive determination of all Church law has its basis in the fact that the Lord Himself, who rules the community as the Head of His body, "came not to be ministered unto, but to minister" (Mk. 10:45). Revealed as such in, His resurrection, and ruling as such by His Holy Spirit, He is the King and Lord of the world and the community as the One who on the cross was defeated and in that way victorious, humbled and in that way exalted. He is the King and Lord as the One who serves His Father, and therefore His own and all men. It is as this One who serves that He rules and requires obedience. He is not, there- fore, one of the lords who do not serve but only rule and leave the serving to others. He is the Lord as He is first the servant of God and all others. The two things cannot be separated or reversed. It is not the case that He rules and at the same time serves, or serves and at the same time rules. It is as He serves that He rules. It is as the humiliated Son of God that He is the exalted Son of Man. Thus the obedience of His community corresponding to His rule can only be service, and the law which obtains in it, in accordance with the basic law which consists in the lordship of Jesus Christ estab- lished within it, can only be the law of service. The community attains its true order as His body when its action is service. And its

---

From Karl Barth, *Church Dogmatics*, IV/2, pp. 690–695. © T. & T. Clark Ltd., Edinburgh. Used by permission of the Publisher.

members, Christians, attain their true order when they serve. In the Christian community, unlike all other human societies, there is no distinction between privileges and duties, claims and obligations, or dignities and burdens. There can be privileges and claims and dignities only in and with the duties and obligations and burdens of service. "And whosoever of you will be the chiefest, shall be the servant of all" (Mk. 10:44). From the point of view of the community and all its members, sanctification means exaltation, but because it is exaltation in fellowship with the One who came to serve it is exaltation to the lowliness in which He served and still serves, and rules as He serves. As in its Lord, and typically for all mankind, the community participates in this exaltation and rules with Him, both as a whole and in each of its members it can only serve, and in the law which obtains within it—Church law—the only real question is that of the correctness of its service.

This determination is (1) unequivocal, non-dialectical and irreversible. In the community it is not at all the case that the law of service carries with it an accompanying law of rule, as if the burden which has to be borne by and within it were bound up with all kinds of dignities, or the obligation laid on it and each of its members authorised all kinds of claims, or its active commitment to service were the basis of all kinds of privileges. This may well be the case, and quite in order, in other human societies. But it is far otherwise in the Christian community. Upon it, and each of its members, there is laid a demand—the demand that it should serve. Its whole law consists and is fulfilled in the fact that it stands under this demand. The question which arises is that of the right form in which both as a whole and in each of its members it must correspond to this demand. For and in the community a demanding which is abstracted from and even in some way conflicts with the fact that it is demanded is quite unlawful. There can be no autonomous demanding. For the community and each of its members legitimate demanding can be only the demanding of that which is necessary to fulfil the common requirement of service. The dignity can be only that of the burden, the claim that of the obligation and the privilege that of the fulfilment of duty. The rule can be only that which in itself and as such is service—and only service. Unequivocally, and unconfused by any speculative end, the freedom of the community and each of the Christians assembled within it is the freedom to serve.

No true church law can hesitate to take into account the unequivocal nature of this determination. No true Church law can follow the example of the law of other societies and give place to a demanding which conflicts with the fact that it stands under a demand; to a rule which is distinct from service. No true Church law can open the door, or leave it open, for this kind of rule. To be sure, there is rule in the community. There are also privileges and claims and dignities. There are demands which the community has to address to its members and its members to the community or to one another. There may even be demands which one community has to make on another, or which have to be made on many communities by a central authority, or which have to be made on the state or other worldly partners. But they must all be closely and strictly scrutinised—and this is where the true Church law that we seek must give guidance and direction—to ensure that it is not a question of the abstract demanding of dominion, or the abstract assertion of privileges and claims and dignities, but only the demanding of service, i.e., that which is made exclusively in the context and fulfilment of service, and expresses only the fact that a demand is laid on the community and all its members. This kind of demanding— and only this—can and should be recognised and regulated and protected in true canon law. On the other hand, the demanding which aims only to assert or secure the community or someone within it is not merely to be checked but eliminated. Neither for the community as such nor for any of its members can true Church law be anything but a law of service. The community knows and takes into account the fact that there are other laws in other spheres. But its own law is a law of service.

This determination is (2) total. That is to say, in the life of the Christian community it is not the case that there is one sphere which is ordered by the law of service but side by side with this there are others in which it does not have the character and intention of service but stands under another determination or is open to many different and even perhaps changing determinations. Service is not just one of the determinations of the being of the community. It is its being in all its functions. Nothing that is done or takes place can escape the question whether and how far within it the community serves its Lord and His work in the world, and its members serve one another by mutual liberation for participation in the service of the whole. That which does not stand the test of this question but is done merely because, even though it does not serve, it has always been done or is regarded as a possible line of action, is quite unlawful, and it must either be jettisoned as ines-

sential and harmful ballast or made to serve (which is often easier
said than done). Either way, there must be no dead corners where
an alien lord pursues his doubtful or at any rate useless way. The
community has neither time nor strength to waste on *allotria*. Nor
must this question of service be put only by way of criticism. It can
be a diviner's rod as well as a measuring rod. There are many old
and disused and unjustifiably obsolete possibilities of service to be
re-discovered and revitalised, and many new and unjustifiably disregarded possibilities to be discovered afresh and realised. When
can the community ever be content with what it is doing, as though
this were the totality of the service required, and that which is right
and lawful for it and within it were either exhausted or on the point
of exhaustion with present-day expansion? It is not the community
itself which constitutes the limits of the totality in which it has to
serve its Lord and its members must serve one another. It is its
living Lord Himself, whose call to halt and advance it has to
follow as His living community. Thus it may never imagine that it
knows already and finally what is the totality in which it has to
serve. It must know only that it has always to serve with the
totality of its being and action.

We may recall in this connexion how futile have been the
attempts to use the terms διακονία and *ministerium* to denote
particular functions within the life of the community: diaconate
to describe the loving assistance extended by the Church to the
sick and the poor, etc.; and ministry the regular preaching office. Surely the freedom to serve granted to the community and
practised by it cannot be narrowed down in this way. Surely its
whole action can and must be a diaconate and the *ministerium
verbi divini*. Surely there are no spheres in which this is not the
case. Surely there can be no new activity, in spheres as yet
undisclosed, which will not necessarily take the form of service.
True Church law must guard against the emergence of these
false distinctions; and where they have been made already it
must remove them. It must declare and maintain the radical
openness of the whole life of the community for its determination to service. To take one or two examples, Church administration (which will largely be concerned with financial questions) is also a question of service, and it cannot therefore be
regarded as self-evidently autonomous and suddenly bureau-
cratised or commercialised. Or again, the Church's scholarship
(theology) is also a question of service, so that though it may
and must claim the widest possible freedom in the choice and

application of its methods there can be no question of any other freedom than that of serving—not the Church, let alone any authority within it, but in the Church. Again, there can be no question of an autonomy of philosophical or historical interests from this standpoint. The same is true of its discipline, in the order and exercise of which the motto: *fiat iustitia et pereat mundus,* is quite illegitimate because it is incompatible with the whole character of this activity as service. And because in the direction of the Church's affairs we are still in the sphere of service, it is better either to avoid altogether terms like monarchy, aristocracy or democracy, with their clear suggestion of the exercise of power, or at any rate to use them in such a way that in the understanding of the rule of the Church on a Christo-cratic basis "rule" is always firmly interpreted as outstanding service.

Finally (3) the determination of the law which obtains in the Church as the law of service is universal. That is to say, as there is no sphere of the Church's activity to which this determination does not apply, there are no individuals within the community who are exempt from service or committed and engaged to serve only to a less serious degree. To be a Christian, and therefore a saint in the communion of saints, is to serve in and with the Christian commu-nity. All Christians do not have to serve equally, i.e., in the same function. But they all have to serve, and to do so in one place with the same eminence and responsibility as others do at other places. As the community exists only as the body of its Head Jesus Christ, so it exists only in the totality of the members of this body, which as the *communio sanctorum* is not a collective where the individual is of no importance because if he dropped out he could at once be replaced by someone else. In the life of the Christian community each individual has his own necessary place, and the service of each individual is indispensable to that of the whole. This service is not the privilege or concern of a few whose selection stands in marked contrast with the exemption of the rest as a lowlier or better portion. Exalted into fellowship with Jesus Christ, each Christian as such is set in the lowliness of His service. How then can he be forced or how can he presume to think that he is set there, and therefore claimed, to a less extent than others? At bot-tom, there is something wrong with the community itself if even one of its members has dropped out of its ministry or never had a share in it. At bottom, all the members suffer if even one defaults in this way. This is something which must be avoided at all costs.

In fact, of course, it may well be the case that when some drop out either totally or partially there are others who will make good the service which is not rendered. But when this happens, it points to an emergency and not to the normal state of affairs in the community. Basically, there is neither discharge nor total or partial leave of absence from this service; nor can there be any question of delegation or substitution. Each one is called, with equal seriousness, to play his part, and to do so as if everything depended on him. And the fact that each has his own particular and different part to play, or service to render, cannot mean that those who are particularly responsible at one point have no responsibility but can leave it to those responsible at another. The service of the community is a differentiated service. But it is a differentiated whole. Hence the concern of one, quite irrespective of the fact that it is his concern in particular, is also the concern of others. None can try to serve in his own small sphere without considering all the other spheres for which his own service will always have indirect significance, and may even acquire and have direct significance as in the pursuit of his concerns he is also involved in the problems of these other spheres as well. It will thus be an emergency and not the normal state if the differentiation and distribution of service leads in practice to disintegration; if it means that the individual and different ministries flourish in mutual unconcern, robbing one another of soil and air and sun like the plants in an ill-tended garden, and generally competing with one another. All Christians equally will constantly need remission of their sins in their cooperation in service. But they must not calculate upon this in advance in the sense that it leads them to regard what is really an emergency as justifiable, and to proclaim it as the normal state. If we ask concerning law and order as we must, we cannot argue that we are even partially discharged from the obligation to serve because others can replace us, or that we have no responsibility for all other spheres because we are competent only in our own. Law and order in the community are never the particular priesthood of a few, but the universal priesthood of all believers.

It will be the task of true Church law to guard and constantly to rescue this truth from distortion and oblivion. Even linguistically, it must avoid the fatal word "office" and replace it by "service," which can be applied to all Christians. Or, if it does use it, it can do so only on the understanding that in the Christian community either all are office-bearers or none; and if all, then only as servants. Even where this is recognised in theory, true canon law will have to be all the more vigilant against practical clericalism: against every distinction between the active and the inactive (or passive) Church; against every separation into the ruling and the ruled, the teaching and the hearing, the confessing and the established, the taxable and the enfranchised community. Whatever may be the actual circumstances in true Church law we cannot regard them as descended from heaven and therefore normative. The unity and universality of the Church's ministry will always be, not a beautiful ideal, but the absolute law of the community, and therefore that which must be maintained as the *conditio sine qua non* of its life. Distinctions of this kind cannot, therefore, be justified and sanctified. On the contrary, there is a constant summons and direction to overcome them: within the limits imposed by time and expedience, but clearly and progressively within these limits; *suaviter in modo,* but *fortiter in re,* uncompromisingly as regards the thing itself. And if it is one of the duties of canon law to regulate the distribution of different functions to different members of the community, clearly declaring that they are qualified and instituted to serve in this or that sphere, in the unavoidable distinctions which this involves it must see to it that there is no possibility of a departmental isolation and autonomy or a struggle for power and prestige; that with all the respect for particular gifts and tasks and their limits the responsibility of all for all and for the whole is maintained and asserted; that the disorder which Paul reproved in 1 Cor. 14 in relation to the gift of speaking with tongues (which had achieved a false preeminence in Corinth) does not arise and gain the upper hand in very different forms which are perhaps more obvious and tempting in different circumstances. It is the task of canon law to guarantee to the community the freedom to obey, and therefore the peace and harmony of service.

26

THOMAS F. TORRANCE

Service in Jesus Christ

THE SCOTTISH DIVINES OF THE SIXTEENTH CENTURY USED TO DIS-
tinguish between what all Christians should do 'of their charity' and
what some have to do 'of authority'. That was a distinction regarding not so much the *kind* of service as the *mode* of service rendered.
All members of the Body of Christ are constrained through love to
bear witness to Him and to pray for others, but some have this
ministry laid upon them as a special task, so that they fulfil it not
only out of love but in obedience to a specific commission from the
Lord and with the definite authority of that commission behind
them. It was this authoritative 'sending', they held, which distinguished the 'solemn' preaching of God's Word, accompanied by
the divine 'seals', from the service of all the faithful in their proclaiming of Christ and His Gospel. While that is no doubt a valuable
distinction, it would be wrong if it were interpreted to mean that,
in contrast to the special ministry within the Church, the service of
all members of the Body of Christ is to be referred back only to the
free movement of their love and to be understood as its spontaneous expression. The great characteristic of all Christian service or
διακονία is that while it is certainly fulfilled under the constraint
of the love of Christ it is a service *commanded* by Him and laid by
Him as a *task* upon every baptized member of His Body.

We must not forget that even love is commanded by God. As
Jesus Himself taught us, the love of God and the love of our
neighbour are the supreme commandments upon which all the
others depend, and in our love to Him we are bound in a relation of
unconditional obedience to His commandments, among which is
the specific commandment to love one another. This is the context

From James I. McCord and T. H. L. Parker, Editors, *Service in Christ,* pp.
1–16. © Epworth Press, 1966; William B. Eerdmans Publishing Company,
Grand Rapids, 1966. Used by permission of the Publishers.

in which διαχονία is to be understood. Christian service is commanded of us. It is to be referred back to the Lordship of Christ and is to be understood as the pure service rendered to the Lord by those who are His servants.

In the New Testament two principal terms are used to speak of the servants of Christ, δοῦλοι and διάχονοι, slaves and waiters. The former refers to status rather than function and describes the relationship that determines the very structures of existence in Christ. The δοῦλος lives under the total claim of God and is completely subordinate to Jesus Christ, to whom he belongs body and soul. The latter refers to function rather than status and describes the service of those who exist in an absolute relationship to Christ as Lord. The διάχονος is one who has been given a task by his Master, and who does only what is commanded by Him, not what he thinks out for himself. The servants of Christ (whether we think of them as δοῦλοι or διάχονοι) are not their own masters, for they belong to Another. They do not carry out their own wishes or minister to their own glory, but they do only what they are told and serve only the glory of their Lord. The way in which the New Testament uses δοῦλος and διάχονος lets us see that Christian service or διαχονία is not something that is accidental to the Christian, but essential to him, for it is rooted in his basic structure of existence as a slave of Jesus Christ. It is a form of service in which he is not partially but completely committed in the whole of his being before God, and which he discharges not occasionally but continuously in the whole of his existence as a follower of Jesus Christ.

We would misunderstand this servant-existence of Christ's followers if we did not see that their servitude in the Lord is the mode of their freedom, and their service of the Lord is the movement of their love, the true freedom and true love into which they have been redeemed. It is Christ's to command and theirs to obey, but both commandment and obedience are modes of the divine love in Jesus Christ in which service and freedom are the obverse of each other. But we would also misunderstand Christian service if we construed it simply as the expression of Christian love, intrinsically intelligible in its own requirement and inherently compelling as an end in itself, for then we would detach Christian service from its heteronomous ground in the Lord Himself and give it a basis in the autonomous existence of the Christian; we would think of it as arising out of himself and explain it as the Christian's self-imposed way of life in which his existence comes to its truest self-expression. Christian service is not the service of love for love's sake, but, service of love though it is, the duty rendered by *servants* to their *Lord* in obedience to His commandment. Hence while it is fulfilled in the form of service to others in the world, it is not fulfilled as something they have freely chosen for themselves but as a task which Christ has laid upon them in the entirely new situation that has overtaken them in Him. Faithful servants do not arrogate to themselves the authority for their actions, nor do they assume responsibility for the results of their service. They act simply as servants who live in subjection to their Lord, but who are free from the necessity, and the anxiety, of having to justify their service. They act responsibly by doing obediently what He commands, and act freely in leaving to their Lord alone the responsibility for the consequences of the service He has laid upon them. Obedience is demanded without any secondary motive, and likewise service is rendered without secondary motive, without any thought of claim upon the Lord and without any thought even of thanks from those to whom service is rendered.

Διακονία is pure service fulfilled in accordance with the requirements of an external Authority, that of the Lord, yet διακονία is intrinsically related to that Authority through its content of love. The content of the commandment and the content of the service in obedience to it derive from the self-giving of God Himself in Jesus Christ the Lord. He gives what He commands and commands what He gives. He commands a service of love, and He gives the love that empowers that service. It is this inner relation between commandment and love, or between 'authority' and 'charity', that is so distinctive of service in Jesus Christ.

Διακονία of this unique kind is possible only because the Lord Himself has come in the form of a servant, incorporating our servant-existence in Himself and incarnating among us the self-giving of God in sheer love and compassion for mankind. He came not to be served but to serve, to live out on earth the life of unconditional obedience to the Father in heaven and the life of pure love poured out to all men in unrestrained mercy. He was Himself the complete embodiment of the commandment of love and of the love commanded within our human existence, and as such He constitutes in Himself the ultimate source for the inner relation between commandment and love and the creative ground of all true Christian service. This is particularly apparent in the Sermon on the Mount, which is at once the self-portrait of our Lord in His life on earth as Son of Man and the promulgation of the will of the Father as unconditionally binding on all men. This is the life of the Servant: 'Be ye therefore perfect as your Father in heaven is perfect.' This is the service of the Lord: 'Be ye therefore merciful as your Father also is merciful.' It is only in this Jesus that we learn what διακονία really is, the loving service in mercy that looks for no reward beyond the knowledge that we do what is commanded of us and looks for no thanks from those to whom mercy is extended, but it is only because this Jesus has made our cause His very own, sharing our existence in servitude and sharing with us His own life of love, that we may and can engage in this kind of διακονία in Him.

Our particular concern here, however, is not with the structure of the Christian's existence as δοῦλος of Jesus Christ and therefore with the general ethos of life in Him, but with the form of the Christian's service as διάκονος of Jesus Christ and therefore with the specific function of life in Him. That is to say, we are concerned with διακονία in its concrete sense as *deaconing,* both as the charge which Christ lays upon the Christian community and as the office to which some are called within the community. Διακονία describes not only the relationship of service to which the whole membership of the Church and specific individuals within it bear to Jesus Christ, but the form which that relationship takes in the mutual service of members to one another and in their service to their fellow men in the world. It is natural that at this point the spotlight, so to speak, should fall upon the *deacon* himself, for it is his specific office, as a humble respresentative of the people of God, to prompt them in their response to Christ and His Gospel and to seek the fruit of that response in their life of deaconing toward their fellow men, and thus in his special vocation as a deacon to fulfil in an exemplary way the kind of διακονία we are all called to exercise in Jesus Christ. It was for this reason that the Early Church saw delineated in the deacon's office more than anywhere else the likeness of Jesus Christ the Servant of God.

II

Before we consider this diaconal ministry we must examine its source and ground in Jesus Christ, for it was the kind of person He was and the kind of ministry He undertook that determined the form and mode of all Christian service. He was sent by the Father to carry out the redemption of human existence, not by dealing with it from the outside but by operating from within it, not by the sheer fiat of divine power but by humble acts of service in all the weakness and frailty of human creaturehood, i.e. as a Man among men, holding messianic office and exercising ministerial function. And so He came qualified by His incarnation to act for the human race within its structures and limitations, and consecrated in His capacity as a humble representative of the people for messianic office within their conditions of alienation and subjection. Hence His mission took both a human and a menial form, the ministry of the Son of Man and of the Servant of the Lord, the *Christos*. Now, we have been accustomed to expound this ministry of Christ in terms of His threefold office as the anointed Prophet, Priest and King, but this has tended to obscure or to discount two essential aspects of His ministry: (*a*) that He fulfilled His ministry as a human office within the conditions of the community which He served and sustained by direct personal and individual acts on His part; and (*b*) that He gave this ministry content and pattern by deeds of love and compassion in the healing and succouring of sick and suffering and outcast human beings. That is to say, the *diaconal* nature and significance of our Lord's ministry of mercy have tended to fall out of the picture, so that the Church throughout history has had great difficulty in relating to their proper source and ground not only the diaconal office within the Church but the deaconing of the whole community.

It is to this neglected aspect of Christ's ministry that we turn our attention in order to lay bare its permanent significance for Christian διακονία. Christ was Himself the διάκονος *par excellence* whose office it was not only to prompt the people of God in their response to the divine mercy and to be merciful themselves, not only to stand out as the perfect model or example of compassionate service to the needy and distressed, but to provide in Himself and in His own deeds of mercy the creative ground and source of all such διακονία. He was able to do that because in Him God Himself condescended to share with men their misery and distress, absorbed the sharpness of their hurt and suffering into Himself, and poured Himself out in infinite love to relieve their need, and He remains able to do that because He is Himself the outgoing of the innermost Being of God toward men in active sympathy and compassion, the boundless mercy of God at work in human existence, unlimited in His capacity to deliver them out of all their troubles. Thus through the Incarnation it is revealed to us that God in His own Being is not closed to us, for He has come to share with us the deepest movement of His divine heart, and so to participate in our human nature that the heart of God beats within it. We know that in the springs of His own eternal Life God is ever open and ready and eager to share the weakness and sorrow and affliction of others and to spend Himself in going to their relief and in saving them. It is the very property of God's nature to be merciful, and in mercy it is that nature that He has come to share with men in Jesus, that they, too, may be merciful as He is merciful.

This is mercy that is quite limitless in its extent, mercy that will not stop short at any point in being merciful. It is not just mercy to man in his creaturely weakness and abject need, but mercy freely and unstintingly extended to him at his wickedest and worst, in his revolt from the divine love and his opposition to the divine grace; mercy that regards man's resistance to God's mercy and man's inability to be merciful as his most desperate affliction and his greatest need. It is in man's proud contradiction of God's love and in his contempt of mercy, in man's sin and guilt, that the real sting of his misery lies, but it is precisely at that point of ultimate extremity, in the terrible sharpness of his distress, that God's mercy is extended and refuses to be limited even by man's arrogant scorn and refusal of it. But this is mercy that operates by stopping to suffer all the worst that man can do and be, by entering into his revolted and alienated existence and by dealing with sin from within the depths of human life, by attacking and vanquishing guilt from the inside of its own movement, imparting itself where there is no mercy, until it begets mercy even where it has been scorned.

Now, what distresses God so deeply as He looks upon man in his fearful condition is not simply his sickness and pain, nor even the torment of anxiety that gnaws at his inner being, but the fact that in his hostility to God man has become possessed of sin in his very mind and is caught in the toils of a vast evil will that extends far beyond him, and what vexes God also is that man's existence breaks up under the pressure of his guilt in it all and under the threat of the divine judgement upon him. In view of this tragic state the mercy of God takes on a dynamic and creative form in miraculous acts of grace and power in which He allies Himself with man against the evil that has entrenched itself within him and against the threat of demolition that has come upon him. That is what we see actually going on in the miracles of Jesus in which He was at work reclaiming lost humanity, not by accusing men in their sickness and sin but by shouldering all their ἀσθένεια upon Himself, i.e. not by throwing the responsibility back upon them but by taking their responsibility on Himself. That is surely the most miraculous thing about the healing acts of Jesus, the fact that in Him God has come into our enslaved existence in such a way as to make Himself responsible for men and even to assume their sin and culpability upon Himself. That is why there took place in Jesus such a struggle with evil, a struggle that was waged between God and evil power not only in the heart and mind of man but in his bodily and historical existence, and a struggle to reclaim the existence of man as human being from its subjection to futility and negation.

That is the pitiful condition of man that lies at the root of his anxiety, for his deepest being is menaced by chaos and slips away from him into corruption and destruction, since his existence is subjected to vanity in its contradiction of God and in its judgement by God. Here God's mercy takes a real form, for it is of the sheer mercy of God that He enters into this very being and existence of man under the dominion of evil power and under the doom of unavoidable destruction, and takes this human being and existence upon Himself. That is to say, God penetrates into the very negation of evil as it is entrenched in man, suffers it in Himself, and so, as it were (how can we find words to express what is so unutterable here?), 'hazards' His own existence and being as God for the sake of man. Moreover, He enters into this banned and sentenced state of man to live in it precisely *as man* under all the assaults of evil, within the entire limitation of the creature exposed to evil power and to the judgement of divine Holiness, in order to struggle with evil and vanquish it just where it has dug itself in so deeply, in the self-will and resistance of the creature toward God, and in the obdurate and brazen character of its hostility gained under God's rejection.

That is the meaning of the incarnate life and ministry of the Son of God and the whole passion of His existence as Man among men, made under the Law, and obedient unto death, where evil pays its fullest wages and delivers its ultimate assault upon God's creatures and where that assault gains its fateful force from the very judgements directed against it. No wonder St Paul insisted that our sin gains its strength from the very Law of God! That is why the 'hazard' to which God submits as He stakes His own being on our behalf and for our salvation comes not from the attack of evil itself but from the judgement and negation of evil—it is that fact that makes the Cross and its *Eli, Eli, lema sabachthani* so indescribably terrible, the sheer anguish of God bowed under His own judgement on sin, a judgement not mitigated in the slightest but utterly fulfilled. Thus the existence of man into which God enters, and within which He lives as Son of Man, is a lost existence that is already breaking up and crumbling away not only under the negation of evil but under the negation of the divine judgement, where the rejection of evil serves to harden and make final the threat to demolish human being. It is into that dark and doomed existence under the divine judgement and into its corruption and destruction under negation that God enters in unutterable mercy in order to save mankind.

Now we can grasp something of the extreme gravity of man's plight, and the nature and extent of his need in the inseparability of his spiritual and physical existence and in the disintegration of his whole creaturely being as man before God. Now we can understand also something of what lay behind the Cross and the descent of the Saviour into our bottomless pit of evil and guilt and death, and so of what was involved in every act of healing and mercy in which Jesus through sharing our human existence sought to release distressed humanity from its subjection to evil and vanity, from its imprisonment in chaos and disorder and disintegration, and sought to restore it to the truth of God's creation, in which God affirms as good that which He has made, and so makes good His own Word in the creation of man.

The miracles of Jesus were concerned, then, with the saving of creation. In them God asserted His claim over the human beings He had made and proclaimed His will to maintain them in integrity of being in face of everything that threatened their existence and to restore them to natural life in the freedom and joy of His creation. The miracles reveal not only that the salvation of man involves a total negation of all that is opposed to God's creative purpose but that it can take place only within the healing and remaking of a human being in his actual physical and spiritual existence. Only through the Creator's full participation with us in our human life on earth can atonement for sin and redemption from evil power issue in the actual restoration of what God has made. The miraculous acts of Jesus are thus the luminous points in His ministry, proleptic to His resurrection from the dead, where it is disclosed that the whole life and sojourn of Jesus Christ among us is the absolute miracle within which and through which the New Creation takes place.

Without the Incarnation of the Creator Word the fallen world would crumble away finally and irretrievably into nothingness, for then God would simply let go of what He has made and it would suffer from sheer privation of being. But the Incarnation has taken place—once and for all the Creator Word has entered into the existence of what He has made and bound it up for ever with His own eternal being and life, yet the Incarnation had to mean, in this union of the Creator and the creature, the final negation by God of all that resists His creative will. That is the stupendous and bewildering miracle of Jesus that just because in Him divine nature and human nature are united in the unity of His one Person, the judgement and expiation of sin had to take place as an inner determination of the life He lived among us from birth to death (and how He was straitened until that inexpressible agony was accomplished!); and the new creation took place in the healing and sanctifying and regenerating of the human nature He assumed from our fallen and corrupt existence (and how joyful and radiant was the fulfilment in His resurrection from the grave!). It was through the sovereign παρουσία of the Creator Word within our flesh at the points of enslavement and disintegration that the integrity and wholeness of man in his spiritual and physical being were restored and that human nature was reclaimed for the heavenly Father. That is what Jesus was in His healing and helping acts. He was the Redeemer at work serving the creature from below and from within his broken and divided existence delivering him from inner bondage, redeeming him from deeply-rooted tension and anxiety; the Creator Himself at work re-creating what He had made by sharing in its humble creaturely existence in all its distress and trouble and futility, and sharing with it the healed and sanctified humanity in the perfect life of the Son of Man.

III

This work Jesus Christ fulfilled from two sides: from the side of God toward man, and from the side of man toward God. He came as God Himself, drawing near to man in all His sovereign freedom and grace, bringing His Kingdom to bear directly upon human life and history. He came as the mighty Son breaking into the realm of darkness to deliver men from their thraldom and shame, and to redeem them from the whole power of evil in triumph over sin and guilt and death and hell itself. Yet, Son of God though He was, He came among us as an infant of days in great humility within the darkness and helplessness and poverty of man, in order to work out through His own human life and deeds among us the faithful answer of man to the saving grace and power of God. Hence He came issuing out of human history as a son of Adam, of the seed of David, in order to wrestle with our perverse human nature from within our disobedient life until He had converted it back in obedience to the Father and offered it to Him in the perfection of filial trust and love.

Within this twofold work Christ came identifying Himself with man in his hopeless misery and abject need and making man's cause His very own. By incarnation and atonement He who had been the ground of man's existence from beyond his existence now forged such a bond of union between man and Himself that He became the ground of man's existence in his existence, undergirding and sustaining it from within and from below, overcoming its vanity and privation of being and giving it meaning and reality in Himself. Hence Christ is to be found wherever there is sickness or hunger or thirst or nakedness or imprisonment, for He has stationed Himself in the concrete actualities of human life where the bounds and structures of existence break down under the onslaught of disease and want, sin and guilt, death and judgement, in order that He may serve man in re-creating his relation to God and realizing his response to the divine mercy. It is thus that Jesus Christ mediates in Himself the healing reconciliation of God with man and man with God in the form, as it were, of a meeting of Himself with Himself in the depths of human need. And it is thus that the Father looks upon every man in his need only by looking at him in and through the atoning presence and suppliance of His incarnate Son that meets Him there, for the incarnate Son is the outgoing of His own divine being toward every man and the pouring out of His own eternal love upon him in unrestrained mercy and grace.

As we have already seen, Jesus ministered this divine mercy as a humble representative of the people into which He had incorporated Himself and within which He had been consecrated to the vocation of the Messiah, the Elect One, the Servant. This office of *Christos* He fulfilled as *Man,* not therefore by a compelling display of mighty power, but by meek and personal service as He went about doing good, helping and healing others, and so through fellowship with men in a shared existence. That was His diaconal ministry to men in their enslavement and disintegration which gave meaning again to human life and sustained it in such a relation to the Father that within it atonement could issue in communion and redemption in new creation. It was indeed only in continuous fulfilment of this diaconal ministry that He went forth at last to offer Himself in sacrificial expiation for the sin of mankind, so that when His atoning work was accomplished in death and resurrection and ascension and the message of reconciliation with God through Christ was freely proclaimed, it could be heard and received by men whose very existence was sustained in its relation to God by the hidden presence of the incarnate and crucified and risen Christ within it. That is the permanent and immense significance of His humble διακονία in the flesh, which has been given continuing effect through the pouring out of Christ's Spirit at Pentecost, for it is that διακονία in the flesh that gives material content to His presence through the Spirit.

Now, in the fulfilment of His earthly ministry Jesus drew to Himself a company of disciples whom He formed and instituted into one Body with Himself as the inner nucleus of the Church, incorporating them into His messianic mission and sending them out to exercise His own διακονία in helping and healing, in preaching and forgiving. He set Himself in their midst as their Lord and their Example in the service of mercy. Through their union and communion with Him in His mission He gave structure to the Church He founded upon them and shaped its ministry of the divine mercy in His Name. That is to say, in constituting them as His Body, baptized with His baptism and partaking of His cup, He so assimilated them into His own diaconal life and service on earth that He made διακονία an essential mark of the Church redeemed by Him and built up round His own Person as the Christ. They were in Him a messianic community anointed for service, through sharing in His own anointing and His own self-consecration for mankind. It cannot be doubted that this diaconal character of life and service in Christ is a basic and permanent sign of the Church sanctified in Him, for it is here that Christ's own image and likeness most clearly appear: in the διακονία of the divine mercy within the spiritual and physical existence of man. The Church cannot be in Christ without being in Him as He is proclaimed to men in their need and without being in Him as He encounters us in and behind the existence of every man in his need. Nor can the Church be recognized as His except in that meeting of Christ with Himself in the depth of human misery, where Christ clothed with His Gospel meets with Christ clothed with the desperate need and plight of men. It is never the διακονία of the Church to be itself the *Christ,* but through its humble service to Christ clothed with His Gospel and its service to Christ clothed with the misery of men to seek and to pray for their meeting and so to be in history the bodily instrument which Christ uses in the proclamation of the divine mercy to mankind and in prompting their responses to that mercy.

Διακονία in this sense is not only the charge which Christ has laid upon the whole membership of His Body but an office to which some within it are specially called and for which He bestows through His Spirit the appropriate χάρισμα. Here Jesus stands among us both as the Κύριος who gives the charge and as the supreme Διάκονος whose example is to be followed in all διακονία of the divine mercy. He would have us minister to one another and to others as He ministered to His fellows in the form of a servant.

What were the distinctive features He exhibited in this ministry?

(i) He served God in His mercy and man in his need with the secret of the Cross in His heart. As He went about doing good, He healed not as a doctor but as a Saviour, and He helped not as a wonder-worker but as the Holy One who absorbed into Himself the affliction of men. Though it was by the Finger or Spirit of God that He brought divine power to bear upon the realm of evil and broke through the thraldom of sin and sickness in miraculous deeds of mercy, He fulfilled His ministry in meekness and lowliness in order to bear the onslaught of evil upon Himself and so to get at the heart of it. It was by living a life of holiness among us in perfect obedience to the Father that He engaged with the inhuman forces of darkness that had encroached upon the bodies and souls of men. Therefore when Jesus healed a man even of a physical affliction He did so only through a struggle with evil will. Nowhere did He heal simply as a kindly physician, but as one who wrestled personally with evil and overcame it through the conflict of His own holy will with the powers of evil spirit. That is why again and again Jesus groaned in agony and grief of spirit as He cured men's bodies and minds and had to renew His strength constantly through prayer, while prayer itself was a battle with the rebellious will of an alienated creation. This was not simply the service of kindness for kindness' sake, but a far profounder service of mercy that dealt with the real sting of evil by penetrating into its sinful motion and undoing its guilt in atonement. It was the kind of service which could not be rendered apart from vicarious divine sorrow for the sin of the world.

(ii) He ministered the mercy of God to man at the sharpest point of his need and misery, where he is not only unmerciful but resents mercy, and is therefore bitterly hostile to this ministry. Although it was the mercy of God freely ministered by Jesus that provoked the resistance of man to its sharpest point of hostility toward God, yet in this ministry of mercy Jesus met the hostility of man by making it the supreme object of His compassion, by accepting it and bearing it in Himself and then by making an end of it in His own death. It is easy enough, as Jesus pointed out, to be merciful to others when it meets with some return, but to be merciful without any hope of return and without ever looking for any return, to go on being merciful in the face of unremitting unthankfulness, and always to make every act of ingratitude, no matter how bitter and obdurate, the very occasion for mercy, is to minister a mercy that is quite limitless. That is real mercy, and that is what it means to be merciful as God is merciful. Such was the mercy ministered by Jesus, triumphant mercy which drew out human unthankfulness and resentment to their ultimate point where He limited it by absorbing it in Himself and put a final end to it in the very death which it inflicted on Him—mercy that cannot be defeated.

(iii) Jesus carried out His ministry as a humble servant on earth in utter reliance upon His Father in heaven, refusing to do anything except what He had been sent to do and refusing to discharge His mission except in the weakness and selflessness of pure service. At no point did He seek to change the nature of His ministry as service, and therefore He rendered it only through constant recourse to prayer in order to let it take effect solely through the good pleasure of the Father. The true and faithful servant does not arrogate authority to himself or build up round him instruments of power or even an aura of prestige through which he may exert pressure to attain his ends; otherwise he would betray the essential nature of his service as *service*. Hence Jesus warned His disciples, as He washed their feet in menial service at the Last Supper, to beware of allowing their service in His name to gather a worldly prestige in which its nature as service would be lost or to take the form of a munificent patronage that could lord it over mankind. Διακονία in the Name of Christ has only one source of power: in prayer and intercession, for Jesus Christ Himself, the supreme *Diakonos,* will rule over the ages and the nations only through the weakness of the Man on the Cross.

Such, then, is the pattern of service which Christ has instituted in Himself for the Church and for all who within it are called to be deacons. It is a charge to be merciful as the Father is merciful and a call to follow Christ in the form of a servant, that all members of the Body of Christ may be fellow labourers in His work and that deacons, reflecting in themselves the pattern of Christ's service, may prompt the whole people of God in the ministry of divine mercy.

IV

Without doubt this is a very difficult charge which Christ has laid upon His Church, and one that is desperately hard for the Church to fulfil in its corporate capacity as Church and therefore in the form of a service rendered by the Community as such. How can it render this service as *service* and render it *effectively* within the power-structures of humanity?

Here the Church is up against a twofold temptation. On the one hand, it is tempted to use worldly power in order to secure the success of its service. As an organized community within the national, social, and economic structures of human life the Church cannot isolate its ministry of the divine mercy from the organized services of the State for the welfare of its people. The Church knows only too well that the need of men is bound up with the injustices inherent in the national, social, and economic structures within which people live, and is often directly traceable to them, and therefore in order to meet human need adequately and rationally attention must be given to the factors that create it and aggravate it. Certainly as far as hunger and poverty and want are concerned, what is required is the application of scientific methods in the production and distribution of goods from the vast wealth with which God has endowed the earth. But how can this be done without economic and political power? And so the Church is constantly tempted not only to institutionalize its service of the divine mercy but to build up power-structures of its own, both through ecclesiastical success and prestige among the people and through social and political instruments, by means of which it can exert pressure to attain its ends and impart power to its service in order to ensure its effectiveness. What church is there that feels deeply the burden of human need, and takes seriously its service of mercy, that does not fall into this temptation?

On the other hand, the Church is tempted to leave the corporate responsibility for the need of men wholly to the State and to restrict itself to the ministry of forgiveness. How can the Church participate in the planned and controlled welfare of mankind without actually compromising its freedom and secularizing its life in the worldly forms of society? And so the Church is tempted to retreat into an area where it could not come into conflict with the power-structures of organized social welfare and where it thinks to avoid the subtle snare of using its success in the relief of human suffering as a means of enhancing its own image or of pressing its own claim upon the people. This could take a quietist and other-worldly form through the restriction of Christian service to inward 'religious' concerns, but it could also take the form of a flight into the anonymity of 'religionless' behaviour or the so-called 'meta-christianity' of the 'new man'. But in either case the Church would decline the burden of human need at its sharpest point and deflect the real force of Christian witness, and so run away from the agony of being merciful as God is merciful.

Whichever alternative the Church chooses, on the one hand or the other, it contracts out of the actual charge Christ has laid upon it and betrays the essential nature of Christian service as *service*. Can the Church engage in the pressure groups of organized society in order to ensure the success of its own enterprise, and so suffer assimilation to the forms of this world, without compromising its real nature as the Body of Jesus Christ? Can it hide its light under the natural forms of man's cultural and scientific development without losing its soul? Can it follow Christ, the Servant of the Lord who steadfastly resisted every temptation to use compelling demonstrations of glory and power to fulfil His ministry, without like Him suffering the hostility and ridicule and ignominy that are heaped by the world on powerless and selfless service of God's mercy? Can the Church really fulfil the charge Christ has laid upon it and therefore take up His Cross without renouncing itself for Him, without, as it were, hazarding its life or losing its identity in recognized historical existence for Christ's sake and the Gospel's? Can the Church go forth from Christ clad with His image in the form of a servant without laying aside the pride and glory and power of the nations, and without taking into its own mouth in triumphant agony His cry before the judgement seat of Pilate: 'My kingdom is not of this world'? And how can the Church go forth from Christ to engage in authentic service in His Name without immersing itself in the need and misery and desperate plight of men in complete solidarity with the world under the judgement and grace of God, without participating deeply in the divine mercy that has put an end in the crucified Body of Christ to our restless striving for power and vain snatching at glory, and to our resentment of meek and humble reliance upon the heavenly Father?

Difficult though it is for the Church as such to carry this burden and fulfil the role of a servant, God in His mercy has instituted within it special ministries to dispense to it the Word of Life and to seek the fruit of it in the lives of its members, to guide the Church and to prompt it in its service. This is the two-fold ministry which we may speak of as 'the service of the Word', and 'the service of response to the Word'. *The service of the Word* is the ministry of Word and Sacrament through which Christ is pleased to be present, offering Himself as Saviour and implementing His salvation by the power of His Spirit. But it is a *service*, a διακονία, in which ministers only *serve* the proclamation of Christ and cannot make that proclamation effective by imparting to it their own strength, and in which they only dispense the Sacraments as *stewards* of the mysteries in utter reliance upon Christ to fulfil His own ministry of Himself in Word and Spirit, in Grace and Power. *The service of response to the Word* is the ministry of the divine mercy to the people in which Christ Himself is pleased to be present, acting as their Representative in lifting them up to the Face of the Father in thanksgiving and worship and in making them His fellow labourers in the pouring out of the divine mercy to all mankind. But it is a *service*, a διακονία, in which deacons only *prompt* the people in their responses of prayer and praise and do not act on their behalf, and in which they guide them in their service to mankind and do not undertake it for them, but in which they remind the people of Christ's own promise to meet them in all their deeds of mercy to the hungry and thirsty and naked and sick and imprisoned, and so to give effect to their service in the depths of human need.

These two ministries are essentially complementary and are mutually dependent, since each requires the other for its proper fulfilment and one is obstructed by the lack of the other. It is through that double ministry that Christ communicates Himself to man by bringing God's presence to bear upon man and by bringing him in his need to receive that presence, by ministering the mercy of God toward man in his guilty estrangement and by freeing him in his desperate need for the response of faith and trust in God, and He does that by incarnating God's love in Himself for man and by sustaining through His own presence the existence of man for fellowship with God. It is thus that Jesus Christ mediates in Himself the healing reconciliation of God with man and man with God in the form of a union of His own presence in the Gospel with His own presence in the depths of human need. The service of the Word serves Christ clothed with His Gospel, so that through it He draws near to man with forgiveness in unconditional grace; and the service of response to the Word serves Christ clothed with the misery of man, so that through it He sustains and upholds man in unutterable compassion until He finds the sheep that is lost and counts that He has found it when it hears His voice and follows Him.

Now, while the New Testament uses the term διακονία both for the service of the Word and for the service of response to the Word, it is especially used and indeed technically used for the service of response to the Word, that is, for the ministry of the *deacon*. We may thus distinguish between the two forms of ministry as the *presbyteral* ministry through which the Word and Sacraments are dispensed and the *diaconal* ministry through which the responses of God's people in worship and witness or intercession and mercy are guided and prompted. The term διαχονία is peculiarly appropriate to the latter ministry, for while the presbyteral ministry is one in which the ministers act not as representatives of the people but only as those sent by Christ and commissioned by Him with authority to dispense His Word of forgiveness, in the proclamation of the Gospel and the administration of the Sacraments, the diaconal ministry is one in which the deacons act as representatives of the people and as examples of the way in which Christ identified Himself with their need, and therefore as sent by Him to engage in a ministry of pure, unassuming service without any commission to exercise authority or pastoral control. They are as necessary and as indispensable to one another as husband and wife, and father and mother, in the same family.

It is an immense tragedy that throughout its history the Church has so often lacked a proper *diaconate* to guide it and prompt it in the ministry of the divine mercy, and to seek the full fruit of that mercy in the activities of the community and in the lives of its members. This has had disastrous consequences for the ministry of Word and Sacrament, for left on its own, without its other half, it has succumbed to the temptation to arrogate to itself a false glory and to fulfil its authoritative commission not by obedient *service* but by usurping control and mastery over the Lord's inheritance. But it has had disastrous consequences also for the service of the Church in its corporate capacity, for without the example of pure service, which it is the office of the deacon to set forth, the Church has fallen into the temptation to give itself out as the patron of goodness and welfare and to assume worldly powers in order to achieve success in its works of relief, and thus has betrayed the very nature of its ministry as service of divine mercy to mankind. This has also meant that the ministry of Christ clothed with His Gospel has been kept apart from the ministry of Christ clothed with the need and plight of men, with the result that the ministry of the Gospel has so often lost its relevance to men in the concrete actualities of their existence, and the ministry of the divine mercy has lacked its penetrating power to strike into the deepest root of human need in man's guilty estrangement from God—thus grave disorder has appeared in the life of the Church and its mission is often fraught with a deep sense of futility.

The Church needs today a massive recovery of authentic *diakonia* if it is to hold forth the image of Christ before mankind and is to minister the mercy of God to the needs of men in the deep root of their evil and in the real sting of their misery. Such a recovery would go far to heal the breaches in the life of the Church and to supply what is lacking in its mission. Three areas in particular call for drastic amendment and far-reaching reform.

(i) *Intercession*.   There is no more basic form of the Church's ministry than prayer, for it is in prayer that it renders its supreme service of worship and thanksgiving to God, and it is only through prayer that the Church can engage in the pure service of divine mercy in utter reliance upon God and in the renunciation of every attempt to put the Word of God into effect through its own cunning or strength. The Church does not minister through the power of its own action but only through the power of its Lord, and therefore it cannot fulfil its *diakonia* on earth without continuous engagement in intercession through its great High Priest at the right hand of God Almighty. The frantic attempts of the Church in modern times to find ways and means of making its message relevant to men, of clothing its ministries with worldly power, or of evolving methods and instruments which will ensure the popularity and success of its enterprise, are open admission that the Church has ceased to believe that the Gospel is really able to effect what it proclaims and of tragic disbelief in the power of intercession, i.e. in the active intervention of the Church's heavenly Mediator which is echoed through the Spirit in the Church's stammering prayers on earth. The intercessory prayer of the Church is direct engagement in the mighty apocalyptic battle between the Kingdom of Christ and the kingdoms of this world and in the triumphant reign of the Enthroned Lamb over all the forces of evil and darkness in history. The Church's greatest need is to *believe again* in the intercession of Christ and to find through prayer the sole source of power in its mission. Nothing can ever take the place of this basic service, the *diakonia* of intercession.

(ii) *Witness*.   Witness is the form which service takes as it moves from worship and intercession in Christ toward men in their estrangement and separation from God. It is open and transparent witness to Jesus Christ as the incarnate love of God, the Lord and Saviour of men, and witness directed above all to the deepest point of man's misery in his guilty alienation from God and to the sharpest point of his need in his hostility to God's grace. It is thus witness in the face of resistance and even persecution. The Christian Church is under constant pressure by the world to conform to its ways and thoughts, to adapt its message to its desires and ambitions, and thus the Church can only bear witness by entering into affliction. It is because the Church is a servant of Christ and is assimilated to His mission in its essential life that it suffers the same hostility as He suffered and shares with Him the weakness and helplessness of His passion. It is because Christ crucified and risen again dwells in the Church and makes it the earthly and historical form of His Body that He leads it into the unavoidable conflict between the mercy of God and the inhumanity of man and between the holiness of God and the sin of mankind. The Church cannot withdraw from the affliction and suffering which this conflict brings without contracting out of its witness and betraying its Lord. Yet this is the very point where the Church today in its faint-heartedness and scepticism seems to have lost its nerve, and where under pressure from the world it makes its message easy and acceptable to human hearing, adapting the Gospel to modern man instead of bringing modern man face to face with the Gospel. But the actual point of relevance and communication lies at the point of offence where the real hurt of man is exposed and divine healing takes place. It is a betrayal of *diakonia* to heal the hurt of God's people lightly, saying peace, peace, where there is no peace. The Church cannot discharge the task which Christ has laid upon it without offering unadulterated witness and engaging in pure evangelism, cost what it may in scorn and ridicule or oppression. If at this point the Church seeks to save its life it will lose it, but here if it is ready to lose it for Christ's sake and the Gospel's it will find it. It still remains true that the blood of the martyrs is the seed of the Church, and that it is through bold and suffering witness that men and women serve Christ most faithfully.

(iii) *Reconciliation*. The Church that is committed to the *diakonia* of the divine mercy must live the reconciled life. It cannot proclaim reconciliation to the world without standing in solidarity with the world under the total grace and judgement of God and without carrying within itself a solidarity of communion in the redemption through the blood of Christ. It cannot offer healing to mankind without being healed in its own body. It cannot minister reconciliation to humanity in its bitter divisions and hostilities without being reconciled in its own membership and purged of its internal bitterness and strife. What can obstruct or damn the service of the Church more than to act a lie against what it proclaims and by perpetuating division within itself to blaspheme the blood of Christ shed to make men at one with God and at one with each other? What is demanded of the Church by Christ is that it should serve the divine mercy in the actualities of physical and spiritual existence where the bounds of human life break up under the divisive forces of evil, and that instead of allowing the divisions of the world to penetrate back into the life of the Church, to make it equivocal and futile, it should live out in the midst of a broken and divided humanity the reconciled life of the one unbroken Body of Jesus Christ—that is διαχονία.

Until the Christian Church heals within itself the division between the service of Christ clothed with His Gospel and the service of Christ clothed with the need and affliction of men, and until it translates its communion in the body and blood of Christ into the unity of its own historical existence in the flesh, it can hardly expect the world to believe, for its *diakonia* would lack elemental integrity. But *diakonia* in which believing active intercession, bold unashamed witness, and the reconciled life are all restored in the mission of the Church will surely be the service with which Jesus Christ is well pleased, for that is the *diakonia* which He has commanded of us and which He has appointed as the mirror through which He reflects before the world His own image in the form of a Servant.

Readers of Karl Barth will be aware of how much this essay owes to him and not least to the last volume of his *Church Dogmatics,* 4.3. It is highly appropriate that *Diakonia* should be the theme of this tribute to him, for rarely has any theologian so consistently directed his theological work to stimulate and prompt the *diakonia* of the divine mercy as the charge which Christ has laid upon the Church as a whole.

27

KARN GRIFFEN

The Church as a Therapeutic Community

IN HIS LECTURE OF SEPTEMBER 25, 1956, DELIVERED BEFORE THE
Swiss Reformed Ministers' Association,[28] theologian Karl Barth
asserted that "the humanity of God," rightly understood, signifies
the God who speaks with man in promise and command; God's
existence, intercession, and activity for man; the intercourse God
holds with man; and the free grace in which God wills to be the
God of man.[29]

Barth reasons that because God reveals Himself as a "partner of
man," albeit a superior one, He is indeed the living God. And it is
His freedom, in which He acts in this man-toward manner, that is
His deity.

> It is the deity which as such also has the character of human-
> ity. In this and only in this form was—and still is—our view
> of the deity of God to be set in opposition to that earlier
> theology. There must be positive acceptance and not uncon-
> sidered rejection of the elements of truth, which one cannot
> possible deny to it even if one sees all its weaknesses. It is
> precisely God's *deity* which, rightly understood, includes his
> *humanity*.[30]

Barth states, however, that there is something even "more concrete" to be seen about God, and that is Jesus Christ, "God's high
freedom."

28. Later published as Karl Barth, *The Humanity of God* (Atlanta: John
Knox, 1960).
29. *Ibid.*, p. 37.
30. *Ibid.*, pp. 45–46.

From Karn Griffen, *The Incarnation: Christian Personhood and the Covenant Community*, pp. 121–139, 142–147. Unpublished Doctor of Ministry Dissertation, Fuller Seminary, 1976. © Karn Griffen, 1976. Used by
permission of the Author.

> The divine capacity which operates and exhibits itself in that superiority and subordination is manifestly also God's capacity to bend downwards, to attach Himself to another and this other to Himself, to be together with him. . . . In that sequence, there arises and continues in Jesus Christ the highest communion of God with man. God's deity is thus no prison in which He can exist only in and for Himself. It is rather His freedom to be in and for Himself but also with and for us. . . .
>
> It is when we look at Jesus Christ that we know decisively that God's deity does not exclude, but includes His *humanity*.[31]

Barth turns to the Scriptures of the New Testament, citing Jesus' teachings and parables, to affirm that in Jesus there is genuine deity which includes within itself "genuine humanity."

> The very One who speaks in these parables takes to His heart the weakness and the perversity, the helplessness and the misery, of the human race surrounding Him. He does not despise men, but in an inconceivable manner esteems them highly just as they are, takes them into His heart and sets Himself in their place.[32]

Thus Barth finds a correspondence between the human rights and dignity of every human being and his place in the eternal Will of God, where Jesus Christ is his Brother and God is his Father. It is on this assumption, says Barth, that we must deal with man. No human being, then, can ever be approached as anyone other than a person whose rightful place is within the divine relationship. The message of the Christian is to transmit this knowledge, bringing it to some for the first time and strengthening it in others.[33]

Therefore, for Karl Barth, there are no real "insiders" and "outsiders" of the community. To all, the message is the same—the Brotherhood of Christ and the Fatherhood of God. Of the Church, Barth says the following:

> We believe the Church is the place where the crown of humanity, namely, man's fellow-humanity, may become visible in Christocratic brotherhood. Moreover, we believe it is the place where God's glory wills to dwell upon earth, that is, where humanity—the humanity of God—wills to assume tan-

31. *Ibid.*, p. 48.
32. *Ibid.*, p. 51.
33. *Ibid.*, p. 53.

gible form in time and here upon earth. Here we celebrate and witness to it. Here we glory in the Immanuel, just as He did who, as He looked at the world, would not cast away the burden of the Church but rather chose to take it upon Himself and bear it in the name of all its members. "If God is for us, who is against us?"[34]

Writing about the community in his *Church Dogmatics,* Barth says that "we cannot avoid the statement that Jesus Christ is the community."[35]

It does not live apart from the mighty work of His self-attestation. It lives as He Himself lives in it in the occurrence of this mighty work; as it is the earthly-historical form of His existence, His body, standing at His disposal, and ruled and impelled by Him, in all its members and their various functions.[36]

Thus, the Church for Barth is that place for man where humanity and deity find a correspondence in man's time and space. This communion, or *communio sanctorum,* for Barth, has as its chief end the proclamation of the kingdom of God. The communion's growth, "intensive growth" which is vertical in height and depth, yet does include the horizontal dimension, is almost a by-product of this chief end. The communion takes place, says Barth, as the divine and human work "in train," as it moves from its origin, a completion in Christ, to its goal, manifestation as a completed fact. "Communion takes place in the sphere of the incomplete between completion and completion, i.e., between union and union."

It is the saints who are and act in this communion. The saints are men who exist in the world, and after the fashion of the world, but who, in virtue of the fact that they come from the union presupposed in the event of their communion and move forward to its revelation, are integrated and engaged in self-integration.[37]

Therefore, according to Barth, the Church is that communion of men who share the same calling, and who, in their common response, are met by Christ who has condescended to live within and

34. *Ibid.,* p. 65.
35. Barth, "The Growth of the Community," *Church Dogmatics* IV/2 (Naperville: Allenson, 1969), p. 655.
36. *Ibid.,* p. 654.
37. *Ibid.,* p. 642.

through the Church, thereby continuing His work and ministry. It is at this point of "meeting," where man's humanity is encountered by God's humanity in Christ, that man recognizes the "partnership of God and, in so recognizing this, realizes his own acceptance and is free to participate fully in the life of the community. Thus, in carrying out the work of his calling, man is "in train" with others of the communion and in partnership with God through the presence of Jesus Christ, who is the community.

Dietrich Bonhoeffer holds that the individual person does not emerge except in community, and that he emerges at the same time that the "collective person" arises, who is the person of the "community of men." Thus, a moment occurs when God's desire for a "community of men" is born *in one* being, the "communion of saints," while being born *from numerous,* similar structures— the individual persons who compose it.

> . . . It is not that many persons, coming together, add up to a collective person, but the person arises only through being embedded in sociality. And when this happens, simultaneously the collective person arises, not before, yet not as a consequence of the arising of the individual. That is, the collective person exists only where persons exist.[38]
> . . . The structures of the individual and the collective unit are the same. Upon these basic relations rests the concept of the religious community and the church.[39]

Bonhoeffer is careful to stipulate that this community, this collective person, is not created by man's intentionality. Rather, the "communion" and hence individual "person" is achieved only in the free "giving of oneself" in surrender to the other. This phenomenon, says Bonhoeffer, "gives us a clear proof that love ultimately seeks not communion, but the other."

> . . . Thus it is precisely in several persons' complete surrender to each other that their new person becomes real and there arises a "community of new persons". Love finds communion without seeking it, or rather precisely because it does not seek it. Whoever loses his life will preserve it. Only thus does the surrender of the individual person to God's will for his neighbor really lead to the communion of saints, for whose realization each man serves as God's instrument.[40]

38. Bonhoeffer, *The Communion of Saints* (New York: Harper & Row, 1964), p. 51.
39. *Ibid.,* p. 52.
40. *Ibid.,* p. 125.

Thus, Bonhoeffer finds that love is at the very core of community and personhood. It is love, he says, that demands that we sacrifice our own interest, even if it puts at risk our own communion with God. The two great biblical examples that he cites for this are Exodus 32:32 and Romans 9:1ff. Moses wishes to be blotted out of the book of life for his people's sin, and Paul wishes that he himself were accursed and cut off from Christ, not in order to be condemned with his brethren, but to win communion with God for them; he wishes to be condemned in their stead.[41]

This kind of communion for the Christian, says Bonhoeffer, is a state established by Christ of "being with one another" and "for one another."

> This active 'being for one another' can be defined from two standpoints: Christ is the measure and standard for our conduct (John 13:15, 34f.; 1 John 3:10), and our conduct is that of a member of the body of Christ, that is, of one equipped with the strength of Christ's love, in which each man can and will become Christ for his fellow-man (1 Cor. 12:12; Rom. 12:4ff.; Eph. 4:4,12ff.; Col. 3:15).[42]

Thus, the community, the collective person, is also an equipping entity. The standard Himself is present to equip His individual instruments and the equipment is Christ Himself, in His love. The gift and the giver are one and the same.

For the Christian counselor, both the *communio sanctorum* of Barth and the *sanctorum communio* of Bonhoeffer offer the same premise, the presence of God Himself, equipping man for his calling, and becoming a "partner" in the undertaking. Deity and humanity correspond at the point of compassion for another. It is no mere individual love and acceptance that the Christian counselor extends to his counselee, but rather the love of Christ Himself. The person that faces the client in hurt and pain is at once individual and collective. The humanity that presents itself in ministry in the Christian counseling chambers, by the suggested models of Barth and Bonhoeffer, is perfect and complete humanity because it is the very humanity of God and is the extension of the Body of Christ, the community.

Within Bonhoeffer's work on the *sanctorum communio* there is a mention of marriage as the smallest "sociological unit" of the *sanctorum communio*.[43] This idea has counseling implications for the counselor who works with marriage partners in "conjoint

41. *Ibid.*, p. 131.
42. *Ibid.*, p. 129.
43. *Ibid.*, p. 155.

therapy,"[44] who views the marriage itself as a "collective person."

Professor Ray S. Anderson argues that the transcendence of God is a reality of the Spirit in which the historical existence of the man in whom the Spirit dwells is reformed to the form of God's Incarnate Word, Jesus Christ. This Jesus is at once the image of the invisible God and the image in which man is created (Col. 1:15; 3:10). The reality of the Spirit, then, Anderson calls the "lived transcendence" which impinges upon the world through the historical life of the man who lives in the Spirit of God. This leads Anderson to say that ". . . lived transcendence is a community of life in the Spirit which takes the form of both a kenotic and ek-static existence." [45]

Anderson finds that the question of *kenosis* (self-emptying) when applied to the community is answered ultimately in Christ's obedience unto death. Therefore, the fundamental character of *kenosis* for the community is conceived as an activity and not an essence.[46] It is found by man in his participation of love toward the "other," who is each man's end and who has become the form of Christ through the working of the Spirit. Thus, says Anderson,

> because I meet my own real existence when I act in love towards the Other, I see beyond his actual existence with its limitations and immaturities. I do not merely tolerate him, I see his reality as a person.[47]

This means for Anderson that the community is composed of actual people who have their place within it, not by virtue of their "capacity to love" or their "maturity of spirit," but by virtue of their common humanity with Christ and the reality of the gift of the Holy Spirit. Thus, it is the community that opens the potential for man to realize his full personhood, "which is the capacity to live in love."[48]

For Anderson, the *kenotic* community is characterized by its recognition of the humanity of all men, the recognition of how sick, how weak, and how unloving acdnunlovable people can be.

---

44. A term applied to a school of marriage therapy that views the marriage dyad, husband and wife, as a third party, a system, and therefore carries out therapy with both parties present. See Virginia Satir, *Conjoint Family Therapy* (Palo Alto: Science and Behavior Books, 1967), pp. 1–8.
45. Anderson, *Historical Transcendence and the Reality of God* (Grand Rapids: Eerdmans, 1975), p. 229.
46. *Ibid.*, p. 232.
47. *Ibid.*, p. 234.
48. *Ibid.*

Its real character, he says, lies in its daring to "include those who have the capacity (and often the compulsion) to destroy the community itself, and even more, in its daring to offer love as a possibility of growth." It is marked, therefore, not by whom it is willing to renounce, but by whom it is willing to receive.

> The one who discovers that he is received into the community by virtue of his common humanity with Christ, and not by virtue of any 'qualifying' efforts of his own, does not stand in the circumference at some distance from the transcendence of God in the community, but is immediately placed in a relation of transcendence through the reality of Spirit who assumes the form of the Other's concrete existence.[49]

Professor Anderson also states that the community is *ek-static*. Here he applies the same meaning to the term as Dr. J. D. Zizioulas does in citing *ek-stasis* as one of two basic aspects of personhood. It is man's "movement towards communion."[50] As Anderson views the "*kenotic* community" it exists in the same flesh as Jesus of Nazareth and is thereby earth-related; yet, it is not earth-bound because it also lives in the same spirit as did Jesus. When Anderson examines the life of Jesus, he finds an unbroken communion with the Father. This dimension to Jesus' person is the *ek-static,* just as His relation to humanity as the eternal logos, as the bearer of human nature in its totality, is the *hypo-static*.

> The idea of Personhood, then, which we are led to consider through this understanding of the person of Christ, includes the reality of Spirit as the ek-static reality of Word. When I have defined lived transcendence as kenotic community, these two aspects of Personhood must be included. That is, the kenotic community is constituted a community through both the hypo-static union of Word and flesh, which is the reality of the Incarnate Word, and ek-static reality of Spirit. The kenotic community is not itself a hypo-static union of Word and flesh, that is, it is not the bearer of humanity in its totality in a unique and unrepeatable existence, it is not another Incarnation; but it is constituted in community with God through its humanity which it has in common with the humanity of the Incarnate Word.[51]

49. *Ibid.*, p. 235.
50. Zizioulas, "Human Capacity and Human Incapacity," unpublished essay presented at the Society for the Study of Theology, Oxford University (April, 1972), p. 410.
51. Anderson, *Historical Transcendence,* p. 241.

Anderson chooses the term *"ek-static"* purposely to avoid any connotation of an introverted experience, that is, of a community "where life is turned back upon itself." This kind of introversion of love, says Anderson, works as a "fragmenting and destructive force" within community, resulting in an intensification of the Ego of personhood in its opposition to other hypostatic entities, and/or it can lead to a tyrannical collectivism which can then become the end towards which personal life exists only as a means towards or as an antecedent for the collective entity.[52]

A final point of Anderson's concerning the *ek-static* community which we will include here, is that this community can serve as the "priest of creation." In the historical transcendence of God through the Incarnation, God meets Himself from the side of creaturehood. Thus, says Anderson, all creation now has the possibility of its *ek-stasis* through the redemption of man from the introversion of the divine image. All creation can now be brought back into relation to God. Thus, says Anderson, "The ek-static community has a cosmic dimension—it is itself the 'horizon of revelation' for all creation."[53]

In the prior section of his work, the discussion of the *kenotic* community, Anderson focuses upon the creation story.

> The kenotic community can be said then to be the 'home of personhood' where man is both received as a person and then, at the same time, receives his personhood. . . . The home, or domicile for man is community with God. There he receives his true personhood. In this sense of the word, domestic refers to the total context in which the Spirit of God works to create man's personhood. The Spirit can be known as the 'domesticating' Spirit of God, who creates the place where man *learns* to receive his personhood. It is not too difficult to interpret the creation story (as given in Genesis) domestically. The world is for man his domicile, his home with God, in which he is a participant with God in the creative process. All the while, man is learning to receive and growing towards his true personhood.[54]

If we accept the conclusion that God began his covenanting condescension prior to the creation story, we can find that Anderson's *"kenotic and ek-static community"* serves as the covenant community to which God joins Himself through Word and flesh in

52. *Ibid.*
53. *Ibid.*, p. 243. See also n. 37, p. 243 for Anderson's remarks concerning Paul's interpretation of the fall, as found in Romans 1:25.
54. *Ibid.*, p. 237.

the Incarnate Jesus, in which man is "met" by the humanity of God (Barth), and in which the "collective person" of Dietrich Bonhoeffer emerges coincident with the individual man finding his "true personhood." Implicit in all three views of the Church is the risk-taking love for the other, the humanity of God present, and the dynamic nature of the community moving forward and outward, not inward, in its calling.

We move now to T. F. Torrance's view of the Church, where we find it is difficult to separate the theology of Torrance from his view of the Church. The two are closely entwined. By the fact of the Incarnation and Torrance's perspective that God has "incorporated" Himself with humanity in Jesus Christ, the ministry of Jesus on earth becomes identified with the human community that bears His name. The Christian Church, therefore, is one and the same with Christ's own ministry. It not only carries on the ministry of Christ, but shares its very life and work with Him. For Torrance, the personal and individual ministry of Jesus is inseparable from His person.

> Because the Person and Work of Christ, what He was and what He did, are inseparable, what the Church is in Him and what it does in proclaiming Him, its being and its ministry, are inseparable. As there is only one Christ and only one Body, so there is only one ministry, that of Christ in His Body.[55]

In this light of inseparability, then, Torrance views the Church as far more than "the holy society founded to perpetuate Christ's memory, observe His teachings, and proclaim His Gospel." It is this, but it is also that which was inherent in His being as the Incarnate Son, was rooted in His humanity as the historical Jesus, and grew out of the fulfillment of His ministry in the flesh.

> The Church of the New Covenant arose out of the indivisible union of the Messiah and the people of God He came to redeem and raise up; it grew out of the concrete way in which He lived His divine life within their human existence thereby transforming their whole way of life; it took shape and form in every act that He performed and derived its essential structure from the way in which He fulfilled His ministry on their behalf.[56]

55. T. F. Torrance, "The Foundation of the Church," *The Scottish Journal of Theology,* XVI (1963), 131.
56. *Ibid.,* p. 123.

This would appear to be a very "high view" of the Church. This inseparable aspect of Jesus and His work together with the Church lifts the Church out of the sphere of "holy society" for Torrance and sets it apart as the "New Covenant Community." For Torrance, the ministry of the Church is integral to its very structure in much the same way as the Messiah, Christ, is "indivisibly united to the structure of the People of God." This union is possible through the Spirit, says Torrance, for in Jesus is found the Church and all ministry: "As there is only one Christ and only one Body, so there is only one ministry, that of Christ in His Body."[57]

For Torrance, as for the apostle Paul, the metaphor of "the Body of Christ" carries a deep significance. Torrance begins with the Person of Christ, who was both Word and Person—Word in the form of personal Being, and Person who was Himself the Word communicated from God to men. That is, Jesus Christ is the One who interprets and authenticates Himself and is the self-communicating, self-authenticating Word of God.

To form the Body, Torrance says, Jesus chose twelve of His followers to be with Him, to be the inner nucleus of His Church. This choice was, according to Torrance, the symbolic act of the gathering of the twelve tribes of Israel, no longer scattered, but joined into one. "Hence he formed and instituted them into one Body with himself. . . ." Jesus prepared His Body, imparted to its members His messianic secret, and inaugurated with them the New Covenant at the Last Supper. This Body then died with Christ at Golgotha. Yet, says Torrance, broken, humbled, scattered though it was, this Body, prepared by Christ, was transformed at Pentecost.

> The Body had already been prepared, the people and the structure he had given them, remained, but the Body was broken and humbled to the dust—it needed to be quickened by the Breath or Spirit of God. That had already happened to Jesus himself, the Head of the Body, for God had not allowed him to see corruption but had raised him bodily from the dead to be the new life-giving Adam, the Head of the new race. Now first upon the apostolic nucleus he breathed his quickening breath and then poured the Spirit out in fulness upon the whole Church, and so the Body prepared for Christ arose and lived. The Christian Church was born, the one Body of Christ incorporating the faithful of all ages before and after the Incarnation.[58]

57. *Ibid.,* p. 131.
58. Torrance, *Theology in Reconstruction* (Grand Rapids: Eerdmans, 1965), p. 204.

Torrance, in considering the apostolic witness to the Word, finds two inextricably woven relationships which correspond to the twofold nature of Christ as Word and Person. First of all, he says, "There is a relationship in word to Christ as Word." This means that the apostolic witness must itself be a "report." It must be derived from and rest upon the Word of Christ in which He interpreted Himself and then communicated Himself to His disciples. The apostolic statements are thus recognition statements which point to Jesus and bring their readers and hearers into a personal encounter with Christ. Secondly, says Torrance, "There is a relationship in person to Christ as Person."

> Because the Word is in the form of personal Being, relationship to the Word cannot be in word and understanding only but must itself be intensely personal. Hence just as through the apostolic witness the Word created understanding of Christ in the mind of the Church, so through the Apostles the Person of Christ creates the community which receives him and which he compacts around himself as his own Body, the Church. Knowledge of Christ and union with Christ went hand in hand together, so that relation to Christ was grounded and mediated through personal and living communion, within which he himself was present, and within which his Word was effectively operative in the lives of men.[59]

Here in these two relationships, Torrance perceives the basic rudiments of the great doctrines of the Church concerning the apostolic foundation of the Church and the Holy Scripture, as well as establishes that this Word is revealed, interpreted, understood, and communicated in community.

Of the apostles Torrance says,

> ... this pure and holy Word of God gathers round him the apostles to be the inner nucleus of his Church, to be in a special way one body with him, the Word made flesh, and to be the receiving end within our sinful history of the complete incarnate revelation.[60]

These men become, in Torrance's words, "recipients of revelation" and "ambassadors of reconciliation." They remain sinners, saved by grace, but are entrusted with the "Word of reconciliation." It is to these redeemed, sinful men that Jesus teaches the mysteries of the kingdom and near the end promises that the Father

59. *Ibid.*, p. 42.
60. *Ibid.*, p. 135.

will send the Spirit to remind them of His teachings and lead them into all truth. Thus it is that

> In the Apostles the mind of the Church is so reconciled and joined to the Mind of Christ that the Mind of Christ is not to be separated out from the mind of the Apostolate, or the *kerygma* of the Apostles to be distinguished from the Word of the Lord (except, of course, in those rare instances where the Apostle himself may do so).[61]

Torrance sees God turning to redeemed humanity to perpetuate this great Incarnate disclosure. He refers to the apostles as the ''hinges'' which fold out the Incarnational revelation horizontally into history. He calls them ''hinges'' in two senses: (1) as disciples hinging the Old Israel with the New Israel, and (2) as apostles through whom the foundation of the Church is laid and through whom the Church is sent out into history.[62] In this foundation can be found the basic doctrine of Holy Scripture, says Torrance, for God has constituted in the apostolic foundation of the Church a creaturely correspondence to His own Word. Through the witness, teaching, and writings of these men, God has effected a union with His Word, which is passed down through the ages as a human expression of the Divine Word.

> The Bible stands above the Church, speaking to the Church the very Word of God, but the Bible also belongs to history which comes under the judgement and the redemption of the Cross. That double place of Holy Scripture must always be fully acknowledged, else we confound the word of man with the Word of God, and substitute the Apostles in the place of Christ.[63]

It would appear that lying at the core of Torrance's view of the Church is Jesus Christ, the Christ of the ''*hypostatic* union,'' of the Chalcedonian doctrine of the two natures, ''*truly God and truly man* ... without confusion, without change, without division, without separation.'' Torrance states that the participation of believers in the Church must be construed in terms of *koinonia* and governed by this great doctrine.

> This is a participation in which the human nature of the participant is not deified but reaffirmed and recreated in its essence as human nature, yet one in which the participant is really

61. *Ibid.*, p. 137.
62. *Ibid.*
63. *Ibid.*, p. 138.

united to the Incarnate Son of God partaking in him in his own appropriate mode of the oneness of the Son and the Father... through the Holy Spirit....[64]

Torrance seems to be saying that the individual who presents himself within the on-going life of the community finds that the acceptance with which he is received is based on nothing but his own humanity. Because Christ is God's own response to Himself within the sphere of human community, man bears within his humanity the potential for this kind of acceptance also. The wholeness which man seeks in his life lies within this sphere of personal acceptance, of accepting and being accepted in community. Torrance says, "Grace is intensely personal."[65] Yet, he also says, it is the mystery of grace which is the mystery of Christ: "... by keeping ourselves within the limits of the great Chalcedonian adverbs we allow that mystery constantly to declare itself to us and impose itself upon us."[66]

Thus, it appears that Torrance is saying that the grace of God is that which "reaffirms and recreates" the human nature of man and unites him with Jesus in the commonality of their humanity. Through God's grace man is enabled to experience the highest kind of affirmation, the acceptance of his being, exactly as he is amid all his human frailty and failings. It is at this point of awareness of one's intrinsic "incapacity," and yet acceptance by the Almighty, that Zizioulas says we find our personhood and ultimately our capacity.

But all this leads to an understanding of Christology in terms of ecclesiology. For by being the initiator of personhood for humanity Christ acquires *a body,* and not only that but he can only be spoken of in terms of this body (Acts 9:5; 1 Cor. 12:12 etc.). At the same time man in relating to Christ in and through personhood affirms his existence only in communion in the *koinonia* of the Spirit. The restoration of personhood in Christ leads thus inevitably to the community of the Church which in its turn offers impersonal nature the possibility of being "referred" to God in its integrity through the personhood of man.[67]

64. *Ibid.,* p. 186.
65. *Ibid.,* p. 181.
66. *Ibid.,* p. 186.
67. Zizioulas, "Human Capacity," pp. 442–443.

CONCLUDING COMMENTS

Professor Torrance brings us back to the Christological ontology of the Church. In the Church man finds he is accepted and is offered the opportunity to enter into a "new humanity," and thereby finds he is in turn able to accept others. Here, also, man is affirmed in his human place, not for what he needs to be, but for what he already is. Here, "compacted" with Christ, prodigal man is truly welcomed home to be who he is really meant to be.

Through our discussion of personhood we can conclude that only the person can truly accept the "other" unconditionally, for only the true person has already sensed this acceptance for himself. Only the person can offer this kind of acceptance because he has recognized the personal in the other human being; therefore, the acceptance he extends is free of conditions and free of the a-personal "its and things" that impede relationships.

The Christian counselor comes to his ministry cloaked in the covenant community, which is at once *kenotic* and *ek-static*. When the *kenosis* is viewed as activity, rather than essence, the very meeting of Christian counselor and client in the therapeutic encounter becomes the work or ministry of the community. Therefore, where the Christian counselor encounters his client, there also is the Church in its activity.

The fact that Jesus Christ and the Church, and Christ's work and the Church's work are inseparable means that the Christian counselor is also united through common humanity with the Incarnate Jesus, and therefore is enabled to trust his own emotions, feelings, and human responses for the "other" whom he meets in the encounter. These human attributes are ascribed a new significance because of the Incarnation and can be viewed as intrinsic to the *ek-static* nature of humanity that moves toward and for the other.

Finally, the Christian counselor is able to face his client in the calm assurance that this person has, by his very humanity, the potential of full and complete personhood. He also has the knowledge that even though the pain may be intense and the problems appear insurmountable, there is a significant task that can be fulfilled by him: complete and unconditional acceptance. This acceptance is possible because the Christian counselor has himself been accepted, and because there is present at every point of human hurt and pain the person of Jesus Christ, in His Spirit, the Advocate.

* * * * *

THE RESOURCES OF THE CHRISTIAN COUNSELOR

It appears to us that what the Christian counselor has working for him above all else in his work is the firm, secure knowledge of God's love for every one of his creatures. This means that God's love and desire for the counselee who confronts the counselor in the therapeutic encounter far surpasses the empathy and the human desire within the counselor to be of help. This can perhaps provide one benefit for the counselor above all else. It can contribute to the alleviation and even prevention of "counselor anxiety," a problem which Howard Clinebell says "produces unawareness of feelings—one's own and the counselee's,"[1] and is one of the blocks to effective counseling.

Because God disclosed Himself to man in humanity, and because Jesus responded in perfect love and obedience to His Father from within this humanity, every human individual shares with Jesus this common ground of being. Therefore, the overflowing love of the Father extends itself to every human, and the Christian who counsels has the assurance of this divine love for his client.

Along with this assurance, the Christian counselor has the assurance of the Father's advocacy for man in Jesus Christ. Torrance has placed a great deal of emphasis upon the fact that "Christ came identifying Himself with man in his hopeless misery and abject need and making man's cause His very own." God, who had created man, by Christ's Incarnation and Atonement "forged" a bond of union between man and Himself by overcoming the human bondages of sin and guilt, death and judgment. He did this in the Incarnate life of Jesus, who "stationed" Himself in the concrete actualities of human life in order to serve God in ministering His mercy and realizing His relation toward men. Thus, says Torrance,

> ... the Father looks upon every man in his need only by looking at him in and through the atoning presence and suppliance of His incarnate Son that meets Him there, for the incarnate Son is the outgoing of His own divine being toward every man and the pouring out of His own eternal love upon him in unrestrained mercy and grace.[2]

1. Howard J. Clinebell, Jr., *Basic Types of Pastoral Counseling* (Nashville: Abingdon Press, 1966), p. 63.
2. Torrance, "Service in Christ," p. 8.

Therefore, the Christian counselor is aware of the presence of Christ throughout the counseling process, serving through the Spirit as common Mediator and Advocate for the counselee and for himself. He need not play god for his client, but rather is able to be more objective in his counseling perspective because of his recognition of the work of the Advocate.

Also working strongly for the Christian counselor is his own personhood and his own awareness that he also is still on the way to personal completeness. Through this recognition, the Christian counselor is preserved from the insidious role of representing embodied wisdom, knowledge, and perfection, a role which can destroy the vital personal encounter and the desired attitudes of correspondence between and within counselor and counselee. It is the genuine recognition on the counselor's part that his own personhood is still in development, and therefore dependent upon the "other," that becomes part of the therapeutic climate and contributes to the healing process. It is this kind of *ek-static* movement, of one person's outgoing concern for another in spite of that person's state of hurt and disorientation, that speaks to the client about his own importance, value, and acceptability. His responses to the therapist may begin at a surface level, but as he grows in security, he too *ek-statically* begins to move toward the "other" in personal sharing of ever-increasing depth.

The sharing by the counselee will, more than likely, come in response to some form of self-disclosure by the counselor. The client's growing awareness of security and self-worth will be enhanced as the counselor discloses himself and exhibits confidence in the counselee by moving toward him with personal information. Psychologist Sidney M. Jourard found in his studies concerning self-disclosure that there existed a significant "correlation between what persons were willing to disclose to other people in their life and what these other people had disclosed to them. There appeared to be a reciprocity in self-disclosure."[3]

There is an aspect to this process that touches upon Ray Anderson's understanding of *kenosis* and the "*kenotic* community." As we have already observed, Professor Anderson conceives of *kenosis* as "activity rather than essence."

> *Kenosis* can be, therefore, another way of understanding the image of God, or of stating the true nature of man. *Kenosis*

3. Sidney M. Jourard, *The Transparent Self,* 2nd ed. (New York: Van Nostrand Reinhold, 1971), p. 13.

means that man has his true nature completed when he participates in the intra-divine transcendence (love), and that this participation does not involve the repudiation or violation of that which is truly human.[4]

As the Christian counselor encounters his client, he is the *kenotic* community in its ministry. The self-disclosure (self-emptying) process contributes to the client's understanding that he is received and fully accepted. The Christian counselor, in turn, already the recipient of acceptance by the *kenotic* community, continues to reveal himself, sometimes in "risk," for his client. What is in process here, then, is not only the interpersonal relationship between two human beings, but also the wider human aspect of community acceptance brought to the counseling chamber by the Christian therapist.

Anderson speaks of "two marks of visibility" for the transcendence of God, present within the community. The first is the Scriptural revelation of God's act in Jesus Christ, which is an audible Word and also a confrontation with the historical existence of the Word as Jesus Christ. "The other form of visibility," says Anderson, "is the presence of the Spirit in the concrete life of the other person in the community, or one could say, in the concrete existence of the community itself." Each of these "two poles of transcendence," says Anderson, "places the person in relation to God's transcendence."[5]

Thus, the open, sharing acceptance by the Christian counselor meets the client at a very personal point of need, that of acceptance and security, self-worth, and personal dignity. Also, according to Anderson, by the counselor's own membership in the Body of Christ, the counselee who is not a Christian is touched at the "crucial point of his own reciprocity," his spiritual autonomy which is his estrangement from God. He runs smack into and tastes of the Spirit of God in what can be a "radical and devastating" encounter.[6]

Where the counseling process will lead, will necessarily depend upon the needs of the client and other variables. But when we accept the conclusion that the Christian counselor is the "community at work," we find we must listen closely to the words of Anderson concerning the character of the *kenotic* community.

4. Anderson, *Historical Transcendence*, pp. 232–233.
5. *Ibid.*, pp. 235–236.
6. *Ibid.*

It seems clear from the character of kenotic community . . . that a conversion 'experience' cannot be demanded as the qualifying act on the part of a person for his belonging to the kenotic community. . . . But it must also immediately be said that participation in the kenotic community does involve receiving as well as being received. And it may well be that only after 'being received' for a considerable length of love (one would naturally say 'time', but these 'lengths' have a duration which only love can measure!) can a person muster the strength and the will to receive. This is, of course, what is entailed in the second aspect of the character of the kenotic community: it offers to each person, to the extent that he is able to bear it, an *actual* growth into the reality of his own personhood, which is the capacity to live in love.[7]

Thus, the very character of his own Christian community is intrinsically entwined within the therapeutic process for the Christian counselor. His own personhood is expressed and strengthened in his movement toward his client in professional, yet personal, regard. His freedom as a person allows him to feel with his client, diminishing the counselee's feelings of remoteness and contributing to a correspondence in personal identity between therapist and client. This correspondence is solidified as the counselor discloses himself to the counselee, working toward a trust-relationship and thereby providing the ground for the client's own sharing of himself.

In all probability, the Christian counselor, whether pastor or layman, is going to have among his counselees a majority of Christians who probably maintain, to a greater or lesser degree, an active Church membership. In these cases the counselor is not the only "visible pole" of God's transcendence, since these clients have been exposed to the Scriptures, the preached Word, and may enjoy a meaningful relationship to Christ. This fact will in no way alter what is working for the counselor, but rather should enhance the potential for effectiveness. T. F. Torrance has pointed out that through the *kerygmatic* Word and the sacraments, the partaker enters into a relationship with Christ. Even though the pain and oppression of the moment may be blocking the benefits of this relationship to the counselees, the counselor is able to take confidence in the love of God and the advocacy of Christ for these individuals.

7. *Ibid.*

EPILOGUE

28

THOMAS F. TORRANCE

The Church in the New Era of Scientific and Cosmological Change

EVERYONE KNOWS THAT WE ARE IN THE MIDST OF AN ERA OF
social and institutional transition and that the changes now taking
place are of critical significance for the Church. But I want to
suggest right away that these are only alterations on the surface of
our existence compared to the profound mutations that have been
taking place in the last fifty years in the foundations of our human
life and thought where a gigantic shift is going on in the basic
structures of thought and in the first principles of knowledge, but
which has only begun to work itself out to the surface. The
changes that Churchmen are mostly concerned about are only indirectly related to this deep-seated shift, for they belong to the transitional period where upheaval below causes fragmentation to set
in on the surface and where often the changes that first take the
field, in spite of being given out as 'liberal' or 'progressive', are
really of a reactionary kind. It is then in connection with these two
levels of change that I wish to discuss the condition of the Church
in the twentieth century and the considerable adjustment it needs if
it is to fulfil the mission in the world with which it has been
entrusted by God, but also to point out what is already going on in
this way behind the scenes or below the surface, which has the
greatest promise for the future.

In order to put things in their proper perspective let me begin by
saying something about the two great mutations in scientific and
cosmological outlook which have already taken place in the history
of our Western culture. The first took place when Greek science

From Thomas F. Torrance, *Theology in Reconciliation*, pp. 267–293. ©
SCM Press 1965; William B. Eerdmans Publishing Company, Grand
Rapids, 1966. Used by permission of the Publishers.

with its sharp distinction between unchanging necessary being and the changing appearances of these things gave rise to *Ptolemaic cosmology* which envisaged a deep split in the cosmos, between the intelligible realm of celestial realities and the sensible realm of terrestrial phenomena. The effect of that was to build a radical dualism into the very fabric of Greek science, philosophy and culture. It was that dualism against which Judaeo-Christianity had to struggle so hard with its message of the God who acts in history and of the Son or Word of God who has become incarnate in our contingent existence. Gnosticism and Arianism, docetism and adoptionism, all stand for hybrid forms of religion which have come to terms with a dualistic outlook in which God remains eternally and immutably detached from the world and does not really interact with it. It is not surprising that they had to be rejected, for they threatened the fundamental basis of the Gospel. It became clear that Christianity could not be maintained or be communicated to the ancient world without a radical reconstruction of the very foundations of Greek science, philosophy and culture, in which its fateful dualism was overthrown. That is what the great Greek theologians in their evangelical concern set themselves to do, and they succeeded so well that they laid Christian theology upon the classical basis upon which the Church has relied ever since; but in so doing they also laid the foundation stone for all modern empirical science, in the doctrine—impossible for Greeks and Orientals alike—of the inherent intelligibility of contingent existence.

Unfortunately, however, the Ptolemaic cosmology, together with the philosophical and cultural dualism between the intelligible and sensible realms, was reintroduced into Christianity through St. Augustine, and has affected the whole of Western Christianity ever since. Instead of counteracting it the introduction of Aristotelian physics, metaphysics and psychology into mediaeval thought had the effect of hardening the dualism between an immutable, impassible Deity and contingent, temporal existence. Thus all ecclesiastical institutions and theological structures of Latin Christianity are profoundly conditioned by that Augustinian tradition.

The second great mutation in scientific and cosmological outlook took place when the changes initiated by Copernicus, Kepler and Galileo were developed by Sir Isaac Newton and mathematically elaborated in his magnificent 'system of the world'. This *Newtonian cosmology* was characterised by a thorough-going dualism between absolute space and time and the contingent events that take place within their embrace, between volume and mass, and primary and secondary qualities, etc. As such it linked on to and took up into itself the Augustinian dualism that passed over into the modern world through the Reformation and took on a distinctively Protestant form. In this way, Newtonian thought built a deep-seated dualism into the whole fabric of Western science, philosophy and culture, which has profoundly conditioned all Protestant institutions and structures. This is just as evident in Protestant scholasticism as in Protestant deism, whereas within the Newtonian framework Protestant philosophy appears to be a sec- ularised form of Augustinianism. Moreover, precisely the same dualism mediated through the writings of John Locke has per- meated all our social institutions as well. The damaging effect of all this nowhere appears more sharply than in the wide gap that opens up between an inert God who cannot be known in himself and the world of phenomena conceived as a closed continuum of cause and effect. That is the source of what Martin Buber used to call 'the conceptual letting go of God' so common in the modern world, but also the source of the wide-spread doubt and difficulties about providence, prayer and worship, for it means that even Christian forms of thought and speech about God are uprooted from any objective ground in the being of God himself and float loose in the vague mists of modern man's vaunted self- understanding. As soon as the ontological reference of our thought and speech is cut off like that, we are shut up to the dismal alternatives of a moralistic existentialism or a sterile linguistic analysis.

Thus the great mutation in thought that took place at the Refor- mation, from the mediaeval to the modern world, was after all only a transition from one form of dualism to another. It should not surprise us therefore that the same problems and the same mistaken answers crop up in the history of Protestant as of Mediaeval Chris- tianity, although they are of course somewhat disguised by being clothed in a rather different idiom and style of thought. But the dualism is more damaging in the modern world because it has been more consistently worked out and because it is no longer a Chris- tian philosophy but natural science that supplies the cultural framework for people's thought. The common ground thus appar- ent in the aberrations of Roman Catholics and Protestants alike, should at least contribute to ecumenical relations between us, if only because the stones we may want to throw at each other inevi- tably rebound upon ourselves!

Now we come to the third great mutation in the scientific and cosmological outlook of Western culture, but compared with the other two, this has the proportions of a *gigantic revolution,* the full implications of which we cannot yet anticipate. The basic character of this new *Einsteinian cosmology* is clear enough: a thorough-going rejection of dualism—not that anything like a monism or a pantheism is envisaged, for we are carried quite beyond that orbit of thought—grounded in the mutual interaction of the space-time metrical field and all matter/energy in the universe: $E = MC^2$. That is to say, here we have a radical reorientation in knowledge in which structure and matter, form and being are inseparably fused together, spelling the end of the analytical era in science. This involves the restoration of a genuine ontology, the replacing of the mechanistic universe with a dynamic universe conceived in onto-relational terms, and the replacing of the old forms of causal connection and natural law with field-structure and field-laws. The vast change that this involves, for example, in the relation of conscious mind to brain, is such that, as Sir John Eccles has recently argued, the revolution of science that must come about will result in an understanding so far transcending our present inadequate concepts that our present science, even in its most sophisticated aspects, will appear as primitive and naive.[1]

There is no need for us to follow this out further, but this must be said: nothing like this has ever appeared before in the whole history of science, philosophy and culture, except in the theology of the pre-Augustinian Greek Fathers, who had to carry through the same kind of revolution in the basis of their culture as modern science is engaged in carrying out today. For the first time, then, in the history of thought, Christian theology finds itself in the throes of a new scientific culture which is not antithetical to it, but which operates with a non-dualistic outlook upon the universe which is not inconsistent with the Christian faith, even at the crucial points of creation and incarnation. This also means that the theology most relevant to the post-Einsteinian world is that of classical Patristic theology, although of course it needs to be recast in the idiom and style of our own era.

A very serious problem faces us today, however: that of the *time-lag* between the inception of the revolution in the foundations of thought and its completion in the restructuring of our forms of thought and life, for the transitional period is full of chaotic ideas,

1. J. C. Eccles, *Facing Reality* (Longman, London, 1970), p. 61.

paranoid anxieties, hybrid solutions and regressive tendencies. This troublesome time-lag is most apparent in three areas: (*a*) the modern (and especially the popular) mind, which is still apparently governed by eighteenth- and nineteenth-century ideas; (*b*) the social sciences, which have been desperately slow to move forward into the realm of fluid field-theories, and still operate with obsolete mechanistic concepts eked out with statistical theory; and (*c*) the technological society, in which the old analytical and instrumentalist science, employed to harness the resources of nature for human ends, has acquired such a momentum of its own that man finds himself being exploited along with nature.

Our day, then, is one of widespread disintegration of form, not least in the arts and humanities, of fragmentation and pluralism in society with corresponding confusion in the social sciences, and of ecological chaos resulting from the technological decomposition of the organised coherences in nature. While all these are features that arise at the phenomenal level, they are not just ways in which modern society is developing and to which we must give expression in the communication of the Christian message, but are symptoms of serious disorder below the surface of human existence, which must be set right and to which the church must address itself. Perhaps the worst thing Churchmen could do would be to lose their nerve at the wide gap opening up between historic Christianity and modern patterns of human behaviour, and allow themselves to be panicked by the *avant-gardes* into translating the Christian message into current social manifestations which are themselves part of the sickness of humanity. That is alas the line so often pursued by reactionary liberals in the name of 'involvement', as though the Church were a sort of religious discotheque, whereas I want to challenge them to follow the example of the Greek Fathers in undertaking the courageous, revolutionary task of a Christian reconstruction of the foundations of culture: nothing less is worthy of the Christian Gospel.

That is the complex situation in which the Church must reexamine the prosecution of its mission. On the phenomenal level, the dissolution of the coherences goes on, while the new combinations, especially noticeable in sound, image and action, fail to produce any substantive order or meaning, and only serve to cut off more poignantly than ever the surface level of human existence from its ontological roots, but in the depths of human existence there is going on an immense revolution which will eventually transform the whole face of human thought and behaviour.

What is the Church to do?

1. THE CHURCH MUST EMANCIPATE ITSELF FROM ITS BUILT-IN OBSOLESCENCE

In his justly famous book, *The Structure of Scientific Revolutions*, Thomas S. Kuhn discusses the serious tension that arises when science comes up with discoveries so novel that the existing structures of thought in normal science require radical alteration. Those existing structures, however, have been built into the mental habits of the community in which normal science operates and constitute what Kuhn calls the paradigms of the community. Hence a scientific revolution calls for a paradigmatic shift in the community rather like a conversion experience, a veritable restructuring of its mind. In its advances, therefore, science has to struggle with the reactionary force of the community, the backward drag of its mental habits, and learn how to break the patterns of current thought in order to assimilate what is really new. Indeed it is only by advancing ahead of the community like that, that science can help the community itself to advance out of the past, but to translate everything back into the existing paradigms would only retard the advance of society.

Now let us be quite frank: the regular tendency of Churchmen has always been to operate within the paradigms of the community and thus to play a role quite the opposite of that fulfilled by scientists. This is most evident of course in popular preaching and folk liturgies. But, in our day, that tendency has been turned into a *regular programme* with the aid of all available media to make the Gospel understandable within the mental habits or current thought-forms which people already have, and thus to eliminate as far as possible any gap between the Gospel and the paradigmatic mould of contemporary society. Quite typical in this respect are the modern slogans: 'the medium is the message', or 'the world writes the agenda'. This is to evade the real mission of communication, for instead of getting to grips with the social consciousness where it stumbles at the Gospel, it allows the Gospel to be merged with the communicative media of a passing phase of human culture and so be swept into the swirl of ideas that float about on the surface of the social consciousness, where it becomes submerged among the debris thrown up from previous generations. By that kind of communication, the Church keeps building into its life a continuing obsolescence, so that, to change the metaphor, when in some sharp crisis a volcanic shift takes place in culture and a serious breach appears between the Church and current social consciousness, its religious utterances converted into cultural expressions are found to be empty of substance, and the cry goes up that God is dead. Yet it is not God who has died out of the Church, but the paradigms of society and the communicative media into which the Gospel had been foolishly merged. In this way crisis after crisis is created for the Church precisely by its Churchmen. Let me put the question bluntly: if the Churches everywhere today suffer from a diminishing membership, and if the ecumenical movement is now losing ground in every country, how far is that due to the fact that the leaders of the Churches, the National Councils and the World Council of Churches, have been fostering a situation in which they are caught by their own self-inflicted obsolescence?

I have been speaking about the present, but what of the historic past which the Church rightly carries over into the present? Sociologists tell us that the theology of every generation is conditioned by the culture through which it passes—and of course they are right. But whereas the sociologists are professedly indifferent to whether such a state of affairs is right or wrong, or whether the concepts concerned are true or false, a scientific theology cannot be indifferent. It is obliged to examine historical doctrines with a view to distinguishing in them what is proper to the authentic substance of the faith and what is foreign to it but which has understandably been merged with it from the paradigms of contemporary society. This kind of clarification is ecumenically as well as evangelically incumbent upon us, but it is also something we owe to the other sciences which are also concerned with questions as to truth and falsity, and which have not a little help to offer us here. Let me select several examples.

Take the principate of St Peter as it is set out in the New Testament and in early Patristic writings such as Cyprian's *De unitate ecclesiae*. When today we compare this with the way in which it was expounded by Leo the Great we find there to be fused with it the pre-Christian Roman law of heredity and legal succession. That is to say, a legal paradigm from non-Christian Latin culture has been grafted on to the original deposit of the faith, and has altered its structure at this point. Thus the difference here between Roman and other Christians is seen to be a difference, not in Christ, nor in St Peter, but in an alien and obsolete non-theological factor.

Or take the doctrine of the *real presence* as defined by Romans and Lutherans in different ways. Scientific analysis of this concept reveals that the real presence is here explained in terms of the

Aristotelian container notion of space (found in the fourth book of the *Physics*), in which there is an inseparable interdependence between the containing vessel and what it contains. This gave rise to serious difficulties and solutions were offered again in obsolete Aristotelian terms. But this container notion of space, which had already been rejected by Patristic theology as alien to the Incarnation, has been discredited by modern science. And it is now quite clear that it is a foreign structure falsely imposed on the real presence which can be expounded more fully and forcefully today without it. Protestant notions of the real presence, on the other hand, have been largely determined by the false dualisms so completely exposed and rejected by relativity theory.

In the third place, let us take the question of *historical succession,* which is such an ecumenical stumbling-block to many Protestants. Scientific analysis shows that if we work separately with space as a three-dimensional continuum and with time as an independent one-dimensional continuum, then the notion of historical succession cannot avoid mechanical connections. Moreover, when this is linked to the container notion of space it cannot avoid the idea of grace being transmitted mechanically from one ecclesiastical vessel or office to another—an idea so disliked by Protestants. On the other hand, if temporal continuity is separated from space, as an inward form of intuition apart from experience, then it relates merely to appearances and is entirely relative to the individual consciousness, and so loses all empirical or objective reality. That is the ground not only for Protestant denigration of historical succession but also for the fateful Protestant difficulties in holding on to the historical Jesus. That is to say, the general Protestant approach to this question is fundamentally distorted by alien notions of time as well as of space and by obsolete paradigmatic structures deriving from the separateness of time and space in European culture. Today, however, the relational concepts of space and time first developed by the Greek Fathers have come into their own, so that with the aid of the invisible but objective structure of space-time, we are able to offer a profounder and more satisfying account of historical continuity in Church and ministry than ever before.

Enough examples have been given to indicate how much the Church can learn today from the immense clarification of some of our basic human concepts achieved by modern science. This does not mean that Christian theology can or should ever be grounded on natural science, but it does mean that as we allow ourselves to be questioned by rigorous scientific analysis we are helped to discriminate what is truly theological, arising on the ground of God's self-revelation, from distorting foreign structures that have so often been grafted on to it but which turn out to be no more than obsolete deposits in the Christian consciousness from some passing phase of human culture.

2. THE CHURCH MUST LEARN AGAIN THE MEANING OF JUSTIFICATION BY GRACE

A few years ago Fr Jock Dalrymple, sometime Roman Catholic chaplain at St Andrews University, remarked, mainly with Edinburgh in mind, that some of our young men being trained for the ministry seemed unable to distinguish between helping a person therapeutically and leading him to Jesus Christ. Such a shrewd evangelical critique of the Church of Scotland, coming from the Roman Catholic Church, seems to indicate that the tables are being turned on the Reformation! It is certainly the case that Protestant Churches everywhere today appear, and want to appear, highly *meritorious,* giving themselves out as the great patrons of goodness: that is, precisely what Jesus warned his disciples against at the Last Supper. How has this come about?

Some of the sharpest thinkers in modern times, coming from Eastern Europe, see us in the West in a way that we cannot easily manage ourselves, and have been warning us against *the moral inversion of the guilty intellectual.* That is, I believe, the insidious infection that has been afflicting western, and particularly Protestant, Churches. Moral inversion (Polanyi's phrase) is a hybrid of idealism and scepticism, of high moral demands on society and individualistic naturalism. It comes about when moral passion is uprooted from its authoritative ground through rationalistic critique of transcendent moral obligation, and becomes embodied in a tangible realm of socio-moral objectives regarded as less open to destructive philosophical analysis. 'The morally inverted person,' Polanyi says, 'has not merely performed a philosophic substitution of moral aims by material purposes, but is acting with the whole force of his homeless moral passions within a purely materialistic framework of purposes.'[2] It is distinctive of moral inver-

2. See *The Logic of Liberty* (Routledge & Kegan Paul, London, 1951), p. 106; *Personal Knowledge* (Routledge & Kegan Paul, London, 1958), pp. 232ff.; *Knowing and Being* (Routledge & Kegan Paul, London, 1969), pp. 14, 16ff., 21f., 44f.; and 'Science and Man', *Proceedings of the Royal Society of Medicine* (1970), vol. 63, pp. 971ff.

sion that it carries with it a strong sense of righteousness and moral superiority, evident in passionate moral indignation against prevailing evils, social injustice, racial discrimination, overpopulation, etc. These are all of course very right and highly laudable causes, but the inflamed moral passion for social betterment that lies behind this, appears to go hand in hand with a guilty detachment from an objective and divine source of moral obligation and a replacement of a personal religious ethic with a naturalistic ethic of self-determination in which man assumes absolute responsibility for himself. This is often accompanied by bitter denunciations of explicit expressions of personal religious morality as hypocritical and dishonest, together with an inverted moral fervour in the alleged 'honesty' that characterises such denunciations. Moreover, this whole approach finds not a little support in the moral nihilism of modern sociology, that is, its deliberate suspension of value in the explanation of human behaviour, without reference to its rightness or wrongness, and therefore apart altogether from moral motives.

There is another important aspect of moral inversion that must be noted. The uprooting of moral passion from its creative source in Christian faith and therefore its lack of Holy Spirit, makes it quite helpless unless it can secure centres of power, from which it can move and change society. Hence it moves into the political arena where it can develop pressure groups and forge the kind of instruments through which it can exert force upon every area of life until its ends are achieved. But this is to move into an area of operations in the technological society where the achievement of social perfection is committed to a political machine which develops its own ideological rationale and generates its own functional momentum, so that inevitably moral motives are submerged in a struggle for power: self-determination is converted into collective power and moral persuasion is replaced by force. In the nature of the case, change one way or the other can take place only through violence of one kind or another. Thus the high moral demands for society geared into a naturalistic concept of man lead paradoxically into inhumanity: that seems to be the case whatever kind of government is in command.

The vast slide of Church leaders in recent times into something like an obsession with socio-moral concerns reflects (does it not?) a nagging sense of guilt over their own personal Christian convictions, which over-compensates for itself, not merely in public demonstrations and loud protests of 'involvement', but in passionate moral extravagances and drives which our modern critics have sometimes described as pathological moralistic excess. Whether that kind of language is justified or not, we must certainly be ready to face up to the criticisms they direct at us. But what concerns me here is that moral inversion of this kind has so infected the Churches, especially Anglo-Saxon Churches, that our evangelical convictions are persistently submerged if not replaced by *consciously meritorious involvement* in socio-political issues, which is associated with a serious degeneration of genuine ethical substance and indeed a widespread moral laxity of the individual in our society. Thus the moralistic externalisation of life in the Churches is concomitant with a fatal loss in spiritual depth. Or perhaps it should be put the other way round: it is an atrophying of the soul, a deep inward emptiness, that forces people outward where they become absorbed in externalities on the surface of existence, but where, as every true pastor knows, the flock of Christ grows weary with the husks of morality and hungers for the sheer grace of God.

I would not like to be misunderstood, for I am not asking for the slightest curtailment of concern for any genuine human, moral or social need anywhere in the world. But I am more and more staggered at two things: *first,* the astonishing *volte-face* that has been taking place in the Churches of the Reformation, in that they reveal a serious lapse from the centrality of the Gospel of Christ, together with a failure to understand that it is justification by grace alone which creates the ethical disturbance that turns the world upside down; and *secondly*, the growing contradiction that the western Churches exhibit to Jesus' total rejection of every value-system based on power, and his proclamation of the new order which cannot be brought about by any form of force, together with a failure to remember that Jesus was crucified by contemporaries who bitterly resented his refusal to have anything whatsoever to do with their political theology.

Let us perform a double thought-experiment. *First,* let us put the Church of today in the place of Jesus in the wilderness where he was tempted of the devil, and ask how it would be able to stand up to those temptations. Would we be able to resist the temptation to turn stones into bread, in face of the vast hunger of mankind? And what of the temptation to have a compelling demonstration of divine, supernatural power in the temple—could we withstand the seduction which religious prestige like that would bring? And the ultimate temptation of political power which would bring into the Church all the kingdoms of the world and their power and glory? Jesus resisted that temptation too and chose instead the way of the servant, with complete renunciation of all power, in order to fulfil his mission in the utter weakness of the man on the Cross. *Then,* let us project the Church of today forward to the last judgment where it will meet Jesus face to face, as he divides the sheep on his right hand from the goats on his left, in the way which he anticipated for us in the parable of Matthew 25. The meritorious Church of today could hardly be placed with the sheep on Christ's right hand, for they did *not* know that they had cared for the hungry and the thirsty, the stranger, the naked, the sick or the imprisoned. That is after all a parable of justification by *grace,* for grace *always* takes us by surprise.

3. THE CHURCH MUST RECOVER ITS MISSION OF HEALING AND RECONCILIATION IN THE DEPTH OF BEING

Shortly after U Thant had been appointed secretary of the United Nations Organisation, some years ago, he gave an interview in this country, in the course of which he was asked what the greatest needs of the East were. He replied at once that the greatest need was spiritual, but added that the East had long since learned that, although it got plenty of material aid from the West, it could get no spiritual help from it. What an indictment of Christian mission! To such an Easterner, evidently, we Westerners are no more than what appears from the outside in our absorption with the material world, for we seem unable to reach beyond the phenomenal level, mistaking superficial tangible actualities for the profound intangible realities. Even the Christian religion seems to become trivialised among us.

We know only too well that there is truth in that: our modern mind lacks ontological depth. Somehow the top of our existence seems to be severed from its roots in a deeper level of reality, so that it lacks a consistent substructure to hold it together, with the result that so often today the creative forces in human life seem to be fighting a losing battle against the forces of fragmentation and disintegration. This has been brilliantly set forth in the Princeton lectures of Erich Kahler, entitled *The Disintegration of Form in the Arts,*[3] in which he shows how in the realms of image, sound and language, forces of decomposition and destruction begin to be at work as soon as the arts cut loose from the underlying structures or

3. George Braziller, New York, 1968.

frames of being, for then the natural coherences dissolve away and a degree of disintegration sets in which is quite frightening, for what happens to artistic form happens sooner or later to man himself.

That fits in completely with the phenomenalist approach to things which has so long dominated our existence in the West. Owing to the profound dualisms at work in our culture, human life and thought have been forced into the mould of observationalist and instrumentalist science, in which structure is abstracted from substance and form is cut off from being, so that external organisation and mechanical connection replace the inner organisation and natural patterns inherent in the created universe. Thus the ability to see things conjunctively has been eroded and displaced by disjunctive processes of analysis, so that fragmentation and decomposition of phenomena result, and they have to be clamped together by means of some artificial framework. But now even artificially contrived coherence is in process of rapid disintegration—that seems to be the message that stares out at us again and again from modern art, as we find painting abandoning first the frame and then any recognisable vestige of pictorial substance.

Where has this been more evident, alas, than in biblical studies? We have a vivid illustration of this in the scientific investigation of the historical Jesus which has been going on for the last hundred and fifty years. There we see, first of all, a phenomenalist bracketing off of the evangelical material from any realm of things in themselves or their internal relations, so that it is approached merely as a collection of appearances relative to observers and detached from any objective sub-structure. Then we have the steady application to it of the methods of observationalist and analytical science, through which the appearances are abstracted from the frame of their natural connectivity in the evangelical witness, so that they inevitably become fragmented like the phenomenal particulars of observationalist natural science. The natural coherence in which the evangelical material has come down to us is explained away as an imposition upon the original appearances through the use of screen images thrown up out of the consciousness and worship of the early Christian community. Nevertheless something is needed to take its place, and so artificial and unnatural frameworks are produced by the scholars, one after the other. At first, of course, the framework used was borrowed from (rather old-fashioned) natural science, the closed continuum of cause and effect used in the construction of the nineteenth-century mechanistic universe. Accordingly, everything in the traditional life of Jesus which could not be causally connected up or explained in that sort of way was excised from the basic collection of phenomena. Then, however, when this scientistic method was found to eliminate virtually everything from the tradition, scholars searched round for some other kind of framework in which some at least of the appearances could be saved by being fitted into a coherent pattern. All this, of course, was still within the phenomenalist game of piecing together what had already been disintegrated through its basic assumptions and methods, so that only one artificially contrived framework after another could be thought up. But now, once again, even that sort of thing is in process of rapid disintegration: the bizarre representations of Jesus offered by some contemporary scholars clearly belong to the same genre as some post nineteen-forty-five painting, devoid of frame and substance alike. Is it any wonder, then, that the Jesus of the modern quest attracts a rapidly diminishing community of worshippers, or that in 'the Jesus Movement' a new counter-cultural approach should be demanded by common people in sharp revulsion from all sophisticated artificiality? Jesus may elude the scholars, but the common people still hear him gladly.

What has gone wrong? Looked at from the perspective of the scientific revolution, the New Testament presentation of Jesus Christ can be construed in terms of observationalist and analytical science even less than the electro-magnetic field. The collapse of classical mechanics at that point forced scientists to realise that the electro-magnetic field can be understood only out of its own innate organisation or dynamic field-structure, which demands of us a drastic change in first principles and methods. That is the significance of the unity of structure and substance, or form and being, that has emerged out of the scientific revolution. Looked at from that point of view, then, two things must be said about the modern quest for the historical Jesus. (*a*) Phenomenal events can only be seen to form a pattern when treated as empirical correlates of a higher level of reality; thus by its initial assumption the phenomenological approach to Jesus doomed itself to futility. (*b*) The divorce of structure from substance or of form from being gives rise to artificial theoretic structures which inevitably break down in face of the empirical reality. That is why the observational quest of Jesus which abstracted structure from substance and form from being could never succeed. Because structure and substance, form and being are already fused together in reality, the only adequate theoretical structures or conceptual forms with which we may operate are those ontologically derived from the empirical field we are investigating.

What does this mean in theological terms? Simply that neither an approach to Jesus starting from his humanity, nor an approach starting from his deity, is in place: we must approach Jesus simultaneously on both levels in the space-time field in which he and we encounter each other; from the very start of our theological interpretation, therefore, we must learn to think conjunctively of him as God and man in the one indivisible fact of Jesus Christ. However convictions about Jesus may arise in us, only when we treat the historical events of his life as empirical correlates of divine acts in an inter-level synthesis, can we do justice to their intrinsic organisation and their inner form as empirical and historical realities. That, paradoxically, is what the phenomenalist and observationalist quest of the historical Jesus has demonstrated, precisely by its failure again and again: as soon as the historical events of Jesus' life are cut off for consideration by themselves as phenomena, they become bafflingly enigmatic and elusive, for they are thereby divested of substance and being, and torn away from their intrinsic structures and coherence.

That should not surprise us in view of what has been happening in modern science, which has demonstrated that only when empirical and phenomenal events are correlated to the space-time metrical field and understood through coordination with its objective framework, can they be explained in the natural forms in which we experience them without mutilation or artificial manipulation. This amounts to a gigantic reversal of the old materialist obsession with perceptible and tangible magnitudes as the exclusively real, for the really objective framework that embraces and regulates the behaviour of all things within the created universe is in fact the imperceptible, intangible magnitude of the space-time metrical field, in which structure and substance, form and being, are inseparably fused together. That is why rigorous scientific method operates from the very start with the closest correlation of theoretical and empirical components in knowledge, the imperceptible and the perceptible, the intangible and the tangible coinhering together at every point.

Why should it be otherwise in theology? I am not implying of course that the experienced imperceptible in natural science is to be identified with the experienced imperceptible in theology, for here we have to do with the imperceptible, intangible reality of the living God who transcends all space-time and is the source of all form and being. But what I am saying is that if natural science today cannot get on without invisible ontological structures, how much more is that the case with theology? Indeed it is precisely because God is the Creator of the whole space-time universe and the transcendent Source of all form and being within it, that Christian theology *above all* must be concerned with the unity of structure and substance, form and being, and therefore with overcoming everything that divides them or tears them apart. That is why the disintegration of form and the loss of substance in the modern world cannot but constitute a standing challenge to the Christian Church. Yet the most impelling reason for this is to be found in the *Incarnation:* the fact that God declined to allow his creation to lapse from him into degeneration and corruption, and entered himself into the disorderly depths of our creaturely and human existence in order to heal it of its profound divisions and recreate its being, reconciling it to himself in the ultimate integration of all things visible and invisible in Jesus Christ.

It follows ineluctably that the Church, which is the Body of Christ in the world, is committed by its union with him, to the mission of healing and reconciliation in the depth of being. To take this seriously would certainly import a radical reversal of our objectives in the Churches, not unlike the reversal that has been taking place in modern science. It amounts to a demand that we set our sights again on the great intangible realities as the primary factors regulating the universe, and find there, in the interaction between God and created being in Jesus Christ, the real solution for the many problems that now absorb us in the realm of tangible and visible actuality. What is supremely needed, therefore, in all the Churches today, is a far profounder understanding of the Incarnation, the coming of God himself into the structures of creaturely and human being, in order to restore the creation to its unity and harmony in himself—that is, a Christology with genuine *substance* in it once more, the theology of the incarnate Son of God, the one Lord Jesus Christ, *'being of one substance with the Father, by whom all things were made'*. And then in intimate correlation with such a Christology, what is supremely needed also is a far profounder understanding of the Church as divine creation within the ontological structures of the universe, entrusted with the mission of healing and reconciliation in the depth of being.

I have had some sharp criticisms to make of the moral, mental and spiritual condition of our Churches today, but my purpose throughout has been to cut away some of the rank growth in the foreground all round us, in order to open up clearly the perspective of the Church's mission in an era of astonishing cosmological change in which basic structures of human science and culture are in process of breaking up but in which new coherences and patterns have been taking firm shape beneath the decay of the old and are already beginning to break through the surface, although as yet they may not be generally recognised. What I would like to do now, is to draw attention to several of these exciting features which seem to me to indicate the shape of change and advance in the years ahead, in the hope that the identification and consideration of them in this way will contribute to the constructive reorientation we need.

(i) It is particularly exciting to find that at last in the development of modern theology, as in the scientific revolution, a reintegration of structure and substance has been taking place, but a rather different kind of structure and substance than that which obtained in the Augustinian-Aristotelian or the Augustinian-Newtonian eras of western theology. The latest evidence for this is to be seen in Professor D. M. Mackinnon's outstanding contribution on 'substance' in Christology in the recent volume of Cambridge studies in Christology.[4] In the scientific revolution, replacing the old mechanistic structure and the discarded 'metaphysical' notion of substance, we have dynamic field-structure and the continuous substance of fused matter and energy, together constituting the indivisible reality of space-time. It is something quite parallel and of course on a different level, that we find struggling to emerge in theology, with the dynamic form and persistent being of a space-time universe in continuous interaction with the living God, the Creator and Redeemer. This is nowhere more evident than in the doctrine of God itself, in which we are learning to think together the being of God *in his acts,* and *the acts of God in his being.* The significance of that can be seen if we glance at the respective problems of theology in the Augustinian-Aristotelian and Augustinian-Newtonian eras. The high Patristic conception of the being of God in his acts tended to suffer severe refraction within mediaeval dualism which led on the one hand to a rather abstract and static concept of God's being and on the other hand to a diminished concept of his acts which tended to be replaced regularly by a metaphysical notion of grace. This led to the reaction of Protestant theology which has increasingly laid the emphasis upon the redemptive acts of God in Christ and in history, but here the high Reformation emphasis upon the acts of God in his being has suffered severe refraction within the Cartesian-Newtonian-Kantian dualism which resulted in the detachment of

4. *Christ and Faith in History,* ed. S. W. Sykes and J. P. Clayton (Cambridge University Press, Cambridge, 1972), pp. 279ff.

the acts of God from his being and their present-day dissolution in the timeless events of the existentialists: the loss of ontology has proved quite fatal. Protestant scholasticism had certainly tried to save theology from all this by encasing the teaching of the Reformation in the static concepts developed by the Newtonian outlook upon the universe, in a way not unlike Newton's strange recasting of his own understanding of the universe in terms of differential law into the axiomatic mould of a geometry of the interrelations of rigid bodies independent of time: but all that is breaking up under the shift from the old cosmology of separated space and time. Now in our own day we see the rise of an Evangelical-Catholic theology in which the patristic understanding of the being of God in his acts and the Reformation understanding of the acts of God in his being are being thought together in such a way that there promises to arise out of it a profound but rather different kind of synthesis from that which arose out of the great mediaeval tradition. Owing not a little to the critical analysis of traditional concepts carried out in the scientific destruction of dualism, Christian theology is now more free and more open for positive reconstruction. The way ahead seems to lie in bringing that critical clarification to bear upon the pioneer work of Karl Barth in his conjunctive rethinking of the being of God in his acts and the acts of God in his being which has so far contributed more than anything else to the advance of theology in recent centuries.

(*ii*) The second outstanding feature to which I wish to draw your attention has also to do with Karl Barth, in his doctrine of the Holy Trinity, which has initiated a reversal of thought in the fundamental grammar of theology, carrying us back through Peter Lombard and John of Damascus, to the great Greek theology of the Early Church. St Augustine had certainly taught that the Trinity bears upon the basic structures of our knowledge of God in such a way that triadic patterns are implied in the human soul, which plays an essential role in our knowledge of God from the very start. But the inherent dualism in Augustinian thought, especially after the collapse of the enlightenment theory of knowledge, tended to separate the knowing soul from the being of God, so that the mediaeval Church brought in Aristotelian modes of thought to help overcome the cleavage. Actually, however, the effect of that measure was to harden the cleavage while only half-overcoming it, so that, as we can see very clearly in the teaching of St Thomas Aquinas, the doctrine of the One God was cut off sharply from the doctrine of the Triune God, the former only being related to the epistemological structure of the knowing mind. Moreover, that carried with it a fateful concept of 'person' which was logically derived from the notions of individuality and rational substance and not derived ontologically from the Trinity, which has seriously affected the whole history of Western thought ever since, Catholic and Protestant alike, and indeed, especially when merged with Newtonian particle-theory through John Locke, gave rise to the atomistic notion of the self-determining personality requiring external political organisation, which has infected the infra-structure of all our social institutions and sciences.

The decisive change in that whole development came with Karl Barth's reconstruction of the doctrine of the Trinity, in which it was essentially related once again to the basic structure of our knowledge of God, so that to know God from the very start is to know him as Triune. But this basic structure is not some Augustinian unchanging triad in the created human soul, but one inseparably bound up with the dynamic interaction of God with man through his self-communication and self-revelation to man. In Roman Catholic theology Karl Barth was first followed here by Michael Schmaus[5] and now in a more succinct and rigorous way by Karl Rahner,[6] although neither seems to have emancipated himself sufficiently from the Boethian-Thomist notion of the person. The work of Karl Rahner, however, has made two things very evident, and this is most exciting: (a) At their deepest point, in the fundamental grammar of Christian theology, the Roman Catholic and Evangelical-Protestant traditions, even in the case of their representative theologians so widely divergent from each other as Rahner and Barth, are merging closely together. The transforming effect of that, eventually, in the superstructures of those traditions can only be enormous. (b) Rahner has also made it explicit that this reconstructed doctrine of the Trinity, in which the *homoousia* is applied to the *self*-communication of God to man, carries over into the Western Church the essential elements of the Eastern Orthodox approach to the Trinity, not least in the way in which the ontological conception of the Trinity follows from the economic conception of the Trinity. The ecumenical implications of that change can hardly be overestimated, provided that East and West, Catholic

---

5. Michael Schmaus, *Katholische Dogmatik 1/2, Gott des Dreieinige* (Max Hueber, München, 1948).
6. In *Mysterium Salutis. Grundriss heilsgeschichtlicher Dogmatik,* edited by J. Feiner and M. Löhrer, vol. 2, ch. 5, 'Der dreifaltige Gott als transzendenter Urgrund der Heilsgeschichte' (Benziger Verlag, Einsiedeln, 1967)—Eng. tr. by J. Donceel, *The Trinity* (Burns & Oates/Herder and Herder, London, 1970).

and Protestant Christians alike, have the courage to work out those implications consistently. But the overall import of this upon the whole of human thought and culture, at least in the West, will be evident from this double fact: that here there is introduced into the ground and frame of our knowledge of God a reconciliation between knowing and being which demands and gives shape to a new grand synthesis; and that here there arises again the distinctively Christian concept of the person, deriving from the community of love in God and defined in onto-relational terms in which the inveterate ego-centricity of the self-determining personality is overcome, which demands and gives shape to a new and open concept of human society.

(*iii*) The third significant feature which I have selected comes from the movement for liturgical renewal in our times, namely, the vicarious role of the *humanity* of Jesus Christ in liturgical prayer and worship. I refer here once again to the work of Josef Andreas Jungmann, perhaps the greatest liturgiologist of the twentieth century. Jungmann has revealed, with meticulous examination and documentation, a process of increasing liturgical monophysitism (as I have called it) in the development of the Church's liturgies in East and West, that is, a movement of greater and greater stress upon the deity and majesty of Christ in worship together with diminishing room for the priesthood of the man Jesus. In the oldest strata of the Church's liturgy, public prayer was regularly directed to the Father only through the mediatorship of Christ, who however was always included with the Spirit and the Father in the trinitarian formulae of adoration and praise. The application of the *homoousia* to Christ and the Holy Spirit arose out of and implied their equal adorability with the Father. But in the prolonged struggles against Arianism, with its notion of the Logos or Son as a semi-divine intermediary between God and the creation, there steadily grew up in reaction the practice of public prayer deliberately directed to Christ in the Eucharistic rite, with the result that precisely there where he is both the offering and the offerer in one, Christ became so pushed into the sheer majesty of God that worshippers lost sight of his humanity in its vicarious and priestly role in human worship of the Father. According to Jungmann this is particularly evident in the mediaeval liturgies, in which there grew up a one-sided emphasis upon awe and fear in the presence of Christ, so that something had to be interposed between him and the sinner. Thus the mass itself and the officiating priest tended to take the place of Christ, a development which has adversely affected the subsequent understanding of public prayer and worship.

So much, then, for Jungmann's historical analysis, but the tracing of this distortion in the growth of the Church's worship and the identification of its grounds, has borne the greatest fruit in the liturgical and religious revival in the Roman Catholic Church leading up to the Second Vatican Council. Yet it is precisely at this point, in the recovered stress upon the vicarious humanity or human priesthood of Christ on the part of Roman Catholic piety, that one can see a profound convergence with Evangelical piety as it is expounded, for example, by Karl Barth who has singled out this aspect of the teaching of John Calvin for special development in his Christology. What we have here, then, is a doctrine of the Incarnation which is not a dualistic account of Christ as *God in man* but one in which Christ is discerned to be *God come as man,* ranging himself on the side of man in order from within man and out of the depth of human being to act from the side of man towards the Father, and not merely to act from the side of the Father towards man, even in the most intimate and deeply human activities of faith, worship and prayer towards God. The crucial issue is thus the vicarious humanity of Jesus, the one everlasting way to the Father.

As we have already seen, Fr. Jungmann has not taken up the important point stressed by Cyril of Alexandria in book after book, that it is Apollinarianism which undermines Christian worship of God the Father through the high-priesthood of Jesus Christ—that is, a subtle form of monophysitism in which creaturely and human nature is readily accorded to Christ but in such a way that his human rational soul is displaced or replaced by the divine mind of the Logos, so that the redemptive role of Christ is reduced to being merely the bodily instrument in the hands of God for man's salvation. That is to destroy at once any saving act by Jesus Christ in the integrity of his humanity from the side of man towards God, and any act of God in the Incarnation by which he takes up our estranged human mind in order to heal and sanctify it in Jesus Christ. But that is to limit salvation to what is merely physical, for 'that which has not been taken up, has not been saved', argued Cyril.[7] On the other hand, if we reject every vestige of Apollinarianism and take seriously the full reality and integrity of the human mind of Jesus in the one person of the Incarnate Son, then we must think of Christ coming among us worshippers as himself a worshipper of the Father, and therefore think of his worship on earth as an essen-

---

7. Cyril of Alexandria, *Commentary on the Gospel according to St. John,* XII:28 (Parker, Oxford, 1874), vol. 2, p. 152.

tial part of his saving and vicarious work in the form of a servant which he fulfilled in life and death and resurrection on our behalf. Thus we think of Christ in his vicarious humanity as Mediator of our salvation in mind as well as body, Advocate who represents us continually before the Father, High Priest who prays in our place and on our behalf, and at the same time through his union and communion with us taking up and sanctifying our prayers in himself, assimilating them into his vicarious prayer, and presenting us in and through his own self-offering to the Father which he makes on behalf of all humanity. Thus it is only in the name of Jesus Christ and not in our own name, through him and no other, that we approach and worship the Father, with no offering but the self-offering of Christ and no prayer or worship but that which he lived and made in his vicarious human life, for in the strictest sense Jesus Christ is himself the prayer and praise and worship with which we appear before the Father. If salvation does not really have to do with the depth of the human mind or rational soul, but only with the physical aspects of human existence involved when the Word was made flesh, then worship in the traditional sense becomes meaningless, for the only relevant worship that could be developed would be one that is an expression of our motivated physical behaviour. If that is the kind of thing to which Protestant worship today is so often reduced, little more than the personal correlate of a social gospel or an expression of political involvement in the world, then it should now become clear that it is riddled through and through with Apollinarianism that sins mightily against the human mind and soul of Jesus. If, on the other hand, we reject every form of monophysite and Apollinarian detraction from the integrity of Jesus' human nature, then we may develop an understanding of Christian worship in which Catholic and Evangelical Christians can be equally at home, for the objective reality of the worship of both lies not in themselves but in Jesus Christ. And that would seem to be the shape of things to come.

(*iv*) The fourth feature we must consider is the most elusive and the most explosive: the resurgence of powerful belief in the Holy Spirit, evident all over the world today in an unparalleled way. Here more obviously than at other points we may see the old institutionalised patterns of existence and behaviour breaking open and new forms of a very different kind arising to take their place, forms that are open to surprising dimensions which we can apprehend only in part but which beckon us to ever deeper and fuller understanding of the ways of God, forms on the boundary between the visible and the invisible, the limited and the unlimited, the expressible and the inexpressible, forms that are *essentially open* and may not be closed. It is of course the open and uncircumscribed character of these forms which extend beyond normal and controlled experience which constitutes their potential danger, for they are open to all kinds of extraneous forces and aims which may invade and pervert them, but that is not what I want to discuss now.

As I understand it, the astonishing movement of the Spirit is, on its negative side, a mighty protest against the determinate forms of the Church's existence in the world which continually arise as the Church yields to the temptation to institutionalise its service of the divine mercy and to build up power-structures of its own both through ecclesiastical success and prestige among the people and through socio-political instruments, by means of which it exerts pressure to attain its ends and impart to its service the kind of efficient power which can recognisably compete with the other power-structures of organised society in the world. But can the Church of Jesus Christ do this sort of thing without becoming assimilated to the worldly forms of human existence where the alienating and enslaving forces of evil and greed and guilt are so deeply entrenched, and therefore without compromising its real nature and mission as the Body of Jesus Christ in the world, thus grieving and quenching the Holy Spirit? What the Church is constantly tempted to do is to substitute worldly power for the power of the Holy Spirit, or, if you like, to generate its own 'holy ghost'. It is against all this that the widespread resurgence of downright belief in the Holy Spirit is a mighty protest in the name of the living God.

How are we to interpret this movement of the Spirit constructively? Here we have a recovery of that orientation in the interrelation of God and the world which was expressed by the Patristic formulation: *From the Father, through the Son, in the Spirit* and *in the Spirit, through the Son, to the Father*.

In the first place, then, this is a stress upon the fact that the mighty acts of God through Jesus Christ are in the Spirit *here and now*, as well as once for all in the Incarnation and at Pentecost. That is to say, it represents a recovery of belief in *God*, not some remote inactive deity, but the mighty living God who acts, and who interacts with the world he has made. That is the kind of God who has been edged out of his creation by the dualistic and deistic concepts embedded in our Western culture and by the obsolete notion of the mechanistic universe, to which the Churches have so sadly succumbed. Looked at in this way, the resurgence of belief in the Spirit is the revolutionary counterpart in the Christian view of God and the world, to the revolutionary understanding of cosmology in the new scientific era with its discovery of the invisible and intangible magnitudes that regulate the open structures within the universe. It imports a realistic and objective understanding of the Kingdom of God breaking into our world through Jesus Christ in such a way that God acts immediately upon the structures of an estranged creation with a view to emancipating creaturely existence, saving it, re-creating it, and harmonising it. It is not surprising, therefore, that Pentecostalists today should interpret the mighty acts of God in the Spirit in the light of the signs and wonders recorded in the Gospels in which we find the incarnate Son of God at work redeeming lost human existence, not by some external fiat, far less by manipulating social, economic and political forces, but by penetrating within the perverted forms of bodily and historical existence and bringing to bear upon men and women in their ontological depths the re-creating activity of the Spirit in deeds of grace and power. It was thus that Jesus reasserted the claim of God's Kingdom over men and women, and proclaimed God's will to maintain them in integrity of being in the face of everything that threatened their existence and to restore them to natural life in the freedom and joy of the creation.

That is the living God who still acts here and now through Jesus Christ in the Spirit, but *in the Spirit* means in God's own distinctive way and with God's own distinctive kind of power, and therefore beyond any realm of human control and manipulation. Just because they really are acts of God, they are acts which are explicable only from the side of God, and not from the side of man. In the nature of the case they are not acts which can be reduced to the phenomenal level where they may be identified with phenomenal events—that is why a Pentecostalist concentration upon phenomena represents, to say the least, a very one-sided understanding of the activity of the Spirit, for there is another and all-important side to this.

In the second place, then, the activity of the Spirit is to be interpreted in terms of the movement described by the Fathers as in the Spirit, through the Son and *to the Father*. Jesus Christ is not only the One through whom the Father gives us his Spirit and acts upon us in the Spirit, but the One through whom, and with whom we have access to the Father in the Spirit, and through whom the Spirit lifts us up to have communion with the Father. The Holy Spirit is sent to us in the name of the Son not in order to concentrate our attention upon our own experiences, either inwardly or outwardly, but to lift up our vision and enable it to embrace a transcendent reality that extends infinitely above and beyond us. At the same time, however, the Holy Spirit endows us with the capacity to know far more than we can tell, for through Christ he establishes us in a communion with the Father that reaches out into the sheer infinity and eternity of God. The fact that in the Spirit we are made to participate in a fulness of life and worship immeasurably greater than ourselves, means that to live in the Spirit is to participate in a movement which constantly lifts us above every phenomenal level of existence to the higher levels of reality in the mystery of God. But that in turn means that we are unable to understand the phenomenal levels aright except as we look away from them to the transcendent levels to which in the activity of the Spirit they are constituted empirical correlates and are therefore made to point us. Regarded, then, from the perspective of the scientific revolution, the activity of the Spirit is to be understood above all as an activity of inter-level coordination and synthesis by means of which the forms of created being are opened to higher levels which endow them with their meaning, since it is only in correlation with them that empirical events on the phenomenal levels can be seen to form patterns of significant depth and intensity. A deeper recognition of this all-important movement of the Spirit through the Son to the Father could do much for the Pentecostalists, for it would help them to direct the focus of their attention away from the phenomena that so often fascinate and absorb them to the mystery of God himself.

The fact that the historical Catholic Churches of East and West have been taking a great interest in the recent movements of the Spirit, would also seem to indicate the shape of things ahead: the characteristic Catholic emphasis, *in the Spirit, through the Son, to the Father* and the characteristic Pentecostalist emphasis, *from the Father, through the Son, in the Spirit,* would then be brought together again. But if so, the decisive factor will surely be played by a deeper understanding of Jesus Christ as the one Mediator between God and man, who through his vicarious humanity mediates to us the Spirit from the Father, and through the same humanity mediates our access in the Spirit to the Father.